Developing
Applications for
Microsoft® Exchange
with C++

Ben Goetter

PUBLISHED BY
Microsoft Press
A Division of Microsoft Corporation
One Microsoft Way
Redmond, Washington 98052-6399

Library of Congress Cataloging-in-Publication Data
Goetter, Ben, 1964-
     Developing Applications for Microsoft Exchange with C++ / Ben Goetter.
        p.   cm.
     Includes index.
     ISBN 1-57231-500-8
     1. Microsoft Exchange.   2. Client/server computing.   3. C++
(Computer program language)   I. Title.
QA76.9.C55G63 1996
005.7'11--dc20   96-28619
                                                                           CIP

Printed and bound in the United States of America.

1 2 3 4 5 6 7 8 9 MLML 1 0 9 8 7 6

Distributed to the book trade in Canada by Macmillan of Canada, a division of Canada
Publishing Corporation.

A CIP catalogue record for this book is available from the British Library.

Microsoft Press books are available through booksellers and distributors worldwide. For further
information about international editions, contact your local Microsoft Corporation office. Or
contact Microsoft Press International directly at fax (206) 936-7329.

Acquisitions Editor: Casey D. Doyle
Project Editors: Patricia N. Wagner, Caroline Pachaud
Technical Editor: Christina Anagnost

CONTENTS

PART THREE   Appendixes

ACKNOWLEDGMENTS

My name appears on the spine and the cover of this book, which is rather like naming only the cow on a cheese wrapper. There is work in the book far beyond the crude raw material that I supplied. Acknowledgments are absolutely due the following people:

- All those at Microsoft Press who handled this manuscript at some point in its gestation, but particularly my long-suffering editors, with love and squalor: Casey Doyle, Caroline Pachaud, Jan Seymour, and Patricia Wagner.

- The developers at Microsoft who took the time to point out errors in my manuscript, flaws in my logic, and deficiencies in my personal character: Scott Briggs, Greg Kramer, Jim Schaad, and Dana Birkby.

- Other helpful members of the Exchange Server development team, for making available resources and information: Brian Valentine, Ken Ewert, Marc Seinfeld, and Alec Dun.

- Steve Maguire for early advice and encouragement, Dr. John Maher for a geochemical reality check, and Gem and Rick Saada for metaphor brainstorming.

- Finally, my wonderful spouse Kathryn Hinsch, for providing crucial program management far above and beyond the call of wifely duty. As Ulysses blessed Nausicaa, so let us be.

9 September 1996
Seattle (Wallingford), Washington, USA

INTRODUCTION

Because Microsoft Exchange was designed as an extensible, customizable system, you, the application author, have a great number of variables available. You can incrementally vary the default behavior of the Exchange client or invent new commands on its tool and menu bars. You can implement a traditional folder application in any of several ways by defining or changing the views, forms, and available verbs. You can leverage Exchange Server–specific features, further customizing folder security options, or modify the automatic message management tasks performed by the inbox assistant on the client. Going still further afield, you can deliver one or more new services to appear within the standard client, or you can write additional client applications to perform message processing outside the standard client. You can even ignore the client altogether, supplanting or replacing it with custom client applications.

Microsoft Exchange and Microsoft Exchange Server make all of these options possible through their open infrastructure.

Who Is the Reader?

As a professional software developer or manager, perhaps you work as a corporate developer seeking to develop an in-house application on top of your company's existing Exchange Server system. Or you could be a corporate solution provider who's evaluating Exchange Server or who's building a custom application for a client already running Exchange Server. Alternatively, you could be an independent software vendor targeting the workgroup market and seeking to leverage Exchange and MAPI in your product. Whoever you are, you are comfortable with messaging concepts, and the notion of workgroup computing is not new to you.

Regardless of the particulars of your professional orientation, you need certain skills to get the most out of this book. You should be conversant with C and have a reading knowledge of C++ sufficient to follow samples presented in that language. Familiarity with the concepts of object-oriented programming will help you understand MAPI and its foundation, the Microsoft Component Object Model (COM). Furthermore, you should have experience in Microsoft Windows and the Win32 API.

You do not need experience with OLE (although it certainly will help) or MAPI. You do, however, need reference materials for each of these technologies, such as those appearing on MSDN (the Microsoft Developer Network) or in the Win32 SDK, since this book does not attempt to recapitulate these lengthy interfaces or their complete documentation. See Appendix B for pointers to some sources of additional information on these and related matters.

Why Read This Book?

Microsoft Exchange Server already contains its own application design environment for building many kinds of information-sharing applications on top of Exchange. So why read this book?

- You need to integrate with Exchange in a manner not possible through the Exchange Server Application Design Environment.

- You prefer C and C++ to Microsoft Visual Basic, the glue language of the Exchange Server Application Design Environment.

- You seek the performance and flexibility available with lower-level languages.

- You are not using Exchange Server but are instead working with Exchange or the Windows Messaging client on other messaging services.

- You program using the Win32 MAPI interfaces and seek to study other MAPI programs.

If any of these statements are true, this book is for you.

This Book's Platform

Every example in this book uses the C++ language on Win32. For writing programs to MAPI, C++ is a concise and expressive choice, since the layout of a COM interface table matches that of the vtable created by most C++ compilers' virtual function implementations. If you use C instead of C++, you can still follow the examples. Chapter 1 contains some notes on interface table and reference-counting implementations that will help C users.

While the examples use C++, they do not use any established class framework such as Borland's OWL or Microsoft Foundation Classes (MFC). Writing an application to a framework is its own art and would only distract from the tutorial purpose at hand: to describe Microsoft Exchange and MAPI. Ignoring the frameworks also improves the portability and palatability of the samples, both to non-Microsoft compilers and to their users.

The examples and code samples all target the Win32 platform. MAPI is part of the extended Win32 APIs and thus is released with each Win32 platform.

On 16-Bit Windows

It is possible to write a 16-bit MAPI application that uses the 16-bit MAPI released with the Win32 SDK and Exchange Server products, but such an application will not run outside the installed Exchange Server client base. For simplicity's sake, then, this book will limit its coverage of 16-bit MAPI development issues to occasional sidebars in the text, each marked with "On 16-Bit Windows."

To build the samples as shipped, you need Microsoft Visual C++ version 2.2 or later. In addition, the full Win32 SDK, as included in MSDN Level 2, contains files useful for MAPI application development. These are unnecessary for building the samples, although they might prove helpful for debugging and testing your application.

The Organization of This Book

Each chapter of this book introduces you to one of the primary technologies that, taken together with its siblings, comprise a Microsoft Exchange application.

Part 1: Architecture

Chapters 1, 2, and 3 provide the foundation necessary for the rest of this book. The Component Object Model articulates a model of software as reusable components. MAPI describes a particular set of component schemas for components related to messaging and workgroup applications. Exchange Server provides the environment in which these messaging components will run.

Part 2: Application

Chapters 4 through 8 discuss the implementation of Microsoft Exchange applications. Simple applications operate entirely within the Exchange client through the client's intrinsic extensibility mechanism. More sophisticated applications will leverage the extensive custom message facilities of MAPI and could alter the message views offered by the Exchange client as well.

Part 3: Appendixes

Appendix A, "A Guide to Sample Applications," discusses the sixteen sample applications found on the accompanying CD-ROM. Appendix B, "For More Information," points you to the latest developments in the world of Exchange.

Along with This Book

This book does not stand alone. Think of it as a guidebook, offering interpretation of the unfamiliar territory of Exchange applications through which you are now traveling. You still need your road maps and automobile user's manual, neither of which this book offers. You might also want to consult other guidebooks.

Your primary road maps lie in the Win32 SDK's "MAPI: The Architecture of Messaging Applications" chapter. As you encounter a new interface or a new technology, take the time to look it up in the MAPI SDK. The online SDK documentation invites you to indulge in hypertext browsing; take advantage of this to learn more about the technology in question.

If you are interested in having your applications run efficiently on Exchange Server or in otherwise exploiting server-specific features, you will want to read the *Microsoft Exchange Server Programmer's Reference,* found in the Microsoft Exchange Server SDK or the BackOffice SDK.

I built the sample programs in this book with Microsoft Visual C++ version 4.0 on both Intel and DEC Alpha platforms. While I've made every effort to keep these programs portable to other platforms and compilers, Murphy's Law guarantees that they contain niggling inconsistencies with other compilers. You might have to tinker with the Makefile, rename a header file, or insert a pragma declaration into the program text to build a sample. Whatever compiler you use, keep its documentation handy.

PART
ONE

Architecture

1

The Microsoft Component Object Model

This chapter introduces the Microsoft Component Object Model (COM). COM, the body of rules by which component software operates, provides the foundation for the Microsoft Messaging Application Programming Interface (MAPI). Therefore, this chapter is also a foundation of the technical knowledge necessary for you to complete the rest of the book. Together with Chapters 2 and 3, it provides a complete introduction to developing applications for Microsoft Exchange. Those versed in OLE or MAPI can skip this chapter.

Any system rests on a set of basic assumptions that dictate the system's behavior. This book's Microsoft Exchange applications all subscribe to a fundamental object model, one that underpins a vision of software as reusable components: COM. To understand the applications of Exchange, you must understand the workings of its components; to understand these components, you must first understand the rules by which they operate.

A Component World

Once upon a time, a battery of programmers would create a single computing machine to perform a single function: multiply a matrix, calculate a standard deviation, or filter a pattern into another pattern. The resulting monolithic computer programs occupied the operation of the entire machine; each program was built specifically from the ground up for its intended purpose and was maintained for the running life of its application. Computers grew more powerful, and the programs they ran became more complex and numerous. The practice of computer programming matured as the demand for programs taxed the state of the art, quickly outstripping the original handcrafting techniques. Still, building programs remained an involved and labor-intensive task. As they addressed the needs of more users, programs became larger and more complex, with their escalating complexity exceeding the progress of software development technology. Despite all manner of advances in procedural verification, code reuse, and successive layers of abstractions, programs got bigger, more expensive, more unwieldy, and more prone to error.

Component software offers a partial solution to this exploding complexity problem. Instead of consisting of a monolithic slab built by its programmers, a component software application consists of a set of specialized subprograms, called *components,* with application-specific logic to coordinate use. Components specialize in particular domains, freeing their users from needing specialized knowledge. Because a component specializes in only one task, it is smaller than a monolithic program and hence is easier to write, maintain, and verify. Once a component exists, it can be used and reused by many client applications, each of which benefits from that component's specialized purpose and freedom from error. The ultimate dream of a component world replaces today's unwieldy one-size-fits-all applications (Swiss Army knives, with more corkscrews than you've ever seen) with specialized collections of components adapted to particular users' requirements. In such an ideal world, users would get what they need without paying for what they didn't need. The effort currently spent in designing, building, and maintaining these omniplex monstrosities would go instead to designing, building, and maintaining repositories of components, each of which could be used and reused in any number of applications.

Consistency in a Component World

For any component system to operate, all components must operate in harmony with one another. Imagine the chaos that would occur if an anesthesiologist in a modern hospital insisted on speaking Russian to a surgical nurse who spoke only German, or if all consulting physicians discarded the notes left by their predecessors. In the same manner, if all components in a system are to form a working whole from their parts, they must subscribe to the same set of operating rules:

- **Component name and address**   How is a component named and loaded by a client? If an application consists of a collection of components, that application's central thread of logic must be able to locate and invoke its constituent components as necessary.

- **Flow-of-control**   How do components in the system intercommunicate? Once it loads a component, the application must send commands to that component.

■ **Role identity**   How does a client know that a particular component can fill a particular role? An application should ensure that a particular component can service a command before making requests of it, particularly if the component in question varies dynamically.

■ **Lifetime**   When is a component's job done? How is the component unloaded? The application must have a way of unloading a component when it has finished its job.

Messaging in a Component World

The intrinsically gigantic scale of a messaging application makes it a prime candidate for a component architecture. Viewed as a whole, messaging systems such as Microsoft Exchange are enormous, spanning multiple types of networks, multiple types of hosts on each network, and multiple types of users on any particular host. On a single host, a messaging application spans problems ranging from document-centered user interface issues to deadlock and contention for shared network resources. Writing an application on this scale truly is impossible; at the very least, maintenance and enhancements must join the running system without necessitating that the entire system be replaced. However, breaking the system down into components allows system specialists to concentrate on messaging system requirements while application specialists concentrate on application and user interface requirements.

Many messaging applications exist as a retrofit or an add-on to another messaging system. When the host system is originally developed under component architecture, such an application need not rewrite portions of this host system; instead, it plugs into the existing system as a component or uses the components of the existing system to build itself. Use of a component architecture also ensures that the application can run on more than one such messaging system without requiring a rewrite for each system. This simplifies application development both by reducing the net development effort and by allowing the application authors to concentrate on the domain they know best, leaving the details of the underlying messaging system to the other components in the system.

A component messaging architecture can benefit applications in domains outside of messaging by providing them with messaging capabilities. If the applications and the document architecture are component-based as well, developers should find it simple to give their applications messaging capabilities, allowing new kinds of applications that share their data with other users.

Microsoft and OLE, the Seeds of a Component World

In late 1990, Microsoft announced a technology called *Object Linking and Embedding*. Originating as a set of extensions to the Dynamic Data Exchange (DDE) protocol, Object Linking and Embedding (almost always called by its acronym, *OLE*) specified a standard for supporting extensible compound documents—that is, documents containing data from other applications. OLE client applications could incorporate data from suitable OLE server applications, allowing this data to be used within the client's own documents as if the client were running the server in question. For example, using OLE, a user could embed a document from a charting application (such as Microsoft Chart) into a Microsoft Word document: Word would save the Chart data in its document file, display that data in its client window just as Chart would, activate the Chart application itself as necessary for editing the embedded document, and update its embedded instance when the launched editing application was terminated. OLE contained a primitive notion of "class" as typing the data stream from a particular server, but it limited its use to within a compound document.

In the following years, Microsoft refined and generalized this basic compound document architecture into a new design that they misleadingly called OLE version 2.0—misleading because OLE 2.0 implies an incremental revision of OLE 1.0. In actuality, OLE 2.0 is a new architecture from the ground up. The new architecture supported a number of user interface enhancements to the compound document model, backing these with new supporting architectures so richly that OLE became a complete application architecture. Most significantly, every participating application now accessed other applications as a set of components through the general, extensible framework that underpins all of OLE. In this generalization, Microsoft had created a component universe for compliant applications. By including OLE[1] in the Microsoft Win32 API set, they planted the seeds of this universe into the operating system.

Microsoft is now gradually adopting the component model for many of its system services. In 1995, several other Microsoft Windows system services—the video capture, speech, messaging services, and, most visibly, the system shell user interface—followed the lead of the OLE services: all operate as and work with component objects. Recently Microsoft has announced *ActiveX,* which will include the ActiveX server framework and will subsume all of what previously included COM and OLE. In future versions of Windows, this architecture will probably be applied to many other services, including the file system, network, and online Help.

---

1. The name "OLE" no longer carries a version number but instead denotes the aggregate of all Microsoft's component object technologies, including the compound document architecture in which the acronym originated.

Justification and Functionality of COM

Underlying all the component systems of Microsoft operating systems is a single architecture: COM. COM is an open architecture for developing client/server applications across platforms. All COM-compatible classes are derived from the *IUnknown* interface.

The Requirements for COM

As discussed above, a component system must subscribe to a set of common operating rules that enable its parts to cooperate. Every component operating within OLE, for example, must have exactly the same characteristics:

Component name and address How does a client application locate the component to handle a particular piece of a compound document? More generally, how does client code locate and instantiate (that is, create an object from a class) a particular component?

Flow-of-control How does the client communicate with that component?

Role identity How does the client confirm that a component can satisfy its request?

Lifetime How does the client application unload the component when it is finished?

By complying with COM operating rules, a component ensures that it addresses these questions with the same answers that all other COM-compliant objects use. The component can then participate in the component architecture of OLE, MAPI, or any other component-based system. Any body of code that participates in these systems must abide by these rules.

When the scope of an architecture broadens, encompassing tens of thousands of components across hundreds of different systems, other characteristics are also important:

Implementation   How are components implemented? What computer language can a developer use in implementing components? Can components developed in one environment work with those developed in another?

Names of components   How does a component claim a name? What prevents a component's name from conflicting with the name of another component?

Scope   What is the scope of a component's operation? Must all components run within the same thread of execution? The same resource-owning process? The same physical host computer? The same web of hosts on a network?

The following sections of this chapter explore how COM addresses these issues.

Objects and Interfaces

In object-oriented design, the basic element of a program is an *object,* with a particular behavior that responds to a certain set of *methods* or commands. Every object has a *class* that defines the object's set of methods and its behavior. An object comes from instantiating such a class, giving it life, so that the new instance can respond to methods and maintain instance data. Classes are said to support *interfaces,* or logical sets of related methods without any particular implementation.[2] Interfaces provide access to OLE objects and define how objects interact. To recapitulate in reverse: a set of methods (commands) is an interface; one or more interfaces with a particular defined behavior, or implementation, makes a class; and a class instantiated makes an object. Figure 1-1 depicts this familiar programming metaphor.

NOTE	While COM shares some terminology with C++, its notions of object and class differ substantially from those of C++. COM lacks constructors and destructors. COM uses object lifetime rules unlike those of C++. COM classes lack a formal type to impose on their objects, unlike C++ classes; instead, a COM object's type results from the union of its interfaces. COM clients interact with interfaces, whereas C++ clients interact with the class. To avoid confusion with any particular object-oriented programming language, then, the following discussions will favor the COM terms *component object, object server,* and *interface.*

---

2. The C++ programming language does not explicitly distinguish between classes and interfaces, although a C++ programmer might model a named interface by defining an abstract base class that consists entirely of pure virtual functions and then uses that class to derive another class.

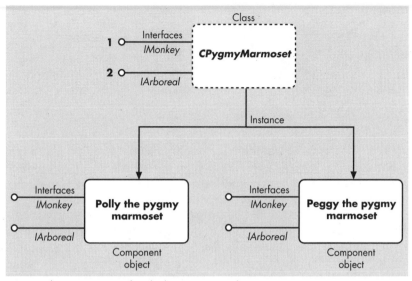

1 Is-a monkey: properties and methods intrinsic to monkeys
2 Is-a tree dweller: properties and methods intrinsic to arboreal animals

Figure 1-1. *Object orientation: interface, class, object. The class* CPygmyMarmoset *supports two defined interfaces:* IMonkey, *representing the class's is-a monkey properties and methods intrinsic to monkeys, and* IArboreal, *representing is-a tree dweller properties and methods intrinsic to arboreal animals. Two instances of* CPygmyMarmoset *appear: Polly and Peggy, the marmosets. Polly is a monkey and a tree dweller, as is Peggy, because both are pygmy marmosets.*

COM roughly follows the object-oriented paradigm. Its basic element is the instantiated component, or *component object*. A component object arises from a class, or *object server,* that supplies the component object's implementation and hence defines its behavior. Clients interact with component objects through *interfaces* that embody logical command sets.

Central to the component architecture is the notion of *interface*. An interface consists of a named set of semantically related methods that a component supports. The client invokes a method on the interface, whereupon the component behind the interface takes some action or makes some other state change. A client communicates with a component object exclusively through the component object's interfaces (shown in Figure 1-2 on the following page); indeed, to the client, the component object *is* its interfaces, since the client holds no handle to any other artifact of the component. A component object can support multiple interfaces.

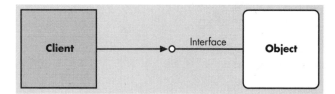

Figure 1-2. *Conventions used for incoming and outgoing interfaces.*

An interface acts like a contract for the component object's behavior: if an interface is present, the component object behaves in a certain way, in accordance with the semantics of the particular interface. A component object might not elect to implement only part of an interface; the component must either implement every detail of the interface or not support that interface. Otherwise, the component object's behavior would break the contract. If an interface ever changes, its name must also change because otherwise there is no guarantee of the semantics of the interface to its clients. A particular name denotes the same interface—the same precise set of semantics—on every component object on which the interface might appear in the universe, forever and ever. Such strongly typed interfaces constitute the foundation of COM's component architecture. When a client recognizes a particular interface on a component, the client knows precisely what to expect from that component: the exact semantics of the recognized interface. Since a client interacts with the component only through this interface, the client can accept any compliant implementation of the interface in its place. This is called polymorphism, which is illustrated in Figure 1-3.

For a client to work with a component, the client must first obtain an interface to that component. Initially every component appears as a black box of unknown potential, with the client holding the interface *IUnknown*—the interface for a component of yet unknown capabilities, which every component must support. Through *IUnknown* (see Table 1-1), the client discovers the capabilities of a particular component by querying it with the names of expected or desired interfaces, using a method appropriately called *IUnknown::QueryInterface*.[3] (*AddRef* and *Release*, which are other *IUnknown* methods, are discussed later in this chapter.) If the component object supports a particular interface, the component hands it back to the interrogator in response to the request; otherwise, the component indicates to the caller that the component does not support that interface, leaving the caller to decide whether to ask for a different interface or leave the component alone.

---

3. This is C++ notation for "the member function *QueryInterface* of the class *IUnknown*." We use it to denote the method *QueryInterface* of the interface *IUnknown*, whether or not the particular implementation was done in C++.

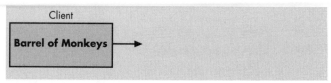

The Barrel of Monkeys client will interact with any component object offering the *IMonkey* interface.

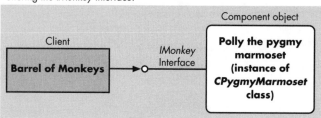

The Barrel of Monkeys client interacts with Polly because this component object offers the *IMonkey* interface.

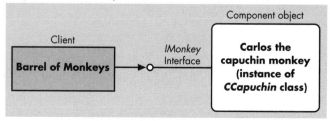

The Barrel of Monkeys client interacts with Carlos, even though this component object was not instantiated from the same class as Polly.

Figure 1-3. *Polymorphism in action.*

Method	Description
QueryInterface	Provides a client with access to other interfaces on an object
AddRef	Increments the reference count for the calling interface on an object
Release	Decrements the reference count for the calling interface on an object

Table 1-1. *Methods on the* IUnknown *interface.*

In the most straightforward scenario, a client obtains access to a component through the component's *IUnknown* interface and asks that component, "I loaded you expecting a particular service. Can you do what I want you to do?" The component responds, "Yes, and here's an interface for performing that service," whereupon the relationship begins. For an example of such a protocol negotiation, see Figure 1-4 on the following page.

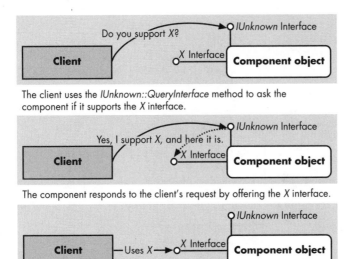

The client uses the *IUnknown::QueryInterface* method to ask the component if it supports the *X* interface.

The component responds to the client's request by offering the *X* interface.

The client now has direct access to the *X* interface.

Figure 1-4. *Negotiating the first protocol.*

A component might support *multiple interfaces.* Indeed, almost all components support multiple interfaces: at the least, *IUnknown,* plus another interface characteristic of the object, with further interfaces possible as well. This simply means that the component can return additional interfaces in response to *QueryInterface* requests for them. Each discrete interface represents a particular semantic contract that the component honors. For instance, a text editor component might support one interface for manipulating text, another for displaying its user interface, and a third for loading and saving data in disk files. An object file editor in the same universe might support an interface for manipulating symbol tables, plus the same user interface and disk-file interfaces supported by the text editor.

FYI

COM uses the interface negotiation mechanism to handle version management of components. Since any modification to an interface results in a different interface with a unique name, a component supports requests for old versions of its functionality by electing to respond to the name of the old version's interface. Likewise, a client supports old components by querying for the name of the old interface when requests for the new one have failed, as shown in Figure 1-5.

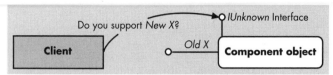

The client uses the *IUnknown::QueryInterface* method to ask the component if it supports the *New X* interface.

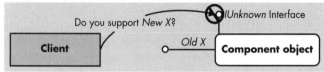

However, the component does not support the *New X* interface and rejects the request.

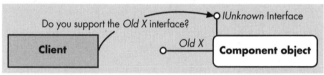

The client then uses the *IUnknown::QueryInterface* method to ask the component if it supports the *Old X* interface.

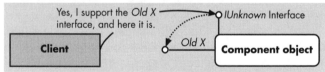

The component responds to the client's request by offering the *Old X* interface.

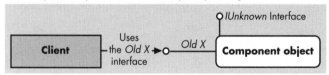

The client drops the *IUnknown* interface and obtains direct access to the *Old X* interface.

Figure 1-5. *Version management between COM interfaces.*

Unlike most object-oriented systems, COM contains no rules for class or interface inheritance. (COM does contain an implementation reuse mechanism called aggregation, the discussion of which falls outside the scope of this book.) An interface is a static raft of semantics; any change to that interface results in another interface with no explicit relationship to its predecessor. In rare instances, however, a particular interface might define itself to include explicitly another interface; in that case, it is part of the semantics of that interface (for example, *IPersistStorage*) that the interface completely subsumes another interface (in this example, *IPersist*). This is very rare, with one important exception: every interface includes *IUnknown* in such a manner that every interface effectively is *IUnknown*, as if it had inherited *IUnknown*. In other words, every interface delivers the mechanism by which a client can request another interface from the component.

Object Naming

For a client to ask a component object for an interface, the client needs to have a name for that interface: a token that the client and component agree represents the interface and that neither can mistake for any other interface. Recall that any change to an interface results in a new interface distinct from the old one.

Every named object in the universe of COM has as its true name a Globally Unique Identifier, or *GUID*. A GUID is a 128-bit integer, spanning a theoretical range from 0 through (2^{128}) −1, or approximately 3.4×10^{38}.

As the name indicates, each GUID value is "globally unique": it exists to uniquely identify one object class in the universe. A GUID must be unique to be valid; once one has been assigned to name something, it must never be reassigned elsewhere,[4] lest two parties hold two different definitions of the same name. Imagine, for example, what might happen if everybody developed a fondness for the GUID value *1* (certainly much easier to remember and type than a chain of 32 hexadecimal digits or 38 decimal digits). Or picture the confusion that would arise in interface negotiations: a man staggers into a room, sees a figure in a white coat, and gasps, "Are you a doctor?" To which the helpful diesel mechanic responds, "Why, yes I *am*. How may I help you?" Bad news, unless the sick man runs SAE 30W for blood!

Developers allocate GUIDs with an algorithm designed to prevent such collisions. The internal structure of a GUID includes 48 bits of machine-specific unique seed, such as an Ethernet or a Token-Ring network address (if available), representing the system that allocated the GUID, together with 64 bits of time in Universal Time Coordinates (UTC) format, representing the time at which the

---

4. Fortunately, with 2^{128} possible GUID values, there's no need to allocate them parsimoniously. This range could accommodate assigning a GUID to every hair on every head on every person in the world. Furthermore, in an echo of *Horton Hears a Who*, every hair on our world could actually accommodate an entire tiny world, equally populous and hirsute as our own, and you'd still have enough GUIDs to assign each tiny hair its own value. Indeed, you could repeat this allocation over 200 million Earth-sized planets, each with hairy inhabitants carrying an inhabited world on each hair, before you'd exhaust the space. Aren't orders of magnitude fun?

system allocated it. This allows each of 2.8 x 10^{14} hosts (the range of the machine-specific identifier) to allocate 10,000,000 GUIDs per second for the next 3000 years (the range of 64-bit UTC).

When a GUID names an interface, the GUID is an interface ID, or *IID*. GUIDs name more than just interfaces, however; everywhere a unique name is necessary, a GUID appears, possibly under a different label. They can name class objects, in which case the GUIDs take the name *CLSIDs,* or they can name remote procedure call (RPC) proxies, in which case they travel as *UUIDs.*[5]

By convention, we write a GUID value as a series of hexadecimal digits, separated with hyphens that demarcate its internal structure and delimited with braces, *{00000000-0000-0000-C000-000000000046}*, with the most volatile time elements to the left and the machine identifier to the right. Because most fleshy, carbon-based people don't work naturally with 128-bit numbers as names, this book uses symbolic constants or shorthand instead of literal GUID values. The quantity listed above, for instance, appears only once in this book and in the API documentation, even though it's the most commonly used interface name in the system: *IUnknown*. Instead of using the literal GUID value, the code refers to the symbol *IID_IUnknown*, while the documents name it as *IUnknown*.

Object Lifespan

Component objects are bodies—logical "objects" in the object-oriented programming sense—that articulate interfaces to their clients. These objects have a life span: they come into existence at a client's demand, fulfill whatever requests are made of them, and finally vanish when they are no longer needed.

The body of code that implements a particular component object is called the *component class*. In the model most common to ActiveX, a client loads the class it needs, passing the system COM library a CLSID—the GUID naming a particular class—and getting in return a class object. A class object (frequently called a *class factory* to reduce overwork of the already grievously abused *o*-word) is itself just a form of component object, one that exports the interface *IClassFactory*; the client interacts with the class factory's offered *IClassFactory* interface to request instances of the component object implemented by the class, as shown in Figure 1-6 on the following page.

---

5. This is the same UUID that the Open Software Foundation (OSF) Distributed Computing Environment (DCE) Remote Procedure Call mechanism uses.

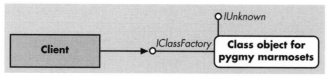

The client uses the *IClassFactory* interface to request a new instance of a pygmy marmoset.

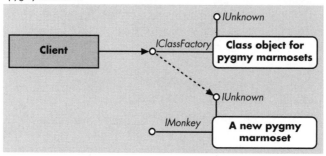

The component responds to the client's request by creating a new instance of pygmy marmoset.

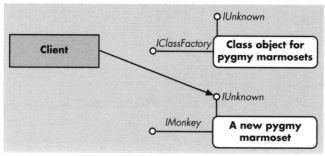

The client uses the *IUnknown::QueryInterface* method to request an interface to the new pygmy marmoset.

Figure 1-6. *A client using a class factory.*

Most of COM lies within the compliant applications themselves. However, systems hosting COM do perform some services, and one of these is maintaining the local repository of components. As shown in Figure 1-7, when the system COM library receives a request with a particular CLSID, it first checks a running object table to see whether it has an instance of that class running and available. If not, it consults the system registry, where it keeps a table associating each known CLSID with its backing body of code and starts the component code as necessary. Once the code is loaded and running, the library passes that class's class factory interface back to the requesting client.

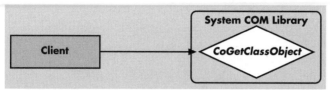

The client supplies a CLSID in its call to the *CoGetClassObject* method to obtain an interface to a class object.

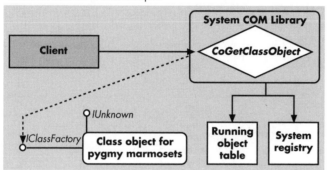

The system COM library checks a running object table to determine whether an instance of the class is available. If not, it consults the system registry and starts the component code. The system COM library returns the *IClassFactory* interface to the class object.

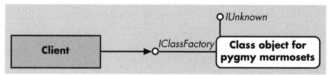

The client obtains direct access to the *IClassFactory* interface.

Figure 1-7. *The system COM library initializes and loads the process by finding the initial class object for a potential client.*

From the class factory interface, a client creates instances of that class's component object. At some point thereafter, the client no longer needs the component, whereupon the object can depart this vale of tears, releasing any associated memory; likewise, at some point, the class itself is no longer necessary, having no outstanding instances of its object to service, and so may depart, allowing the system to unload its code. The problem is knowing when no part of the client has any reference to an object. Because the client itself is built of components, it might well pass one component's interface to another component, which in turn might pass the interface further along. The original logic that loaded the component has no way of knowing how many other components made reference to the component and so cannot make the decision to unload the component on its own.

To address this, COM uses a pervasive system of manual reference counting. Every time a client makes a new reference to a component, it informs the component of the fact. ("Hey, I just gave your address to Charlie here—he's going to need you to stick around.") Conversely, every time a client is finished with such a reference, it takes the trouble to inform the component before discarding the reference. ("I'm all done. I no longer need you. Of course, I can't necessarily speak for anybody else.") Armed with this information, the component itself tracks the number of references it has outstanding, as shown in Figure 1-8; when the component sees that number fall to 0, it knows it should retire. Reference counting takes place through the methods *IUnknown::AddRef* and *IUnknown-::Release*. More on the rules of reference counting a bit later in this chapter.

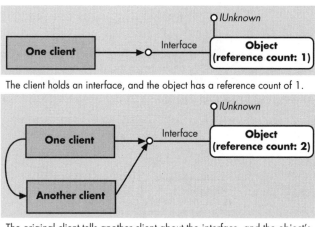

The client holds an interface, and the object has a reference count of 1.

The original client tells another client about the interface, and the object's reference count increases to 2.

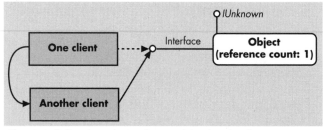

The original client drops the interface, and the object's reference count decreases to 1.

Figure 1-8. *Objects track the number of references that clients make to them.*

Object Encapsulation

Clients access and reference all objects exclusively through their interfaces. This encapsulation shields the clients from many extraneous details about the object, including precisely where the component is hosted. The component might operate within the client's own process,[6] either in code already resident or in a dynamic-link library (DLL) loaded by the system COM library. Alternatively, the component might operate in a separate process running on the machine, communicating with the client process using an RPC interface. In the next release of Windows, the component object might not be required to reside on the client's computer at all but instead might host itself on a different machine, with the two machines linked by a network. From the client's perspective, it acts in all scenarios by invoking methods on an interface; what happens thereafter depends on the implementation of the component, with the system COM library transparently applying different communication mechanisms to connect the two ends.

The simplest model of object encapsulation is the in-process (or *inproc*) server model. (The body of code constituting the component class is frequently called the *server*, in contrast with client code, because the server services the requests made of its objects.) In-process servers reside in DLLs that the system COM library loads on the client's behalf for accessing the server's class object. Once the server has been loaded into the client process, the server can hand interfaces directly to the client code. The system COM library involves itself only in loading, unloading, and establishing the initial connection between the two; thereafter, client and component communicate directly. Figure 1-9 offers an example of an in-process server.

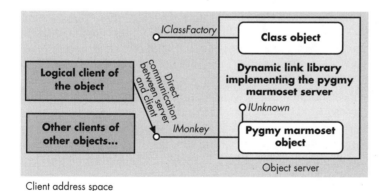

Client address space

Figure 1-9. *An in-process server embeds the code implementing its objects within the same process as that hosting the code of its clients' objects. The system locates a DLL encapsulating the desired class, loading it on behalf of the client process.*

---

6. In a Windows-based system, the *process* is a basic element of resource ownership. Every executable file (.EXE) loads its code into its own process, whereas a dynamic-link library file (.DLL) loads its code into another existing process.

The other model of object encapsulation is the out-of-process (or *local*) server model.[7] Local servers reside in .EXE files that the system COM library loads on the client's behalf, resulting in a separate process to host the component. Once the server process has been loaded or (if it was running already) located, the system COM library establishes a connection between it and the requesting client process and then maintains the connection across the interprocess boundary. Each time the client invokes a method on the component's interface, the system transforms this into an RPC to the server. Although this involves considerable overhead per call, it enables the client to use component objects implemented by stand-alone applications or by other independently running services.

From the perspective of the client, all method invocations appear to be in-process. When a client requests a particular class object from the system COM library, the system takes different steps, depending on whether that class's server is implemented in-process or out-of-process. If the class works in-process, the system has a simple job: load the server code, set up the connection, and get out of the way, leaving the interface in the hands of the client. If the class works out-of-process, however, the system has more work to do to maintain the transparency of the model. As the system loads the server code, it gives that server a *stub* (used as a placeholder for code) that the server keeps in its own process, interacting with the stub as if the stub were the client making requests. After setting up the server with a stub, the system returns a *proxy* to the client for its process in the place of the interface that the client expected. The client interacts with this proxy just as if it were the promised component object's interface. When the client invokes a method on this pseudo-interface proxy, that proxy takes the client-supplied parameters, marshals them into a transportable format, and invokes a system-supplied RPC channel to transport the parameters to the server. On the other end, the system stub manager receives the parameters from the RPC channel and relays them to the appropriate stub, which unmarshals the parameters and uses them to invoke the server's object in its own address space. The results of the method invocation are returned to the client in the same manner, except in reverse: the stub takes the received results, marshals them, and passes them to the RPC channel, which in turn relays them back to the proxy for unmarshaling and eventual presentation to the client. Figure 1-10 shows the players in this method.

---

7. "Local" servers are so called because while they host remote procedure calls, they actually run local to the client's machine, as opposed to a truly remote (in the networking sense) server running on some other machine. New releases of Windows support truly remote component objects through Distributed COM, or DCOM, making out-of-process no longer synonymous with "local."

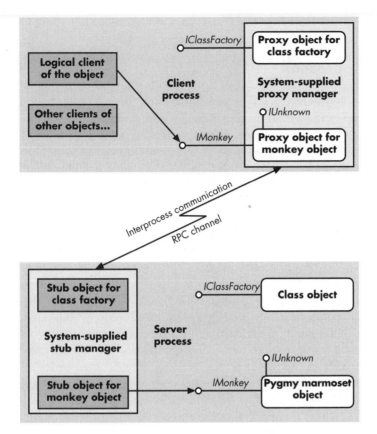

Figure 1-10. *Interprocess communication to an out-of-process server. All method invocations to out-of-process objects travel across process boundaries transparently to the client.*

Implementation Within COM

That's COM at 1000 meters. Let's now examine how implementation in the COM universe works. We can't discuss any more COM without writing code.

Common Standards

Beyond the high-level standards set forth above, COM specifies much finer details of the operations of compliant components. All the fancy *o*-word component architecture in the world won't help much if two components don't precisely agree on what happens when one invokes a method on the other's interface. These standards allow for established and recognizable behavior of its components.

The binary interface standard

The first "components" were libraries of collected code fragments. A library traditionally specifies its interfaces as a source code standard. The library is written in one particular language, or more specifically one particular implementation of the language, and expects its clients to use that same language or something compatible with it. Microsoft libraries don't work with Borland compilers. Pascal libraries typically require either Pascal clients or clients that know how to pretend to be written in Pascal for the purposes of calling the library. If a library doesn't work with a particular client, the solution is to rebuild the library for that client.

Such source code standards are unacceptable in a component world. Once released into a system, a component must operate with every suitably cooperative client that it meets; the component doesn't have the luxury of being recompiled for a particular use. Software developers use an enormous number of different development systems, each optimized for a particular set of strengths; no power on earth could force those developers to adopt a single standard. Instead, COM facilitates the language and implementation independence of its components by defining a *binary* standard—one specified at the object-code level, at which all the different development systems eventually meet[8]—for its interfaces. Such a binary standard allows different components to use different implementation systems and yet still work together.

COM components implement interfaces as linear arrays of function addresses, with each element in the array representing a particular method on the interface. Such an array is called a *vtable,* or "virtual function table," after the construct that many C++ compilers use to implement virtual class member function calls. A client holds and manipulates this interface through a pointer to a pointer to its first element, called an *interface pointer.* The definition of a particular interface guarantees the layout of the methods within that interface's vtable. Clients invoke methods by their offset within the vtable. For example, invoking the *IUnknown::AddRef* method on an object yields a call to the function named as the second element in the object's vtable.

---

8. Additional rules cover interoperability for components that do not share this binary standard, such as 16-bit Windows components running on Win32 systems or Microsoft Windows NT DEC Alpha Clients using components hosted on a PowerPC system.

FYI

The binary standard detailed here applies to Win32 operating systems running on Intel microprocessors. The COM standard spans many different host architectures; clearly, a binary standard depends on the identity of the host and the object code standards thereon. The precise details of interface vtable layout and function calling sequence thus can vary between platforms; consider the rules for stack usage when you make function calls on a RISC processor that contains many registers, or the layout of a vtable in memory on a non-Intel byte-ordered architecture. When out-of-process servers make interplatform interoperability possible, the in-process proxies and stubs will conform to the standards of each host process's platform, with the intervening connectivity layers translating as necessary.

Each method typically honors a standard calling sequence. The caller pushes the parameters to the method onto the stack in right-to-left order and then pushes the interface pointer itself as an additional parameter, which the call can use to locate per-object instance data. The called function pops the arguments off the stack unless it takes a variable number of arguments, in which case the caller must pop the arguments off the stack upon return. The function leaves a system standard status code in the EAX register upon returning.

Fortunately, every development system provides higher-level abstractions with which to automate this rubbish. That's why high-level computer languages exist, after all. Since this book presents all of its examples in C++, I'll discuss the implementation and usage of vtables in Microsoft's C++ development system and then translate the example into straight C.

By design, a vtable mimics the layout of a C++ class virtual function table, as generated by several companies' compilers. The following class declaration will generate the signature of *IUnknown* when it is instantiated.

```
class CThisClassImplementsUnknown
{
public:
    virtual HRESULT __stdcall QueryInterface(REFIID iid, void**
        ppv);
    virtual ULONG __stdcall AddRef();
    virtual ULONG __stdcall Release();
};
```

(For the moment, ignore the types HRESULT and REFIID; all you need to know is that HRESULT, like ULONG, is a 32-bit quantity that fits nicely in the register EAX.) The *IUnknown* vtable will contain the three methods of the interface *IUnknown* at the correct offsets and with the correct calling sequences, as shown in Figure 1-11.

A client with a pointer to an object of this class can invoke its methods by calling virtual member functions through the pointer. However, a client will never have such a pointer; what it will have is an interface pointer, which works like a pointer to a C++ abstract base class. The client sees the interface as follows:

```
struct IUnknown
{
    virtual HRESULT __stdcall QueryInterface(REFIID iid, void** ppv)
        = 0;
    virtual ULONG __stdcall AddRef() = 0;
    virtual ULONG __stdcall Release() = 0;
};
class CThisClassImplementsUnknown: public IUnknown { };
```

When the client calls a method through this pointer, it invokes the method implementation of the component object that implements the interface. In the following example, the *AddRef* function is called using the pointer *punk*:

```
IUnknown* punk = /* Never mind from where for now */;
punk->AddRef();
```

Since the COM interface standard is a binary standard, any environment that can generate compliant object code can implement or use an interface. In straight, non-syntactically-sugared C, the equivalent interface definition is as follows:

```
typedef struct IUnknownVtbl
{
    HRESULT ( __stdcall *QueryInterface )(
    struct IUnknown* This,
    REFIID riid,
    void** ppvObject);
    ULONG ( __stdcall *AddRef )(IUnknown* This);
    ULONG ( __stdcall *Release )(IUnknown* This);

} IUnknownVtbl;
typedef struct IUnknown
{
    struct IUnknownVtbl* pvtbl;
} IUnknown;
```

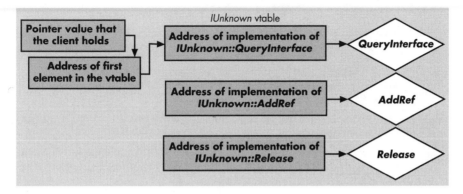

Figure 1-11. *Layout of an* IUnknown *interface vtable. In a flat-model x86 environment, each of the pointers is 4 bytes long. The 12-byte table containing the addresses of the method implementations is the vtable proper.*

A component object supplies a compliant vtable by building a table of function pointers, while the client invokes the object's methods by calling through that table, passing the interface pointer as the first argument, as shown in the following call to the *AddRef* function:

```
IUnknown* punk = /* Ditto */;
(*(punk->pvtbl->AddRef))(punk);
```

The C and C++ examples here are equivalent, as both adhere to COM's binary standard for interfaces.

The error return standard
Beyond the calling sequence, COM defines some of the rules for interface method function returns as well. All interface methods return a 32-bit value, and almost all of these are HRESULTs. An HRESULT allows the returning routine to indicate any one of a number of outcomes of success or failure.

> **NOTE** COM strictly forbids methods from throwing error exceptions across interface boundaries. Every method must return to its caller.

The structure of an HRESULT comprises three significant fields:

■ The most significant bit (bit 31) is the *severity,* which denotes whether the code indicates success or failure. A severity of 1 (*SEVERITY_ERROR*—that is, an HRESULT with the most significant bit set) denotes an error that prevented the method from completing. A severity of 0 (*SEVERITY_SUCCESS*) indicates that the method completed successfully.

■ Bits 16 through 26 (the lower 11 bits of the upper word) constitute the *facility,* which indicates which logical subsystem allocated the result code. In effect, the facility groups result codes into logical families.

■ Bits 15 through 0 (the lower word) constitute the *code,* which describes what happened in the method.

Success codes are part of the intrinsic semantics of the method. If there are three ways in which a particular method can succeed, the interface must explicitly define those three ways. However, very few distinct success codes actually exist. Most commonly, a method will return *NOERROR*, the code that indicates "Command completed successfully—look at its output parameters or other side effects." Alternatively, a method can elect to return a Boolean value using the two codes *S_OK* and *S_FALSE*.

Since more than one success code exists, using the common idiom *if (hr !=NOERROR)* or *if (hr)* to check the return result against *NOERROR* might not yield useful information. Code should instead check the most significant bit of the HRESULT through the macros *SUCCEEDED* and *FAILED*, as in the following example:

```
HRESULT hr = p->Something();
if (FAILED(hr))
    // Take action.
```

In contrast to success codes, the range of error codes need not be fixed when the interface is defined. An interface can specify certain error codes as expected but usually cannot forbid others, since different implementations of the interface might encounter different error exception states that they want to signal. Error codes are legion, then, since every subsystem and every component used by the interface has a score of ways in which it can fail. If a method encounters an error while it is executing, it can return its own error code if it understands the error and can define it more precisely in an interface-specific fashion; otherwise, it cascades the encountered error back to its caller as best it can.

Two facilities hold semantic interest beyond their contents:

FACILITY_WIN32 A mapped Win32 API error code was returned—that is, a code returned by the Win32 *GetLastError* API. A method that fails and would reflect an error from this API should compose an HRESULT in this facility with the code set to the API error code.

FACILITY_ITF The error is specific to the current interface. A method cannot blindly cascade a result in this facility back to its caller if the method isn't part of the same interface family that generated the result, since that result might have a completely different meaning in its new context. If an interface must generate its own family of result codes, it must use this facility.

Further, within a third facility, called *FACILITY_NULL*, lie many codes of general utility. Methods have recourse to all of these to indicate common errors.

E_NOINTERFACE A component object does not support a particular requested interface.

E_NOTIMPL The interface did not implement the current method. No released component can ever return this result.

E_POINTER* and *E_HANDLE The method did some parameter validation and found a pointer or handle parameter invalid.

E_INVALIDARG The caller supplied the method with an invalid argument.

E_UNEXPECTED The method called some other method and received a result that it didn't know how to handle.

E_ABORT The user intervened in order to prevent the method from completing successfully.

E_ACCESSDENIED The caller lacked some sort of privilege necessary for the method to succeed.

E_OUTOFMEMORY The method failed to allocate enough memory to satisfy the caller's request.

E_FAIL The method failed for no specific reason.

On 16-Bit Windows

The old 16-bit platforms differentiated between HRESULT, "handle to a result," which was the abstract result type returned by methods, and a literal integer SCODE, "status code" value, which encoded the actual error code embedded within the result. Code written to those platforms uses *GetScode* to extract the SCODE from an HRESULT and uses *ResultFromScode* to take an SCODE value and construct an HRESULT suitable for returning.

The memory management standard

A final standard that COM places on its components is a set of rules for memory allocation and call-by-reference methods. Any function that allocates memory and passes the results back to the caller begs the question: who takes responsibility for releasing this memory?

As with method returns, COM standardizes rules for memory allocation and call-by-reference method parameters. One class of allocated objects is interface pointers. COM directs these through the semantics of *IUnknown* and reference counting. All other call-by-reference parameters in COM fall into one of three classes:

- An *in*-parameter has its storage both allocated and freed by the caller. Any call-by-value parameter is a degenerate case of a call-by-reference in-parameter.

- An *out*-parameter has its storage allocated by the method but is freed by the caller. If the method fails, it will set the out-parameter to NULL so that the caller does not need to take further action.

- An *in/out* parameter has its storage initially allocated by the caller but leaves the method free to release and reallocate additional storage as necessary; as with an out-parameter, the caller takes final responsibility for freeing the storage. If the method fails, it must leave the caller's given value untouched. If the method fails after irrevocable action has been taken, the method sets the parameter to NULL.

When an out-parameter or an in/out parameter is used, ownership of the memory crosses the interface boundary. It follows that both sides of the interface must agree to use the same allocator to manipulate that memory.

COM provides a standard memory allocator through its system library function *CoGetMalloc*, which returns an object implementing the *IMalloc* interface. However, certain subsystems—notably, MAPI—elect to use their own allocators to this end.

IMalloc

The *IMalloc* interface describes the system-supplied memory allocator used in COM and ActiveX. Using it enables clients to call system interfaces with out-parameters and in/out-parameters. The *IMalloc* methods *Alloc*, *Free*, and *Realloc* are similar to the C library functions *malloc*, *free*, and *realloc*.

As a Client

Now we go on to see how all these concepts and standards apply in the client world. A client's role is to interact with components. Its jobs are to get access to the component, get the interfaces that it wants to use on the component, and interact with those interfaces. All the while, it must honor the reference-counting system that controls the life span of the object.

How a client uses an interface

A C++ client treats an interface as if it were a pointer to some class's abstract base class, simply invoking the member functions of this abstract base:

```
HRESULT hr = pobj->Method();
```

A C client treats an interface as a pointer to a jump table, by calling through the function pointer at the appropriate offset:

```
    HRESULT hr;
    hr = *(pobj->pVtbl->Method)(pobj);
```

In each case, the client must check the result returned before making any subsequent assumptions about side effects of the method:

```
if (SUCCEEDED(hr))
{
    /* Method succeeded. */
}
```

How a client gets an object

There are two ways a client can get access to an object. The first is to ask some other component or subsystem, which will get the object (or perhaps already has the object) for it. The client calls a function, passing as an out-parameter a pointer to an interface pointer, and the called function returns an interface for the object in the out-parameter. The system COM library function *CoGetMalloc* works in just this way, providing clients with access to the task allocator object, and therefore is a fine example. Use of the *CoGetMalloc* function is shown in the following example:

```
    void* pv = NULL;
    IMalloc* pmall;
    HRESULT hr = CoGetMalloc(1L, &pmall);
    if (SUCCEEDED(hr))
        pv = pmall->Alloc( /* … */ );
```

Note that the client sees nothing of the object other than the returned interface pointer, through which all interaction takes place. From the client's perspective, the object is some anonymous implementation of the interface *IMalloc*; of course, *CoGetMalloc* makes certain guarantees about that implementation. Note also that the client does not use the interface pointer unless the call to instantiate it succeeded.

The second way to access an object is if the client doesn't know anybody who already has the object; it then has to bring it to life itself. First the client gets the class factory for the class of the component object in question, and then it interacts with the class factory to create an instance of the object.

COM identifies a class by its CLSID, a GUID distinguishing that class from all other classes in the universe. Recall that a class embodies a particular component object, the implementation of a set of interfaces. Armed with the CLSID of the class it wants, the client goes to the system COM library and asks it for the class or, more specifically, the class factory interface of that class. At one level, this is just what happened in the previous example: the client didn't know where to get the object, but it knew a call that did, so it passed that call an out-parameter for an interface pointer.

In the following code fragment, *CoGetClassObject* returns a value for *&pfactory*, which is a pointer to the location of an interface pointer.

```
IClassFactory* pfactory;
HRESULT hr = CoGetClassObject(CLSID_MonkeyHouse,
    CLSCTX_INPROC_SERVER|CLSCTX_LOCAL_SERVER,
    NULL,
    IID_IClassFactory,
    (void**)&pfactory);
```

As shown in this example, *CLSID_MonkeyHouse* is the CLSID of some class I've (whimsically) named *MonkeyHouse*; in the code, it's really a symbol naming the external storage of a particular 16-byte GUID structure, one with the value of the CLSID in question. *CoGetClassObject* needs this CLSID to determine which class object the client wants. The CLSID isn't the only GUID needed. *IID_IClass-Factory* is the IID, the GUID identifying a particular interface, for the *IClassFactory* interface. *CoGetClassObject* requires that the client specify which factory interface it wants on the class object; if the client supplied some other IID, the API would look for that interface (*IMonkeyFactory*) from the class. The cast to *void**** of the interface pointer out-parameter satisfies the requirement that the out-parameter remains generic: since *CoGetClassObject* can return any one of many different interfaces, its out-parameter must remain generic. Finally, the conjunction of *CLSCTX* constants specifies only that the client doesn't care where COM loads the server, in-process or out-of-process.

To satisfy this call, the system COM library looks both in-process and out-of-process for an already loaded *MonkeyHouse* class. Failing to find that, it consults the system registry, looking for a server for a CLSID installed on this machine; if COM finds such a server, COM starts it, either loading it in-process or launching it out-of-process as the server's implementation mandates. Having found the server, COM then requests a class factory from it. At this point, an out-of-process server requires establishing the suitable remote connections between its process and that of the client, with an in-process proxy for the class factory in the client and an in-process stub in the new server.

Once *CoGetClassObject* returns the class factory, the client can request an object from the class by using the *IClassFactory::CreateInstance* function, as shown in the following code fragment:

```
IHungryMonkey* pmnk;
hr = pfactory->CreateInstance(NULL, IID_IHungryMonkey,
    (void**)&pmnk);
if (SUCCEEDED(hr))
    ⋮
```

Like *CoGetClassObject*, the *CreateInstance* function is generic, requiring an IID to specify the interface that it will place into its generic out-parameter. To satisfy this call to the *CreateInstance* function, the class constructs a new, uninitialized object, returning it to the client with an interface of the requested type.[9] (Presumably some method on the requested *IHungryMonkey* interface, perhaps *Feed*, will initialize the new monkey.)

IClassFactory::CreateInstance

Purpose
Use the *IClassFactory::CreateInstance* method to create an uninitialized object.

Syntax
```
HRESULT CreateInstance ( IUnknown * pUnkOuter, REFIID riid,
    void ** ppvObject );
```

Parameters	Parameter Type	Description
IUnknown * pUnkOuter	In-parameter	Pointer to the controlling unknown of the aggregate (if the object to be created is part of an aggregate); otherwise, this value is NULL.
REFIID riid	In-parameter	The IID of the interface to be used in creating the object.
void ** ppvObject	Out-parameter	Pointer to an interface pointer location.

---

9. I had previously stated that every component first appears to the client as a raw *IUnknown* interface. That was an oversimplification. It actually first appears as an initialization interface that includes *IUnknown*.

Beyond maintaining any remote connections between out-of-process components, the system COM library is now out of the loop. The interaction through the *IClassFactory* interface takes place completely between the client and the component server. Figure 1-12 shows the client interacting first with the system and then with the class.

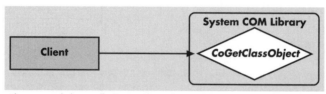

The potential client calls *CoGetClassObject* to request a class object associated with *CLSID_MonkeyHouse*.

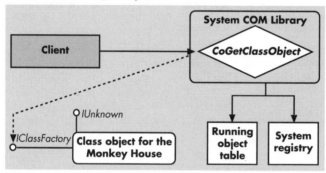

The system COM library checks a running object table to determine whether an instance of the class is available. If not, it consults the system registry and starts the compound code. The system COM library returns the *IClassFactory* interface to the class object.

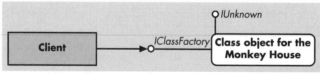

The client calls *IClassFactory::CreateInstance* to create a new object from the Monkey House with the initial interface.

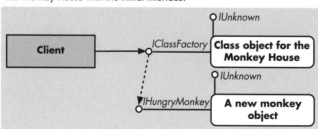

The class object returns the requested interface on a new instance.

Figure 1-12. *A client gets new instances of its objects.*

IClassFactory

The *IClassFactory* interface articulates how a class constructs new instances of its objects. It is implemented by the class object but not by the class's component objects.

How a client gets an interface

A client has access to an object only by holding an interface pointer on that object. To get any other interface, the client must call *IUnknown::QueryInterface* from another interface, as illustrated in Figure 1-13.

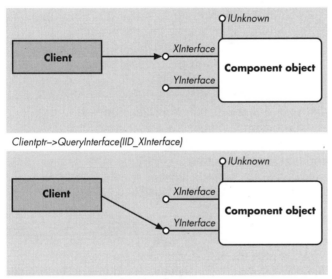

Clientptr–>QueryInterface(IID_XInterface)

Clientptr–>QueryInterface(IID_YInterface)

Figure 1-13. *To get an interface, a client must query for that interface at run time. This client holds a pointer to* X Interface; *if it wants* Y Interface, *it must call* IUnknown::QueryInterface *for* IID_YInterface *on its known* X Interface. *If the implementation of* X *also supports* Y, *as it does in this diagram, the call returns a pointer to* Y Interface.

QueryInterface and its type algebra (involving symmetric, reflexive, and transitive operations) lies at the heart of the COM.

■ All interfaces include the *IUnknown* interface. More precisely, all interfaces contain the methods of the *IUnknown* interface at the same offsets as those used in that interface: 0 for *QueryInterface*, 1 for *AddRef*, and 2 for *Release*. Hence, a client can interact with a particular object's *IUnknown* interface through any interface on that object.

■ From any interface on an object, a client can use *QueryInterface* to obtain access to any other interface on that object. The *QueryInterface* operation is symmetric, reflexive, and transitive.

■ Although all interfaces support the methods of the *IUnknown* interface, only one of them will return in response to a direct query for *IID_IUnknown*. A particular object will always return the same binary value of this *IUnknown* interface pointer for the life of the object. This is the COM component object identity rule: two objects are identical if they return the same binary value to an explicit call to the *QueryInterface* method for the *IUnknown* interface.

■ The set of interfaces that an object supports is fixed for the life of the object. If an object ever denies support for an interface—that is, returns *E_NOINTERFACE* to a call to the *QueryInterface* method for that interface's IID—that object does not support that interface and will similarly refuse all subsequent requests for that interface. If an object ever admits support for an interface—that is, returns *NOERROR* to that call to *QueryInterface*—that object supports that interface and will satisfy all subsequent requests for it as well. These rules apply to object identity, not to class identity; by the laws of COM, it is theoretically possible for one class to instantiate two objects and have them support two divergent sets of interfaces. In other words, type is an attribute of an object, not of a class.

The following sequence continues my Monkey House example and illustrates how to use the *QueryInterface* function to obtain a pointer on an interface specified by *IID_IZooAnimal*. From the initial interface *IHungryMonkey*, the client queries for the interface *IZooAnimal*, representing the functionality it wants in the inhabitants of the Monkey House.

```
IHungryMonkey* pmnk = /* Set as per above.... */
IZooAnimal* panimal;
HRESULT hr = pmnk->QueryInterface(IID_IZooAnimal,
    (void**)&panimal);
if (SUCCEEDED(hr))
    ⋮
```

Since every interface is polymorphic with the *IUnknown* interface, the client invokes the *QueryInterface* function on the interface pointer that it currently holds, *IHungryMonkey*. Like *CoGetClassObject* and *IClassFactory::CreateInstance* before it, the *QueryInterface* function accepts an IID as an in-parameter, using that to set the type of the interface pointer in its returned out-parameter. (Perhaps it would be more accurate to describe the previous two examples presented for the *CoGetClassObject* and *CreateInstance* functions as being like *QueryInterface*, since the *QueryInterface* function is the archetype.)

The result returned by the *QueryInterface* function should be discussed further. If the queried object supports the requested interface, it returns a pointer to that interface in the out-parameter and yields a *NOERROR* result—that is, *SUCCEEDED*. However, if it does not support that interface, it clears the out-parameter (by the rules of COM memory management) and returns *E_NOINTER-FACE*. For example, in the following code fragment, the *QueryInterface* function returns *E_NOINTERFACE* because the *IDieselEngine* interface is not supported by the object *pmnk*:

```
IDieselEngine* pdiesel;
hr = pmnk->QueryInterface(IID_IDieselEngine, (void**)&pdiesel);
ASSERT(hr == E_NOINTERFACE);
```

FYI

The four requirements for implementing *QueryInterface* are as follows:

1. The set of interfaces accessed through *QueryInterface* on an object must be static. A call to *QueryInterface* for a pointer to an interface must succeed in all future calls if it succeeded on the first call, or if it failed on the first call, it must fail in all future calls.

2. It must be symmetric. If the client holds a pointer to *ptr1* and the IID of the interface is *IID_Interface1*, the call *ptr1->QueryInterface(IID_Interface1)* must succeed.

3. It must be reflexive. If a client holds a second pointer *ptr2* from *ptr1->QueryInterface(IID_Interface2), ptr2->QueryInterface(IID_Interface1)* must also succeed.

4. It must be transitive. If a client holds a pointer ptr2 from *ptr1->QueryInterface(IID_Interface2)* and a pointer *ptr3* from *ptr2->QueryInterface(IID_Interface3), ptr3->QueryInterface(IID_Interface1)* must also succeed.

A successful call to the *QueryInterface* function yields a new interface pointer, through which the client can invoke the methods of that interface on the object, as shown in the following example:

```
panimal->DepictOnPicturePostcard();  // New zoo animal activity
pmnk->Feed(banana);  // N.B. the old interface is still valid.
```

The old interface pointer remains available for further interaction if necessary.

The rules for reference counting

Until now, we've been ignoring the rules for managing the life span of an object. In practice, this would be a recipe for disaster: objects would come into existence but never depart, leading eventually to a general collapse where system tables fill, heaps grow to consume all available swap space, file handles are never flushed and closed, object servers never unload, network connections linger forever, and the smirking ghost of Malthus presides over the smoldering ruins of your computer. The converse is even worse: if an object departs while any client keeps an interface pointer to that object and if the client subsequently attempts to invoke a method through that interface, somebody's going to be very disappointed.

The goal of reference counting is to keep an object around only as long as any client has a reference to that object. Every object tracks the number of references made to it by clients; clients participate by informing any component when a new reference appears or an old one lapses. When the component sees its last reference vanish, it knows that no client depends on its existence any longer and so is free to retire.

Because clients can manipulate components only through interface pointers, a reference maps fundamentally to an interface pointer. With every new copy of an interface pointer created, either by a method such as *IClassFactory::Create-Instance* or *IUnknown::QueryInterface* or by making a simple binary copy of the pointer variable, a new reference to that object comes into being. With every copy of an interface pointer that is destroyed, a reference vanishes. This occurs when a copy of the pointer variable is overwritten or is just forgotten or when the copy of the pointer goes out of scope on the stack.

The essential rules of reference counting are simple:

- New objects come into the world with a reference count of 1, since *CreateInstance* hands its caller the only reference to that new object.

- Every new interface pointer or copy of an interface pointer created requires that the client call *IUnknown::AddRef* through that pointer, thus incrementing the object's reference count.

- Every interface pointer or copy of an interface pointer destroyed requires that the client call *IUnknown::Release* through that pointer, thus decrementing the object's reference count.

- The object can expire if the reference count falls to 0.

- A section of code can omit *AddRef/Release* pairs if it has special knowledge that the interface's reference count will remain correct over its lifetime.

This last clause is the optimization clause, yielding the following corollaries:

- Function in-parameters can omit their *AddRef/Release* pairs, because their lifetime is a subset of that of the caller's copy of the pointer, used to instantiate their value.

- Function out-parameters and return values can omit their *AddRef* calls, so long as the function local interface pointer copy that instantiates these parameters is stable and omits its own *Release* at function's end. This transfers reference ownership from the function to its caller.

- Functions can omit *AddRef/Release* pairs where the scoping of local variables clearly makes them redundant.

- A nested object can maintain a back-pointer to its container without reference-counting this pointer at all.

Let's see these rules in action by sending a client to the jungle and reference-counting some monkeys:

```
IClassFactory* pfact;
HRESULT hr = CoGetClassObject (CLSID_MonkeyJungle,
    CLS_INPROC_SERVER|CLSCTX_LOCAL_SERVER,
    NULL,
    IID_IClassFactory,
    (void**) &pfact);
ASSERT (SUCCEEDED(hr));
    /* Since CoGetClassObject is not always successful,
        don't try this at home, kids. */
```

As illustrated in Figure 1-14, the *CoGetClassObject* call returns a class factory interface pointer to the client. The reference count of this Jungle Server class factory is 1, since this client code holds its only interface. The client received the interface in an out-parameter and thus does not need to use the *AddRef* function to increment the reference count, since interfaces received in out-parameters have been stabilized by their creators. Note that the client code does not discriminate between in-process and out-of-process servers—from the client's perspective, they are equivalent.

```
IClassFactory* pfact;
HRESULT hr = CoGetClassObject (CLSID_MonkeyJungle,
    CLSCTX_INPROC_SERVER|CLSCTX_LOCAL_SERVER,
    NULL,
    IID_IClassFactory,
    (void**) &pfact);
```

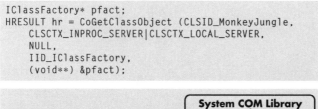

The client code calls *CoGetClassObject* to obtain a pointer to the class object associated with *CLSID_MonkeyJungle*.

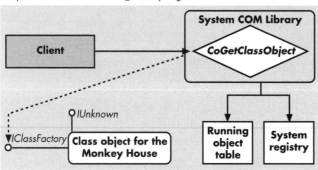

The system COM library returns an interface to the class object.

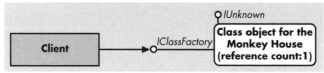

The client code obtains direct access to *IClassFactory*. The reference count is incremented to 1, without a call to *IUnknown::AddRef*.

Figure 1-14. *The client goes to the system to get a class object using* CoGetClassObject.

Figure 1-15 continues the example. The *IClassFactory::CreateInstance* call returns a baby monkey interface pointer to the client. The Jungle Server monkey object has a reference count of 1, because it is a new object and this client holds its only interface. Again, the client code does not need to use the *AddRef* method to set the reference count for this interface pointer.

```
IBabyMonkey* pbaby;
hr = pfact->CreateInstance(NULL, IID_IBabyMonkey, (void**) &pbaby);
```

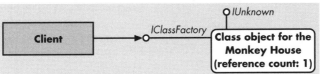

The client code calls *IClassFactory::CreateInstance* to obtain a pointer to the class object associated with *IID_IBabyMonkey*.

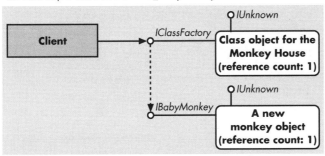

The class object returns the requested interface on a new instance.

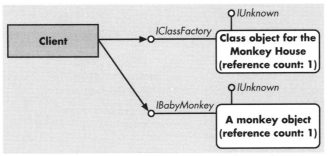

The client code obtains direct access to the *IBabyMonkey* interface.

Figure 1-15. *The client gets an object instance from the class factory by using* IClassFactory::CreateInstance.

Figure 1-16 on the following page shows some trivial use of the new object. The *IUnknown::QueryInterface* call returns a new interface pointer to the client, one embodying the more tourist-oriented aspects of our by now very well fed baby monkey. The monkey object now has a reference count of 2. The client code still does not need to call the *AddRef* method.

```
pbaby->Feed(banana, 100);        // Make it grow up big and strong.
IZooAnimal* panimal;
hr = pbaby->QueryInterface(IID_IZooAnimal, (void**) &panimal);
```

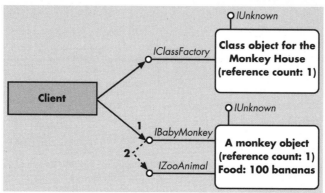

The client code calls (1) *IUnknown::QueryInterface* on the *IBabyMonkey* interface and then (2) *IUnknown::QueryInterface*.

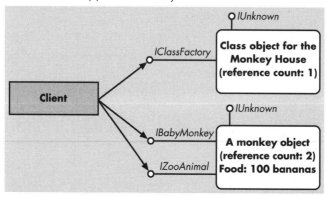

The *IUnknown::QueryInterface* call returns a new interface pointer to the client, thus incrementing the reference count to 2.

Figure 1-16. *The client supplies the monkey with some instance data through its* Feed *method and then requests an additional interface on the object by using the* IUnknown::QueryInterface *function, which it calls through the existing* IBaby-Monkey *interface. This increments the object's reference count.*

Figure 1-17 introduces multiple monkey instances, with the client code creating a new monkey object. Since it reused the baby monkey interface pointer, it destroyed the pointer, thus removing a reference to the first hundred-banana monkey. The client code informs the component of this by calling *IUnknown-::Release* on the pointer before overwriting it. If the out-parameter to *CreateInstance* had been an in/out parameter, calling *Release* would have been the responsibility of the class factory implementation instead of the responsibility of the client; if this is unclear, review the memory management rules for in/out parameters discussed earlier in this chapter. Each monkey object has a reference count of 1.

```
pbaby->Release();
hr = pfact->CreateInstance(NULL, IID_IBabyMonkey, (void**) &pbaby);
pbaby->Feed(lettuce, 50);        // A different diet for this monkey
```

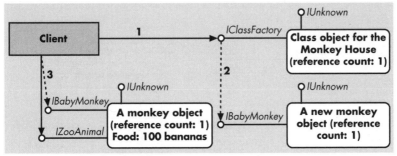

1   The client code calls *IClassFactory::CreateInstance* to obtain a pointer to a new object from the Monkey House.

2   The class object returns the requested interface on a new instance.

3   The client releases the *IBabyMonkey* interface pointer on the first instance.

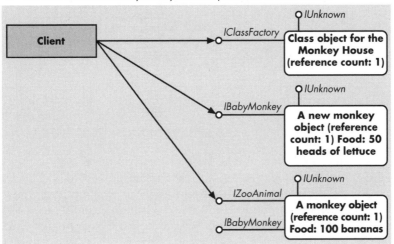

The client code calls *IBabyMonkey::Feed* on the new interface pointer.

Figure 1-17. *The client now requests a second object of the same class as the first and initializes it.*

Figure 1-18 continues our jungle saga. Having fed the second monkey, the client code decides to view it as a zoo animal just like the first monkey. Now the second monkey has 2 outstanding references. Because the client code does not need to create more monkeys (it being a very small zoo), it releases the class factory. The class factory's reference count drops to 0, allowing it to retire. As a point of good form, the client code clears the interface pointer after releasing it, a practice that flushes a certain class of stray-reference bugs.

```
IZooAnimal* panimal2;
hr = pbaby->QueryInterface(IID_IZooAnimal (void**) &panimal2);
pfact->Release();
pfact = NULL
```

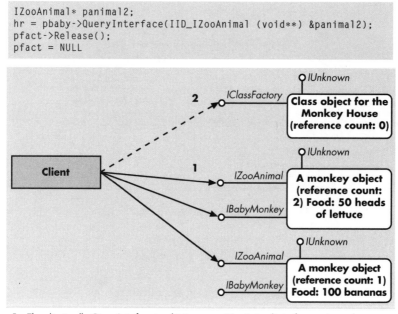

1 The client calls *QueryInterface* to obtain a new *IZooAnimal* interface pointer, thus incrementing the reference count to 2.

2 The client releases the class factory.

Figure 1-18. *When the client no longer needs the class object for creating objects, it releases it.*

Figure 1-19 concludes our zoo story. Having finished with the baby monkey interface, the client code releases it and then sets the pointer to NULL to prevent errors. Finally, the client demonstrates an obvious local optimization as it swaps its two pointers to zoo animal interfaces through a temporary pointer. Even though it copies interface pointers several times, it calls neither *AddRef* nor *Release* on any of these, since the life span of the new copy lies completely within the scope of the already stable interface pointers.

```
pbaby->Release();
pbaby = NULL;
IZooAnimal* panimalSwap;
panimalSwap = panimal;
panimal = panimal2;
panimal2 = panimalSwap;
panimalSwap = NULL;
```

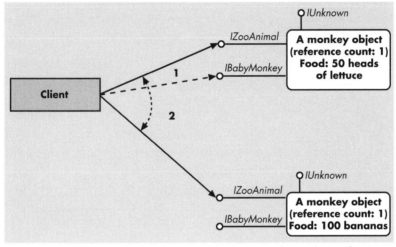

The client code (1) releases the pointer to the *IBabyMonkey* interface and (2) performs local optimization of the pointers.

Figure 1-19. *The reference count is preserved through a local manipulation.*

Automating reference counting

Like so many repetitive, mechanical tasks, reference counting is tedious and prone to error. The following function displays several instances of the *Request, Use, Release* idiom used repeatedly:

```
BOOL Demonstration()
{
    IClassFactory* pfact;
    HRESULT hr = CoGetClassObject(CLSID_MonkeyJungle,
        CLSCTX_INPROC_SERVER|CLSCTX_LOCAL_SERVER,
        NULL,
        IID_IClassFactory,
        (void**)&pfact);
```

(continued)

```
if (FAILED(hr))
    return FALSE;
IBabyMonkey* pbaby;
hr = pfact->CreateInstance(NULL, IID_IBabyMonkey,
    (void**)&pbaby);
if (FAILED(hr))
{
    pfact->Release();
    return FALSE;
}
pfact->Release(); /* No longer need the class factory */
pfact = NULL;
hr = pbaby->Feed(banana, 100);
if (FAILED(hr))
{
    pbaby->Release();
    return FALSE;
}
IZooAnimal* panimal;
hr = pbaby->QueryInterface(IID_IZooAnimal, (void**)&panimal);
if (FAILED(hr))
{
    pbaby->Release();
    return FALSE;
}
hr = panimal->SomeOtherMethod();
if (FAILED(hr))
{
    panimal->Release();
    pbaby->Release();
    return FALSE;
}
hr = pbaby->YetAnotherMethod();
if (FAILED(hr))
{
    panimal->Release();
    pbaby->Release();
    return FALSE;
}
panimal->Release();
pbaby->Release();
return TRUE;
}
```

Request, Use, Release

The life cycle of the class factory illustrates a common idiom in COM client coding: *Request, Use, Release*. The client code initially requests an interface pointer to some object, gaining a reference to the object. It uses that interface for a while. (Since it has a reference and that reference has been counted by the request code—for example, *QueryInterface*—the object will remain for the duration of the client's usage.) Finally, when the client code no longer needs the object, it releases the interface, signaling to the object that it is doing so using *IUnknown::Release*.

```
Interface* pi;
hr = Request(&pi);
if (SUCCEEDED(hr))
{
    pi->Use();
    /* … */
    pi->Release();
    pi = NULL;
}
```

This extremely simple example spent more programmer bandwidth on unwinding its state and sequencing various calls to *IUnknown::Release* than it did on program logic. The resulting maze is difficult to read and prone to error, particularly during code maintenance, because the maintainer can confirm that any particular exit point unwinds the function's references only by tracing the lifetime of each interface pointer.

Reordering the code's flow-of-control can collapse the myriad exit paths into one, as shown in the following example:

```
BOOL Demonstration2()
{
    IClassFactory* pfact = NULL;
    IBabyMonkey* pbaby = NULL;
    IZooAnimal* panimal = NULL;

    HRESULT hr = CoGetClassObject(CLSID_MonkeyJungle,
        CLSCTX_INPROC_SERVER|CLSCTX_LOCAL_SERVER,
```

(continued)

```
        NULL,
        IID_IClassFactory,
        (void**)&pfact);
    if (FAILED(hr))
        goto unwind;
    hr = pfact->CreateInstance(NULL, IID_IBabyMonkey,
        (void**)&pbaby);
    if (FAILED(hr))
        goto unwind;
    hr = pbaby->Feed(banana, 100);
    if (FAILED(hr))
        goto unwind;
    hr = pbaby->QueryInterface(IID_IZooAnimal, (void**)&panimal);
    if (FAILED(hr))
        goto unwind;
    hr = panimal->SomeOtherMethod();
    if (FAILED(hr))
        goto unwind;
    hr = pbaby->YetAnotherMethod();
    if (FAILED(hr))
        goto unwind;

unwind:
    if (panimal)
        panimal->Release();
    if (pbaby)
        pbaby->Release();
    if (pfact)
        pfact->Release();
    return (SUCCEEDED(hr));
}
```

This rolls all of the state unwinding logic into a single compact block, taking advantage of the code's close association between fetching an interface pointer and getting a new reference on the backing object. (It differs slightly from the first example in that it holds the class factory reference until the end of the function.) Maintenance programmers can easily verify that every implicit *IUnknown::AddRef* has its single matching call to *Release*. The block of interface pointer variables declared at the function's opening exactly matches the set of *Release* calls at the end.

Anti-*goto* activists will object to this pattern's flurry of *goto* statements. (Although the program could also contain a sequence of nested *if* statements, the resulting cascade is extremely difficult to read and write.) More substantively, C++ stylists will observe that these statements change the data declaration pattern, forcing every local variable definition to take place before the first *goto* statement. Defining a local variable later in a block allows the programmer to create it correctly initialized, eliminating the unsafe period in which the variable is defined but has no value. Also, many class locals have constructors with useful side effects, which activate when the flow-of-control reaches the local's definition in the block. This *goto*-laden idiom thus negates some very useful features of the C++ language.

The following example uses the results of each method invocation as a flag to permit subsequent invocations:

```
BOOL Demonstration3()
{
    IClassFactory* pfact = NULL;
    IBabyMonkey* pbaby = NULL;
    IZooAnimal* panimal = NULL;

    HRESULT hr = CoGetClassObject(CLSID_MonkeyJungle,
        CLSCTX_INPROC_SERVER|CLSCTX_LOCAL_SERVER,
        NULL,
        IID_IClassFactory,
        (void**)&pfact);

    if (SUCCEEDED(hr))
        hr = pfact->CreateInstance(NULL, IID_IBabyMonkey,
            (void**)&pbaby);
    if (SUCCEEDED(hr))
        hr = pbaby->Feed(banana, 100);
    if (SUCCEEDED(hr))
        hr = pbaby->QueryInterface(IID_IZooAnimal,
            (void**)&panimal);
    if (SUCCEEDED(hr))
        hr = panimal->SomeOtherMethod();
    if (SUCCEEDED(hr))
        hr = pbaby->YetAnotherMethod();

    if (panimal)
        panimal->Release();
    if (pbaby)
        pbaby->Release();
    if (pfact)
        pfact->Release();

    return (SUCCEEDED(hr));
}
```

This still doesn't work well if the function needs to construct local class objects in midstream, because each such object would be constrained to the scope of its bounding *if* statement.

NOTE When an object is constructed within a block of code (for example, within an *if* statement), the scope of that object is limited to that block of code and to the blocks of code nested inside of it. This is called *local scope*. When a pointer is declared inside of a class, the scope of that pointer is the class in which the pointer was declared. This is called *class scope*.

This uniquely C++ problem demands a C++ solution. By embedding each of the interface pointers in a class wrapper and then defining that class wrapper to call *Release* in its destructor, we can guarantee that each reference is released when the pointer goes out of scope. While this doesn't address every permutation of reference counting, the following example handles *Request, Use, Release* very nicely, completely automating this common idiom:

```
BOOL Demonstration4()
{
    SafeIPtr<IClassFactory> spfact;
    HRESULT hr = CoGetClassObject(CLSID_MonkeyJungle,
        CLSCTX_INPROC_SERVER|CLSCTX_LOCAL_SERVER,
        NULL,
        IID_IClassFactory,
        spfact.Adopt());
    if (FAILED(hr))
        return FALSE;

    SafeIPtr<IBabyMonkey> spbaby;
    hr = spfact->CreateInstance(NULL, IID_IBabyMonkey,
        spbaby.Adopt());
    if (FAILED(hr))
        return FALSE;
    hr = spbaby->Feed(banana, 100);
    if (FAILED(hr))
        return FALSE;

    SafeIPtr<IZooAnimal> spanimal;
    hr = spbaby->QueryInterface(IID_IZooAnimal, spanimal.Adopt());
    if (FAILED(hr))
        return FALSE;
    hr = spanimal->SomeOtherMethod();
    if (FAILED(hr))
```

```
            return FALSE;
        hr = spbaby->YetAnotherMethod();
        if (FAILED(hr))
            return FALSE;

        return TRUE;
    }

template <class Interface>
class SafeIPtr
{
private:
    Interface* _pi;

    void SafeAddRef()
        { if (0 != _pi) _pi->AddRef(); }
    void SafeRelease()
        { if (0 != _pi) _pi->Release(); }

public:
    SafeIPtr(): _pi(0) {}
    SafeIPtr(const SafeIPtr& r) : _pi(r._pi)
        { SafeAddRef(); }
    SafeIPtr(Interface* p, BOOL fAdopt = FALSE): _pi(p)
        { if (!fAdopt) SafeAddRef(); }
    ~SafeIPtr()
        { SafeRelease(); }

    const SafeIPtr& operator=(const SafeIPtr& r)
        { if (this != &r)
            { SafeRelease(); _pi = r._pi; SafeAddRef(); }
        return *this; }
    const Interface*& operator=(const Interface*& p)
        { SafeRelease(); _pi = p; SafeAddRef(); return p; }

    operator Interface*() const    { return _pi; }
    Interface* operator->() const  { return _pi; }

    void** Adopt()          { SafeRelease(); _pi = 0; return &_pi; }
    void Adopt(Interface* pi) { SafeRelease(); _pi = pi; }
    void Abandon() { _pi = 0; }
};

#define DECLARE_SAFE_INTERFACE(i) typedef SafeIPtr<i> Sp##i
```

Instead of using interface pointers, this fragment uses a *smart pointer* template class that builds a suitably typed wrapper on the fly. The smart pointer overloads its pointer-indirection operator to reference the embedded interface pointer, allowing clients to treat the smart pointer as an interface pointer for most purposes. When it proves necessary to graft such a safe interface wrapper on an existing reference, the *SafeIPtr::Adopt* and *SafeIPtr::Abandon* methods (shown in the preceding code sample) provide a mechanism to short-circuit the class's precise pairing of *AddRef* calls with *Release* calls.

More sophisticated and complete approaches to automating reference counting are certainly possible. In general, the more extensive the framework, the more thoroughly the environment can automate the process.[10]

> **NOTE** The various samples in this book adopt differing reference count management strategies, as befits their differing degrees of complexity. Code with little use of local class objects may use the jump-to-common-unwind-clause strategy, as seen in the *CStubPostForm::HrRespondForm* function of the file Chap06\Poststub\FORM.CPP. More complex code uses smart pointers, as seen in the *CTargetMessage::WrapInto* function of the file Chap07\Fwd-asatt\WORK.CPP. Given the simple nature of most tutorial code, however, most samples simply release all references with every exit path.

As a Server

Now we move on to see the functionality of the server in the COM world. A server's role is to offer components to prospective clients. Thus, a server is a body of code that implements interfaces, component objects, and class objects.

As discussed early in this chapter, servers come in two flavors: in-process and out-of-process. The mechanics of implementing objects remain the same for these two models, however. Their implementations differ only in the framework surrounding the class object—the code that returns a class object to the system COM library—and in the details of keeping a server running.

Implementing an interface

An interface is nothing more than a table of functions that adheres to the COM binary interface standard. The server must provide an implementation for each

10. Don Box presents an extremely sophisticated example of a class framework to automate reference counting in "Building C++ Components Using OLE2," which appeared in the *C++ Report*, Volume 7, Number 3. See also his *combind* library at *http://www.develop.com/combind.htm*.

of these functions, build the table, and supply access to the table on demand—that is, whenever a client or an RPC stub acting on behalf of a client needs to invoke a method.

The easiest way to build an interface is to describe it as a C++ abstract base class. This defines the structure of the backing table, giving each row in the table a name and a type. The resulting abstract base class definition can serve to guide both the implementation and any clients of the class. In the following example, the *Feed* method is declared as a method on the *IBabyMonkey* interface:

```
struct IBabyMonkey: public Iunknown
{
    virtual HRESULT __stdcall Feed(enum FOOD food, int c) = 0;
};
```

The following interface definition inherits from the definition of *IUnknown*, which reads something like this:

```
struct Iunknown
{
    virtual HRESULT __stdcall QueryInterface(REFIID iid, void**ppv)
        = 0;
    virtual ULONG __stdcall AddRef() = 0;
    virtual ULONG __stdcall Release() = 0;
};
```

Taking into account the polymorphism of class *IBabyMonkey* with class *IUnknown*, the *IBabyMonkey* vtable actually looks like this:

```
struct IBabyMonkey
{
    virtual HRESULT __stdcall QueryInterface(REFIID iid, void**ppv)
        = 0;
    virtual ULONG __stdcall AddRef() = 0;
    virtual ULONG __stdcall Release() = 0;

    virtual HRESULT __stdcall Feed(enum FOOD food, int c) = 0;
};
```

NOTE Since every COM interface inherits from the *IUnknown* interface, the first three elements of every component object's vtable must contain the above function definitions, referencing implementations of the *IUnknown* interface methods for the object.

More typically, we use macros to increase the portability of the code to other platforms. These macros include *STDMETHOD*, *STDMETHOD_*, *THIS*, *THIS_*, *PURE*, and *DECLARE_INTERFACE_*, defined in the header files of the Win32 SDK (OBJBASE.H) and included with most C-based development environments, to abstract over the calling sequence. A definition that uses these macros can deliver its services to C and C++ clients.[11] In the following example, some of these macros are used:

```
#undef INTERFACE
#define INTERFACE IBabyMonkey
DECLARE_INTERFACE_(IBabyMonkey, IUnknown)
{
    STDMETHODIMP(Feed)(THIS_ enum FOOD food, int c) PURE;
};
```

The inventor of an interface—as opposed to the author of a particular implementation of the interface—must allocate an IID, a GUID, naming the interface. This is the true name of the interface, the one that *IUnknown::QueryInterface* and other such methods will recognize; anything else is just syntactic sugaring for the programmer's sake. The tool UUIDGEN.EXE will generate a correct GUID, as will GUIDGEN.EXE.

NOTE Both UUIDGEN.EXE and GUIDGEN.EXE are available in Microsoft Visual C++ version 4. Other development environments may offer the same or equivalent tools.

Most servers implement already existing interfaces, in which case they use the existing GUID and the existing abstract base class definition for the interface. Implementing the interface consists of defining a class that inherits from this abstract base class and then supplying an implementation for the class, as follows:

```
class CBabyMonkeyImpl: public IBabyMonkey { /* … */ };
```

This class has a member function implementing each method on the interface. A server hands out base pointers to instances of this class as interface pointers. When the client calls through this base pointer, it executes the member function that corresponds to the requested method.

---

11. Without such a portable definition, the interface's author would either have to maintain a separate header file for potential C-language clients or leave those clients to generate their own definition.

Implementing a component object

A component object is a set of available interfaces and their implementations, together with some instance data. The server hands back a pointer to one of its interfaces to the client; from that interface, the client can request any number of other interfaces on the same object. The basic problem here is one of interface management: tracking those interfaces, handing back the correct pointers to clients, and having each of those interfaces find its per-object instance data as necessary.

If the component object offers only a single interface (plus, of course, *IUnknown*), its implementation is straightforward. The server author defines a class that inherits from the interface in question and then implements the class. A pointer to the class is isomorphic with an interface pointer to the class so long as the class first inherits from its interface before any other classes containing virtual functions. Since every interface is polymorphic with *IUnknown*, the object does not need to carry an extra vtable in requests for *IUnknown*. It can simply return that of its primary interface.

In the following example, the class *CBabyMonkeyImpl* is defined:

```
class CBabyMonkeyImpl: public IBabyMonkey
{
private:
    ULONG _cRef;
    ⋮
public:
    // IUnknown methods
    STDMETHODIMP(QueryInterface)(REFIID iid, void**ppv);
    STDMETHODIMP_(ULONG, AddRef)();
    STDMETHODIMP_(ULONG, Release)();
    // IBabyMonkey methods
    STDMETHODIMP(Feed)(enum FOOD food, int c);

    CBabyMonkeyImpl();
};
```

The class keeps the component object's instance data as private member variables and implements each method as a member function. The following functions show an object's implementations of *AddRef* and *Release*:

```
STDMETHODIMP_(ULONG) CBabyMonkeyImpl::AddRef()
{
    return ++_cRef;
}
```

(continued)

```
STDMETHODIMP_(ULONG) CBabyMonkeyImpl::Release()
{
    ULONG cTmp =--_cRef;
    if (cTmp == 0)
        delete this;
    return cTmp;
}


CBabyMonkeyImpl::CBabyMonkeyImpl() : _cRef(1){}
```

These accepted implementations of *AddRef* and *Release* are frequently written
in line. An object—a component object, which this class implements—is created with a reference count of 1. Each new reference increments the count,
whereas each removed reference decrements it. When the object sees that no
client holds any more references to it, or rather when it assumes as much from
its reference count falling to 0, it invokes its own destructor and returns its dynamically allocated memory to the server's heap.

The following function shows how an object's implementation of *QueryInterface*
assigns pointers to interfaces.

```
STDMETHODIMP CBabyMonkeyImpl::QueryInterface(REFIID riid,void**
    ppvObj)
{
    HRESULT hr = S_OK;
    *ppvObj = NULL;

    if ( (IID_IUnknown == riid) || (IID_IBabyMonkey == riid) )
        *ppvObj = (IBabyMonkey*)this;
    else
        hr = E_NOINTERFACE;

    if (NULL != *ppvObj)
        ((IUnknown*)*ppvObj)->AddRef();
    return hr;
}
```

Since this simple monkey object supports only one interface, its interface management requirements are simple. If it recognizes the interface, it passes back a
pointer to the implementation's vtable; otherwise, it returns a result signifying
that the caller requested an interface not supported by the component. Since
IUnknown and *IBabyMonkey* have their first three methods in common, any
request for *IUnknown* simply returns the vtable for *IBabyMonkey*. Note that
QueryInterface increments the interface's reference count before it returns. In

this class, the interface is one with the class, so it did not need to do so through the interface pointer; it could have simply called its own *AddRef* member or even incremented the counter member directly. The indirection is a legacy of other interface management architectures where separate interfaces operate as separate subobjects.

The comparison statements bear further discussion, because they are actually hiding beneath a couple of layers of syntactic camouflage. The caller passes *QueryInterface* a REFIID, or "reference to an IID," which is really just a pointer to a GUID structure or, in C++, a reference to that structure. The object implementation compares that REFIID against the IIDs of the interfaces that it supports: both *IID_IUnknown* and *IID_IBabyMonkey* are the names of static GUID structures in the implementing server's image. The Win32 SDK overloads the C++ equality operator to compare two IIDs with the API *IsEqualIID*.

During development, *E_NOTIMPLEMENTED* should be returned by any incomplete method, as follows:

```
STDMETHODIMP CBabyMonkeyImpl::Feed(enum FOOD food, int c)
{ return E_NOTIMPLEMENTED; }
```

In a shipping component, this would constitute a bug, since by including an incomplete method, a component violates the contract that it signed when it returned *S_OK* to a *QueryInterface* for that component.

Complex component objects

A component object that supports more than one interface requires a slightly more sophisticated interface management scheme. It cannot depend on passing out raw pointers to its vtable to clients, since its vtable no longer matches any interface. Instead, it must return pointers to different vtables, as needed.

The simplest approach starts with the scheme of a simple component object (uses the class's vtable as that of the interface) and generalizes it to handle multiple interfaces. Taking each of the different vtables of the interfaces, it concatenates them into one master vtable and then uses that vtable as the backbone of a C++ class. When clients call for an interface, it returns pointers offset into the class's master vtable.

Multiple inheritance of interface base classes suffices to build the master vtable. The following line of code shows how a class can inherit these base classes:

```
class CBabyMonkeyImpl: public IBabyMonkey, public IZooAnimal
```

Then the *QueryInterface* implementation must return an offset pointer, as follows:

```
STDMETHODIMP CBabyMonkeyImpl::QueryInterface(REFIID riid,
    void** ppvObj)
{
    HRESULT hr = S_OK;
    *ppvObj = NULL;

    if ( (IID_IUnknown == riid) || (IID_IBabyMonkey == riid) )
        *ppvObj = (IBabyMonkey*)this;
    else if (IID_IZooAnimal == riid)
        *ppvObj = (IZooAnimal*)this;
    else
        hr = E_NOINTERFACE;

    if (NULL != *ppvObj)
        ((IUnknown*)*ppvObj)->AddRef();
    return hr;
}
```

Note the cast operators applied to the *this* pointer in each case. These are significant because they return offsets into the vtable that corresponds to the base class of each cast.

Both interfaces supported are derived from *IUnknown*. It does not matter which is returned in response to queries for *IUnknown* so long as the choice is consistent. (Recall that this is the identity test for component objects.) The C++ compiler sets both of the *IUnknown* slots in the vtable—there are indeed two, one for *IBabyMonkey* and one for *IZooAnimal*—with the address of the suitably named members of *CBabyMonkeyImpl*. However, if the base classes share other member functions with the same name and if those twin functions have different semantics—that is, they cannot share a single implementation in the class—the component object cannot use multiple inheritance in this manner.

Another approach to supporting multiple interfaces encapsulates each interface in its own subclass, contained within a master class embodying the object as a whole. This allows a component developer to reference count each interface separately, a technique that can prove useful for managing large components. Encapsulation of the *IBabyMonkey* and *IZooAnimal* interfaces is shown in the following example:

```
class CBabyMonkeyImpl: public IUnknown
{
private:
    class CBabyImpl: public IBabyMonkey { /* … */ }
    class CZooImpl: public IZooAnimal { /* … */ }
public:
    ⋮
};
```

The class might keep private instances of each of these classes, or it might allocate them dynamically. In either case, it returns a pointer to the suitable subobject in response to *QueryInterface* requests. Such an implementation must ensure that any subobject has access to the other interfaces and that reference counting on subobjects is correctly reflected in the master object.

In some cases, a component object might need to implement an interface through *aggregation*—that is, including a whole other component object to supply the interface. For more on that topic, see the *OLE Programmer's Guide*.

Implementing a class object in-process

Any component that a client finds through the system COM library requires a class factory. Recall that a class factory is a particular flavor of component object, one that makes itself available through a distinguished interface on the server code. Although this interface differs between in-process and out-of-process servers, the basic class factory itself works the same way.

Class factories are simple component objects derived from the *IClassFactory* interface. Once a client has hold of a factory, which it obtains by calling the system API *CoGetClassObject*, it uses that factory to create new instances of the class's component object using *IClassFactory::CreateInstance*, as shown in the following example:

```
class CJungleFactory: public IClassFactory
{
public:
    static UINT cObjs;
    static UINT cLocks;

private:
    ULONG _cRef;
    :
public:
    // IUnknown methods
    STDMETHOD(QueryInterface)(REFIID iid, void**ppv);
    STDMETHOD_(ULONG, AddRef)();
    STDMETHOD_(ULONG, Release)();
    // IClassFactory methods
    STDMETHOD(CreateInstance)(IUnknown* punkOuter, REFIID iid,
        void** ppv);
    STDMETHOD(LockServer)(BOOL fLock);

    CJungleFactory() : _cRef(1) {}
    ~CJungleFactory() {}
```

(continued)

```
    static void OnObjectCreated();
    static void OnObjectDestroyed();
};

UINT CJungleFactory::cObjs = 0;
UINT CJungleFactory::cLocks = 0;

STDMETHODIMP CJungleFactory::CreateInstance(IUnknown* punkOuter,
    REFIID iid, void** ppv)
{
    if (NULL != punkOuter)
        return CLASS_E_NOAGGREGATION;
    if (NULL == ppv)
        return E_INVALIDARG;
    CBabyMonkeyImpl* pmnk = new CBabyMonkeyImpl;
    if (NULL == pmnk)
        return E_OUTOFMEMORY;
    HRESULT hr = pmnk->QueryInterface(iid, ppv);
    pmnk->Release();
    return hr;
}
```

The first parameter to *CreateInstance* is used only in aggregation, which this server does not support. (Again, if this interests you, see the *OLE Programmer's Guide.*) The rest is simple. It creates a new instance of the component object and then queries the interface that it needs off of it. If that succeeds, the code will have two references to the object—one from the first allocation and one from the additional interface that it holds—so it has to discard one through *Release.* If that fails, it will have only one reference, and this *Release* will let the object vanish completely. The *QueryInterface* function has passed an interface pointer from the component object back to the caller, and that pointer serves as the caller's initial handle to the object.

The rest of the details of a class factory depend on the server that implements it: in-process or out-of-process.

Implementing an in-process server

As noted, servers are the bodies of code that implement class objects. The registry associates a particular server with a CLSID, as in the example shown in Figure 1-20. This shows the system COM library what code to load when a client requests a class object through *CoGetClassObject.*

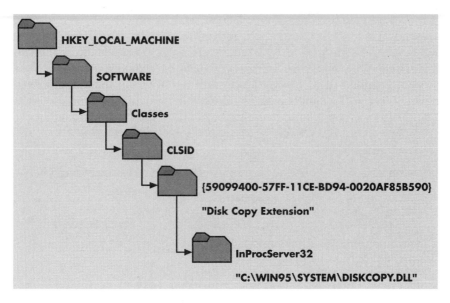

Figure 1-20. *Registry information for a registered server.*

An in-process server operates as a DLL that COM loads to access its component objects. Once the system has loaded the server, it needs some entry into that server to locate the class object. By convention, every in-process server exports an entry point *DllGetClassObject*. The following function does nothing more than return an interface to the class object for a particular CLSID:

```
STDAPI DllGetClassObject(REFCLSID clsid, REFIID iid, void** ppv)
{
    if (CLSID_MonkeyJungle != clsid)
        return CLASS_E_CLASSNOTAVAILABLE;
    if (NULL == ppv)
        return E_INVALIDARG;
    CJungleFactory* pjung = new CJungleFactory;
    if (NULL == pjung)
        return E_OUTOFMEMORY;
    HRESULT hr = pjung->QueryInterface(iid, ppv);
    pjung->Release();
    return hr;
}
```

A server can implement more than one class, so the entry point *DllGetClassObject* specifies the CLSID of the particular class sought by the client. Beyond that, the routine acts like *IClassFactory::CreateInstance* in its particulars.

Ideally the system unloads the server DLL when it is no longer needed. The server signals that it is safe to unload by returning *S_OK* from another exported entry point, *DllCanUnloadNow*, which the system calls periodically, usually in response to a client *CoFreeUnusedLibraries* call. *DllCanUnloadNow* should refuse permission to unload the DLL—that is, return *S_FALSE*—if the server is still running any objects. The simplest way to track objects involves keeping a count of outstanding objects, similar to the reference counts that most component objects keep. Every managed object's constructor should increment the count, and every destructor should decrement it.

The following sample code shows how the system unloads the server DLL:

```
void CJungleFactory::OnObjectCreated()
{ ++CJungleFactory::cObjs; }

void CJungleFactory::OnObjectDestroyed()
{ --CJungleFactory::cObjs; }

CBabyMonkeyImpl::CBabyMonkeyImpl()
{
    ⋮
    CJungleFactory::OnObjectCreated();
}

CBabyMonkeyImpl::~CBabyMonkeyImpl()
{
    ⋮
    CJungleFactory::OnObjectDestroyed();
}

STDAPI DllCanUnloadNow()
{
    return ((CJungleFactory::cObjs) == 0 &&
        (CJungleFactory::cLocks == 0)) ? S_OK : S_FALSE;
```

If the server changes its implementation to be out-of-process, it might want to take more action when the object count falls to 0; hence, all object counts are manipulated through an intermediary call.

A client might want to keep a server in memory even through periods when it does not service any objects. It does that by calling *IClassFactory::LockServer*, which sets a server lock that lasts until the client unlocks it. Note that *DllCanUnloadNow* checks a lock count as well as an object count. The corresponding implementation of the interface method merely increments and decrements this count, as follows:

```
STDMETHODIMP CJungleFactory::LockServer(BOOL fLock)
{
    if (fLock)
        ++cLocks;
    else
        --cLocks;
    return S_OK;
}
```

As long as any server locks or active objects are outstanding, the server DLL refuses to allow COM to unload it. Once all activity in the server ceases, however, the server grants permission the next time it is asked.

Implementing an out-of-process server

Like an in-process server, an out-of-process server (Figure 1-21) appears in the registry, indexed under the CLSID of the class it implements. When the system finds that it has to load such a server, it looks up the path of the executable code module necessary and then *spawns* that image—that is, creates a process/task to host a particular code image—using *CreateProcess*.

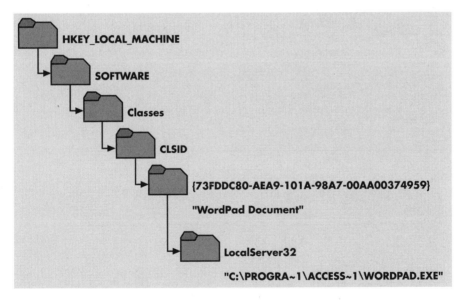

HKEY_LOCAL_MACHINE

SOFTWARE

Classes

CLSID

{73FDDC80-AEA9-101A-98A7-00AA00374959}

"WordPad Document"

LocalServer32

"C:\PROGRA~1\ACCESS~1\WORDPAD.EXE"

Figure 1-21. *Registry information for an out-of-process server.*

Unlike in-process servers, however, the out-of-process server is running in its own process (obviously), not under the direct control of the system COM library. COM cannot call into the server and get its class object; instead, it must wait for the server to call it back with a class object. COM then sets up the remote connection needed between client and server.

A server executable knows that COM has spawned it by the presence of the */Embedding* switch on the command line. When it sees this, it must create a class factory for each of its classes and then register that class factory by calling back to COM with *CoRegisterClassObject*. The server runs until it sees its object and lock counts drop to zero, whereupon it exits.

We'll return to out-of-process server implementation issues in Chapters 5 and 6, when we examine MAPI form servers.

Alternative class object designs

The preceding pages describe a design where a CLSID identifies a class of component objects. Some objects limit themselves to a particular working domain and so forgo CLSIDs and class objects in favor of a different naming and location scheme. Such objects are not true component objects, because they work by a different set of rules and so cannot fully interoperate with other objects. Within their own domain, however, they behave as components.

Most of MAPI implements individual classes in such a deviant manner. We will examine MAPI and its idiosyncrasies in the next chapter.

2

The Win32 Messaging API

Chapter 2 provides the second of three parts of the complete technical introduction to developing applications for Microsoft Exchange. If you are already familiar with MAPI and ActiveX (formerly called OLE), you can proceed to the next chapter.

MAPI: The Architecture of Messaging Applications

At a very abstract level, COM describes how objects work together to construct a component architecture. These rules can describe how a word processing application runs accessory applications, how an automated kitchen interacts with household appliances, or how a computer game loads and describes different virtual worlds. COM contains no intrinsic content; there is no domain to COM itself. COM promises only to let components work together based on its rules. Built on top of COM, the Microsoft Messaging Application Programming Interface (MAPI) provides the next necessary layer of structure. Components must all agree on what interfaces they will use. Using the rules laid down by COM, MAPI defines standard interfaces, roles, and relationships for *messaging* objects and describes an overall architecture for messaging on the desktop.

Such applications will have a wide platform base because MAPI is available on all Windows-based desktops. Windows 95 and Windows NT 4.0 contain support for MAPI applications that are part of the included Windows Messaging Subsystem, while previous versions of Windows—Windows NT 3.51 and the MS-DOS–based Windows for Workgroups 3.11—support MAPI through an installable set of components.[1]

---

1. See ftp://ftp.microsoft.com/developr/MAPI/redist.

Standardization of Messaging Architecture

First and foremost, MAPI is valuable because it provides a standard in its messaging architecture. Programmers need not study a myriad of different interfaces and need not spend effort developing applications and services for each interface. This simplifies the development of new messaging applications. Furthermore, it encourages extension of conventional applications with messaging and information-sharing functions. With so many competing standards, messaging application developers faced with a new one must ask themselves the question: why bother with another one? Why MAPI? In short, whereas most messaging standards concern themselves with a particular underlying messaging system, MAPI focuses on the applications that use those systems.

Users benefit from the interoperability of components that are written to MAPI, as well as from the greater number of applications that results from simplifying development.

Extensible Component Architecture

MAPI inherits all the virtues[2] of COM, its object foundation. Every MAPI service describes itself as a component and is accessible as one (with some variations that I'll describe shortly). Available to all MAPI applications is a world of components offering their services. If an application needs the services of other objects in the system, the application finds that all those objects obey the same rules of object interaction, protocol negotiation, lifespan, and return codes.

An application receives the services of any installed component willing to play the desired role; there is no need to limit an application to work with one messaging system unless that application seeks services unique to that system. MAPI goes beyond the normal generic object access mechanisms of COM in supporting a couple of different notions of *object sets*. For example, installed message stores or address books make it easier for applications to interact with all the objects in a particular set in parallel. With MAPI, a service can extend the desktop messaging architecture by adding a component without necessarily replacing other components in that role.

Although COM doesn't sufficiently address all differences between the various messaging systems, MAPI interfaces are designed for extensibility, minimizing any changes necessary in an application.

This means that users can receive a class of messaging applications that can interact with multiple underlying messaging systems—for example, a mail client that can handle both CompuServe and MCI Mail, or a document library that works against both Mesa Conferences Plus and Exchange Server public folders.

---

2. Yes, it inherits its vices too.

Separation of Application and Messaging System

The MAPI architecture defines a number of distinct roles that its components play and, in doing so, separates client applications from the underlying message services.

Both application and service authors benefit from this separation. Application authors gain a layer of abstraction, allowing their products to run against a number of messaging systems. As long as the applications conform to the features common to all MAPI service providers, authors need release only a single version of the application; they can address a specific feature of a backing messaging system while retaining a common implementation for the majority of the application's function. For service (or messaging system) authors, this layer of abstraction means they need not invent their own user interface and application support. Both application and service authors remain free to work within their own area of expertise. Users gain the ability to utilize their familiar desktop applications against whatever messaging system fate—or their Information Systems department—thrusts upon them.

Rich API

Unlike most generic service APIs, MAPI is quite rich, perfectly able to support document-intensive workgroup and messaging applications within the generic confines of the interface. Although this presents a challenge for prospective authors of MAPI-compliant messaging services, it allows client applications more interesting functionality, while remaining portable across messaging platforms. Users gain a class of portable applications more interesting than "Hello, world" or "Scribble."

The User Features of the Windows Messaging Subsystem (WMS)

WMS, the Windows Messaging Subsystem, is MAPI's standard user interface. It provides a mechanism for grouping sets of desired messaging services into "profiles" that it can run simultaneously, a standard desktop application for viewing those services, and a standard set of basic services, such as an address book for e-mail addresses and a folder for storing received messages. All users of Microsoft Windows 95 or Microsoft Windows NT have WMS on their desktops.

WMS frees service developers from having to write a user interface layer to host their messaging system on Windows 95 or Windows NT. Application developers have the features of this client, plus those of its ancillary services, to call upon in their own applications.

Users benefit from seeing the same interface within the context of any messaging system they might use and from that interface's effective integration of all their services used into a single "Universal Inbox," courtesy of its generic treatment of messaging objects.

The MAPI Architecture

Like any complicated structure, MAPI offers a number of different architectural perspectives on itself, depending on the vantage point of the viewer. In this section, three perspectives are discussed: the component model, the process model, and the object model.

In the *component model,* MAPI consists of layers of components that call each other through a broker layer that acts as a mediator. This broker layer, which is implemented in MAPI32.DLL, manages the relationship between applications and messaging services. On one side, MAPI32.DLL acts as a broker for service providers—components that provide services for message transport, persistent storage, and address directories. On the other side, MAPI32.DLL acts as a broker for the applications that use those services. The client applications contact the broker, which in turn sets them up with the services they need.

A second view offers an alternative form of the component view, the *process model.* It examines MAPI as a collection of processes on the desktop. Each process contains a number of the layers described above.

By a third view, the *object model,* MAPI is a hierarchy of objects offered to its clients. The MAPI universe consists of component objects; but instead of clients requesting these objects individually from the system COM library, they establish contact with the MAPI32.DLL broker layer, which gives them a root object. From this root object, called a *session,* the clients access other objects in turn.

Component Model

The MAPI architecture divides its players into three classes. There are the *clients:* messaging and workgroup applications that call MAPI to make requests of available messaging services. There are the *service providers:* proxies for messaging services that exist to provide application access to some messaging system. And, of course, there is MAPI itself, the middleware glue that binds everything together. Figure 2-1 shows a MAPI sandwich.

Client component

A client defines itself by its client relationship to MAPI. If a piece of software calls MAPI to access messaging services, that software is a client. All user-oriented messaging applications are clients, as are other workgroup applications that use MAPI to store, exchange, and share data. The Exchange mail client itself is a MAPI client. So is Schedule+ 7.0 from Microsoft Office when it is running in workgroup-enabled mode, or Visio 4.0 when it executes its File - Send command.

Clients

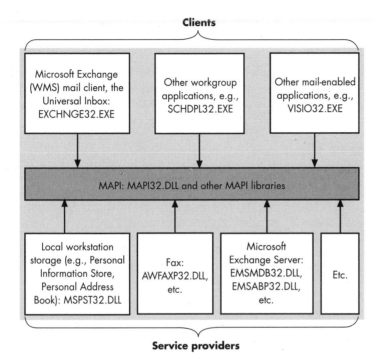

Service providers

Figure 2-1. *All MAPI is divided into three parts: the clients, the service providers, and the MAPI middleware. By standing between the clients and the service providers, MAPI enforces generic plug-and-play interfaces between them.*

The heart of MAPI is the resource brokerage DLL, MAPI32.DLL. Service providers register themselves with MAPI, which loads them in response to user requests; clients call MAPI to secure the services of the providers. MAPI itself provides a number of supporting services to both providers and clients, such as rafts of common user interface code, configuration management services, utility functions for implementing some common idioms of the MAPI API, and a process that ferries messages between services, the MAPI *spooler*. MAPI can satisfy some client requests on its own, such as requests for configuration management; MAPI answers others by collating information from a number of different service providers; and it serves still others by simply passing the call through to a particular service provider, often doing no more than changing the name of the interface as it passes through the MAPI layer.

Service provider component

The service providers are driver libraries that provide the services of a particular messaging system to MAPI applications. When a client program begins a messaging session, MAPI loads a set of service providers and calls those service providers as is necessary to satisfy the requests of the client. Different classes of service providers encapsulate different aspects of a messaging system, such as its directory services, its persistent message storage services, or its message addressing and delivery services. A messaging system's developers typically integrate all the system's MAPI service providers into a single package, a *messaging service*. Adding a messaging service to a MAPI installation enables the client applications to use the service's system. In addition to messaging services, MAPI can load one or more standalone service providers to supply services associated with no particular messaging system, such as a personal address book or storage local to the user's workstation.

Each service provider essentially acts as an in-process component object server, implementing a set of objects whose services MAPI then brokers to its clients. The different classes of providers, discussed in the following sections, implement different types of objects, each of which fulfill a different role in the functioning messaging subsystem.

Transport providers   Transport providers handle the submission and reception of messages to and from a particular message system. Client programs almost never interact directly with a transport provider or its objects; instead, the clients work with the objects of a message store, where they see messages come and go courtesy of a transport provider. The transport provider works through a separate process known as the MAPI spooler.

A transport provider registers itself as responsible for recipients on a particular system, represented by the *e-mail address type*—a short string identifying the type of a mail address, such as Simple Mail Transfer Protocol (SMTP) for *user@host.dom* or *MSMAIL* for *POSTOFFICE/USER*. After a client composes and submits a message, MAPI uses the MAPI spooler to hand that message to each transport provider that corresponds to one of that message's recipients. The transport provider transforms the message from MAPI format into the format for its particular system and submits it to the recipient's messaging system.

When a transport provider detects a new message for you on a system, the transport provider alerts the MAPI spooler, which has the option of processing that message, typically copying it to your default message store. Transport providers frequently work closely with an associated message store provider in the messaging service, particularly when new messages from the service simply appear in the store of that same service.

Message store providers   Message store providers represent a facility for storing messages, such as the .MMF files of Microsoft Mail, the folders of QuickMail on the Apple Macintosh, or the mailbox disk files of many UNIX mailers. They provide the initial point of composition for a client's outgoing message as well as a destination for incoming messages. Since a user might amass a great number of messages, the message store supports grouping the messages in a hierarchical structure, as well as searching for messages matching a predicate. Clients frequently interact with message stores in a manner similar to navigating through a file system or manipulating a database.

The MAPI message store hierarchy resembles the Windows 95 file system in its hierarchical structure, as depicted in Figure 2-2 on the following page. A messaging system describes its storage structure as a set of top-level *message stores,* which MAPI subdivides into a tree of *folders.* Folders can contain other folders and/or messages. MAPI describes the set of all message stores offered by all loaded message store providers in a single *message store table,* which it offers to clients. The standard WMS mail client, Exchange, uses this message store table when it displays the set of known stores in its left-hand pane, the folder list.

A MAPI message store also strongly resembles a traditional database. MAPI further subdivides its messages into *properties,* which a client can access within a message. Each property within a message has its own type, such as integer, character string, or binary object. A client can request a *table* from MAPI describing the contents of any folder. This returns a database-style construct with each message corresponding to a row and each property within a message corresponding to a column. Tables support *restrictions,* which limit their contents to only those rows matching a given predicate, as in a database query operation.

Note that unlike the file system, MAPI message stores have no notion of a pathname. Instead, most objects in the store—be they folders or messages—keep an *entryid* (entry identifier), or name, corresponding to a database record key. A client discovers this entry identifier initially by viewing the contents of that object's containing folder and subsequently can use it to access that object directly. Whereas a pathname embeds the names of the object's containers in that object's name, an entry identifier suffers no such constraint and can retain the same value even if the object is moved within the store, at the discretion of the message store provider implementing the entry identifier in question. A message store provider remains free to maintain a pathname as an informational property on an object.

A message store provider can appear in a messaging service, representing that system's storage facilities, or it can appear as a standalone provider, independent of any messaging system. Such standalone providers are useful to allow MAPI access to external databases or to provide a system-independent message storage. An example of an independent message store provider is the WMS Personal Folders provider. It allows MAPI clients to maintain messages and folders in a disk file on their personal workstations, without regard to the message's system of origin.

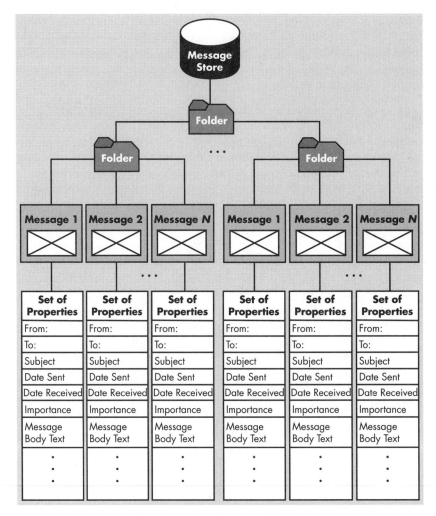

Figure 2-2. *Structure of a single message store hierarchy. A client discovers the message stores available to it by examining the MAPI message store table, which lists all stores currently known.*

Address book providers Address book providers supply client access to directory information—that is, a list of known recipients accessible on a particular mail system. A *recipient* is anything to which a user can direct a message; this can be either a single user on the system or a *distribution list,* a named list of such users. An address book provider might present all of its entries as a single list, or it might subdivide them into containers, with the containers arranged hierarchically like the folders in a message store. Figure 2-3 illustrates this. Address book providers share a great number of concepts with message store providers, including the container hierarchy, entry identifier, property, table, and restriction. MAPI manipulates them differently from message stores, however: instead of assembling a table of all top-level containers, it actually merges the contents of the top-level address book containers into a single master table, which it offers to clients as the topmost object.

Clients typically interact with address book providers either when they are addressing messages or when they are fetching information about a particular recipient. For addressing messages, address book entries keep appropriate properties, such as the display name, a displayable string used in the user interface to represent the recipient; the e-mail address, a string specific to the underlying structure of the messaging system; and the e-mail address type, indicating which transport provider will carry the message to this recipient.

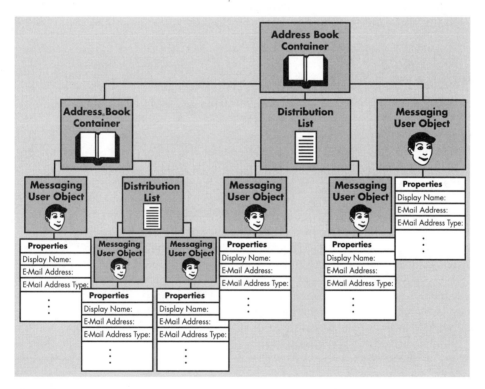

Figure 2-3. *Structure of an address book.*

Most client interactions with address book providers are read-only; indeed, many address book providers do not offer write access to their underlying directory. The most significant exception to this is the WMS Personal Address Book provider, which allows MAPI clients to keep a local list of known recipients and associated data in a disk file on their personal workstation. The Personal Address Book (PAB) also hosts a couple of special services necessary to the correct operation of MAPI, such as the *one-off table,* a temporary address book through which the client can manipulate addresses.

Sets of providers   When a client starts a session with MAPI, it provides MAPI with a string naming the *profile* to use for that session. The profile is a bundle of configuration data kept by MAPI that specifies the providers to load for that particular session, plus configuration data for each provider loaded. A workstation can host multiple profiles, each corresponding to a different running configuration of MAPI, either loading different providers or just keeping different user preferences for the same providers. For Windows 95 systems, MAPI stores each profile in the system registry under the key

```
HKEY_CURRENT_USER\Software\Microsoft\Windows Messaging System\Profiles
```

For Windows NT systems, this key is

```
HKEY_CURRENT_USER\Software\Microsoft\Windows NT\Current Version
    \Windows Messaging System\Profiles
```

Available API sets   MAPI links its clients to its providers by defining two different programming interfaces, as shown in Figure 2-4. Clients write to API, where the *A* denotes *Application.* Providers write to the Service Provider Interface (SPI); some portions of this interface are simply mirror images of portions of the MAPI interface, acting to channel a component's implementation in ways suitable to MAPI, whereas others are special interfaces for SPI clients themselves to call or implement. Between these API and SPI interface boundaries, MAPI itself lies. When the API matches the SPI, MAPI just passes the interface pointer from the service provider up to the client, leaving the client and provider to complete their business without interference, with the client making calls directly into the provider's component implementation. Elsewhere MAPI interprets calls to the client API as a set of commands to the SPI.

On 16-Bit Windows

Lacking a system registry, the 16-bit MAPI implementation stores the data found in profiles in an .INI file in the Windows\System folder.

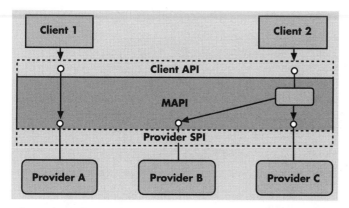

The two faces of MAPI: client API vs. provider SPI. Client 1 calls an API that matches the SPI exported by provider A. MAPI plays matchmaker between the two and then leaves the client calling directly to the provider. Contrast this against client 2, where MAPI implements its API call by in turn making a number of calls to the SPI on providers B and C and then synthesizing the results.

Figure 2-4. *The two faces of MAPI: client API vs. provider SPI.*

As shown in Figure 2-5 on the following page, MAPI actually offers four distinct client APIs, each addressed to the needs of a different class of client. First there is its essential client API, MAPI itself (commonly referred to as *full* or *Extended* MAPI). It is available to any client capable of using COM and offers the greatest degree of power and freedom in exchange for significant programming effort. On top of Extended MAPI are three other APIs: Simple MAPI, Common Messaging Calls (CMC), and ActiveX/Messaging. Each simplifies raw MAPI, trading a loss in expressive power for greater programming convenience.

Simple MAPI provides a simple function-call–based interface suitable for mail-enabling a Windows-based application—for example, implementing a send item on the application's File menu through the high-level *MAPISendMail* API—with minimal effort. CMC provides an equally simple interface set of high-level functions suitable for mail-enabling applications. However, unlike Simple MAPI, applications making CMC calls are portable to non-Windows-based platforms since CMC, being the product of an X.400 API Association (XAPIA) standardization effort, might be available on those platforms. Finally, ActiveX/Messaging exposes MAPI constructs as objects from ActiveX components (formerly called OLE Automation Server), making it the API of choice for contemporary Microsoft Visual Basic clients. It offers more power than Simple MAPI or CMC but considerably less power than Extended MAPI.

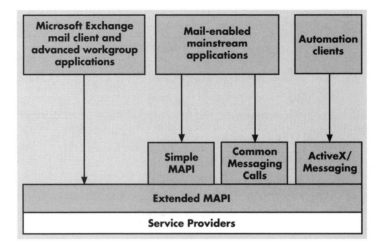

Figure 2-5. *MAPI offers several secondary API sets that hide the complexity of its component architecture.*

ActiveX/Messaging allows Visual Basic clients to deliver a variety of messaging solutions. However, for this book's class of applications, Extended MAPI is the only API worth considering.

Process Model

Now consider the different tasks that host the components—clients, service providers, and MAPI—discussed above. With no client logged onto MAPI, the Windows Messaging Subsystem lies completely inactive, being nothing more

---

Simple vs. Extended MAPI

Simple MAPI first appeared in Microsoft Mail 3.0 under the name *MAPI,* the Messaging Application Programming Interface. At that time, it acquired the label *Simple MAPI* to distinguish it from so-called *MAPI 0,* a richer set of undocumented APIs internal to Microsoft Mail, which Microsoft elected not to publish in favor of a planned, more-complete API set. That more-complete set became *MAPI 1.0,* also called *Extended MAPI* (or occasionally *MAPIX*) to differentiate it from its Simple cousin, and is today's Win32 MAPI.

So beware: today the term MAPI is ambiguous. An application that claims to "support MAPI" might make Simple MAPI calls, might make use of the full Win32 MAPI facilities, or if it is a Win16 e-mail client, might even implement all Simple MAPI calls itself, as did Microsoft Mail 3.0.

Throughout this book, the term MAPI denotes the WIN32 API Extended MAPI.

than a set of image files and registry data on disk. Once a client logs onto MAPI, though, the subsystem springs to life. The client has MAPI32.DLL loaded already; as part of the logon operation, MAPI reads the named profile (which the client specifies by name when it requests a logon), checks each of the services named therein, and loads those services' own providers. MAPI also starts the spooler process to handle background message processing and might launch still other processes, such as the forms servers (described later), to handle various client requests, as illustrated in Figure 2-6.

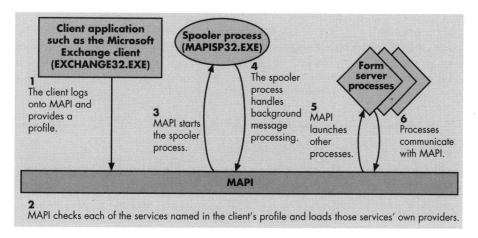

Figure 2-6. *The processes within an active MAPI subsystem.*

The spooler

The MAPI spooler process, MAPISP32.EXE, works in the background of any client, ferrying messages to and from transport providers for delivery to and from a messaging system, as shown in Figure 2-7 on page 77. For receiving incoming messages, the spooler receives notice of the new message from a loaded transport provider. The spooler is then responsible for copying the message to the default message store and invoking any installed *message hook providers* for post-download message processing, such as possibly mirroring all messages to a printer or maintaining a running tally of message arrivals. Once the newly arrived message reaches the message store, MAPI brings the message to the attention of clients. To send outgoing messages, the spooler accepts the message from the message store, invokes message hook providers on the message, and passes the message to each transport provider that accepts responsibility for one or more of the message's recipients. However, when a message store and a transport provider are tightly coupled, delivery can effectively take place between the two without the spooler's intervention. Exchange Server couples its store and XP in just this fashion.

A message hook provider is used to process messages before the MAPI spooler sends them to the transport provider (called *outbound hook provider*) or to intercept and reroute the messages (called *inbound hook provider*).

A client can elect to start MAPI without launching the spooler, in which case delivery takes place only between tightly coupled providers and no message hook processing will occur. This is useful when the client wants only to browse the contents of the message stores or must run completely without user supervision, as would happen within a Windows NT service. Otherwise, MAPI spawns the spooler process on behalf of the first client to request a session with mail delivery services.

Playing Voyeur with the MAPI DLLs

If you watch a process loading and initializing MAPI in the debugger, you might see it connect to a number of the following DLLs:

MAPI32.DLL implements the functions and interfaces of MAPI itself.

OLE32.DLL implements the in-process COM system support required by every client and component object.

RPCRT4.DLL implements the default cross-process interface marshaling, used to let clients interact with components in foreign processes.

WMSUI32.DLL implements the user interface components of the Windows Messaging Subsystem. This includes the address book interface, much of the standard note forms, and even most of the Windows Messaging client itself. On systems with Microsoft Exchange, Exchange replaces this DLL to supply its own interfaces.

WMSFR32.DLL implements the MAPI Forms Manager, described in Chapter 5. On systems with Microsoft Exchange, Exchange installs an additional DLL, EMSUIX32.DLL, which supplants it.

MSPST32.DLL implements the service providers for the Personal Address Book and Personal Folders services, standard to every WMS installation.

You might see other DLLs implement other service providers, or they might implement in-process extensions to the Exchange client, described in Chapter 4.

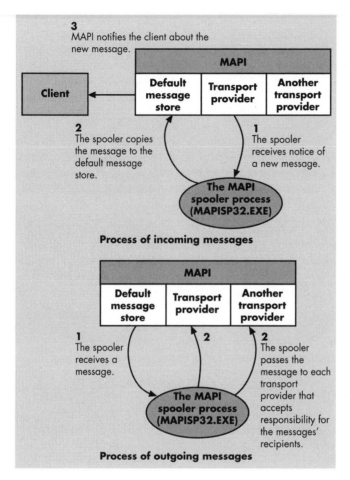

3
MAPI notifies the client about the new message.

2
The spooler copies the message to the default message store.

1
The spooler receives notice of a new message.

Process of incoming messages

1
The spooler receives a message.

2
The spooler passes the message to each transport provider that accepts responsibility for the messages' recipients.

Process of outgoing messages

Figure 2-7. *The MAPI spooler process.*

Only one instance of the spooler process runs at a time on a single computer. When multiple clients operate multiple sessions with MAPI, those clients share the services of the spooler.

The client applications   A MAPI client process explicitly loads MAPI32.DLL and then calls entry points in that DLL to start MAPI and get a session running. MAPI in turn loads its other DLL components as it needs them, possibly including WMSUI32.DLL, WMSFR.DLL, various controls, and OLE32.DLL and RPCRT4.DLL if the client didn't already have COM loaded (which might be the case for a client using only the Simple MAPI or CMC API sets). The client must supply the name of a profile to get a session; MAPI takes that profile and loads every service provider DLL, such as MSPST32.DLL, that the profile names. In short, every MAPI client contains all of MAPI, while every MAPI client with its own session contains the images of the necessary providers as well, as shown in Figure 2-8.

Form servers   Under certain circumstances, a client can operate using the session of another client process instead of requesting its own session. Such a client does not access MAPI objects in-process; instead, the client operates against a set of out-of-process MAPI objects, using the COM interprocess object access mechanisms as discussed in the "Object Encapsulation" section of Chapter 1. The address space of such a remote client resembles that of a conventional client before logon in that the remote client does not load the images—effectively, the in-process object servers—of the providers it uses.

One common variety of client that does not use its own session is the *form server*. Recall that each message in a message store consists of a set of typed properties. The set of properties can vary from message to message within the same store or even within the same folder. Although one message carries the properties *From, To, Subject,* and *Message Text,* another might carry *Received By, Call For, Call From, Is Urgent,* and *Call Back Phone Number.* These two messages are said to have a different *message class.* The form server is the component that implements the *form,* the piece of user interface and associated executable code that sends and reads a message of a particular class.

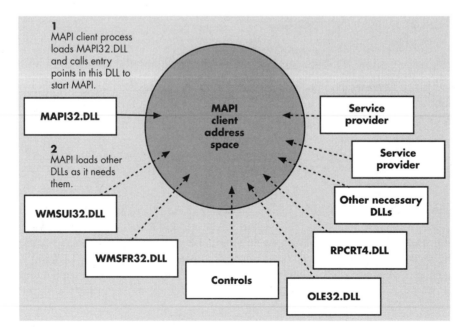

Figure 2-8. *Cross section of a MAPI client process.*

When a client asks MAPI to display a message, MAPI locates the correct form server for that message's message class and spawns it. The form server does not log onto MAPI itself but instead uses the active session object of the originating client. (See Figure 2-9.) This allows the form server to send and read the message under the certification of the client.

For more detail about forms and their servers, see Chapter 5.

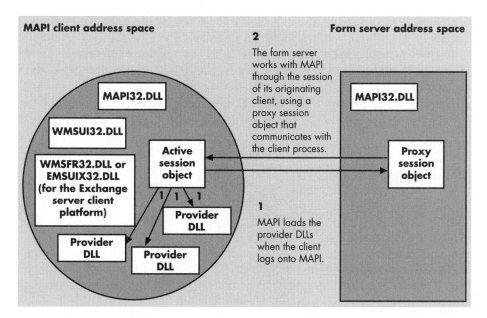

Figure 2-9. *Cross section of a running form server. Note that the form server process does not include an active session object or providers of its own.*

The ActiveX/Messaging server MAPI offers the ActiveX/Messaging interface to any application with recourse to Automation. Applications request an automation object with the name MAPI.Session and subsequently interact through the properties and methods of that object. MAPI implements these automation objects through the ActiveX/Messaging server, MDISP32.EXE.

The ActiveX/Messaging server operates much like any other ActiveX components. It articulates a set of automation objects, which in this case represent messaging concepts, to clients of Automation through the *IDispatch* interface, which ActiveX makes available through cross-process. The server then describes the objects to automation clients through a type library. It implements these messaging objects through client calls to MAPI that the server makes on its clients' behalf. ActiveX will start and stop this server through the usual automation server protocols in response to client requests. In Figure 2-10, the client process holds a proxy MAPI.Session Automation object, which communicates with the actual MAPI.Session Automation object in the Automation server through a remote *IDispatch* interface. To implement this object, the Automation server runs an actual MAPI client. When the Automation client invokes a method on its MAPI-.Session object, the Automation server manipulates the actual MAPI session backing that object and returns the results to the client. Thus, the client keeps the illusion of manipulating MAPI without keeping the MAPI image in its own address space.

As a MAPI client process itself, the ActiveX/Messaging server process contains the image of MAPI as well as the images of various providers that the ActiveX components load on behalf of their clients. However, note that the server's clients need not contain the MAPI subsystem image, but only ActiveX, since the server performs all the actual interaction with MAPI.

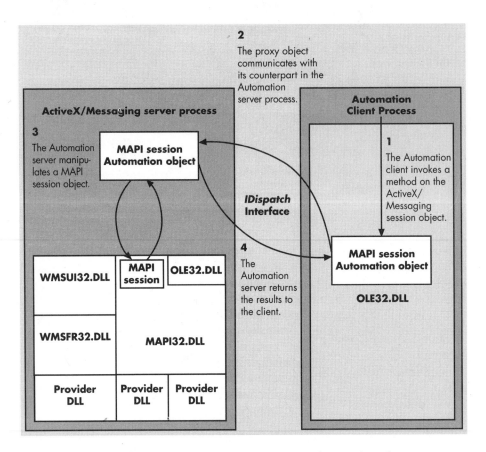

Figure 2-10. *The ActiveX/Messaging server corresponding with a client.*

> ### IDispatch
>
> The *IDispatch* interface is used to allow access to the methods and properties of an application so that other applications can use them.

Object Model

As mentioned earlier, MAPI is a COM-based component architecture. Therefore, any client operates within MAPI by gaining access to and manipulating various objects within the subsystem.

MAPI implements some types of component objects itself. It takes responsibility for all objects that encapsulate the configuration and administration of the subsystem and its profiles. MAPI builds tables derived from its loaded providers, such as status tables, message store tables, and, most notably, the address book. It also offers a number of objects to its providers, most of which remain invisible to clients; these become interesting to clients only when the provider uses them to construct objects for clients. The most prominent MAPI-implemented object is the session, through which every client action ultimately takes place.

From an underlying provider, MAPI simply passes back most objects. If the client is already holding a provider-implemented object and gains access to a new object by using some interface on the previous object, MAPI remains completely out of the loop and the transaction takes place exclusively between the client and the provider. (If the client does not have a session of its own, MAPI will intervene to the point of maintaining the interprocess connection.) Provider-hosted objects include messages, folders, stores, and attachments of message store providers; mail recipients, distribution lists, and address book containers of address book providers; and any number of status objects, plus tables of each of everything.

Many clients also implement a few objects that they delegate to MAPI in some fashion, allowing MAPI to call them in response to various events. *Advise sinks* give MAPI a channel of communication to a client, while *progress indicator objects* let the client define how a provider marks time during a lengthy operation. Both objects are discussed in more detail later in this chapter.

Differences from COM

COM has a strong model for object registration and creation. Based on what we know about COM and MAPI so far, we *think* we could easily predict how a client uses MAPI and how MAPI in turn loads providers for the client.

In our prediction, a client starts a session with MAPI by giving the system COM library its CLSID, *CLSID_MAPI,* so that COM locates the implementation of that class object, the in-process server MAPI32.DLL, loads it, and returns an interface to its class factory. The client then invokes *IClassFactory::CreateInstance* for *IID_IMAPISession* to get an interface on a new session object. Finally the client invokes *IMAPISession::Logon* to associate the session with a particular user profile, load the necessary service providers, and generally initialize the session to be ready for use. MAPI in turn implements the *Logon* method on its session object by opening the named profile, fetching the CLSIDs of the service providers named there, and loading each in-process server in turn. Once MAPI holds all the objects for a particular session, it can deliver the various methods on the *IMAPISession* interface, providing access to each provider's objects for the client as necessary.

Perfectly logical, right? Now forget all of that. The preceding paragraph is a complete fantasy. MAPI doesn't quite work that way since it doesn't use the COM object registration and creation mechanism.

A client actually starts a session with MAPI by explicitly loading the system MAPI DLL, MAPI32.DLL, finding the required entry points in that DLL and calling the API *MAPIInitialize*. (See Table 2-1.) It then calls *MAPILogonEx*, passing that entry point the name of the profile the client wants to use and receiving in return an interface on a session object through which it gains access to any loaded providers. MAPI implements logon by opening the named profile, retrieving the provider names and types from there, and loading and initializing each in a manner specific to the MAPI Service Provider Interface (SPI). Once the client holds the session, all of its subsequent interactions obey COM with regard to interface discipline and object lifetimes. A loaded service provider continues to deviate from COM throughout its running lifetime since MAPI requests new objects through an interface other than a class factory and controls its lifetime through a mechanism other than *DllCanUnloadNow*.

Method	Description
MAPIAllocateBuffer	Allocates a memory buffer
MAPIAllocateMore	Allocates an additional memory buffer associated with an existing buffer that was allocated using the *MAPIAllocateBuffer* method
MAPIFreeBuffer	Frees a memory buffer allocated with the *MAPIAllocateBuffer* or *MAPIAllocateMore* method
MAPIInitialize	Increments the reference count of an object and initializes per-instance global data for the Extended MAPI Dynamic Link Library
MAPILogonEx	Logs a client application onto a session
MAPIUninitialize	Decrements the reference count, cleans up, and deletes per-instance global data for the Extended MAPI DLL

Table 2-1. *Methods used to implement a MAPI Session.*

MAPI also differs slightly from vanilla COM in its memory management particulars. Instead of the ActiveX default memory allocator, it uses its own memory allocation package, which offers a function call interface specific to MAPI—*MAPIAllocateBuffer*, *MAPIAllocateMore*, and *MAPIFreeBuffer*—in addition to the conventional *IMalloc* interface. These function call interfaces let a caller request additional buffers of memory, which the memory allocator chains onto the first buffer such that freeing the first buffer frees all the memory in the chain.

Using such memory chaining, providers can extend structures initially allocated and supplied by the caller. Once finished with the structure, the caller can release the memory while remaining ignorant of precisely which buffers a provider modified.

Session, the root object

A process with MAPI loaded and initialized is ready to become a client of MAPI. To do so, it calls the *MAPILogonEx* API and names a profile that specifies the precise set of providers and configuration for MAPI to use. MAPI opens that profile and loads each provider there named, using the configuration data in the profile for each provider and passing along user credentials for providers that need them, such as a message store that encrypts its data to prevent unauthorized users from viewing it. If the client has specified no profile, MAPI presents the user with a dialog box for selecting one; likewise, if any provider needs additional credentials or configuration information, MAPI presents the necessary user interface. When MAPI completes this logon process, it returns to the calling client an interface on a new session object.

A client does not need to demand a new session to operate. MAPI allows a client to create its session as "shared," which allows any other client on the workstation to log on; request the use of the shared session; and, therefore, use the same providers, configuration, and credentials as the first client. This allows a group of programs to run without burying the user in an avalanche of redundant logon prompts since, after the first client logs on, each subsequent client uses the same results as the first. If a client requests a shared session and none exists, that client must create a new session. Only a single shared session is ever available. Similarly, MAPI allows clients to export their sessions to form servers that they invoke; rather than logging on separately, the form server operates against the session of the client controlling it by using a COM remote interface to communicate with the client.

All MAPI client activity takes place through a session with MAPI, whether that session is new, shared, or remote: either directly in the case of methods invoked on the session interface itself or indirectly through secondary objects acquired through the session. We describe the session as *containing* those secondary objects since a client must interact with the session—that is, "open" it, look "within" it—to access its contained objects. Likewise, stores and folders contain folders and messages, messages contain attachments, and address books contain various types of addressing entries, plus further nested containers of the same. To access any contained object, a client must first access its container. Figure 2-11 depicts a hierarchy of contained objects, with the ultimate root container, the session, as the outermost object.

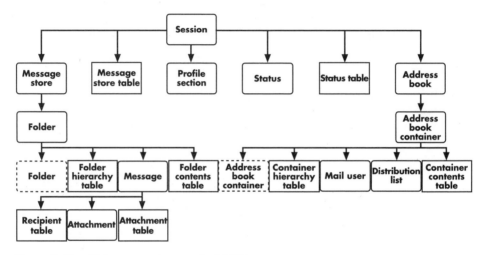

Figure 2-11. *Object containment in MAPI.*

Table 2-2 presents more information about each of the objects in this diagram, describing the name of their primary MAPI interface and the method used to find them. Some objects have entry identifiers (entryids), which, once discovered, can be used to reach the object from any level of enclosing container, all the way to the outermost object, the session. Entry identifiers usually first appear to the client in a descriptive table, listing a number of sibling objects in a container. Some other objects, listed in Table 2-3 on page 86, are implemented by the client and, in a sense, lie outside the diagram, although the client still must present them to MAPI through the session.

Object Type	Interface Name	Contents of Table	Method Used to Locate the Object
Session	*IMAPISession*		*MAPILogonEx*
Message store table	*IMAPITable*	Message store	*IMAPISession::GetMsgStoresTable* on a session
Message store[1]	*IMsgStore*		*IMAPISession::OpenMsgStore* or *MAPISession::OpenEntry* on a session

1. The object type has an entry identifier.

Table 2-2. *Objects commonly used by MAPI clients.*

Object Type	Interface Name	Contents of Table	Method Used to Locate the Object
Folder[1]	*IMAPIFolder*		*IMsgStore::OpenEntry* on a store, *IMAPIContainer::OpenEntry* on a folder, or *IMAPISession::OpenEntry* on a session
Folder contents table	*IMAPITable*	Message	*IMAPIFolder::GetContentsTable* on a folder
Folder hierarchy table	*IMAPITable*	Folder	*IMAPIFolder::GetHierarchyTable* on a folder
Message[1]	*IMessage*		*IMsgStore::OpenEntry* on a store, or *IMAPIContainer::OpenEntry* on a folder, or *IMAPISession::OpenEntry* on a session
Attachment table	*IMAPITable*	Attachment	*IMessage::GetAttachmentTable* on a message
Attachment	*IAttach*		*IMessage::OpenAttach* on a message
Recipient table	*IMAPITable*	Recipient	*IMessage::GetRecipientTable* on a message
Address book	*IAddrBook*		*IMAPISession::OpenAddressBook* on a session
Address book container[1]	*IABContainer*		*IAddrBook::OpenEntry* on an address book or a container
Container contents table	*IMAPITable*	Mail user, distribution list	*IMAPIContainer::GetContentsTable* on a container
Container hierarchy table	*IMAPITable*	Address book container	*IMAPIContainer::GetHierarchyTable* on a container
Mail user[1]	*IMailUser*		*IMAPIContainer::OpenEntry* on an address book or a container
Distribution list[1]	*IDistList*		*IMAPIContainer::OpenEntry* on an address book or a container
Status table	*IMAPITable*	Status	*IMAPISession::GetStatusTable* on a session
Status[1]	*IMAPIStatus*		*IMAPISession::OpenEntry* on a row of a table
Profile section	*IProfSect*		*IMAPISession::OpenProfileSection* on a session

1. The object type has an entry identifier.

Object Type	Interface Name
Advise sink	*IMAPIAdviseSink*
Progress indicator	*IMAPIProgress*

Table 2-3. *Objects commonly implemented by MAPI clients.*

Properties

MAPI describes many of its objects as having a set of *properties,* or attributes, of a particular type. Such objects have an interface that inherits from—that is, is polymorphic with—*IMAPIProp.*

A property superficially resembles a C++ class data member: it is a piece of per-object instance data of a particular type accessible with a particular name, as shown in the C++ example in Figure 2-12. However, unlike C++ data members, the set of MAPI properties available on an object of a given class is not determined at compile time and is not necessarily fixed; a client must check and query for each of an object's members at run time and, in some instances, might even add and remove members at run time. This aspect of MAPI properties strongly resembles the "property list" construct of many languages, including several dialects of LISP, in which any object can carry a dynamic list of name-value pairs. On objects that disallow dynamic variation of the set of properties, a property resembles instead a single field in a single SQL record: although a particular object's schema is fixed, the client still must query for it at run time.

The set of properties on an object might vary, depending on that object's type, implementing provider, or life history.

Some properties are mandatory on objects of a particular type. For example, every mail user has a mailing address, every message has a message length, and every folder has the entry identifier of its parent folder. A provider that implements such an object must deliver each of its required properties since these are essential to the successful operation of code that manipulates the object. Client code must fetch the properties at run time but might treat their absence as an error exception case, similar to running out of memory during an operation. Such mandatory properties do not preclude the presence of other properties.

Some properties are standard but optional on any particular object. A message might carry a value representing its urgency, while a mail user might have properties for the user's home telephone number, business telephone number, and fax number. Client code that would use these properties must handle their absence in a nonexceptional manner since any particular instance of the object can lack them.

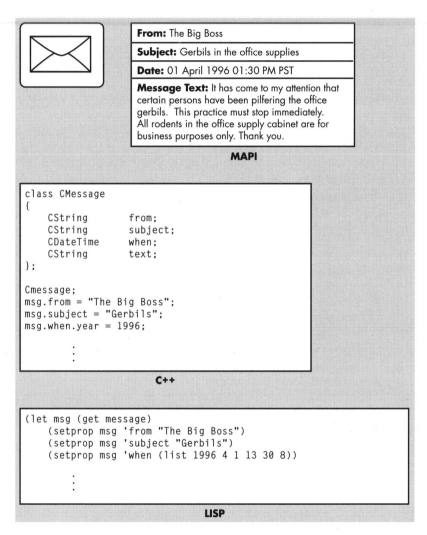

From: The Big Boss

Subject: Gerbils in the office supplies

Date: 01 April 1996 01:30 PM PST

Message Text: It has come to my attention that certain persons have been pilfering the office gerbils. This practice must stop immediately. All rodents in the office supply cabinet are for business purposes only. Thank you.

MAPI

```
class CMessage
{
    CString        from;
    CString        subject;
    CDateTime      when;
    CString        text;
};

Cmessage;
msg.from = "The Big Boss";
msg.subject = "Gerbils";
msg.when.year = 1996;

          .
          .
          .
```

C++

```
(let msg (get message)
    (setprop msg 'from "The Big Boss")
    (setprop msg 'subject "Gerbils")
    (setprop msg 'when (list 1996 4 1 13 30 8))

          .
          .
          .
```

LISP

Figure 2-12. *MAPI properties resemble LISP property lists or database fields more than C++ data members. A C++ object carries a fixed set of members, statically determined by the object's type. Contrast that with a property list bearing any number of name-value tuples, which might vary dynamically between instances of an object.*

Some properties appear as a value added by a particular provider. A secure message store provider might include the name and public encryption key of a message's creator in the message itself, while an address book provider might include a property representing the X.400 Distinguished-Name of any object it implements. Client code using these properties has special knowledge that it is running against a particular provider and interprets the semantics of the provider's properties accordingly. Such clients must balance the cost of sacrificing MAPI component generality against the value they add.

Finally, some properties appear added by a particular client.   Most message store providers allow client code to add and remove arbitrary properties on a message dynamically, tagging the message with client-specified data. To ensure that two pieces of client code use the same semantics when doing so, each message carries a special property, its *message class,* by which client code associates a particular message with a particular set of properties, or *schema.* MAPI contains mechanisms for associating a message class with a form server dedicated to creating, rendering, and otherwise manipulating messages of that class. Chapter 5 discusses these mechanisms further.

MAPI manipulates every property using its *property tag,* which consists of a property *identifier* and a property *type.* The property identifiers are 16-bit integers partitioned into various subranges for properties on objects in particular domains; from the subranges, MAPI assigns particular values to denote certain MAPI standard properties, such as 0x0037 for the identifier of *PR_SUBJECT,* the subject of a message. MAPI reserves all the property identifiers with the high bit set (that is, having a value of 0x8000 or greater) for *named properties,* in which MAPI takes a client-supplied GUID and subidentifier and hashes that into a locally unique 15-bit value; such named properties allow multiple components to tag a shared object—for example, a message in the store—without interfering with one another's tags. The property type is an opcode (operation code) denoting the format of a property's value—for example, string, integer, or time and date. The type of *PR_SUBJECT* is PT_TSTRING—that is, 0x001F, a transmutable string value that uses Windows ANSI characters in some environments and Unicode standard in others.

NOTE   A complete breakdown of standard property tags and their ranges appears in the include file MAPITAGS.H. The values of the property type opcodes appear in MAPIDEFS.H.

Most concrete objects in the MAPI universe, such as messages, folders, file attachments, and so forth, describe themselves with properties, as do a few more abstract objects that find the extensibility of the interface useful. Table 2-4 summarizes the objects visible to clients that have interfaces that inherit either directly or indirectly from *IMAPIProp.*

Name	Interface
Message store object	*IMsgStore*
Folder object	*IMAPIFolder*
Message object	*IMessage*
Attachment object	*IAttach*
Address book object	*IAddrBook*
Address book container object	*IABContainer*
Mail user object	*IMailUser*
Distribution list object	*IDistList*
Profile section object	*IProfSect*
Status object	*IMAPIStatus*

Table 2-4. *Objects offering properties to clients.*

A client can request the properties for a number of objects in parallel through a table.

Tables

A *table* object presents the properties for many objects at once. Continuing the analogy in which *IMAPIProp* corresponds to a single database record, *IMAPI-Table* represents a table in the database, with each row representing a particular object and each column, or field, representing a particular property (a single property tag value) on that object. Clients can specify the columns in a table, restrict the rows in the table to those matching some condition, or sort the table on a column or columns. The provider implementing the table can limit sorts and restrictions to accommodate its underlying database engine.

A client gains access to a table by invoking the appropriate method on the table's enclosing object. In Figure 2-13 on the following page, the client opened the folder's contents table by invoking *IMAPIContainer::GetContentsTable* to retrieve a table of messages within the folder. Logically, the table is an attribute of that enclosing object, providing access to a number of other objects contained within that object. Table 2-5 on page 91 lists a variety of objects with tables. The client can use the property information contained in the table; if the client needs more properties than the table contains or if the client needs to interact directly with one of the table's objects, it must open the object directly.

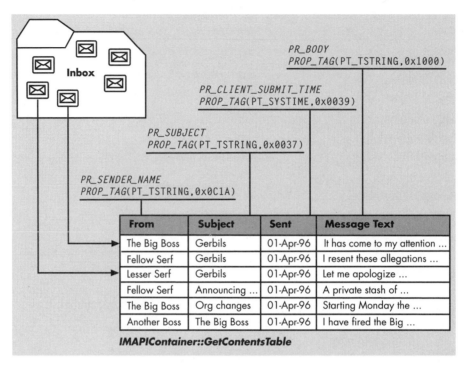

Figure 2-13. *A folder's contents table summarizes the messages within the folder. Here the folder contains six messages and so has a contents table with six rows. Each row contains properties pertaining to a particular message.*

Objects available through tables have in the table a single property that acts as a key, enabling direct access to the object. For most MAPI objects, that is the object's entry identifier, *PR_ENTRYID*. To access that object, the client must extract its entry identifier value from the *PR_ENTRYID* column of the table and then pass this entry identifier value to the *OpenEntry* method on the object that manifested the table, receiving in return an interface on the identified object. If the object is a message store, the table's containing object, the session, offers a method *IMAPISession::OpenMsgStore* with slightly different semantics but functionally equivalent to *OpenEntry*. Attachments lack entry identifiers; their tables contain an attachment number, which the client must pass to *IMessage-::OpenAttach* on the enclosing message to access the attachment.

NOTE The entry identifier might be valid only when the table is open.

Containing Object	Table	Method
Session	Status table containing status objects	*IMAPISession::GetStatusTable*
Session	Message store table containing message stores	*IMAPISession::GetMsgStoresTable*
Folder	Folder hierarchy table containing folders	*IMAPIContainer::GetHierarchyTable*
Folder	Folder contents table containing messages	*IMAPIContainer::GetContentsTable*
Message	Attachment table containing attachments	*IMessage::GetAttachmentTable*
Message	Recipient table containing recipients	*IMessage::GetRecipientTable*
Address book container	Container hierarchy table containing address book containers	*IMAPIContainer::GetHierarchyTable*
Address book container	Container contents table containing mail users and distribution lists	*IMAPIContainer::GetContentsTable*
Distribution list	Distribution list hierarchy table containing distribution lists	*IMAPIContainer::GetHierarchyTable*
Distribution list	Distribution list contents table containing mail users	*IMAPIContainer::GetContentsTable*

Table 2-5. *Objects offering tables of their contained objects to clients.*

Tables commonly represent the contents of a particular MAPI container.

Containers

MAPI interacts with hierarchies of containers through the *IMAPIContainer* interface. Message folders, address book containers, and distribution lists all share the trait of containing both child items—that is, messages and mail users—and further container items like themselves. (This is similar to a hierarchical file system, in which a directory can contain either a file or a subdirectory.) Hence, all have interfaces that derive from *IMAPIContainer*. Note that the *IMAPIContainer* interface itself subsumes the *IMAPIProp* and, of course, *IUnknown* interfaces.

The majority of the tables shown in Table 2-5 appear through the graces of the methods *GetHierarchyTable* and *GetContentsTable*, methods that appear through their object's interfaces incorporating *IMAPIContainer*. *GetHierarchyTable* returns a table of containers contained within the object; *GetContentsTable* returns noncontainer items. For example, if invoked on a folder, *GetHierarchyTable* returns a table of other folders that the original folder contains, whereas *GetContentsTable* returns a table of contained messages.

Additional Objects Implemented by Clients

On occasion clients do have the ability to implement objects of their own. Whereas most client code obtains interfaces on objects and makes imperative commands of those interfaces, sometimes a client needs to take a more passive role, responding to an event that originates or is otherwise propagated from within MAPI. Similar to a client's window procedures, which it hands to the user interface subsystem of Windows, clients build these objects and delegate them to the messaging subsystem to receive control in certain circumstances.

Advise sink objects supply MAPI with a locus through which to notify the client of various events on an object. The client implements the advise sink and registers it with MAPI through the *IMAPISession::Advise* method on a session, address book, message store, or table. Whenever MAPI sees changes take place on the item of interest, it notifies each outstanding advise sink on the object. User interface code can refresh its contents in the face of changes in a table's backing data; user notification functions can fire on the receipt of new mail; message store browsers can change a view on a displayed folder when it moves in the folder hierarchy; and running applications can shut down gracefully when the underlying shared session closes.

Progress indicator objects allow the client to define an application-specific user interface that runs during lengthy operations. As the extended operation progresses, the client can update the displayed interface to reflect the client's degree of progress toward completion. For example, a client might draw a graphical thermometer that fills itself as a folder copy operation progresses. To update this display while the messages store provider implements the copy, the client hands a progress indicator object to the provider.

NOTE	Note that this section does not discuss two major species of client-supplied objects and their associated interfaces, deferring each to later chapters. Chapter 4 discusses Exchange client extension objects, which supplant, redefine, or otherwise extend the standard WMS mail client. Chapters 5 through 7 discuss form objects, which define and implement new types of messages.

The Applications Within the MAPI Architecture

Within the MAPI architecture, user applications typically operate as MAPI client applications. The applications load MAPI, make calls to the objects that MAPI exposes, and generally leverage any MAPI service providers installed on the system. For example, if the system contains providers to access a user's mailbox on Hewlett-Packard OpenMail, a MAPI application sends its messages through OpenMail and manipulates the items it finds in the OpenMail store. If the system contains providers for Microsoft Mail or Exchange Server, a MAPI application operates within the context of these messaging systems.

Different varieties of applications use the resources of client MAPI in different ways. A program that sits on a mailbox, reading incoming messages and ordering pizzas to specification, operates quite differently from a program that browses the address book.

Most of this book consists of MAPI code fragments, both large and small. This introductory section therefore omits most implementation details, deferring them to samples throughout the remaining chapters. However, it does present one sample just to promote understanding.

A Taxonomy of Applications

Most MAPI applications involve the exchange of information in some fashion—that being the manifest purpose of MAPI. An application approaches information exchange by one of four categories: system, report, mailbox, or folder. Each category of application uses MAPI in a slightly different manner. However, these categories are neither exhaustive nor exclusive. They're only guides to thinking about MAPI.

A system application

A system application does not involve itself in information exchange at all; instead, it manipulates the MAPI system itself for the benefit of the system's user and other applications. System applications log onto MAPI and get a session but rarely open any stores or address books. Instead they open status tables, profile sections, and various administrative objects of the session. System applications that involve themselves exclusively with configuring the profile and messaging services might elect not to start the spooler.

A provider's setup program is a system application: it manipulates MAPI, writing entries into the provider's profile section and possibly loading the provider itself to present its administrative options; it never exchanges data with another host, even in so limited a fashion as reading archived messages. Likewise, the Control Panel pane (called either Mail or Mail and Fax) that administers local MAPI profiles is a system application, starting up just enough MAPI to perform maintenance and cleanup.

A report application

A report application does not move information either; instead it passively consumes information that is already available. Report MAPI applications strongly resemble database browsing and report-generation applications—a resemblance strengthened by the store-centric nature of much of MAPI. Report applications log onto MAPI and get a session and might elect not to start the spooler. Once they have the session, either they lunge straight for the message store table or address book or they use a persistent entry identifier to open their container of interest directly. They spend much time building tables.

Applications that browse or process the contents of address books and message stores are report applications. An application dedicated to archiving sent messages would fall into this category as well.

A mailbox application

A mailbox application moves information by sending messages to the mailboxes of mail users or by watching its mailbox for new messages. Mailbox applications always start the spooler unless they limit themselves to running on systems with tightly coupled stores and transports. They monitor advise sinks for new mail notifications. They compose new messages, address them, and submit them to the spooler and transports for transmission. They can invoke form servers to send or read custom message types.

Traditional messaging clients are mailbox applications, with the entire application devoted to sending outgoing messages and to receiving and filing incoming messages. A mail-enabled mainstream application is a mailbox application, caring only that its package of data goes forth or that the mailbox delivers some incoming data package. An unattended process that monitors a mailbox for activity and processes each new arrival is a mailbox application also.

A folder application

A folder application moves information by creating messages in a folder or by interacting with the existing messages in a folder. Folder applications have no need of the services of the spooler. They monitor advise sinks for changes in the contents tables of their folder. They compose new messages and save them to a folder, usually invoking form servers to manage nonstandard (that is, nonmessaging) message types. Like report applications, they spend much time building and manipulating tables.

Traditional database applications are folder applications, as are most conferencing and bulletin board applications. Each of these uses the shared facilities of the common database to exchange information. The message store provider might implement a truly shared database, in which other users simultaneously access the same set of records, or it might implement a private database in which only one user at a time ever sees the data.

Nonspecific and heterogeneous applications

Many extensions or application add-ons are nonspecific. They take no explicit approach to information exchange; instead, they participate in whatever their host does.

The taxonomy isn't hard and fast; it's only a tool to describe an application's messaging philosophy. An application that simply logs onto a shared session and holds it open for other applications would be a system application, unless it was intended to run the spooler and pump mail from the transport mailbox into the default store. In this case, it would be acting more as a mailbox-centric application. The Exchange mail client is a mailbox-centric application, but it hosts any number of folder-centric applications as well. Some applications are heterogeneous—they fit into multiple categories.

An Example Application

To conclude this discussion of MAPI, let's examine a sample client application. We will review just the basics: initializing MAPI, getting a session, invoking methods on the session, counting references, and checking and handling errors. (If you haven't been cross-referencing the interfaces and methods named so far in the *MAPI Programmer's Guide,* now is a good time to start.)

The Exchange client itself contains no notion of scheduling message transmission, deferring that responsibility to its loaded MAPI transport providers. If users want to retrieve messages from three different message services at midnight (or whenever the phone tolls are the least expensive), they must build a profile naming the transport provider for each of those message services, configure each transport provider to schedule its message transmission at midnight, and then leave the Exchange client running overnight. This won't work if one of the transport providers does not support scheduled transmission, if it does not support the kind of scheduling desired (for example, every other Sunday at midnight), or if the user does not want to leave the Exchange mail client constantly running.

To address this, I will provide the user with a utility that downloads all of the messages from the services in a particular profile, making the utility suitable for spawning from an external scheduling program, such as WinCRON, the Windows 95 System Agent, or any one of several tickler utilities. The utility accepts the name of a profile on its command line, making the utility suitable for accessing the services in various profiles while the utility is unattended. When the utility finishes its task, the program terminates. It works with any scheduler favored by the user since it contains no scheduling logic itself.[3]

---

3. It's not a shortcoming—it's a feature! I love marketing.

Source code for the program

On this book's companion disk, see the directory *Chap02\Mfetch* for the source code for this sample program. The MFETCH.CPP file contains the code for all the interesting MAPI activity. Other files included in the Mfetch folder encapsulate user interface support, command line parsing, and similarly uninteresting matters.

Checking for MAPI

The Mfetch application statically links with MAPI32.DLL, which provides the top-level messaging services of MAPI. Therefore, the application will not run on systems without MAPI where the system loader presents a diagnostic such as "Undefined call to dynalink: MAPI32.DLL." However, in situations in which an application program must run on such systems, it should instead load the MAPI library dynamically by using a sequence of *LoadLibrary* and *GetProcAddress* system calls.

The registry key HKEY_LOCAL_MACHINE\SOFTWARE\Microsoft\Windows Messaging Subsystem contains a number of values that define the messaging API sets installed on the local machine. These value names are MAPI (Simple MAPI), MAPIX (Extended MAPI), ActiveX/Messaging, and CMC. If CMC is enabled, CMCDLLNAME and CMCDLLNAME32 will be used to specify the 16-bit and 32-bit DLLs hosting CMC. An application dynamically loading messaging APIs should first check for the keys pertaining to the API it uses. If it fails to find that value set to 1, it should disable its messaging functions.

Starting and stopping MAPI

The application starts by initializing the MAPI subsystem within its address space. *MAPIInitialize* takes a single parameter in which the caller can specify certain special states for MAPI's benefit, such as whether the program has a user interface service on Windows NT or whether it wants all notifications to take place in a separate thread. In the following code from the file Chap02\Mfetch\MFETCH.CPP, passing NULL as a parameter to the *MAPIInitialize* function is a convenient shorthand to decline all of these options.

```
    ⋮
MAPIINIT_0 mapiinit = { MAPI_INIT_VERSION,
    MAPI_MULTITHREAD_NOTIFICATIONS };
HRESULT hr = MAPIInitialize(&mapiinit);
if (FAILED(hr))
{
    ui.Message(IDS_MAPI_INIT_FAILED);
    return 1;
}
    ⋮
```

NOTE The Mfetch program calls *MAPIInitialize* and *MAPIUninitialize* once each in its *WinMain* function.

If MAPI starts successfully, the application has recourse to all the interfaces of MAPI. As a side effect, MAPI initializes the COM subsystem through *CoInitialize* since it needs the object management facilities of COM. MAPI clients can therefore skip calling *CoInitialize* (and *CoUninitialize*) themselves.

When the application no longer needs MAPI, it must call *MAPIUninitialize*. MAPI reference counts itself and its own constituent components, allowing multiple components to use MAPI without explicit knowledge of one another's activity. Therefore, every call to *MAPIInitialize* must have a corresponding call to *MAPIUninitialize*. This lets MAPI manage its per-instance global structures and state.

On 16-Bit Windows

16-bit MAPI applications look for registry keys associated with the dynamically loaded API under the section [Mail] in the initialization file WIN.INI.

Managing a session

Mfetch performs session management in its *WinMain* function. After MAPI has been initialized, the application next must get a session using the profile specified on the application's command line. All interaction with the message services named in the profile will take place through the session object. To get a session, the application calls *MAPILogonEx* from the *WinMain* function in the MFETCH.CPP file, as shown in the following code:

```
    ⋮
IMAPISession* psess = NULL;
hr = MAPILogonEx((ULONG)ui.GetHwndVisible(),
    (TCHAR*)(cmdline.HasPFlag() ? cmdline.GetPParm() : NULL),
    (TCHAR*)(cmdline.HasCFlag() ? cmdline.GetCParm() : NULL),
    MAPI_NEW_SESSION|fMapiUnicode,
    &psess);
if (FAILED(hr))
{
    ui.Message(IDS_MAPI_LOGON_FAILED);
    MAPIUninitialize();
    return 1;
}
    ⋮
```

Building Sample Applications

As written, the files in the Mfetch folder compile with Microsoft Visual C++ versions 2.2 and 4.0, although any compiler that includes the MAPI support files from the Win32 SDK will suffice. You can either offer the "external" makefile MAKEFILE directly to the *nmake* build tool (for example, *nmake /f Makefile*) or build a Visual C++ version 4.0 workspace around the shell makefile MFETCH.MAK.

The first parameter to *MAPILogonEx* specifies a window handle for the caller's user interface parent window. If the function that called the *MAPILogonEx* function specifies either *MAPI_LOGON_UI* (to prompt the user for logon information) or *MAPI_PASSWORD_UI* (to prompt the user for a password) in the *flFlags* parameter, MAPI presents the user interface on behalf of the caller, allowing the user to select the profile desired and the credential string to use with that profile; that user interface needs a parent window to deliver the best window activation behavior. However, since we designed this application to run unattended, this invocation passes neither of those flags in the *flFlags* parameter, and so MAPI will present no such user interface; the caller could pass NULL in the *ulUIParam* parameter for the parent window without any ill effect. Instead, MAPI receives the profile name and the credential string in the *lpszProfileName* and *lpszPassword* parameters specified on the application's command line, which the code sample encapsulates in the *cmdline* object. If either of those two parameters is incorrect, the API returns a failure code, whereupon the program terminates with an error message.

The *flFlags* parameter to *MAPILogonEx* consists of a set of flags that controls aspects of the logon. *MAPI_NEW_SESSION* tells MAPI that it must create a new session instead of acquiring the shared session. Without this flag, if any other client had already created a shareable session (using *MAPI_ALLOW_OTHERS*), MAPI would return that session to the application, even if that existing session did not use the profile specified in the calling API *MAPILogonEx* function (appropriate behavior for an interactive application, perhaps, but not for our utility). The flags also contain the manifest constant *fMapiUnicode*. When the program is built for a Unicode text environment (*#define _UNICODE 1*), this manifest expands to include the value *MAPI_UNICODE* in the flags, specifying to the MAPI subsystem that all string parameters use 16-bit UNICODE characters instead of 8-bit Windows ANSI characters. We have already mentioned *MAPI_LOGON_UI* and *MAPI_PASSWORD_UI*. For other possible flags, see the API documentation.

The *lplhsession* parameter of the *MAPILogonEx* function is an out-parameter, which returns the interface pointer of the acquired session. All subsequent MAPI activity will take place through this session object.

Note the explicit and ugly casts to TCHAR* in the code. The *GetPParm* and *GetCParm* methods on our C++ command line object return CONST pointers, informing clients of the class that they cannot write through that pointer. Unfortunately, none of the prototypes for the MAPI interfaces or functions honor the CONST directive, necessitating this cast to remove the CONST attribute of the parameter. Any client code that uses CONST must do this often when it invokes MAPI.

MAPILogonEx

Purpose

Use the *MAPILogonEx* function to log a client application onto a session.

Syntax

```
ULONG MAPILogonEx(ULONG ulUIParam,
    LPTSTR lpszProfileName, LPTSTR lpszPassword,
    FLAGS flFlags, ULONG unreserved,
    LPLHANDLE lplhSession)
```

Parameters	Parameter Type	Description
ULONG *ulUIParam*	In-parameter	Handle to the window associated with the modal logon dialog box
LPTSTR *lpszProfileName*	In-parameter	Pointer to a string that identifies the profile name after logon
LPTSTR *lpszPassword*	In-parameter	Pointer to a string that identifies the profile password
FLAGS *flFlags*	In-parameter	Flag bitmask that controls the logon process
ULONG *ulReserved*	Reserved	Set to 0
LPLHANDLE *lplhSession*	Out-parameter	Pointer to a handle associated with a MAPI session

MAPI and Unicode

Throughout these code samples, you will see the type TCHAR used for characters. Like other aspects of the Win32 API set, the MAPI interfaces accept and return strings in either ANSI or Unicode formats. ANSI strings consist of traditional 8-bit characters, which are assumed to occupy the current code page setting of the client's process. In contrast, Unicode strings consist of 16-bit values denoting points in the unified Unicode character set, which subsumes most previous code pages, including the variable-length multibyte character sets traditionally used to represent many Asian languages. A TCHAR can represent either an 8-bit or a 16-bit character, depending on the language preprocessor _UNICODE symbol, which selects its definition as either UNSIGNED CHAR or UNSIGNED SHORT.

However, unlike the other Win32 APIs, the MAPI interfaces do not keep two entry points for every function, with one accepting ANSI and the other Unicode input. Instead, their methods and functions expect a flag *MAPI_UNICODE* in a bit-flags parameter. If that flag is set, the methods and functions interpret any strings as consisting of 16-bit characters and any pointers to strings as pointing to strings of 16-bit characters. Also, they return any string data in Unicode. Contrast this to the conventions of the ActiveX interfaces, which expect all of their input to consist of Unicode strings. Non-Unicode clients of ActiveX frequently must use various translation layers that thunk ANSI input into Unicode parameters for the API, and vice versa on output.

Although the MAPI interfaces all support Unicode data in this fashion, no particular implementation of an interface necessarily supports Unicode. If a function or an interface method is not able to honor *MAPI_UNICODE*, it returns *MAPI_E_BAD_CHARWIDTH* to the caller. Conversely, it is possible that a MAPI provider hosted on a DEC Alpha AXP running Windows NT might accept only Unicode strings, in which case any method not specifying *MAPI_UNICODE* would return *MAPI_E_BAD_CHARWIDTH*.

These code samples extensively use the transmutable type TCHAR, together with the property type PT_TSTRING and the transmutable string functions of TCHAR.H, all in the expectation of easing a future port to a platform fully supporting Unicode. Always use the manifest constant *fMapiUnicode* in method flags when using these transmutable types so that the method will receive the *MAPI_UNICODE* when it receives real 16-bit characters.

If the call succeeds, the client has an interface to the new session in its *psess* variable. However, the call might fail for any number of reasons. Perhaps the client specified a nonexistent or invalid profile name or credential string. In this case, since the call did not allow access to a user interface, MAPI cannot prompt you for the correct profile name or password and, therefore, must fail the call. If the call had allowed access to a user interface, you could have canceled the logon operation by choosing Cancel in the Choose A Profile dialog box. Or perhaps the system simply could not host any more sessions. Whatever the reason, if the call fails, it returns an error value in its HRESULT variable. The client tests this return value through its use of the *FAILED* macro.

Once the client finishes working with the message services of a session, it must shut down the session in an orderly fashion, instructing MAPI of its intentions and giving MAPI a chance to present any logoff user interface that an underlying messaging service might require. *IMAPISession::Logoff* gives MAPI just this notification, passing a window handle for any such user interface, although here the call does not include the *MAPI_LOGOFF_UI* flag that would give MAPI permission to use the handle. (A *MAPI_LOGOFF_UI* flag would complement a *MAPI_LOGON_UI* flag in the *flFlags* parameter to *MAPILogonEx*.)

After the client calls the *Logoff* method, it releases the session object, decrementing its reference count and informing MAPI that the client no longer uses the object. After the client has released the session, the object effectively no longer exists. Robust client code will clear an interface pointer variable after calling its *IUnknown::Release* method to ensure that it does not reference the object illegally; the following code (from the *WinMain* function of the MFETCH.CPP file) omits that step since it has no subsequent lifetime in which to make such a reference, being in the final stages of termination.

```
    ⋮
if (psess)
{
    hr = psess->Logoff((ULONG)ui.GetHwndVisible(), 0, 0);
    if (HR_FAILED(hr))
        ui.ErrorMessage(psess, hr, "Disconnecting from
            session");
    psess->Release();
}

MAPIUninitialize();
    ⋮
```

Managing notifications

Typically, an application registers for notifications on its session or other objects to learn of interesting state changes. For a session, MAPI advertises only two events. An application using the shared session can pass *MAPI_LOGOFF-_SHARED* in the *ulFlags* parameter to *IMAPISession::Logoff*, indicating that every client of that session should abandon the session, in which case MAPI relays the news to all users of that session. (This is how an application such as the Exchange mail client or Microsoft Schedule+ implements its File - Exit and File - Exit And Log Off menu commands.) Alternatively, MAPI can succumb to a critical error, in which case it attempts to inform all of its running clients to let them terminate gracefully.

MAPI implements notifications by posting messages to a hidden window in the process, the *MAPI notification window,* which it creates during the client's initial call to *MAPIInitialize.* The thread owning this window must have a working message pump for MAPI to deliver the notification successfully. MAPI creates its notification window on the calling thread unless the caller specifies *MAPI-_MULTITHREAD_NOTIFICATIONS* in the *MAPIInitialize* call, in which case MAPI creates a new thread to host the notification window.

NOTE

Notifications are of little use to the Mfetch application, which does not use the shared session and does not run persistently. Nevertheless, Mfetch goes through some of the motions for demonstration's sake. Note that Mfetch neither specifies *MAPI_MULTITHREAD_NOTIFICATIONS* nor contains its own message pump and so will not reliably receive notifications from MAPI.

In the following code excerpt from the file MFETCH.CPP, a client requests notifications on an object by implementing an advise sink object and then registering that object with MAPI. The MAPI notification window procedure calls an advise sink's *IMAPIAdviseSink::OnNotify* method whenever it receives notice of an event of interest to that sink.

```
class CAdviseSink: public IMAPIAdviseSink
{
public:
    MAPI_IUNKNOWN_METHODS(IMPL);
    MAPI_IMAPIADVISESINK_METHODS(IMPL);

    static IMAPIAdviseSink* Create(CUICommon* pui)
        { return new CAdviseSink(pui); }
```

```
private:
    CAdviseSink(CUICommon* pui) : _cRefs(1), _pui(pui) { }
    ~CAdviseSink() { }

    ULONG _cRefs;
    CUICommon* _pui;
};
    ⋮
STDMETHODIMP CAdviseSink::QueryInterface(REFIID riid, void** ppvObj)
{
    HRESULT hr = NOERROR;

    *ppvObj = NULL;

    if ((IID_IUnknown == riid) || (IID_IMAPIAdviseSink == riid))
    {
        *ppvObj = (IMAPIAdviseSink*)this;
        AddRef();
    }
    else
        hr = E_NOINTERFACE;

    return hr;
}


STDMETHODIMP_(ULONG) CAdviseSink::AddRef()
{
    return ++_cRefs;
}


STDMETHODIMP_(ULONG) CAdviseSink::Release()
{
    ULONG ulCount = --_cRefs;
    if (0L == ulCount)
        delete this;
    return ulCount;
}

// N.B. - A bug in MAPIDEFS.H makes this ULONG, not HRESULT.

STDMETHODIMP_(ULONG) CAdviseSink::OnNotify(ULONG cNotif,
    LPNOTIFICATION pNotif)
```

(continued)

```
{
    for (unsigned i = 0; i < cNotif; i++)
    {
        if (pNotif[i].ulEventType == fnevCriticalError)
        {
            // ERROR_NOTIFICATION err = pNotif[i].info.err;

            _pui->Message("Critical MAPI error - terminating");
            PostQuitMessage(1);
        }
    }

    return (ULONG)NOERROR;
}
```

Optionally, a client can elect to call the *HrAllocAdviseSink* function, which provides a system-supplied *IUnknown* template implementation around a caller-supplied *OnNotify* function.

> **NOTE**   MAPI defines its individual error codes in the header file MAPICODE.H and might have access to any of the Win32 error codes defined in WINERROR.H as well. A program should use these values to respond to particular failure codes, such as the value *MAPI_E_USER_CANCEL* returned by MAPI when you choose Cancel to a MAPI-supplied dialog box.

Once Mfetch has a session, it creates an advise sink and then registers that sink with the session through *IMAPISession::Advise*, specifying the kind of event that it wishes to follow. A session accepts requests for *fnevCriticalError*, specifying (obviously) critical errors, and *fnevExtendedError*, which subsumes shared session logoff notifications. Other types of objects support other types of notifications, such as *fnevNewMail*, reported by message store objects. If MAPI accepts the sink and the registration, Mfetch receives in return a connection number to use in subsequent sink management. Mfetch then releases the created sink object, since MAPI has added its own reference to the object, and manages the sink's subsequent lifetime through the *IUnknown* protocol. This process is shown in the following excerpt from the *WinMain* function:

```
⋮
#if USE_PREFAB_ADVISE_SINK
    IMAPIAdviseSink* psink = NULL;
    hr = HrAllocAdviseSink(NotifyCallback, &ui, &psink);
    if (FAILED(hr))
```

```
        {
            ui.Message("Failed to allocate advise sink");
            fOk = FALSE;
        }
#else
        IMAPIAdviseSink* psink = CAdviseSink::Create(&ui);
        if (NULL == psink)
        {
            ui.Message("Failed to allocate advise sink");
            fOk = FALSE;
        }
#endif

        ULONG nCookie = 0L;
        if (psink)
        {
            hr = psess->Advise(0, NULL, fnevCriticalError, psink,
                &nCookie);
            if (FAILED(hr))
            {
                ui.ErrorMessage(psess, hr, "Registering advise sink");
                fOk = FALSE;
            }
        }
    ⋮
```

When a client no longer needs to track events on an object, or before the client releases the object in any case, it should signal its lack of interest to MAPI, passing the connection number back to *IMAPISession::Unadvise*. MAPI in turn removes the sink from its internal tables, releasing its references, as shown in the following code from the *WinMain* function of Mfetch:

```
    ⋮
    if (nCookie != 0L)
        psess->Unadvise(nCookie);
    if (psink)
        psink->Release();
    ⋮
```

The default message store

Next Mfetch must mount the session's default message store. The MAPI spooler downloads a message by contacting a transport, accepting a message from the transport, and moving that message into the current session's default message store. Since a session starts with no active message stores, it cannot receive delivered messages until the caller mounts the default store.

When a client initially acquires a session, all the store providers named in the session's profile lie dormant. MAPI compiles the message store table from the provider data kept in the profile, offering this table as a property of the session. To activate a message store provider, the client must read a row of the message store table, extract the entry identifier (entryid) of the message store from the row, and call *IMAPISession::OpenMsgStore*. MAPI in turn loads the appropriate provider, which validates the caller's access privileges and then returns a store object.

Mfetch starts by examining the message store table on the session. *IMAPISession::GetMsgStoresTable,* called in the *OpenDefaultMDB* function, returns a MAPI table of message store information, as follows:

```
    ⋮
IMAPITable* ptblStores;
HRESULT hr = psess->GetMsgStoresTable(0L, &ptblStores);
if (FAILED(hr))
{
    ui.ErrorMessage(psess, hr, IDS_E_FIND_DEFAULT_STORE);
    return FALSE;
}
    ⋮
```

The MAPI table abstraction supports a wide range of database operations on its virtual structure. However, for a table that has very few rows, such as a message store table, it is most efficient simply to bring the entire structure into memory at once. MAPI provides the *HrQueryAllRows* function to do this as economically as possible. The caller specifies the columns desired in the table through a counted array, encapsulated in the type *SPropTagArray*. Here the caller requests only two columns in the table: *PR_ENTRYID*, the entry identifier, allowing the caller to get an interface on the object corresponding to the row; and *PR_DEFAULT_STORE*, which will be set on the row corresponding to the default message store—that is, what we're seeking. *HrQueryAllRows* performs a series of *IMAPITable* manipulations, saving the caller a lot of work; these have the effect of allocating storage for *SRowSet* to contain all the rows of the table. MAPI allocates storage for *SRowSet* and returns the rows of the table, as shown in the following excerpt from the *OpenDefaultMDB* function in the MFETCH.CPP file.

```
    ⋮
enum {ivalEid = 0, ivalDefault, cvalTotal};
SizedSPropTagArray(cvalTotal, taga) =
```

```
        { cvalTotal,
        { PR_ENTRYID, PR_DEFAULT_STORE } };

    SRowSet* prs;
    hr = HrQueryAllRows(ptblStores, (SPropTagArray*)&taga, NULL, NULL, 0,
        &prs);
    if (FAILED(hr))
    {
        ui.ErrorMessage(ptblStores, hr, IDS_E_FIND_DEFAULT_STORE);
        ptblStores->Release();
        return FALSE;
    }
    ⋮
```

With all the rows of the table in memory, Mfetch now can search for the single row corresponding to the default message store. The application iterates through the row set, seeking the row with a *PR_DEFAULT_STORE* column present and set to *TRUE*; once it finds that, it extracts the entry identifier column from the row for use by *OpenMsgStore*. *OpenMsgStore* returns to the caller an interface pointer to the mounted message store. This is shown in the following code extracted from the *OpenDefaultMBD* function in the MFETCH.CPP file:

```
    ⋮
    IMsgStore* pmdb = NULL;
    for (unsigned i = 0; i < prs->cRows; i++)
    {
        SPropValue* pval = prs->aRow[i].lpProps;

        assert(pval != NULL);
        assert(pval[ivalEid].ulPropTag == PR_ENTRYID);

        if ((pval[ivalDefault].ulPropTag == PR_DEFAULT_STORE)
            && (pval[ivalDefault].Value.b == 1))
        {
            hr = psess->OpenMsgStore((ULONG)ui.GetHwndVisible(),
                pval[ivalEid].Value.bin.cb,
                (LPENTRYID)pval[ivalEid].Value.bin.lpb,
                NULL, ulFlags, &pmdb);
            if (FAILED(hr))
                ui.ErrorMessage(psess, hr,
                    IDS_E_FIND_DEFAULT_STORE);
            break;
        }
    }
    ⋮
```

Once Mfetch has opened the store, it no longer needs the message store table or its saved row set. As shown in the following excerpt from the *OpenDefault-MBD* function, MAPI supplies a helper function *FreeProws* to release the memory allocated for the row set structure:

```
    ⋮
FreeProws(prs);
ptblStores->Release();
    ⋮
```

With the default store mounted, Mfetch can proceed to download messages from the transport. Once the transmission completes, the program closes down the store and the store's provider. The *IMsgStore::StoreLogoff* call allows the caller to close down the provider gracefully, specifying what the provider should do with any pending transport activity during logoff since conceivably a message might be arriving or departing asynchronously to the program's operation. This is shown in the following excerpt from the *WinMain* function:

```
    ⋮
    ULONG ulParms = LOGOFF_ORDERLY;
    hr = pmdb->StoreLogoff (&ulParms);
    if (FAILED(hr))
        ui.ErrorMessage (pmdb, hr, "Disconnecting from store");
    pmdb->Release();
    ⋮
```

NOTE   Mfetch opens the message store in its *OpenDefaultMDB* function and closes the store in the *WinMain* function.

The spooler

With the session established and the default store loaded, MAPI is ready to download messages. The application now has only to give the spooler a little push in the right direction.

All the active components of a running MAPI subsystem report their status in the status table, which MAPI offers as a property of the session object, similar to the message store table. An application can locate the spooler in the status table, open the spooler's status object, and through the status object, perform certain limited communications with the spooler, including telling it to download any messages it sees on the transports. This process strongly resembles that of manipulating the message store table.

First, in the *DownLoadMessages* function, the Mfetch program retrieves the status table from the session.

```
    ⋮
IMAPITable* ptbl = NULL;
HRESULT hr = psess->GetStatusTable(0L, &ptbl);
if (FAILED(hr))
{
    ui.ErrorMessage(psess, hr, IDS_E_FIND_SPOOLER);
    return FALSE;
}
    ⋮
```

Next, since status tables are small, the *DownLoadMessages* function brings the contents of the entire table into memory, as shown below. Except for the identity of one requested column, this could be the message store table.

```
    ⋮
enum {ivalEid = 0, ivalType, cvalTotal};
SizedSPropTagArray(cvalTotal, taga) =
    { cvalTotal,
    { PR_ENTRYID, PR_RESOURCE_TYPE } };
SRowSet* prs;
hr = HrQueryAllRows(ptbl, (SPropTagArray*)&taga, NULL, NULL, 0,
    &prs);
if (FAILED(hr))
{
    // Bail out.
}
    ⋮
```

With all the rows of the status table in memory, the application now searches for the row corresponding to the spooler. Once Mfetch finds that row, it extracts the entry identifier and passes it to *OpenEntry*, which returns an interface on the spooler status object. This process is shown in the following code excerpt:

```
    ⋮
IMAPIStatus* pstat = NULL;
for (unsigned i = 0; i < prs->cRows; i++)
{
    SPropValue* pval = prs->aRow[i].lpProps;

    assert(pval != NULL);
    assert(pval[ivalEid].ulPropTag == PR_ENTRYID);
```

(continued)

```
        if ((pval[ivalType].ulPropTag == PR_RESOURCE_TYPE)
            && (pval[ivalType].Value.ul == MAPI_SPOOLER))
        {
            ULONG ulType;
            hr = psess->OpenEntry(pval[ivalEid].Value.bin.cb,
                (LPENTRYID)pval[ivalEid].Value.bin.lpb,
                &IID_IMAPIStatus, MAPI_BEST_ACCESS, &ulType,
                (IUnknown**)&pstat);
            if (FAILED(hr))
                ui.ErrorMessage(psess, hr, IDS_E_FIND_SPOOLER);
                break;
        }
        ⋮
```

Observe the continuing similarity to the message store table manipulation code. Such table manipulation is fundamental to MAPI programming.

Finally, with the status object in hand, the *DownLoadMessages* function asks the spooler to flush its incoming message queue, as shown in the code below. This causes the spooler to contact each message transport and check for incoming messages, with all activity taking place synchronously to the caller.

```
    ⋮
hr = pstat->FlushQueues((ULONG)ui.GetHwndVisible(), 0,
    NULL, FLUSH_DOWNLOAD|FLUSH_FORCE);
if (FAILED(hr))
    ui.ErrorMessage(pstat, hr, IDS_E_FLUSH_SPOOLER);
pstat->Release();
    ⋮
```

The results

When Mfetch is launched, it opens a profile, examines its contents, and moves any incoming messages from the transports named in the profile to the default message store. Insulated by MAPI's generic approach to underlying messaging systems, this simple application will operate correctly within the context of any underlying configuration: from a simple mailbox on a Mail or POP3 host to much more sophisticated hosts, such as the Exchange Server.

3

Exchange Server: The Messaging System

MAPI provides an abstraction that allows an application to interact with an underlying messaging system, without becoming too deeply embroiled in the mechanics of such a system. Nevertheless, as the saying goes, the devil is in the details. When a program crashes or otherwise malfunctions, layers of abstraction go flying like pieces of an exploding Hollywood stunt car, leaving the development staff to pick through the smoldering ruins and determine what went wrong. A program hosted on a particular system might want to take special advantage of that system's features or otherwise optimize itself for good behavior and performance while running thereon. Even if they never plan the topology of an organization's messaging infrastructure or play administrator for an evening, application developers should have a solid command of the architecture and operation of their host system.

To that end, a short presentation of the facilities of Microsoft Exchange Server is in order. I will first examine the different components appearing in a site running Exchange Server: the various servers that cooperate to provide messaging services within an enterprise, and the manner in which clients communicate with those servers to exchange messages and other forms of information. Next I will change focus to examine Exchange Server from the perspective of MAPI since that is how client applications will view it. Finally I will dissect the typical "Exchange application," presenting its anatomy as a client of MAPI that interacts with the services of Exchange Server.

Component and Process/Data Model of Exchange Server

From the perspective of an organization with messaging needs, the most compelling feature of Exchange Server is its scalable client/server architecture. This means that its architecture can handle a site of 100,000 users as well as a site of 100 users. Logically, a working Exchange Server installation consists of a set of one or more servers, offering a suite of services[1] between them and a set of clients that request the services of those servers. To understand Exchange Server, one must understand its constituent services and how they work together.

Figure 3-1 depicts many of the services of Exchange running within a single messaging site. An Exchange installation might distribute these among multiple Microsoft Windows NT servers to spread the load among different hosts. High-demand services such as the *message store* can run on many servers simultaneously to distribute the load still further and bring more hardware into play. Clients interact directly with some services, such as the message store that hosts their messages, while they see other services only through the side effects of the service running in the system, such as the *message transfer agent* that ferries messages between instances of the store.

Everybody and Their Grandmother Is a Client/Server

"Client/server," like "object," is one of those overused buzzwords that don't provide any useful information about a system. After all, Microsoft Mail keeps its post office files on a server, right? And client workstations access those post offices on the server, right? So what's the big deal? The difference lies in how a client accesses the server, the types of services that the client expects from the server, and the manner in which the servers intercommunicate.

In Microsoft Mail, the server is nothing more than a shared file point. It acts like a large storage medium, a sort of common scratch pad, that every participant knows how to access by name. For client 1 to send a message to client 2, client 1 opens the file corresponding to client 2's mailbox, locks the file open, appends data to the file, unlocks the file, and closes the file handle; subsequently, client 2 checks its mailbox file, finds new data therein, opens the file, locks the file open, reads the new data from the file, resets the file pointer to eliminate the old data, unlocks the file, and closes the file. Client 1 has complete access to the contents of client 2's mailbox. The server sees nothing more than a sequence of file operations on its file services: open, close, read, write, lock, unlock, seek, reset, and query attributes.

In Exchange Server, each server actually articulates a remote interface with message-oriented semantics. To send a message to a particular mailbox, a client must submit the message as a single logical object together with its intended destination. The server takes responsibility for getting that message to

---

1. In Windows NT parlance, the computer hosting the code is the *server,* while the logical body of code responding to client requests is the *service.* In the parlance of RPC discussed later in this chapter, the requesting agency is the *client,* and the responding agency is the *server.* A Windows NT server can host multiple RPC servers, each implemented as a Windows NT service running on the server.

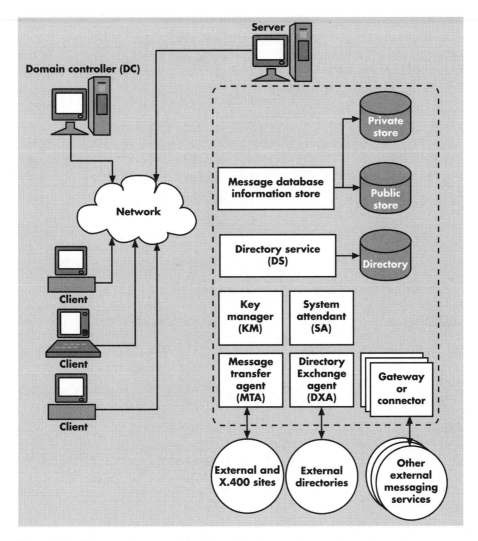

Figure 3-1. *The services running in an Exchange Server messaging site.*

its destination's mailbox. The client has no notion of where its destination lies and certainly has no power to open the destination mailbox's storage directly. Not only does this protect the data on the server, but also it allows the server to apply levels of indirection, such as consulting a directory, to determine where the destination mailbox might actually lie.

Servers communicate among themselves using similar but more structured protocols, consulting the directory to learn the names of their partners. The results are more secure since clients always work through a third party; more scalable since clients and servers defer location decisions to RPC bind requests and directory consultations; and more robust since any server deals with requests on a logical per-message request rather than per-file access, making their heuristics more easily tunable and their computed statistics more directly applicable to determining future server requirements.

In a sense, then, both systems are client/server; they simply differ as to the services they offer in a client/server fashion. Mail is a shared-file messaging system built on top of the client/server file-sharing system offered by Novell Netware or Microsoft LAN Manager. Exchange is a client/server messaging system built on top of the advanced networking capabilities of Windows NT.

The Windows NT Domain Controller

The *domain controller* (DC) is a Windows NT Advanced Server computer that holds the security database for a domain, authenticating users and checking security tokens. A domain contains at least one domain controller, and possibly more than one; one domain controller is designated the *primary* domain controller and replicates the contents of its database to the other *backup* domain controller servers in the domain. Together, the primary and backup domain controllers oversee all logon activity in the domain. When a user logs onto the network, a domain controller validates the offered user name and password and supplies the user with a security access token, which Windows NT subsequently uses on any attempt by the user to access an object.

Exchange Server operates within the security framework of the Windows NT domain architecture. It uses this mechanism to authenticate a user sending a message, ensuring that one user does not send mail impersonating another user without explicit authorization on the part of the impersonated user. It also controls the set of folders and directory objects that a user can access. Users without a security access token have no privileges within Exchange Server. All permissions ultimately depend on a user's properly validated identity within a domain.

A single Windows NT domain can host approximately 10,000 user accounts. Organizations that support very large numbers of messaging users must build structures of multiple domains linked by domain trust relationships to host them all. Each of those domains will have its own set of domain controllers.

The Exchange Server Information Store

The Exchange Server *information store* (message database, or MDB) is a Windows NT service containing a database of user-originated information, encompassing mailboxes for sending and receiving data, private user folders for storing private data, and public folders for storing and exchanging data among multiple users simultaneously. This information store service runs on a Windows NT server computer that hosts the storage backing the database. It stores and organizes its contained messages, documents, and other data, and it provides browsing and query facilities for locating and retrieving them. It originates all messages sent from the system and receives messages on behalf of its users with mailboxes. When a user on the system sends a message to another user with a mailbox in the same database, the information store manages all aspects of transmitting the message.

A single information store is limited to the size of its hosting computer's backing storage, or 2 GB maximum for each of its constituent databases: one for public data and one for private mailbox data, together totaling 4 GB maximum. When an organization's number of users or its data requirements tax this limit, a messaging site must offer multiple information stores hosted on multiple server computers to accommodate it all. A site might also offer multiple information stores to distribute the computational or communications load across multiple sets of hardware.

An organization might elect to *replicate* public folder data between databases on different servers. This allows multiple databases to host the same set of public data, thus distributing the load of hosting it among different computers. Periodically, each instance of the database, or *replica,* sends a synopsis of its local changes to the other replicas. When an item undergoes changes in multiple replicas simultaneously, the system attempts to reconcile the changes to keep the replicas identical.

The Exchange Server Directory Service

The Exchange Server *directory service* (DS) is a Windows NT service containing a database of systemwide administration and configuration data. The database contains the identities of mail users and their recipient mailboxes, message distribution lists, available public folders and the servers hosting them, data replication patterns and schedules, and relationships to other messaging sites, including other Exchange sites and external message gateways. Like the information store, the directory service runs on a Windows NT server computer that hosts the storage backing the database. The directory service follows much of the ISO X.500 directory specification, describing all objects in the system as members of a hierarchy of classes, with each class adhering to a schema of properties. Whenever a component in the Exchange Server needs to learn an attribute of some object in the site, whether the component is a client or a server, it consults the directory service.

Every server offering Exchange Server services runs an instance of the directory service. The directory service replicates its contents with every other instance of the directory service in the system, making its contents a universal common resource. A basic element of Exchange Server topology is the *messaging site,* a term used rather freely in this text until now but which actually denotes a set of servers that share the contents of a single logical directory. Note that a single messaging site might span multiple domains. However, if it does, the administrators must take special care to ensure that users from one domain have access to servers in another domain.

The directory service and the information store complement one another. Every directory service offers a mirror replica of every other directory, whereas information stores have varied contents, with replication of public stores set up as a special case. Directory services contain addresses, references, and configuration metainformation; information stores contain user-supplied or contributed information. Directory service contents change rarely; information store contents change often. With a few exceptions, only administrators can change the contents of the directory service, but all sorts of users have write privileges to various portions of the information store.

Components Invisible to Applications

Applications primarily interact with the domain controller, directory service, and information store. An application gets its authorization from the domain controller, looks up information in the directory service, and then reads and writes to and from the information store. However, many other components operate in an Exchange Server installation; these interact only with other services and therefore are invisible to applications, except when they fail.

The message transfer agent

The Exchange Server *message transfer agent* (MTA) ferries messages between instances of the information store, gateways, external message transfer agents, and Exchange Server message sites. It handles message delivery whenever a message must leave a particular store database—that is, when it cannot be handled by message transfer agent local delivery. In communicating with foreign systems, the message transfer agent translates a message as necessary between the Exchange Server's native MAPI format and the industry standard X.400 format.

The system attendant

The Exchange Server *system attendant* (SA) automates a number of tasks involved in maintaining the messaging system. It monitors communications between servers, assists in routine administration of replication, tracks key maintenance for public key encryption, and performs many other miscellaneous tasks that keep the overall system functioning smoothly.

The directory synchronizer

The Exchange Server *directory synchronizer* (directory Exchange agent, or DXA) exchanges directory service information with certain external directories, using the Microsoft Mail 3.*x* directory synchronization protocol. This ensures that one system's directory accurately reflects mail recipients contained in another system's directory so that clients of the local directory service can correctly address messages to clients of the external system.

The key manager

The Exchange Server *key manager* (KM) implements a number of aspects of public-key cryptography as used in Exchange Server. It generates the initial keys, both public and private; stores public keys as necessary; and configures the encryption features on a particular mailbox. The key manager interacts mostly with the administrator program and the system attendant service, publishing its data in the directory for the use of clients and other services.

The connectors and gateways

The Exchange Server can support any number of *connectors* and *gateways* that allow it to exchange information with external messaging systems. A connector is nothing more than a gateway that offers tight integration with all the services of Exchange.

The Clients

Users can communicate with Exchange Server through several flavors of the client program.

The Exchange Server Administrator program is one such client. Users with sufficient privileges run this program to view and modify the configuration of the system. It primarily operates by manipulating the schema and contents of the directory, but it also modifies various sensitive zones of information stores as necessary and communicates with both the key manager and the system attendant services. Any administrator works with Exchange through this program.

Standalone application programs provide another variety of client. Exchange Server offers a couple of different application programming interfaces, or APIs, with which an application can communicate with Exchange. Foremost among these is MAPI, Microsoft's standard message-oriented programming interface. A program can also use DAPI, the Directory Access Programming Interface, for importing and exporting data to and from the directory.

Most typically, users experience Exchange Server through the facilities of a mail client (messaging user agent, or MUA), an application designed to submit and receive messages to and from a messaging system—here, Exchange Server. On the various Microsoft Windows–based platforms, Exchange delivers its clients as MAPI applications, leveraging both the richness of MAPI and Exchange

Server's support for it. These clients run on more than the server platform Windows NT; they run on workstation versions of Windows NT and on Microsoft Windows 95 as well since MAPI appears on all Microsoft Win32 platforms. Furthermore, they run on 16-bit Windows through the graces of a special 16-bit version of MAPI. Beyond Windows platforms, Exchange Server makes clients available for MS-DOS and Apple Macintosh System 7, although these non-Windows-based clients do not have MAPI.

Whatever their operating system platform, clients run on workstation computers separate from the servers hosting the messaging system. They access the services of Exchange Server through a protocol called *remote procedure call.*

RPC in Exchange

Remote procedure call (RPC) is a protocol for client/server computer communication. In RPC, the client makes a procedure call and the server implements it. Client and server can run on different computers and in different operating environments, so long as they share network connectivity and have compliant RPC run-time environment support. Each end's application code sees only a procedure call out or in; the intervening RPC run-time support handles transferring the flow-of-control across the network, including function parameters and return values. RPC is part of the Open Software Foundation's Distributed Computing Environment.

Figure 3-2 demonstrates the difference between a regular procedure call and a remote procedure call. In a regular procedure call, the caller pushes arguments and its return address on the stack, jumps to the subroutine address, and then transfers control to the subroutine. After the subroutine has finished executing, the system uses the information pushed on the stack to return control to the caller's return address. In contrast, a remote procedure call transfers control to a client stub (what COM calls a proxy), which extracts the passed parameters from the client's address space, marshals them into a network-standard format, and submits the results to the system RPC run times for transmission across the network. Across the network on the server's side, the server's system RPC run times receive the data from the network transport and pass it to a server stub (what COM calls a stub), which unmarshals the parameters from network-standard format into the format expected by the server's code within the server's address space and then calls the actual server procedure. When the called server procedure returns, the intervening layers perform exactly the same steps to return values to the client caller. Whereas a regular procedure call takes place within a single address space, a remote procedure call connects two address spaces, imposing layers of abstraction that preserve the procedure call metaphor.

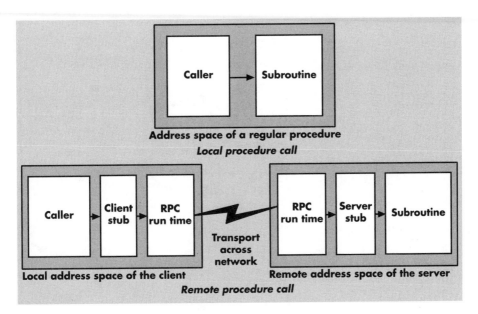

Figure 3-2. *A regular procedure call takes place within a single address space. Compare this to a remote procedure call, which interposes layers of abstraction to extract the parameters from one address space, transfer them across the network, and reassemble the parameters in a different address space.*

All Exchange Server services operate as RPC servers. Any client must contact a server with a security access token (courtesy of a previous user validation by a domain controller); the server uses that token to determine whether the client can receive the services it requests. Messaging clients act as RPC clients, requesting the contents of a particular mailbox or folder of a particular server, as shown in Figure 3-3 on the following page. Services also intercommunicate using RPC, in which case they can act as clients when contacting their neighbor services.

RPC offers two different models by which clients locate their server. A client can consult a name service, requesting any server that can satisfy a particular requirement, or it might bind to a server by name. In Exchange Server, all RPC clients bind to their servers by server name. The services use information published in the directory to identify their neighbors, whereas the messaging clients require the name of the server hosting a mailbox as initial configuration data.

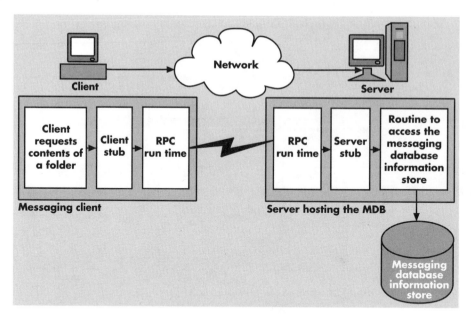

Figure 3-3. *RPC connects Exchange clients to their servers.*

Exchange Server as Seen by MAPI

Any MAPI application has a specific client perspective with respect to the services of Exchange Server. MAPI provides a generic interface to the facilities of any messaging system and maps the facilities of Exchange Server, as rendered through its service providers, into MAPI's own metaphor. At the same time, Exchange retains a number of distinguishing features that remain apparent even through MAPI.

All Exchange clients communicate with servers using RPC. The RPC binding and calling takes place in the MAPI providers, doing so transparently to the MAPI client application. The providers keep the name of the server hosting the user's mailbox in the configuration section of the profile and then use that data when they initialize themselves to bind to the servers. Any call into the provider might result in a remote procedure call to a server, as illustrated in Figure 3-4. For the sake of improved performance, a provider attempts to minimize the number of RPCs it generates. Still, clients should structure their code to allow the provider to work with a minimum of RPC traffic—for example, merging calls to *IMAPI-Prop::GetProps* so that a provider can fetch the data in one RPC instead of two and using the *MAPI_DEFERRED_ERRORS* flag wherever possible, such as in calls to *IMAPIContainer::OpenEntry*.

The MAPI providers depict Exchange as a set of generic MAPI objects. Folders from the Exchange Server information store support *IMAPIFolder*, and user records from the Exchange Server directory service support *IMailUser*, just as if

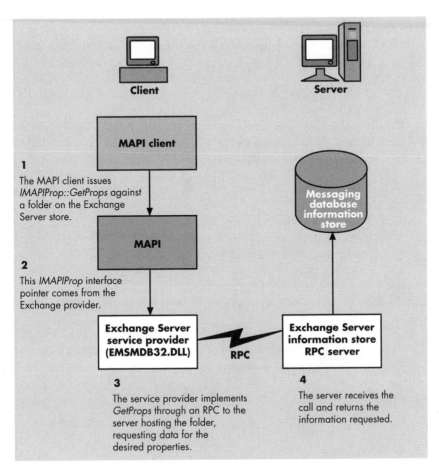

Figure 3-4. *The Exchange providers make remote procedure calls on behalf of their clients.*

they had come from any other provider. However, Exchange marks its objects when possible; clients that want to take special advantage of Exchange can look for these distinguishing marks on an object and manipulate those objects accordingly. In a status table, the status objects corresponding to the services of Exchange Server name the Exchange DLLs as their MAPI providers, with either EMSABP32.DLL or EMSMDB32.DLL in the column *PR_PROVIDER_DLL_NAME.* More usefully, Exchange flags its stores in the message store table in the *PR-_PROVIDER_MDB* column; this value indicates whether the store is an Exchange store and, if so, whether it is a mailbox, delegate mailbox, or public folder store. Exchange also flags objects from its directory in the address book hierarchy in a similar fashion, using the column *PR_AB_PROVIDER_ID.* Once a client knows that an object originates with Exchange Server, it can anticipate any special inherent semantics.

Through the extensible *IMAPIProp* interface, a MAPI object from Exchange usually offers a number of properties specific to the implementation in addition to the standard properties of the object type. Figure 3-5 demonstrates this with a folder object from the Exchange information store. (Tables 3-1 and 3-2 describe properties standard to all MAPI objects and properties specific to Exchange, respectively.) Some of these properties simply represent information kept by Exchange that it associates with the object. For example, the Exchange store retains the identity of the user that originally created a particular message as *PR_CREATOR_NAME* and *PR_CREATOR_ENTRYID* on that message. Other properties represent special facilities delivered by Exchange, such as *PR_OOF-_STATE* on a mailbox, to indicate a user's out-of-office state, or they might have special semantics, such as *PR_TEST_LINE_SPEED*, that always yield an RPC for a fixed amount of data when the client requests it, the better to test the speed of the connection from client to server. Finally some properties offer a complete Exchange-specific interface from server to client, such as *PR_RULES_TABLE*. When this is opened using *IMAPIProp::OpenProperty*, it returns an interface pointer to a custom interface for manipulating the rules on a folder or it returns *PR_ACL_TABLE*, which provides an interface to manipulate the access control list on a folder.

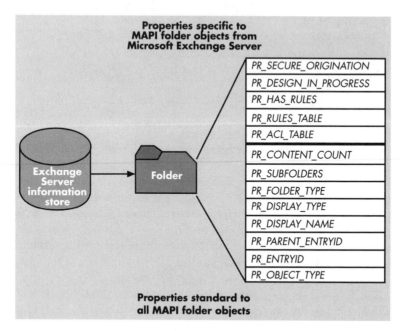

Figure 3-5. *Objects from Exchange Server providers carry additional properties. If a client knows that the object comes from Exchange Server, it can query and use those properties.*

Property	Type	Description
PR_AB_PROVIDER_ID	PT_BINARY	A unique value used to identify the address book provider that supplies the address book container in the hierarchy
PR_CONTENT_COUNT	PT_LONG	The number of entries in the address book container
PR_DISPLAY_NAME	PT_TSTRING	The display name for a particular MAPI object
PR_DISPLAY_TYPE	PT_LONG	A value used to associate a display element (such as a folder, messaging user, or distribution list) with a row of an address book or table hierarchy
PR_ENTRYID	PT_BINARY	An entry identifier used to open and edit properties of MAPI objects, such as a mail user, message, distribution list, address book container, folder, message store, or status object
PR_FOLDER_TYPE	PT_LONG	A constant that indicates the folder type, such as a generic folder, root folder, or search-results folder
PR_IDENTITY_DISPLAY	PT_TSTRING	The display name associated with the unique identifier (UID) of a messaging user
PR_IDENTITY_ENTRYID	PT_BINARY	The provider's entry identifier for the user
PR_INSTANCE_KEY	PT_BINARY	A unique value used to identify a row in a table such as a contents table or categorization table, but not a display table
PR_OBJECT_TYPE	PT_LONG	The type for an object (such as an address book container, address book object, distribution list, folder, or message attachment) that corresponds to the primary interface available for the object
PR_PARENT_ENTRYID	PT_BINARY	The entry identifier of the folder where a message was located during a search

Table 3-1. *Properties standard to all MAPI folder objects*   *(continued)*
(defined in the MAPITAGS.H file).

Table 3-1. *continued*

Property	Type	Description
PR_PROVIDER_DISPLAY	PT_TSTRING	The display name defined by a vendor for a service provider
PR_PROVIDER_DLL_NAME	PT_TSTRING	The filename of a DLL representing the MAPI service provider
PR_RESOURCE_FLAGS	PT_LONG	The flag that appears on message services and providers to represent information about the messaging service, messaging service table, and profile
PR_RESOURCE_METHODS	PT_LONG	A bitmask used to signify the methods supported for status objects
PR_RESOURCE_TYPE	PT_LONG	A constant used to identify the type of service provider (such as address book, spooler hook, profile, message store, and transport providers)
PR_ROWID	PT_LONG	A unique identifier that specifies a particular recipient in a status or recipient table
PR_STATUS_CODE	PT_LONG	A bitmask representing the status of a service provider
PR_STATUS_STRING	PT_TSTRING	A string indicating the current status of a service provider (such as whether the service provider is processing a message)
PR_SUBFOLDERS	PT_BOOLEAN	A Boolean value indicating whether a folder contains subfolders

Property	Type	Description
PR_ACL_TABLE	PT_OBJECT	A table used for reading and modifying access control lists
PR_CREATOR_ENTRYID	PT_BINARY	An entry identifier in an address book that identifies the user who created a message

Table 3-2. *Properties specific to Exchange server (defined in the EDKMDB.H file).*

Property	Type	Description
PR_CREATOR_NAME	PT_TSTRING	A read-only property identifying the display name of the user who created a message
PR_DESIGN_IN_PROGRESS	PT_BOOLEAN	A Boolean value indicating whether all users or only owners have access to a public folder object
PR_HAS_RULES	PT_BOOLEAN	A Boolean value indicating whether a folder has rules
PR_OOF_STATE	PT_BOOLEAN	A Boolean value used to indicate a user's out-of-office state
PR_RULES_TABLE	PT_OBJECT	Property used to read and modify rules on a folder
PR_SECURE_ORIGINATION	PT_BOOLEAN	A Boolean value used to indicate whether the externally generated messages in an Exchange folder were altered to appear like messages generated by Exchange
PR_TEST_LINE_SPEED	PT_BINARY	A property that forces the underlying Exchange Server message provider to execute a single remote procedure call against the server

Address Book Provider

The Exchange Server address book provider renders the contents of portions of the Exchange directory for MAPI. It supplies mail recipients and containers for the address book, allowing the addressing of messages to various entities in the directory. In addition to the usual mail users and distribution lists, it presents recipients for public folders; users can address messages to public folder recipients, thus placing a copy of the message in the folder. It also presents recipients for any custom mailboxes in the enterprise—that is, any programs that solicit a sent message as input, such as a gateway to a fax machine.

The Exchange Server address book provider supports hierarchical address book containers. These containers distinguish themselves with a special *PR_AB_PROVIDER_ID* value.

The Exchange directory can handle in excess of 100,000 users. To manipulate such large data sets efficiently, its underlying database keeps a fixed set of keys and sorts available on its contents and will not honor requests that would require a new key or sort. Its address book provider reflects this limitation and will fail requests for contents tables sorted on arbitrary columns.

Transport Provider

The Exchange Server transport provider handles aspects of message delivery and interaction with the MAPI spooler. It is tightly coupled with the message store provider since the Exchange information store handles message transmission and delivery itself.

If a user configures a personal information store as the default store in his or her profile, the MAPI spooler contacts the Exchange transport provider and pumps messages from the server store into the personal store. This allows a user to keep all Exchange messages in local storage on a workstation instead of on the server. However, if the user configures the Exchange Server store as the default store in the user's profile, Exchange handles all transmission and delivery without spooler intervention.

Message Store Provider

The Exchange Server message store provider renders the contents of the Exchange information store for MAPI. It defines a number of rows in the message store table: one for the user's default mailbox and private mail folders, one for the public folder store, and one for each mailbox for which the user can act as a delegate. Each such store distinguishes itself with a special *PR_PROVIDER-_MDB* value.

A user's mailbox store receives mail delivered to that user. It contains personal mail folders for organizing the user's personal messages and data, organized in the usual hierarchy of folders and messages. A user can offer another user delegate access to this mailbox by altering the Exchange *access control list* (ACL) on the mailbox to grant the other user permission; the store then appears in the other user's message store table as a delegate store.

The public folder store provides access to all the public folders in the organization's Exchange Server system. The visible public folder hierarchy comes from the directory service, whereas the contents of individual folders come from a server hosting a replica of that public folder and its data. Each folder offers a number of special properties that support the design of a database-style application within the folder. The access control list on a public folder allows its designer to grant or forbid access to the folder by particular users or groups of users. Figure 3-6 shows a client's view of the personal and public message stores and how the Exchange Server information store backs them.

For the most part, message store replication takes place transparently to MAPI clients. A client changes the contents of a folder, whereupon the server takes care of replicating the changes to all other mirror images of that folder. If a user

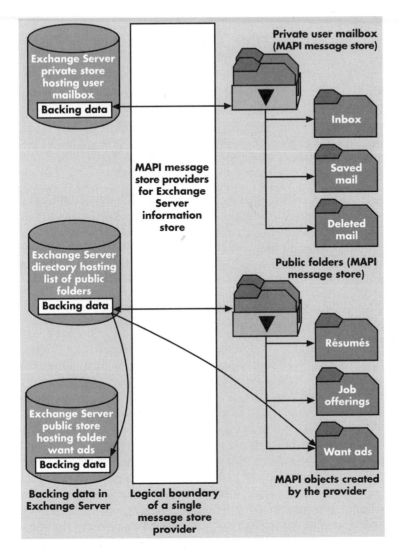

Figure 3-6. *The personal and public message stores as depicted by MAPI. By default, Exchange Server depicts two message stores to its MAPI clients: one corresponding to the user's mailbox and one containing all visible public folders.*

makes a change that conflicts with another user's simultaneous change on a different replica, the server either picks a dominant version itself or bounces the decision back to the users, depending on the setting of an Exchange-specific folder property. If the server bounces the decision, the clients see a message consisting of a composite of all the various message states and must select one version as the victor. Client code never sees this composite message unless it expects it since by default the Exchange Server supplies a standard user interface for resolving such replication conflicts.

The message store hosts a special library of form servers in a public folder that it replicates throughout the organization. The Exchange Server providers extend MAPI's form lookup mechanism to use this additional global library, enabling the organization to implement a standard set of forms for interpersonal messaging.

Every folder in the store supports a rules mechanism. A folder optionally lists a set of predicates, which the store evaluates upon delivering a message to that folder; if a predicate matches the message, the store applies to the message a set of actions associated with the predicate. Set on a mailbox, this mechanism allows a user to filter incoming messages; set on a public folder, it allows an application to take automated actions on submissions. Clients manipulate the rules mechanism by opening a special interface on the folder object.

Client User Interface Extensions

Exchange Server offers a good deal of dedicated client/user interface that extends the facilities of the standard Windows Messaging System (WMS) Exchange client, reflecting the various special properties and interfaces offered by Exchange's MAPI objects. It puts many custom commands on the Exchange client's menu bar and property pages, offering access to access control lists, rules, and many special properties. It supplies an extended MAPI Forms Manager, plus a form to handle most messages in conflict. In short, these client extensions translate Exchange's features into added value for the user. Figure 3-7 shows the user interface extensions in action. The Exchange Server MAPI providers render Exchange Server objects as generic MAPI quantities, with extra features reflected through extra properties and interfaces; the Exchange client uses these generic objects, and the extensions to the Exchange client make it nongeneric by interpreting the nongeneric object properties.

An Exchange Application as a MAPI Application

The services offered by the Exchange Server information store create a center for organizational information exchange. A public folder is visible throughout the organization, with its name advertised in the global Exchange directory service. From the name of the folder, a client can access the folder without reference to the name of the server hosting the folder; in fact, multiple servers can host the folder, with the system maintaining multiple replicas of the same folder to distribute the load across multiple hardware platforms or to make it available at different points of the network topology. The system replicates any

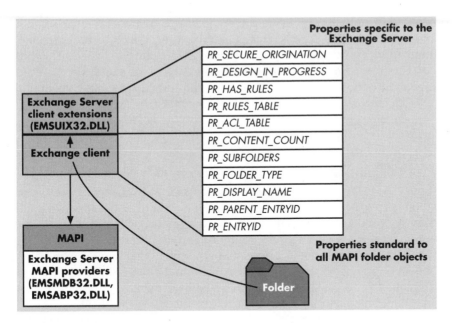

Figure 3-7. *Through extensions to the generic Exchange client, Exchange Server depicts the extensions that it makes to its MAPI objects.*

changes made to one folder to other images of the folder as necessary. The store can contain any kind of data and supports the indexing and searching functions of MAPI, along with the MAPI standards for associating a particular user interface with a particular data set. The folder can exercise strict control over the set of users allowed to view or modify its contents by applying the security features of Exchange Server, and the folder can optionally take automatic actions on its contents.

When a designer builds a solution for collaborative or cooperative work around the information-sharing facilities of an Exchange Server folder, the result is an Exchange *application*.

The Application as a MAPI Client

Every Exchange application is a MAPI client application. These applications in Exchange are presented as folders. By default, an application takes advantage of the Exchange client user interface, which provides the user with a standard interface for discovering, browsing, and manipulating the application. The Exchange client displays the folder hierarchy table in its left-hand pane (the folder list); when the user is browsing the public folder store, this displays the names and hierarchy of public folders as registered in the Exchange directory. Once the user selects an item from the folder list, the Exchange client requests a contents table of that item, using the results to populate its right-hand pane (the folder contents list). The Exchange client allows a user to request different summary views of that contents table, corresponding to different column sets in the requested folder contents table, and abides by the MAPI discipline for associating custom message classes with the form servers that manipulate those classes. Although it is natural and convenient for an Exchange application to use the facilities of the mail client for this, any dedicated MAPI client application can do the same. In fact, the features it is exploiting are MAPI generic. A class of applications that limits itself to these facilities will operate from a *set of personal folders* as well as from the Exchange Server store.

Many applications depend on further features specific to Exchange Server. Folder replication takes place transparently to the client; an administrator performs the necessary system configuration through the administrator client, and the system handles everything else from there. Folder rules and folder security are configured through special client extensions that work with Exchange Server objects and, of course, only work on folders hosted within the server information store. A folder may offer different user-selectable summary views of its contents; while contents tables with variable columns are a feature of generic MAPI, the mechanism for naming and storing different descriptions of the columns comes only through an Exchange Server–specific client extension. Likewise, the folder property that names a folder's default view is not a generic MAPI property, nor are the other properties that specify different aspects of the application's behavior. A sufficiently dedicated client MAPI application could deliver user-selectable column sets itself, but other features depend exclusively on activity of the backing Exchange Server information store.

The Exchange Client as an Application

Hosting an application through the Exchange client offers a number of immediate advantages to both the developer and the user. Most obviously, it provides a user interface framework for the application as a ready-to-run component, with no development effort required. Also it gives every user of the application a familiar user interface and allows each user to discover and run the application as necessary. Finally many such folder applications can operate completely self-contained, requiring no components outside those contained in the applications folder itself; an application can be copied between stores, with the user needing no setup effort to use it in any place. It does have a couple of disadvantages, which are fairly obvious as the counterpart of its strengths. Its users must be able to locate the name of the public folder in the folder hierarchy. Also, the folder application inherits the user interface limitations of the Exchange client framework.

The simplest Exchange application consists of nothing more than the Exchange client running against a message store, preferably the Exchange Server information store. The Exchange client contains its own default forms with which it can add, remove, and modify information in a folder. It allows an application designer to specify custom views for the folder and allows a client of the application to select one of those column sets when the client views the folder's contents. It also allows the designer to specify certain automatic actions on the folder's contents and to control the set of users with access to the folder. These applications originate completely within the native facilities of the Exchange client.

Transcending the Exchange Client

As a single application, the Exchange client is necessarily limited in what it can do by itself. However, the Exchange client rests on top of a rich universe of component objects, an entire environment specifically designed for flexibility and extensibility; by diving into this universe, a developer can build a system that better addresses the requirements of the particular application, transcending the trade-offs and limitations of Exchange's native application development environment.

The rest of this book is about transcending the limitations that the Exchange client places on its applications. Each successive chapter in the book extends or replaces the native facilities of Exchange with custom developer-supplied components, through which an application author can perform the following tasks:

- Modify the commands on the menu bar of the Exchange client

- Alter the behavior of the client's native forms

- Supplant the forms used by the client with a custom user interface manipulating custom message types

- Change the columns displayed by the client

- Specify additional named column sets that the client will honor

- Replace the client with a viewer that handles columns and forms

All the objects of MAPI and Exchange await your application's command.

PART

TWO

Application

4

Extending the Exchange Client

This chapter discusses the simplest variety of Microsoft Exchange application. Most of the applications in this book use the Exchange client as their container. These applications either use the client's own forms or they do not use the form/ view application architecture entirely.

The Client and Its Extensions

Every user's Exchange experience centers around the standard WMS (Windows Messaging Subsystem) mail client application, the "exchange" that hosts the universal Inbox, a file folder system for storing received messages and documents, and a view of the folders on the shared Exchange Server desktop. Applications written for Exchange operate within many folders, which the user accesses by navigating the store using the Exchange client. Exchange supplies most of the implementation of these applications itself; to build more advanced applications, the application author must replace or supplement Exchange's own implementation with extensions.

The Client

Our first applications consist of little more than embellishments of the Exchange client. Some applications add functionality through new commands on the client menu or toolbar, whereas others act to alter the effects of existing commands. Before building any of these, let's study their foundation.

Gross anatomy of the client

The Exchange client consists of a single process containing a single user-interface thread. From its single message loop, Exchange hosts multiple independent top-level windows, each of which uses the desktop as its parent window. There are two kinds of top-level windows: viewers and forms. Taken together, these windows offer the *form/view application architecture* characteristic of the Exchange client and its derivative applications. Top-level windows contain their own menu bars and can invoke any number of child windows beneath them.

Viewers   The viewer is a window that presents a *view* of multiple items to the user. A view consists of a tabular display of a set of items with select properties, such as *From, Subject,* and *Received*, with each discrete property occupying its own column in the table and each item occupying its own row. The view sorts the set of items by one or more of the displayed properties and might restrict the set further to display only those items matching some criterion, such as "Only unread items" or "Only items with attachments."

The set of items in the view might come from one of several sources. Most frequently, the view shows the contents of a particular folder, either the Inbox or some other folder, in the message store. A viewer displaying such a view is called the message viewer, or simply the viewer. If the user is using the Exchange Remote Mail feature, it is called the remote viewer, and if the view comprises the results of a search within the message store, it is called the search viewer.[1] Examples of a message viewer, remote viewer, and search viewer are shown in Figure 4-1.

Upon first starting the Exchange client, the user sees a single viewer, with items displayed in the user's Inbox folder. At the user's command, such as View - New Window, Tools - Remote Mail, or Tools - Find, the client can present multiple such viewers, each potentially rendering a different view of a different set of items. Each viewer then operates as an independent top-level window, subject to the constraints of the single message loop of the Exchange client hosting these windows. Many viewers allow the user to change the set of items being viewed: a message viewer displays the contents of any folder that the user selects, while a search viewer allows the user to specify a new set of criteria for the search operation. Message viewers also allow the user to change the characteristics of their view by choosing the Columns, Group By, Sort, or Filter command from the View menu.

---

1. An address book resembles a viewer in many respects, too, since it renders the entries of an address book in a view, much as a message viewer does its messages. However, address books cannot host applications because they cannot be customized like other viewers and use backing stores optimized for directory services. Thus they offer only peripheral interest to the application author.

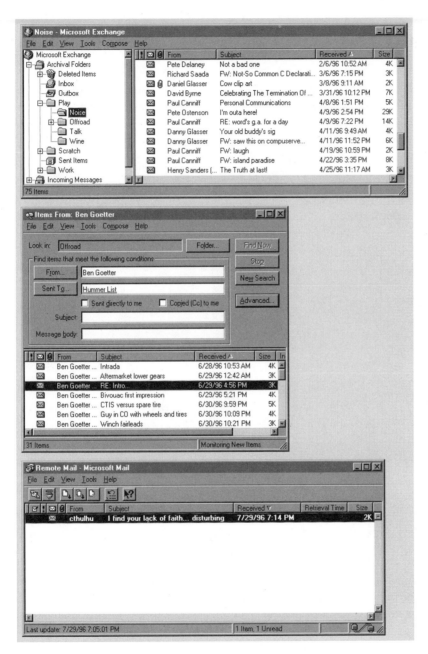

Figure 4-1. *Message viewer, search viewer, and remote viewer.*

Forms   The form is a window that displays the contents of a single item to the user. The presentation of the form varies depending on the type of item. Forms representing interpersonal e-mail messages (shown in Figure 4-2) display the message's sender, date of composition, recipients, and subject in the message heading area, and the body of the message in the message body area. A form representing a stock price might display the name of the company; its ticker symbol and the name of its stock exchange; the date of the price quoted in the message header; the volume of shares traded that day; and the high, low, and closing prices for the day in the message body. The Exchange client implements all the forms for its predefined item types, such as interpersonal messages, various forms of receipts, messages posted to a folder, and documents embedded within a folder. Other types of items require custom forms that an application author implements.

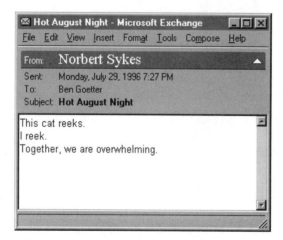

Figure 4-2. *Standard note form.*

A form appears when a user opens any item visible in a view or exercises any offered verb—any command that appears on a context-sensitive menu when the users right-click on an item, or on the Compose menu of the viewer—against an item. A form also appears when the user elects to create a new item, such as what happens when the user issues a Compose - New Message command. In each case, the form that appears corresponds to the type of item, whether it is activated or newly created.

Child windows   Each form and viewer contains its own menu bar, from which the user can invoke commands that yield child windows such as progress indicators, property sheets, or intramessage search dialog boxes. These child windows might operate modally to their host window, depending on the particular command. At any one time, the Exchange client can host multiple viewer windows, each displaying the contents of a folder or results of a search, and can host multiple form windows of its own as well, each displaying the contents of an item. Since Exchange implements child windows with a single user-interface thread and message loop, any window operating modally to its parent window blocks user access to every other window in the client. In effect, a property sheet is modal to every top-level Exchange window, not just to the window spawning it.

The client described as a MAPI application

The Exchange client is a MAPI application. We must understand some of its activity within MAPI if we are to make changes to that activity.

When the client starts, it logs onto MAPI, requesting the shared session. If another application has already created a shareable session, the client receives a handle to that session, obviating all prompting from MAPI for logon information; otherwise, it creates the shareable session, thus allowing other MAPI work group applications (such as Microsoft Schedule+) subsequently to log onto that session without redundantly prompting the user. If the client has been configured to use the default profile always (specified on the General tab displayed when you choose Tools - Options), it specifies this preference at its logon, which suppresses the profile selection user interface even if a shareable session doesn't yet exist.

Viewers within MAPI   Once started, the client displays a viewer focused on the user's Inbox, the default delivery folder for message class "IPM" on the default store of the profile. As shown in Figure 4-3 on the following page, the left-hand pane of the viewer contains a displayed store row for every row in the profile's message store table, plus a displayed hierarchy tree gleaned from the hierarchy tables of the opened folders of opened message stores. The right-hand pane of the viewer displays the contents table of the currently opened folder, as rendered through the parameters of the current view (by choosing the Columns, Group By, Sort, or Filter command from the View menu).

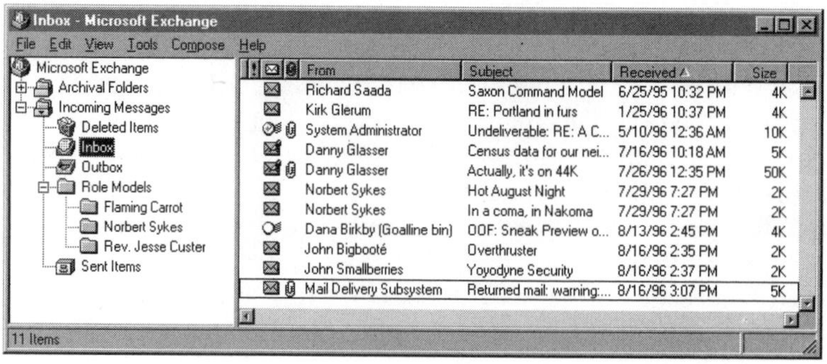

Figure 4-3. *A viewer, focused on the user's inbox. The left-hand pane contains a store and folder hierarchy, and the right-hand pane contains a contents table.*

The remote viewer operates in a manner similar to the regular message viewer. However, instead of directly mounting and traversing the message stores, the remote viewer depends on a folder contents table from the remote transport provider to populate its view. The search viewer also populates its view from the rows of a folder contents table—only in this case, the folder is the special search-results folder of message stores.

Whether remote or normal, every viewer in the Exchange client populates its view from a backing folder contents table. The viewer requests notifications through MAPI whenever changes take place within the table, such as would happen when a new message arrives in a user's Inbox folder or an item changes in a public folder. Upon receiving a notification of a change, the viewer changes the contents of its displayed window to reflect the change.

Forms within MAPI   A command from the viewer's context-sensitive menu or Compose menu results in Exchange locating and activating the correct form for the selected message or, in the case of creating a new message, the selected message class.[2] For all default behavior, the Exchange client itself implements the form. Exchange's intrinsic message types include interpersonal messages, which are the traditional point-to-point notes of e-mail; re-sent messages, which

---

2. The next chapter discusses this process in detail. For now, never mind how it happens.

Exchange generates when it sees that a transport failed to deliver a submitted message; posted messages, notes posted in public folders within which other users will read and reply; document messages, which wrap application documents so that the user can store them in a message folder; and four types of message status reports: delivered, not delivered, read, or never read.[3] When processing interpersonal and posted messages, Exchange enables the "unsent" message flag *(MSGFLAG_UNSENT)* in the *PR_MESSAGE_FLAGS* bitmask.

The *PR_MESSAGE_FLAGS* bitmask specifies the current status of a message object. The flags for this bitmask are shown in Table 4-1.

Flag	Description
MSGFLAG_ASSOCIATED	The message is associated with a folder.
MSGFLAG_FROMME	The message sender is also the message receiver.
MSGFLAG_HASATTACH	The message has an attachment.
MSGFLAG_READ	The message has been read.
MSGFLAG_RESEND	The message will be re-sent if it could not be delivered.
MSGFLAG_SUBMIT	The message has been identified as ready for sending.
MSGFLAG_UNMODIFIED	The message has not been revised since it was received.
MSGFLAG_UNSENT	The message has been saved but has not been sent.

Table 4-1. *Bitmask flags associated with* PR_MESSAGE_FLAGS.

---

3. Clients running under Exchange Server might also see signed messages, sealed messages, out-of-office notifications, and automatic responses from the Inbox Manager. Exchange implements each of these intrinsically by reusing its implementation of one of the existing intrinsic message types. Exchange implements other Exchange Server message types externally, as described in later chapters.

When the user composes a new interpersonal message, Exchange creates a new message in the Inbox of the default store and then produces a form for the unsent message—standard send note—with all its fields blank, leaving the user to enter the necessary message and destination information into the form. Once finished, the user can take one of the following three possible actions:

1. The user can discard the note, in which case Exchange releases the message without ever committing its changes to the store; because the message was new, this results in the message never appearing at all.

2. The user can save the note without sending it, in which case Exchange writes its data into the store and commits the changes, thus creating the message in the store for other clients to find. Since the note was never sent, Exchange ensures that the note has the *MSGFLAG_UNSENT* flag, which ensures that future attempts to read the message yield a send note as well.

3. The user can ask to send the note to its destination. Here, Exchange saves the message and then moves it to the special Outbox folder, from where it will submit the message to the MAPI spooler for subsequent delivery. Posted messages work in a fashion similar to interpersonal messages, except that the Exchange client immediately creates the message in its destination folder and, hence, never needs to submit it to the spooler.

When the user opens an existing received message, Exchange reads the data from the message and then produces a sent message form, a standard read note, with its fields set to the values of the properties read from the message. The user can make changes to this data and save it back to the message in the store.

When the user opens a message to respond to it, as would happen by choosing the command Compose - Reply To Sender, Exchange creates a new message, and then produces a send note containing information derived from the original message. From there, all proceeds as if the user were composing a new message.

When the user opens an existing unsent message, such as might happen if a new message had been saved in the Inbox before submission, Exchange produces a send note and then sets its fields to the contents of the saved message. The user can make changes to the data and either save it back to the message in the store or submit the message for delivery to its recipients.

Client Extensions

More interesting than the precise actions of the Exchange client is its willingness to let an application author change those actions. An Exchange client extension allows the application author to alter certain aspects of the behavior of components intrinsic to the Exchange client: its viewers and intrinsic forms and the associated commands. The application author supplies a component that delivers the desired side effects and then arranges for the client to invoke that component at the appropriate times.

The extension as a component

An Exchange client extension is a component object that implements the *IExchExt* interface, which is defined in the Win32 SDK header file EXCHEXT.H. The client loads the object server and then creates an instance of the object for every extensible context of the client. Client contexts include the entire application, the different viewers and the address book, the different versions of a note form, and property sheets. (EXCHEXT.H defines constants for the complete set of extension contexts denoted as *EECONTEXT_* followed by a context name such as *SESSION* or *VIEWER*. For more information on these extension contexts, see the section "Different extensibility contexts.") Each instance of the pertinent object results in a separate client context, so two separate viewer windows would constitute two separate viewer extensibility contexts, and the Exchange client would create an extension object for each. Through the *IExchExt::Install* method, the client asks the created object whether it wants to operate in the current context; if it does, the client then asks the object for additional interfaces that specify extension functionality.

Differences from COM   An Exchange client extension strongly resembles a standard COM in-process server; however, it differs from the standard in its details of class identification, server registration, and class factory operation (that is, object creation). By deviating from the object registration standard, client extensions limit themselves to operating in the domain of the Exchange client.

Exchange client extensions do not identify their class with a CLSID, do not register their servers under the HKEY_CLASSES_ROOT key of the system registry, do not implement the *IClassFactory* interface, and do not export the COM-compliant *DllGetClassObject* or *DllCanUnloadNow* entry point. Instead of a CLSID, an extension class identifies itself with a printable string that serves to tag its registration string under the registry key HKEY_LOCAL_MACHINE-\SOFTWARE\Microsoft\Exchange\Client\Extensions. (See Figure 4–4.) Instead of exporting the standard entry point and implementing a class factory, an extension server exports an entry point that returns a new instance of an extension object. The client queries additional interfaces off this object as needed.

In all other details, Exchange client extensions adhere to the conventions of COM. They count references, negotiate interfaces, manage memory, and return error codes just as any other component object does.

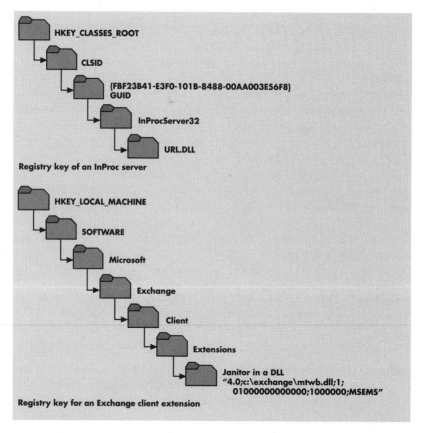

Figure 4-4. *Registry keys for an inproc server and for an Exchange client extension.*

Viewing the anatomy of an extension

On this book's companion CD-ROM, the directory Chap04\Eeminim contains the very simplest extension object possible. If registered in HKEY_LOCAL-_MACHINE\Software\Microsoft\Exchange\Client\Extensions, the Eeminim extension allows the Exchange client to load it. Once loaded, the extension does nothing except announce when Exchange creates and installs new extension objects. While this is not the most exciting application imaginable, it lets us view the basic anatomy of an Exchange client extension. If you prefer to follow the source code in the text editor of your preference,[4] all the activity of interest takes place in the source file EXT.CPP.

All extension objects operate within the address space of the Exchange client. A DLL hosts the server that implements these objects. The entry point of our simplest extension's server does nothing more than save the instance handle of the module corresponding to the loaded DLL. The server needs this handle to load its resources from the correct file (although our minimal extension never needs to load anything). The code required to save the instance handle is shown in the following function:

```
BOOL WINAPI DllMain(HINSTANCE hinstDll, DWORD fdwReason, LPVOID)
{
    if (DLL_PROCESS_ATTACH == fdwReason)
    {
        CUICommon::Init(hinstDll);
    }
    return TRUE;
}
```

As mentioned above, Exchange client extensions do not implement *Dll-GetClassObject* entry points or proper class factories but instead simply export an entry point that returns a new instance of an extension object, as shown in Figure 4-5 on the following page. An entry point always returns an extension of a single class (in the COM sense). Note that the server declares the entry point as having type *extern "C";* this is not strictly necessary but greatly simplifies the process of exporting the entry point by ordinal, since the author need not enter a C++ decorated symbol name in the export definition file. Where a COM in-process server exports its entry points by name, Exchange client extensions always export their entry points by ordinal, naming that ordinal in their registry entries.

---

4. I've been alternating between the MSVC editor and Alan Phillip's freeware PFE.

The actual entry point is implemented in EXT.CPP as follows:

```
⋮
extern "C" IExchExt* CALLBACK ExchEntryPoint();
⋮
// Exchange client extension entry point

IExchExt* CALLBACK ExchEntryPoint()
{
    return new CExtImpl;
}
```

1 Exchange loads the extension DLL.

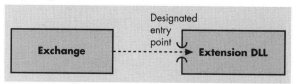

2 Exchange acquires the entry point into the extension DLL.

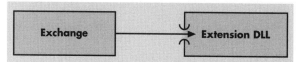

3 Exchange calls the entry point.

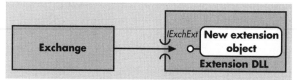

4 The extension library creates and returns a new object.

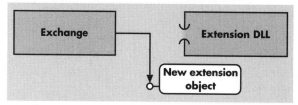

5 Exchange acquires a new extension object.

Figure 4-5. *Exchange acquires a new extension object.*

The class *CExtImpl* implements the extension object. Here it singly inherits from the abstract C++ base class *IExchExt*, guaranteeing that its vtable matches that of the desired interface.[5] Like all interfaces, *IExchExt* inherits from *IUnknown*, so *CExtImpl* must supply an implementation for the members of *IUnknown* as well. In addition, the class declaration shows the single additional member of *IExchExt*, plus some instrumentation that we'll discuss shortly. The implementation of the *CExtImpl* class is included in the EXT.CPP file, as follows:

```
class CExtImpl : public IExchExt
{
public:
    CExtImpl();
    ~CExtImpl();

    // The methods of IUnknown

    STDMETHODIMP QueryInterface(REFIID riid, void** ppvObj);
    inline STDMETHODIMP_(ULONG) AddRef()
        { ++_cRef; return _cRef; }
    inline STDMETHODIMP_(ULONG) Release()
    {
        ULONG ulCount = --_cRef;
        if (!ulCount) { delete this; }
            return ulCount;
    }

    // The methods of IExchExt

    STDMETHODIMP Install(IExchExtCallback* pmecb, ULONG mecontext,
        ULONG ulFlags);

private:
    ULONG _cRef;
    UINT  _context;

    static UINT nSeqNext;
    UINT  _nSeq;

    void Trace(const TCHAR* pszMsg) const;
};
```

---

5. If this technique is unfamiliar to you, take a moment to review the section on implementing servers in Chapter 1, "The Microsoft Component Object Model."

The implementation of *IUnknown* is standard. Since this simplest of extensions does nothing, it offers none of the interfaces through which an extension does real work. It admits to being an extension, *IExchExt*, but it does nothing more, declining requests for other interfaces with the return code *E_NOINTERFACE*. This is implemented in the following code:

```
STDMETHODIMP CExtImpl::QueryInterface(REFIID riid, void** ppvObj)
{
    *ppvObj = NULL;

    HRESULT hr = S_OK;
    IUnknown* punk = NULL;

    if ( (IID_IUnknown == riid) || (IID_IExchExt == riid) )
    {
        punk = (IExchExt*)this;
    }
    else
        hr = E_NOINTERFACE;

    if (NULL != punk)
    {
        *ppvObj = punk;
        AddRef();
    }

    return hr;
}
```

Once the Exchange client has the new extension object, it attempts to install that object into a particular client context (more on those in a moment) by calling the extension's *IExchExt::Install* method. As shown in the following implementation of the *CExtImpl::Install* method, the extension responds with the return code *S_OK* to indicate that it is willing to operate in the current context, or with *S_FALSE* to refuse (in which case the client releases the object).

```
STDMETHODIMP CExtImpl::Install(IExchExtCallback* peecb,
    ULONG eecontext, ULONG ulFlags)
{
    static BOOL fWarnOnce = FALSE;
    static BOOL fMinorBuildOk = FALSE;

    ULONG ulBuildVer;
    ULONG ulProductVer;
    HRESULT hr;

    _context = eecontext;
```

```
    Trace("Calling IExchExt::Install");

    // Ensure that this is the right version.
    CUICommon ui;

    hr = peecb->GetVersion(&ulProductVer, EECBGV_GETVIRTUALVERSION);
    if (SUCCEEDED(hr))
        hr = peecb->GetVersion(&ulBuildVer, EECBGV_GETBUILDVERSION);
    if (FAILED(hr))
    {
        ui.Message(IDS_E_EECBGLITCH);
        return S_FALSE;
    }

    if ( (CURRENT_PRODUCT_CODE != (ulProductVer &
        EECBGV_VERSION_PRODUCT_MASK))
        ||(EECBGV_BUILDVERSION_MAJOR !=
        (ulBuildVer & EECBGV_BUILDVERSION_MAJOR_MASK)) )
    {
        // The first time, explain why we aren't loading.
        // Subsequently, remain silent.

        if (!fWarnOnce)
        {
            fWarnOnce = TRUE;
            ui.Message(IDS_E_INCOMPATIBLE_VERSION);
        }
        return S_FALSE;
    }
    if ( (LAST_MAJVER_SUPPORTED < (ulProductVer &
        EECBGV_VERSION_MAJOR_MASK)) ||(LAST_MINVER_SUPPORTED
        < (ulProductVer & EECBGV_VERSION_MINOR_MASK))
        ||(LAST_BUILD_SUPPORTED < (ulBuildVer &
        EECBGV_BUILDVERSION_MINOR_MASK)) )
    {
        // The first time, make a note of it.
        // Subsequently, abide by user's decision.

        if (!fWarnOnce)
        {
            fWarnOnce = TRUE;
            fMinorBuildOk = (ui.Query(IDS_Q_LATER_BUILD,
                MB_YESNO) == IDYES);
        }
        if (!fMinorBuildOk)
            return S_FALSE;
    }

    return S_OK;
}
```

NOTE To compile and install the applications described in this book, see Appendix A.

If the extension agrees to installation, the client subsequently queries for additional interfaces that provide the useful function of the extension. As we saw in the previous *CExtImpl::QueryInterface* example, this trivial extension supports no such interfaces, so it will contribute nothing further to the client.

In addition to the above, I have written the Eeminim extension to report the identity of each new extension object, along with the context into which Exchange loaded the object. The extension tracks each object by assigning it a sequential integer in its *_nSeq* member variable. When run under the debugger, this extension displays the sequence of extension objects requested by the client, along with the context into which each was loaded.

```
⋮
UINT CExtImpl::nSeqNext = 0;
⋮
CExtImpl::CExtImpl()
    : _cRef(1), _context(0),
    _nSeq(nSeqNext++)
{
    // Nothing else to do at this time.
}
⋮
void CExtImpl::Trace(const TCHAR* pszMsg) const
{
    TCHAR szBuf[128];
    wsprintf(szBuf, "Sequence: %u, context: %u.  ", _nSeq,
        _context);
    ::OutputDebugString(szBuf);
    ::OutputDebugString(pszMsg);
    ::OutputDebugString("\n");
}
```

The extension interfaces

Once loaded into the Exchange client, an extension can offer many sorts of services, each of which the extension embodies in an interface. After successfully calling the *CExtImpl::Install* method on the extension to confirm its operation, the client queries the extension for each of these interfaces (see Figure 4-6); should the object acknowledge an interface, the client uses that interface to request services of the object. An extension can support multiple such interfaces and can use them even within a single instance of the extension object. Like the master extension interface *IExchExt*, each of these interfaces appears in the Win32 SDK header file EXCHEXT.H.

TIP To see the client query the extension for each interface, install Eeminim again, run EXCHNG32.EXE under the debugger, and within EEMINIM.DLL set a breakpoint on *CExtImpl::Query-Interface*. Watch the client first install an extension object, and then query that object for each interface listed on the following page. In each case, the client passes the interface *IID* to *Query-Interface*, which returns the volley *E_NOINTERFACE*.

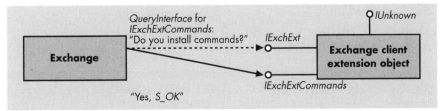

1 Exchange successfully requests the *IExchExtCommands* interface, and *QueryInterface* returns *S_OK*.

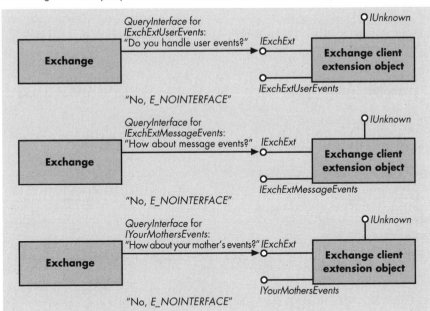

2 Exchange's requests for other interfaces are denied, and *QueryInterface* returns *E_NOINTERFACE*.

Figure 4-6. *The client, having loaded an extension, queries it for all the possible extensibility interfaces. The extension returns references to the interfaces that it supports.*

IExchExtCommands: This most common extension interface allows an extension to create new commands on the menus and toolbars of the Exchange client or to intercept and redefine existing such commands.

IExchExtUserEvents: This interface allows an extension to take action in response to user-made changes to the current selection in a view. Used together with *IExchExtCommands*, it allows menu commands to change in response to user activity.

IExchExtSessionEvents: This little-used interface allows an extension to take action when the Exchange client sees a new message arrive. Since messages might arrive when the client is not running, an application should never rely on this interface to process all incoming messages.

IExchExtMessageEvents: This interface allows an extension to react to the message processing of forms intrinsic to the Exchange client. It does not give an extension any leverage over an external form because such a form isn't part of the client.

IExchExtAttachedFileEvents: This interface allows an extension to react to the attachment processing of the forms intrinsic to the Exchange client. Like its sister interface *IExchExtMessageEvents*, it does not give an extension any leverage over an external form.

IExchExtPropertySheets: This interface allows an extension to define additional pages on the property sheets of the Exchange client.

IExchExtAdvancedCriteria: This little-used interface allows an extension to alter the contents of the Exchange client's Find dialog boxes.

The methods available on the extension interfaces are described in Table 4-2.

Interface Method	Method Description
IExchExtCommands interface	
InstallCommands	Used by the extension to install new menu commands or toolbar buttons
InitMenu	Used by the extension to update the items in a menu when the user activates the menu bar
DoCommand	Executes a menu or toolbar command after the user has chosen it
Help	Provides the user with information on a command
QueryHelpText	Provides the user with information on a status bar or tool tip for a command

Table 4-2. *Methods available on extension interfaces.*

Interface Method	Method Description
QueryButtonInfo	Provides the user with information about the extension's toolbar buttons
ResetToolbar	Used by the extension to return the toolbar buttons to the default positions
IExchExtUserEvents interface	
OnSelectionChange	Used by the extension to receive control when the user changes the selection in the Exchange client
OnObjectChange	Used by the extension to receive control when changes occur in the container objects displayed by the Exchange window (such as a folder whose contents are displayed)
IExchExtSessionEvents interface	
OnDelivery	Allows the extension to take action when a new message arrives
IExchExtMessageEvents interface	
OnRead	Allows an extension to take action before Exchange reads the properties of a message to be displayed to the user
OnReadComplete	Allows an extension to undo its implementation of the *OnRead* method when an error has occurred or to release resources allocated by *OnRead*
OnWrite	Allows the extension to take action before Exchange writes the contents of a standard form to the properties of a message
OnWriteComplete	Allows an extension to undo its implementation of the *OnWrite* method when an error has occurred or to release resources allocated by *OnWrite*
OnCheckNames	Allows the extension to take action before Exchange converts user-specified recipient names to address book entries
OnCheckNamesComplete	Allows an extension to undo its implementation of the *OnCheckNames* method when an error has occurred or to release resources allocated by *OnCheckNames*
OnSubmit	Allows the extension to take action just before Exchange submits an already created message
OnSubmitComplete	Allows an extension to undo its implementation of the *OnSubmit* method when an error has occurred or to release resources allocated by *OnSubmit*

(continued)

Table 4-2. *continued*

Interface Method	Method Description
IExchExtAttachedFileEvents interface	
OnReadPattFromSzFile	Allows an extension to take action just before Exchange reads the data contained in the attached file
OnWritePattToSzFile	Allows an extension to take action just before Exchange writes attachments from a message to a file (such as when the user chooses the File - Save or File - Open command)
QueryDisallowOpenPatt	Prevents a file attachment from being opened directly without storing it first to an intermediate file, particularly when an encrypted file needs to be decoded or when the contents of a modified file need to be restored
OnOpenPatt	Replaces or enhances the functionality of Exchange just before it opens a file attachment without writing it to an intermediate file
OnOpenSzFile	Replaces or enhances the functionality of Exchange just before it opens an intermediate file containing data from an attached file that could not be opened directly
IExchExtPropertySheets interface	
GetMaxPageCount	Returns the maximum number of pages that the extension might add to the property sheet
GetPages	Adds property sheet pages to the current list of pages when Exchange is building a property sheet and needs each extension object to fill in any added pages
FreePages	Frees resources allocated by the *GetPages* method, particularly used when the user closes the properties dialog box and the extension objects need to free pages
IExchExtAdvancedCriteria interface	
InstallAdvancedCriteria	Allows an extension to implement the Advanced Criteria dialog box within Exchange
DoDialog	Displays the Advanced Criteria dialog box defined by an extension
Clear	Prompts all Advanced Criteria defined by an extension to be cleared by it
SetFolders	Notifies an extension object when the folders that the search criteria will be applied to have been changed
QueryRestriction	Provides an object representation and a readable record of the information that the user entered in the Advanced Criteria dialog box
UninstallAdvancedCriteria	Allows an extension to release resources after the criteria user interface is closed

Life within the client

An Exchange client extension operates in a sensitive world. Running within the process space of the Exchange client, the extension can damage data structures internal to the client with a stray write. An extension can tie up the single working thread of the client or starve its message loop. When an extension disables its present window while the interface is modal, it prevents access to all other windows in the client because of the client's single message loop architecture. Finally, an extension can cause the client to leak or lose MAPI objects through mismanaging the reference counts on objects handed to it.

How the Client Calls Extensions

Now that the Exchange client and the structure of its extensions have been examined, let's see how they work together. From the preceding discussion of the simple extension Eeminim, we know the basic sequence of events. The Exchange client loads a client extension server and then creates and attempts to install an extension object into every available extensibility context. From each extension installed, the client queries for the extensibility interfaces, using the interfaces returned by the extension to change client behavior.

We still haven't seen how the client finds an extension server in the first place or defined these frequently mentioned "extensibility contexts" of the client. To do so, let's examine again the extensibility process from the client's point of view.

How extensions appear in the registry

Most component objects identify themselves with a unique CLSID, using this CLSID to register themselves with the System COM library. A prospective client of such a component object consults the System COM library to locate and load these objects' servers.

Instead of using the COM mechanisms, the Exchange client finds its extension components by examining a private registry key, namely HKEY_LOCAL-_MACHINE\SOFTWARE\Microsoft\Exchange\Client\Extensions. As the key name indicates, the set of installed client extensions is not a per-user attribute but is fixed per workstation. Each string value within this key constitutes a single client extension. When the client starts, it reads the contents of this key to find all the extensions available to the client.

Contents of an extension entry   Figure 4-7 on the following page displays a sample client extension registry entry. This is a string value consisting of a series of semicolon-separated fields. The Exchange client requires only the first two fields in the entry; if any other fields are empty, the client supplies a suitable default value for each empty field. Empty fields consist of one field-delimiting semicolon followed immediately by another. An entry can omit any trailing empty fields by removing all remaining semicolons.

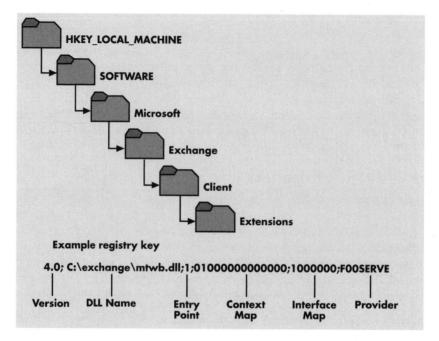

Figure 4-7. *Sample extension key. This key describes an extension in the library at pathname C:\exchange\MTWB.DLL, with its entry point at ordinal 1. The extension also works only within a message viewer, exports only* IExchExtCommands, *and requires the presence of the Microsoft Exchange Server service providers in order to operate.*

As shown in Figure 4-7, the registry entry consists of the following fields:

Version   The first field consists of the string "4.0". This is the version number of the registry entry. It serves to differentiate the entry syntax from that of a Microsoft Mail 3.*x* extension.

DLL name   The second field contains the pathname of the server hosting the client extension. It can contain a fully qualified pathname to the DLL, or only the name of the DLL. In the latter case, the Exchange client depends on the default load path to locate the library correctly. If this entry contains the string *<ExtsDir>*, the client substitutes the name of the configured *shared extensions directory,* specified in the registry value HKEY_LOCAL_MACHINE\SOFTWARE-\Microsoft\Exchange\Client\Options\SharedExtsDir.

Ordinal entry point The third field names the ordinal of the extension's entry point as a decimal integer. If this field is empty, the client seeks the entry point at ordinal 1.

Context map The fourth field contains a string of 0s and 1s specifying which extensibility contexts the extension will handle. If this field is empty, the client creates an instance of the extension for every context; otherwise, it creates instances only for those types of context flagged with a 1. Table 4-3 shows the order of the flags contained in the context map string. Exchange reads the map from left to right, treating missing entries as 0s. For a description of these contexts, see the section "Different extensibility contexts" later in this chapter.

Interface map The fifth field contains a string of 0s and 1s similar to the context map, but here specifying which interfaces the extension offers. If this field is empty, the client queries the extension object for every interface germane to the context in which it installs the extension; otherwise, it queries only for those interfaces flagged with a 1. Table 4-4 on the following page shows the order of the flags contained in the interface map string. For a description of these interfaces, see the section "The extension interfaces."

Position in Map (Left to Right)	Client Extensibility Context
1	EECONTEXT_SESSION
2	EECONTEXT_VIEWER
3	EECONTEXT_REMOTEVIEWER
4	EECONTEXT_SEARCHVIEWER
5	EECONTEXT_ADDRBOOK
6	EECONTEXT_SENDNOTEMESSAGE
7	EECONTEXT_READNOTEMESSAGE
8	EECONTEXT_SENDPOSTMESSAGE
9	EECONTEXT_READPOSTMESSAGE
10	EECONTEXT_READREPORTMESSAGE
11	EECONTEXT_SENDRESENDMESSAGE
12	EECONTEXT_PROPERTYSHEETS
13	EECONTEXT_ADVANCEDCRITERIA
14	EECONTEXT_TASK

Table 4-3. *Context map flags.*

Position in Map (Left to Right)	Extension Interface Supported
1	IExchExtCommands
2	IExchExtUserEvents
3	IExchExtSessionEvents
4	IExchExtMessageEvents
5	IExchExtAttachedFileEvents
6	IExchExtPropertySheets
7	IExchExtAdvancedCriteria

Table 4-4. *Interface map flags.*

Provider   The sixth and final field contains the service name of a service provider accompanying the client extension. (Note that a *PR_SERVICE_NAME* such as "MSEMS" is sometimes used rather than the display name *PR_DISPLAY-_NAME* such as "Microsoft Exchange Server"; examine the file %SystemRoot-%\MAPISVC.INF for the association of service provider names with display names.) If this field is empty, the Exchange client considers the extension suitable for all providers; otherwise, it loads the extension only if the currently loaded profile contains the named service provider.

Identifying an extension registry entry   Each extension registry entry differentiates itself from its fellow entries with a tag name. This tag serves only to differentiate the entry from the other values beneath the registry key. Although the Exchange client does not use this tag in any way, it is important. If it is not unique within the key, a client extension overwrites another extension's registration information, effectively removing the other extension from the client. Also, the extension must remember this tag if it is to uninstall itself correctly.

How the client reads entries   By default, the Exchange client reads the extension registry key when it starts and loads every extension named there. Having loaded every extension library, the client creates an extension object from each of these libraries for every extensibility context that it encounters unless the extension library has specified in its context map that it does not handle a particular context.

NOTE   While traditionally the tags have a short, readable name, nothing prevents an extension from using the printable form of a GUID for its tag. This solves the uniqueness problem at a stroke.

Some extensions operate only in the presence of certain MAPI service providers. For example, the Microsoft Exchange Server Advanced Security client extension ETEXCH32.DLL requires that the session contain the Microsoft Exchange Server providers. An extension could conceivably handle this in its *IExchExt::Install* method by looking for the provider on the current session and refusing to load in the provider's absence, but that would still require that the Exchange client load the extension DLL, and such loads are slow, particularly when they necessitate other library loads, process image fix-ups, and so forth. More efficiently, the registry entry of such an extension will include the name of the provider that the extension requires. When the Exchange client reads the extension registry key, it skips any entries that name a provider not loaded in the current profile.

Most extensions can identify in advance which client extensibility contexts they will find of interest and which interfaces they will and will not offer. By communicating this knowledge to the Exchange client, these extensions can decrease the load on the memory manager and reduce the total working set. The registration entries of such extensions will include explicit context map and interface map strings. When the client reads the extension registry key, it saves the context and interface maps of any extension library that it loads. Within a particular context, the client requests extension objects only from those extensions that have advertised their willingness to handle the context; likewise, the client requests from the object only those interfaces that the extension advertises.

Registering the simplest extension, revisited   Let's return to the simplest Exchange client extension Eeminim for a moment. You registered it by merging the contents of the source file Chap04\Eeminim\EEMINIM.REG into the System registry, thus giving the Exchange client the information it needed to locate and load the extension. Now examine the following contents of EEMINIM.REG:

```
REGEDIT4

[HKEY_LOCAL_MACHINE\SOFTWARE\Microsoft\Exchange\Client\Extensions]
@=" "
"Stub"="4.0;c:\\chap04\\eeminim\\eeminim.dll;1"
```

The file directs that REGEDIT create a value called "Stub" under the key for Exchange client extensions. This value specifies the name of the extension DLL. Without a fully qualified pathname, the client depends on the default load path semantics of *LoadLibrary*, which is why we copied the DLL into the system directory. The registry entry specifies an entry point at ordinal 1; since this is the default value, the entry could omit this value with the same effects.

NOTE　REG files require two consecutive backslashes to insert a single backslash character into a string literal. Therefore, to place the file EEMINIM.DLL for this example into a directory C:\Exchange, the tag would have to read as follows:

```
"Stub"="4.0;c:\\chap04\\eeminim\\eeminim.dll;1"
```

Although "Stub" is a very poor choice for a tag name, it is a little better than the name *Extension* or even *foo*. Still, it will work until the first time somebody installs a client extension on this workstation with a registry entry generated by cut-and-paste from EEMINIM.REG.

Lacking a context map, interface map, or provider name for this entry, Exchange loads the extension in every context and requests it for every interface. Of course, the extension declines every interface request other than *IExchExt* or *IUnknown*, but the client doesn't know that, since it found no interface map in the extension's registry entry.

Different extensibility contexts

Once the client holds the entry point for an extension library, it calls through that entry point to request a separate extension object for every extensible locus occurring within the client. Each discrete viewer window constitutes such a locus, as does every instance of the intrinsic note form, every property sheet, and every address book. The client identifies the type of locus—viewer, form, or whatever—by classifying its context through its extensibility context ID, appearing as the set of manifest constants *EECONTEXT* in EXCHEXT.H

Table 4-5 shows the Exchange windows and interfaces associated with each extensibility context ID.

Extensibility Context	Exchange Window	Interfaces
EECONTEXT_TASK	None	*IExchExt::Install,* *IUnknown::Release*
EECONTEXT_SESSION	None	*IExchExtSessionEvents*
EECONTEXT_VIEWER	The main viewer containing two panes: the folder hierarchy in the left pane and the folder contents in the right pane	*IExchExtCommands,* *IExchExtUserEvents,* *IExchExtPropertySheets*
EECONTEXT-_REMOTEVIEWER	The Remote Mail window displayed after the user issues the Remote Mail command	*IExchExtCommands,* *IExchExtUserEvents,* *IExchExtPropertySheets*

Table 4-5. *Exchange windows and interfaces associated with their extensibility context IDs.*

Extensibility Context	Exchange Window	Interfaces
EECONTEXT-_SEARCHVIEWER	The Find window displayed after the user issues the Find command	IExchExtCommands, IExchExtUserEvents, IExchExtPropertySheets
EECONTEXT-_ADDRBOOK	The address book window displayed after the user issues the address book command	IExchExtCommands, IExchExtUserEvents
EECONTEXT-_READNOTEMESSAGE	The read note window where the user reads received messages	IExchExtCommands, IExchExtUserEvents, IExchExtMessageEvents, IExchExtAttachedFileEvents, IExchExtPropertySheets
EECONTEXT-_SENDNOTEMESSAGE	The standard compose note window where the user composes messages	IExchExtCommands, IExchExtUserEvents, IExchExtMessageEvents, IExchExtAttachedFileEvents, IExchExtPropertySheets
EECONTEXT-_READPOSTMESSAGE	The standard posting window where the user reads posting messages	IExchExtCommands, IExchExtUserEvents, IExchExtMessageEvents, IExchExtAttachedFileEvents, IExchExtPropertySheets
EECONTEXT-_SENDPOSTMESSAGE	The window where the user composes posting messages	IExchExtCommands, IExchExtUserEvents, IExchExtMessageEvents, IExchExtAttachedFileEvents, IExchExtPropertySheets
EECONTEXT-_READREPORTMESSAGE	The read report message window where the user reads received report messages	IExchExtCommands, IExchExtUserEvents, IExchExtMessageEvents, IExchExtAttachedFileEvents, IExchExtPropertySheets
EECONTEXT-_SENDRESENDMESSAGE	The send resend message window displayed after the user issues the Send Again command when a nondelivery report has been received	IExchExtCommands, IExchExtUserEvents, IExchExtMessageEvents, IExchExtAttachedFileEvents, IExchExtPropertySheets
EECONTEXT-_PROPERTYSHEETS	A property sheet window	IExchExtPropertySheets
EECONTEXT-_ADVANCEDCRITERIA	The dialog box where the user defines advanced search criteria	IExchExtAdvancedCriteria

Few extensions have an interest in all contexts. If the extension publishes a context map in its registry, the client first consults that context map to see whether the extension handles a particular context; should the extension refuse, the client does not create an instance of the extension for that context. Otherwise, the client calls through the extension library's entry point to get a new extension object for the context and then provides the context ID to the object's *IExchExt::Install* method. The extension here has a second chance to decline interest in the context by returning *S_FALSE* from this method.

These extensibility context IDs are defined within the Microsoft Exchange client:

EECONTEXT_TASK   When the Exchange client first starts, it offers a task context to any extensions it finds before it ever calls *MAPILogonEx*. This context is associated with no particular window and has no MAPI session available to it. The duration of this context begins when the program is started and ends when the client exits. The task context can span several logons.

EECONTEXT_SESSION   Once the Exchange client obtains a session from its call to *MAPILogonEx*, it offers a session context to its extensions. Like the task context, *EECONTEXT_SESSION* has no associated visible window on the screen. This context does have a session, however. The session context begins at session logon and ends when the client exits, terminating the session (and, incidentally, the client).

EECONTEXT_VIEWER   Every standard message viewer window has a viewer extensibility context that will remain for the lifetime of the window. In the left pane, the standard message viewer displays the folder hierarchy as the default; in the right pane, it displays the folder contents. Viewer contexts have access to the menu, toolbar, and window of their associated viewer window and can track user activity within that window. They can also alter property sheets accessed through the viewer.

EECONTEXT_REMOTEVIEWER   Remote viewers have an extensibility context that functions similarly to that for a standard message viewer, except that it operates within a remote context. The remote viewer context begins when the user chooses Tools - Remote Mail.

EECONTEXT_SEARCHVIEWER   The search viewer window has its own extensibility context and greatly resembles that of the standard message viewers. The search viewer context begins when the user chooses the Tools - Find command and ends when the user closes the search results window.

EECONTEXT_ADDRBOOK The address book window has its own extensibility context as well. The duration of the address book context begins when the user chooses the Tools - Address Book command and ends when the user closes the address book.

EECONTEXT_READNOTEMESSAGE Every window of the forms intrinsic to the Exchange client has an extensibility context that exists for the lifetime of the window. Like viewer contexts, read note form contexts have access to the menu, toolbar, and window of their associated form; can track user activity within the form's window; and can alter the property sheets of the form. They can also react as the form retrieves and saves the message from and to its backing store and as the user manipulates file attachments within the form.

EECONTEXT_SENDNOTEMESSAGE A send note form has its own extensibility context. Send note form contexts greatly resemble read note form contexts, having access to the menu, toolbar, and window of their associated form; tracking user activity; and altering property sheets. A new send form, such as originally appears from a new message in a Compose - Reply To Sender command, does not see any message retrieval since the message retrieval implicit in a reply takes place outside the form. However, they can react when the form saves the message back to the store and can track name resolution (Tools - Check Names) and message submission (File - Send).

EECONTEXT_READPOSTMESSAGE The Exchange client gives messages posted in a folder their own message class, their own form, and hence, their own extensibility context. The context of a read post message is nearly identical to that of a read note message, although the backing form will be different.

EECONTEXT_SENDPOSTMESSAGE As in the read forms, the context of a posted message under composition resembles an interpersonal message under composition, although it will not track name resolution because posted messages don't use recipients but instead save themselves directly to the destination folder.

EECONTEXT_READREPORTMESSAGE The Exchange client renders the four classes of MAPI report message—read, never read, delivered, and not delivered—with a report form, supporting that form with a report form extensibility context. There is little that an extension can do in this context, although the context has the usual access to the form's menu, toolbar, window, and property sheet.

EECONTEXT_SENDRESENDMESSAGE   When the user invokes the Send Again command from a nondelivery report form, the Exchange client presents its resend form, which it supports with a resend form extensibility context. This context strongly resembles that of the standard send note, although the actual form differs considerably in its read-only treatment of the message.

EECONTEXT_PROPERTYSHEETS   For every property sheet dialog that it creates, the Exchange client creates a property sheet extension context, inviting extensions to amend their own pages to the property sheet. This is a separate context from the context of the window hosting the property sheet. The client offers the opportunity to modify a property sheet both to the property sheet's own context and to the context of the hosting window.

EECONTEXT_ADVANCEDCRITERIA   For the rare extension interested in altering the contents of the Advanced dialog box accessed through the Find or Filter dialog box, the Exchange client offers this context.

Figure 4-8 shows four extensibility contexts: *EECONTEXT_VIEWER*, *EECONTEXT_SENDNOTEMESSAGE*, *EECONTEXT_TASK*, and *EECONTEXT_SESSION*.

Interface offered to an extension

With most calls to the extension, the Exchange client supplies a pointer to an object implementing the *IExchExtCallback* interface. An extension uses this interface to retrieve more information about the client or the current client context. As the callback object is valid only for the duration of the client's call into the extension object, the extension should not call the *AddRef* method and cache this interface but instead should always use the interface pointer passed on each call into the extension.

Use of the *IExchExtCallback* interface during installation   An extension first sees the *IExchExtCallback* interface when the client calls its *IExchExt::Install* method, requesting permission to install it in a particular client extensibility context. In the following example, the client passes a pointer to the callback object as the first parameter to this method.

```
STDMETHODIMP CExtImpl::Install(IExchExtCallback* peecb,
    ULONG eecontext, ULONG ulFlags)
{
    // Call through the "peecb" parameter to talk to the client.
    ⋮
}
```

At object installation time, the client offers the extension three pieces of information with which to make its load/no load decision.

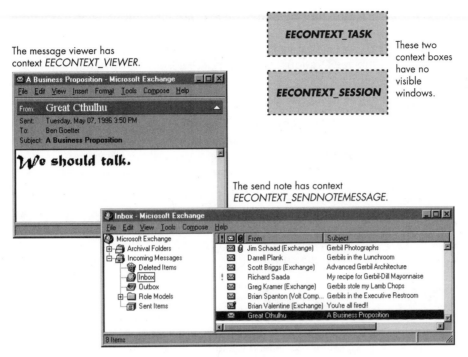

The message viewer has context *EECONTEXT_VIEWER*.

EECONTEXT_TASK

EECONTEXT_SESSION

These two context boxes have no visible windows.

The send note has context *EECONTEXT_SENDNOTEMESSAGE*.

Figure 4-8. *As shown in this display, Exchange has four extensibility contexts currently active. The message viewer has a context* EECONTEXT_VIEWER, *and the send note under composition has* EECONTEXT_SENDNOTEMESSAGE. *In addition, two contexts are not associated with visible windows:* EECONTEXT_TASK *and* EECONTEXT_SESSION. *If the user stopped composing the current message and dashed off another message, Exchange would create another* EECONTEXT_SENDNOTEMESSAGE *for the duration of the note form of the new message.*

Callback interface: This interface offers several methods that the extension can use to determine whether it should work within the current context. If the context is any context other than *EECONTEXT_TASK, IExchExtCallback::GetSession* returns an interface pointer to the current MAPI session of the client, through which the extension can examine the current MAPI environment to see whether the extension's presence is warranted. Many contexts support *IExchExtCallback-::GetObject* to return an interface pointer to the current MAPI object pertinent to the context (folder, message, or store). However, the most universally useful install-time method is *IExchExtCallback::GetVersion*.

Context ID: This value indicates the context into which the extension would load. It matches one of the *EECONTEXT* manifest constants described in the section entitled "Different extensibility contexts." If the extension has supplied a context map in its registration information, the context ID matches one of the flags set in the map.

Flags setting: If the *EE_MODAL* flag of the *Install* method is set, it indicates that the client is requesting permission to load the extension into an environment that supports only modal windows. While most extensions can safely ignore this parameter, an extension that presents modeless windows must either present those windows in a modal form or refuse to load.

Every extension should call the *GetVersion* method at least once to determine whether the extension will run in the current version of Exchange. An extension can use its retrieved information to change its behavior to accommodate the known vagaries of past versions or might simply want to guard itself against unanticipated future changes in the client.

> **NOTE** The Exchange client will happily install one instance of an extension into a form or viewer context and another into a property sheet context and then offer both instances of the same extension the opportunity to amend the form's or viewer's property sheet. This causes two copies of the extension's additions to appear in the property sheet in question—a common bug. Caveat programmer.

The following excerpt from Eeminim illustrates one version-checking strategy. (You can find this fragment, or one much like it, in any sample appearing in this chapter.)

```
STDMETHODIMP CExtImpl::Install(IExchExtCallback* peecb,
    ULONG eecontext, ULONG ulFlags)
{
    static BOOL fWarnOnce = FALSE;
    static BOOL fMinorBuildOk = FALSE;

    ULONG ulBuildVer;
    ULONG ulProductVer;
    HRESULT hr;

    _context = eecontext;

    Trace("Calling IExchExt::Install");

    // Ensure that this is the right version.

    CUICommon ui;
```

```
hr = peecb->GetVersion(&ulProductVer, EECBGV_GETVIRTUALVERSION);
if (SUCCEEDED(hr))
    hr = peecb->GetVersion(&ulBuildVer, EECBGV_GETBUILDVERSION);
if (FAILED(hr))
{
    ui.Message(IDS_E_EECBGLITCH);
    return S_FALSE;
}

if ( (CURRENT_PRODUCT_CODE != (ulProductVer &
    EECBGV_VERSION_PRODUCT_MASK))
    ||(EECBGV_BUILDVERSION_MAJOR != (ulBuildVer &
    EECBGV_BUILDVERSION_MAJOR_MASK)) )
{
    // The first time, explain why we aren't loading.
    // Subsequently, remain silent.

    if (!fWarnOnce)
    {
        fWarnOnce = TRUE;
        ui.Message(IDS_E_INCOMPATIBLE_VERSION);
    }
    return S_FALSE;
}
if ( (LAST_MAJVER_SUPPORTED < (ulProductVer &
    EECBGV_VERSION_MAJOR_MASK))
    ||(LAST_MINVER_SUPPORTED < (ulProductVer &
    EECBGV_VERSION_MINOR_MASK))
    ||(LAST_BUILD_SUPPORTED  < (ulBuildVer &
    EECBGV_BUILDVERSION_MINOR_MASK)) )
{
    // The first time, make a note of it.
    // Subsequently, abide by user's decision.

    if (!fWarnOnce)
    {
        fWarnOnce = TRUE;
        fMinorBuildOk =
            ui.Query(IDS_Q_LATER_BUILD, MB_YESNO) == IDYES);
    }
    if (!fMinorBuildOk)
        return S_FALSE;
}

return S_OK;
}
```

The extension makes two calls back to the Exchange client, asking what kind of client is hosting it (using the *IExchExtCallback::GetVersion* method with *EECBGV_GETVIRTUALVERSION*) and what build of that client is running (with *EECBGV_GETBUILDVERSION*). First the extension checks to ensure that it is actually running within the product called Microsoft Exchange, as claimed by the product code in the returned version. At the same time, it confirms that it is using the same interface definitions as the version of Exchange hosting it, through the major build version code. If it finds that either of these two versions does not match its expected value, it reports the problem to the user and refuses to load. Observe that it caches a note to the effect that it already reported the problem, so as not to deluge the user with redundant "This extension refused to load" message boxes.

After checking the major version, the extension compares the minor build number against the build number of WMS, on which the extension was last tested. Table 4-6 shows some of these numbers that an extension might encounter in the field. If the version of Exchange postdates the last version tested, the extension asks the user to make the call and then caches the results of the request.

WMS Build Number	Released Platform
410	Retail Windows 95
611	Exchange Server 4.0 release candidate 1
736	Exchange Server 4.0 release candidate 2
837	Exchange Server 4.0 released version
839	Windows 95 update—"Windows Messaging"

Table 4-6. *Build numbers of some released versions of WMS.*

Since the Exchange client typically creates and installs extension objects before creating the hosting window, certain methods on the callback interface might not always return useful results. For example, the *IExchExtCallback::GetWindow* method will return *S_FALSE* (with a NULL *lphwnd* in its out-parameter) if it is called at this time since no window yet exists to return a value.

Other uses of the *IExchExtCallback* interface   An extension has frequent recourse to the *IExchExtCallback* interface during its running life. Table 4-7 describes the methods available through the *IExchExtCallback* interface.

Method	Description
GetVersion	Gets the version number of Exchange
GetWindow	Gets a handle associated with the current Exchange window
GetMenu	Gets a handle associated with the menu for the current Exchange window
GetToolbar	Gets a toolbar window handle
GetSession	Gets an interface to the currently open MAPI session and associated address book
GetObject	Gets an interface for a specific object and the store containing the object
GetSelectionCount	Gets the number of objects selected in an active window that displays containers
GetSelectionItem	Gets the entry identifier and the associated information of a currently selected item in an Exchange window
GetMenuPos	Gets the location of a menu or command or set of commands on the Exchange menu for the currently active context
GetSharedExtsDir	Gets the location of the directory containing extensions shared in Exchange
GetRecipients	Gets a pointer associated with the recipient list of the currently selected item
SetRecipients	Defines the items in an address list for the currently selected item
GetNewMessageSite	Gets interface pointers to the message, site of the message, or view context of the selected message
RegisterModeless	Allows extension objects to coordinate between the modeless windows and modal windows displayed by the Exchange client
ChooseFolder	Displays a dialog box used to select a message store and folder

Table 4-7. *Methods available on the* IExchExtCallback *interface.*

An extension uses *IExchExtCallback::GetMenu* and *IExchExtCallback::GetToolbar* to add and manipulate commands and *IExchExtCallback::GetMenuPos* to locate a particular command on the Exchange client's menu. It uses *IExchExtCallback::GetWindow* to get a parent for its dialog boxes; more ambitious extensions might delve into the window hierarchy beneath this window to manipulate the contents of the host form or viewer, although this sort of usage tends to break with new releases of Exchange and certainly isn't supported or endorsed by Microsoft.

An extension calls *IExchExtCallback::GetSession* to work against the Exchange client's current session or *IExchExtCallback::GetObject* to work with the object currently open in the client context. In form contexts, it calls *IExchExtCallback::GetRecipients* and *IExchExtCallback::SetRecipients* to alter the addressing of the form. In viewer contexts, it calls *IExchExtCallback::GetSelectionCount* and *IExchExtCallback::GetSelectionItem* to retrieve the MAPI entry identifiers and other information about the currently selected items in the viewer.

Creating New Commands

Most commonly, an extension serves to add a new command to the Exchange client. This command might do no more than launch an external application such as the Windows Help engine WINHLP32.EXE, or it might contain significant functionality of its own. It can appear completely integrated within the client, appearing on the menu with an accompanying toolbar button, status bar and tooltip Help text, and Help available by pressing F1 with the menu command selected. It can examine the current selection in the client's viewer windows and can enable or disable its commands in response to the type of object selected. It can present the user with a dialog box for input or can append pages to the standard property sheets of the client, such as the ones that appear when the user chooses Tools - Options.

Most of the code samples in this section originate from a single program, the simple client extension Mtwb, available on this book's companion CD-ROM disc in the directory Chap04\Mtwb. On the File menu of the client's viewer windows, Mtwb installs a command that empties the client's Deleted Items folders. We will follow several excerpts from this program, all of which appear in the file EXT.CPP.

Extending the Menu and the Toolbar

The first step in creating a new command is to have it appear on the command menu of the Exchange client so that the user can find and invoke it. To appear here in the client's user interface, an extension implements the *IExchExtCommands* interface. An extension hosting this interface receives an invitation to install its own commands into Exchange and subsequently learns of all command activity, both its own and that intrinsic to the client. Any extensibility context associated with a window containing a menu bar is fair game for the *IExchExtCommands* interface.

Extending the menu

As soon as the hosting context has a menu and window, Exchange will invoke the *IExchExtCommands::InstallCommands* method on the installed extension. This happens almost immediately after installation: the extension sees a call to *IExchExt::Install* (to which it presumably accedes), next invokes a flurry of *IUnknown::QueryInterface* calls as the client learns the capabilities of this extension, and finally issues the *InstallCommands* invitation. Within the scope of the *InstallCommands* call, the extension must add its commands to the menu and toolbar of the client.

Vtable management   The sample extension Mtwb must implement two different interfaces, *IExchExt* and *IExchExtCommands*. It simply concatenates the two vtables in the vtable of its implementation class, with its *IUnknown::QueryInterface* implementation returning correctly offset vtable pointers[6] to the object's clients. Thus, the following implementation class singularly delivers two interfaces:

```
class CExtImpl : public IExchExt, IExchExtCommands
{
public:
    CExtImpl();
    ~CExtImpl();

    // The methods of IUnknown

    STDMETHODIMP QueryInterface(REFIID riid, void** ppvObj);
    inline STDMETHODIMP_(ULONG) AddRef()
        { ++_cRef; return _cRef; }
    inline STDMETHODIMP_(ULONG) Release()
        { ULONG ulCount = --_cRef;
          if (!ulCount) { delete this; }
          return ulCount;
        }

    // The methods of IExchExt

    STDMETHODIMP Install(IExchExtCallback* pmecb, ULONG mecontext,
        ULONG ulFlags);

    // The methods of IExchExtCommands
```

(continued)

---

6. If these C++ casts look like magic, take a moment to review the section on implementing complex component objects in Chapter 1, "The Microsoft Component Object Model."

```
    STDMETHODIMP InstallCommands(IExchExtCallback* pmecb, HWND hwnd,
        HMENU hmenu, UINT * cmdidBase, LPTBENTRY lptbeArray, UINT ctbe,
        ULONG ulFlags);
    STDMETHODIMP DoCommand(IExchExtCallback* pmecb, UINT mni);
    STDMETHODIMP_(VOID) InitMenu(IExchExtCallback* pmecb);
    STDMETHODIMP Help(IExchExtCallback* pmecb, UINT mni);
    STDMETHODIMP QueryHelpText(UINT mni, ULONG ulFlags, LPTSTR sz,
        UINT cch);
    STDMETHODIMP QueryButtonInfo(ULONG tbid, UINT itbb,
        LPTBBUTTON ptbb, LPTSTR lpsz, UINT cch, ULONG ulFlags);
    STDMETHODIMP ResetToolbar(ULONG tbid, ULONG ulFlags);

private:
    ULONG _cRef;
    UINT  _context;
    UINT  _cmdidWaste;
    UINT  _itbb;
    UINT  _itbm;
};
    ⋮
STDMETHODIMP CExtImpl::QueryInterface(REFIID riid, void** ppvObj)
{
    *ppvObj = NULL;

    HRESULT hr = S_OK;
    IUnknown* punk = NULL;

    if ( (IID_IUnknown == riid) || (IID_IExchExt == riid) )
    {
        punk = (IExchExt*)this;
    }
    else if (IID_IExchExtCommands == riid)
    {
        punk = (IExchExtCommands*)this;
    }
    else
        hr = E_NOINTERFACE;

    if (NULL != punk)
    {
        *ppvObj = punk;
        AddRef();
    }

    return hr;
}
```

Installing the commands The extension's implementation of its *IExchExtCommands::InstallCommands* method must place the extension's commands into the menu structure of the calling client. The extension must directly alter the structure of the client's menu by using the native menu-manipulation facilities of the host operating system, such as the *InsertMenuItem* API on Windows 95 and Microsoft Windows NT 4.0 or *AppendMenu* and *InsertMenu* on Microsoft Windows 3.11 and Microsoft Windows NT 3.51.

While an extension receives a handle to the menu bar of its host context window directly as a parameter (also available through the *IExchExtCallback::GetMenu* method), usually instead it uses the *IExchExtCallback::GetMenuPos* method to find the pop-up menu and position of an existing Exchange client command. This allows the extension to position its command relative to the other commands on the menu. Remember that other extensions might also be adding commands to the menu at the same time, so absolute locations ("I am the fourth command on the Tools pop-up menu") do not work. The *GetMenuPos* method takes as its first parameter the command ID of the existing menu item, which the now familiar header file EXCHEXT.H publishes as a manifest constant prefixed with *EECMDID_* followed by the name of the menu command, as shown in Figure 4-9.

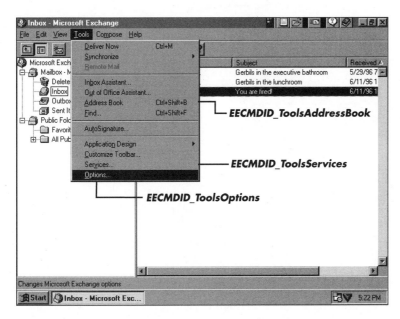

Figure 4-9. *The Exchange client publishes the menu IDs of its menu items in EXCHEXT.H. An extension can position its commands relative to existing commands by passing these menu IDs as parameters to* IExchExtCallback::GetMenuPos.

Another possible bone of contention between extensions is the command ID of each respective menu command. To help resolve this, the client gives the extension the first command ID available to the extension as an in-out parameter. The extension must record the command ID values that it uses since the client will subsequently use this value in calls requesting the extension command. To ensure that no other extension attempts to use the same command ID values, the extension must update the parameter in the call to reflect the next available value; the client then uses that value as the first command ID available to the next extension it loads in that context, as shown in Figure 4-10.

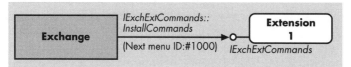

1 Exchange calls *IExchExtCommands::InstallCommands* to install the menu commands and toolbar buttons of Extension 1.

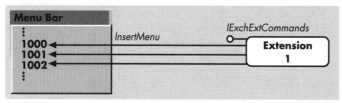

2 The extension needs three menu IDs for the three menu items that it must add: #1000, #1001, #1002.

3 The call returns with menu ID #1003 in an in-out parameter.

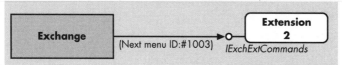

4 The cycle continues: Exchange calls *IExchExtCommands::InstallCommands* to install the menu commands and toolbar buttons of Extension 2.

Figure 4-10. *Exchange coordinates its extensions so that no two extensions attempt to claim the same ID for their own menu items.*

The following extract from the *IExchExtCommands::InstallCommands* implementation of Mtwb does all of this:

```
STDMETHODIMP CExtImpl::InstallCommands(IExchExtCallback* pmecb,
    HWND hWnd, HMENU hMenu, UINT * pcmdidBase,
    LPTBENTRY lptbeArray,UINT ctbe, ULONG ulFlags)
{
    assert(EECONTEXT_VIEWER == _context); // Per Install above

    // First, the menu

    HMENU hmenuFile;
    ULONG nMenuPos;
    HRESULT hr = pmecb->GetMenuPos(EECMDID_FileExit, &hmenuFile,
        &nMenuPos, NULL, 0);
    assert(SUCCEEDED(hr));
    if (FAILED(hr))
        return S_FALSE;

    TCHAR szCommand[80];
    GetString(szCommand, sizeof(szCommand)/sizeof(TCHAR),
        IDS_WASTE_CMD);
    InsertMenu(hmenuFile, nMenuPos, MF_BYPOSITION | MF_SEPARATOR, 0,
        NULL);
    InsertMenu(hmenuFile, nMenuPos, MF_BYPOSITION | MF_STRING,
        *pcmdidBase, szCommand);
    _cmdidWaste = *pcmdidBase;
    ++(*pcmdidBase);
    ⋮

    return S_OK;
}
```

The *InstallCommands* function requests the submenu and position of the space immediately preceding the menu's File - Exit command. Using the utility function *GetString* (from the file Chap04\Mtwb\UI.CPP), it fetches the text of the menu command from the extension library's resource file into a local buffer and then adds that text to the menu at the correct place. Finally, it saves the command ID that it used into a member variable, incrementing the out-parameter so that the next extension loaded doesn't step on its toes.

The Mtwb extension created its command on the File menu immediately preceding the Exit command and demarcated the command on the menu with a separator. Given the function of the command, the command on the menu is in a reasonable location. Extension commands by their nature frequently appear on the Tools menu; there by convention, they should leave the Services and Options commands as the last items on the menu. A place to avoid is the end of the Compose menu since the Exchange client appends the commands intrinsic to selected custom forms here.

Supporting the menu command   Now the command is on the menu. To complete support for this menu command, it needs Help and appropriate text in the Exchange client's status bar. The extension specifies each of these through a method on the *IExchExtCommands* interface.

The *IExchExtCommands::QueryHelpText* method returns status bar text to the client. Since the same method returns tooltip text, the extension checks the "flags" parameter (which, contrary to the API documentation and parameter name, is actually an opcode) for the value *EECQHT_STATUS* before returning the status text, which the extension copies into the buffer passed to the method. The length of the copied text must not exceed the size of the buffer, which the client specifies as a count of characters.

When the client needs status bar text for a particular command, it calls every extension loaded in the context, passing that extension the command ID of the command in question. Each extension should examine the given value and return *S_FALSE* if it does not handle that command, in which case the client proceeds to the next extension. Otherwise, the extension should return *S_OK* to indicate that it has taken care of the request. The client performs this dispatching action for its intrinsic commands as well as for those commands added by extensions, allowing an extension to supplant the client's own status bar text for intrinsic commands. This command dispatching is shown in Figure 4-11.

The following *IExtImp::QueryHelpText* method of the Mtwb application checks the flags parameter to determine whether it is necessary to retrieve status bar and tooltip text:

```
STDMETHODIMP CExtImpl::QueryHelpText(UINT cmdid, ULONG ulFlags,
    LPTSTR psz, UINT cch)
{
    assert(EECONTEXT_VIEWER == _context); // Per Install above

    if (cmdid != _cmdidWaste)
        return S_FALSE;

    if (ulFlags == EECQHT_STATUS)
    {
        GetString(psz, cch, IDS_WASTE_STATUS);
    }
    else if (ulFlags == EECQHT_TOOLTIP)
    {
        GetString(psz, cch, IDS_WASTE_TOOLTIP);
    }

    return S_OK;
}
```

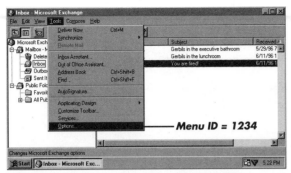

1 The user selects a command with a menu ID of 1234.

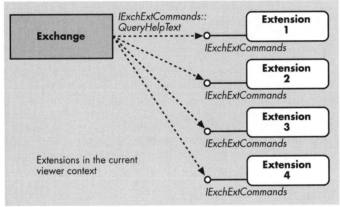

2 Exchange offers the menu ID to every extension loaded into the context for this window.

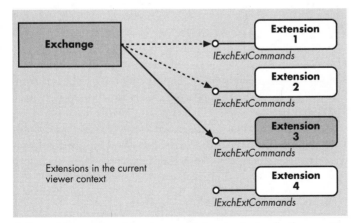

3 If one of the extensions claims the menu ID, the extension handles the menu ID; otherwise, Exchange handles the menu ID itself.

Figure 4-11. *Command dispatch in Exchange. Every extension installed in the context for a particular window gets a chance to handle any menu item on that window.*

Since Mtwb keeps only a single command ID, its dispatch handling need check against only a single value. A utility function fetches the requested status bar text from the extension library's resource file into the buffer of the Exchange client.

Assertions and Error Paths

Observe the careful use of the assert macro in the *CExtImpl::InstallCommands* function. The first assertion checks that the context (saved into a class member variable in the implementation of *IExchExt::Install*) is in fact *EECONTEXT-_VIEWER*. This is guaranteed by the context map of the extension's registration (see Chap04\Mtwb\MTWB.REG) and beyond that (should some malign force have damaged the registry entry) by a check in the *Install* implementation; the assertion serves as documentation and an internal check to help make maintenance more robust, but not as an error path. The second assertion guarantees that the callback to *IExchExtCallback::GetMenuPos* succeeds since it is using a manifest *EECMDID* constant from the header file in a context known to support that menu item; however, it does not serve as an error path either, that being the role of the following *FAILED* check and return.

The moral of this pious little homily: client extensions run within the process space of the Exchange client and thus must be like Caesar's wife in their rectitude, since they will bring down the entire client should they throw any sort of fatal exception.

Command Dispatch Bugs

While the command dispatch mechanism is flexible, it is not especially robust in the face of misbehaving components. Every extension must take care to respond only to the correct command IDs since otherwise it might steal a command from the Exchange client or from another extension. If you ever find yourself pursuing a bug where your extension is not seeing one of the dispatched methods of the *IExchExtCommands* interface, that is, the *QueryHelpText, Help, DoCommand*, or *QueryButtonInfo* method, keep this in mind. You might find that another extension, loaded before your extension, is stealing your command from you. (Of course, *YOU* would never introduce such a bug, would you?)

Similarly, if an extension returns a failure code other than *S_FALSE*, the client terminates its search through the extensions. This too can rob your extension of its command.

The *IExchExtCommands::Help* method should display help for a particular command, such as might appear in response to pressing F1 with the command's menu item selected. As it does with the *QueryHelpText* method, the Exchange client iterates through all extensions installed in the current context when it seeks the extension to handle a particular command ID. In the following example from the EXT.CPP file of Mtwb, note the use of the supplied callback interface to retrieve a parent window for the invocation of the Help engine:

```
STDMETHODIMP CExtImpl::Help(IExchExtCallback* pmecb, UINT cmdid)
{
    assert(EECONTEXT_VIEWER == _context); // Per Install above

    if (cmdid != _cmdidWaste)
        return S_FALSE;

    HWND hwnd = NULL;
    pmecb->GetWindow(&hwnd);
    CUICommon(hwnd).Message(IDS_NO_HELP_AVAILABLE);
    return S_OK;
}
```

Extending the toolbar

Extensions add toolbar buttons for their commands at the same time that they add menu items: in their *InstallCommands* implementation. Extensions add toolbar bitmaps and buttons through the standard system facilities like they manipulate menu items.

On 16-Bit Windows

Since 16-bit Windows (and release 3.51 of Windows NT, for that matter) lacks a system standard toolbar control, the Exchange client includes on these platforms a clone of the Windows 95/Windows NT 4.0 control. Extension toolbar code might treat all platforms identically and ignores changes that handle the 16-bit differentiation between HRESULT method return codes and the SCODE constants *S_OK* and *S_FALSE*.

Note that most 16-bit development environments lack the structure and message definitions necessary for client code to communicate with the toolbar control. The author of a 16-bit application must privately define these as necessary, porting them from the Win32 include file COMMCTRL.H.

Adding the button The following code fragment from Mtwb—this time, omitting the menu code for clarity—adds the bitmap for this extension's single command to the pool of bitmaps used by the viewer toolbar:

```
STDMETHODIMP CExtImpl::InstallCommands(IExchExtCallback* pmecb,
    HWND hWnd, HMENU hMenu, UINT * pcmdidBase, LPTBENTRY lptbeArray,
    UINT ctbe, ULONG ulFlags)
{
    ⋮
    int tbindx;
    HWND hwndToolbar = NULL;
    for (tbindx = ctbe-1; (int) tbindx > -1; --tbindx)
    {
        if (EETBID_STANDARD == lptbeArray[tbindx].tbid)
        {
            hwndToolbar = lptbeArray[tbindx].hwnd;
            _itbb = lptbeArray[tbindx].itbbBase++;
            break;
        }
    }

    if (hwndToolbar)
    {
        TBADDBITMAP tbab;

        tbab.hInst = CUICommon::GetHinst();
        tbab.nID = IDB_EMPTYWASTE;
        _itbm = SendMessage(hwndToolbar, TB_ADDBITMAP, 1,
            (LPARAM)&tbab);

        ResetToolbar(EETBID_STANDARD, 0L);
    }

    return S_OK;
}
```

The first section of *CExtImpl::InstallCommands* steps you through the supplied array of toolbars, looking for the standard toolbar in the array;[7] as soon as it finds the toolbar, it reserves a toolbar button index, incrementing the index so that the next extension in line doesn't receive the same index. (This works just like the menu command ID allocation scheme.) With the handle to the toolbar, the second section adds a bitmap for the command to match the just-retrieved index.

---

7. In the Exchange client version 4, this is a degenerate array of only a single member. We retain the loop construct for form's sake.

This code adds a potential button rather than an actual button. The resulting button appears in the Customize Toolbar dialog box so that the user can choose to place it on the toolbar.

Extensions should add only an actual button to the toolbar in the extension's implementation of the *IExchExtCommands::ResetToolbar* method, and then only if the extension wants its button to appear on the toolbar by default. As the following example shows, Mtwb leaves the choice of toolbar buttons up to the user. The Exchange client invokes the following method when it needs to initialize a fresh toolbar or when the user chooses the Reset button in the Customize Toolbar dialog box that appears when the Tools - Customize Toolbar command is selected:

```
STDMETHODIMP CExtImpl::ResetToolbar(ULONG tbid, ULONG ulFlags)
{
    // To implement this method,
    // the extension must cache the results of a prior call
    // to IExchExtCallback::GetToolbar.

    if (EECONTEXT_VIEWER != _context)
        return S_FALSE;

    if (EETBID_STANDARD != tbid)
        return S_FALSE;

    // Nothing to do

    return S_OK;
}
```

Notice that the *ResetToolbar* method lacks an *IExchExtCallback* parameter; extensions implementing it must cache the results of an earlier call to the *IExchExtCallback::GetToolbar* method to have a destination for the *TB_INSERTBUTTON* message.

Supporting the button   Toolbar buttons, like menu items, need support from the extension's *QueryHelpText* and *Help* methods to support tooltip text and F1 Help. While the already-listed *Help* function suffices to support a toolbar button, *CExtImpl::QueryHelpText* requires a clause to handle the *EECQHT_TOOLTIP* opcode. With that addition, here's the unabridged Mtwb implementation:

```
STDMETHODIMP CExtImpl::QueryHelpText(UINT cmdid, ULONG ulFlags,
    LPTSTR psz, UINT cch)
{
    assert(EECONTEXT_VIEWER == _context); // Per Install above
```

(continued)

```
        if (cmdid != _cmdidWaste)
            return S_FALSE;

        if (ulFlags == EECQHT_STATUS)
        {
            GetString(psz, cch, IDS_WASTE_STATUS);
        }
        else if (ulFlags == EECQHT_TOOLTIP)
        {
            GetString(psz, cch, IDS_WASTE_TOOLTIP);
        }

        return S_OK;
}
```

In addition, a toolbar button needs an implementation of the *IExchExtCommands::QueryButtonInfo* method in its extension. From this method, the Exchange client retrieves additional information necessary to satisfy the *TBN_GETBUTTON-INFO* and *TB_INSERTBUTTON* toolbar messages that it will use. In the following code excerpt, the client dispatches *QueryButtonInfo* calls in a manner similar to *QueryHelpText* and other methods but uses a toolbar button index instead of a command ID:

```
STDMETHODIMP CExtImpl::QueryButtonInfo (ULONG tbid, UINT itbb,
    LPTBBUTTON ptbb, LPTSTR lpsz, UINT cch, ULONG ulFlags)
{
    assert(EECONTEXT_VIEWER == _context); // Per Install above

    HRESULT hr = S_FALSE;

    if (_itbb == itbb)
    {
        ptbb->iBitmap = _itbm;
        ptbb->idCommand = _cmdidWaste;
        ptbb->fsState = TBSTATE_ENABLED;
        ptbb->fsStyle = TBSTYLE_BUTTON;
        ptbb->dwData = 0;
        ptbb->iString = -1;
        GetString(lpsz, cch, IDS_WASTE_TBBUTTON);

        hr = S_OK;
    }
    return hr;
}
```

Enabling the command

An extension controls the state of its menu items and toolbar buttons through its implementation of the *IExchExtCommands::InitMenu* method. The Exchange client invokes this method on all loaded extensions each time the user accesses the menu, giving the extensions the opportunity to make appropriate state changes. The extension can here enable, disable, set check marks, or otherwise alter the state of these controls to reflect the state elsewhere.

The *InitMenu* method has to execute quickly; otherwise the user experiences a frustrating delay before the menu appears. Perform only the least demanding calculations in an extension's *InitMenu* implementation. For best performance, cache the results of state calculations in another method and then use those results here to dictate the state of the command controls.

Since Mtwb never changes the state of its command controls, the code for the *Init-Menu* function is simple, as follows:

```
STDMETHODIMP_(VOID) CExtImpl::InitMenu(IExchExtCallback* pmecb)
{
    HMENU hmenu;
    HRESULT hr = pmecb->GetMenu(&hmenu);
    if (FAILED(hr))
        return;

    EnableMenuItem(hmenu, _cmdidWaste, MF_ENABLED);

    HWND hwndToolbar;
    hr = pmecb->GetToolbar(EETBID_STANDARD, &hwndToolbar);
    if (FAILED(hr))
        return;

    SendMessage(hwndToolbar, TB_ENABLEBUTTON, _cmdidWaste,
        MAKELONG(TRUE, 0));
}
```

> **NOTE** If you've been dutifully reading the interface definitions in the MAPI SDK documentation *Extending the Microsoft Exchange Client,* you probably wonder why *CExtImpl::InitMenu* explicitly enables the toolbar button, given the official assertion that the client "...intercepts the *EnableMenuItem* message and applies the same enabled or disabled state to the associated toolbar button." Unfortunately, the client does no such thing. *Caveat lector.*

Invoking the command

Finally, with a command item on the menu and a button on the toolbar—both enabled and ready to go—our extension is ready to service a user command. Upon the user activating a menu item or toolbar button, the Exchange client dispatches the command ID of the activated command item through the *IExch-ExtCommands::DoCommand* method of each extension loaded in the context. Any extension can claim the command by responding in the affirmative, thus ending the dispatch process.

After all the preceding work, the following Mtwb implementation of the *DoCommand* method is anticlimactic:

```
STDMETHODIMP CExtImpl::DoCommand(IExchExtCallback* pmecb,
    UINT cmdid)
{
    assert(EECONTEXT_VIEWER == _context); // Per Install above

    if (cmdid != _cmdidWaste)
        return S_FALSE;

    EmptyWastebasket(pmecb);
    return S_OK;
}
```

To visit the function that does all the work, see Chap04\Mtwb\WORK.CPP. In this file, *EmptyWastebasket* uses its *IExchExtCallback* parameter twice: first to get a parent window to host any user interface needed, using the *IExchExtCallback::GetWindow* method, and then to get a pointer to the client's current MAPI session, using the *IExchExtCallback::GetSession* method. Thereafter Mtwb operates against the found session like any other MAPI client application.

Getting Input from Exchange

The Mtwb extension enjoys a luxury rare among Exchange client extensions: it has no need for user input at all. The user simply chooses the extension's Expunge Deleted Items command from Exchange's File menu, and Mtwb takes off from there, operating against the current state it discovers in the current session. Most extensions, however, need some additional direction. They might implement a transitive command against a particular object, in the manner of most existing commands on the File and Edit menus. They might offer different options in their operation, in the manner of the Options dialog box; or they might need additional information from the user to complete a command, in the manner of the Copy, Move, and Save As options on the File menu. Exchange makes it possible to obtain information about its current state and get input from the user.

Getting the current selection

Exchange commonly provides input by giving the extensions a target. An extension can either use the item currently open in the client or use the set of selected items. In whichever way that the extension gets its selection, it should enable or disable menu items appropriately.

Currently open item   The simplest way to provide direction to an extension is to have it use Exchange's currently open item as its own object. (See Figure 4-12.) To do this, you use the method *IExchExtCallback::GetObject*. The *GetObject* callback returns a reference to an interface on the currently opened object. The precise type of the object and interface retrieved varies depending on the extensibility context and the time of the call. The extension might then use this object as the target of its own action. For example, a command might use the currently open folder when creating a new message or when posting a new message to that folder.

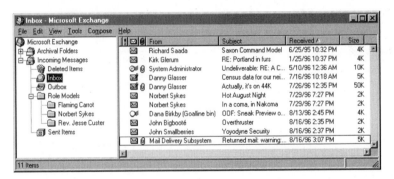

Figure 4-12. *Within the extensibility context corresponding to this viewer window, Exchange returns a reference to the MAPI folder object from* IExchExtCallback::GetObject. *Any extension invoked within that context can use this reference as its target.*

The following fragment, if called from an implementation of *IExchExtCommands-::DoCommand* in *EECONTEXT_VIEWER*, retrieves a reference to the current folder:

```
IExchExtCallback* peecb = ... ;
IMAPIFolder* pfld;
HRESULT hr = peecb->GetObject(NULL, (IUnknown**)&pfld);
if (SUCCEEDED(hr))
{
    ⋮
    pfld->Release();
}
```

Set of selected items   If the extension will operate from within an Exchange client container object, such as a viewer, it can use the methods *IExchExtCallback::GetSelectionCount* and *IExchExtCallback::GetSelectionItem* to ask the client for the set of objects currently selected in the container. (See Figure 4-13.) The extension first calls *GetSelectionCount* to retrieve the total number of items selected and then calls *GetSelectionItem* once for each item found. Instead of a reference to an existing open MAPI interface, *GetSelectionItem* returns an entry ID for the item requested, which the caller must open itself.

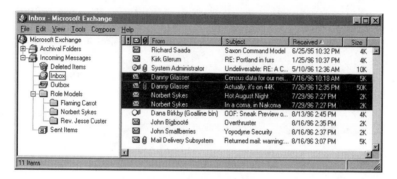

Figure 4-13. *Extensibility contexts within containers also allow an extension to use the set of currently selected items as their target.*

The following fragment visits every message selected in the current folder. All code that handles error exceptions has been removed for clarity.

```
    ⋮
IExchExtCallback* peecb = ...;
IMsgStore* pmdb;
HRESULT hr = peecb->GetObject(&pmdb, NULL);
if (FAILED(hr))
    ⋮
ULONG cElements;
hr = peecb->GetSelectionCount(&cElements);
if (FAILED(hr))
    ⋮
for (ULONG iElement = 0; iElement < cElements; iElement++)
{
    ULONG nType;
    LPENTRYID peid;
    ULONG cbEid;
    hr = peecb->GetSelectionItem(iElement, &peid, &cbEid,
        &nType, NULL, 0L, NULL, 0L);
    if (FAILED(hr) || (nType != MAPI_MESSAGE))
```

```
    ⋮
    IMAPIMessage* pmsg;
    hr = pmdb->OpenEntry(cbEid, peid, (LPIID)&IID_IMAPIMessage,
        0, &nType, (IUnknown**)&pmsg);
    if (FAILED(hr))
    ⋮
    pmsg->Release();
    MAPIFreeBuffer(peid);
}
pmdb->Release();
```

Enabling and disabling menu items   The preceding fragment operates only on selected messages. Any extension that limits itself to operating on a particular type of item—on only messages, only message stores, only Schedule+ meeting requests, and so forth—should control the state of its menu commands such that they are disabled when the user selects ineligible items. For example, the interface should not invite the user to reply to a folder object or to create a subfolder within a message.

The most straightforward technique for controlling a menu item state involves setting the state in the extension's *IExchExtCommands::InitMenu* method. The client calls this method on its extensions every time the user activates the client menu bar. At that time, the extension can check the types of items selected and enable or disable its menu commands as appropriate. You should ensure that the extension doesn't undertake long operations; otherwise, the client/user interface responsiveness could suffer. A couple of calls to *IExchExtCallback::GetSelectionCount* and *IExchExtCallback::GetSelectionItem* at this time will cause no trouble; a couple thousand such calls might slow operation unacceptably, as might a series of *OpenEntry* and *GetProps* operations, particularly if the message in question resided on an Exchange Server message store requiring remote procedure call activity.

If the extension offers a toolbar button, you should modify the state of this command item as well. Unlike the commands on a menu, the buttons on a toolbar always remain visible, so adding logic within the *IExchExtCommands::InitMenu* method will not suffice as a solution. In this case, the extension must implement an additional interface, *IExchExtUserEvents*, informing the client that the extension wants to track user activity. When the client finds this interface on an extension, it calls the extension's implementation of the method *IExchExtUserEvents::OnSelectionChange* every time the set of selected items changes in the client. By coordinating this method with the *InitMenu* method, an extension can keep accurate states for all its command items.

The code sample Chap04\Eetrans demonstrates an extension using this tactic for tracking command item status. The Eetrans application consists of little more than the Mtwb sample, stripped of all function and then enhanced to track the current selection and offer itself only when the user selects message items.

The vtable management for Eetrans derives trivially from that for Mtwb, adding the new interface in an additional clause of the *CExtImpl::QueryInterface* implementation (located in the file EXT.CPP) as follows:

```
class CExtImpl : public IExchExt,
    IExchExtCommands, IExchExtUserEvents
{
public:
    ⋮
    // The methods of IUnknown
    ⋮
    // The methods of IExchExt
    ⋮
    // The methods of IExchExtCommands
    ⋮
    // The methods of IExchExtUserEvents

    STDMETHODIMP_(VOID) OnSelectionChange(IExchExtCallback* peecb);
    STDMETHODIMP_(VOID) OnObjectChange(IExchExtCallback* peecb);

private:
    ⋮
#if defined(DEBUG)
    BOOL    _fInitSelection;
#endif
    BOOL    _fValidSelection; // Set on OnSelChange
};
    ⋮


STDMETHODIMP CExtImpl::QueryInterface(REFIID riid, void** ppvObj)
{
    *ppvObj = NULL;

    HRESULT hr = S_OK;
    IUnknown* punk = NULL;

    if ( (IID_IUnknown == riid) || (IID_IExchExt == riid) )
    {
        punk = (IExchExt*)this;
    }
```

```
    else if (IID_IExchExtCommands == riid)
    {
        punk = (IExchExtCommands*)this;
    }
    else if (IID_IExchExtUserEvents == riid)
    {
        punk = (IExchExtUserEvents*)this;
    }
    else
        hr = E_NOINTERFACE;

    if (NULL != punk)
    {
        *ppvObj = punk;
        AddRef();
    }

    return hr;
}
```

In response to every notification of the selection changing, the extension reexamines the current selection to determine the type of the items selected. In the interest of performance, the extension examines only the first element to determine its type, noting the results of its discovery in the _fValidSelection_ member variable. Since the toolbar remains visible at all times, the extension updates its state immediately. Updating the menu state can wait until the user indicates some interest in the menu. In the EXT.CPP file of the Eetrans application, these updates are performed in the *CExtImpl::OnSelectionChange* function, as follows:

```
STDMETHODIMP_(VOID) CExtImpl::OnSelectionChange(
    IExchExtCallback* peecb)
{
    assert(EECONTEXT_VIEWER == _context); // Per Install above

    BOOL fValid = FALSE;
    ULONG cElements;
    HRESULT hr = peecb->GetSelectionCount(&cElements);
    if (SUCCEEDED(hr) && (cElements > 0))
    {
        // Just check first element.

        ULONG nType;
        hr = peecb->GetSelectionItem(0L, NULL, NULL, &nType, NULL,
```

(continued)

```
                    0L, NULL, 0L);
            if (SUCCEEDED(hr) && (nType == MAPI_MESSAGE))
                fValid = TRUE;
        }

        _fValidSelection = fValid;

#if defined(DEBUG)
        if (!_fInitSelection)
            _fInitSelection = TRUE;
#endif

        // Update the toolbar immediately.

        HWND hwndToolbar;
        hr = peecb->GetToolbar(EETBID_STANDARD, &hwndToolbar);
        if (FAILED(hr))
            return;

        SendMessage(hwndToolbar, TB_ENABLEBUTTON, _cmdidStub,
            MAKELONG(fValid, 0));
    }
```

The following code for the *IExchExtCommands::InitMenu* method uses the state that the selection tracking code left in a member variable. Note that the very first *InitMenu* was preceded by the first *OnSelectionChange*.

```
STDMETHODIMP_(VOID) CExtImpl::InitMenu(IExchExtCallback* peecb)
{
    assert(EECONTEXT_VIEWER == _context); // Per Install above

#if defined(DEBUG)

    // Confirm that the first SelChange precedes the first
    // InitMenu.

    assert(_fInitSelection);
#endif

    HMENU hmenu;
    HRESULT hr = peecb->GetMenu(&hmenu);
    if (FAILED(hr))
        return;

    EnableMenuItem(hmenu, _cmdidStub,
        (_fValidSelection ? MF_ENABLED : MF_GRAYED));
}
```

Extending a property sheet

The Exchange client allows its extensions to append pages to any of its property sheet dialog boxes, as shown in Figure 4-14. When the currently open or selected item doesn't provide sufficient direction, an extension might take a more direct approach to user input. This allows the extension to integrate tightly with the Exchange user interface. If a client extension implements the *IExchExt-PropertySheets* interface, the client contacts that extension whenever the client creates a property sheet dialog box from a window in the current extensibility context. For example, if the extension supports the property sheet extension interface, any extension installed into the context of a particular viewer window sees the property sheets summoned from the window that appears when the user chooses the File - Properties or the Tools - Options command. In addition to the usual contexts, the client creates a new context of type *EECONTEXT-_PROPERTYSHEETS* with every property sheet dialog box and loads an instance of any willing extension into this context.

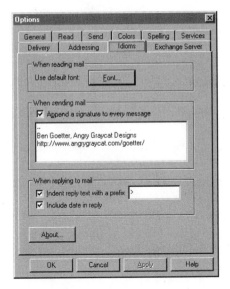

Figure 4-14. *Tools - Options property sheet. An extension can add pages to any property sheet dialog in Exchange. Here the extension has amended the Tools - Options dialog box to include a page for its own configuration data.*

An extension recognizes the type of property sheet from the value in the *ulFlags* parameter passed to the methods of the *IExchExtPropertySheets* interface. The values *EEPS_MESSAGE*, *EEPS_FOLDER*, and *EEPS_STORE* (all manifest constants defined in EXCHEXT.H) indicate that the property sheet originated from a File - Properties command on a message, folder, or store object, respectively.

Each of these property sheets works on the currently selected object (implicitly selected, in the case of *EEPS_MESSAGE*, within a note form extensibility context) and offers loaded extensions access to this object through the *IExchExtCallback::GetObject* callback. The value *EEPS_TOOLSOPTIONS* indicates that the property sheet originated from the Tools - Options command. Options property sheets have no associated selected object, instead describing global states; their extensions favor *IExchExtCallback::GetSession*.

On 16-Bit Windows

Since 16-bit Windows (and release 3.51 of Windows NT, for that matter) lacks a system property sheet, the Exchange client includes on these platforms a clone of the Windows 95/Windows NT 4.0 facility. Extension property sheet code might treat all platforms identically and ignore changes that handle the 16-bit differentiation between HRESULT method return codes and the SCODE constants *S_OK* and *S_FALSE*.

Note that most 16-bit development environments lack the structure and message definitions necessary for client code to communicate with the property sheet. The author of a 16-bit application must privately define these as necessary, porting them from the Win32 include file PRSHT.H, which contains variable declarations and constants associated with property sheets.

Vtable management   The remaining code samples in this chapter appear in the sample program Chap04\Inetxidm.[8] Most of this sample program appears in the last section on enhancing the standard forms of Microsoft Exchange. Here we observe instead the single configuration page that Inetxidm installs into the property page that appears after the user chooses Tools - Options.

The extension must implement *IExchExtPropertySheets* and return that interface to the client when requested. Its vtable management, here excerpted from Chap04\Inetxidm\EXT.CPP, presents no surprises:

```
class CExtImpl : public IExchExt, IExchExtPropertySheets,
    IExchExtMessageEvents, IExchExtCommands
{
public:
    CExtImpl();
```

---

8. Inetxidm is a fairly busy program. If, while tracing through it, you have trouble seeing the forest for all the trees, take a look at the sample Chap04\Eestub—I've clearcut all the functionality there, leaving nothing more than a skeleton of an Exchange extension.

```
    ~CExtImpl();

    // The methods of IUnknown
    ⋮
    // The methods of IExchExt
    ⋮
    // The methods of IExchExtPropertySheets

    STDMETHODIMP_(ULONG) GetMaxPageCount(ULONG ulFlags);
    STDMETHODIMP GetPages(IExchExtCallback* peecb,ULONG ulFlags,
        LPPROPSHEETPAGE ppsp, ULONG * pcpsp);
    STDMETHODIMP_(VOID) FreePages(LPPROPSHEETPAGE ppsp,
        ULONG ulFlags, ULONG cpsp);

    // The methods of IExchExtMessageEvents
    ⋮
    // The methods of IExchExtCommands
    ⋮
};
STDMETHODIMP CExtImpl::QueryInterface(REFIID riid, void** ppvObj)
{
    ⋮
    else if (IID_IExchExtPropertySheets == riid)
    {
        punk = (IExchExtPropertySheets*)this;
    }
    ⋮
}
```

Indicating interest   The client calls the *IExchExtPropertySheets::GetMaxPage-Count* method of the extension when it wants to give the extension a chance to modify a property sheet. In response, the extension must return the number of pages that it wants to append to the dialog box. If the extension has no interest in this particular property sheet, it returns 0, indicating that it has no pages.

The code for the *GetMaxPageCount* method is shown in the following code excerpt from EXT.CPP:

```
STDMETHODIMP_(ULONG) CExtImpl::GetMaxPageCount(ULONG ulFlags)
{
    // In a message, Exchange is calling the extension once for
    // property sheets and once for the note form.  Respond only
    // once.
```

(continued)

```
if (_context != EECONTEXT_PROPERTYSHEETS)
    return 0;
// Note that "ulFlags" is actually an opcode, not a word of
// flags.

if (ulFlags == EEPS_TOOLSOPTIONS)
    return 1;

// Ignore all other property sheets.

return 0;
}
```

In the Inetxidm sample, the extension allows the client to load instances of the extension into several different extensibility contexts. This can result in the client contacting multiple instances of the extension to modify a single property sheet: one for the context of the hosting window and one for the property sheet context itself. The extension checks the current context (which it saved into a member variable in its implementation of the *IExchExt::Install* method) and offers pages only if the context is that of the property sheet.

The client contacts the extension to extend any property sheet. Since the extension wants its pages to appear only when the Tools - Options command is issued, it checks the flags parameter of the method, indicating interest only for the opcode *EEPS_TOOLSOPTIONS*.

Defining the property sheet   If the extension returns a nonzero page count from *IExchExtPropertySheets::GetMaxPageCount*, the client returns for the promised pages, calling the extension's *IExchExtPropertySheets::GetPages* method. The code for this method is as follows:

```
STDMETHODIMP CExtImpl::GetPages(IExchExtCallback* peecb,
    ULONG ulFlags, LPPROPSHEETPAGE ppsp, ULONG * pcpsp)
{
    if (_context != EECONTEXT_PROPERTYSHEETS)
        return S_FALSE;

    if (ulFlags != EEPS_TOOLSOPTIONS)
        return S_FALSE;

    ppsp[0].dwSize = sizeof (PROPSHEETPAGE);
    ppsp[0].dwFlags = PSP_DEFAULT|PSP_HASHELP;
    ppsp[0].hInstance = CUICommon::GetHinst();
    ppsp[0].pszTemplate = MAKEINTRESOURCE(IDD_MAINPROP);
    ppsp[0].hIcon = NULL;      // Not used in this sample
```

```
ppsp[0].pszTitle = NULL;  // Not used in this sample
ppsp[0].pfnDlgProc = (DLGPROC)MainPropPageDlgProc;

// Give the property page a reference to the session to use.

IMAPISession* psess;
HRESULT hr = peecb->GetSession(&psess, NULL);
if (FAILED(hr))
{
    CUICommon().Message(IDS_E_NOSESSION);
    return S_FALSE;
}

// Inherits AddRef in GetSession

ppsp[0].lParam = (DWORD)psess;
ppsp[0].pfnCallback = NULL;
ppsp[0].pcRefParent = NULL; // Not used in this sample

*pcpsp = 1; // Only a single page

return S_OK;
}
```

The client passes an array of Win32 *PROPSHEETPAGE* structures to the *Get-Pages* method. This array contains as many elements as the extension indicated that it had pages. The extension should set these structures to define the pages that it will create, returning the number of pages that it actually defined—that is, the number of elements in the array that it set—in the last out-parameter.

In the *CExtImpl::GetPages* method of the Inetxidm application, the extension describes a perfectly conventional property sheet page. The client looks on the module of the extension DLL for a dialog box resource *IDD_MAINPROP*, using the *MainPropPageDlgProc* procedure (see the file PRSHT.CPP of the Inetxidm application and the following section) as that page's dialog box procedure.

The value passed in the *lParam* parameter is of particular interest. When the Exchange client activates the property sheet page, that page will not have any reference to *IExchExtCallback* with which to retrieve information about the client. By sending a reference to the session in the dialog box application-defined data parameter, the dialog box has access to the current MAPI session and so can query and set values thereon as needed. The extension releases this reference in its *IExchExtPropertySheets::FreePages* member.

Implementing the property sheet An extension must supply a dialog box procedure to control the behavior of its property sheet page.

The Inetxidm sample (see Chap04\Inetxidm\PRSHT.CPP) has a fairly involved property sheet. You can escape to the simpler property sheet of Chap04\Eestub, but then you will miss the most interesting feature of this example—its session management.

The *WM_INITDIALOG* clause retrieves the session reference passed in the *IExchExtPropertySheets::GetPages* method above, storing the interface pointer in an auxiliary structure *SPropPageAux* (not shown here) created for the purpose. The procedure then saves that auxiliary structure in the dialog box user data DWORD (*GWL_USERDATA*). This keeps the auxiliary data unique for each instance.

The following code, extracted from PRSHT.CPP, is used to control the behavior of the extension's single property sheet page:

```
BOOL CALLBACK MainPropPageDlgProc(HWND hdlg, UINT nMsg,
    WPARAM wParam, LPARAM lParam)
{
    BOOL fMsgResult;

    switch (nMsg)
    {
    case WM_INITDIALOG:
    {
        PROPSHEETPAGE* ppsp = (PROPSHEETPAGE*)lParam;
        SPropPageAux *paux =
            new SPropPageAux((IMAPISession*)(ppsp->lParam));
        paux->sig.Init();
        paux->cf.Init();
        paux->prefix.Init();
        SetWindowLong(hdlg, GWL_USERDATA, (DWORD)paux);
```

```
CheckDlgButton(hdlg, IDC_USESIG, paux->sig.WillUseSig());
SetDlgItemText(hdlg, IDC_EDITSIG, paux->sig.GetSig());
SendDlgItemMessage(hdlg, IDC_EDITSIG, EM_SETLIMITTEXT,
    (WPARAM)(MAXSIGLENGTH*sizeof(TCHAR)), 0L);
EnableWindow(GetDlgItem(hdlg, IDC_EDITSIG),
    paux->sig.WillUseSig());

CheckDlgButton(hdlg, IDC_USEPREFIX,
    paux->prefix.WillUsePrefix());
CheckDlgButton(hdlg, IDC_LONGINTRO,
    paux->prefix.UseLongForm());
SetDlgItemText(hdlg, IDC_EDITPREFIX,
    paux->prefix.GetPrefix());
SendDlgItemMessage(hdlg, IDC_EDITPREFIX, EM_SETLIMITTEXT,
    (WPARAM)(MAXPREFIXLENGTH*sizeof(TCHAR)), 0L);
EnableWindow(GetDlgItem(hdlg, IDC_EDITPREFIX),
    paux->prefix.WillUsePrefix());
EnableWindow(GetDlgItem(hdlg, IDC_LONGINTRO),
    paux->prefix.WillUsePrefix());
return TRUE;
}
break;
```

When the dialog box is terminated, the *WM_DESTROY* clause releases the auxiliary structure containing the interface pointer. Note that additional reference counting does not need to take place on the contained session interface pointer because *MainPropPageDlgProc* does not add any references. *MainPropPageDlgProc* manipulates only the single reference obtained in the *GetPages* method. The code for the *WM_DESTROY* clause is as follows:

```
⋮
case WM_DESTROY:
{
    SPropPageAux *paux =
        (SPropPageAux*)GetWindowLong(hdlg, GWL_USERDATA);
    delete paux;
    SetWindowLong(hdlg, GWL_USERDATA, 0L);
}
return TRUE;
⋮
```

The following *WM_COMMAND* clause dictates the behavior of the page in response to user activity in each of the controls in the page, as listed in Table 4-8 on page 200:

```
case WM_COMMAND:
{
    switch (LOWORD(wParam))
    {
    case IDC_ABOUT:
        DialogBox(CUICommon::GetHinst(),
            MAKEINTRESOURCE(IDD_ABOUT), hdlg,
            (DLGPROC)AboutDlgProc);
    return TRUE;

    case IDC_FONT:
    {
        SPropPageAux *paux =
            (SPropPageAux *)GetWindowLong(hdlg, GWL_USERDATA);
        if (DefineDefaultFont(hdlg, &paux->cf))
        {
            paux->fDirty = TRUE;
            PropSheet_Changed(GetParent(hdlg), hdlg);
        }
    }
    return TRUE;

    case IDC_USESIG:
    {
        const BOOL fCheck =
            IsDlgButtonChecked(hdlg, IDC_USESIG);
        EnableWindow(GetDlgItem(hdlg, IDC_EDITSIG), fCheck);
        SPropPageAux *paux =
            (SPropPageAux *)GetWindowLong(hdlg, GWL_USERDATA);
        paux->fDirty = TRUE;
        paux->sig.SetWillUseSig(fCheck);
        PropSheet_Changed(GetParent(hdlg), hdlg);
    }
    return TRUE;

    case IDC_EDITSIG:
        if (HIWORD(wParam) == EN_KILLFOCUS)
        {
            if (SendMessage((HWND)lParam, EM_GETMODIFY, 0, 0))
            {
                SPropPageAux *paux = (SPropPageAux *)
                    GetWindowLong(hdlg, GWL_USERDATA);
```

```
                paux->fDirty = TRUE;
                paux->sig.SetSigFromWindow((HWND)lParam);

                PropSheet_Changed(GetParent(hdlg), hdlg);

                SendMessage((HWND)lParam, EM_SETMODIFY,
                    (WPARAM)0, 0);
            }
        }
        else if (HIWORD(wParam) == EN_MAXTEXT)
        {
            CUICommon(hdlg).Message(IDS_E_EXCEEDEDSIGLENGTH);
        }
    return TRUE;

    case IDC_USEPREFIX:
    {
        const BOOL fCheck = IsDlgButtonChecked(hdlg,
            IDC_USEPREFIX);
        EnableWindow(GetDlgItem(hdlg, IDC_EDITPREFIX), fCheck);
        EnableWindow(GetDlgItem(hdlg, IDC_LONGINTRO), fCheck);
        SPropPageAux *paux =
            (SPropPageAux *)GetWindowLong(hdlg, GWL_USERDATA);
        paux->fDirty = TRUE;
        paux->prefix.SetWillUsePrefix(fCheck);
        PropSheet_Changed(GetParent(hdlg), hdlg);
    }
    return TRUE;

    case IDC_LONGINTRO:
    {
        const BOOL fCheck = IsDlgButtonChecked(hdlg,
            IDC_LONGINTRO);
        SPropPageAux *paux =
            (SPropPageAux *)GetWindowLong(hdlg,
            GWL_USERDATA);
        paux->fDirty = TRUE;
        paux->prefix.SetUseLongForm(fCheck);
        PropSheet_Changed(GetParent(hdlg), hdlg);
    }
    return TRUE;

    case IDC_EDITPREFIX:
        if (HIWORD(wParam) == EN_KILLFOCUS)
```

(continued)

199

```
        {
            if (SendMessage((HWND)lParam, EM_GETMODIFY, 0, 0))
            {
                SPropPageAux *paux =
                    (SPropPageAux *)GetWindowLong(hdlg,
                    GWL_USERDATA);
                paux->fDirty = TRUE;
                paux->prefix.SetPrefixFromWindow((HWND)lParam);
                PropSheet_Changed(GetParent(hdlg), hdlg);

                SendMessage((HWND)lParam, EM_SETMODIFY,
                    (WPARAM)0, 0);
            }
        }
        else if (HIWORD(wParam) == EN_MAXTEXT)
        {
            CUICommon(hdlg).Message(IDS_E_EXCEEDEDPREFIXLENGTH);
        }
        return TRUE;
    }
}
break;
```

Control ID	Control
IDC_ABOUT	Button to invoke the "About This Extension . . ." dialog box
IDC_FONT	Button to invoke the "Choose Font" dialog box
IDC_USESIG	Check box indicating whether to use the signature
IDC_EDITSIG	Edit control containing the contents of the signature
IDC_USEPREFIX	Check box indicating whether to prefix replies
IDC_LONGINTRO	Check box indicating whether to use a long prefix introduction
IDC_EDITPREFIX	Edit control containing the prefix string for replies

Table 4-8. *Controls used in the property sheet page dialog procedure of the Inetxidm sample.*

The following *WM_NOTIFY* clause dictates the page's behavior within the property sheet as a whole. For more information about each of the messages handled within this clause, read the Win32 SDK.

```
case WM_NOTIFY:
{
    switch (((LPNMHDR) lParam)->code)
    {
    case PSN_KILLACTIVE:
        // Allow this page to receive PSN_APPLY.
        fMsgResult = FALSE;
    break;

    case PSN_SETACTIVE:
        // Fill the controls in the page with information....

        fMsgResult = FALSE;  // Accepts activation
    break;

    case PSN_APPLY:
    {
        SPropPageAux *paux =
            (SPropPageAux *)GetWindowLong(hdlg, GWL_USERDATA);
        if (paux->fDirty)
        {
            paux->cf.Save();
            paux->sig.Save();
            paux->prefix.Save();
            paux->fDirty = FALSE;
        }
    }
    fMsgResult = PSNRET_NOERROR;
    break;

    case PSN_HELP:

        // Fake an About command.
        PostMessage(hdlg, WM_COMMAND, IDC_ABOUT, 0);

        // Doesn't matter on this notification
        fMsgResult = TRUE;
    break;
```

(continued)

```
            case PSN_QUERYCANCEL:
            {
                SPropPageAux *paux =
                    (SPropPageAux *)GetWindowLong(hdlg, GWL_USERDATA);
                if (paux->fDirty)
                {
                    CUICommon ui(hdlg);
                    fMsgResult = (ui.Query(IDS_Q_DISCARDCHANGES,
                        MB_YESNO) == IDNO);

                    // Return TRUE (i.e., IDNO) to cancel.
                    // Return FALSE (i.e., IDYES) to proceed,
                    // discarding changes.
                }
                else
                {
                    fMsgResult = FALSE;
                }
            }
            break;

            default:
                fMsgResult = FALSE;
            break;
            } // Switch

            SetWindowLong(hdlg, DWL_MSGRESULT, fMsgResult);
            break;
        } // Case WM_NOTIFY

        default:
            fMsgResult = FALSE;
        break;
        } // Switch

    return fMsgResult;
}
```

Releasing the property sheet   After the user has dismissed the property sheet dialog box, the client calls the extension's *IExchExtPropertySheets::FreePages* implementation to unwind any state or release memory allocated in its *GetPages* method. In the following excerpt from the EXT.CPP file of the Inextidm application, the extension releases the reference to the session that it obtained in *GetPages*:

```
STDMETHODIMP_(VOID) CExtImpl::FreePages(LPPROPSHEETPAGE ppsp,
    ULONG ulFlags, ULONG cpsp)
{
    if (_context != EECONTEXT_PROPERTYSHEETS)
        return;

    if (ulFlags != EEPS_TOOLSOPTIONS)
        return;

    // Release the session reference that the property page held.

    IMAPISession* psess = (IMAPISession*)ppsp[0].lParam;
    psess->Release();
}
```

Prompt the user for input

Finally, an extension can display its own dialog box for input or output. Such an extension uses *IExchExtCallback::GetWindow* to determine the parent window of the dialog box that it presents.

If the dialog box involves selecting a source or destination folder from the set of mounted message stores, the extension can use the client-supplied *IExchExtCallback::ChooseFolder* facility as a starting point.

Modal vs. modeless user interface in Exchange extensions

Any Exchange extension implementing a modal user interface should keep the message pump architecture of the client in mind. While superficially the client resembles a multithreaded application with multiple top-level windows all apparently running independently, in fact the client implements all of these windows from a single message loop. You can observe this by opening two view windows, requesting a modal dialog box from one of the windows (by choosing a command such as Tools - Options), and then attempting to activate the other window. In the same fashion, an extension that displays a modal dialog box can lock up the entire application.

An extension with a long-lived user interface window needs to implement that window as modeless. The extension must implement the *IExchExtModeless* interface on an object associated with the window, passing that object to *IExchExtCallback::RegisterModeless* when the client first installs the extension. The client will subsequently call *IExchExtModelessCallback::AddWindow* whenever the user creates a new modeless window.

Extensions loaded into contexts associated with modal Exchange user interface windows, such as property sheets, must not display modeless windows. Such extensions will see *EE_MODAL* set when they receive their call to *IExchExt-::Install*. They can either elect to suppress or change their own user interface or decline installation at that time.

Changing Client Behavior

An Exchange client extension can also change the existing behavior of the Exchange client. The extension can work within the client menu, intercepting or disabling altogether existing commands on the menu. It can also work within the forms intrinsic to the client, both creating new commands on those forms' menus and changing the forms' handling of their underlying messages and file attachments.

Changing Existing Menu Commands

The Exchange client's command dispatch mechanism gives client extensions the power to intercept any command from the menu or toolbar, whether the command is intrinsic to the client or is supplied by an extension. For any command, when the client needs to execute it or just display the status bar text, tooltip text, or help for that command, the client calls every extension loaded in the current context, passing each extension the command ID of the command in question. If an extension claims a command, the client lets that extension handle the command and will not pass it to any other extension or supply the information itself. It is up to the extension to refuse commands not owned by the extension.

Redefining existing commands

A client extension can easily redefine an additional command by intercepting the *DoCommand*, *Help*, and *QueryHelpText* calls through *IExchExtCommands* for that command's ID. The EXCHEXT.H header file publishes the command IDs for the client's default menu commands; a client can use these values as parameters to *IExchExtCallback::GetMenuPos*, as was demonstrated above, or can use them when the client is subclassing that command. For example, an extension might want to intercept the client's File - Delete command to perform some additional validation and warning when a user deletes a message. Such an extension would watch for dispatches with the command ID value *EECMDID_FileDelete*. (See Figure 4-15.)

An implementation of *IExchExtCommands::DoCommand* can easily revert to the behavior of the default Exchange client by returning *S_FALSE* from the method. The client will see that return value, conclude that the extension wasn't interested in the command, and continue chaining down the list of installed extensions. Once the client runs out of extensions, it supplies the default command implementation itself.

Disabling existing commands

Client extensions disable existing commands in much the same manner that they disable their own commands. If they disable a command unconditionally, they add code to *IExchExtCommands::InitMenu* disabling the menu item with the command ID in question. If they disable commands in response to particular user selections, they track *InitMenu* and optionally *IExchExtUserEvents::OnSelectionChange*, modifying the menu and toolbar state as they find appropriate.

Even with the menu item disabled, the command accelerator can still function. A client extension disabling a particular command should thus intercept *IExchExtCommands::DoCommand* requests for that command to incapacitate its accelerator keys, if any.

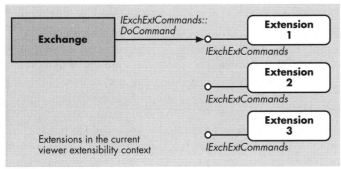

1 Exchange dispatches the File - Delete command (having a menu ID of *EECMDID_FileDelete*).

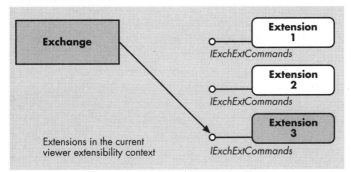

2 Extension 3 claims this command to implement the command itself.

Figure 4-15. *Here* EECMDID_FileDelete *is snagged before Exchange gets to handle it.*

Enhancing the Standard Forms

Until now we haven't discussed the extensibility contexts associated with the forms intrinsic to Exchange, focusing instead on the viewer contexts. The form contexts offer most of the same possibilities available from the viewer contexts, along with a number of new ones.

Keep in mind that this section applies only to those forms intrinsic to the Exchange client. Exchange users could encounter many other types of forms, such as the meeting request forms of Schedule+, the "WordMail" feature of Microsoft Office 95, the custom forms created with the Exchange Forms Designer, the Exchange Server public folder conflict notification form, or even the form applications appearing later in this book. Those forms will not support Exchange client extensions since they are not implemented by the Exchange client.

Altering the form menu

Most of the preceding section that discusses adding commands to the Exchange client menu and toolbar applies equally well to the form contexts as to the view contexts. Every form has its own menu and toolbar, onto which an extension installed in the form's context could append custom commands. Forms support property sheets under both the commands File - Properties and Tools - Options; the former sheet reflects the properties of the current message onto which an extension is free to append its own information, while the latter is the same as that displayed in the viewer.

Instead of a viewer displaying a set of objects, forms display a single object; thus the callback interface in a form extensibility context does not support the *IExch-ExtCallback::GetSelectionCount* and *IExchExtCallback::GetSelectionItem* methods. Likewise, rather than watch *IExchExtUserEvents::OnSelectionChange*, an extension in a form context will watch *IExchExtUserEvents::OnObjectChange*, through which the Exchange client notifies the extension that the current form now displays a different message, as can happen through the View - Next or View - Previous commands. Form commands have recourse to the *IExchExtCall-back::GetRecipients* and *IExchExtCallback::SetRecipients* callbacks, which manipulate the contents of the recipients fields on the form.

Within the form context, the *IExchExtCallback::GetObject* method always returns a reference to the current message.

If you would like to analyze some code, take a look at the EXT.CPP files of the samples Chap04\Inetxidm and Chap04\Eestub, which demonstrate installing a command on the menu and toolbar of a form.

Altering a read message

A client extension can alter the message-handling behavior of Exchange forms by implementing the *IExchExtMessageEvents* interface. When the Exchange client finds this interface on an extension installed in a form context, it notifies the extension whenever the form reads a message from the store, writes the message back to the store, submits the message for transmission, or resolves names typed in the form recipients fields against address books.

The Exchange client invokes *IExchExtMessageEvents::OnRead* when the user opens a standard read note form, reading the message from the store, or when the user opens a standard send note form for an unsent message that the user had previously saved to the store without sending it. At that time, the extension examines the backing message using the reference retrieved from *IExchExt-Callback::GetObject*. Since the form has not yet read the backing message, a call to *IExchExtCallback::GetRecipients* made at this time will find nothing. The extension could elect to provide its own user interface in the place of the Exchange form, in which case the extension should return *S_OK* to override Exchange's user interface, or else could return *S_FALSE* to allow Exchange to proceed, potentially invoking other extensions. This works in a manner similar to the menu command dispatch mechanism.

After the form reads the message, Exchange invokes *IExchExtMessageEvents-::OnReadComplete*. If the extension had previously returned an error from its *On-Read* method, Exchange passes *EEME_FAILED* in the flags parameter to *OnReadComplete*, signaling that the extension should take this opportunity to clean up any state it left from the previous call. Otherwise, the extension could work on the completed form. A call to *IExchExtCallback::GetRecipients* at this time can be used to enable the form to read the recipients from the message. For more adventurous people, *IExchExtCallback::GetWindow* returns the topmost window in the form window itself. From this topmost window, the extension might walk the last of the child windows, examining and possibly modifying those windows. Again, the extension should return *S_FALSE* or *S_OK* to disallow or permit further processing. Should the extension return an error code here, Exchange invokes *OnReadComplete* once more, this time passing *EEME_COM-PLETE_FAILED* in the flags parameter.

Note that a new send note form does not call the *OnRead* method, since it is not reading a message. Less intuitively, a new send note created in response to an existing message does not read the original message; instead, the client reads the message and then creates the send note, populating that send note with the response text in its message body. An extension that wants to receive control within a new send note should implement *IExchExtCommands::InitMenu*, setting a flag such that the extension performs the desired processing on the first call to *InitMenu* since this is the first extensibility call to be fired when the note is completely initialized.

The Inetxidm sample performs several tasks, including setting the default font of the read note form and changing the default format of included reply text. To set the default read font, the extension finds the form's RichEdit control and sets that control's default font before the form adds any text to the control; to modify the reply text, the extension works in the control after the form has added the text.

The member variable *_hwndRE* contains a handle to the RichEdit control. The extension locates this[9] when the client first installs it into the form context, in its implementation of *IExchExt::Install*; at the same time, it checks the current build version of Exchange, setting a member variable *_fOldEEME*.[10] The class *CCharFormat*, located in PRSHT.CPP, encapsulates the character format setting needed to set the RichEdit control; since the class needs a session to determine the initial character format, the extension requests a reference to the session from the extension callback and then releases that reference once it constructs the character format object. The member variable *_msgtype* is an instance of *CMsgType*, which you can find in EXT.CPP; it uses a heuristic to guess the type and history of the message.

The code for the *OnRead*, *OnReadComplete*, and *InitMenu* methods (from the file EXT.CPP) is as follows:

```
STDMETHODIMP CExtImpl::OnRead(IExchExtCallback* peecb)
{
    // The preread handler delivers default font mapping
    // for forms that can render monospace-formatted Internet mail.

    switch (_context)
    {
    case EECONTEXT_SENDPOSTMESSAGE:
    case EECONTEXT_SENDNOTEMESSAGE:
```

---

9. Code such as that delivering the RichEdit control location heuristic depends on assumptions outside of the contract of *IExchExtCallback*. Nothing prevents it from breaking in Microsoft Exchange version 5. This is exactly why every *IExchExt::Install* implementation should call *GetVersion*! See the function *FindREOnNote* in the file Chap04\Inetxidm\STDNOTE.CPP to see the dirty deed done.

10. This stands for "Old *IExchExtMessageEvents*." Older builds of the Microsoft Exchange client, including the version released with retail Windows 95, call *OnRead* in new send note forms. The Inetxidm sample changes its behavior to suit the current build.

```
        // Not sure what to do about remapping these first two.
        // If we set this font, we lose the "send" font setting.
        // If we don't, we don't get reply text defaulted correctly.
        // (TODO: save original read setting, set the default for
        // the insertion of the reply text, and then reset to the
        // original.)

        // In post-611 builds, this will do the right thing,
        // since new reply notes never see OnRead.

    case EECONTEXT_READNOTEMESSAGE:
    case EECONTEXT_READPOSTMESSAGE:
        break;

    default:
        // This way, the function defends itself against unknown
        // future variants, as FindREOnNote is less robust than it
        // might be.
        return S_FALSE;
    }

    IMAPISession* psess;
    HRESULT hr = peecb->GetSession(&psess, NULL);
    if (FAILED(hr))
    {
        CUICommon().Message(IDS_E_NOSESSION);
        return S_FALSE;
    }

    CCharFormat cf(psess);
    psess->Release();
    cf.Load();
    SendMessage(_hwndRE, EM_SETCHARFORMAT, 0, (LPARAM)(void*)&cf);

    // Can't yet detect whether it's a reply, since recipients
    // are unavailable.  (Pre-611)

    return S_FALSE;
}

STDMETHODIMP CExtImpl::OnReadComplete(IExchExtCallback* peecb,
    ULONG ulFlags)
{
    // Note: post-611, this will not fire on new reply notes, since
    // they aren't reading the message themselves.  (Should still
```

(continued)

```
    // fire on initialization of saved notes, though.)  Hence
    // this takes place in InitMenu instead.

    // The post-read handler converts replies into Internet standard
    // format, where necessary.  It also checks to see whether
    // we're forwarding a possibly already signed message,
    // suppressing the signature setting in that case.

    if (_context != EECONTEXT_SENDNOTEMESSAGE)
        return S_FALSE;

    if (ulFlags == EEME_COMPLETE_FAILED) // Nothing to unwind
        return S_FALSE;

    if (_fOldEEME) // Only on builds before 611 (RC1)
    {
        HRESULT hr = _msgtype.Read(peecb);
        if (FAILED(hr))
        {
            return S_FALSE;
        }

        // If it's a new reply, and the sender's willing,
        // work on the message body.

        if (_msgtype.IsNew() && _msgtype.IsReply())
        {
            IMAPISession* psess;
            HRESULT hr = peecb->GetSession(&psess, NULL);
            if (FAILED(hr))
            {
                CUICommon().Message(IDS_E_NOSESSION);
                return S_FALSE;
            }

            CPrefixSetting prefix(psess);
            prefix.Init();
            if (prefix.WillUsePrefix() && prefix.HasPrefix())
            {
                MungeReplyBody(_hwndRE, prefix);
            }

            psess->Release();
        }
```

```
        else if (_msgtype.IsForward())
        {
            // By default, turn off signatures on forwards...

            _fUseSig = FALSE;
        }
        else if (_msgtype.WasSubmittedOnce())
        {
            // ...and messages opened from the Outbox.

            _fUseSig = FALSE;
        }
    }

    return S_FALSE;
}
    ⋮
STDMETHODIMP_(VOID) CExtImpl::InitMenu(IExchExtCallback* pmecb)
{
    if (EECONTEXT_SENDNOTEMESSAGE != _context)
        return;

    // This is the first look that the extension gets at the
    // completed reply note, so it's the best place to munge reply
    // text.  (OnReadComplete doesn't fire on new reply notes
    // after build 611.)

    if (!_fInitMenuOnce)
    {
        if (!_fOldEEME)
        {
            HRESULT hr = _msgtype.Read(pmecb);
            assert(SUCCEEDED(hr));

            if (_msgtype.IsNew() && _msgtype.IsReply())
            {
                IMAPISession* psess;
                HRESULT hr = pmecb->GetSession(&psess, NULL);
                if (FAILED(hr))
                {
                    CUICommon().Message(IDS_E_NOSESSION);
                    return;
                }
```

(continued)

```
                    CPrefixSetting prefix(psess);
                    prefix.Init();
                    if (prefix.WillUsePrefix() && prefix.HasPrefix())
                    {
                        MungeReplyBody(_hwndRE, prefix);
                    }

                    psess->Release();
                }
                else if (_msgtype.IsForward())
                {
                    // By default, turn off signatures on forwards...

                    _fUseSig = FALSE;
                }
                else if (_msgtype.WasSubmittedOnce())
                {
                    // ...and messages opened from the Outbox.

                    _fUseSig = FALSE;
                }
            }

            // Only look at the above sequence once.

            _fInitMenuOnce = TRUE;
        }


        // Now to the real menu business

        HMENU hmenu;
        HRESULT hr = pmecb->GetMenu(&hmenu);
        if (FAILED(hr))
            return;

        const BOOL fHasSig = _sig.HasSig();
        EnableMenuItem(hmenu, _cmdidSign, (fHasSig ?
            MF_ENABLED : MF_GRAYED));
        if (fHasSig)
            CheckMenuItem(hmenu, _cmdidSign, (_fUseSig ?
                MF_CHECKED : MF_UNCHECKED));

        HWND hwndToolbar;
        hr = pmecb->GetToolbar(EETBID_STANDARD, &hwndToolbar);
```

```
    if (hr != S_OK)
        return;

    SendMessage(hwndToolbar, TB_ENABLEBUTTON, _cmdidSign,
        MAKELONG(fHasSig, 0));
    if (fHasSig)
        SendMessage(hwndToolbar, TB_CHECKBUTTON, _cmdidSign,
            MAKELONG(_fUseSig, 0));
}
```

Altering a sent message

The *IExchExtMessageEvents* interface treats its other events (writing the message to the store, submitting the message to the spooler, and checking the entered names of message recipients) in the same way that it treats message reads. In response to each event, the client calls one method immediately before the event, a companion method immediately after the event, and possibly the companion method a second time, passing *EEME_FAILED* or *EEME_COMPLETE_FAILED* as appropriate.

When the user saves the message back to the store, the client calls *IExchExt-MessageEvents::OnWrite* and *IExchExtMessageEvents::OnWriteComplete*. When the user submits a message for transmission, the client calls *IExchExtMessage-Events::OnSubmit* and *IExchExtMessageEvents::OnSubmitComplete*; these calls precede and follow the actual writing of the outgoing message to the store so that the extension sees the call sequence *OnSubmit, OnWrite, OnWriteComplete*, and *OnSubmitComplete*. An extension can easily discriminate between the two types of writing—for transmission and for saving—by setting a flag in the *On-Submit* method.

The following code sample, again from Chap04\Inetxidm\EXT.CPP, comprises the remainder of the sample's *IExchExtMessageEvents* implementation. Inetxidm does not concern itself with the process of resolving the contents of the addressing fields into recipients, deferring the *IExchExtMessagesEvents::OnCheckNames* member pair with stub implementations. Within the *OnSubmit* method, the extension sets and clears only a flag modifying the behavior of the *OnWrite* method. The *OnWriteComplete* method modifies the written message body to include some boilerplate text, while the *OnWrite* method inserts a custom property to ensure that the extension doesn't add the boilerplate twice, should the message ever return (for example, if the message returns in a nondelivery report and subsequently is resubmitted).

The code for the *OnWrite, OnWriteComplete, OnCheckNames, OnCheckNames-Complete, OnSubmit,* and *OnSubmitComplete* methods is as follows:

213

```
STDMETHODIMP CExtImpl::OnWrite(IExchExtCallback* pecb)
{
    // The prewrite handler stamps this message as having been
    // processed.  This prevents the extension from munging the
    // message body twice.

    if (_context != EECONTEXT_SENDNOTEMESSAGE)
        return S_FALSE;

    CWaitCursor wait; // Mark busy
    HRESULT hr = _msgtype.Write(pecb, _fInSubmitState);
    if (FAILED(hr))
        return hr;

    return S_FALSE;
}

STDMETHODIMP CExtImpl::OnWriteComplete(IExchExtCallback* pecb,
    ULONG ulFlags)
{
    // The postwrite handler appends signatures onto outgoing
    // messages.

    if (_context != EECONTEXT_SENDNOTEMESSAGE)
        return S_FALSE;

    if (ulFlags == EEME_COMPLETE_FAILED) // Nothing to unwind
        return S_FALSE;

    if (!_fInSubmitState)      // This is not a submission.
        return S_FALSE;

    // Suppressed on this message, or else not present

    if (!_fUseSig)
        return S_FALSE;

    AppendSignature(pecb, _sig);

    // I don't really care whether the signing failed or not.

    return S_FALSE;
}
```

```
STDMETHODIMP CExtImpl::OnCheckNames(IExchExtCallback*)
{
    return S_FALSE;
}

STDMETHODIMP CExtImpl::OnCheckNamesComplete(
    IExchExtCallback*, ULONG)
{
    return S_FALSE;
}

STDMETHODIMP CExtImpl::OnSubmit(IExchExtCallback*)
{
    // Differentiate save from send, for signatures' sake.  When I
    // see this set in OnWrite/Complete, I know that I'm ready to
    // work on an outgoing message.

    // An alternative for signing the message would locate the RTF
    // control at this time, pasting the signature text at the end
    // of the control.  Or it could paste it in at on-read-complete
    // time.

    _fInSubmitState = TRUE;
    return S_FALSE;
}

STDMETHODIMP_(VOID) CExtImpl::OnSubmitComplete(
    IExchExtCallback*, ULONG)
{
    _fInSubmitState = FALSE;
    return;
}
```

This extension changes the message twice as the client writes that message: once before the write and once after the write if the write took place as part of a submission. In each case, the extension operates on the same MAPI message object that the Exchange client uses, since the extension requested a reference to that object through *IExchExtCallback::GetObject*. While the extension can set as many properties as it wants, it can never call *IMAPIProp::SaveChanges*; that is the exclusive prerogative of the client, which effectively brokers the use of its single message object between all its extensions.

The following code appends boilerplate text to the end of the message body from Chap04\Inetxidm\SIG.CPP:

```
void AppendSignature(IExchExtCallback* peecb,
    const CSigSetting& sig)
{
    assert(sig.HasSig()); // Otherwise, never called
    if (!sig.HasSig())
        return;

    const TCHAR* pszSig = sig.GetSig();
    const UINT cchSig = _tcslen(pszSig);
    if (0 == cchSig)
        return;

    HWND hwnd = NULL;
    peecb->GetWindow(&hwnd);
    CUICommon ui(hwnd);

    CWaitCursor wait; // Mark busy

    IMessage *pmsg = 0;
    HRESULT hr = peecb->GetObject(NULL, (IMAPIProp**)&pmsg);
    if (FAILED(hr))
    {
        ui.Message(IDS_E_FINDMSGSIGN);
        return;
    }

    IStream *pstrmBody = 0;
    hr = pmsg->OpenProperty(PR_BODY, &IID_IStream, STGM_WRITE,
        MAPI_MODIFY, (IUnknown**)&pstrmBody);
    if (FAILED(hr))
    {
        if (hr == MAPI_E_NOT_FOUND)
        {
            // The message had no body.  It came about either
            // through dragging a file into the "Mail Recipient"
            // target or through mailing a message with an
            // explicitly empty body.

            // Ideal behavior would probably be to prompt the user
            // to specify whether to create a body.
            // Instead, just bail out quietly.
        }
        else
```

```
        {
            ui.ErrorMessage(pmsg, hr, IDS_E_WHILESIGNINGBODY);
        }
        pmsg->Release();
        return;
    }

    LARGE_INTEGER li = {0,0};
    hr = pstrmBody->Seek(li, STREAM_SEEK_END, NULL);
    if (SUCCEEDED(hr) && *pszSig != '\r')
        hr = pstrmBody->Write(_T("\r\n"), 2*sizeof(TCHAR), NULL);
    if (SUCCEEDED(hr))
        hr = pstrmBody->Write(pszSig, sizeof(TCHAR)*cchSig, NULL);
    if (SUCCEEDED(hr) && pszSig[cchSig-1] != '\n')
        hr = pstrmBody->Write(_T("\r\n"), 2*sizeof(TCHAR), NULL);
    if (SUCCEEDED(hr))
        hr = pstrmBody->Commit(STGC_DEFAULT);
    if (FAILED(hr))
    {
        ui.Message(IDS_E_SIGNMSGBODY);
        pstrmBody->Release();
        pmsg->Release();
        return;
    }

    pstrmBody->Release();
    pstrmBody = 0;

    BOOL fPartied;
    hr = RTFSync(pmsg, RTF_SYNC_BODY_CHANGED, &fPartied);
    if (FAILED(hr))
    {
        ui.Message(IDS_E_SYNCMSGBODY);
        pmsg->Release();
        return;
    }

    // All client extensions operate as parasites within the
    // client.  Only the client gets the privilege of calling
    // SaveChanges.

    pmsg->Release();
    pmsg = 0;
}
```

This function takes the desired boilerplate text from an instance of the class *CSig-Setting*, gets a reference to the form's message object, locates the plain text message body property that the form has already written to the message (this being called from *OnWriteComplete*, as shown in the method implementation listing above), appends the boilerplate text to the message body, and finally invokes the MAPI RTF engine to synchronize the rich text with the changed body text.

Do not confuse the call to *IStream::Commit* with committing the changes to the message. The stream call commits the changes only within the scope of the single stream in question.

Automatically processing attached files   The Exchange forms also allow client extensions to modify Exchange's native file attachment processing. Such an extension will implement the *IExchExtAttachedFileEvents* interface, inviting Exchange to call the extension whenever a user of the form opens an attached file or saves a file to a message. The obvious uses of this interface include automatic virus detection and attachment size policy enforcement.

For more information on this interface and others, see the book *Extending the Microsoft Exchange Client* in the MAPI SDK documentation.

5

Forms: Theory and Environment

This chapter discusses the MAPI forms mechanism, through which an application can introduce a new type of message with its own user interface. Specifically, it describes the architecture of the forms environment, the operation of the MAPI Forms Manager, and the means through which a client gets information about a particular form. Subsequent chapters discuss implementing and interacting with such forms.

Forms and Messages

In the last chapter, we discussed the form and view windows of the Exchange client and examined applications that extended those windows in various ways. By leveraging the Exchange client extensibility interfaces, you can use an application to add or change commands on a form or on a view window's menu bar, alter the contents of the form window, and change the way that the form reads and sends messages. Such an application is still working from the basic functionality supplied in the Exchange client: either a point-to-point message to carry a body of rich message text between users (the send form) or a posted message to save a body of rich message text in a particular folder (the post form).

Many messaging and workgroup applications resemble the basic Exchange client functions in only the most general way. Consider an application for coordinating appointments between its users. Instead of message text, such a scheduling program can carry the time, date, and duration of an appointment to its destination. Instead of an edit control for entering and viewing a message, the scheduler might contain a calendar and clock readout on which to schedule the appointment, plus a small edit control in which to describe the appointment. A user of such an application, faced with a set of appointment requests, might want to see its pertinent attributes (that is, time, date, duration) in any view of that set and might also want to see the commands germane to those requests (such as Accept This Appointment, Decline This Appointment, or Check My Schedule) on a context menu that appears when the right mouse button is clicked. Such applications use the Exchange client as a framework for browsing and viewing their own application-specific items. The Exchange client supports these applications through the MAPI forms management facilities.

The Role of Forms in MAPI

Technically speaking, MAPI defines forms as constructs that create and display messages of a particular type as defined by the *message class* string property (*PR_MESSAGE_CLASS*) of the message. With forms, an application author can define a completely new message type, embedding its own data within an instance of that type of message, and can supply that message type with its own commands, view columns, and user interface.

The Exchange client tightly integrates these defined MAPI forms into the Exchange user interface. When you open a message, the Exchange client examines that message to determine its correct form and then invokes that form on your behalf. Even if you select a message without opening it, the Exchange client makes available to you the commands pertinent to that message's form. The Compose - New Form command of Exchange allows you to select a form from a forms library. If you open a folder containing its own forms library, the Exchange client lists the forms from that library directly on the Compose menu. It also consults those forms for custom columns to use within the folder, offering those columns when you choose the Tools - Inbox Assistant, Tools - Find, and View - Columns commands.

Figure 5-1 shows a view window from the Exchange client that demonstrates this integration. The application in the view has defined its own message type to create its own item, with a form that supplies a custom icon and columns for the view. Those columns also appear when you choose the Tools - Inbox Assistant and Tools - Find commands. The form also defines the commands that apply to the item, both on the viewer's Compose menu and on any context menu on the item. When the user chooses one of the form's commands, the form displays its own user interface, distinct from that of the Exchange client, as shown in Figure 5-2.

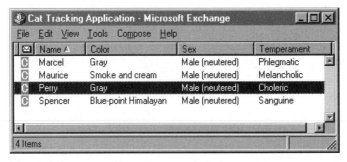

Figure 5-1. *View of a custom application.*

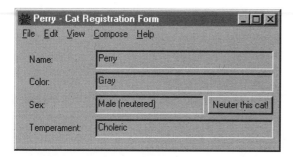

Figure 5-2. *Form of a custom application.*

Exchange Client Features

If you are working on a Windows Messaging Subsystem (WMS) that appears only on an Exchange Server platform that does not include Microsoft Exchange Server, you might not see client features such as the Tools - Inbox Assistant and Tools - Out Of Office Assistant since these features originate from Exchange Server. The client implements its support for those features in a library of Exchange client extensions, EMSUIX32.DLL, using the mechanisms described in the last chapter. The setup program that installs the Exchange Server MAPI service providers also installs this client extension library. A client lacking this library will not contain those features; a client with this library but running against a profile that does not name the Exchange Server providers displays the features as disabled menu items.

Other features, such as most of the commands in the View menu, originate from the Exchange client itself. Certain versions of the Exchange client lack those features—for example, versions that were released on the retail Windows 95 platform and those that were included in the redistributable copy of WMS. The setup program that installs the Exchange Server MAPI service providers replaces portions of WMS to enable these features.

Regardless of the presence of particular client features, all of the underlying MAPI mechanisms operate in the same fashion on each platform.

Send vs. Post Forms

Forms fall naturally into two classes, based on the means by which their messages reach their destinations: send forms and post forms. Each of these will be discussed in the following sections.

Send forms

Send forms embody what you typically imagine as e-mail. They create a message that travels to a destination mailbox through the services of a message transport service. All interpersonal messages fall into this category, including those created by the standard Exchange note form, as do routed documents and custom point-to-point message types. In general, all applications that depend on a transport provider to carry their messages to their ultimate destinations are send forms.

The message of a send form starts in the sender's mailbox, where the sender creates it. At the sender's request, the form submits the message to the MAPI message spooler, which in turn hands it to the loaded MAPI transport providers. The MAPI transport providers interpret the e-mail addresses in the message's recipient table and send the message to its final destination. If that destination is a system with MAPI, the message ends up in a folder such as the inbox of a recipient's mailbox or another folder in a message store.

Post forms

Post forms embody the database-style interaction that takes place in many folder-hosted Exchange applications. This class of forms includes the standard Exchange post-to-folder form, bulletin boards, and most of the sample applications included in Exchange Server.

A post form creates a message and then saves (or *posts,* to use the bulletin board metaphor) that message directly into a destination folder. These post form messages lack many of the envelope attributes of a send form message, such as a recipient table, since post form messages never pass through a message transport. This makes post forms considerably simpler than send forms.

Some Standard Exchange Forms

The Exchange client delivers all of its intrinsic messaging functionality in a number of forms that it implements itself. Some standard Exchange forms include *IPM.Note, IPM.Post, IPM.Document, IPM.Resend,* reports, and application-defined forms. These forms are discussed in the following sections.

IPM.Note

The most commonly encountered send form is the Exchange standard send note. It appears in response to the command Compose - New Message, which creates messages of class *IPM.Note.* (See Figure 5-3.) These messages carry a body of user-specified rich text and attachments addressed to one or more recipients listed in the form's To and Cc fields.

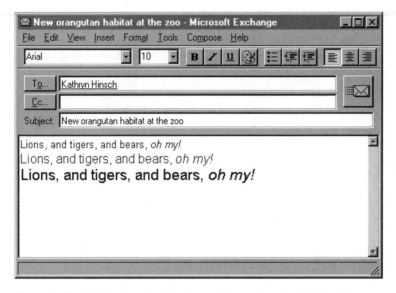

Figure 5-3. *Exchange standard send form invoked by the Compose - New Message command.*

IPM.Post

The most commonly encountered post form is the Exchange standard interpersonal message (IPM) post to folder form. It appears in response to the command Compose - New Post In This Folder, which creates messages of class *IPM.Post*. (See Figure 5-4 on the following page.) These messages resemble messages of class *IPM.Note* in their visible content, although they lack most artifacts of the message envelope such as address fields; in their place are some additional bulletin-board type fields for classifying discussions.

IPM.Document

When you drag a file from the Explorer into an Exchange viewer window, Exchange stores a copy of the document in the viewed folder. To do this, Exchange creates a message of class *IPM.Document*,[1] stores the copied file as an attachment on the message, and saves this message in the destination folder. If Exchange recognizes the file as one that uses the compound document structure, Exchange stores the summary properties from the document in the message as named

---

1. Actually, Exchange creates a subclass of this class, as described in the section "Resolution of a Form" later in this chapter.

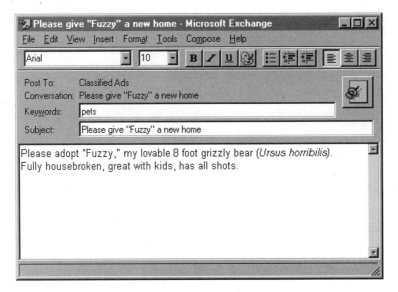

Figure 5-4. *Exchange standard post form invoked by the Compose - New Post In This Folder command.*

properties in the *PS_PUBLIC_STRINGS* property set, allowing those properties to appear in searches and views on the folder. Requests to open the item do so with the document's application; if that application operates as an ActiveX component, it is embedded OLE-fashion. This document wrapper is an example of a post form with very little user interface of its own—but a post form nevertheless.

IPM.Resend

When Exchange resends a send note message (*IPM.Note*) that has previously failed to be delivered, it uses the send form *IPM.Resend*. The *IPM.Resend* form comes from the Exchange-supplied form for *Report.IPM.Note.NDR* when you click the Resend button. The *IPM.Resend* form displays the original message body but does not allow you to change this message body, offering only editable To and Cc fields with which to redirect the failed message.

Reports

The spooler and service providers of MAPI generate report messages to inform clients of various events: a message being read, a message deleted without being read, a message delivered successfully, or one failing delivery. These messages are not created by forms, but they still need forms if you are to display and view them. Exchange provides a default form that will display each of these different report types. You most frequently see it when a send note fails delivery for some reason (*Report.IPM.Note.NDR*).

Standard Application-Defined Forms

To go beyond the standard Exchange functionality, an application can define forms to augment or replace those native to Exchange. Some examples of standard application-defined forms are described in the following sections.

Microsoft Office 95

When installed on a system containing Microsoft Exchange and MAPI, Microsoft Word 7 includes the WordMail feature, with which you can use Word to edit e-mail messages. Word implements this feature by installing its own form to handle messages of class *IPM.Note*, replacing the standard form supplied by the Exchange client. Having installed its own form, Word can supply all the user interfaces for creating and rendering messages of this class.

Microsoft Schedule+ 7

Users of Microsoft Schedule+ 7 (included in both Microsoft Office 95 and Microsoft Exchange Server) running in workgroup mode can send, receive, and acknowledge meeting requests through e-mail. These meeting requests appear in the Microsoft Exchange Inbox folder as discrete items with a Schedule+ icon. Schedule+ implements these items as a message containing the data for the meeting request and supplies a number of forms that allow you to open or acknowledge the request from within Exchange. The message types defined by Schedule+ are shown in Table 5-1.

Message Type	Description
IPM.Schedule.Meeting.Request	Meeting Request
IPM.Schedule.Meeting.Resp.Pos	Positive Meeting Response
IPM.Schedule.Meeting.Resp.Neg	Negative Meeting Response
IPM.Schedule.Meeting.Resp.Tent	Tentative Meeting Response
IPM.Schedule.Meeting.Canceled	Meeting Cancellation

Table 5-1. *Message types defined by Schedule+.*

Microsoft Exchange Server

Microsoft Exchange Server generates several varieties of message beyond those intrinsic to the generic Exchange client. For example, Exchange Server can duplicate a public folder, thus distributing the load of hosting user access to that public folder across multiple servers. The system duplicates changes made to any one instance of the folder—any one replica—to all other instances of that folder. In doing so, if the system finds that changes made at one replica conflict with changes made at another, it announces the conflict by sending a message of class *IPM.Conflict.Message* to the users responsible for those changes, as well as to any designated contact users of the public folder, so that somebody can resolve it. A special form renders this message type.

Microsoft Exchange Forms Designer

A number of electronic forms packages, such as Delrina Formflow, Jetform Design, and Caere Omniform, allow you to design and develop custom message types in Exchange, either for sending messages to other users or for posting messages as part of a folder application. To this end, Microsoft Exchange Server includes the Microsoft Exchange Forms Designer package, which generates form applications using Microsoft Visual Basic 4 and includes a number of sample applications. When you use Exchange Forms Designer, you lay out the form in an environment similar to the development environment of Visual Basic and give the form's item type the same name as the message class of the form's underlying message.

Form as Component Object

In terms of the Microsoft Component Object Model (COM), a MAPI form is a component object that implements the *IMAPIForm* interface plus the *IPersistMessage* interface to read and save the contents of a form to and from MAPI messages. Unlike the extension objects of the Exchange client application, a MAPI form object adheres to all the rules of COM. Every form has a CLSID that uniquely identifies the form's class; this CLSID indexes an entry that locates the server implementing that class, beneath the HKEY_CLASSES_ROOT key of the system registry. Once loaded, form servers register their class objects (or class factories) just as any other object server registers class objects; as shown in Figure 5-5, those class objects build instances of form objects just as any other class object creates instances.

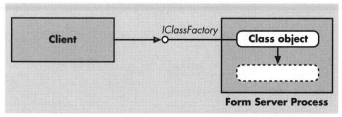

1 The client requests a new form object from the *IClassFactory* interface.

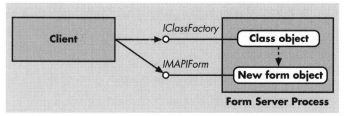

2 The client drops the *IClassFactory* interface and obtains direct access to the new form object.

Figure 5-5. *The class object creates the form objects.*

Analogy Between Forms and ActiveX Server Applications

Roughly speaking, forms are to messages as ActiveX server applications are to files.

In OLE, a document has a type, which is made explicit by the CLSID of the application that created it. (See Figure 5-6 on the following page.) The CLSID is determined either from a literal CLSID appearing in a stream on the root storage of the document's host file (if the file uses OLE-structured storage), by pattern matching the file's contents, or by association with the filename extension. When a particular application creates a document, it is associated forever with that document unless it is converted to another object type by another application. An OLE container is responsible for determining the correct CLSID of an embedded document's server (with help from the OLE run-time support) and for passing control to that server at the appropriate times. In a sense, Windows Explorer acts as the ultimate container, invoking the correct application for open requests on visible files, although it differs in the gross mechanical details from the OLE container proper.

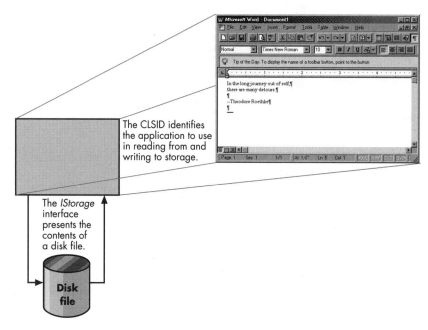

The CLSID identifies the application to use in reading from and writing to storage.

The *IStorage* interface presents the contents of a disk file.

Disk file

Figure 5-6. *File document implemented by the application server.*

In MAPI, a message has a type, made explicit by the value of its message class property. When a particular form creates a message, it is associated forever with that message, unless the message type is emulated by another form. (See Figure 5-7.) A container of messages is responsible for determining the correct CLSID of a message's form (with help from MAPI) and passing control to that form at the appropriate times. The Exchange Inbox is the prototypical container and does just this, loading and invoking the appropriate form for a message's class when you choose a command related to that message.

The form is not the message, any more than the application is the file. However, a document-centered user interface displays the two as one, allowing you to manipulate documents or custom messages without thinking of the server application implementing a particular form. When you open an item in Windows Explorer, the shell invokes the correct application on your behalf; when you open an item in the Exchange viewer, Exchange invokes the correct form on your behalf. An application author sees a form server and a message, but the user sees only an item.

Since messages identify their type by the value of their message class property, and forms identify themselves by their CLSID, some utility is needed to

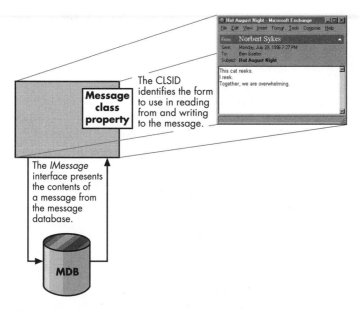

Figure 5-7. *Message document implemented by the form server.*

translate the message class to a form CLSID. A MAPI component called the *Forms Manager* performs this translation by a process called *resolution*. The program that installs a MAPI form server must provide to MAPI the message classes of that server's forms. The MAPI Forms Manager will store that information, using it when it needs to locate the correct form.

CLSID vs. Message Class

A CLSID identifies a single form, which is capable of handling only a single message class. A particular form always creates a message of its associated message class. However, do not confuse the form with the server implementing the form. The form is the class, implemented by some server; the server is simply an executable image, that is, the body of running code that supplies the class. Nothing prevents a single server from implementing multiple forms, each with its own CLSID.

More than one CLSID can claim a single message class. Think of the relationship between the Exchange standard send note and the Microsoft Office Word-Mail send note. As two discrete classes of form object, each has its own CLSID; however, they both emit messages with the class *IPM.Note*, allowing one form to replace another. One Exchange user might use WordMail to send a message to a recipient who uses out-of-the-box Exchange; since both users' send forms emit messages with this standard message class, they can communicate freely.

Scope of a Valid CLSID

Imagine a corporate messaging site, most likely running Microsoft Exchange Server, that encompasses 20,000 or so users. Such a site might host over a thousand different workgroup and messaging applications, each with its own custom message types and accompanying forms. Many of those forms will constitute folder applications written by other users, which the public folder architecture of Exchange Server makes available for browsing and discovery. It would be impossible for users to install all of those form servers or even to track the changes made to the forms in different applications.

Since a form is a component object, it must have a valid entry listing its CLSID in the system registry. To avoid forcing a workstation to install every form it might ever encounter, MAPI allows a form server to reside in a *forms library,* which is further described in the section "Storage for a Form" later in this chapter. When a client contacts the Forms Manager to invoke the correct form for a given message class, the Forms Manager consults its forms libraries and from them installs the correct form server for the message class. As part of installing the form, the Forms Manager adds entries to the workstation's system registry, describing the CLSID of the form. This lets the workstation virtually host the myriad forms available.

As MAPI gives, MAPI can take away. If the workstation lacks sufficient storage to host the needed form server, MAPI attempts to free sufficient storage by purging the files of the least recently used transient form server. This might result in system registry entries for each CLSID that no longer has its server local to the workstation. A client accessing a CLSID of such a form must always check with MAPI first to ensure that the form's CLSID is valid.

Convergence with Compound Documents

The analogy between the MAPI form and the ActiveX component application continues because MAPI uses the compound document activation technology for activating its forms. MAPI treats messages like embedded document instances and treats its forms like document servers that don't support in-place activation. Substitute *IMAPIForm* for *IOleObject* and *IPersistMessage* for *IPersistStorage*, keep in mind MAPI's mediator role in determining the correct CLSID of a form from the message class, and you're in business.

Form viewers

The object from which you invoke the form is called a *form viewer.* Typically, a form viewer displays a set of items in iconic fashion. From this compact representation, you can activate one of the items, whereupon the form viewer will contact MAPI to invoke the correct form for the item. Because of the similarity between compound document activation and MAPI form activation, form viewers are sometimes called containers, after their OLE counterpart.[2]

The most common form viewers are the viewer windows of the Exchange client. Less obviously, the Exchange standard note form is also a viewer when it contains embedded message instances. For more about MAPI form viewers, see Chapter 7.

Verbs

Like a compound document object, every form offers a set of *verbs*—actions that it performs in response to a request to activate the item, either from the Exchange client or from any other viewer item container. The Exchange client displays the verbs for a form in one of two ways: on an item's context menu when the user right-clicks on an item in the viewer window or on the Compose menu.

All forms support the default verb Open (known in OLE as "Show") to display themselves. When you double-click, invoke File - Open, or press Enter on a highlighted item in Exchange, the viewer activates the item's form with this Open verb. The form then leaps into view for the user, displaying the contents of the message in a visible window. Some custom forms might offer different verbs to render themselves in different fashions. For example, a form representing the price of a traded stock on a given day might offer a version (Graph) that displays a graph of the day's trading activity on that stock, allowing you to select between different displays of the item by choosing different open commands. Many forms will also support Print and Save As operations as verbs, sending the contents of the form to a printer or to a disk file.

In one common pattern of verb usage, a form creates a new instance of the form in response to the verb. The originally activated form activates the new form and then closes itself, leaving you working in the response form. This *response form* model appears in many of the standard Exchange client forms: Reply To Sender, Reply To All, Reply In This Folder, and Forward are all response forms. Other forms might support these standard verbs if they resemble the standard forms in their general operation, or they might implement completely different response verbs. A meeting request form might offer Accept Meeting and Decline Meeting verbs, each of which creates a form for responding to the original request, while a stock price form might offer Buy and Sell.

Further discussion of activation must wait until the next chapter, when the form server takes center stage.

---

2. These containers should not be confused with true MAPI containers. Unlike true OLE containers, MAPI containers do not fully support linking. No moniker type exists for message references.

Do not confuse verbs with the commands in the form's user interface or with any commands that a form server application might expose through ActiveX. A verb conveys a command from the viewer to the form, activating the form in the process. A form typically supports only a few verbs, since there are only so many ways in which to activate the object.

Creating Structured Messages with Forms

As described by the naked MAPI interface, a message is an unstructured, untyped bag of properties. It consists of *IMAPIProp*, an interface describing each object as a bag of MAPI properties; methods to manipulate a message's attachment and recipient tables; and methods to send the message on a trip through the message transports. Given a message by itself, no client has a guarantee of that message having any particular content. It's like passing a raw file handle; it could contain anything.

Forms take this unstructured bag and impose structure on it. An application that creates messages with a subject line, message body, and comment field wants any agent reading that message to expect a subject line, message body, and comment field. Conversely, code that expects those three properties need recognize only messages that fulfill the criteria. To do this, we must impose type on the untyped basic message.

Description of Message Classes

The mandatory *message class* property (*PR_MESSAGE_CLASS* in header file MAPITAGS.H) identifies the type of a message. Message class properties are readable strings, such as *IPM.Note* or *IPM.Purchase.Req.Corporate*. Character case distinctions are not significant in a message class, appearing only to improve the readability of the string. The MAPI Forms Manager uses the message class to locate the correct form for handling the message.

Message classes are hierarchical. The periods in a message class string serve to delimit the class into hierarchical components, with each component, as you move right to left through the string, constituting a distinct message class that subsumes all message classes to its right. Thus the message class *IPM.Note.Secure* comprises the classes *IPM.Note.Secure*, *IPM.Note*, and *IPM*. Such leading message classes are known as *superclasses* of the total class string. Conversely, *IPM.Note.Secure* is called a *subclass* of *IPM.Note*.

The message class describes the message's *schema*, or set of properties and property semantics common to all messages of that class. For example, all messages of class *IPM.Note* have a subject (*PR_SUBJECT*) unless the subject field is empty and body text (*PR_BODY*) unless the message body is left empty, and might carry a number of other properties related to rich text in the message body. (See Table 5-2.)

NOTE   Every message class you've seen so far has been a subclass of the *IPM* message class. *IPM* denotes Interpersonal Message, or a message meant for human consumption. Another high-level superclass, *IPC*, encompasses messages destined for automatic consumption by software—interprocess communication. By default, the MAPI message spooler delivers interpersonal messages to the Inbox folder. See the *GetReceiveFolder*, *GetReceiveFolder-Table*, and *SetReceiveFolder* methods of *IMsgStore* for further examples of message classes used to control inbound message classification.

Property	Type	Description
PR_SUBJECT	String	The subject of a message
PR_BODY	String	The text of the message body
PR_RTF_COMPRESSED	Binary	The compressed rich text version of the message body
PR_RTF_SYNC_BODY_CRC	Long	The cyclical redundancy check for the text body
PR_RTF_SYNC_BODY_COUNT	Long	The number of significant characters in the message body
PR_RTF_SYNC_BODY_TAG	String	The significant characters appearing at the beginning of the message body
PR_RTF_SYNC_PREFIX_COUNT	Long	The number of insignificant characters preceding the significant characters
PR_RTF_SYNC_TRAILING_COUNT	Long	The number of insignificant characters appearing after the significant characters of the message

Table 5-2. *Properties for messages of class* IPM.Note. *These properties form only a subset of the full schema of the message class.*

A subclass inherits the schema of its superclass and might embellish this further. Thus, as shown in Figure 5-8, a message of the hypothetical class *IPM.Note.-Secure* abides by the schema of *IPM.Note* but also carries a schema uniquely its own, in this case properties that describe the digital signature of the sender.

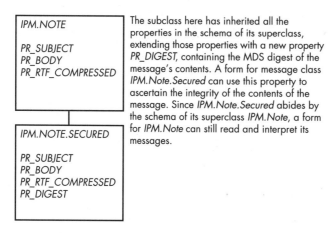

The subclass here has inherited all the properties in the schema of its superclass, extending those properties with a new property *PR_DIGEST*, containing the MDS digest of the message's contents. A form for message class *IPM.Note.Secured* can use this property to ascertain the integrity of the contents of the message. Since *IPM.Note.Secured* abides by the schema of its superclass *IPM.Note*, a form for *IPM.Note* can still read and interpret its messages.

Figure 5-8. *Comparison of the* IPM.Note *message class with a hypothetical* IPM.Note.Secure *message class.*

MAPI does not enforce or even define the schema of a message class, leaving that job to the individual forms creating the messages.

> **NOTE** Even if a schema includes a particular property, client code and forms should gracefully handle the absence of that property. Many properties in a schema are optional; witness both the subject and the body of *IPM.Note*, either of which might be absent from the message in certain circumstances. It's also possible that an application from outside your jurisdiction might send messages using your form's message class.

Properties of a Message Class

Through the MAPI Forms Manager, a form might advertise, or publish, a subset of the properties in the schema of its message class. A client application can use this information to generate meaningful views and searches across bodies of messages found at run time.

For example, the form for the message class *IPM.Letter.Business* might elect to publish the salutation and closing properties of its business letter form messages.

Client code that builds MAPI tables could look at the message class of the messages in the folder, find the form for that message class, and learn what custom properties the form published, adding those properties to the column set of the table. When that code encountered a folder of business letters, it would create a table, including the salutation and closing attributes of each item.

The application publishes only those properties that would prove meaningful in a search or a view. A message might contain many properties of no interest to the end user. For example, there is no point in *IPM.Note* publishing the various RTF synchronization properties—what would a user do with them? A client truly dedicated to exposing every property in a message can always call *IMAPIProp::GetPropList* on the message.

Property Sets in MAPI

When form designers create a new message class, they must lay out the schema for the properties of that class. Starting with the schema of the form's superclass, designers choose new properties in which to carry the form's data, selecting a type (Boolean, integer, string, or binary) for each new property, and a property ID.

MAPI reserves all the property IDs from 0x6800 through 0x7fff for use in new message classes, so form designers can freely choose from the values in this range as long as they do not conflict with uses of the same values in the superclass.[3] Note that the second half of this range contains nontransmittable properties, that is, properties that a message transport provider will discard before transmitting the message. Hence a send form should not use this latter range for any properties that need to reach the destination in one piece.

Since every message class can use the range from 0x6800 through 0x7fff for its properties, a contents table that includes these properties in its columns might contain some surprises. For example, a business letter form *IPM.Letter.Business* might use the string property with ID 0x6801 for storing its salutation ("Dear Sir or Madam"), while the love letter *IPM.Letter.Love* might use that property ID for a saccharine endearment ("Oh, how I adore your ears, my precious darling"). A search folder seeking a value on this property would generate amusing results if it came across both types of item, because MAPI knows nothing about the per-message-class semantics of the property; it just passes the query to the search engines of its message store providers. To prevent unintentional humor caused by such a property collision (see Figure 5-9 on the following page), such a contents table should restrict its rows to those matching the current message class.

---

3. This is a problem only when an existing custom message type is placed in a subclass.

NAME	Customer Name
Anthony, Elosie	002
Hector, James	004
<<Kathryn, have you seen my toothbrush?>>	
Mondigiloni, Martha	009
Thompson, Lee	013
Winer, Marion	020

The unfortunately humorous results of two
unrelated message classes sharing a common
property ID. *IPM.Note.Harmony.Marital* and
IPM.Record.Customer both use the string
property ID 0x6801. A query for the contents
of all 0x6801 values picked up a value that
does not belong to any mailing list.

Figure 5-9. *Property collision.*

MAPI property sets make it possible for a form to reserve a property that no other form will use. An application reserves a property set through a GUID allocated by the application author. This GUID identifies a unique name space of properties, within which the application can allocate its properties. The resulting properties will not collide with the properties of any other messages on the host message store. Cross-message class searches on these properties will not turn up any hits on inappropriate data.

NOTE The easiest way to allocate a property set is to reuse the CLSID of the form as the property set's GUID. This also gives you one less 128-bit number to recognize in the debugger at three o'clock in the morning.

A group of cooperating message classes might want to share one or more property definitions so that, for example, *IPM.Stock.Ask*, *IPM.Stock.Bid*, and *IPM.-Stock.Info* all share a common stock name property on which you can query. (See Figure 5-10.) Such a suite of forms should allocate a single MAPI property set to reserve a space for their properties and then use the same property definitions within that single name space.

NOTE Do not confuse MAPI property sets with OLE property sets. They share little more than a name.

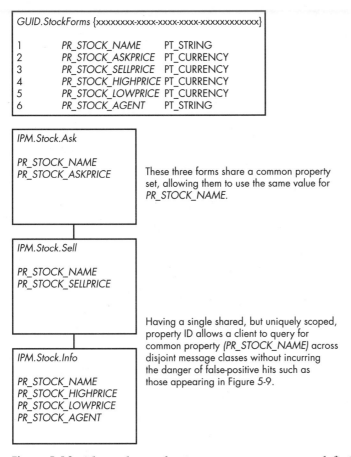

```
GUID.StockForms {xxxxxxxx-xxxx-xxxx-xxxx-xxxxxxxxxxxx}

1        PR_STOCK_NAME       PT_STRING
2        PR_STOCK_ASKPRICE   PT_CURRENCY
3        PR_STOCK_SELLPRICE  PT_CURRENCY
4        PR_STOCK_HIGHPRICE  PT_CURRENCY
5        PR_STOCK_LOWPRICE   PT_CURRENCY
6        PR_STOCK_AGENT      PT_STRING
```

```
IPM.Stock.Ask

PR_STOCK_NAME
PR_STOCK_ASKPRICE
```

These three forms share a common property set, allowing them to use the same value for PR_STOCK_NAME.

```
IPM.Stock.Sell

PR_STOCK_NAME
PR_STOCK_SELLPRICE
```

Having a single shared, but uniquely scoped, property ID allows a client to query for common property (PR_STOCK_NAME) across disjoint message classes without incurring the danger of false-positive hits such as those appearing in Figure 5-9.

```
IPM.Stock.Info

PR_STOCK_NAME
PR_STOCK_HIGHPRICE
PR_STOCK_LOWPRICE
PR_STOCK_AGENT
```

Figure 5-10. *Three classes sharing a common property definition.*

The MAPI Forms Manager

Any discussion of forms and messages keeps returning to the role of MAPI in tying all the pieces together. Although much of MAPI consists only of pass-through middleware, which takes client calls and relays them to service providers, MAPI takes a more active role in forms management. Here MAPI implements an engine called the *Forms Manager* to play its role.

The Forms Manager performs three essential tasks for MAPI:

■ It maintains information about installed forms so that clients can access the characteristics of a form and its messages without firing up the form directly.

- It manages storage of forms through its forms library constructs, enabling an enterprise to host more form applications than would fit on a single workstation, and organizes the forms for convenient maintenance.

- It resolves a message class to the correct form, using its database of form information and storage.

Interface to the Forms Manager

To talk to the Forms Manager, a MAPI client calls the *MAPIOpenFormMgr* function. This API locates the MAPI Forms Manager, returning an *IMAPIFormMgr* interface through which the client can work. To use the Forms Manager, the client must have logged onto MAPI and have a valid session. This is illustrated in the following code sample:

```
IMAPISession* psess = /* … */;
IMAPIFormMgr FAR* pfrmmgr;
HRESULT hr = MAPIOpenLocalFormMgr(psess, &pfrmmgr);
if (SUCCEEDED(hr))
{
    ⋮
    pfrmmgr->Release();
}
```

Figure 5-11 shows the results of having successfully opened the Forms Manager. Once the client has a reference to *IMAPIFormMgr*, the client can avail itself of the services of the Forms Manager through that interface. Most client interactions need go no further than this interface.

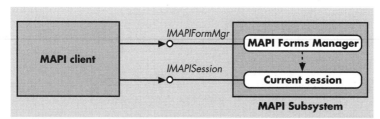

The MAPI client calls the *IMAPIFormMgr* method to acquire an interface on the MAPI Forms Manager component. The client has already called *IMAPILogonEx* to hold a session.

Figure 5-11. *Client communication with MAPI.*

Information About a Form

Think of all the times that an application needs the following information about a form or a message class:

■ A search definition user interface must present the user with meaningful options for the properties it will specify when building a query: it needs to know the pertinent properties for a particular message class or classes to avoid offering "Shoe size" as a potential parameter when searching legal briefs.

■ A viewer should be able to identify and display only columns germane to the current set of items in the view.

■ A viewer should be able to identify the correct icon for displaying a form.

■ A viewer must know the verbs offered by a given form if it is to give a user any way of activating a form other than Open.

If an application had to load a form to get this information, things would get ugly very quickly. Imagine installing and invoking six form servers just to get the icons in a folder, or a set of potential columns. Instead, an application can ask the MAPI Forms Manager for all of this information.

The MAPI Forms Manager maintains a directory of information about each form and uses this directory when it resolves a message class to find the correct form and form class identifier. The entries in this directory store other information as well: properties, verbs, icons, display names, and descriptions. Once the Forms Manager locates the entry for a form, it can return all of this information to any interested client.

Properties of a Form

A client looks up the form entry for a particular message class by calling *IMAPIFormMgr::ResolveMessageClass*. In response to this call, the Forms Manager resolves the message class, returning a form information object—an *IMAPIFormInfo* interface—that describes the form found.

IMAPIFormInfo describes a form as a set of properties, exposed through the methods of *IMAPIProp*, from which *IMAPIFormInfo* inherits. These are not the properties of the form's message class; rather, these are properties describing the characteristics of the form itself. This property interface is read-only, existing only to export form information to clients. Attempts to call *IMAPIProp::SetProps*, *IMAPIProp::DeleteProps*, or any other method will return *MAPI_E_NO_ACCESS*.

Table 5-3 on the following page describes the properties that a client might find on a form information object. Any one form information object might not necessarily have all of these properties.

Property Name	Type	Description
PR_MESSAGE_CLASS	String	The message class of the form's messages
PR_FORM_CLSID	CLSID	The CLSID of the form server
PR_DISPLAY_NAME	String	The display name of the form
PR_COMMENT	String	A descriptive comment about the purpose or content of a form
PR_ICON	Binary	A full-sized (32 x 32 pixel) icon for the form's items
PR_MINI_ICON	Binary	A small (16 x 16 pixel) icon for the form's items
PR_FORM_VERSION	String	The version number of the form
PR_FORM_CONTACT_NAME	String	The name of a contact person for the form
PR_FORM_DESIGNER_NAME	String	The display name of the tool used to design the form
PR_FORM_DESIGNER_GUID	CLSID	A GUID uniquely identifying the tool used to design the form
PR_FORM_CATEGORY	String	A category of the form
PR_FORM_CATEGORY_SUB	String	A subcategory within the form category
PR_FORM_HIDDEN	Boolean	Indication of whether the user can compose an instance of the form
PR_FORM_HOST_MAP	Long	A multivalued integer property associated with a set of environments supported by the form
PR_FORM_MESSAGE_BEHAVIOR	Long	An opcode describing the form's behavior in handling messages

Table 5-3. *Form information properties.*

Message class

PR_MESSAGE_CLASS contains the message class that the form handles. This string is the primary key of the form database, the column that indexes every entry; *IMAPIFormMgr::ResolveMessageClass* uses this string when it looks up the form information. A client can detect whether the Forms Manager resolved its message class with a superclass of the desired message class[4] by comparing the PR_MESSAGE_CLASS string against the parameter given to the API.

---

4. This can happen. See "Message Superclassing" later in this chapter.

Form CLSID

PR_FORM_CLSID contains the CLSID of the form's class object, by which clients can request an instance of the form from the System COM Library.

Since resolving a message class to a form does not force the Forms Manager to install the form from its forms library, this CLSID might not yet be valid in the local workstation's system registry. A client that would avail itself of this CLSID must first call *IMAPIFormMgr::PrepareForm*, forcing the Forms Manager to download the form if necessary.

Display name

PR_DISPLAY_NAME contains the user-readable display name of the form, such as "Standard message form" for the form handling *IPM.Note*, or "Meeting Request" for the form handling *IPM.Schedule.Meeting.Request* (the Microsoft Schedule+ meeting request message). Applications typically use this value as a display name for the message type, either when offering to compose new instances of the message (as from the Compose - New Form command) or when searching the message store (for example, "Find all items of type so-and-so"). The dialog boxes of *IMAPIFormMgr::SelectForm* and *IMAPIFormMgr::SelectMultipleForms* use this value to identify each form.

Comment

PR_COMMENT contains a user-readable string further describing the purpose or content of a form. It appears in user interfaces to help users select the correct form.

Icon and mini-icon

PR_ICON and *PR_MINI_ICON* contain large (32 x 32 pixel) and small (16 x 16 pixel) icons for items of this form. As returned in an *IMAPIProp::GetProps* call, these entries have no use other than to signal that the form in fact has an icon. Instead, a client must invoke the *IMAPIFormInfo::MakeIconFromBinary* method on the form information object, passing the method the property ID of the desired icon. From that, the Forms Manager returns the handle of a working icon, which the client can display through the usual graphics device interface (GDI) calls.

A client should destroy the icon returned by using the *DestroyIcon* function after the client has finished with it.

Version

PR_FORM_VERSION contains a user-readable string naming the version number of the form, such as 2.0.1. It appears in user interfaces to tell you which version of a form application is being used. Since it is a string, your application can use any version organization format that you like.

Contact name

PR_FORM_CONTACT_NAME contains a user-readable string naming an individual responsible for supporting the form application. It appears with the version string in user interfaces.

Designer name and GUID

PR_FORM_DESIGNER_NAME contains a user-readable string naming the design environment used to develop a particular form application—for example, Microsoft Exchange Forms Designer. *PR_FORM_DESIGNER_GUID* stores a GUID uniquely identifying this design environment. A design environment can use this code to find the forms created within it, ensuring that the design environment does not offer to modify form applications from some other environment.

Category and subcategory

PR_FORM_CATEGORY and *PR_FORM_CATEGORY_SUB* contain user-readable strings that classify the form into a category and subcategory. User interfaces, such as those presented by *IMAPIFormMgr::SelectForm*, can use these values to organize the contents of large forms libraries.

Hidden

PR_FORM_HIDDEN contains a Boolean value. If it is set, a viewer should not offer to create instances of a form. The dialog box presented by *IMAPIFormMgr-::SelectForm* will not display hidden forms.

Hidden forms have several uses. Some forms, such as those rendering the *Report* message classes, cannot be composed; they exist only to read these messages and so should not appear in any interface invoked by issuing the Compose - New Form command. Other forms could be composable but obsolete. A site might retain the forms so that users could read old messages created with those forms, but the site would want to prevent users from creating new instances of those obsolete messages and so would mark the form as hidden.

Despite the name, a hidden form should still appear in code that displays forms for specifying columns and queries. Hence *IMAPIFormMgr::SelectMultipleForms* still shows these.

Host map

PR_FORM_HOST_MAP contains a host map of available forms. It is a multivalued integer property, with each value representing one of the platforms supported by a particular form.

Many forms libraries are shared among multiple users, not all of whom will be running on the same hardware or operating system platform. Some could use Microsoft Windows 95, others Microsoft Windows NT on one of its many available hardware platforms, and still others an Apple Macintosh or Microsoft Windows 3.1 operating system platform. A forms library could contain server implementations for multiple platforms, allowing the Forms Manager to fetch the correct version of the form's server for the current platform. The host map indicates which platforms have support.

Each integer entry in the host map represents one of the platforms supported by the form. (See Table 5-4.) An entry consists of the opcode for the processor architecture and the opcode for the operating system.

Opcode	Description
MAPIFORM_CPU_X86	Intel x86 architecture
MAPIFORM_CPU_AXP	DEC Alpha architecture
MAPIFORM_CPU_MIP	MIPS architecture
MAPIFORM_CPU_PPC	PowerPC architecture
MAPIFORM_CPU_M68	Motorola 68xxx architecture
MAPIFORM_OS_WIN_31	16-bit Microsoft Windows over MS-DOS
MAPIFORM_OS_WIN_95	Windows 95
MAPIFORM_OS_WINNT_35	Windows NT 3.5 and 3.51
MAPIFORM_OS_WINNT_40	Windows NT 4.0
MAPIFORM_OS_MAC_7X	Apple Macintosh System 7

Table 5-4. *Each entry in the host map represents an available form server binary, as encoded by the intended processor architecture and operating system. The* MAPIFORM_PLATFORM *macro in* MAPIFORM.H *conjoins the CPU and OS opcodes for the target platform into a host map entry.*

Message behavior
PR_FORM_MESSAGE_BEHAVIOR contains an integer property encoding the form's behavior when the form is handling its messages. This could have one of two values: either *MAPI_MESSAGE_BEHAVIOR_FOLDER*, indicating a post form, or *MAPI_MESSAGE_BEHAVIOR_IPM*, indicating a send form.

Extensions
A form can extend the set of properties on its information object by using MAPI-named properties. By adding a named property, a client and a form can communicate a private behavioral contract outside the standard MAPI interfaces.

The most common such named property has property identifier 1 in the property set *PS_EXCHFORM*. (The Win32 SDK header file EXCHFORM.H names these as *lidOpMap* and *psOpMap*, respectively.) The Exchange client checks for this property on any form that it invokes; should it find the property, it will use the value of this property to pass the verbs of Exchange's own forms to the custom form.

Example of Viewing Form Properties

Take a look at the sample program in the directory Chap05\Frminf on the companion CD-ROM. This is an Exchange client extension that talks to the MAPI Forms Manager to learn the different attributes of the form of the currently selected message. To show the results of that form in action, the extension can also display the set of properties constituting the message.[5] Take a moment to install this utility, as described in Appendix A. To look around your message store at the forms backing a few different types of messages, select a form and choose the File - Form Information command. All the action of interest takes place in the source file Chap05\Frminf\WORK.CPP.

The function *ListboxFormInfo* in Chap05\Frminf\WORK.CPP populates the user interface with the properties of the information object for the form of the selected message. It starts with context provided by the Exchange client: interfaces to the current MAPI session and folder in the message store, plus the message class of the selected message. Before doing anything, the function posts a wait cursor. Many Forms Manager operations can take an appreciable interval of time to complete, particularly if they involve consulting the contents of a forms library on an Exchange server message store over a slow network link, or if they involve installing the server for a form from such a library.

In the following excerpt, *ListboxFormInfo* posts a wait cursor (using a helper class defined in FRMINF.H) and resets the contents of the list box:

```
void ListboxFormInfo(HWND hwndList, IMAPISession* psess,
    IMAPIFolder* pfld, const TCHAR* pszMsgClass)
{
    CUICommon ui(GetWindow(hwndList, GW_OWNER));
    CWaitCursor wait;
    ListBox_ResetContent(hwndList);
    ⋮
```

---

5. The versions of the Win32 SDK on the Microsoft Developer Network contain a highly versatile tool for viewing messages, MDBVU32.EXE. Use it for examining messages instead of Frminf if you have access to it.

The function needs an interface to the Forms Manager, so it requests one. In an Exchange extension, the call to open the Forms Manager completes much more quickly than it would in a standalone MAPI client application, since the extension is running within the process of the Exchange client, which already has this component loaded. A standalone application might do better to keep this interface around for a while instead of opening and closing the Forms Manager with every click on a radio button, as does Frminf.

In the following excerpt, the *ListboxFormInfo* function requests an interface to the Forms Manager:

```
⋮
IMAPIFormMgr* pfrmmgr;
HRESULT hr = MAPIOpenFormMgr(psess, &pfrmmgr);
if (FAILED(hr))
{
    ui.ErrorMessage(psess, hr, "Opening Forms Manager");
    return;
}
```

NOTE   In the last chapter, we would have been more interested in Chap05\Frminf\EXT.CPP on the companion CD-ROM, where the extension interfaces with its Exchange client host. Feel free to browse that file if you just can't get enough extension examples. You might want to compare this file and the last chapter's skeleton Chap04\Eetrans\EXT.CPP. I like WinDiff for this, although many text editors contain this function as well—highly enlightening. Can you say "template"?

Once the function has a handle to the Forms Manager, it immediately asks the Forms Manager to resolve the message class in question. The Forms Manager consults its forms libraries for a form that handles the message class, returning to the client an information object describing the form that it found. Note that the Forms Manager uses the folder containing the message to help it determine the correct forms library to use. (More on this later.)

In the following code excerpt from the *ListboxFormInfo* function, the Forms Manager resolves the message class:

```
⋮
IMAPIFormInfo* pfrminf;
hr = pfrmmgr->ResolveMessageClass(pszMsgClass, 0, pfld,
    &pfrminf);
```

(continued)

```
if (FAILED(hr))
{
    ui.ErrorMessage(pfrmmgr, hr, "Resolving message class");
    pfrmmgr->Release();
    return;
}
⋮
```

The client requests all the properties describing the form from the information object and then displays each of those properties in the form's list box. What could be easier? Were the function seeking a particular property, say, *PR_DISPLAY-_NAME* or *PR_COMMENT*, with which to populate some sort of textual user interface, it would build a property tag array (*SPropTagArray*) describing the tags of the properties it sought and would then pass that array to the form information object's *IMAPIProp::GetProps* method in the first parameter.

As shown in the following code, the *ListboxFormInfo* function invokes the *GetProps* method to request the properties describing the form and then calls the *DecodeProperty* function to display these properties in the form's list box:

```
⋮
ULONG cval;
SPropValue* pval;
hr = pfrminf->GetProps(NULL, 0L, &cval, &pval);
if (FAILED(hr))
{
    ui.ErrorMessage(pfrminf, hr, "Getting properties");
    pfrminf->Release();
    pfrmmgr->Release();
    return;
}
⋮
for (unsigned i = 0; i < cval; i++)
{
    DecodeProperty(hwndList, pval+i, pfrminf);
}

MAPIFreeBuffer(pval);
⋮
pfrminf->Release();
pfrmmgr->Release();
}
```

Actually, It Could Be Easier...

Any implementation of the *IMAPIProp* interface comes from some provider. When you call *IMAPIProp::GetProps* on a message, you execute code from the message store provider hosting that message, be it the Personal Folders provider (MSPST32.DLL), the Exchange Server provider (EMSMDB32.DLL), or some other provider. Likewise, *GetProps* on an object from the address book comes courtesy of an address book provider. Unfortunately, not all providers are as flexible. A form information object is actually implemented by a system library called the *Forms Manager provider*.

The Forms Manager provider released in Exchange Server 4 does not implement *IMAPIProp* as fully as do the standard MAPI service providers in the Windows Messaging System. Named property handling in particular offers problems. The Forms Manager provider does not return correctly mapped values for extension properties in response to any of the get-all-properties forms of *GetProps*, *IMAPIProp::GetIDsFromNames*, or *IMAPIProp::GetNamesFromIDs*, specifically those that pass NULL as their property tag array and request all available properties. As a result, the code you see in the previous code excerpt returns some incorrect information.

To work around this, avoid the get-all-properties forms with the named property methods and watch for invalid elements returned from *IMAPIProp::GetProps*. They will have property IDs of 0 or 0xffff, which mark them as invalid. Caveat programmer!

Requesting the form extension property for special Exchange client semantics is just as easy. Recall that form extension properties use MAPI named properties to control the property name space. A client checking for these semantics in a form builds a *MAPINAMEID* structure describing the property, submits that structure to the form information object to get the correct property tag to use, and uses that tag to get the extension value. If the extension does not exist, the final call to *IMAPIProp::GetProps* will return *MAPI_W_ERRORS_RETURNED*, with *PT_ERROR* in the property value of *MAPI_E_NOT_FOUND*. The following example from the *ListboxFormInfo* function presumes that you didn't yet release your interfaces to the form information object and Forms Manager as shown above.

```
    ⋮
    MAPINAMEID nmid = { /*deconst*/ (GUID*)&psOpMap, ulKindOpMap,
        { lidOpMap } };
```

(continued)

```
MAPINAMEID* pnmid = &nmid;

SPropTagArray* ptagary;
hr = pfrminf->GetIDsFromNames(1, &pnmid, 0, &ptagary);
assert(SUCCEEDED(hr));
hr = pfrminf->GetProps(ptagary, 0, &cval, &pval);
assert(SUCCEEDED(hr));
⋮
MAPIFreeBuffer(pval);
MAPIFreeBuffer(ptagary);
⋮
```

NOTE To see some code that picks apart the property values returned in the Frminf program, trace through the *DecodeProperty* function in the Chap05\Frminf\WORK.CPP source file on the companion CD-ROM.

Published Properties

Remember that the properties on an information object describe the form, not the form's messages. To describe the properties available on the form's messages to prospective clients, an information object offers its *IMAPIFormInfo::CalcFormPropSet* method. The *CalcFormPropSet* method returns to the caller the set of properties that the form has elected to publish—that is, to advertise itself as available on its messages. A client will typically use these when setting the columns of a table, on either a folder containing items of the form's class or on a search folder seeking such items. This ensures that the client's queries and restrictions will be germane to the type of the items the client seeks.

The sample Chap05\Frminf on the companion CD-ROM also displays published properties. Browsing the properties published by the standard Exchange forms reveals that there aren't any. The standard Exchange forms don't publish their properties. Instead, the Exchange client knows the properties related to its message classes (*IPM.Note, IPM.Post*, and friends) and includes them in its property browsing interfaces as defaults. If your client implements its own property browser, you must do likewise.

Another tack that some forms take is to deliver all of their properties as named string properties in the *PS_PUBLIC_STRINGS* property set. Since this property set contains all the summary properties promoted in *IPM.Document* messages, the Exchange client queries for all the public string properties known to a message store, displaying them in its property browser. This works well for document messages since they have a widely variable schema.

Example of viewing published properties

Back into Chap05\Frminf\WORK.CPP we go, this time diving into the function *ListboxPublishedProperties*. This function populates the form's list box with the set of properties that the form has explicitly published. It does not take into account any special knowledge of the *IPM.Note* schema, nor does it browse the public strings name space. The function resets the form's list box, opens an interface onto the Forms Manager, and resolves the message class into a form information object just like its sister function *ListboxFormInfo*. The *ListboxFormInfo* function uses the generic methods of *IMAPIProp*, which returns an *SPropTagArray* structure containing a list of property tags. In contrast, the *ListPublishedProperties* function uses *IMAPIFormInfo::CalcFormPropSet*, which returns a list of the form's published properties in the *SMAPIFormPropArray* structure. This is shown in the following example:

```
    ⋮
IMAPIFormMgr* pfrmmgr;
HRESULT hr = MAPIOpenFormMgr(psess, &pfrmmgr);
if (FAILED(hr))
{
    ui.ErrorMessage(psess, hr, "Opening the Forms Manager");
    return;
}


IMAPIFormInfo* pfrminf;
hr = pfrmmgr->ResolveMessageClass(pszMsgClass, 0, pfld,
    &pfrminf);
if (FAILED(hr))
{
    ui.ErrorMessage(pfrmmgr, hr, "Resolving message class");
    pfrmmgr->Release();
    return;
}

SMAPIFormPropArray* pfrmprpary;
hr = pfrminf->CalcFormPropSet(0, &pfrmprpary);
if (FAILED(hr))
{
    ui.ErrorMessage(pfrminf, hr, "Getting published
        properties");
    pfrminf->Release();
    pfrmmgr->Release();
    return;
}
    ⋮
```

The *SMAPIFormPropArray* returned by *IMAPIFormInfo* works like any number of other variable-length arrays in MAPI, containing a count followed by a variable number of records. Once the client finishes with the array, the following call to *MAPIFreeBuffer* returns to the pool the resources allocated for the array:

```
    :
    for (unsigned i = 0; i < pfrmprpary->cProps; i++)
    {
        DecodePublishedProp(hwndList, pfrmprpary->aFormProp+i);
    }

    MAPIFreeBuffer(pfrmprpary);
    :
```

The format of a published property record is unique within MAPI and deserves further examination. It comprises four parts: a display name for the benefit of property browsers and view column headings; a MAPI named property entry, listing where instances of the property might be found on a message; a property type code, describing the format of that property; and a magical extension cookie, the *FORMPROPSPECIALTYPE*, allowing clients to build browsable property structures beyond those intrisic to generic MAPI. If a published property record uses the property type of generic MAPI, it declares its special type as *FPST_VANILLA*,[6] in which case the advertised property type code tells all.

In the client software and Forms Manager provider accompanying Microsoft Exchange Server 4, only one special type exists: *FPST_ENUM_PROP*. Such a type includes an enumeration of string-integer pairs constituting possible values for the property and advertises a second named property, an integer (*PT_I4*) record, as its index property. Browsers honoring this type must display the strings in the ascending order of their integer index. Setting any one value sets both the string value and the associated integer index. While a view containing this column displays the regular string value, a sort on this column would use the special type's index property to ensure that sorts appear in a logical order. The Exchange 4.0 client does not do this; instead, it sorts enumerated types by their display values.

For example, consider a T-shirt order form. Unless the form is for a software project T-shirt (you know, the "I SURVIVED THE BLAZEMONGER 4.0 PROJECT"

---

6. This is a hideous calumny against vanilla lovers! I encourage everybody to define it as *FPST_TAPIOCA*.

variety), in which case it will always be size XL, such a form needs a field for specifying the size of the shirt: extra small (XS), small (S), medium (M), large (L), extra large (XL), heroic (XXL), silverback gorilla (XXXL). By specifying this field as a special enumeration property, the form lets browsers offer logical choices when building a search.

Returning to the sample code, we see that the *DecodePublishedProp* function of Chap05\Frminf\WORK.CPP shows the structure of a published property record. This doesn't crack the enumeration structure, limiting itself to describing whether the property is a special type. In the following excerpt, the *Decode-PublishedProp* function calls *DecodePropType* to identify the type of the property and then determines whether it is enumerated (*FPST_ENUM_PROP*):

```
void DecodePublishedProp(HWND hwndList, SMAPIFormProp* pfrmprp)
{
    TCHAR szType[64];
    DecodePropType(pfrmprp->nPropType, szType,
        sizeof(szType)/sizeof(TCHAR));
    switch (pfrmprp->nSpecialType)
    {
    case FPST_VANILLA:
        // Don't touch it.
        break;
    case FPST_ENUM_PROP:
        _tcscat(szType, " (enum)");
        break;
    default:
        _tcscat(szType, " (unknown special)");
        break;
    }

    TCHAR szNMID[192];
    DecodeNamedProperty(pfrmprp->nmid, szNMID,
        sizeof(szNMID)/sizeof(TCHAR));
    ⋮
```

In the following conclusion of the *DecodePublishedProp* function, note the handling of *MAPI_UNICODE* in the flags field of the record. Actually, the provider would return Unicode only if the client requested it by passing *MAPI-_UNICODE* in the originating call to *CalcFormPropEnum*.

```
        ⋮
    TCHAR szLine[256];
    if (pfrmprp->ulFlags & MAPI_UNICODE)
        wsprintf(szLine, "%ws %s %s",
        (WCHAR*)pfrmprp->pszDisplayName, szType, szNMID);
    else
        wsprintf(szLine, "%s %s %s",
        (CHAR*)pfrmprp->pszDisplayName, szType, szNMID);

    ListBox_AddString(hwndList, szLine);
}
```

As a browser, this sample just takes the named property definition and dumps it into the list box. In practice, client code would resolve the name into a property tag for a given message store and then use that tag when the client code constructed the MAPI table for a search or a view.

Obtaining published properties of multiple forms

At times, an application might need to fetch the published properties for several forms at once. How the application will treat the resulting set of property IDs depends on what it wants with them. The application might want the set of possible columns in a folder view; it would start with the set of message classes of the items in that folder, get the properties of the forms of each message class, and take the union of these as its set of possible columns. If some rows of the resulting folder contents table contain some *PT_ERROR* cells, the application would render those as blank; they correspond to items that didn't have one of the properties. Alternatively, the application might want to obtain the intersection of two sets of possible properties, in which case an advanced AND-search would be implemented. It would start with a set of message classes as the first clause of the search, get the properties of the forms of each, and find the intersection of these properties, since every possible clause must be germane to each item being examined.

Figure 5-12 shows the results of performing intersections and unions on the properties of the *IPM.Stock.Ask*, *IPM.Stock.Sell*, and *IPM.Stock.Info* message classes. In calculating either an intersection or a union, an application has recourse to the Forms Manager method *IMAPIFormMgr::CalcFormPropSet*. This function is similar to the *IMAPIFormInfo::CalcFormPropSet* function, but it works with an array of form information structures and derives either the intersection or the union over each form's published properties.

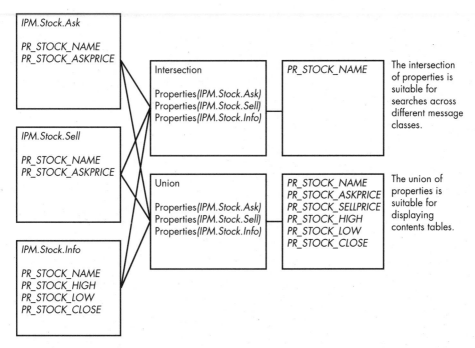

Figure 5-12. *Union and intersection of the properties of the* IPM.Stock.Ask, IPM.Stock.Sell, *and* IPM.Stock.Info *message classes.*

Published Verbs

A client implementing a viewer can retrieve the verbs for a form in much the same manner as it retrieves a form's published properties. In this case, the method to use is *IMAPIFormInfo::CalcVerbSet*, which returns the form's verbs in a *SMAPIVerbArray* structure. The *SMAPIVerbArray* structure is another counted array of *SMAPIVerb* structures that contains the form's verbs. A client uses these verbs in its user interface, presenting options for activating a form, just as an OLE container would use the *OLEVERB* structure. Indeed, a MAPI verb is identical to an OLE verb except that a service provider has the option of returning a non-Unicode display name when the client does not specify *MAPI_UNICODE* in the *ulFlags* parameter. A client should honor the MAPI verb's *fuFlags* field when displaying verbs on an item's context menu and should check the *OLE-VERBATTRIB_ONCONTAINERMENU* attribute flag in its *grfAttribs* field as well, displaying the verb only if it has that attribute.

The sample Chap05\Frminf, in addition to its many other talents, displays the published verbs of a form.

Example of viewing published verbs

In addition to enumerating the name of the method and the type of the structure returned, the following excerpt from the *ListboxFormVerbs* function is used for enumerating published properties:

```
    ⋮
IMAPIFormMgr* pfrmmgr;
HRESULT hr = MAPIOpenFormMgr(psess, &pfrmmgr);
if (FAILED(hr))
{
    ui.ErrorMessage(psess, hr, "Opening the Forms Manager");
    return;
}

IMAPIFormInfo* pfrminf;
hr = pfrmmgr->ResolveMessageClass(pszMsgClass, 0, pfld,
    &pfrminf);
if (FAILED(hr))
{
    ui.ErrorMessage(pfrmmgr, hr, "Resolving a message class");
    pfrmmgr->Release();
    return;
}

SMAPIVerbArray* pvbary;
hr = pfrminf->CalcVerbSet(0, &pvbary);
if (FAILED(hr))
{
    ui.ErrorMessage(pfrminf, hr, "Getting verbs");
    pfrminf->Release();
    pfrmmgr->Release();
    return;
}

for (unsigned i = 0; i < pvbary->cMAPIVerb; i++)
{
    DecodePublishedVerb(hwndList, pvbary->aMAPIVerb+i);
}

MAPIFreeBuffer(pvbary);
    ⋮
```

Again, the error checking in the preceding code is redundant since this code does not pass *MAPI_UNICODE* in the first parameter of *CalcVerbSet*—not even in the transmutable *fUnicode* form. There isn't much to decoding the MAPI verb structure. As you can see in the following code, the *DecodePublishedVerb* function takes the same approach to wide characters in the display name as the published property structure:

```
void DecodePublishedVerb(HWND hwndList, SMAPIVerb* pvb)
{
    TCHAR szLine[128];
    if (pvb->ulFlags & MAPI_UNICODE)
        wsprintf(szLine, "<%ws> index=%lu flags=0x%lx attrs=0x%lx",
            (WCHAR*)pvb->szVerbname, pvb->lVerb, pvb->fuFlags,
            pvb->grfAttribs);
    else
        wsprintf(szLine, "<%s> index=%lu flags=0x%lx attrs=0x%lx",
            (CHAR*)pvb->szVerbname, pvb->lVerb, pvb->fuFlags,
            pvb->grfAttribs);

    ListBox_AddString(hwndList, szLine);
}
```

Storage for a Form

MAPI stores and organizes its forms through a construct called a *forms library*. A forms library stores the files implementing a form and records all the information necessary for the Forms Manager to locate and use its forms, including all of the properties it offers on a form information object. Forms libraries also scope the act of message class resolution, allowing each folder application to define its own world of forms without interfering with the operation of other folder applications.

There are four types of forms libraries: local (or application) forms library, folder forms library, personal forms library, and organizational forms library. Each of these will be discussed in the following sections.

Most clients interact with forms libraries passively, through the *IMAPIFormMgr* interface to the Forms Manager, which handles the libraries on their behalf. They resolve message classes into form information objects through *IMAPIFormMgr-::ResolveMessageClass*, create form instances through *IMAPIFormMgr::CreateForm* and *IMAPIFormMgr::LoadForm*, and even select a form, picking it from the forms libraries through the user interface *IMAPIFormMgr::SelectForm* or *IMAPIForm-Mgr::SelectMultipleForms*. For those rare scenarios in which a client application truly needs direct communication with a forms library, such as when the client application is installing or uninstalling a form, the client can obtain an *IMAPI-FormContainer* interface through either *IMAPIFormMgr::OpenFormContainer* or *IMAPIFormMgr::SelectFormContainer*.

When resolving a message class into a form, the Forms Manager consults a series of forms libraries (shown in Figure 5-13) to find a definition for the form. Local applications get the first crack at satisfying a form request, then any library associated with the current folder. Next comes the user's own collection of forms in the personal forms library. Finally users of Microsoft Exchange Server have recourse to the replicated enterprise-wide organization forms library.

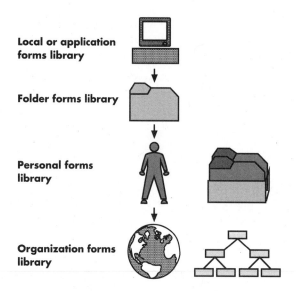

Local or application forms library

Folder forms library

Personal forms library

Organization forms library

Figure 5-13. *Forms libraries.*

Local (Application) Forms Library

An application already installed on a workstation neither wants nor needs the storage management services of MAPI. Such applications use the local (or application) forms library. (See Figure 5-14.) Unlike the other types of forms libraries, the local forms library does not store the files of its forms, depending instead on the workstation's own file system and system registry entries. Forms in the local forms library get first crack at every request to resolve a message class.

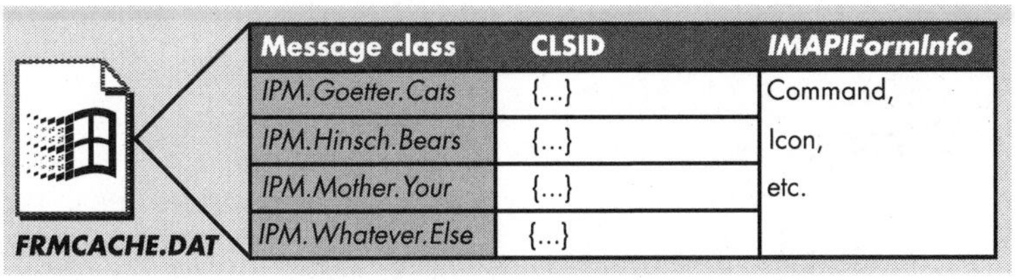

Message class	CLSID	IMAPIFormInfo
IPM.Goetter.Cats	{...}	Command,
IPM.Hinsch.Bears	{...}	Icon,
IPM.Mother.Your	{...}	etc.
IPM.Whatever.Else	{...}	

The local forms library contains only what is necessary to associate a message
class with an existing CLSID, plus the rest of the form information. The CLSID
is that of an already registered application.

Figure 5-14. *Contents of the local forms library. This instance contains records
for form entries.*

The local forms library is not intended for general form application usage; rather,
it serves the needs of the locally installed application that happens to manifest
certain forms. *IMAPIFormMgr::SelectFormContainer* will not offer the local forms
library as a destination. Instead, a program must open it explicitly, as shown in
the following example:

```
IMAPIFormMgr* pfrmmgr;
IMAPIFormContainer* pfrmcnt = NULL;
HRESULT hr = pfrmmgr->OpenFormContainer(HFRMREG_LOCAL, NULL,
    &pfrmcnt);
if (SUCCEEDED(hr))
{
    ⋮
    pfrmcnt->Release();
}
```

The local forms library is the only forms library accessible without an active MAPI
session. *MAPIOpenLocalFormContainer* returns a form container interface on
the local library, allowing application setup programs to install their MAPI form
entries without logging onto MAPI. This special, sessionless form container
does not support any form of message class resolution—only adding and removing forms.

In the following example, a call to the *MAPIOpenLocalFormContainer* returns
a form container interface:

```
IMAPIFormContainer* pfrmcnt = NULL;
HRESULT hr = MAPIOpenLocalFormContainer(&pfrmcnt);
if (SUCCEEDED(hr))
{
    ⋮
    pfrmcnt->Release();
}
```

The local forms library data resides in the file Windows\Forms\FRMCACHE.DAT, which it shares with the MAPI Forms Manager's *local forms cache*.

Folder Forms Library

Much of the flexibility of the Exchange workgroup application model lies in the self-contained nature of its folder applications (shown in Figure 5-15). The MAPI Forms Manager allows each folder to host its own forms library. When a client specifies a folder in a message class resolution, MAPI puts that folder's library first in line to resolve the request, preceded only by the application form registry. This lets folder owners define their own message classes within that folder without too much worry over conflicts with the message class definitions of other folders.[7] The folder encompasses the complete application, with clients using the folder's form definitions to create items within the folder and other clients reading those items with the same forms.

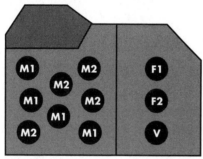

This folder contains messages from two different classes (M1 and M2) as well as the forms definitions for each of these classes (F1 and F2) and a single view definition.

Figure 5-15. *Self-contained folder applications.*

Unlike entries in the application library, an entry in a folder forms library contains the complete definition of the form, including any executable files and their registration information. The Forms Manager copies this information to your workstation file system when necessary.

A form container interface on a folder forms library can be quite useful. A setup program might want to add or remove forms from a particular folder application. An application might want to restrict a particular message class resolution to within a folder application, thus preventing forms from any other library from

---

7. However, if the user copies any items out of the folder, all bets are off.

satisfying the request. Most commonly, an application might simply want the set of all properties published from within the folder, which it can obtain with a single call to the *IMAPIFormMgr::CalcFormPropSet* method on the form container in question. Note that to open a folder's forms library with *IMAPIForm-Mgr::OpenFormContainer*, the client must first open an *IMAPIFolder* interface on the folder in question.

In the following code example, a form container interface is obtained in a call to the *OpenFormContainer* function:

```
IMAPIFormMgr* pfrmmgr;
IMAPIFolder* pfld;
IMAPIFormContainer* pfrmcnt = NULL;
HRESULT hr = pfrmmgr->OpenFormContainer(HFRMREG_FOLDER, pfld,
    &pfrmcnt);
if (SUCCEEDED(hr))
{
    ⋮
    pfrmcnt->Release();
}
```

Once the application has a form container, only a few lines of code need to be added to obtain the intersection or union of all the forms' properties published within the folder. The following example requests the union (*FORMPROP-SET_UNION*), which would be suitable for building a contents table to view the item within the folder:

```
IMAPIFormContainer* pfrmcnt = …; // See above.
SMAPIFormPropArray* pfrmprpary;
hr = pfrmcnt->CalcFormPropSet(FORMPROPSET_UNION, &pfrmprpary);
for (unsigned i = 0; i < pfrmprpary->cProps; i++)
{
    DecodePublishedProp(hwndList, pfrmprpary->aFormProp+i);
    // Or whatever
}
MAPIFreeBuffer(pfrmprpary);
```

Folder forms library data resides in the alternative contents table of the folder, that is, the table returned by passing the *MAPI_ASSOCIATED* flag to *IMAPICon-tainer::GetContentsTable*. This table is sometimes called the folder-associated information table, or FAI. Here the Forms Manager serializes the data into messages, one form definition per message. These form definition messages (or FDMs), shown along with the rest of the contents of the forms library in Figure 5-16 on the following page, have class *IPM.Microsoft.FolderDesign.Form-*

Description to distinguish them from other per-folder nonmessage data associated with the folder. (See Chapter 8 for more uses of the FAI table, such as storing folder-specific view descriptors.) One form definition can encompass implementations for multiple platforms, as reflected in the multivalued *PR-_FORM_HOST_MAP* property on a form's information object; the Forms Manager will fetch the correct implementation version for the platform of the requesting client as necessary. Since the forms, or rather the messages containing the forms, actually occupy the folder, a copied folder will retain copies of all the forms within it. Folders on message stores that do not support this FAI table cannot host forms libraries.

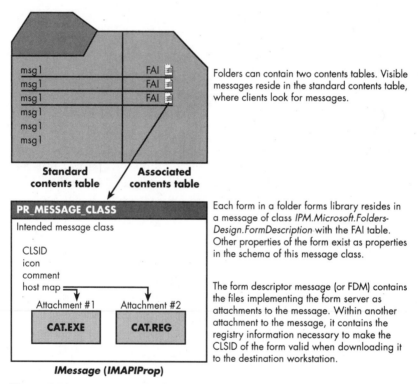

Folders can contain two contents tables. Visible messages reside in the standard contents table, where clients look for messages.

Standard contents table   **Associated contents table**

Each form in a folder forms library resides in a message of class *IPM.Microsoft.Folders-Design.FormDescription* with the FAI table. Other properties of the form exist as properties in the schema of this message class.

The form descriptor message (or FDM) contains the files implementing the form server as attachments to the message. Within another attachment to the message, it contains the registry information necessary to make the CLSID of the form valid when downloading it to the destination workstation.

PR_MESSAGE_CLASS

Intended message class

CLSID
icon
comment
host map

Attachment #1   Attachment #2

CAT.EXE   **CAT.REG**

IMessage (IMAPIProp)

Figure 5-16. *Structure of a folder forms library.*

Personal Forms Library

The personal forms library provides a forms library associated with no one particular folder. It stays in your default message store, where you have full read and write privileges over its contents and where it remains accessible to you at all times.

When resolving a message class to a form, the Forms Manager checks the personal forms library after checking for a folder forms library, if any. In point-to-point send form scenarios, a client might choose to pass a NULL in the *pFolderFocus* parameter to *IMAPIFormMgr::ResolveMessageClass*, in which case the Forms Manager will check the personal forms library immediately after checking local applications.

In practice, the personal forms library has several uses:

- Since you have full read and write privileges over its contents, you can keep personally written or privately used form applications in it. It provides an excellent test environment for point-to-point forms before those forms are installed in a shared library somewhere.

- Since they are associated with no particular folders, forms in the personal forms library are checked by every client resolution request. This makes the personal forms library a good place to keep copies of forms with which to read items copied out of their host applications' folders.

- Since it resides on the default store, the personal forms library can roam with you if you keep that store local. You might elect to copy some forms from another library to the personal library so that they remain available when the user goes off line or when traffic on the network slows to a crawl.

Applications open the personal forms library by passing *HFRMREG_PERSONAL* in the *hfrmreg* parameter to *IMAPIFormMgr::OpenFormContainer*. Typically, this is done only during the installation of a form because there is little practical need for restricting a message class resolution to the personal forms library or for requesting the union of all of its forms' properties. The personal forms library makes a suitable default destination for installing send forms.

The personal forms library data resides on the current session's default message store in the alternative contents table of the *IPM_COMMON_VIEWS* folder. This folder is outside the visible folder hierarchy, so it is relatively safe from intentional or accidental deletion. In all other aspects, it resembles a folder forms library.

Exchange Server Organization Forms Library

Microsoft Exchange Server delivers an additional forms library: the organization forms library, which is replicated throughout the enterprise by the public folder machinery of Exchange Server. Every user in the enterprise can resolve a message class against the organization forms library, although only designated administrators have sufficient authority to modify its contents. This lets system administrators distribute and maintain forms through a single secured locus. When resolving a message class, the Forms Manager checks the organization forms library only after checking every other possible library.

Writing Code Specific to Microsoft Exchange Server

Applications manipulate the services of Microsoft Exchange Server using a number of symbols that do not appear in the generic Win32 MAPI header files because they describe the facilities of a single MAPI service provider. These header files—EXCHCLI.H, EDKMDB.H, and others—appear in the Exchange Server SDK, which is part of the Microsoft BackOffice SDK. To use these symbols, you will need to install the header files of the BackOffice SDK or define them privately to your application.

Applications open the organization forms library by passing *HFRMREG_ENTER-PRISE* (defined in the Exchange Server header file EXCHCLI.H) to *IMAPIFormMgr-::OpenFormContainer*. Passing this value for the *hfrmreg* parameter is used to specify the organization's Microsoft Exchange Server registry in the public store. The only purpose for opening the organization form registry is to install a form into it. Organization forms libraries can be huge, spanning many hundreds of installed forms. Because they host the forms of an entire organization, it would be atypical for an organization forms library to contain only the forms of a single application; hence, calculating a joint property set over the contents of the library would be both agonizingly slow and nonsensical. Therefore, the library does not support *IMAPIFormContainer::CalcFormPropSet*.

Forms Manager Provider

The MAPI Forms Manager actually resides in a provider library that MAPI loads from the registry value HKEY_LOCAL_MACHINE\SOFTWARE\Microsoft\Exchange\Forms Registry\Provider. As indicated by the registry key path, a given installation of WMS uses but a single Forms Manager provider library, currently loaded profile notwithstanding. Generic WMS installations use the Forms Manager provider WMSFR32.DLL. However, installations containing Exchange Server use a Forms Manager implemented in the library EMSUIX32.DLL, which is how those clients gain the additional features of Exchange Server forms support. Platforms with different provider libraries might also offer a different user interface and additional properties on *IMAPIFormInfo*.

The organization forms library for any particular client actually is a public folder, albeit one that does not appear in the visible public folder hierarchy. Exchange Server keeps a separate subtree of folders in its public folder store, called the non-IPM subtree, which the server replicates but never makes visible. Clients can obtain the entry identifier of this subtree by requesting the property *PR_NON-_IPM_SUBTREE_ENTRYID* (defined in the Exchange Server SDK header file EDKMDB.H) from the public folder message store object in just the manner that a more generic MAPI application might locate the wastebasket folder on a message store. Somewhere beneath the non-IPM subtree, the folder identified by *PR_EFORMS_REGISTRY_ENTRYID* in turn contains a number of child folders. Every programming language supported in the organization owns one of those child folders—its own folder beneath the master folder—and delivers the organization forms library for clients using that language. Each forms library folder has a property *PR_EFORMS_LOCALE_ID* (again, from EDKMDB.H) that identifies the locales of the clients it supports. (See Figure 5-17.)

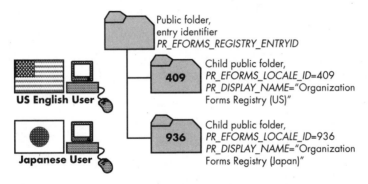

Figure 5-17. *Form registry folders in the public folder.*

Rather than enumerate and search this set of folders by hand, an administrative or otherwise superpowered client could retrieve the entry identifier of the folder that hosts the organization forms library for its language through the Exchange-Server specific *PR_EFORMS_FOR_LOCALE_ENTRYID* property, calculated on its behalf by the message store provider. The following code example illustrates this technique:

```
IMsgStore* pmdb;
SPropTagArray taga = { 2, {
    PR_MDB_PROVIDER,PR_EFORMS_FOR_LOCALE_ENTRYID } };
enum { ivalMDBProvider, ivalLibEid, cvalMax };
```

(continued)

```
ULONG cval = 0;
SPropValue* pval = NULL;
HRESULT hr = pmdb->GetProps( &taga, 0L, &cval, &pval );
if (FAILED(hr))
    return;
if (hr == MAPI_W_ERRORS_RETURNED) // Give up.
    return;

assert(cval == (ULONG)cvalMax);

if ( (PROP_TYPE(pval[ivalMDBProvider].ulPropTag) !=PT_BINARY)||
    (PROP_TYPE(pval[ivalMDBProvider].Value.bin.cb) != 16) ||
    (!IsEqualGUID((REFGUID)pval[ivalMDBProvider].Value.bin.lpb,
    pbExchangeProviderPublicGuid) )
    return;

assert(PROP_TYPE(pval[ivalLibEid].ulPropTag) == PT_BINARY);

IMAPIFolder* pfld = NULL;
ULONG ulType = 0L;
hr = pmdb->OpenEntry(
    pval[ivalLibEid].Value.bin.cb,
    (LPENTRYID)pval[ivalLibEid].Value.bin.lpb,
    (LPIID)&IID_IMAPIFolder,
    // Assuming that you're the administrator
    MAPI_MODIFY|MAPI_DEFERRED_ERRORS,&ulType,
    (IUnknown**)&pfld );
⋮
```

Note that the client must first ensure that the information store (MDB) is in fact the public folder store by comparing the value of *PR_MDB_PROVIDER* with the GUID *pbExchangeProviderPublicGuid*, defined in EDKMDB.H. Were this store not the public folder store of Microsoft Exchange Server, the client could make no assumptions as to the type and semantics of the property at the *PR_EFORMS-_FOR_LOCALE_ENTRYID* tag.

NOTE   The previous code sample makes no assumptions as to the message store it receives. Since message store providers publish the *PR_MDB_PROVIDER* property in the message store table, it would be more efficient for the code that originally opens the message store to search the message store table for the row with the proper GUID and open that one.

No forms library user need ever bother with this sort of manipulation, of course, since the standard MAPI form management and resolution interfaces provide all the access to the organization forms library necessary.

Resolution of a Form

Now we come to the crux of the Forms Manager's operation, the process by which it digs through its managed storage to locate information about a form: *form resolution*. The Forms Manager translates message classes to form CLSIDs, returns form information objects for the found forms, and subsequently makes those forms local to the requesting client as necessary to make the CLSID usable.

Steps of Resolution

The process starts when a client comes to the Forms Manager with a message class seeking information about that form. This is accomplished either explicitly through a call to the *IMAPIFormMgr::ResolveMessageClass* function or implicitly through a call to the *IMAPIFormMgr::LoadForm* function, which needs form information to locate and activate the necessary form. The following code is an example of a call to the *ResolveMessageClass* function:

```
CHAR* pszMsgClass;
IMAPIFolder* pfld;
IMAPIFormMgr* pfrmmgr;
IMAPIFormInfo* pfrminf = NULL;
hr = pfrmmgr->ResolveMessageClass(pszMsgClass, 0, pfld,
    &pfrminf);
```

The Forms Manager receives this request and in turn examines each of its forms libraries for a match for the message class sought. Since the request specifies a folder, the Forms Manager includes that folder's forms library in the search. Optionally, the client could pass NULL for the folder, indicating that no folder library is pertinent.

First the Forms Manager looks to see whether the form for the message class already exists local to the calling client. This might be the case for one of two reasons: either an application on the client's computer has installed itself as a form in the local application forms library, or else the Forms Manager has already made the form local as part of a previous resolution and activation. In either case, the Forms Manager will have a record for the form in its local form cache database, Windows\Forms\FRMCACHE.DAT. The Forms Manager reads the data from the local form cache, assembles a form information object, and returns that object to the caller.

265

If no entry exists locally, the Forms Manager searches a series of remote forms libraries. As shown in Figure 5-18, if the resolution request specifies a folder, the Forms Manager checks that folder's forms library first. If that fails to find a match for the message class, the Forms Manager checks the personal forms library. If both the folder and personal forms libraries fail to find a match, the Forms Manager finally consults the Exchange Server organization forms library.

To match a message class, a form must match the message class in question (that is, the *PR_MESSAGE_CLASS* property on an instance of *IMAPIFormInfo*) and support the current operating system platform of the checking Forms Manager (*PR_FORM_HOST_MAP*). From the FDM backing the form definition in the library, the Forms Manager builds a form information object for the caller.

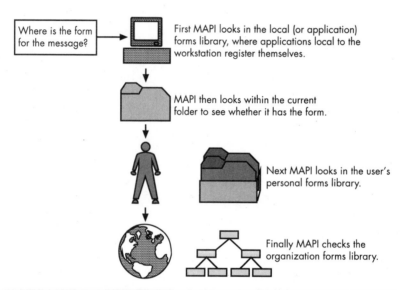

Figure 5-18. *Sequence of libraries check.*

If no entry handling the message class exists either locally or in a library, the Forms Manager replies to the request for resolution with *MAPI_E_NOT_FOUND*.

Message Superclassing

Message class resolution requests usually don't fail completely. In the event that the Forms Manager finds no exact match for the message class in any library, it proceeds to seek a match for each superclass of the sought class. A client can suppress this behavior only by specifying *MAPIFORM_EXACTMATCH* in its resolution request.

Through message superclassing, a single form can handle many message classes. For example, the document wrapper form can handle *IPM.Document*. No wrapped document message ever has that exact message class; instead, they take a message class such as *IPM.Document.Word.Document.6*, reflecting the type of their wrapped document. When no form claims to handle the exact message class *IPM.Document.Word.Document.6*, the Forms Manager checks for superclasses, finding a match for *IPM.Document* within the local application forms library.

Report form handling depends extensively on message superclassing. The Microsoft Exchange client registers a form to handle only the base message class report. By default, all MAPI message reports then go to this form. When MAPI returns a nondelivery message for a standard send note with the message class *Report.IPM.Note.NDR*, the report form ends up handling this class. However, if a custom form *IPM.Criticism.Constructive* wanted to handle its own report messages, as it might well want to do, it would register itself as handling the message class *Report.IPM.Criticism.Constructive*, whereupon it would satisfy all resolutions for *Report.IPM.Criticism.Constructive.NDR*.

By convention, all interpersonal message classes are subclasses of the base message class *IPM*. The Microsoft Exchange client registers a default form for this message class. You might try to resolve a message class for which the Forms Manager can find no form; this can happen if an item from a folder application is copied to another folder without its accompanying form, or if someone else uses a custom form installed only in a personal forms library. Nevertheless, as long as that message class descends from *IPM*, the user will at least get the default *IPM* form. If you are attempting to read the message, that default form will display the *PR_BODY* property of the mystery message, which usually contains a warning such as, "You need the Giant Robot form to read these schemes for total world domination," or the like.

Making a Form Local to the Client

Before anybody can read a message, the form for that message must be local to the client so that the client can use the form's CLSID to request an instance of a form object and do the deed. This isn't a problem for forms from the application local forms library; by definition, they are already local, with valid entries in the system CLSID registry pointing to ready-to-run servers. However, a form from a remote forms library might not yet exist on the caller's computer. It might not have an entry in the system CLSID registry, or it might have an invalid entry. If so, the Forms Manager must remedy the situation to make the form callable by the client.

A client requests the Forms Manager to ensure that a form is local and has a valid CLSID. This is done by calling the *IMAPIFormMgr::PrepareForm* function and passing a form information object describing the desired form to the Forms Manager. More often, however, the client will call the *IMAPIFormMgr::Create-Form* or *IMAPIFormMgr::LoadForm* function, both of which call the *PrepareForm* function in the course of their form creation duties. If the form is already local, the *PrepareForm* function confirms this fact. If the form is already local but came from some remote forms library, the *PrepareForm* function confirms that the local version of the form matches the version in the forms library. If the form is not local, the Forms Manager makes it so.

When the Forms Manager makes a form local, it first checks to see how much file system space it has already claimed for making other forms local. If necessary, it removes the files of the form least recently used or, if unused, the least recently resolved and activated through the Forms Manager. Once it has sufficient space, it creates a subdirectory beneath the Forms directory to host the files it will extract. Next it extracts the files for the current operating system and platform from the forms library of origin, copying those files to the new subdirectory. Finally it inserts the registry text into the system registry, correcting the registry entry to indicate the actual destination directory.

Once the Forms Manager returns control to the caller, the form is ready to run, just a CLSID away.

6

Implementing and Installing the Form

From the theory of Chapter 5, this chapter introduces the practice of implementing and installing forms. Application authors deliver forms as component objects that offer the MAPI form interfaces. MAPI forms libraries store the servers implementing these objects, indexing them so that a client can locate the form for a given message class as necessary.

Form as Component Object, Revisited

Recall from the last chapter: a form in MAPI is a component object that implements the *IMAPIForm* interface plus the *IPersistMessage* interface to load and save a form's contents to and from MAPI messages. When a MAPI client contacts the Forms Manager to get the form for handling a particular message, the Forms Manager locates the correct class for handling that message, extracting the class's server from a forms library and setting it up as necessary. The Forms Manager then creates an instance of the form object from that class for the requesting client. Finally the MAPI client works through the object's exposed form interfaces to create or manipulate the desired message.

Implementing a form, then, consists of writing a server that supplies these objects, including that server in a forms library, and tagging the server with the correct information. That's all.

The Interfaces of the Object

A form object must implement at least two interfaces: its initialization interface *IPersistMessage*, through which the form interacts with the messages that back the form's persistent data (which is data that can be serialized for later instantiation), and its activation interface *IMAPIForm*, through which the form responds to commands from the viewer application that requested the form's services. In addition, most forms supply an ancillary sink object to expose the *IMAPIForm-AdviseSink* interface, which notifies form objects of changes or activity within the view hosting the form.

If you are familiar with the interfaces of ActiveX containers and embedded objects, you can easily understand the MAPI form interfaces. The *IPersistMessage* interface works like the *IPersist-Storage* interface by allowing the viewer to pass a message object to the form, while the *IMAPIForm* interface works like a simplified *IOleObject* interface that has no notion of object linking or in-place editing.

IPersistMessage

Every form exists to create or display some message. Through the methods on the form's *IPersistMessage* initialization interface, the viewer supplies the form with a message in which to work and subsequently instructs the form to make its changes to the message. The methods available on the *IPersistMessage* interface are shown in Table 6-1.

Method	Description
QueryInterface	Returns the specified interface on an object
AddRef	Increments the object's reference count.
Release	Releases a reference to an object
GetLastError	Returns information about the last error to befall the form
GetClassID	Returns an identifier for the form's message class
IsDirty	Checks whether changes were made to a form since it was last saved
InitNew	Provides a form with a message that will serve as a base for creating a new message
Load	Loads a form from an already existing message
Save	Saves revisions of a form to an already existing message
SaveCompleted	Returns a message to a form after a save has been completed
HandsOffMessage	Releases a form

Table 6-1. *Methods on the* IPersistMessage *interface.*

A form cannot assume that it has complete control over the object backing its message; its message could very well reside within some other object. Imagine that a form opens a message that is embedded (inner message) within another message (outer message). Also suppose that the message is under the control of another form rendering the outer message. Any time that the outer form saves its message, the inner form must write out changes to its inner message. If the outer form abandons its changes, the inner form must revert back to its original version as well. (See Figure 6-1.) A form, therefore, must work indirectly when reading and writing to and from the message. The viewer hosting the form takes responsibility for obtaining the message from either the message store, file, or enclosing message and gives the form its initial *IMessage* interface, which manages the message. Likewise, when the time comes to save the form's changes to its message, the form must wait for a command from the viewer before writing its changes. Furthermore, the form must release all references to its message upon command, trusting the viewer to restore the reference to the proper message when it is needed later. By implementing the *IPersistMessage* interface, a form accommodates this indirection, working by rules that let the viewer maintain messages within messages.

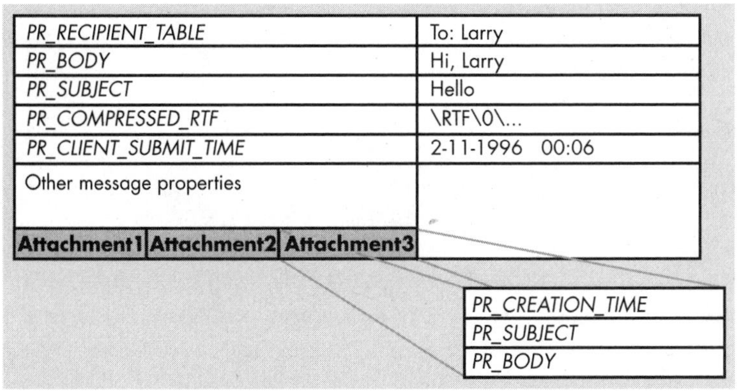

PR_RECIPIENT_TABLE	To: Larry
PR_BODY	Hi, Larry
PR_SUBJECT	Hello
PR_COMPRESSED_RTF	\RTF\0\...
PR_CLIENT_SUBMIT_TIME	2-11-1996 00:06
Other message properties	
Attachment1 **Attachment2** **Attachment3**	

| PR_CREATION_TIME |
| PR_SUBJECT |
| PR_BODY |

Figure 6-1. *Schematic of a message embedded within another message.*

The simplest way to follow the rules of the *IPersistMessage* interface is to consider the form as occupying one of a series of five distinct states: Uninitialized, Normal, No Scribble, Hands Off From Normal, or Hands Off After Save. A form takes a particular state in response to calls to its *IPersistMessage* implementation. The current state of the form dictates the manner in which the form handles its current message, if there is one, as well as how it responds to subsequent *IPersistMessage* commands.

Uninitialized state Every form object originally leaves its class factory in the Uninitialized state, as illustrated in Figure 6-2. Such an embryonic form can do little other than await initialization, when the viewer gives the form its message.

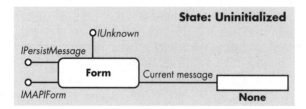

Figure 6-2. *Uninitialized state of a form object.*

Viewers initialize forms with messages in one of two ways. If the viewer is associating the form with a completely new message instance, such as takes place when a user initially requests to compose an instance of the form, then the viewer invokes the *IPersistMessage::InitNew* method. (See Figure 6-3.) In response to the *InitNew* method, the form accepts a reference to the message that it uses for subsequent storage, then sets its own default values. Otherwise, if the viewer is associating the form with an already existing message instance, the viewer invokes the *IPersistMessage::Load* method to request that the form read its persistent data from the given message. Successful initialization through either the *InitNew* or *Load* method leaves the form in the Normal state, holding a reference to a message.

Normal state In the Normal state, the form holds references against a message backing the persistent data of the form. If the form's data differs from the contents of the message (as shown in the example in Figure 6-4 on page 274), the form indicates this by calling the *IPersistMessage::IsDirty* method, which checks for changes in the form since the form was last saved. No other client of the message makes any changes to the message at this time. The form is free to hold references to objects embedded within the message because those objects will not move or change.

Although the form occupies this state, the viewer can demand to make changes to the message. The viewer requests that the form release all of its references to the message and to objects within the message by calling the *IPersistMessage-::HandsOffMessage* method. In response, the form immediately releases all such references, dirty state notwithstanding, recursively calling the *HandsOffMessage* method to release message objects or the *IPersistStorage::HandsOffStorage* method to release embedded objects, as necessary. (See Figure 6-5 on the following page.) The form then enters the Hands Off From Normal state, which leaves the viewer free to make its own changes to the previously held message. Should the viewer choose, it can later restore the message (either the same message or its equivalent) to the form through a call to the *IPersistMessage-::SaveCompleted* method, as will be discussed in the section "Hands Off From Normal state."

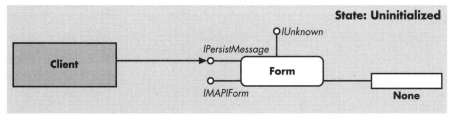

The client code calls *IPersistMessage::InitNew* or *IPersistMessage::Load* to initialize the form.

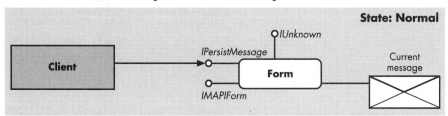

After the form is initialized, the form holds a reference to the message, which is now in the Normal state.

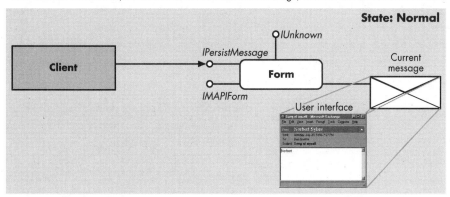

The client code calls *IMAPIForm::DoVerb* to display the current message.

Figure 6-3. *A form receives a message after initialization.*

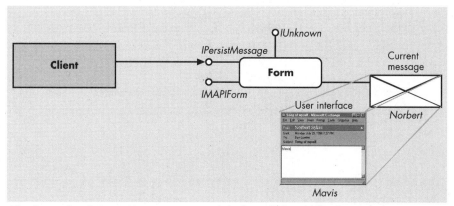

The client code calls *IPersistMessage::IsDirty* to ask the form whether it differs from the message backing that form. The message contains *Norbert*, but the user interface contains *Mavis*.

Figure 6-4. *The form holds a reference to the message that it read. Because the user has changed the edit control, the contents of the form differ from the contents of the message, so the form reports its state as "dirty."*

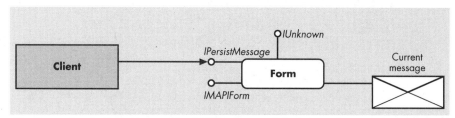

The client code calls *IPersistMessage::HandsOffMessage* to ask the form to release its reference to the message so that the client can modify the message.

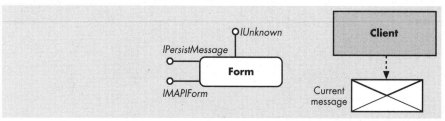

In response, the form releases the message, leaving the client holding the only reference to the message. The client is now free to modify the message.

Figure 6-5. *The form releases a reference.*

Alternatively, the viewer can command the form to save its own changes to a message with a call to the *IPersistMessage::Save* method. The viewer can have the form write its data to a different message from that originally supplied in the initialization (*InitNew* or *Load*) call, or it can have the form save the changes to the original message. (See Figure 6-6.) The latter is possible if the form has indicated through the *IPersistMessage::IsDirty* method that it has changes to make persistent. Upon successfully writing data to the specified message, the form enters the No Scribble state, where it can retain its references to embedded objects but is forbidden from making any further changes to them.

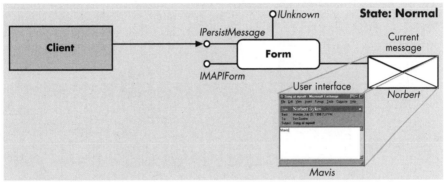

The client code calls *IPersistMessage::Save* to request that the form write its changes to the message. The message contains *Norbert,* but the user interface contains *Mavis.*

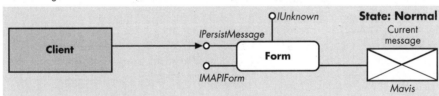

The form writes *Mavis* to the message.

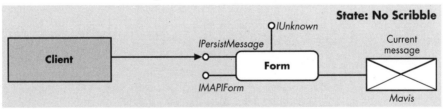

After setting its changes to the message, the form enters the Scribble state, in which it continues to hold reference to its message but refrains from making further changes. It is awaiting further orders from its client as to the eventual disposition of its message.

Figure 6-6. *The form saves changes.*

No Scribble state   In the No Scribble[1] state, the form has just completed a call to the *IPersistMessage::Save* method and is awaiting further directions. The form continues to hold references to its message and any embedded objects within the message.

Having told the form to save itself, the viewer can take one of two directions: have the form drop its references, or signal that the save operation is at an end. To drop the references, the viewer calls the *IPersistMessage::HandsOffMessage* method. (See Figure 6-7.) This puts the form into the Hands Off After Save state, which is similar to the Hands Off From Normal state except that it originates in the No Scribble state instead of in the Normal state, and leaves the viewer free to manipulate the message further.

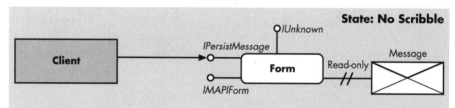

With the form in the No Scribble state, the client calls *IPersistMessage::HandsOffMessage*.

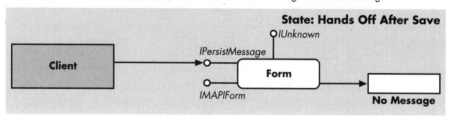

The form releases its reference to the message and enters the Hands Off After Save state.

Figure 6-7. *The form releases references in response to a call to* IPersistMessage::HandsOffMessage.

Alternatively, the viewer can now call the *IPersistMessage::SaveCompleted* method, which immediately returns the form to the Normal state (see Figure 6-8), signaling that the save operation is at an end.

---

1. This is colorfully called the "zombie" state in old versions of the OLE-structured storage API documentation.

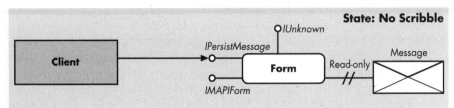

With the form in the No Scribble state, the client calls *IPersistMessage::SaveCompleted* to return a message to the form.

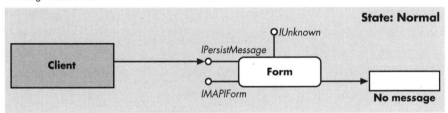

The form then resumes full ownership of the message and reenters the Normal state.

Figure 6-8. *The form leaves the No Scribble state and returns to the Normal state.*

Objects implementing the *IPersistStorage* interface make more of a distinction between their Normal (Scribble) and No Scribble states than do MAPI forms. *IPersistStorage* implementations are free to write to their backing storage objects anytime they occupy the Normal state; for them, the period following an *IPersistStorage::Save* command is unusual in that they must refrain from writing into their storage objects until they receive a call to the *IPersistStorage::SaveCompleted* method. In contrast, *IPersistMessage* implementations are not so free to mark up their backing message; they must defer all their writes until they receive a call to the *IPersistMessage::Save* method, which is the only time during their Normal state that they can write to the backing message. Thus MAPI forms don't really differentiate between the Scribble and No Scribble states. A better name for the No Scribble state might therefore be the "Just Saved, Now What?" state.

Hands Off From Normal state   In the Hands Off From Normal state, the form has no backing message, having dropped all references to its message in response to the viewer's *IPersistMessage::HandsOffMessage* command. The form should make no changes to its data that it would want to make persistent, since it has no message into which to save that data and no guarantee of receiving such a message before its demise.

There are two ways to return the form to the Normal state. The viewer can call the *IPersistMessage::SaveCompleted* method, which returns a message for the form's use. (See Figure 6-9.) While this message might not be exactly the same message that the form held before obeying the *HandsOffMessage* command, the message will contain the same data. For example, the viewer might have ordered the form to release its message so that the viewer would be free to relocate the underlying message elsewhere. The form should retain this reference, opening embedded objects within the message as necessary, and then should return to the Normal state.

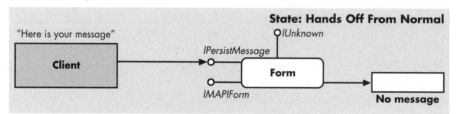

With the form in the Hands Off From Normal state, the client calls *IPersistMessage::SaveCompleted* to hand a message to the form.

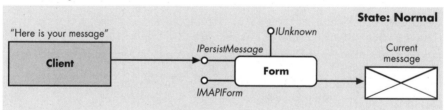

The form holds the message reference that brought on the call and enters the Normal state.

Figure 6-9. *The form returns to the Normal state in response to a call to* IPersistMessage::SaveCompleted.

Alternatively, the viewer can give the form an entirely new message against which to work by calling one of its initialization methods, either the *IPersistMessage-::InitNew* method or the *IPersistMessage::Load* method. (See Figure 6-10.) Being in a hands-off state, the form has no other message reference outstanding. As with any other initialization, the form can start a new life with the new message, changing its contents to reflect the content of the new message. This reinitialization returns the form to the Normal state.

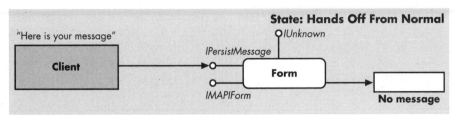

With the form in Hands Off From Normal state, the client calls *IPersistMessage::InitNew* or *IPersistMessage::Load* to hand a message to the form.

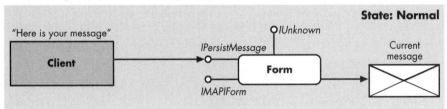

The form holds the message reference that brought on the call and enters the Normal state.

Figure 6-10. *The form receives a new message in response to a call to* IPersist-Message::InitNew *or* IPersistMessage::Load.

Hands Off After Save state   The Hands Off After Save state resembles the Hands Off From Normal state in almost every respect. A form enters the Hands Off From Normal state when it receives the *IPersistMessage::HandsOffMessage* command while in the Normal state. In contrast, a form enters the Hands Off After Save state when it receives the *HandsOffMessage* command while in the No Scribble state, which it enters after successfully performing the *IPersistMessage::Save* method. Regardless of which state it is in, the form awaits a call to its *IPersistMessage::SaveCompleted* method to provide its "Get Out Of Jail Free card."

A form discriminates between the Hands Off After Save state and the Hands Off From Normal state so that it knows when to notify clients that a save has taken place. Receiving the *SaveCompleted* command while in the Hands Off After Save state indicates that the form received a *HandsOffMessage* command while it was in the No Scribble state, that is, after successfully completing a *Save* command; receiving the *SaveCompleted* command while in this state therefore indicates that the form completed a save action, just as if the save-concluding call had arrived during the No Scribble state. Compare this to the Hands Off From Normal state, where a call to the *SaveCompleted* method does not indicate any sort of save, but simply returns the message to the state it was in prior to whatever action (rename, etc.) mandated the temporary hands-off state. The form will notify interested parties by invoking the *IPersistMessage::OnSaved* method on their registered view advise sinks.

State diagram   Any form implementing the *IPersistMessage* interface promises to behave in a certain fashion and in turn expects a certain kind of treatment from its client viewer. Calls to the *IPersistMessage* interface always arrive in precisely defined sequences. If successful, the calls leave the form in a particular state, depending on the call and the previous state of the form. The form states that are possible and the transitions between them are depicted in Figure 6-11.

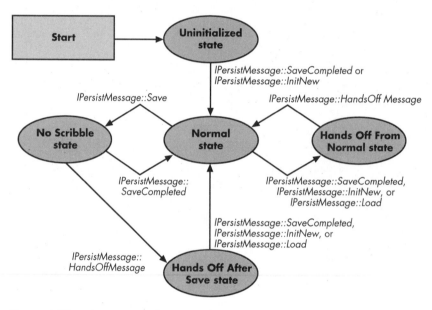

Figure 6-11. *Master state diagram.*

The form must do its part to uphold this contract by returning *E_UNEXPECTED* to any client attempting a transition outside of those depicted in Figure 6-11. For example, a faulty viewer might attempt to save a message that it had never loaded. The form sees a call to the *IPersistMessage::HandsOffMessage* method when it is in the Uninitialized state and returns *E_UNEXPECTED* to the buggy client, which will hopefully then die of embarrassment.

Some methods of the *IPersistMessage* interface (not included in this diagram) are always available to callers. A form makes its last error code available, regardless of the state of its relationship with its message, and does not change state in response to a client requesting its last error. For this reason, forms should make the *IPersistMessage::GetLastError* command available at all times. Likewise, a form will not change state in response to any client that requests its CLSID or its relationship to its message; therefore a form should make its *IPersistMessage::GetClassID* and *IPersistMessage::IsDirty* methods always available as well.

Message site A form cannot assume that the message it receives is residing in the Inbox folder of some user's message store. It can work on conventional messages having entry identifiers that locate the message with a message store. It can work on a message embedded within another message, which can happen when one message includes another message as an attachment. It can work on messages that do not reside in message stores at all, whether they are serialized onto a disk file or block of memory, or appear within a compound document rendered by some OLE container application. Whatever the source of the message, the viewer will present the message to the form, expecting the form to supply the correct user interface for the message while accommodating the following limitations of the backing message: an embedded message cannot be submitted; a message in a read-only folder cannot be deleted; and a parent folder cannot exist for a message contained in a file or embedded within a compound document.

To encapsulate the many possible sources of a message, the viewer provides the form with a *message site object* on its initialization methods, *IPersistMethod::InitNew* and *IPersistMethod::Load*. Whereas the message interface typically comes from a MAPI message store provider, the message site interface always comes from the viewer, which implements the message site object itself. Therefore the form must call the message site for any operations that might vary due to the actual site hosting the message. Since the viewer implements the message site, it can make the correct allowances on the form's behalf.

The message site interface offers many methods, falling roughly into two families. First, it offers a number of *Get* methods on the *IMAPIMessageSite* interface (shown in Table 6-2 on the following page), which serve to fetch information pertinent to the site hosting a particular message: *GetSession*, *GetStore*, *GetFolder*, *GetMessage* (redundant with the *IMessage* parameter provided to *IPersistMessage*), and *GetFormManager*. Some of this information is available elsewhere in the message. For example, a client could query the message for its *PR_PARENT_ENTRYID* property and then open the entry identifier that is returned to get the object containing the message. The client would then handle the lack of this property or the return of an object of a type other than *MAPI_FOLDER* appropriately, possibly changing its interface to reflect that its message does not reside within a folder. Using the equivalent method on the message site object provides the same information with fewer transactions against the underlying message database, since the viewer already had to obtain that information for its own operation. When running against a distributed system such as Microsoft Exchange Server, this results in fewer remote procedure calls, with greatly improved responsiveness to the user.

Method	Description
QueryInterface	Returns the specified interface on an object
AddRef	Increments the object's reference count
Release	Releases a reference to an object
GetLastError	Returns information about the last error to befall the form
GetSession	Obtains the MAPI session for the current message
GetStore	Obtains the message store for the current message
GetFolder	Obtains the folder where the current message was created or opened
GetMessage	Obtains the current message
GetFormManager	Obtains a Forms Manager interface that the form can use to launch another form
NewMessage	Initiates a new message
CopyMessage	Copies the current message to a folder
MoveMessage	Moves the current message to a folder
DeleteMessage	Deletes the current message
SaveMessage	Requests that the current message be saved
SubmitMessage	Requests that the current message be submitted to the MAPI spooler
GetSiteStatus	Obtains the status of the message site object with respect to the capabilities of the message site on the message

Table 6-2. *Methods on the* IMAPIMessageSite *interface.*

The other family of methods on the *IMAPIMessageSite* interface offers message-specific actions—*NewMessage, CopyMessage, MoveMessage, DeleteMessage, Save-Message, SubmitMessage*—applied to the current message, or, as appropriate, to the site of the current message. An additional *Get* method, *IMAPIMessage-Site::GetSiteStatus*, returns a bit vector indicating which of these methods is currently applicable. This allows a form to disable its File - Delete and File - Move commands. The File - Delete command is disabled when the form is operating in a folder where the current user lacks delete privileges; the File - Move command is disabled when it is invoked on a message embedded within another message. Calls to these methods result in the viewer taking action appropriate to the actual site of the message. In the case of many methods, this generates subsequent calls to the form. For example, a form calling the *IMAPIMessageSite::SaveMessage* method should expect to see calls to several methods of the *IPersistMessage* interface because the viewer requests that the form save its changes to the backing message. The viewer can also use the *IMAPIMessageSite* interface to ensure that the form conforms with viewer behavior: for example, the *DeleteMessage* method can move a message into a Deleted Items container, while the *NewMessage* method can create its new message in a particular default folder and set certain default properties, such as *PR_SENTMAIL_ENTRYID* or *PR_DELETE_AFTER_SUBMIT*.

IPersistMessage vs. IPersistStorage   The *IPersistMessage* interface works very much like the structured storage interface *IPersistStorage*. If you are familiar with ActiveX and OLE, you are probably already pretty familiar with the *IPersistMessage* interface. There are, however, a few differences.

Structured storage lets a server write freely into a storage during its Normal state. MAPI requires that forms write only their changes in their *IPersistMessage::Save* implementation.

Structured storage has only a single hands-off storage state. MAPI differentiates between two different hands-off states: Hands Off From Normal and Hands Off After Save.

The *IPersistStorage* interface inherits from another interface, *IPersist*, thus guaranteeing that *IPersistStorage* keeps its *IPersist::GetClassID* method in the same vtable location as the methods of the *IPersistFile, IPersistStream,* and *IPersistStreamInit* interfaces. Despite its name, the MAPI *IPersistMessage* interface does not inherit from the *IPersist* interface; instead, it keeps the MAPI-specific *GetLastError* method at that offset. Hence, if a MAPI form server wants to implement

IPersist,[2] it cannot return a pointer to its *IPersistMessage* vtable but must instead return a pointer to a separate vtable that correctly delivers that interface. Also, unlike the *IPersistStorage* interface, implementations of *IPersistMessage* must deliver the full MAPI *GetLastError* method.

IMAPIForm

After the viewer has given the form a message to play with, it must give the form its marching orders. Most commonly this is "show yourself." The form appears at the suggested location, displays the contents of the given message (or in the case of new message, the default contents), and interacts with the user until either the user or the viewer dismisses the form. Alternatively, the viewer can give one of three commands: ask a form to render its message to a printer or to a file, create a response to its given message, or display itself in some alternative format. Whatever the command, in each case the viewer takes an initialized form and activates it through the form's *IMAPIForm* interface. The methods available on this interface are shown in Table 6-3.

Method	Description
QueryInterface	Returns the specified interface on an object
AddRef	Increments the object's reference count
Release	Releases a reference to an object
GetLastError	Returns information about the last error to befall the form
SetViewContext	Defines the form view as the current view context
GetViewContext	Returns the current view context
ShutdownForm	Closes a form object
DoVerb	Performs the action defined for the specified verb
Advise	Specifies that a form viewer is to be notified about changes to a form
Unadvise	Disables a form viewer's registration for notification of form object changes

Table 6-3. *Methods on the* IMAPIForm *interface.*

---

2. Note that MAPI does not require that forms implement the *IPersist* interface. Conceivably, an object might implement both *IPersistMessage* and one of the ActiveX persistence interfaces, however, and then this would become an issue. If a form implemented *IPersistStorage*, it would have to implement *IPersist* as well. Many objects implementing *IPersist* actually return a pointer to a derived interface, such as *IPersistStorage*. A form implementing *IPersist* would have to take care not to return a pointer to *IPersistMessage* in such a case, but instead to return a pointer to *IPersistStorage*, since contrary to the implication of its name, *IPersistMessage* does not properly subsume *IPersist*.

Form activation with a verb Viewers activate forms by invoking the form's *IMAPIForm::DoVerb* method. The viewer provides the form with either a number representing the verb or the initial action for the form to take upon its activation. It also provides information describing the form's working environment, including a handle to its parent window and a rectangle delimiting the dimensions that the form's window should occupy. Upon receiving the request, the form displays its user interface at the requested location (see Figure 6-12) and performs the action indicated by the given verb.

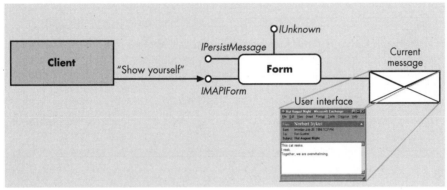

The client calls *IMAPIForm::DoVerb* to display the message.

Figure 6-12. *The viewer displays the form.*

Each form defines the verbs that it supports, since it must recognize the integer code for its verbs as parameters to its *DoVerb* method. A form delivering standard Exchange-style messaging functionality can use the verbs of the Exchange client, as defined in the header file EXCHFORM.H.[3] (See Table 6-4 on the following page.) In addition to this, a form is free to define its own verb codes private to the form; these should start at 1 and ascend incrementally to avoid colliding with the codes standard to Exchange. In addition, all forms should respond to the standard verbs defined by the *IOleObject* interface OLEIVERB_PRIMARY[4] for the default action and *OLEIVERB_SHOW, OLEIVERB_OPEN*, and *OLEIVERB_HIDE* for showing, opening, and hiding the form's user interface. With the exception of those verbs defined by the *IOleObject* interface, the form lists all the verbs to which it responds in the registration entry of its forms library so that the viewer can populate its user interface with options germane to the form.

---

3. Versions of the Win32 SDK prior to July 1996 do not include EXCHFORM.H.

4. The verb *OLEIVERB_PRIMARY* is the same as the verb *EXCHIVERB_OPEN*.

Name	Value	Action
EXCHIVERB_OPEN	0	Show the message in the form
EXCHIVERB_REPLYTOSENDER	102	Generate a response form addressed to the message's sender
EXCHIVERB_REPLYTOALL	103	Generate a response form addressed to the message's sender and all its original recipients
EXCHIVERB_FORWARD	104	Generate an unaddressed response form incorporating the contents of the original message
EXCHIVERB_PRINT	105	Render the message to the current printer
EXCHIVERB_SAVEAS	106	Save the message into the specified file, optionally rendering it as plain or rich text
EXCHIVERB_REPLYTOFOLDER	108	Generate a response form, posting it into the current folder

Table 6-4. *Verb codes.*

After initially activating the form, a viewer can continue to communicate with a form through additional calls to the *DoVerb* method. A viewer can elect to hide all forms when it hides itself, by sending the verb *OLEIVERB_HIDE* to all its running forms. Such a viewer would subsequently make its forms reappear through *OLEIVERB_SHOW*. When the user opens an item in the view already open, the viewer typically brings that item's existing form to the foreground by sending it *OLEIVERB_SHOW* instead of opening a new instance of the form.

View contexts Before the viewer activates the form, it gives that form a reference to a *view context* object. The viewer implements a view context that includes the current sequence of items visible in the view of the user-activated form, other parameters describing the context of the viewer application, and the viewer's expectations of the form. These expectations are defined by the answers to the following questions: Will the form present a read-only user interface? Will it present a user interface at all, or will it go quietly about its business (for example, rendering the form to a printer)? Should the form operate modal to the viewer or can it operate as a top-level window?

The form can request that the viewer activate the next message in a view by calling the *IMAPIViewContext::ActivateNext* method on its view context with the next item defined as whatever appears next in the current view. (See Figure 6-13.) This might result in the viewer closing the current form. Through the *IMAPIViewContext::GetViewStatus* method, the form can ask the view context whether any items lie before or after the current item in the view sequence, as well as ask about other characteristics of the view status (such as whether the form is modal or interactive). The form can then use this status to enable or disable buttons and commands of its user interface, such as the arrow buttons on the standard Microsoft Exchange read note for moving between elements in the current view.

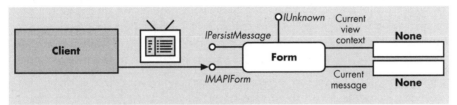

The client code calls *IMAPIForm::SetViewContextMessage* to supply the form with a view context.

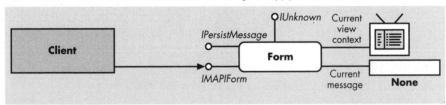

The view context represents the logical sequence of messages, within which the client will activate the form on a message.

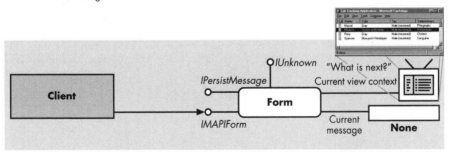

Any message given to the form will correspond to a position in the sequence of messages.

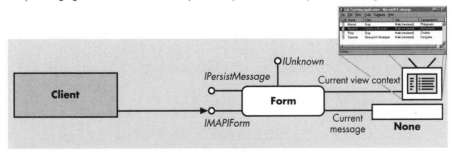

To determine the next or previous message, the form asks its view context.

Figure 6-13. *Activation of the next and previous messages.*

A form receives the view context through a call to its *IMAPIForm::SetViewContext* method. At any given time, a particular form has only one view context to represent the context within which that form interprets any View - Next and View - Previous commands made to it. If a viewer gives the form another view context, the form releases the previous context and uses the new one instead. A form gives its current view context a form advise sink through the *IMAPIViewContext::SetAdviseSink* method so that the form is notified of changes that take place within the view context. Before releasing a view context, the form revokes its advise sink from the view context by calling the *IMAPIViewContext::SetAdviseSink* method and specifying a NULL advise sink as a parameter.

A form can also receive a view context as a parameter to the *IMAPIForm::DoVerb* method. If given, this per-verb context does not replace the current context of the form; rather, the form uses it for the duration of the verb's operation. A viewer provides a per-verb context for two reasons: to bring up an instance of the form modal to its parent window or to run the form invisibly for certain tasks, such as printing or saving its contents to a file.

View advise sinks   A viewer can implement one or more *view advise sink* objects to receive notifications of changes or other events within the form.

A form receives a view advise sink through a call to its *IMAPIForm::Advise* method. While a form has only one view context at any time, it can host many view advise sinks, with each sink representing some viewer interested in the fate of the form. The form holds each sink until the viewer makes the correct call to *IMAPIForm::Unadvise*, whereupon the form releases the indicated sink and forgets about it. A form notifies all of its held view advise sinks as follows:

■ Upon any initialization (that is, after completing *IPersistMessage::InitNew* or *IPersistMessage::Load*), the form should call *IMAPIViewAdviseSink::OnNewMessage* to notify a form viewer that a message has been loaded in a form.

■ Upon shutdown (that is, after completing *IMAPIForm::ShutdownForm*), the form should call *IMAPIViewAdviseSink::OnShutdown* to notify a form viewer that a form is being closed.

■ Upon submitting the message to the MAPI message spooler (that is, after invoking *IMAPIMessageSite::SubmitMessage*), the form should call *IMAPIViewAdviseSink::OnSubmitted* to notify a form viewer that a current message has been submitted to the MAPI spooler.

- Upon rendering a page to the printer or ending a print job, either normally or abnormally, the form should call *IMAPIViewAdviseSink::OnPrint* to notify a form viewer of the printing status of a form.

- Upon saving changes to the current message (that is, after completing *IPersistMessage::SaveCompleted* from either the Hands Off After Save state or the No Scribble state [if the original save was not to a different message]), the form should call *IMAPIViewAdviseSink::OnSaved* to notify a form viewer that the message in the form object has been saved.

How to shut down a form   Having activated the form through *IMAPIForm::DoVerb*, the viewer typically leaves the form to run until the user closes or otherwise dismisses it, or until the form completes its assigned task and closes itself, such as might happen when the viewer activates the form to print an item. Once the user closes the viewer, the viewer must mop up any instances of forms that are still running. Viewers close forms from without by calling *IMAPIForm::ShutdownForm*, specifying whether to save any outstanding changes in the method's input save options parameter. These save options are shown in Table 6-5.

Flag	Description
SAVEOPTS_NOSAVE	Does not save the form data
SAVEOPTS_PROMPTSAVE	Prompts the user to determine whether changes to the form data will be saved
SAVEOPTS_SAVEIFDIRTY	Saves the form if the form has been changed

Table 6-5. *Mutually exclusive flags for the* ulSaveOptions *parameter of the* ShutdownForm *method.*

A form implements *IMAPIForm::ShutdownForm* by calling *IMAPIMessageSite::SaveMessage* in accordance with its dirty state and the specified save options parameter, then tearing down the internals of the form, releasing all pending references to other objects, and otherwise cleaning up its state. Once the form has completely shut down, it is no longer a working form object; such a dead form responds only to *IMAPIForm::IUnknown*.

IMAPIForm vs. IOleObject   To a certain degree, the *IMAPIForm* interface resembles the *IOleObject* interface, which ActiveX uses for servers that represent objects embedded within a container. If you imagine the viewer as a container render-ing a set of embedded items, this simile begins to work. The *IMAPIForm* inter-face, however, is much simpler than the *IOleObject* interface.

Most obviously, MAPI and its forms support no notions of linking or monikers. All form objects work against a message site object given to them by the viewer; that message site contains an open message interface. In addition, MAPI con-tains no notion of client sites within a container, either for static display of a form or for in-place editing. There is no view object and no in-place editing. Forms always appear within their own windows. Containers render inactive items using only their own logic, aided by information published by the form in the forms library.

Where ActiveX differentiates among three states of a server—passive, loaded, and running—MAPI considers its forms as either active or inactive. *IOleObject-::Close* moves the object from the running (active) state to the loaded state, while *IMAPIForm::ShutdownForm* makes the form inactive and, in fact, tears down the form to where it is no longer even a form.[5]

Another difference between the *IMAPIForm* and *IOleObject* interfaces is that MAPI form objects offer no interface for enumerating verbs. Any client want-ing to learn the verbs supported by a particular form object must locate a corresponding form information object from a forms library and then query that object for verbs, as shown in the previous chapter.

Finally, like the *IPersistMessage* interface, the *IMAPIForm* interface offers the MAPI *GetLastError* method, a function unknown to the ActiveX activation interfaces.

IMAPIFormAdviseSink
By registering a view advise sink with a form, a viewer learns of events taking place within that form. Conversely, a form learns of certain form-relevant events in a viewer by implementing a *form advise sink* object. This is a separate ob-ject from the form object; the object supporting the *IMAPIForm* and *IPersist-Message* interfaces need not support the *IMAPIFormAdviseSink* interface, and vice versa. The methods available on the *IMAPIFormAdviseSink* interface are shown in Table 6-6.

---

5. In the object sense, it is no longer a form, since it no longer honors or responds to the *IMAPI-Form* interface.

Method	Description
QueryInterface	Returns the specified interface on an object
AddRef	Increments the object's reference count
Release	Releases a reference to an object
OnChange	Notifies a form object about modifications in the status of a viewer
OnActivateNext	Identifies whether the current form object can handle the class of the next message to be displayed

Table 6-6. *Methods on the* IMAPIFormAdviseSink *interface.*

The form registers its advise sink with the viewer by calling *IMAPIViewContext- ::SetAdviseSink* when the viewer sets the form's view context. Should the viewer change the view context, the form removes its form advise sink from the first context before registering it with the second one. Since a view context hosts only a single form advise sink, the form sets a view context's held advise sink (in the *pmvns* parameter of the call to the *SetAdviseSink* method) to NULL to make it release its current form advise sink.

When the view status changes in a view context, the view context notifies its held form advise sink by calling the *IMAPIFormAdviseSink::OnChange* method on that sink. (The flags that can be used in the call to *OnChange* are shown in Table 6-7.) This signals to the form that the setting of flags *VCSTATUS_NEXT* and *VCSTATUS_PREV* has possibly changed and merits reexamination. Based on these flags' settings, the form enables or disables any user interface for Go To Previous Message and Go To Next Message commands that it offers.

Flag	Description
VCSTATUS_READONLY	The delete, submit, and move commands are disabled
VCSTATUS_NEXT	The viewer includes a next message
VCSTATUS_PREV	The viewer includes a previous message
VCSTATUS_INTERACTIVE	The form displays the user interface
VCSTATUS_MODAL	The form is modal to the viewer

Table 6-7. *Flags used in the parameter to the* IMAPIFormAdviseSink::OnChange *method.*

More important, the view context uses the form advise sink to check whether the sink's form can handle the next (or previous) message in the sequence. When the form calls the *IMAPIViewContext::ActivateNext* method, the viewer calls back to the *IMAPIFormAdviseSink::OnActivateNext* method on its form advise sink, giving the sink certain parameters about the message in question: its message class, its message status, and its message flags. If the sink agrees to the request, the viewer either reinitializes the form with the new message, if the form permits, or uses a new form interface offered by the sink. Otherwise, the viewer shuts down the current form and creates a new form to handle the new message, resolving and launching that new form through the MAPI Forms Manager. For best performance, a form should agree to handle the new message if it can.

Different Advise Sinks

The advise sinks of the MAPI form interfaces differ from those used elsewhere in MAPI.

The conventional MAPI advise sink, the *IMAPIAdviseSink* interface, establishes communication between MAPI service providers and clients. The MAPI form advise sinks, the *IMAPIFormAdviseSink* and *IMAPIViewAdviseSink* interfaces, establish communication between forms and viewers—both of which are MAPI clients—and act more like the ActiveX *IAdviseSink* interface than like the MAPI construct. They do not use the MAPI notification engine or any of the *NOTIFICATION* structures defined by MAPI. Caveat programmer!

Synthesis

Let's bring all these interfaces together. As shown in Figure 6-14, the form object implements the *IPersistMessage* and *IMAPIForm* interfaces. A viewer holds a reference to this form, which it obtained through the MAPI Forms Manager.

The form object holds a message site, which it received at its initialization (*IPersistMessage::InitNew* method or *IPersistMessage::Load* method), and a view context, which it received shortly thereafter (*IMAPIForm::SetViewContext* method). (See Figure 6-15.) The viewer implements both of these interfaces. Through the viewer-supplied message site object, the form has access to interfaces on many other objects. Foremost among these is *IMessage*, which usually (but not always)[6] comes from a message object in a MAPI message store provider, opened by the client. In addition, the message site offers the client's session, the MAPI Forms Manager object, and the message's enclosing folder and store objects, if applicable.

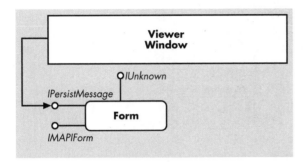

Figure 6-14. *The viewer holds a reference to the form.*

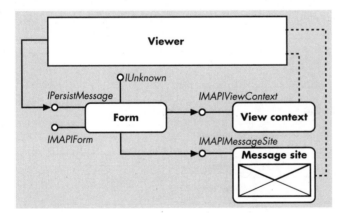

Figure 6-15. *The form object holds a message site and a view context.*

As shown in Figure 6-16 on the following page, the form object holds one or more view advise sinks, which are received through a call to *IMAPIForm::Advise*. When the form completes certain events, it announces the fact to every view sink that it holds, thus notifying any interested views.

---

6. Nothing limits messages to coming from message store providers. Imagine a client calling the *OpenIMsgOnIStg* utility function to get a message interface backed by a file.

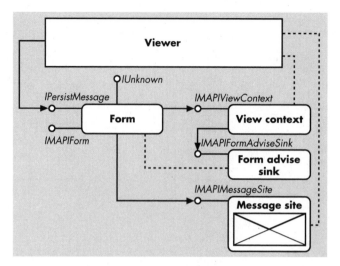

Figure 6-16. *The form object holds view advise sinks.*

As shown in Figure 6-17, the view context holds a form advise sink, which it received through a call to *IMAPIViewContext::SetAdviseSink,* made immediately in response to *IMAPIForm::SetViewContext.* The form advise sink holds some unspecified relation to the form object, sufficient to let it perform the duties of *IMAPIFormAdviseSink::OnChange* and *IMAPIFormAdviseSink::OnActivateNext.*

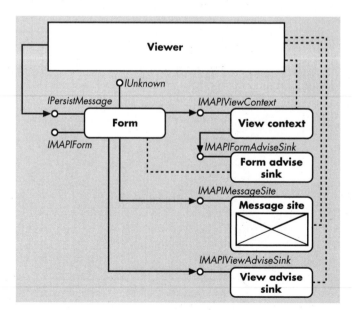

Figure 6-17. *The view context holds a form advise sink.*

The Server Hosting the Form Object

Every form object originates in a class object hosted by a server, which MAPI loads in response to client demands for a particular form. (See Figure 6-18.) All of the usual COM mechanics regarding class objects and object instances apply.

```
IBabyMonkey* pbaby
hr = pfact->CreateInstance (Null, IID_IPersistMessage, (void**) &pbaby);
```

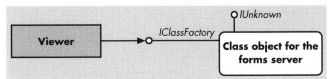

The client code calls *IClassFactory::CreateInstance* to obtain a pointer to the class object associated with *IID_IPersistMessage*.

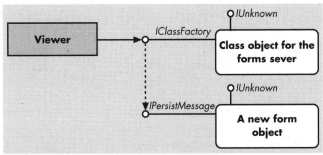

The class object returns the requested interface on a new instance.

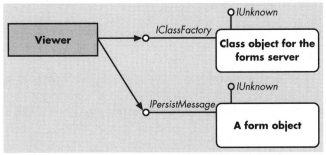

The client code obtains direct access to the *IPersistMessage* interface.

Figure 6-18. *The client acquires a form object.*

Process model

Forms and viewers communicate through the COM cross-process procedure call architecture, with MAPI providing the necessary interface remoting code that is needed to link proxies to stubs (Figure 6-19). When a viewer invokes the *IMAPI-Form::DoVerb* method on a form interface that it holds, that viewer is actually calling a MAPI-supplied proxy for the form object in its own address space. MAPI transforms this into a remote procedure call to the form server hosting the form object and calls out of a stub within the form server process to execute the form object's actual implementation of the *DoVerb* method. Conversely, when a form invokes the *IMAPIMessageSite::GetSession* method on the message site interface that it received at its initialization, that form is actually calling a MAPI-supplied in-process proxy for the message site object. Furthermore, this latter interface returns yet another proxy to the form so that when the form calls the session interface that it receives, MAPI effectively executes them against the session of the viewer. It should also be noted that MAPI does not support in-process form servers; every form server must run in its own process, separate from the viewer.[7]

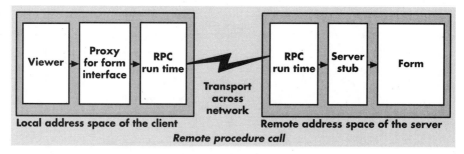

Figure 6-19. *Calls passing through the proxy/stub interface.*

Performance implications   Forbidding in-process form servers creates the following corollaries for Exchange application performance:

- Creating the first instance of a form object will be very slow because the system COM library must load its image from disk, create a process to house the server, and establish the cross-process bookkeeping. An application should do anything it can to increase startup speed and reduce the number of times that the system must load its server. Registering the server's class object as *REGCLS_MULTIPLEUSE* (which specifies that multiple applications can connect to the class object) is a good step in this direction. Another step is properly supporting MAPI's server caching, as described in the section "Server Caching."

---

7. As an exception, the Exchange 4.0 client shares one process between its viewers and its forms. Nothing prevents a particular MAPI client from implementing both a client viewer and a form server. Such a client would register the class object or objects for its forms at application startup, then subsequently access its form objects through the usual COM and MAPI mechanisms.

■ Transactions between viewer and form are relatively slow, since each call must pass through the MAPI interface remoting mechanism. (See Figure 6-19.)

■ A form need not keep the images of the MAPI service providers—or much of MAPI—within its process and need not log on to MAPI itself. It is riding piggyback on the session of the viewer. (See Figure 6-20.)

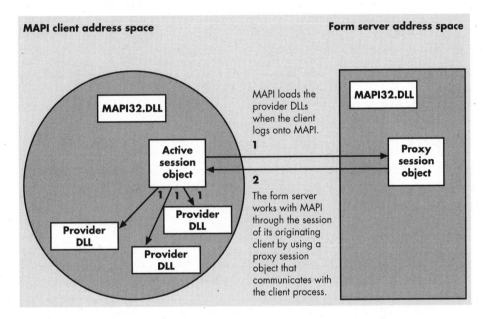

Figure 6-20. *The form server uses the session of another process.*

■ Because every MAPI call that the form makes takes place against an interface that the form receives from the viewer, every MAPI call passes through the interface remoting mechanism. A form should bundle its actions into as few MAPI calls as possible. This is similar to the usual advice for making an application run efficiently against the service providers for Microsoft Exchange Server, and indeed the goal of each is ultimately the same: to minimize the total number of remote procedure calls[8] needed.

---

8. Of course, the COM remote procedure call mechanisms that connect MAPI forms to their MAPI viewer clients are quite different from those that connect Exchange workstations with Exchange servers.

Server caching

To prevent a workstation from spending all its cycles loading and unloading form servers, the MAPI Forms Manager implements a couple of different levels of cache: one in memory and one on disk.

Since loading a class object can be a time-consuming process, MAPI makes it possible for the developer to reduce the total number of server loads, locking a few of its most recently loaded form servers into memory through the *IClass-Factory::LockServer* method on the form's class object. Servers so locked should honor their client's request and remain running until their lock count drops to zero, even if they have no active objects outstanding.

If loading a class object is slow, extracting a server's files from a forms library onto a workstation is even slower. As described at the end of the previous chapter, MAPI keeps a local disk cache of recently invoked form servers. To maintain such a cache, the MAPI Forms Manager must know when it can remove a form's server files from the cache. By convention, a running form server creates a global atom consisting of the CLSID of its form, expressed as a string; before purging a server from the cache, MAPI first checks for the server's CLSID in the global atom table and stays its hand if it finds that atom.

The form factory

For form implementations that can share most of their code in a common run-time package, a form factory offers an efficient alternative to individual form server files. Instead of the forms library containing every file, a form factory contains only the files necessary to a particular form. In addition to the CLSID of the form, the library names the CLSID of the *form factory*—a run-time server already installed on the host workstation—which it received at installation time from the *DesignerRuntimeGuid* key of the form's configuration (CFG) file. The presence of this run-time CLSID in a forms library entry marks that form as using a form factory.

The MAPI Forms Manager installs a factory-using form from the forms library just as it does any other form: by copying the form's files onto the local disk form cache and by copying the form's registry text into the system registry. However, when a client requests to activate such a form, MAPI does not ask the System COM Library for the form's class object. Instead MAPI asks COM for the named form factory, using the CLSID of the run time specified in the form's registration; on that form factory object, MAPI calls the *IMAPIFormFactory-::CreateClassFactory* method to obtain the class object for the desired form. For the run time to return the correct class object, it must either know all of its potential CLSIDs a priori or use data in the registry, presumably the data downloaded as part of installing the factory-using form. Once MAPI has the form's class object, activation proceeds as usual.

MAPI caches form factory objects in memory in a manner similar to class objects. All other forms of caching still apply as well.

Note that MAPI does not store form factories in a forms library. All form factories must be installed on host workstations prior to resolution and activation of factory-using forms.

Implementing a Form Server

First Questions

The very first step of implementing any form is deciding just what the form is. A form's identity lies tightly bound to its property schema, which describes the current structure of data and views of the form such as the columns, data types of the columns, and the relationships between views. Therefore the form's identity is also tightly bound to the message class of the messages that the form will display as its items.

If the form exists to fill an existing niche, property schema might be less important than the message class. A form that must replace the standard note form will necessarily have the message class *IPM.Note*, and will adopt a message schema closely mimicking that of the Exchange client's note form. Similarly, a form that extends an existing class must start with the schema of that class; thus a bulletin board posting with an attached digital signature might take the class *IPM.Post.Signed*. Taking this class indicates that if another client lacked the correct form, that client could still coerce the message into a working *IPM.Post*, albeit at the price of losing some information, namely the additional properties of *IPM.Post.Signed* that are not present in *IPM.Post*, plus any semantics by which the form sets those or other properties.

If instead the form exists to provide shape to some new application and does not fill an existing niche, the message class might be less important than the precise property schema. You can have an application for animal husbandry in the dairy industry and specify the columns of your data set in a business proposal: the application must track the breed, age, health, stud history, and number of DWI citations (or whatever) of a particular bull. Given those, the precise value of the message class is less important, since it isn't accommodating the schema of any other message class, though it should take a few pains not to collide with other known message classes such as *IPM.YourNameHere.Old-MacDonaldFarm.Bull.Record*.

Class identifier (CLSID)

In a sense, the property schema defines the application, reducing the application to the persistent signature of its properties. By this reckoning, two different forms could implement the same application by supporting identical property schemes and message classes. The two different forms would nevertheless have different CLSIDs, as the CLSID identifies a particular implementation of an application—that inherent to a particular form server.

The distinguishing property of a CLSID is its uniqueness (hence the *U* in GUID). The very first step in developing a form server should therefore be to generate a unique GUID to use as this CLSID. Resist the temptation to reuse the CLSID of another server by cutting and pasting from that server's source files!

To generate the GUID, run one of the tools for GUID generation, such as UUID-GEN.EXE or GUIDGEN.EXE, supplied with many development environments and the Microsoft Win32 SDK. You can use these programs to allocate a block of contiguous GUIDs, which makes it easier to recognize your own GUID in the debugger. The sample source file Samples\GUIDS.TXT shows where I've done this for the sample applications of this book. If you run these tools on a system that contains a network adapter, they will use the Ethernet address on that network adapter to ensure the uniqueness of the resulting GUIDs.

Example of a send form application

Let's visit the sample program Chap06\Sendstub. The Sendstub folder directory houses an extremely simple form server that will occupy our initial attention. As the name implies, the form is a send form, creating a message that it addresses and hands to the MAPI message spooler and transport providers for delivery.

Examine the value of the following manifest constant *SZ_FORM_MESSAGE-_CLASS* that appears at the very beginning of the source file Chap06\Sendstub-\FORM.H:

```
// The value of the SZ_FORM_MESSAGE_CLASS must match that of the
// MessageClass in the SENDSTUB.CFG file.

#define SZ_FORM_MESSAGE_CLASS "IPM.Note.StubTest"
```

In the file Chap06\Sendstub\SENDSTUB.CPP, the value of the *MessageClass* field in the Description section must match that of *SZ_FORM_MESSAGE_CLASS*. The stub send form adheres to the property schema of the standard send note, making a few changes in the interest of simplifying the example. It therefore takes the message class *IPM.Note.StubTest*, implying that if for some reason the stub send form is missing, the standard send note form can handle it.

While the sample send form essentially reuses an existing property schema, it still needs its own CLSID. The source file Chap06\Sendstub\GUIDS.H uses the *DEFINE_GUID* macro to define a GUID for this program. The following macro is lifted from the block in the GUIDS.TXT file common to all this book's samples:

```
// CLSID of the stub send form
// **You must change this if you use this form as a template!**
// {da32e202-97b8-11cf-b6a6-08002b2b3625}

DEFINE_GUID(CLSID_StubSendForm, 0xda32e202, 0x97b8, 0x11cf, 0xb6,
    0xa6, 0x08, 0x00, 0x2b, 0x2b, 0x36, 0x25);
```

Getting GUID Definitions

Getting GUIDs defined correctly in a program can be confusing. Why is it that you can reference *IID_IStorage* in your program and link successfully, yet reference *IID_IMessage* and fail to find its definition?

Everything centers around the definition of the *DEFINE_GUID* macro. You want one module in your program to define the GUID, and every other module to reference a declaration. (Think of the difference between *int x = 0* and *extern int x* in C.)

A number of GUIDs have definitions for their storage in a library (for example, UUIDX.LIB). To use those GUIDs, include a *DEFINE_GUID* for that GUID in your program and then link with the library. Depending on the header file in question, you may need to define an advisory symbol *USES_IID_YourMother* to get the GUID declaration (for example, *IID_YourMother*) or you may just be able to include the <YOURMOTHER.H> header file. Eyeball the header file and see. This is why a program can reference *IID_IStorage* and link without further ado: the programming environment's build options probably include UUID.LIB or UUID2.LIB in their default libraries.

Other GUIDs, such as those of MAPI, do not have such a library available. For such GUIDs, you need to include the definition (as opposed to the declaration) yourself in one module. The easiest way to do this is to include <INITGUID.H> after <OBJBASE.H> in the module that you will use to contain those storage definitions. INITGUID.H redefines *DEFINE_GUID* to emit storage. You will then have an .OBJ file containing the GUID storage, which when linked into your program will resolve the pending references of the external declarations elsewhere in your program, just as would the version included from a library.

This becomes complicated only when you include precompiled headers (PCH) in the mix. Since the PCH will include a definition of *DEFINE_GUID* that does not emit storage, you need to eschew PCH for the scope of the single module that will define the GUID. I typically create a single GUIDS.CPP file that includes OBJBASE.H, INITGUID.H, MAPIGUID.H, and my GUID definitions, then compile that file without PCH.

MAPIGUID.H is a very clean header file: you can create a file of OBJBASE.H, INITGUID.H, and MAPIGUID.H, and it will compile without errors. I like that because GUIDS.CPP takes long enough to compile without including every header file in the Win32/MAPI/OLE/ActiveX/YOURMOTHER universe. Unfortunately, EXCHEXT.H is not as clean. Therefore, if your GUIDS.CPP must include EXCHEXT.H, it has other requirements that slow your builds. For that reason, I cut and paste the necessary *DEFINE_GUID* clauses from EXCHEXT.H into my GUIDS.CPP instead of including the file as usual.

The *DEFINE_GUID* macro, defined in the Win32 SDK header files OBJBASE.H and INITGUID.H, uses the symbol *INITGUID* to switch between two forms: one form of the macro emits static data definitions, suitable for linking into a program, whereas the other emits declarations for references to that data definition. Most source files in this sample form project include this local header file when it is necessary to resolve a reference to the symbol *CLSID_StubSendForm*. The source file must remain small, because the project cannot compile the source file while using precompiled headers. Only a single source file, Chap06\Sendstub-\GUIDS.CPP, defines the *INITGUID* symbol. That same source file contains the definitions of all other GUID symbols not imported from libraries such as UUID.LIB. In the following excerpt from the GUID.CPP file, you see the use of symbols such as *USES_IID_IMessage* plus the MAPIGUID.H header file to obtain a local definition of an *IID* (interface identifier GUID):

```
#define INITGUID

#include <objbase.h>
#include <initguid.h>

#define USES_IID_IMAPIProp
#define USES_IID_IMessage
#define USES_IID_IMAPIFormAdviseSink
#define USES_IID_IMAPIForm
#define USES_IID_IPersistMessage

#include <mapiguid.h>
#include "guids.h"
```

Just as it does with its message class, the form presents its CLSID to the forms library at its installation time. The field CLSID in the Description section of SENDSTUB.CFG shows this. Also examine the file SENDSTUB.REG, which contains a sample system registry entry for the form server. Ordinarily the MAPI Forms Manager generates this registry entry by using information supplied in the forms library registration. However, any application that installs its form server in the local forms library container—or any developer who would test that form server with minimum interference from the MAPI Forms Manager—must also completely install that form server in the system registry. The following registry entry (from the SENDSTUB.REG file) provides template information for such an installation:

```
REGEDIT

HKEY_CLASSES_ROOT\CLSID\{da32e202-97b8-11cf-b6a6-08002b2b3625} =
    IPM.Note.StubTest
```

```
HKEY_CLASSES_ROOT\CLSID\{da32e202-97b8-11cf-b6a6-08002b2b3625}
    \InprocHandler32 = mapi32.dll
HKEY_CLASSES_ROOT\CLSID\{da32e202-97b8-11cf-b6a6-08002b2b3625}
    \LocalServer32 = c:\Chap06\sendstub\sendstub.exe
```

The discussion of interfaces and registration of forms has prepared us to discuss the structure of a form server.

Common Scaffolding

Every MAPI form server must conform to the out-of-process model. Such a form server needs a certain structure to occupy its own process: a *WinMain* entry point (with a strategy for cracking a command line and for initializing MAPI), a message pump on its primary thread, the registration and eventual revocation of the class object, and finally the implementation of the class object itself. While this section examines this structure as implemented in Chap06\Sendstub, the other samples in this chapter—the stub post form Poststub and the somewhat more complex Catform—use the same structure as well.

Entry point

The stub send form has a very simple structure. Upon entry, it registers a number of window classes and loads some strings from its resources so that it can display error messages if a disaster occurs. The source file Chap06\Sendstub\MAIN.CPP contains the canonical *WinMain* function, which calls a number of classes declared in Chap06\Sendstub\UI.H that encapsulate all window support. The following code excerpt from the *WinMain* function of the MAIN.CPP file shows the registration of the window classes and the loading of strings:

```
int WINAPI WinMain(HINSTANCE hInstance, HINSTANCE, LPSTR pszCmd,
    int)
{
    // Load strings, register window classes.

    if ( !CUICommon::Init(hInstance) || !CUIMain::Init() ||
        !CUISendForm::Init() || !CUIReadForm::Init() )
        return 1;

    // Create a top-level window for the server.

    CUIMain ui;
    if (!ui.Start())
        return 1;
    CClassFactory::SetServerUI(&ui);
    ⋮
```

Once enough infrastructure exists that the server can display a message box, it examines the command line for parameters that have been passed, using a utility class *CCmdLine* (defined in Chap06\Sendstub\CMDLINE.CPP and CMDLINE.H). Ordinarily, only the System COM Library launches the server; hence the presence of any command line switches other than */Embedding* indicates an error, as does the absence of that switch. As a special case, the following code excerpt from the *WinMain* function contains some code to install and uninstall the server in debugging scenarios:

```
    :
    CCmdLine cmdline;
    if (!cmdline.Parse(pszCmd))
    {
        ui.Message(IDS_USAGE);
        return 1;
    }
    if (cmdline.HasHelpFlag())
    {
        ui.About();
        return 0;
    }
#if defined(TEST_LOCAL_FORM_LIBRARY)
    if (cmdline.HasInstallFlag() && cmdline.HasUninstallFlag())
    {
        ui.Message("Make up your mind!");
        return 1;
    }
    if (cmdline.HasInstallFlag())
    {
        return Install(ui);
    }
    if (cmdline.HasUninstallFlag())
    {
        return Uninstall(ui);
    }
#endif
    if (!cmdline.HasCOMFlag())
    {
        ui.Message(IDS_USAGE);
        return 1;
    }
    :
```

MAPI initialization

As discussed previously, MAPI forms always operate against the session of the viewer that launched the form. A form server therefore dispenses with the usual call to *MAPILogonEx* that obtains a session;[9] instead, the server's forms receive the session and every other necessary MAPI artifact from the message site object handed to their *IPersistMessage* interface. Nevertheless, like every other process that uses MAPI,[10] the form server initializes the MAPI subsystem within its own process before it avails itself of any MAPI interfaces.

In the following continuation of the *WinMain* function, the stub send form passes the gauntlet of command line parsing and can initialize MAPI, undoing this step shortly before terminating.

```
    ⋮
    HRESULT hr = MAPIInitialize(NULL);
    if (FAILED(hr))
    {
        ui.Message(IDS_MAPI_INIT_FAILED);
        return 1;
    }

    int nRet = 3;
    {
        CStubFactory factory;
        assert(SUCCEEDED(factory.HrGetError()));

        if (SUCCEEDED(factory.HrGetError()))
            nRet = ui.RunMessagePump();
    }

    MAPIUninitialize();
    return nRet;
}
```

---

9. You last saw this in Chap02\Mfetch\MFETCH.CPP. Yes, it's been a while, hasn't it?

10. Contrast this to the in-process client extensions of Chapter 4, which dispense with this step by virtue of operating within another process—the Exchange client—that has already initialized MAPI.

Class object

When the System COM Library spawns a server process, it expects that server process to return a class object for each of that server's objects. Once the system recognizes that class object, the system can establish the necessary interprocess communication channels for clients to use the objects of the server process. Every form server must therefore register a class object for its supported forms as soon as possible after starting; otherwise, the system assumes that the server spawn failed and, after a couple of retries, reports failure to the requesting client.

The stub send form creates and registers its class object immediately after initializing MAPI. For a form server, the action of initializing MAPI will not take an unduly long time, since some other MAPI client—if nothing else, the viewer requesting the presence of the form—will already have loaded MAPI. If the server requires some more lengthy initialization sequence, you might want to defer that until after registering its class objects, setting a flag in the class object to wait for the remainder of the necessary process setup before servicing object creation requests. As shown in the following excerpt from the MAIN.CPP file, the class object operates within the scope of the *CStubFactory* object, which remains until the server terminates its message pump:

```
    ⋮
    {
        CStubFactory factory;
        assert(SUCCEEDED(factory.HrGetError()));

        if (SUCCEEDED(factory.HrGetError()))
            nRet = ui.RunMessagePump();
    }
    ⋮
```

The *CStubFactory* object is declared in the source file FACTORY.H, as follows:

```
class CStubFactory: public CClassFactory
{
public:
    CStubFactory();
    ~CStubFactory();
protected:
    virtual HRESULT NewObject(IUnknown** ppunk);
};
```

The source file Chap06\Sendstub\FACTORY.CPP contains the following implementation of this *CStubFactory* object:

```
// Derived methods

HRESULT CStubFactory::NewObject(IUnknown** ppunk)
{
    if (NULL == ppunk)
        return E_INVALIDARG;

    IUnknown* punk = CStubSendForm::Create(this);

    if (NULL == punk)
        return E_OUTOFMEMORY;

    *ppunk = punk;
    return NOERROR;
}


CStubFactory::CStubFactory(): CClassFactory(CLSID_StubSendForm)
{
    // ...
}


CStubFactory::~CStubFactory()
{
    // ...
}
```

To facilitate code reuse between the different form server examples, *CStubFactory* uses a base C++ class, *CClassFactory*, that embodies most of its COM class object functionality.

In the previous excerpt, note that *CStubFactory* was derived from *CClassFactory*. The constructor of this derived class passes the CLSID of the class object *StubSendForm* to the base C++ class *CClassFactory*. To create instances of *CStubSendForm* component objects, the functions of the *CStubSendForm* class call the virtual function *NewObject*, which calls the static member function *CStubSendForm::Create*.

All the interesting class object manipulation and activity takes place in the base C++ class *CClassFactory*. Every instance of this object represents a particular class object. As shown above in the constructor of its derived C++ class *CStubFactory*, *CClassFactory* accepts the CLSID of its class as a parameter to its constructor.

When the stub send form server constructs its instance of its class object, the *CClassFactory* base class first translates its given CLSID into a string, then registers that string in the global atom table. Declaration of the methods and variables required to do this are shown in the following excerpt from the FACTORY.H file:

```
class CClassFactory: public IClassFactory
{
private:
    ATOM _atmRunning;
    ULONG _nRegistered;
    ULONG _cRef;              // Count of references
    HRESULT _hrInit;

    static void CALLBACK CloseServerCheck();
    static ULONG _cObjs;      // Count of active objects
    static ULONG _cLocks;     // Count of active locks

    // Lets the module shut down the server
    static CUICommon* _puiServer;

public:
    CClassFactory(REFCLSID clsid);
    ~CClassFactory();
    HRESULT HrGetError() const
    { return _hrInit; }

    // The methods of IUnknown

    STDMETHODIMP QueryInterface (REFIID riid, void** ppvObj);
    STDMETHODIMP_(ULONG) AddRef();
    STDMETHODIMP_(ULONG) Release();

    // The methods of IClassFactory

    STDMETHODIMP CreateInstance(IUnknown* punkOuter, REFIID riid,
        void** ppvObject);
    STDMETHODIMP LockServer(BOOL fLock);
```

```
    // Called by any object from a derived factory
    static void CALLBACK ObjDestroyedCallback();

    // Called once, at application startup
    static void SetServerUI(CUICommon* pui)
        { _puiServer = pui; }

protected:
    // Define this method per factory.
    virtual HRESULT NewObject(IUnknown** ppunk) = 0;
};
```

Registration of the CLSID in the atom table and error checking to determine the validity of the newly created class object are shown in the following excerpt from the FACTORY.CPP file:

```
CClassFactory::CClassFactory(REFCLSID clsid)
    : _cRef(1), _hrInit(NOERROR), _atmRunning(0), _nRegistered(0)
{
    TCHAR szCLSID[40];
#ifdef _UNICODE
    StringFromGUID2(clsid, szCLSID, sizeof(szCLSID));
#else
    {
        WCHAR wszCLSID[40];
        int nRet = StringFromGUID2(clsid, wszCLSID,
            sizeof(wszCLSID));
    assert(nRet > 0);
    BOOL fOk = WideCharToMultiByte(CP_ACP, 0, wszCLSID, -1,
        szCLSID, sizeof(szCLSID)/sizeof(TCHAR), NULL, NULL);
    if (!fOk)
    {
        _hrInit = HRESULT_FROM_WIN32(::GetLastError());
        return;
    }
    }
#endif

    // The MAPI Forms Manager uses this atom to detect whether a
    // factory is running.
    _atmRunning = ::GlobalAddAtom(szCLSID);
    :
```

After the CLSID is registered in the global atom table, the MAPI Forms Manager checks for the presence of that atom to determine whether a server is running. This checking is necessary so that the Forms Manager does not try to delete the files that implement a running server. This deletion might occur when the Forms Manager tries to make room in the local computer's storage for the files of a new MAPI form server that will be downloaded from a forms library. In the preceding example, also note that the Win32 error code is converted to an HRESULT when a COM Unicode string cannot be converted into the correct character set of the process. Clients of *CClassFactory* (and by public C++ inheritance, *CStub-Factory*) use the *_hrInit* member variable and its corresponding accessor member function *HrGetError* to determine the validity of the newly created class object.

After adding this atom, the server registers its COM class object, saving the returned cookie in a member variable for the eventual revocation of the object. Because the C++ class inherits from *IClassFactory*, the object itself contains the vtable necessary for implementing the COM class object, with the C++ class containing the methods of the COM interface as virtual member functions. (This is very similar to the way in which the C++ classes implemented the Exchange client extensions in Chapter 4.) The class object makes itself available for multiple use, allowing MAPI to load the server once for many instances of the form; details of this will follow when we examine the form server's message pump. The following excerpt from the *CClassFactory::CClassFactory* function shows the registration of the class factory:

```
    ⋮
// Register the class factory.
HRESULT hr = ::CoRegisterClassObject(clsid,
    (IClassFactory*)this, CLSCTX_LOCAL_SERVER,
    REGCLS_MULTIPLEUSE, &_nRegistered);
if (FAILED(hr))
{
    _hrInit = hr;
    return;
}
}
```

When the server terminates, it revokes this class object so that no clients attempt to use it. The server then removes the global atom to free MAPI to delete its files. This takes place in the destructor of the C++ base class, as shown in the following excerpt from the FACTORY.CPP file:

```
CClassFactory::~CClassFactory()

// There may be a few references left.
// They are from COM itself and will disappear
```

```
    // after the factory revokes the class object.

{
    if (_nRegistered)
    {
        ::CoRevokeClassObject(_nRegistered);
        _nRegistered = 0;
    }

    if (_atmRunning != 0)
        ::GlobalDeleteAtom(_atmRunning);
}
```

While the class object supports *IUnknown*, its reference-counting implementation works a little differently than usual. Most C++ classes implementing COM objects follow a canonical reference-counting technique. As shown in the following functions from the FACTORY.CPP file, the COM objects increment a counter variable upon *IUnknown::AddRef* and decrement it upon *IUnknown-::Release*, committing object suicide in response to the *delete this* line of code when the reference count falls to zero:

```
STDMETHODIMP_(ULONG) CClassFactory::AddRef()
{
    ++_cRef;
    return _cRef;
}

STDMETHODIMP_(ULONG) CClassFactory::Release()
{
    // COM will not release its final references until
    // the server revokes its class object.

    ULONG ulCount = --_cRef;
    if (1L == ulCount)
    {
        // Instead of "delete this," check the server
        // and shut it down if possible.
        CloseServerCheck();
    }
    return ulCount;
}
```

However, the reference count of a COM class factory never falls to zero within its lifetime, since upon the server registering its class object, COM establishes one or more references to that object in the course of establishing interprocess communication. COM does not release those references until the server revokes the class object.

To resolve this mutual embrace, we ignore the factory's reference count when determining object lifetime. Instead, we terminate the server when it is servicing no objects and when no client has locked it into memory. The class factory implementation therefore keeps its reference count (*_cRef*) strictly as an advisory counter, depending on the count of outstanding objects (*_cObjs*) and locks (*_cLocks*) to control its lifespan. The FACTORY.CPP file contains the following *CClassFactory::CloseServerCheck* function, which is called at suitable occasions to signal the hosting server process to close.

```
void CClassFactory::CloseServerCheck()
{
    if ((CClassFactory::_cLocks == 0) &&
        (CClassFactory::_cObjs == 0))
    {
        if (CClassFactory::_puiServer)
            CClassFactory::_puiServer->Close();
    }
}
```

Upon the termination of the server's message pump, the factory C++ object, which is created on the stack, unlike most C++ objects implementing component objects, goes out of scope and, in its destructor, revokes its class object.

Every time an object from this factory self-destructs, that object calls back to the class factory. The class factory adjusts its counter of outstanding objects and considers whether its life work is done. (Class factories lead a very angst-ridden existence.) This is shown in the following *CClassFactory::ObjDestroyedCallback* function from the FACTORY.CPP file:

```
void CALLBACK CClassFactory::ObjDestroyedCallback()
{
    assert(CClassFactory::_cObjs > 0);
    --CClassFactory::_cObjs;

    CloseServerCheck();
}
```

A class factory supports the notion of a server lock through the following *IClass-Factory::LockServer* method from the FACTORY.CPP file:

```
STDMETHODIMP CClassFactory::LockServer(BOOL fLock)
{
    if (fLock)
    {
        ++CClassFactory::_cLocks;
    }
```

```
    else
    {
        assert(CClassFactory::_cLocks > 0);
        --CClassFactory::_cLocks;

        CloseServerCheck();
    }
    return NOERROR;
}
```

This method allows the client to keep its server in memory even while the server is hosting no objects. MAPI uses server locks to leave its last few form servers cached in memory, thus speeding the invocation of subsequent instances of those forms. This stub send form server supports server lock requests with a counter member variable, _cLocks_, that the form server checks whenever it considers terminating.

The *LockServer* supports the class object so that the class object can offer its primary method, *IClassFactory::CreateInstance*. A client invokes this method on a class object to get a new instance of the object of that class, in this case, a MAPI form object. The C++ base class of this sample calls down to a virtual member function to create the instance of the actual form object, then dynamically queries that object for the precise interface desired by the client. Since querying a new interface results in a new reference against the object, this function must release the original interface before returning the new interface to the client. In the following *CreateInstance* function from the FACTORY.CPP file, note the maintenance of the _cObjs_ counter that controls the lifetime of the server:

```
STDMETHODIMP CClassFactory::CreateInstance(IUnknown* punkOuter,
    REFIID riid, void** ppvObject)
{
    if (NULL == ppvObject)
        return E_INVALIDARG;
    *ppvObject = 0;

    // Aggregation is not supported.

    if (NULL != punkOuter)
        return CLASS_E_NOAGGREGATION;

    IUnknown* punk = NULL;
    HRESULT hr = NewObject(&punk);
    if (FAILED(hr))
        return hr;
```

(continued)

```
    hr = punk->QueryInterface(riid, ppvObject);
    punk->Release();
    if (FAILED(hr))
        return hr;

    ++CClassFactory::_cObjs;
    return NOERROR;
}
```

After the class object is registered in the constructor of *CClassFactory*, it awaits requests through the methods of its *IClassFactory* interface. The class factory creates new instances of form objects and returns them to callers, with the System COM Library and MAPI's remote interface code ensuring that those objects span the cross-process void.

Message pump

The stub send form uses a single main thread, hosting a single message pump. Off of this single thread, it can host multiple form objects, just as it promises in the *REGCLS_MULTIPLEUSE* parameter that it specifies when registering its class object. Each of these form objects offers its own top-level frame window for a user interface.

During its life, the server maintains a single invisible top-level window to host its message pump and to receive interprocess communications from COM and MAPI. The server creates this window in the *WinMain* function, immediately after registering all window classes. The class factory code uses this window to close down the server when it is idle and unlocked, as shown above in the *CClassFactory::CloseServerCheck* function.

In the following excerpt from the *WinMain* function (see the file Chap06\Send-stub\MAIN.CPP), the top-level window for the server is created where it subsequently hosts the message pump:

```
⋮
// Create the top-level window for the server.

CUIMain ui;
if (!ui.Start())
    return 1;
CClassFactory::SetServerUI(&ui);
⋮
int nRet = 3;
{
    CStubFactory factory;
    assert(SUCCEEDED(factory.HrGetError()));

    if (SUCCEEDED(factory.HrGetError()))
        nRet = ui.RunMessagePump();
}
```

```
    MAPIUninitialize();
    return nRet;
}
```

Through interprocess communication brokered through the top-level window, the server receives the cross-process requests for new form objects, which, in turn, it controls through additional interprocess communication. For each form object, the server can create a corresponding form user interface object, depending on the frame window of that form. This is accomplished either through the *CUISendForm* or *CUIReadForm* interfaces from the UI.CPP file of the Sendstub project. Since the server can host multiple form objects, it also can host multiple frame windows, each possibly with a different parent window, or frame windows modal to some parent window. To correctly dispatch windowing messages through the accelerator tables and embedded controls of each of these windows, the server maintains a list of all its form user interface objects and peruses that list at message dispatch time. This multiplexing message pump resides in Chap06\Sendstub\UI.CPP along with all the other windowing code. Because *CUIMain* inherits from *CUICommon*, the main server message pump (called in the *WinMain* function) is defined by the following *CUICommon::RunMessagePump* function:

```
int CUICommon::RunMessagePump()
{
    MSG msg;

    while (::GetMessage(&msg, 0, 0, 0))
    {
        CUIForm* pui;

        // Dispatch to correct form window.

        for (pui = ::PuiFirst; pui != NULL; pui = pui->GetNext())
        {
            if (pui->TranslateMessage(&msg))
                break;
        }

        if (pui == NULL)
        {
            ::TranslateMessage(&msg);
            ::DispatchMessage(&msg);
        }
    }
    return (msg.wParam);
}
```

Limited by its single message pump thread, the server can host only a single modal form user interface object at a time. When a form client requests this modal user interface, the server sets the global flags *::FModalUp* and *::HwndUp*, then drops into a modal message loop for that single user interface window. These global flags, referenced throughout UI.CPP, control whether the server will allow another form object to present its user interface. The single thread and message pump of the server require this limitation.

```
void CUIForm::RunModalMessagePump()
{
    _fIsModal = TRUE;

    const BOOL fOldModalUp = ::FModalUp;
    const HWND hwndOldUp = ::HwndUp;

    ::FModalUp = TRUE;
    ::HwndUp = _hwnd;

    const HWND hwndOwner = ::GetWindow(_hwnd, GW_OWNER);
    const BOOL fEnableOwner = ::IsWindowEnabled(hwndOwner);
    ::EnableWindow(hwndOwner, FALSE);

    // Assume that the enabled state of the first sibling we find
    // is the same as that of all other siblings.

    const CUIForm *puiSibling =
        (::PuiFirst == this) ? GetNext() : ::PuiFirst;
    const BOOL fEnableSiblings =
        (puiSibling == NULL) ? TRUE:
        ::IsWindowEnabled(puiSibling->_hwnd);
    CUIForm *pui;
    for (pui = ::PuiFirst; pui != NULL; pui = pui->GetNext())
    {
        if (this != pui)
            ::EnableWindow(pui->_hwnd, FALSE);
    }

    MSG msg;
    while (!_fDeletePending && (::GetMessage(&msg, NULL, 0, 0)))
    {
        // Instead of running down the form chain,
        // look only at its own form.

        if (!TranslateMessage(&msg))
        {
            ::TranslateMessage(&msg);
```

```
        ::DispatchMessage(&msg);
    }
}

// Reenable siblings and owner as appropriate.

for (pui = ::PuiFirst; pui != NULL; pui = pui->GetNext())
{
    if (this != pui)
        ::EnableWindow(pui->_hwnd, fEnableSiblings);
}

::EnableWindow(hwndOwner, fEnableOwner);

::FModalUp = fOldModalUp;
::HwndUp = hwndOldUp;

delete this;
}
```

Subsequent calls into the server to display the user interface first check the state of the global flags. If any modal form is running, calls to the *CUIForm::IsLocked-OutByModalForm* function will return the error code *OLEOBJ_S_CANNOT_DO-VERB_NOW*, which indicates that the object cannot perform the requested action, even though the request was valid. Once the modal form closes, the server clears the *::FModalUp* and *::HwndUp* flags. For more information on the context of these calls, see the *IsLockedOutByModalForm* function (in the file Chap06\Sendstub\UI.CPP), which was called at the beginning of the *CStubSend-Form::HrOpenForm* function (in the file Chap06\Sendstub\FORM.CPP).

Implementing a Basic Send Form

For our first form, we'll examine the stub send form server discussed in all the examples in this chapter so far. The stub send form implements an exceptionally simple, yet still addressable and sendable form. As its message class *IPM-.Note.StubTest* indicates, the stub send form is essentially compatible with the standard send note *IPM.Note*, starting with the functionality of the standard send note, then subtracting functions when possible. Therefore, the stub send form has the following limitations:

- It supports no rich text and no form of attachment.

- It displays no Cc or Bcc fields in its addressing header.

- It has no Move, Copy, or Save As commands in its user interface.

- It implements Print and Save As commands from the client in only the most rudimentary manner.

- It defers Forward and Reply To All commands from the client to the standard send note as implemented by the Exchange client.

- It creates a message without conversation indexes, the properties that support the conversation grouping features of the Exchange client.

Most of the stub send form's properties are created in the source files Chap06-\Sendstub\FORM.H and FORM.CPP. These files contain declaration and implementation of the object returned by the *CreateInstance* method of the server's class factory. This object is an instance of the C++ class *CStubSendForm*, the anatomy of which we will dissect later in this section.

Object creation

The C++ class *CStubSendForm* declares its constructor as protected, forcing clients to use its static member function *CStubSendForm::Create* to create instances of the class. You saw this called above, within the function *CStubFactory::NewObject*. Primarily, this ensures that the server always creates instances of the class on the heap, allowing the class to use the *delete this* self-destruction idiom safely. In the following *CStubSendForm::Create* function, the object is returned to the caller with a reference count of 1:

```
IUnknown* CStubSendForm::Create(IClassFactory* pfact)
{
    CStubSendForm* pfrm = new CStubSendForm(pfact);
    if (NULL == pfrm) // If the task allocator failed
        return NULL;

    // When created, the object has a reference count of 0 the
    // constructor. This indirection returns the object to the
    // caller with a reference count of 1, ensuring that the AddRef
    // will be external if we're enforcing that, and allowing
    // the IUnknown to manage separate vtables, again, if we're
    // enforcing that (USE_SEPARATE_VTABLE_REFCOUNTS).

    IUnknown* punk = NULL;
    (void)pfrm->QueryInterface(IID_IUnknown, (void**)&punk);
    return punk;
}
```

Construction and destruction contain few surprises. When the form object is created, it saves a reference to its class factory,[11] so that the form can create additional copies of itself for implementing the Compose - Reply command. When destroyed, the form object releases this reference and then notifies the class factory so that it can perform its close-server check.

---

11. See the arguments to the operator *new* for an example of this.

The form class uses the standard reference-counting idiom. When the last client of the form releases its references, the form object terminates its own existence. The following *AddRef* and *Release* functions implement the reference-counting idiom:

```
STDMETHODIMP_(ULONG) CStubSendForm::AddRef()
{
    ++_cRef;
    return _cRef;
}

STDMETHODIMP_(ULONG) CStubSendForm::Release()
{
    ULONG ulCount = --_cRef;
    if (!ulCount)
        delete this;

    return ulCount;
}
```

Managing vtables

The central form object inherits from three interfaces: *IMAPIForm*, *IPersist-Message*, and *IMAPIFormAdviseSink*, implementing the methods of all three as members of a single C++ class. This greatly simplifies both managing the state of the form object and having the methods of one interface return information from another, because all three can share member variables. This is shown in the following excerpt from the FORM.H header file:

```
class CStubSendForm : public IPersistMessage, public IMAPIForm,
    public IMAPIFormAdviseSink
{
private:
    ULONG _cRef;

    CLastError      _lasterr;
    CViewNotifier   _viewnotify;
    :
```

However, debugging can be made easier if each interface maintains its own reference counts, so that you, the developer, can precisely target interface leaks. To this end, FORM.CPP and FORM.H implement separate vtable objects that consist of nothing more than the vtable of a particular interface, a separate reference count, and a pointer to the actual implementation of the interface methods, which are all built conditionally on *USE_SEPARATE_VTABLE_REF-COUNTS*. As shown in the following excerpt from FORM.H, the form object class declares each auxiliary vtable, such as that for the *IPersistMessage* interface, as classes private to the form object class.

```
          ⋮
#if defined(USE_SEPARATE_VTABLE_REFCOUNTS)

    // Keep separate reference counts and interface objects
    // for each interface supported.

    class CTablePM: public IPersistMessage
    {
    private:
        ULONG _cRef;
        IPersistMessage* _pImplementation;

    public:
        CTablePM(IPersistMessage*);

        MAPI_IUNKNOWN_METHODS(IMPL);
        MAPI_GETLASTERROR_METHOD(IMPL);
        MAPI_IPERSISTMESSAGE_METHODS(IMPL);
    } _tablePM;
```

The implementation of the vtable object forwards all its calls to the actual implementation in the class, maintaining its own additional reference count for debugging interest only. As shown in the following functions (see the FORM.CPP file), the form object gives each embedded vtable object a pointer to the outer form object when the form constructs its contained objects:

```
CStubSendForm::CTablePM::CTablePM(IPersistMessage* pImpl)
    : _cRef(0), _pImplementation(pImpl)
{ }

STDMETHODIMP CStubSendForm::CTablePM::QueryInterface(REFIID riid,
    void** ppvObj)
{
    return _pImplementation->QueryInterface(riid, ppvObj);
}

STDMETHODIMP_(ULONG) CStubSendForm::CTablePM::AddRef()
{
    ++_cRef;
    return _pImplementation->AddRef();
}

STDMETHODIMP_(ULONG) CStubSendForm::CTablePM::Release()
{
    --_cRef;
    return _pImplementation->Release();
}
```

```
STDMETHODIMP CStubSendForm::CTablePM::GetLastError(HRESULT hr,
    ULONG ulFlags, MAPIERROR** pperr)
{
    return _pImplementation->GetLastError(hr, ulFlags, pperr);
}


STDMETHODIMP CStubSendForm::CTablePM::GetClassID(CLSID* pclsid)
{
    return _pImplementation->GetClassID(pclsid);
}


STDMETHODIMP CStubSendForm::CTablePM::IsDirty()
{
    return _pImplementation->IsDirty();
}


STDMETHODIMP CStubSendForm::CTablePM::InitNew(
    IMAPIMessageSite* pmsgsite, IMessage* pmsg)
{
    return _pImplementation->InitNew(pmsgsite, pmsg);
}


STDMETHODIMP CStubSendForm::CTablePM::Load(
    IMAPIMessageSite* pmsgsite, IMessage* pmsg,
    ULONG ulMessageStatus, ULONG ulMessageFlags)
{
    return _pImplementation->Load(pmsgsite, pmsg,
        ulMessageStatus, ulMessageFlags);
}


STDMETHODIMP CStubSendForm::CTablePM::Save(IMessage* pmsg,
    ULONG fSameAsLoad)
{
    return _pImplementation->Save(pmsg, fSameAsLoad);
}


STDMETHODIMP CStubSendForm::CTablePM::SaveCompleted(IMessage* pmsg)
{
    return _pImplementation->SaveCompleted(pmsg);
}


STDMETHODIMP CStubSendForm::CTablePM::HandsOffMessage()
{
    return _pImplementation->HandsOffMessage();
}
```

Finally, the form object's implementation of *IUnknown::QueryInterface* returns pointers to these separate vtable objects when needed. As a result, external clients always call through one of the embedded vtable objects when these clients invoke methods on form interfaces, including *AddRef* and *Release*. This lets the developer track references to each interface and track internal references against external references. This tracking is possible because internal references—those made as calls against the *IUnknown* implementation of *CStubSendForm* itself (instead of against its embedded auxiliary vtables)—appear as the difference between the reference count of the form and the sum of the reference counts of its embedded tables.

Note here the special use of the class member variable *_state*. Ordinarily that variable tracks the *IPersistMessage* state, such as the Normal or No Scribble state, of a particular form object. After a form has been forcibly closed, however, it is dead to the world and can only respond to *IUnknown*. In COM terms, it is no longer a form. The form object uses an additional form state value *stateDead* to enforce this distinction.

Note also that the form implements the form advise sink (through the *IMAPIFormAdviseSink* interface) in the same object as the form proper (through the *IMAPIForm* and *IPersistMessage* interfaces). Although a client is not supposed to query from a form to a sink or vice versa because the two are separate objects, the following implementation of *QueryInterface* (from the FORM.CPP file) does not prevent it:

```
STDMETHODIMP CStubSendForm::QueryInterface(REFIID riid, void** ppvObj)
{
    *ppvObj = NULL;

    HRESULT hr = S_OK;
    IUnknown* punk = NULL;

    // After shutdown, this object is d-e-a-d.
    // Ensure that it responds only to IUnknown.

    if (stateDead == _state && IID_IUnknown != riid)
        return _lasterr.Set(E_NOINTERFACE);

    if (( IID_IUnknown == riid) || ( IID_IPersistMessage == riid))
    {
#if defined(USE_SEPARATE_VTABLE_REFCOUNTS)
        punk = (IPersistMessage*)&_tablePM;
#else
        punk = (IPersistMessage*)this;
#endif
    }
```

```
        else if (IID_IMAPIForm == riid)
        {
#if defined(USE_SEPARATE_VTABLE_REFCOUNTS)
            punk = (IMAPIForm*)&_tableMF;
#else
            punk = (IMAPIForm*)this;
#endif
        }
        else if (IID_IMAPIFormAdviseSink == riid)
        {
#if defined(USE_SEPARATE_VTABLE_REFCOUNTS)
            punk = (IMAPIFormAdviseSink*)&_tableMFAS;
#else
            // The baseform object implements both the form and the sink.
            punk = (IMAPIFormAdviseSink*)this;
#endif
        }
        else
            hr = _lasterr.Set(E_NOINTERFACE);

        if (NULL != punk)
        {
            *ppvObj = punk;
            punk->AddRef();
        }

        return hr;
}
```

Implementing *IPersistMessage*

Whether or not the form server uses separate vtable reference counts, every call
to a method on an interface ends up in the implementation on the C++ class
itself.

IPersistMessage::GetLastError   The class *CStubSendForm*, along with every
other form sample in this book, defers all error state management to its member
variable *_lasterr*, an embedded instance of *CLastError*. The use of this variable is shown in the following *CStubSendForm::GetLastError* function (see the
FORM.CPP file):

```
STDMETHODIMP CStubSendForm::GetLastError(HRESULT hr, ULONG ulFlags,
    MAPIERROR** pperr)
{
    // Delegated to the helper class.

    return _lasterr.HrGetLastError(hr, ulFlags, pperr);
}
```

The class *CLastError* is defined in the header file Chap06\Sendstub\LASTERR.H, with its implementation appearing in LASTERR.CPP. The *CLastError* interface is responsible for keeping track of the last error to befall the form object so that a client, upon invoking a failed method on the form, can query the form for additional information about why the method failed. Throughout its implementation of the interfaces *IPersistMessage* and *IMAPIForm*, the form object will make note of errors by calling *CLastError::Set* on its embedded instance of this class, recording the error for posterity.

IPersistMessage::GetClassID   There is little for a form server's *IPersistMessage-::GetClassID* method to do. Since this form object knows the CLSID of itself at compile time, the form object copies that value into its out-parameter after validating that out-parameter as writable. In the following implementation of the *GetClassID* method, note the use of the *CLastError::Set* to record errors:

```
STDMETHODIMP CStubSendForm::GetClassID(CLSID* pclsid)
{
    // Validate the out-parameter.
    if (IsBadWritePtr(pclsid, sizeof(CLSID)))
        return _lasterr.Set(E_INVALIDARG);

    *pclsid = CLSID_StubSendForm;
    return NOERROR;
}
```

If a NULL parameter somehow sneaks through this or any other method, or if the server crashes for any other reason, the client receives the error code *RPC-_E_SERVERFAULT* in response to its method invocation. The client continues to operate, its integrity protected by the process boundary, as depicted in Figure 6-21. Only the form server would die. Compare this to the much less graceful death that the Exchange client suffers when one of its in-process client extensions decides to divide by 0.

IPersistMessage::IsDirty   The viewer calls the *IPersistMessage::IsDirty* method to determine whether a form contains any changes that it needs to write to its backing message. The stub send form example contains two possible loci of dirtiness: the user interface, where the user could have changed the contents of a control through typing, or the addressing fields, which, while visible in the user interface, are actually managed by the form object itself. The *IsDirty* method is shown in the following code from the FORM.CPP file:

```
STDMETHODIMP CStubSendForm::IsDirty()
{
    // If the dirty state is known, return that.

    if (_fDirty)
        return S_OK;

    // If AdrList has been set, propagate its dirty state.
    if (_fDirtyAdrlist)
    {
        _fDirty = TRUE;
        return S_OK;
    }

    // Nothing form-side is dirty... check the user interface.

    if (NULL == _pui)
    {
        _fDirty = FALSE;
        return S_FALSE;
    }

    _fDirty = _pui->IsDirty();
    return _fDirty ? S_OK : S_FALSE;
}
```

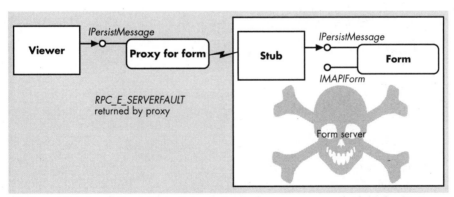

The form object attempted to divide by 0, terminating the form server process that hosts the object.

Figure 6-21. *The viewing client learns of a fault in a form server through an error code from the remote procedure call layer.*

Note the member variable *_pui*, which the form object has set to the user interface object, if the form has any user interface. This member variable is a pointer to an instance of the class *CUIForm*, as declared in the header file Chap06-\Sendstub\UI.H. Where different flavors of user interface are possible, the *CUIForm* class uses virtual member functions to abstract these differences to its client, the form object. The *CUIForm::IsDirty* function is one such virtual member function, since the version of the form that appears for a delivered message does not allow the user to modify the subject field.

IPersistMessage::InitNew   When the viewer wishes to associate a form with a brand new, unsent message (for example, when the user requests to compose a new instance of the message), the viewer invokes the *IPersistMessage::InitNew* method on the form.

As shown in the following example from the FORM.CPP file, *InitNew* has a very straightforward implementation:

```
STDMETHODIMP CStubSendForm::InitNew(IMAPIMessageSite* pmsgsite,
    IMessage* pmsg)
{
    // Refuse the call if the state is invalid for an InitNew
    // transition. Returns E_UNEXPECTED rather than
    // CO_E_ALREADYINITIALIZED, etc.

    switch (_state)
    {
    case stateUninit:
    case stateHandsOffAfterSave:
    case stateHandsOffFromNormal:
        break;

    default:
        return _lasterr.Set(E_UNEXPECTED);
    }

    // Validate arguments (trivially).

    if (NULL == pmsgsite || NULL == pmsg)
        return _lasterr.Set(E_INVALIDARG);
    ⋮
```

First the server verifies that the form is in a state that can accept this call, returning *E_UNEXPECTED* if this is not the case. Next it performs some trivial validation of the parameters passed: a reference to a message site object plus a reference to the message embedded within the message site object. The latter prevents the form from having to call back immediately through the message site.

Seeing that these two references are valid (or at least that they are not NULL), the form increments their reference count and saves them in member variables. This allows subsequent functions to reference the objects for reading and writing as necessary in accordance with other method invocations on the form. If those member variables held any previous object references, the form releases those previous references before overwriting the contents of the member variables with the new references; this is a standard defensive programming idiom, theoretically unnecessary in the form, since a call to *InitNew* should arrive only when the form is in a state where it has no such pending references to other messages and messages sites. Once the form has the new references saved safely away, it fetches a couple of additional parameters that it knows it will need soon from the message site.

After adding a couple of additional default values, the form has all its internal data in the correct initial state. There remains only to clear the form's dirty state and reset any user interface present; the member function *PutDataIntoUI* knows to treat any NULLs in instance variables as empty strings or the like. This is shown in the following continuation of the *InitNew* method:

```
    ⋮
// Grab the current message site, etc., from the caller.

pmsgsite->AddRef();
pmsg->AddRef();
ReleaseEverything();
_pmsgsite = pmsgsite;
_pmsg = pmsg;
pmsgsite->GetSiteStatus(&_ulSiteStatus);
pmsgsite->GetSession(&_psess);

// Create initial default values.

_ulMsgStatus = 0;
_ulMsgFlags = MSGFLAG_UNSENT;


// Some properties to consider for default values:

// PR_DELETE_AFTER_SUBMIT
// PR_IMPORTANCE
```

(continued)

```
// PR_ORIGINATOR_DELIVERY_REPORT_REQUESTED
// PR_PRIORITY
// PR_READ_RECEIPT_REQUESTED
// PR_SENSITIVITY
// PR_SENTMAIL_ENTRYID


// A new message is clean until it is explicitly dirtied
// by the user.

ClearDirty();

if (_pui)
    PutDataIntoUI();
    ⋮
```

Finally, as shown in the following conclusion of the *InitNew* method, the form completes initialization by passing into the Normal state and then notifying any registered view advise sinks that it is working with a new message:

```
    ⋮
// State transition: -> Normal

_state = stateNormal;

// Notify any registered view advise sinks.

_viewnotify.OnNewMessage();

return S_OK;
}
```

The member *_viewnotify* consists of an instance of a helper class *CViewNotifier*, declared in Chap06\Sendstub\VIEWNTFY.H. Like the *CLastError* class, the *CViewNotifier* helper class exists to implement a piece of repetitive functionality, here the *IMAPIForm::Advise* function, plus all maintenance and notification of view advise sinks given to it.

IPersistMessage::Load   The method *IPersistMessage::Load* works very much like the *IPersistMessage::InitNew* function, except that it is given more information about the message and makes the form read its values from the given message instead of accepting defaults. While the form passes a couple of those values as parameters, the form digs other values out of the properties on the passed message interface, as shown in the following excerpt from the FORM.CPP file:

```
STDMETHODIMP CStubSendForm::Load(IMAPIMessageSite* pmsgsite,
    IMessage* pmsg, ULONG ulMsgStatus, ULONG ulMsgFlags)
{
    // Refuse the call if the state is invalid for an InitNew
    // transition.

    // Returns E_UNEXPECTED rather than CO_E_ALREADYINITIALIZED,
    // etc.

    switch (_state)
    {
    case stateUninit:
    case stateHandsOffAfterSave:
    case stateHandsOffFromNormal:
        break;

    default:
        return _lasterr.Set(E_UNEXPECTED);
    }

    // Validate arguments (trivially).

    if (NULL == pmsgsite || NULL == pmsg)
        return _lasterr.Set(E_INVALIDARG);

    // Grab the current message site, etc., from the caller.

    pmsgsite->AddRef();
    pmsg->AddRef();
    ReleaseEverything();
    _pmsgsite = pmsgsite;
    _pmsg = pmsg;
    pmsgsite->GetSiteStatus(&_ulSiteStatus);
    pmsgsite->GetSession(&_psess);

    _ulMsgStatus = ulMsgStatus;
    _ulMsgFlags = ulMsgFlags;
```

(continued)

```
        // Dig into the message....

        HRESULT hr = HrLoadFrom(pmsg, ulMsgFlags);
        if (FAILED(hr))
            return hr; // Cascade--already set

        // A newly loaded message is clean until it is explicitly
        // dirtied by user.

        ClearDirty();

        // State transition: -> Normal.

        _state = stateNormal;


        if (_pui)
            PutDataIntoUI();

        // Notify any registered view advise sinks.

        _viewnotify.OnNewMessage();

        return S_OK;
    }
```

The stub form server digs into a message in the following *CStubSendForm-::HrLoadFrom* member function:

```
HRESULT CStubSendForm::HrLoadFrom(IMessage* pmsg, ULONG ulMsgFlags)
{
    HRESULT hr = HrLoadValFrom(pmsg);
    if (FAILED(hr))
        return hr;

    if (ulMsgFlags & MSGFLAG_UNSENT)
        hr = HrLoadAdrlistFrom(pmsg);

    return hr;
}
```

HRLoadFrom first reads the message to retrieve a number of properties that it uses to populate the user interface, keeping the results in a vector of *SPropValue* pointers. What happens next depends on whether the message has been sent or not. If the message was never sent, the form reads whatever address list currently exists on the message so that it can populate the displayed user interface and allow the user to continue modifying the recipient table. If the message was already sent, the form can avoid opening the address list, making do with the property *PR_DISPLAY_TO* read into the property value vector.

Examining the server's code to read properties from a message reveals a couple of common idioms. The function declares, in parallel, a sized property tag array, like the one used in a call to *IMAPIProp::GetProps*, and an enumeration. Each element in the enumeration indexing is an element in the property tag array, and the last element in the enumeration indexes the total number of items in the array. If the call to *GetProps* returns successfully, each element in the enumeration also indexes the appropriate item in the returned property value array. The code also expects the *PR_BODY* property to prove too large to read back in a single column of the set, so it makes allowance to stream that large property into memory and then patch the property value array. This is shown in the following implementation of the *HrLoadValFrom* method of the FORM.CPP file:

```
HRESULT CStubSendForm::HrLoadValFrom(IMessage* pmsg)
{
    assert(pmsg);

    MAPIFreeBuffer(_pval);
    _pval = NULL;

    enum {ivalMsgFlags, ivalSubject, ivalNormSubject, ivalClass,
        ivalFrom, ivalDate, ivalBody, ivalTo, cvalMsg };

    SizedSPropTagArray(cvalMsg, tagaRead) = { cvalMsg, \
        { PR_MESSAGE_FLAGS, PR_SUBJECT, PR_NORMALIZED_SUBJECT, \
        PR_MESSAGE_CLASS, PR_SENDER_NAME, PR_CLIENT_SUBMIT_TIME,
        PR_BODY, PR_DISPLAY_TO } };

    ULONG cval = 0L;
    HRESULT hr = pmsg->GetProps((SPropTagArray*)&tagaRead, 0,
        &cval, &_pval);
    if (FAILED(hr))
        return _lasterr.Set(hr, pmsg);

    if (PROP_TYPE(_pval[ivalBody].ulPropTag) == PT_ERROR &&
        _pval[ivalBody].Value.l == MAPI_E_NOT_ENOUGH_MEMORY)
```

(continued)

```
    {
        hr = HrStreamInAux(pmsg, PR_BODY, _pval,
            &_pval[ivalBody].Value.LPSZ);
        if (FAILED(hr))
        {
            MAPIFreeBuffer(_pval);
            _pval = NULL;

            return hr; // Cascade back--lasterr already set in form.
        }
        else
        {
            // Fixed it, so patch proptag to remove PT_ERROR.
            _pval[ivalBody].ulPropTag = PR_BODY;
        }
    }
}

assert(cval == cvalMsg);
_cvalMax = cval;
    ⋮
```

Note that the function saves the indexes of successfully retrieved values into member variables for future reference. It examines the property tag at the index corresponding to a particular property to determine whether that tag matches the expected value; if it fails to match (for example, when the call to *GetProps* returns a PT_ERROR type in that column), the function sets the index to *IVAL-_INVALID*, denoting that no such property exists in the array. The object retains the property value array in its member *_pval*, saving much complexity in copying and memory allocation. When the time comes to free this array, the client need only call *MAPIFreeBuffer* on the topmost pointer to the array; MAPI takes care of the rest, having chained the storage for every subject within the array onto the first buffer using the *MAPIAllocateMore* function. This works even if the caller had to stream in data from the message body because the server's stream-in function *CStubSendForm::HrStreamInAux* uses a similar technique, taking the name of the buffer onto which to append newly allocated memory as well as the name of the buffer into which to stream.

The *HrLoadValFrom* is continued in the following excerpt:

```
    ⋮
// Set indices into pval.

_ivalBody = (_pval[ivalBody].ulPropTag == PR_BODY)
    ? ivalBody : IVAL_INVALID;
_ivalFrom = (_pval[ivalFrom].ulPropTag == PR_SENDER_NAME)
    ? ivalFrom : IVAL_INVALID;
```

```
    _ivalSubject = (_pval[ivalSubject].ulPropTag == PR_SUBJECT)
        ? ivalSubject : IVAL_INVALID;
    _ivalNormSubject = (_pval[ivalNormSubject].ulPropTag ==
        PR_NORMALIZED_SUBJECT)
        ? ivalNormSubject : IVAL_INVALID;
    _ivalClass = (_pval[ivalClass].ulPropTag == PR_MESSAGE_CLASS)
        ? ivalClass : IVAL_INVALID;
    _ivalDate = (_pval[ivalDate].ulPropTag == PR_CLIENT_SUBMIT_TIME)
        ? ivalDate : IVAL_INVALID;
    _ivalTo = (_pval[ivalTo].ulPropTag == PR_DISPLAY_TO)
        ? ivalTo : IVAL_INVALID;

    return NOERROR;
}
```

A look at the function that reads the address list is less enlightening, if only because it requires less code. Note that the MAPI utility function *HrQueryAllRows* can treat an address list as a row set. Note also that *FreePadrlist*, like all the other MAPI functions for releasing memory including *FreeProws* and *MAPIFreeBuffer*, does nothing when passed a NULL parameter.[12]

The following implementation of the *HrLoadAdrlistFrom* function (from the FORM.CPP file) reads the address list:

```
HRESULT CStubSendForm::HrLoadAdrlistFrom(IMessage* pmsg)
{
    assert(pmsg);

    ::FreePadrlist(_padrlist);
    _padrlist = NULL;

    IMAPITable* ptbl = NULL;
    HRESULT hr = pmsg->GetRecipientTable(0, &ptbl);
    if (FAILED(hr))
        return _lasterr.Set(hr, pmsg);

    // Address lists are isomorphic with Rowsets.
    hr = HrQueryAllRows(ptbl, NULL, NULL, NULL, 0,
        (SRowSet**)&_padrlist);
```

(continued)

---

12. If you're as used to the *if (p) free(p), if (punk) punk->Release()* idiom as I am, you may find this jarring. I certainly do.

```
        if (FAILED(hr))
        {
            _lasterr.Set(hr, ptbl);
        }

        ptbl->Release();
        return hr;
}
```

IPersistMessage::Save   When the client calls the *IPersistMessage::Save* method (and only then)[13] the form writes its data into the specified message. The client specifies whether it is calling the *Save* method to save the form's data back into the same message from which the form loaded its data. In this case, the form can assume that the message contains all fixed properties and needs only incremental changes. Otherwise, if the form is saving its data to a message other than the one from which the form was loaded, the form needs to create a complete copy of its message, adhering to the message class schema of the message specified in a parameter to the *Save* function. The *CStubSendForm::Save* method of the Chap06\Sendstub\FORM.CPP file implements both courses of action through two calls to the utility function *CStubSendForm::HrSaveInto*. As shown in the following excerpt, the second call to the *HrSaveInto* function saves a cloned version of the original message, thus inducing a full-save scenario.

```
STDMETHODIMP CStubSendForm::Save(IMessage* pmsg,
    ULONG fSameAsLoad)
{
    // Only forms in the Normal state can be saved.
    if (stateNormal != _state)
        return _lasterr.Set(E_UNEXPECTED);

    // Validate arguments (trivially).
    // A NULL message is legitimate when it is saving into the same
    // message as loaded.

    if (!fSameAsLoad && NULL == pmsg)
        return _lasterr.Set(E_INVALIDARG);
```

---

13. Contrast this to *IPersistStorage*, where the server remains free to write into its storage at any time during the Normal state.

```
    HRESULT hr;
    if (fSameAsLoad)
    {
        // If pmsg is non-NULL, this indicates an emergency
        // low-memory save situation. No special handling is
        // indicated for this stub form.

        // Save in-place.
        hr = HrSaveInto(_pmsg);
    }
    ⋮
```

The function knows that the *HrSaveInto* member function has already set the last error for any error return. Hence, as shown in the following lines of the *Save* function, it simply cascades back the error return, without needing to call *_lasterr.Set* redundantly:[14]

```
    ⋮
    if (FAILED(hr))
        return hr; // Cascade--already set
    ⋮
```

If the function succeeds, the form passes into the No Scribble state, where it waits for a call to either the *IPersistMessage::SaveCompleted* or the *IPersistMessage-::HandsOffMessage* function. The *Save* function also saves the *fSameAsLoad* flag to help determine the correct course of action if the viewer next calls the *IPersistMessage::SaveCompleted* function. This is shown in the concluding lines of the *Save* function:

```
    ⋮
    _state = stateNoScribble;
    _fSameAsLoaded = fSameAsLoad;
    return S_OK;
}
```

---

14. The member variable *_lasterr* is an instance of the class *CLastError* (declared in LASTERR.H) that tracks the last error state for subsequent use in implementing the form's *GetLastError* method. Its *CLastError::Set* function records the last error state.

In the Sendstub example, the *HrSaveInto* function contains all the logic for writing properties into a message, providing the logical complement to the *CStubSendForm::HrLoadFrom* function. This simple example of a form makes no attempt to differentiate a new save from an incremental save; instead, it continuously writes all its properties that can be set. If the form has an *ADRLIST* structure and has set the flag indicating changes therein, the form replaces the recipient table on the message with its own address list. After that, the form goes to its user interface to update the contents of its value array *_pval* and then builds an array (*rgvalToWrite*) of the property values that it wants to write into the message from the values at specific indexes (for example, *_ivalSubject*). As shown in the following excerpt, the function copies each *SPropValue* structure from its value array into the *rgvalToWrite* array without regard for reference counts or pointer duplication; since the array harmlessly passes out of scope at the end of the function, this is fine.

> **NOTE** The ADRLIST structure contains information describing the recipients on an address list, including the recipients' display names, messaging system types, messaging system addresses, and entry identifiers.

```
HRESULT CStubSendForm::HrSaveInto(IMessage* pmsg)
{
    HRESULT hr = NOERROR;

    // If we have an address list and have modified it,
    // write it into the message.

    if (_padrlist && _fDirtyAdrlist)
    {
        hr = pmsg->ModifyRecipients(0, _padrlist);
        if (FAILED(hr))
        {
            _lasterr.Set(hr, pmsg);
            return hr;
        }
    }

    // Get the array that we'll use for outgoing data.

    SPropValue rgvalToWrite[20];
    int ival = 0;

    // From the user interface, set data into pval array.
```

```
GetDataFromUI();
assert(IsValidIval(_ivalSubject));
assert(IsValidIval(_ivalBody));
rgvalToWrite[ival++] = _pval[_ivalSubject];
rgvalToWrite[ival++] = _pval[_ivalBody];
⋮
```

During a save operation, the form always writes its own message class into the message, regardless of the original message class. To understand why, imagine a scenario in which this form handles a message for a subclass of its intended message class, such as *IPM.Note.StubTest.Example.Unconvincing*. As demonstrated in Figure 6-22, if this form sets its own properties on that message, the schema of the actual subclass could be violated, creating a hybrid message with the original message class, but with the property semantics of the superclass.

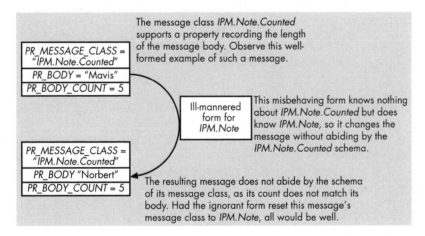

Figure 6-22. *If a form changes a message that has a subclass of its intended message class, that form must coerce the message into its own message class, lest the resulting message violate the schema of the subclass.*

Therefore, as shown in the following excerpt from the *HrSaveInto* function, the sample form coerces all messages into its own class:

```
⋮
// Coerce the message into this form's message class
// to avoid the "object slicing" problem.

rgvalToWrite[ival].ulPropTag = PR_MESSAGE_CLASS;
rgvalToWrite[ival++].Value.lpszA = SZ_FORM_MESSAGE_CLASS;
⋮
```

When the form saves an unsent message, it sets the message delivery time property itself to have the last-saved time appear in the viewer for that message. At other times, the spooler provides the correct setting for this value, as shown in the following lines from the *HrSaveInto* function:

```
      ⋮
    // Generate timestamps as needed.
    // Most of the time, the spooler handles this.
    // Set a "message delivery time" property on a saved message
    // so that it appears sorted in a useful order.

    FILETIME ft;
    GetSystemTimeAsFileTime(&ft);

#if 0 // Send form doesn't need this one.
    rgvalToWrite[ival].ulPropTag = PR_CLIENT_SUBMIT_TIME;
    rgvalToWrite[ival++].Value.ft = ft;
#endif
    rgvalToWrite[ival].ulPropTag = PR_MESSAGE_DELIVERY_TIME;
    rgvalToWrite[ival++].Value.ft = ft;
      ⋮
```

With the value array built, the *HrSaveInto* function calls *IMAPIProp::SetProps* on the given message to set the new values into the message. However, just as *IPersistStorage::Save* does not commit any changes it makes to its storage, the form defers to its caller the committing of property changes using the *Save-Changes* method. If the message body proves too large to write out, the *HrSave-Into* function calls the *CStubSendForm::HrStreamOutAux* function (sister to the *CStubSendForm::HrStreamInAux* function) to finish the job. This is shown in the concluding lines of the *HrSaveInto* function:

```
    // Everything to set is now in rgvalToWrite.
    // The variable ival, indexing the next available cell
    // in the array, works here as the count.

    SPropProblemArray* pProblems = NULL;
    hr = pmsg->SetProps(ival, rgvalToWrite, &pProblems);
    if (FAILED(hr))
    {
        _lasterr.Set(hr, pmsg);
        return hr;
    }

    // Expected problem: PR_BODY is too big to set this way.
    // Workaround: stream it out if we must.
```

```
    if (pProblems)
    {
        for (unsigned i = 0; i < pProblems->cProblem; ++i)
        {
            // Run down the array until we find the body property.

            if (PR_BODY == pProblems->aProblem[i].ulPropTag &&
                MAPI_E_NOT_ENOUGH_MEMORY ==
                pProblems->aProblem[i].scode)
            {
                hr = HrStreamOutAux(pmsg, PR_BODY,
                    _pval[_ivalBody].Value.LPSZ);
                // lasterr already set
                break;
            }
        }

        MAPIFreeBuffer(pProblems);
        pProblems = NULL;
    }

    return hr;
}
```

IPersistMessage::SaveCompleted   With the *IPersistMessage::SaveCompleted* method, the caller takes a form out of limbo. The form could have serviced an *IPersistMessage::Save* call, an *IPersistMessage::HandsOffMessage* call, or a *Save* call followed by a *HandsOffMessage* call. Typically, this method has very little to do. It hangs onto the new message interface, if such was provided; completes the save by clearing its dirty state and notifying clients if its past history (current state, plus possibly the *fSameAsLoaded* parameter from the last call to the *IPersistMessage::Save* function) so mandates; and moves back to the Normal state. The Sendstub form example is completely typical in this regard, as shown in the following *SaveCompleted* function from the Chap06\Sendstub\FORM.CPP file:

```
STDMETHODIMP CStubSendForm::SaveCompleted(IMessage* pmsgNew)
{
    // State validation.
    // SaveCompleted takes the object from the Hands Off or No
    // Scribble state back to normal mode. It is illegal at any
    // other time.

    switch ( _state )
    {
    case stateHandsOffFromNormal:
```

(continued)

```
        case stateHandsOffAfterSave:
        case stateNoScribble:
            break;

        default:
            return _lasterr.Set(E_UNEXPECTED);
        }


        // Parameter validation.
        // If the object is reverting from Hands Off state,
        // it must receive a storage to use.

        if (stateNoScribble != _state && NULL == pmsgNew)
            return _lasterr.Set(E_INVALIDARG);

        // If the caller supplies a new message interface, use it.
        // Unless the form has to open subobjects on the new message,
        // this cannot fail.

        // If this somehow failed, we'd return E_OUTOFMEMORY and remain
        // in the Hands Off or No Scribble state.

        if (NULL != pmsgNew)
        {
            // Call AddRef before release, in case pmsg == _pmsg.
            pmsgNew->AddRef();
            if (NULL != _pmsg)
            {
                // The form will have dropped this reference in a Hands
                // Off state.
                assert(_state == stateNoScribble);
                _pmsg->Release();
            }
            _pmsg = pmsgNew;
        }


        switch (_state)
        {
        default:
            assert(FALSE);
        case stateHandsOffFromNormal:
            // This SaveCompleted did not complete a save, but instead
            // completed a rename or move or the like.
            // Picking up the new storage was all the activity needed.
            break;
```

```
        case stateNoScribble:
            // This SaveCompleted completed a save without an intervening
            // HandsOffStorage.
            if (pmsgNew == NULL && !_fSameAsLoaded)
            {
                // Saved to another storage. The current form is
                // still dirty.
                break;
            }
            // Otherwise, saved to current storage.
            // Fall through to next case....

        case stateHandsOffAfterSave:
            // This SaveCompleted completed a save with an intervening
            // HandsOffStorage.
            _viewnotify.OnSaved();

            // Reset the dirty bits.
            ClearDirty();

            break;
    }

    _state = stateNormal;
    return S_OK;
}
```

IPersistMessage::HandsOffMessage   An implementation of the *IPersistMessage-::HandsOffMessage* method has even less to do than the *IPersistMessage::Save-Completed* method: it must release any message interfaces that it holds, first recursively calling the *IPersistStorage::HandsOffStorage* function and the *IPersist-Message::HandsOffMessage* function on any embedded persistent storage and message objects, and then transitioning into the appropriate state of catatonia. Again, the following *HandsOffMessage* function from the FORM.CPP file is completely typical, not even having any embedded objects to manage.

```
STDMETHODIMP CStubSendForm::HandsOffMessage()
{
    // State validation.
    // Since this function is so simple, handle the state transition
    // here as well.
```

(continued)

```
    switch ( _state )
    {
    case stateNormal:
        _state = stateHandsOffFromNormal;
        break;
    case stateNoScribble:
        state = stateHandsOffAfterSave;
        break;
    default:
        return _lasterr.Set(E_UNEXPECTED);
    }

    // "Freeze! Drop your message!"

    // All forms in the Normal/No Scribble state will have
    // a message.

    assert(_pmsg != NULL);
    if (_pmsg != NULL)
    {
        _pmsg->Release();
        _pmsg = NULL;
    }

    // The form is now in Hands Off mode, where it can do almost
    // nothing other than close.
    return S_OK;
}
```

Recycling the *IPersistMessage* implementation   Much of the stub send form's *IPersistMessage* implementation can be reused with only a little more work than renaming the class from *CStubSendForm* to *CYourNameHere*.

■ First and foremost, the new form must have a unique CLSID.

■ The auxiliary member functions *CStubSendForm::HrLoadFrom* and *CStubSendForm::HrSaveInto* must reflect the schema of the new form.

■ The new form must correct the saved indexes to reflect the new schema and to update the places where those indexes are set and reset. The indexes are set and reset in methods other than in the *HrLoadFrom* and *HrSaveInto* methods, such as in the *CStubSend-Form::ResetPval* method or in the *CStubSendForm* constructor.

- The stub send form uses the *CStubSendForm::GetDataFromUI* and *CStubSendForm::PutDataIntoUI* functions to glue its user interface object to its backing data. Any change in either the schema or the user interface mandates a change in these functions, which serve as the bindings of a sort of poor man's model-view-controller framework.

Implementing *IMAPIForm*

As with the *IPersistMessage* implementation, the major part of a form server's *IMAPIForm* implementation consists of rote presentations of standard method implementations.

IMAPIForm::GetLastError   Because the vtable entry point for *IMAPIForm::GetLastError* points to the same function as *IPersistMessage::GetLastError*, see the section "*IPersistMessage::GetLast Error*" on page 323 for further details of its implementation.

IMAPIForm::SetViewContext   The viewer calls the *IMAPIForm::SetViewContext* method to give the form a view context within which to operate. The form will use this view context for determining the previous and next messages in the currently viewed sequence and for determining certain other attributes of the form's working environment.

The stub send form has a completely canonical implementation of the *SetViewContext* method. It saves a reference to the given view context, along with the status DWORD of that context. If this view context indicates that the form is operating in an interactive manner—in other words, if the form appears to the user in a window that must be dismissed by some action—the form gives that view context the form's advise sink. This enables the form to learn of certain kinds of activity within the view. Finally, if the form has any user interface showing, it updates that user interface to reflect the status of the new view.

The code for the *CStubsendForm::SetViewContext* function in the Chap06\Sendstub\FORM.CPP file is as follows:

```
STDMETHODIMP CStubSendForm::SetViewContext(IMAPIViewContext *pvwctx)
{
    if (pvwctx != NULL) // Do this before the release.
        pvwctx->AddRef();

    if (_pvwctx != NULL)
    {
        // Remove the form's advise sink from the previous
        // view context.
```

(continued)

343

```
_pvwctx->SetAdviseSink(NULL);
        _pvwctx->Release();
    }
    _pvwctx = pvwctx;

    _ulViewStatus = 0;
    if (pvwctx != NULL)
    {
        pvwctx->GetViewStatus(&_ulViewStatus);

        // Give form's advise sink to the new view context
        // if (and only if) we're in an interactive context.

        if (!(_ulViewStatus & VCSTATUS_INTERACTIVE))
        {
            // Note that the form object implements its own sink
            // object, and, therefore, simply passes "this" to
            // SetAdviseSink. When the proxy manager uses
            // QueryInterface for the expected interface to send
            // remotely, it will generate an external AddRef.

            pvwctx->SetAdviseSink(this);
        }
    }

    // Update the user interface with a new status.

    if (_pui)
        _pui->Update(_ulSiteStatus, _ulViewStatus);

    return S_OK;
}
```

IMAPIForm::GetViewContext   The sample form's implementation of the *IMAPI-Form::GetViewContext* method is even more canonical—and less interesting—than that of the *IMAPIForm::SetViewContext* method, returning a reference only to whatever view context the form has saved in its *_pvwctx* variable member. This is shown in the following *GetViewContext* method:

```
STDMETHODIMP CStubSendForm::GetViewContext(
    IMAPIViewContext** ppvwctxOut)
{
    // Validate the out-parameter.

    if (IsBadWritePtr(ppvwctxOut, sizeof(IMAPIViewContext*)))
        return _lasterr.Set(E_INVALIDARG);
```

```
    *ppvwctxOut = _pvwctx;

    if (_pvwctx == NULL)
    {
        return S_FALSE;
    }
    else
    {
        _pvwctx->AddRef();
            return S_OK;
    }
}
```

IMAPIForm::ShutdownForm   A client calls the *IMAPIForm::ShutdownForm* function to yield much the same result as calling the *IOleObject::Close* function on
an active embedded object. Under program control, the *ShutdownForm* function
closes the running form; whether or not the data in the form is saved depends
on the parameters passed to the method, which can be any of the *SAVEOPTS*
enumerations supported by the *IOleObject::Close* function. (See Table 6-8.) In
contrast, a closed embedded object remains an OLE object and could be re-
opened, but a form that has been shut down is no longer a form; it is a stub—
a smoking, burned-out shell of an object, fit only for the bit bucket. The
ShutdownForm method has two main types of client: viewers that are shutting down and need to bring down all open forms with them, and forms that
wish to close themselves for whatever reason, such as when the user invokes
the File - Delete or Compose - Reply To Sender commands on the form.

Enumeration	Description
SAVEOPTS_NOSAVE	Form data will not be saved
SAVEOPTS_PROMPTSAVE	The user will be prompted to save data related to the form
SAVEOPTS_SAVEIFDIRTY	Form data will be saved if the form has changed

Table 6-8. SAVEOPTS *enumerations that can be used in the* ulSaveOptions
parameter of the IMAPIForm::ShutdownForm *method.*

The shutdown implementation in the stub send form first validates its parameters and checks whether the form has already been shut down. As a special case,
the form supports calling *ShutdownForm* on a form already dead, since presumably any client doing so must have missed the original form-is-closing notification, which the form frequently rebroadcasts. A call to the server's auxiliary

345

member function *HrQuerySave* (discussed below) performs whatever save is specified in the *ulSaveOptions* parameter of the *ShutdownForm* function. If the caller specifies *SAVEOPTS_PROMPTSAVE* and the user presses Cancel, this function returns *MAPI_E_USER_CANCEL*, which the *ShutdownForm* function then relays to its caller. A caller receiving *MAPI_E_USER_CANCEL* from the *ShutdownForm* function should cease its own shutdown sequence in the face of the user's mandate.

Validation of the *ShutdownForm* method parameters and state is shown in the following excerpt from the Chap06\Sendstub\FORM.CPP file:

```
STDMETHODIMP CStubSendForm::ShutdownForm(ULONG ulSaveOptions)
{
    // Validate parameters.

    switch (ulSaveOptions)
    {
    default:
        return _lasterr.Set(E_INVALIDARG);
    case SAVEOPTS_NOSAVE:
    case SAVEOPTS_PROMPTSAVE:
    case SAVEOPTS_SAVEIFDIRTY:
        break;
    }

    // Validate state.

    switch (_state)
    {
    default:
    case stateDead:
        // Catch the case where the form has already shut down.
        _viewnotify.OnShutdown();
        return _lasterr.Set(E_UNEXPECTED);

    case stateUninit:
    case stateNormal:
    case stateNoScribble:
    case stateHandsOffAfterSave:
    case stateHandsOffFromNormal:
        break;
    }

    HRESULT hr = HrQuerySave(ulSaveOptions);
    if (FAILED(hr))
        return hr;
```

⋮

Having saved anything that needed saving, the form now turns its attention to shutting itself down. First, as shown in the following line of code, the form temporarily increments its own reference count by calling *IUnknown::AddRef*:

```
    ⋮
// Avoid self-destruction in any callbacks.
AddRef();
    ⋮
```

This is necessary to prevent premature self-destruction; as the form spreads the word of its impending demise, the various agencies that hold references to the form release those references, which might well result in the reference count dropping to 0 before the form gracefully destroys its own internal data structures.

Next, as shown in the following code, the form announces its coming shutdown to every view that registered for such notifications:

```
    ⋮
// Notify any views with an advise sink that we're shutting down.
// The preceding AddRef protects us against immolating ourselves
// when those views in turn release us.

_viewnotify.OnShutdown();
    ⋮
```

This results in each of those views releasing any references that they hold on this form.

Then the form releases every internal reference and frees every buffer that it holds. In the case of the example form, this includes revoking its own form advise sink on the currently saved view context before releasing that view context. Since the example form implements the form advise sink as part of the form object, this triggers the release of yet another reference against the form object. Next the form disposes of any outstanding user interface windows, which in turn causes the release of an internal reference that the user interface object held on the form object. This is shown in the following excerpt from the *ShutdownForm* function:

```
    ⋮
// Drop our own advise sinks, etc.

ReleaseEverything();

// Forcibly tear down the user interface.
// Note that the user interface holds (held) a reference to us.
```

(continued)

347

```
if (NULL != _pui)
{
    _pui->DeferredDelete(); // Delayed blast delete, for modal.
    _pui = NULL;
}
    ⋮
```

At this point, everything is dead. The form holds no references to any other object, and any object that was paying attention no longer holds references against the form. In the most common scenario of this form being launched and run by the Microsoft Exchange client, the form will have but one reference remaining: the one created initially by calling the *AddRef* function to prevent premature self-immolation. Revoking that reference results in the immediate destruction of the form object. Before doing this, however, the form marks itself as dead, so that it behaves properly[15] in the event that some other agency still holds a reference.

```
    ⋮
// "He's dead, Jim."
// From this point, the form responds only to IUnknown.

_state = stateDead;

// All clear! Release internal reference.
Release();

    return S_OK;
}
```

This is as good a time as any to describe the example's *CStubSendForm::HrQuerySave* member function. The *HrQuerySave* function interprets the given *SAVEOPTS* enumeration in light of the presence or absence of the form's user interface window, the form's dirty state, and, as appropriate, the will of the user. If the function deems a save necessary, it calls back through the current message site object to request that the viewer save the current message. This results in several reentries of the form server, because the viewer invokes the methods of the *IPersistMessage* interface to have the form make its data persistent within its own piece of the message.

---

15. The proper behavior of all dead things, including forms, is to lie very still and do nothing, other than slowly decompose. I do not advocate any sort of undead activity. Resurrection lies beyond the scope of this work.

The code for the *HrQuerySave* function is as follows:

```
HRESULT CStubSendForm::HrQuerySave(ULONG ulSaveOptions)
{

    // Do nothing.
    if (ulSaveOptions == SAVEOPTS_NOSAVE)
        return S_OK;

    // If clean, nothing to do--return immediately.
    if (IsDirty() != S_OK)
        return S_OK;

    if (ulSaveOptions == SAVEOPTS_PROMPTSAVE && NULL != _pui)
    {
        int nAnswer = _pui->Query(IDS_SAVECHANGES,
            (MB_ICONEXCLAMATION | MB_YESNOCANCEL));
        switch (nAnswer)
        {
        case IDCANCEL:
            return MAPI_E_USER_CANCEL;
        default:
            assert(FALSE);
        case IDNO:
            return S_OK;
        case IDYES:
            break;
        }
    }

    // This might result in a callback through IPersistMessage.

    HRESULT hr = _pmsgsite->SaveMessage();
    if (FAILED(hr))
        _lasterr.Set(hr, _pmsgsite);

    return hr;
}
```

IMAPIForm::DoVerb Everything that a form can do, it offers to the viewer through its *IMAPIForm::DoVerb* method. At the very least this includes showing itself, hiding itself, and opening itself to present the default user interface. For forms that implement anything even remotely resembling e-mail, this also includes forwarding and replying to a message. For forms that wish to interact richly with the viewer of the Microsoft Exchange client, this also includes saving the form to a disk file and sending the form to a printer so that the File - Print and File - Save As commands operate transparently against the form in the same manner as they do against Exchange's own intrinsic message types. With all of these different functions under its canopy, the *DoVerb* method tends to be the complicated member of the *IMAPIForm* interface family.

The viewer always supplies a rectangle specifying the desired size and position of the form's user interface window. The Microsoft Exchange client positions all the forms it displays with the current dimensions that it uses. Unfortunately, while Exchange changes those dimensions in response to the user moving and resizing those forms intrinsic to Exchange, Exchange offers no interface by which an external form server can tell the viewer that a user resized it. Hence, form objects always receive the size of the last Exchange note form in their *DoVerb* calls.

A viewer can also supply a pointer to a view context; if given, this view context overrides the form's currently set view context for the duration of the call to the *DoVerb* method. Typically, a viewer uses this view context to display a particular form modally or noninteractively. The stub send example form implements this by keeping two view contexts, one global (*_pvwctx*) and one per-verb (*_pvwctxPerVerb*), along with two corresponding view context status words, and by always using the per-verb view context if the *_pvwctx* variable is set. This is shown in the following excerpt from the *CStubSendForm::DoVerb* function of FORM.CPP:

```
STDMETHODIMP CStubSendForm::DoVerb(LONG iVerb,
    IMAPIViewContext* pvwctx, ULONG hwndParent,
    LPCRECT prcPosRect)
{
    if (NULL == prcPosRect)
        return _lasterr.Set(E_INVALIDARG);

    // The view context parameter overrides the form's default
    // context for the duration of the verb.

    if (pvwctx != NULL)
    {
        pvwctx->AddRef();
        _pvwctxPerVerb = pvwctx;
        pvwctx->GetViewStatus(&_ulViewStatusPerVerb);
    }

    HRESULT hr = S_OK;
    :
```

The heart of a *DoVerb* call typically consists of a *switch* statement used to select between the different verb codes recognized by the form. The stub send form uses two such *switch* constructs. One *switch* statement handles the verbs, mapping most of them to *EXCHIVERB_OPEN* while at the same time implementing *OLEIVERB_HIDE* in line and rejecting any inappropriate in-place activation verbs. This *switch* statement is shown in the following code from the *DoVerb* function:

```
    ⋮
// Handle the OLE default verbs: open, show, hide.

if (iVerb < 0L)
{
    switch (iVerb)
    {
    case OLEIVERB_OPEN:
    case OLEIVERB_SHOW:
        // Map each of these to the standard action.
        iVerb = EXCHIVERB_OPEN;
        break;

    case OLEIVERB_HIDE:
        if (_pui)
            pui->HideForm();
            break;

    default:
        // An in-place activation verb. Tell the container
        // to bug off.
        hr = _lasterr.Set(E_NOTIMPL);
        break;
    }
}
    ⋮
```

The other *switch* statement discriminates between the different verb codes assigned by the Exchange client and offers its own unique verb code as well: 1, which it implements as a synonym for *EXCHIVERB_REPLYTOSENDER*, albeit a synonym with its own listing on the client's Compose and per-item context menus. This *switch* statement is shown in the following code from the *DoVerb* function:

```
    ⋮
// Handle MAPI and form verbs, which might be a remapping
// of an OLE verb.
```

(continued)

```
BOOL fUnrecognized = FALSE;
if (iVerb >= 0)
{
    switch (iVerb)
    {
    case EXCHIVERB_FORWARD:
    case EXCHIVERB_REPLYTOALL:
    case EXCHIVERB_REPLYTOFOLDER:
        // The viewer should never ask these of us.
        assert(FALSE);
        // Fall through to the default.

    default:
        // An unrecognized verb. Treat as primary, then
        // complain.
        fUnrecognized = TRUE;
        // Fall through to the default.

    case EXCHIVERB_OPEN:
        hr = HrOpenForm((HWND)hwndParent, prcPosRect,
            CurrentViewStatus());
        if (SUCCEEDED(hr) && fUnrecognized)
            hr = _lasterr.Set(OLEOBJ_S_INVALIDVERB);
        break;

    case EXCHIVERB_REPLYTOSENDER:
    case 1: // "Respond"
        hr = HrRespondForm((HWND)hwndParent, prcPosRect);
        if (SUCCEEDED(hr))
        {
            _pvwctxPerVerb = NULL;
            ShutdownForm(SAVEOPTS_NOSAVE);
        }
        break;

    case EXCHIVERB_PRINT:
        hr = HrPrintForm();
        break;

    case EXCHIVERB_SAVEAS:
        hr = HrSaveAsForm();
        break;
    }
}
⋮
```

A more ambitious form might implement unique verb codes for delivering different views on its item, or else compose different forms in response to the current form.

A form object receives the verb codes of the standard Exchange client by listing a special extension property in its forms library registration. Since this form advertises itself as not implementing the Forward, Reply All, or Reply To Folder commands of the Compose menu, the verb *switch* statement flags the receipt of those verbs with an assertion check because the Exchange client should never send them to the form. However, as nothing prevents some other ill-behaved client from passing one of these codes to the form in a call to the *DoVerb* method, the flow-of-control upon receipt of these verbs falls through to the default case, which executes the default Open verb, then complains that the client requested an unknown verb.

In the concluding lines of the *DoVerb* function, the original view context is restored:

```
    :
    // Restore the original view context.

    if (NULL != _pvwctxPerVerb)
    {
        _pvwctxPerVerb->Release();
        _pvwctxPerVerb = NULL;
    }

    // Get the current status of the original context.

    _ulViewStatus = 0;
    if (_pvwctx != NULL)
    {
        _pvwctx->GetViewStatus(&_ulViewStatus);

        // Update the user interface with the new status.

        if (_pui)
            _pui->Update(_ulSiteStatus, _ulViewStatus);
    }

    return hr;
}
```

The stub send form server implements opening and showing the form's default view in its member function *CStubSendForm::HrOpenForm*. First the form server checks whether some other form is already running modal to another window; if so, this form server cannot deliver the goods, having but its single thread and message pump, so it regretfully declines the client's request. Next the form server checks whether the form already has some user interface; if so, it moves that window to the correct coordinates and then displays the window. This is shown in the following excerpt from the *HrOpenForm* function of the FORM.CPP file:

```
HRESULT CStubSendForm::HrOpenForm(HWND hwndParent,
    LPCRECT prcPosRect, ULONG ulViewFlags)
{
    // A modal form locks out all other forms until it closes.

    if (CUIForm::IsLockedOutByModalForm(hwndParent))
        return _lasterr.Set(OLEOBJ_S_CANNOT_DOVERB_NOW);

    // If this form already has a window,
    // move it to the specified coordinates and show it.

    if (_pui)
    {
        _pui->ShowFormHere(prcPosRect);
        return S_OK;
    }
    ⋮
```

After the form server displays the window, it must create the user interface object for the form. Because all the forms of this server operate as top-level windows, the server ignores the specified parent window unless the view context (either set on the form or per-verb) specifies modal operation. This is shown in the following lines from the *HrOpenForm* function:

```
    ⋮
    if (!(ulViewFlags & VCSTATUS_MODAL))
    {
        // If we are not modal, the parent becomes the desktop.
        hwndParent = NULL;
    }
    ⋮
```

When the form creates its user interface object, it uses the "unsent" message flag to differentiate between the two flavors of user interface that it offers: compose note and read note. A compose note appears when the message has not yet been sent; this note contains an editable subject line, allows the user to add and remove recipients from its address field, and offers the File - Submit command to deliver its message to the MAPI message spooler for processing and delivery. The other flavor of note, the read note, appears on messages lacking this flag; intended for viewing delivered messages, this note displays its subject and recipients in read-only controls, and lacks the File - Send command. Depending on the type of note it delivers, the form creates an instance of either *CUISend-Form* or *CUIReadForm* and saves a pointer to the resulting user interface object in its *_pui* member variable. It also notes the decision in its *_formtype* variable for use when the form must select different behaviors for the different note types in places other than in the user interface. After creating the actual window through the virtual member function *CUIForm::Start*, the form sets its controls with the proper values, moves the window to the correct location, and finally displays it. This is shown in the following continuation of the *HrOpen-Form* function:

```
    ⋮
// Must create a window for its user interface.
// _formtype discriminates between the two available window types.

if (_ulMsgFlags & MSGFLAG_UNSENT)
{
    _formtype = formtypeCompose;
    _pui = (CUIForm*) new CUISendForm(this);
}
else
{
    _formtype = formtypeRead;
    _pui = (CUIForm*) new CUIReadForm(this);
}

if (_pui == NULL)
    return _lasterr.Set(E_OUTOFMEMORY);

if (!_pui->Start(hwndParent))
    return _lasterr.Set(E_OUTOFMEMORY);

PutDataIntoUI();
_pui->ShowFormHere(prcPosRect);
    ⋮
```

If the form window is to be modal, the form drops into a modal message loop that repeats until either the user closes the window or the viewer shuts it down. Otherwise, the server returns here, leaving the window of the new user interface object visible on the display, where the user can interact with it through the server's main message loop. This is shown in the concluding lines of the *HrOpenForm* function:

```
    ⋮
    // If we are modal, we loop until the form is closed.
    if (ulViewFlags & VCSTATUS_MODAL)
    {
        _pui->RunModalMessagePump();
        // The modal message loop ended upon the death
        // of the window.
        // _pui is kaput.
    }

    return S_OK;
}
```

<table>
<tr><td>**NOTE**</td><td>For information on how the stub send note implements the other verbs, see the section "How to inherit the implementation of the Exchange client's standard form verbs" later in this chapter. We will not explore response forms until the next chapter, however, which discusses creating and manipulating form objects.</td></tr>
</table>

IMAPIForm::Advise   Viewers register a view advise sink with a form through the *IMAPIForm::Advise* method to receive notifications of changes that the viewer makes. The stub send form sample implements this method in a manner similar to its implementation of the *IMAPIForm::GetLastError* method—by delegating the call to an instance of a helper class. Here the instance is *_viewnotify*, and the helper class *CViewNotifier*.

```
STDMETHODIMP CStubSendForm::Advise(IMAPIViewAdviseSink * psink,
    ULONG* pnCookie)
{
    // Delegate advise requests to notify the helper.

    HRESULT hr = _viewnotify.Advise(psink, pnCookie);
    if (FAILED(hr))
    {
        hr = _lasterr.Set(hr);
    }
    return hr;
}
```

Declared in Chap06\Sendstub\VIEWNTFR.H, the view notifier helper stores the view advise sinks of the view contexts that request to register for notifications from the form and subsequently dispatches notifications to its sinks as the form dictates. Its implementation, as contained in VIEWNTFR.CPP, is simple, saving references to the given sinks in a small private array *_rgpsink*, and returning a 1-based index into that array as the connection number, with 0 being an invalid connection number. The code for the *CViewNotifier::Advise* function is as follows:

```
HRESULT CViewNotifier::Advise(IMAPIViewAdviseSink* psink,
    ULONG* pnCookie)
{
    if (NULL == psink)
        return E_INVALIDARG;
    if (IsBadWritePtr(pnCookie, sizeof(ULONG)))
        return E_INVALIDARG;

    for (int i = 0; i < MAXSINKS; ++i)
    {
        if (NULL == _rgpsink[i])
        {
            _rgpsink[i] = psink;
            _rgpsink[i]->AddRef();
            *pnCookie = (ULONG)(i+1); // 1-based cookie
            return S_OK;
        }
    }

    return E_OUTOFMEMORY;
}
```

IMAPIForm::Unadvise In the same way that it does the *IMAPIForm::Advise* call, the stub send form delegates *IMAPIForm::Unadvise* to the view notifier helper. Given the implementation of the *Advise* method, the *Unadvise* method contains no surprises. The following *CStubSendForm::Unadvise* function calls the *CViewNotifier::Unadvise* function:

```
STDMETHODIMP CStubSendForm::Unadvise(ULONG nCookie)
{
    // Like advise requests, the stub send form delegates to the
    // notify helper.

    HRESULT hr = _viewnotify.Unadvise(nCookie);
    if (FAILED(hr))
    {
        hr = _lasterr.Set(hr);
    }

    return hr;
}
```

The advise sink is actually released in the *CViewNotifier::Unadvise* function from the VIEWNTFR.CPP file:

```
HRESULT CViewNotifier::Unadvise(ULONG nCookie)
{
    if (nCookie == 0)
        return E_INVALIDARG;

    int i = (int)(nCookie-1);

    if (i >= MAXSINKS)
        return E_INVALIDARG;
    if (NULL == _rgpsink[i])
        return E_INVALIDARG;

    _rgpsink[i]->Release();
    _rgpsink[i] = NULL;
    return S_OK;
}
```

Having seen the *Advise* and *Unadvise* functions, you can no doubt predict how the view notifier helper dispatches notifications: by iterating across its small array of sinks and announcing the notification to any valid references that it finds. The following *CViewNotifier::OnShutdown* function from the VIEWNTFR.CPP file works just like any other dispatcher:

```
void CViewNotifier::OnShutdown()
{
    for (int i = 0; i < MAXSINKS; ++i)
    {
        if (NULL != _rgpsink[i])
        {
            _rgpsink[i]->OnShutdown();
        }
    }
}
```

Recycling the implementation of the *IPersistMessage* interface   As with its *IPersistMessage* implementation, much of the stub send form's *IMAPIForm* implementation invites convenient reuse. After adjusting the auxiliary member function *CStubSendForm::ReleaseEverything*, used elsewhere in the destructor and methods of *IPersistMessage*, *ShutdownForm* should work without further modification. You might also need to adjust the *CStubSendForm::IsDirty* function to reflect the new form's data and user interface structure.

The only real modification to *IMAPIForm* will take place within the many-tentacled monster *CStubSendForm::DoVerb* function, which must support the diverse verbs of the new form. All the auxiliary functions referenced by the *DoVerb* function might require extensive modification in the new form as well.

Implementing *IMAPIFormAdviseSink*

Forms can optionally implement a form advise sink object to receive notifications from viewers regarding activity in the view context. The form advise sink interface need not be on the form object; conceptually, the two are different objects with no requirement that one object support the interfaces of the other. Nevertheless, it is frequently convenient to implement the form advise sink within the form object, where it has full access to the members of the form object. For this reason, the stub send form delivers a single object that plays both roles, responding to *IUnknown::QueryInterface* requests for *IPersistMessage*, *IMAPIForm*, and *IMAPIFormAdviseSink* interfaces as well.

IMAPIFormAdviseSink::OnChange   Should the view context change the setting of the *VCSTATUS_PREV* or *VCSTATUS_NEXT* flags in its status, it will notify the form by calling the *IMAPIFormAdviseSink::OnChange* method of the form advise sink. The form responds to this by updating its user interface to reflect the new viewer status. The following implementation of the *CStubSendForm::OnChange* method is used to update the interface of the stub send form example:

```
STDMETHODIMP CStubSendForm::OnChange(ULONG ulFlags)
{
    // What's new in the view?

    if (_pvwctxPerVerb == NULL)
    {
        // Ignore OnChange notifications if operating in a per-verb
        // view context (i.e., as happens in a response).

        _ulViewStatus = ulFlags;

        // Update the user interface with the new status.

        if (_pui)
            _pui->Update(_ulSiteStatus, _ulViewStatus);
    }

    return S_OK;
}
```

Most of what's interesting in this function (okay, perhaps "interesting" is over-stating things a little) takes place in the following *CUIForm::Update* and *CUISendForm::AdjustMenu* functions (from the Chap06\Sendstub\UI.CPP file):

```
void CUIForm::Update(ULONG ulSiteStatus, ULONG ulViewStatus)
{
    AdjustMenu(GetMenu(GetHwnd()), ulSiteStatus, ulViewStatus);
}
    ⋮
void CUISendForm::AdjustMenu(HMENU hmenu, ULONG ulSiteStatus,
    ULONG ulViewStatus)
{
    EnableMenuItem(hmenu, ID_FILE_SUBMIT,
        MF_BYCOMMAND|((ulSiteStatus & VCSTATUS_SUBMIT) ?
        MF_ENABLED:MF_GRAYED));

    EnableMenuItem(hmenu, ID_FILE_DELETE,
        MF_BYCOMMAND| (!(ulViewStatus & VCSTATUS_READONLY) &&
        (ulSiteStatus & VCSTATUS_DELETE) ? MF_ENABLED:MF_GRAYED));
#if 0¹⁶
    EnableMenuItem(hmenu, ID_FILE_COPY,
        MF_BYCOMMAND| (!(ulViewStatus & VCSTATUS_READONLY) &&
        (ulSiteStatus & VCSTATUS_COPY) ? MF_ENABLED:MF_GRAYED));
    EnableMenuItem(hmenu, ID_FILE_MOVE,
        MF_BYCOMMAND| (!(ulViewStatus & VCSTATUS_READONLY) &&
        (ulSiteStatus & VCSTATUS_MOVE) ? MF_ENABLED:MF_GRAYED));
#endif
}
```

The stub send form keeps a very simple user interface, so its user interface object can update itself merely by calling its own virtual member function *AdjustMenu*. A particular flavor (compose or read) of the user interface object ends up exe-cuting the correct menu adjustment code (*CUISendForm::AdjustMenu* or *CUIRead-Form::AdjustMenu*). Each function examines the flags of the message site and view context status DWORD and enables or disables controls accordingly. The *CUIReadForm::AdjustMenu* function follows:

---

16. Even though the stub send form does not implement the Copy and Move commands, I include them here to demonstrate the correct message site and view context status handling.

```
void CUIReadForm::AdjustMenu(HMENU hmenu, ULONG ulSiteStatus,
    ULONG ulViewStatus)
{
    EnableMenuItem(hmenu, ID_FILE_SAVE,
        MF_BYCOMMAND| ((ulSiteStatus & VCSTATUS_SAVE)?
        MF_ENABLED:MF_GRAYED));
    EnableMenuItem(hmenu, ID_FILE_DELETE,
        MF_BYCOMMAND| (!(ulViewStatus & VCSTATUS_READONLY) &&
        (ulSiteStatus & VCSTATUS_DELETE) ? MF_ENABLED:MF_GRAYED));
#if 0
    EnableMenuItem(hmenu, ID_MESSAGE_COPY,
        MF_BYCOMMAND| (!(ulViewStatus & VCSTATUS_READONLY) &&
        (ulSiteStatus & VCSTATUS_COPY) ? MF_ENABLED:MF_GRAYED));
    EnableMenuItem(hmenu, ID_MESSAGE_MOVE,
        MF_BYCOMMAND| (!(ulViewStatus & VCSTATUS_READONLY) &&
        (ulSiteStatus & VCSTATUS_MOVE) ? MF_ENABLED:MF_GRAYED));
#endif
    EnableMenuItem(hmenu, ID_VIEW_ITEMABOVE,
        MF_BYCOMMAND|(ulViewStatus & VCSTATUS_PREV ?
        MF_ENABLED:MF_GRAYED));
    EnableMenuItem(hmenu, ID_VIEW_ITEMBELOW,
        MF_BYCOMMAND|(ulViewStatus & VCSTATUS_NEXT ?
        MF_ENABLED:MF_GRAYED));
    EnableMenuItem(hmenu, ID_COMPOSE_REPLY,
        MF_BYCOMMAND|(ulSiteStatus & VCSTATUS_NEW_MESSAGE ?
        MF_ENABLED:MF_GRAYED));
}
```

IMAPIFormAdviseSink::OnActivateNext When a viewer is executing its *IMAPIViewContext::ActivateNext* method, it calls back to the form advise sink of its current form to determine whether that form can handle the next message. If the form accedes, it will handle the new message, either in the current form object itself or else in a new form object that it returns.

The stub send form takes a common approach to handling activate next requests. If the message class of the new message precisely matches that of the form's own messages, the form agrees to take the new message. Otherwise, if the message class of the new message matches that of the message that the form is currently rendering, the form agrees to take the new message. If the form can handle the new message using the same user interface object as it uses for the current message, it will offer to let the viewer reuse the current object, by simply returning *S_OK*. Otherwise, the form acquires a new instance of itself and returns that to the caller. To get that new instance, the form returns to its own class factory; while this approach might seem inefficient, it ensures that the class factory retains a correct outstanding object count, and greatly simplifies the flow-of-control by preserving the existing object creation paths. The following *CStubSendForm::OnActivateNext* function shows how the stub send form handles activate next requests:

```
STDMETHODIMP CStubSendForm::OnActivateNext(LPCSTR pszMessageClass,
    ULONG ulMessageStatus, ULONG ulMessageFlags,
    IPersistMessage** ppPersistOut)
{
    // Validate the out-parameter.

    if (IsBadWritePtr(ppPersistOut, sizeof(IPersistMessage*)))
        return _lasterr.Set(E_INVALIDARG);

    *ppPersistOut = NULL;

    // Compare the class in question with this form's default
    // class. Note that message class comparisons are case
    // insensitive.

    if (lstrcmpi(SZ_FORM_MESSAGE_CLASS, pszMessageClass) != 0)
    {
        // Failed, yet it gets a second chance.

        if (IsValidIval(_ivalClass))
        {
            // If this form has a message loaded, compare that
            // message's class with the class in question. This
            // lets the form safely respond to handle superclasses
            // of its intended message class.

            assert(PR_MESSAGE_CLASS == _pval[_ivalClass].ulPropTag);
            if (lstrcmpi(_pval[_ivalClass].Value.lpszA,
                pszMessageClass) != 0)
                return S_FALSE;
        }
        else
        {
            // Lacking a message, we can't safely say that we're
            // the right choice. Let the viewer resolve this
            // message class to find the correct form.

            return S_FALSE;
        }
    }
```

```
    // Okay, it's possible that this form can handle the message.

    // If the message matches the composition state of the current
    // message, let the viewer reuse this form.

    if ((_ulMsgFlags & MSGFLAG_UNSENT) == (ulMessageFlags &
        MSGFLAG_UNSENT))
        return S_OK;

    // We can handle it, but we don't want to use the current form.
    // Instead, offer a new form to the viewer.

    HRESULT hr = _pfactory->CreateInstance(NULL,
        IID_IPersistMessage, (void**)ppPersistOut);

    // Do NOT set last error here--
    // IMAPIFormAdviseSink does not support GetLastError.
    if (FAILED(hr))
        return hr;

    return S_OK;
}
```

Note that message classes are always ANSI strings (never Unicode) and that comparisons of these strings are always insensitive to case. Note also that none of this method's error return paths invokes the last error helper object, since the form advise sink is a separate object from the form object—and, unlike the interfaces *IMAPIForm* and *IPersistMessage* of the form itself, *IMAPIFormAdviseSink* does not contain a *GetLastError* method.

Implementing form commands

The stub send form demonstrates a number of other common form idioms. I list some of these here to pull them out of the *IMAPIForm::DoVerb* method. Other idioms take place in response to commands in the form's user interface rather than in response to verbs from the viewer.

How to reply to the current message   Implementing an e-mail Compose - Reply command falls under the category of a *response form verb:* a command that examines the current message, creates a new message based on the contents of the old message, and invokes a form—not necessarily the same form as the one offering the response form verb—to render the new message. Reply To All, Reply To Sender, and Forward are all examples of response form verbs, as is Reply To Folder in a post form.

Implementation of either a true form verb or a command on the form's menu requires the ability to create and manipulate form objects, which is covered in

Chapter 7. If you're on fire to see this now, trace the code path from the *EXCHIVERB_REPLYTOSENDER* case through the call to *CStubSendForm::HrRespondForm* in the *CStubSendForm::DoVerb* function of the Chap06\Sendstub-\FORM.CPP file. Within the confines of this chapter, you can always reuse the implementation of the reply function in the Exchange client's standard form.

How to inherit the implementation of the Exchange client's standard form verbs

In the last chapter, we discussed the mechanism for extending the form information object with additional extension properties. A form can supply a string, called an *operation map*, that describes the Exchange-standard verbs that it supports, by listing the form information extension property #1 in the property set PS_EXCHFORM (defined in the header file EXCHFORM.H). This operation map consists of a vector of decimal digits, with each position in the vector (listed in Table 6-9) representing a different Exchange-standard verb, and the value of each digit therein (listed in Table 6-10) representing the action that the form would take in response to that verb.

Index	Verb
0	(Reserved for Microsoft Exchange)
1	Open
2	Reply To Sender
3	Reply To All
4	Forward
5	Print
6	Save As
7	(Reserved for Microsoft Exchange)
8	Reply To Folder

Table 6-9. *Indexes in the Exchange client operation map.*

Value	Meaning
0	Verb supported, implemented entirely by Exchange client
1	Verb supported, passed to *IMAPIForm::DoVerb* as usual
2	Verb not supported, menu item disabled

Table 6-10. *Possible values in the Exchange client operation map.*

Each position represents a different Exchange-standard verb. Thus, by specifying a *0* in the fifth element of this vector of digits in the value field, a form requests that the Exchange client enable the Forward command when it selects messages of this type. Should the user invoke this command, the Exchange client will pass the message to its own form, implementing *IPM.Note*. If the message conforms to enough of the *IPM.Note* property schema, Exchange can generate a response form for forwarding the message to another user.

The following example shows the Exchange client operation map from the stub send form, as it appears in Chap06\Sendstub\SENDSTUB.CFG:

```
[Extensions]
Extensions1=Exchange_Client

[Extension.Exchange_Client]
Type=30
NmidPropset={00020D0C-0000-0000-C000-000000000046}
NmidInteger=1
Value=111201112
```

As denoted by the *1*s in the Value field of this configuration file, we support Exchange-compatible Open, Reply To Sender, Print, and Save As verbs, expecting to receive the *EXCHIVERB* code for each of these in our *IMAPIForm::DoVerb* method when these verbs are selected. The *0* in the Value field is used to request that the client implement the Forward verb on our behalf as just described. Finally, the Exchange client enables all of its intrinsic verbs except for the verbs Reply To All and Reply To Folder, each of which the form's configuration file marks with a *2* in the operation map.

How to support printing from the Exchange client   A form supports requests from the client to print that form by specifying *0* or *1* in the sixth element of the Exchange client operation map, as described above. With *0*, the Exchange client attempts to render the message itself. With *1,* however, the client passes *EXCHIVERB_PRINT* to *IMAPIForm::DoVerb*.

The following bogus code from the stub send form example demonstrates how a form should respond to such a Print command:

```
HRESULT CStubSendForm::HrPrintForm()
{
    FORMPRINTSETUP* pfps;
    HRESULT hr = CurrentViewContext()->GetPrintSetup(fMapiUnicode,
        &pfps);
    if (FAILED(hr))
        return _lasterr.Set(hr, CurrentViewContext());
```

(continued)

```
DEVMODE* pdmode = (DEVMODE*)::GlobalLock(pfps->hDevMode);
if (!pdmode)
{
    MAPIFreeBuffer(pfps);
    _viewnotify.OnPrint(0, E_FAIL);
    return _lasterr.Set(E_FAIL);
}
DEVNAMES* pdnames = (DEVNAMES*) ::GlobalLock(pfps->hDevNames);
if (!pdnames)
{
    ::GlobalUnlock(pdmode);
    ::GlobalFree(pfps->hDevMode);
    MAPIFreeBuffer(pfps);
    _viewnotify.OnPrint(0, E_FAIL);
    return _lasterr.Set(E_FAIL);
}

HDC hdc = ::CreateDC(
    (LPCTSTR)pdnames + pdnames->wDriverOffset,
    (LPCTSTR)pdnames + pdnames->wDeviceOffset,
    (LPCTSTR)pdnames + pdnames->wOutputOffset,
    pdmode);
if (NULL == hdc)
{
    ::GlobalUnlock(pdnames);
    ::GlobalFree(pfps->hDevNames);
    ::GlobalUnlock(pdmode);
    ::GlobalFree(pfps->hDevMode);
    MAPIFreeBuffer(pfps);
    _viewnotify.OnPrint(0, E_FAIL);
    return _lasterr.Set(E_FAIL);
}

DOCINFO di;
ZeroMemory((void*)&di, sizeof(di));
di.cbSize = sizeof(DOCINFO);
di.lpszDocName = "Stub Send Form";
di.lpszOutput = NULL;
di.lpszDatatype = NULL;
di.fwType = 0;

::StartDoc(hdc, (LPDOCINFO)&di);
::StartPage(hdc);

// Actual output to the printer should go here.
::TextOut(hdc, 0, 0, szBogus,
    (sizeof(szBogus)/sizeof(TCHAR))-1);
```

```
    ::EndPage(hdc);
    ::EndDoc(hdc);

    _viewnotify.OnPrint(1, S_FALSE);

    ::DeleteDC(hdc);
    ::GlobalUnlock(pdnames);
    ::GlobalFree(pfps->hDevNames);
    ::GlobalUnlock(pdmode);
    ::GlobalFree(pfps->hDevMode);
    MAPIFreeBuffer(pfps);

    return NOERROR;
}
```

The current view context—almost certainly per-verb because the client will want to invoke the form in noninteractive mode—supports a method, *IMAPIView-Context::GetPrintSetup*, for the form to retrieve the current printer settings of the client. The form creates a printer device context using this information, then renders each page of the document onto the device context using the suitable calls to the Windows GDI. After each page, and at the end of the document, the form notifies its view context of its printing progress through *OnPrint* notifications. At the end, the form cleans up the device context and returns.

How to support saving to a file from the Exchange client   A form supports requests from the client to save that form to a text file in a manner very similar to printing: by specifying *0* or *1* in the seventh element of the Exchange client operation map, as described above. With *0*, the Exchange client attempts to render the message itself. With *1*, however, the client passes *EXCHIVERB_SAVEAS* to *IMAPIForm::DoVerb*.

The following code from the file FORM.CPP of the send form application—even more bogus than its printing code, if such a thing is possible—delivers the basic skeleton of Save As support:

```
HRESULT CStubSendForm::HrSaveAsForm()
{
    ULONG ulFlags;
    ULONG ulFormat;
    IStream* pstrm;

    HRESULT hr = CurrentViewContext()->GetSaveStream(&ulFlags,
        &ulFormat, &pstrm);
    if (FAILED(hr))
        return _lasterr.Set(hr, CurrentViewContext());
```

(continued)

367

```
        if (fMapiUnicode != (ulFlags & MAPI_UNICODE))
        {
            pstrm->Release();
            return _lasterr.Set(MAPI_E_BAD_CHARWIDTH);
        }

        // Ignore format.

        // Actual output to the stream should go here.
        hr = pstrm->Write(szBogus, (sizeof(szBogus)/sizeof(TCHAR))-1,
            NULL);
        if (FAILED(hr))
        {
            pstrm->Release();
            return _lasterr.Set(hr);
        }

        pstrm->Release();
        return NOERROR;
}
```

Here the form uses *IMAPIViewContext::GetSaveStream* to obtain an *IStream* interface on the desired output file, which the user has already selected from a dialog box in the Exchange client. Since the stub send form does not support rich text, it ignores the setting of the format parameter, whether *SAVE_FOR-MAT_RICHTEXT* or *SAVE_FORMAT_TEXT*. A form properly supporting *SAVE_FORMAT_RICHTEXT* should instead emit its contents in RTF format. The simplest way to do this is to create a private, hidden instance of the Windows standard Rich Edit control (class name *RichEdit*), stream the form's text-format data into that control using *EM_STREAMIN*, and then stream the data out in RTF format using *EM_STREAMOUT*.

How to save a message, sent or unsent When the user selects the File - Save menu command, the form saves all changes to the current message. If the message is new, it appears in the inbox; otherwise, the message remains in whatever folder held the message. A saved message retains the state of its flag *MSGFLAGS-_UNSENT* so that subsequent requests to open it continue to use the correct version of the form: the compose (send) flavor for unsent messages or the read flavor for delivered messages.

The stub send form implements the File - Save command very simply. The *CStub-SendForm::CmdSave* function is called in response to the message *WM_COM-MAND* on the menu item *ID_FILE_SAVE* of the *CUIForm::WndProc* function, which is located in the Chap06\Sendstub\UI.CPP file. As shown in the following code from the *CmdSave* function, the form object asks the message site to save the message and then notifies any view advise sinks of the change:

```
void CStubSendForm::CmdSave()
{
    HRESULT hr = _pmsgsite->SaveMessage();
    if (FAILED(hr))
    {
        _lasterr.Set(hr, _pmsgsite);
        _pui->ErrorMessage((IPersistMessage*)this, hr,
            IDS_WHILE_SAVING);
    }
    else
    {
        _viewnotify.OnSaved();
    }
}
```

How to submit a message for delivery From the perspective of the form, submitting a message for delivery differs only slightly from saving it, although of course the result is completely different. Once again, when the user interface object sees the command (in response to the *WM_COMMAND* message on the menu item *ID_FILE_SUBMIT* of the window procedure *CUIForm::WndProc*, which is located in the Chap06\Sendstub\UI.CPP file), it calls into the form object (Chap06\Sendstub\FORM.CPP). The form object first checks to ensure that the message contains at least one recipient, calls the message site to submit the message for delivery, then notifies any view advise sinks of the submission. Finally the form shuts itself down. This sequence of actions is exemplified in the following *CStubSendForm::CmdSubmit* function:

```
void CStubSendForm::CmdSubmit()
{
    assert(_formtype == formtypeCompose);

    if (NULL == _padrlist)
    {
        // This will be set if the user has ever visited the
        // address book.
        _pui->Message(IDS_NO_RECIPIENT);
        return;
    }
```

(continued)

369

```
HRESULT hr = _pmsgsite->SubmitMessage(0);
if (FAILED(hr))
{
    _lasterr.Set(hr, _pmsgsite);
    _pui->ErrorMessage((IPersistMessage*)this, hr,
        IDS_WHILE_SENDING);
}
else
{
    _viewnotify.OnSubmitted();
}

ShutdownForm(SAVEOPTS_NOSAVE);
}
```

How to address a message for delivery   For MAPI to hand a message to a messaging system, the message must have a recipient table containing at least one recipient. MAPI differentiates between primary (To), carbon copy (Cc), and blind carbon copy (Bcc) recipients, and recipients of re-sent messages. From all of these, the stub send form supports only primary recipients, forcing the user to enter a modal instance of the address book user interface to change the recipients of the message. These rudimentary addressing facilities nevertheless will suffice to demonstrate the essentials of addressing a message.

When the user interface object sees the user hit the address button (thus activating the *WM_COMMAND* message on the control *IDC_ADDRESS* of the dialog box procedure *CUISendForm::DlgProc*, which is located in the Chap06\Sendstub-\UI.CPP file), it calls into the form object (the *CStubSendForm::CmdAddress* function of the Chap06\Sendstub\FORM.CPP file). If the form object doesn't yet have a reference to the address book on the session, it rectifies the situation, saving the reference in the member variable *_pab*. The form object then invokes the address book modally to modify the form's *_padrlist* member variable, where the form keeps the ADRLIST structure that it will blast onto the message's recipient table when the *IPersistMessage::Save* function is called. (You might want to review *CStubSendForm::Save* at this point.) This sequence of events is exemplified in the following *CStubSendForm::CmdAddress* function:

```
void CStubSendForm::CmdAddress()
{
    assert(_formtype == formtypeCompose);
    assert(_psess);
```

```
    ULONG ulHwnd = (ULONG)_pui->GetHwndUI();
    if (NULL == _pab)
    {
        HRESULT hr = _psess->OpenAddressBook(ulHwnd, NULL, 0,
            &_pab);
        if (FAILED(hr) || MAPI_W_ERRORS_RETURNED == hr)
        {
            // I want to report MAPI_W_ERRORS_RETURNED as well.

            _lasterr.Set(hr, _psess);
            _pui->ErrorMessage((IPersistMessage*)this, hr,
                IDS_WHILE_ADDRESSING);
            if (FAILED(hr))
                return;
        }
    }
    assert(_pab);

    // BUGBUG INTL¹⁷
    ADRPARM adrparm = { 0, NULL, AB_RESOLVE | DIALOG_MODAL,
        NULL, 0L, NULL, NULL, NULL, NULL, "Address Book",
        NULL, "Send Note To", 1, 0, NULL, NULL, NULL, NULL };

    HRESULT hr = _pab->Address(&ulHwnd, &adrparm, &_padrlist);
    if (SUCCEEDED(hr))
    {
        _fDirtyAdrlist = TRUE;
        ((CUISendForm*)_pui)->SetRecipients(_padrlist);
    }
    else if (MAPI_E_USER_CANCEL != hr)
    {
        _lasterr.Set(hr, _pab);
        _pui->ErrorMessage((IPersistMessage*)this, hr,
            IDS_WHILE_ADDRESSING);
    }
}
```

---

17. "BUGBUG INTL" denotes that this code cannot be localized because of hardcoded language-specific data. It's just another way of saying, "Beware!"

As its last act in the *CmdAddress* function, the form updates the user interface object to show the new contents of the ADRLIST structure. The user interface code in the read form could use the *PR_DISPLAY_TO* property (containing the list of primary recipients) for the message's string property; this, however, will not suffice for the compose note, since the message store cannot calculate this value until the client changes the message's recipient table and commits those changes to the store. Therefore, the compose note *CUISendForm* interface must do it the hard way.

Any hope (instilled by the ease of the call to the *IAddrBook::Address* function) of treating the ADRLIST structure as a black box should be dispelled by a look at the implementation of *CUISendForm::SetRecipients* (located in the file Chap06-\Sendstub\UI.CPP). Although the stub send form user interface is primitive, it still needs to display the names of the recipients. This entails perusing the AD-RENTRY rows of the ADRLIST pseudo-SRowSet, finding the display name of every entry of recipient type MAPI_TO, and concatenating them all into the character buffer *szRendered*. Finally, the contents of that buffer will be used to set the window text of a read-only edit control. This is exemplified in the following *CUISendForm::SetRecipients* function:

```
void CUISendForm::SetRecipients(const ADRLIST* padrlist)
{
    // BUGBUG INTL
    static const TCHAR szEllipsis[] = "...";
    const int cchEllipsis = sizeof(szEllipsis)/sizeof(TCHAR)-1;
    static const TCHAR szSeparator[] = "; ";
    const int cchSeparator = sizeof(szSeparator)/sizeof(TCHAR)-1;

    // Find and reset control contents.

    HWND hwnd = ::GetDlgItem(GetHwndUI(), IDC_TO);
    Edit_SetText(hwnd, "");

    if (padrlist == NULL || padrlist->cEntries == 0)
        return;

    // Render recipients into a character buffer.

    TCHAR szRendered[512];
    szRendered[0] = 0;
    int ichCurrent = 0;
    int cchRemaining = sizeof(szRendered)/sizeof(TCHAR)-1;

    const ADRENTRY* padre;
    for (padre = padrlist->aEntries;
        padre < padrlist->aEntries + padrlist->cEntries;
        ++padre)
```

```
    {
        if (NULL == padre->rgPropVals)
            continue;

        // Find display name of this recipient.

        TCHAR* pszName = NULL;
        BOOL fIsTo = FALSE;

        SPropValue* pval;
        for (pval = padre->rgPropVals;
            pval < (padre->rgPropVals + padre->cValues);
            ++pval)
        {
            if (pval->ulPropTag == PR_RECIPIENT_TYPE)
            {
                // Render only TO values--skip all others.
                if (pval->Value.l == MAPI_TO)
                    fIsTo = TRUE;
                else
                {
                    pszName = NULL;
                    break;
                }
            }
            else if (pval->ulPropTag == PR_DISPLAY_NAME)
            {
                // Found it!
                pszName = pval->Value.LPSZ;
            }
            if (NULL != pszName && fIsTo)
                break;
        }

        // Append display name (if found) to buffer.

        if (NULL != pszName)
        {
            const int cchName = _tcslen(pszName);
            if (cchSeparator+cchName+cchEllipsis <= cchRemaining)
            {
                if (ichCurrent > 0)
                {
                    // Separate this element from its predecessor.
                    _tcscpy(szRendered+ichCurrent, szSeparator);
                    cchRemaining -= cchSeparator;
                    ichCurrent += cchSeparator;
                }
```

(continued)

```
                    _tcscpy(szRendered+ichCurrent, pszName);
                    cchRemaining -= cchName;
                    ichCurrent += cchName;
                }
                else
                {
                    // Guaranteed by previous comparison
                    assert(cchEllipsis <= cchRemaining);
                    _tcscpy(szRendered+ichCurrent, szEllipsis);

                    // No more formatting possible--out of room
                    break;
                }
            }
        }

    Edit_SetText(hwnd, szRendered);
}
```

Implementing a Basic Post Form

A post form differs from a send form in the manner through which it reaches its destination. Rather than entrusting a message transport to carry its message, the post form saves the message directly into the destination folder, bypassing both message spooler and transport provider. Post forms therefore dispense with addressing and recipient tables. In turn, they themselves must set certain properties that a send form's message receives from the MAPI message spooler.

Our example of a post form (located in the directory Chap06\Poststub) is derived directly from the stub send form, with only a few changes necessary to switch between the two. Indeed, if you munge the source of the stub post form, renaming its class (*CStubPostForm*), its message class *IPM.Post.StubTest*, and its CLSID back to the values of the stub send form, then compare the projects with a file comparator such as WinDiff, you will find only minute differences between the two.

Obvious differences from the send form

Since post forms are saved, not sent, the stub post form lacks every trace of addressing. The form object CStubPostForm, declared in Chap06\Poststub-\FORM.H, lacks the *_padrlist* member variable in which the sendstub keeps its rudimentary recipient list, the *_pab* member variable used to keep the address book, and even the index *_ivalTo* variable in which the send form object keeps the offset of the displayable *To* list. The calculations for the *IPersistMessage-::IsDirty* function are also somewhat simpler, since they need not allow for any address list and can reside entirely within the user interface object.

This lack of addressing support yields a greater simplification than it first might seem from comparing these stub form samples. Most send forms must implement much more sophisticated addressing support than that delivered in *CStubSendForm*: think of the multiple, freely editable addressing fields of the Exchange client's notes, appearing in different combinations, each one able to resolve recipients dynamically, display resolved recipients as single glyphs, and perform other friendly yet code-intensive actions.

How to post a message

There is little difference between the code to save the changes back to an existing post form and code to save the first version of the post form.

Posting a new message   Post forms post themselves to their destination in a manner similar to the way in which the send form saves itself, or even submits itself. Naturally, the post form calls the *IMAPIMessageSite::SaveMessage* function on its message site rather than the *IMAPIMessageSite::SubmitMessage* function, and there is no address list to check; instead, the client creates the message given to the form within the correct folder when the client first launches the post form.

The *CStubPostForm::CmdPost* function sets a flag to change its *IPersistMessage::Save* behavior, which is used during the calls back into the form, instigated by calling the *SaveMessage* function on the message site; at that time, the form writes additional timestamp properties onto the message, compensating for the lack of a message spooler to set those properties. After saving the new form, the form shuts itself down. This sequence of actions is exemplified in the following *CStubPostForm::CmdPost* function (located in the Chap06\Poststub\FORM.CPP file):

```
void CStubPostForm::CmdPost()
{
    assert(_formtype == formtypeCompose);

    // Request a "Posted" timestamp.

    _fTimeStampNeeded = TRUE;

    HRESULT hr = _pmsgsite->SaveMessage();
    if (FAILED(hr))
    {
        _lasterr.Set(hr, _pmsgsite);
        _pui->ErrorMessage((IPersistMessage*)this, hr,
            IDS_WHILE_POSTING);
    }
```

(continued)

```
    else
    {
        _viewnotify.OnSaved();
    }

    ShutdownForm(SAVEOPTS_NOSAVE);
}
```

Saving an existing message   The stub post form does not offer the File - Save command to new messages to differentiate it from the File - Post command, which functions almost identically. Saving the file consists of nothing more than asking the message site to save its message, then boasting about one's success. Since the message has already been posted, the form does not request the timestamp property and does not shut itself down after it has saved the message. This is shown in the following *CStubPostForm::CmdSave* function from the Chap06\Poststub\FORM.CPP file:

```
void CStubPostForm::CmdSave()
{
    assert(_formtype == formtypeRead);

    HRESULT hr = _pmsgsite->SaveMessage();
    if (FAILED(hr))
    {
        _lasterr.Set(hr, _pmsgsite);
        _pui->ErrorMessage((IPersistMessage*)this, hr,
            IDS_WHILE_SAVING);
    }
    else
    {
        _viewnotify.OnSaved();
    }
}
```

Adding the properties ordinarily set by the message spooler

Messages of class *IPM.Post* appear in the default views of the Exchange client and therefore share many of the same properties as those of *IPM.Note*. In the note form, however, the MAPI message spooler creates many of these properties, such as *PR_MESSAGE_DELIVERY_TIME* (containing the date and time when the message was delivered) appearing in the Exchange client's Received view column, and *PR_SENDER_NAME* (containing the message sender's display name) appearing in the From column. To have meaningful entries in those columns, the post form creates them itself. Thus, when the post form implements the

IPersistMessage::Save method, its behavior differs substantially from that of the note form, even allowing for the lack of a call to the *IMessage::ModifyRecipients* function.

Just as in the stub send form, the stub post form contains the heart of its *IPersist-Message::Save* activity in a helper function, *CStubPostForm::HrSaveInto*, appearing in the Chap06\Poststub\FORM.CPP file. The function opens identically to its send form sibling.

```
HRESULT CStubPostForm::HrSaveInto(IMessage* pmsg)
{
    // Get the array that we'll use for outgoing data.

    SPropValue rgvalToWrite[20];
    int ival = 0;

    // From the user interface, set data into pval array.

    GetDataFromUI();
    assert(IsValidIval(_ivalSubject));
    assert(IsValidIval(_ivalBody));
    rgvalToWrite[ival++] = _pval[_ivalSubject];
    rgvalToWrite[ival++] = _pval[_ivalBody];

    // Coerce the message to this form's message class.
    // Necessary to avoid the "object slicing" problem.

    rgvalToWrite[ival].ulPropTag = PR_MESSAGE_CLASS;
    rgvalToWrite[ival++].Value.lpszA = SZ_FORM_MESSAGE_CLASS;
    ⋮
```

The first deviation from the implementation of the send form appears in the post form's handling of the *MSGFLAG_UNSENT* flag. The send form leaves this flag to the message spooler, so that any attempt to open an unsent message will give the correct "under composition" flavor of the form; when the message spooler claims the outgoing message, it creates a new copy of the message with the flag cleared in such locations as the *Sent Items* folder and, on the other end of the transaction, ensures that this flag is clear on any incoming messages. In a post form, however, this will not work so simply, since the first copy of the message created in the destination folder is the same object that will appear in the folder as the posted message; once the flag is set, it will remain set for the life of the message object. The post form can conceivably create a new copy of the message in the folder upon "posting," deleting the original message under composition or keeping the message under composition in another location.

Rather than resorting to such extremes, the post form doesn't support the "unsent" attribute; it clears the flag before the first save of the message. This post form therefore does not support the "saved but unsent, saved yet incomplete" state of send forms. Once the user has saved a posted message, the message is part of the folder. In the following excerpt from the *HrSaveInto* function, the message flags are explicitly set, and the unsent flag is cleared:

```
    ⋮
// Need to set message flags explicitly, clearing the unsent
// flag. Subsequent invocations of the form on the message
// will bring up the read mode rather than the compose mode.

// In a point-to-point form, we are interested in preserving
// the sent vs. unsent distinction. Here, however, we
// aren't.

rgvalToWrite[ival].ulPropTag = PR_MESSAGE_FLAGS;
rgvalToWrite[ival++].Value.ul = (_ulMsgFlags &
    (~MSGFLAG_UNSENT));
    ⋮
```

Since the message spooler never touches the posted message, the post form must set its own timestamps, as shown in the following excerpt from the *HrSaveInto* function:

```
    ⋮
// Generate timestamps as needed.
// (In a point-to-point form, the spooler would take care of
// this.)

if (_fTimeStampNeeded)
{
    FILETIME ft;
    GetSystemTimeAsFileTime(&ft);

    rgvalToWrite[ival].ulPropTag = PR_CLIENT_SUBMIT_TIME;
    rgvalToWrite[ival++].Value.ft = ft;
    rgvalToWrite[ival].ulPropTag = PR_MESSAGE_DELIVERY_TIME;
    rgvalToWrite[ival++].Value.ft = ft;

    _fTimeStampNeeded = FALSE;
}
    ⋮
```

The post form must also set its own values for derivations of the *PR_SENDER* and *PR_SENT_REPRESENTING* properties. From the session, the post form queries for the current notion of the sender's "identity;" this returns a value from the transport provider loaded in the session. Ordinarily, the MAPI transport that carries the message gets to declare this: for example, a message arriving through an SMTP transport would consider me "Ben Goetter" at "goetter@angrygraycat-.com," while a message on my Microsoft Mail shared-file system sometimes comes from "Ben" with a mailbox "goetter" on the server \\CTHULHU. Since no transport carries this message, the post form lets MAPI select the primary transport to use its notion of identity, then propagates the values of this identity on to the message.

```
    ⋮
// To get the SENDER and SENT_REPRESENTING values:
// QueryIdentity.
// (In a point-to-point form, the spooler would take care of
// this.)

ULONG cbEid;
ENTRYID* peid;
assert(_psess);
if (NULL == _psess)
    return _lasterr.Set(E_FAIL);
HRESULT hr = _psess->QueryIdentity(&cbEid, &peid);
if (FAILED(hr))
{
    _lasterr.Set(hr, _psess);
    return hr;
}

ULONG ulType;
IMAPIProp* pmprp = NULL;
hr = _psess->OpenEntry(cbEid, peid, &IID_IMAPIProp, 0,
    &ulType, (IUnknown**)&pmprp);
if (FAILED(hr))
{
    _lasterr.Set(hr, _psess);
    MAPIFreeBuffer(peid);
    return hr;
}
assert(ulType == MAPI_MAILUSER);
```

(continued)

```
enum { ivalEid, ivalDisplayName, ivalMailAddr, ivalAddrType,
    ivalSearchKey, cvalIdentity };

SizedSPropTagArray(cvalIdentity, tagaReadIdentity) =
    { cvalIdentity, \ { PR_ENTRYID, PR_DISPLAY_NAME,
    PR_EMAIL_ADDRESS, PR_ADDRTYPE, PR_SEARCH_KEY } };

ULONG cval = 0L;
SPropValue* pvalIdentity;
hr = pmprp->GetProps((SPropTagArray*)&tagaReadIdentity, 0,
    &cval, &pvalIdentity);
if (FAILED(hr))
{
    _lasterr.Set(hr, pmprp);
    pmprp->Release();
    MAPIFreeBuffer(peid);
    return hr;
}

if (PR_ENTRYID == pvalIdentity[ivalEid].ulPropTag)
{
    assert(ival <
        sizeof(rgvalToWrite)/sizeof(rgvalToWrite[0]));
    rgvalToWrite[ival].ulPropTag = PR_SENDER_ENTRYID;
    rgvalToWrite[ival++].Value = pvalIdentity[ivalEid].Value;
    assert(ival <
        sizeof(rgvalToWrite)/sizeof(rgvalToWrite[0]));
    rgvalToWrite[ival].ulPropTag = PR_SENT_REPRESENTING_ENTRYID;
    rgvalToWrite[ival++].Value = pvalIdentity[ivalEid].Value;
}
if (PR_DISPLAY_NAME == pvalIdentity[ivalDisplayName].ulPropTag)
{
    assert(ival <
        sizeof(rgvalToWrite)/sizeof(rgvalToWrite[0]));
    rgvalToWrite[ival].ulPropTag = PR_SENDER_NAME;
    rgvalToWrite[ival++].Value =
        pvalIdentity[ivalDisplayName].Value;
    assert(ival <
        sizeof(rgvalToWrite)/sizeof(rgvalToWrite[0]));
    rgvalToWrite[ival].ulPropTag =
        PR_SENT_REPRESENTING_NAME;
    rgvalToWrite[ival++].Value =
        pvalIdentity[ivalDisplayName].Value;
}
```

```
if (PR_EMAIL_ADDRESS ==
    pvalIdentity[ivalMailAddr].ulPropTag)
{
    assert(ival <
        sizeof(rgvalToWrite)/sizeof(rgvalToWrite[0]));
    rgvalToWrite[ival].ulPropTag = PR_SENDER_EMAIL_ADDRESS;
    rgvalToWrite[ival++].Value =
        pvalIdentity[ivalMailAddr].Value;
    assert(ival <
        sizeof(rgvalToWrite)/sizeof(rgvalToWrite[0]));
    rgvalToWrite[ival].ulPropTag =
        PR_SENT_REPRESENTING_EMAIL_ADDRESS;
    rgvalToWrite[ival++].Value =
        pvalIdentity[ivalMailAddr].Value;
}
if (PR_ADDRTYPE == pvalIdentity[ivalAddrType].ulPropTag)
{
    assert(ival <
        sizeof(rgvalToWrite)/sizeof(rgvalToWrite[0]));
    rgvalToWrite[ival].ulPropTag = PR_SENDER_ADDRTYPE;
    rgvalToWrite[ival++].Value =
        pvalIdentity[ivalAddrType].Value;
    assert(ival <
        sizeof(rgvalToWrite)/sizeof(rgvalToWrite[0]));
    rgvalToWrite[ival].ulPropTag =
        PR_SENT_REPRESENTING_ADDRTYPE;
    rgvalToWrite[ival++].Value =
        pvalIdentity[ivalAddrType].Value;
}
if (PR_SEARCH_KEY == pvalIdentity[ivalSearchKey].ulPropTag)
{
    assert(ival <
        sizeof(rgvalToWrite)/sizeof(rgvalToWrite[0]));
    rgvalToWrite[ival].ulPropTag = PR_SENDER_SEARCH_KEY;
    rgvalToWrite[ival++].Value =
        pvalIdentity[ivalSearchKey].Value;
    assert(ival <
        sizeof(rgvalToWrite)/sizeof(rgvalToWrite[0]));
    rgvalToWrite[ival].ulPropTag =
        PR_SENT_REPRESENTING_SEARCH_KEY;
    rgvalToWrite[ival++].Value =
        pvalIdentity[ivalSearchKey].Value;
}
```

(continued)

```
// Everything to set is now in rgvalToWrite.
// The variable ival, indexing the next available cell in the
// array, works here as the count.

SPropProblemArray* pProblems = NULL;
hr = pmsg->SetProps(ival, rgvalToWrite, &pProblems);
if (FAILED(hr))
{
    _lasterr.Set(hr, pmsg);
    MAPIFreeBuffer(pvalIdentity);
    pmprp->Release();
    MAPIFreeBuffer(peid);
    return hr;
}

// Expected problem: PR_BODY is too big to set this way.
// Workaround: stream it out if we must.

if (pProblems)
{
    for (unsigned i = 0; i < pProblems->cProblem; ++i)
    {
        // Run down the array until we find the body property.

        if (PR_BODY == pProblems->aProblem[i].ulPropTag &&
            MAPI_E_NOT_ENOUGH_MEMORY ==
            pProblems->aProblem[i].scode)
        {
            hr = HrStreamOutAux(pmsg, PR_BODY,
                _pval[_ivalBody].Value.LPSZ);
                // Lasterr already set
                break;
        }
    }

    MAPIFreeBuffer(pProblems);
    pProblems = NULL;
}

MAPIFreeBuffer(pvalIdentity);
pmprp->Release();
MAPIFreeBuffer(peid);
return hr;
}
```

Distinctive post form verbs

Working without addresses, the stub post form naturally supports the Reply To Folder command rather than the Reply To Sender command. The *switch* statement at the heart of its *IMAPIForm::DoVerb* implementation reflects as much, with the form's solo custom verb—verb code 1, just as in the stub send form—duplicating the *EXCHIVERB_REPLYTOFOLDER* verb. Later on during this call, the function *CStubPostForm::HrRespondForm* acts much as does its sibling in the *CStubSendForm* interface; notably, however, it creates the new message in the correct location for a posted response and completely lacks the call to the *CStubSendForm::HrAddressResponseForm* function responsible for addressing replies in the stub send form.

A quick look at the operations map appearing in Chap06\Poststub\POST-STUB.CFG shows support for the Exchange-compatible Open, Print, Save As, and Reply To Folder verbs, each expecting to receive the *EXCHIVERB* code for each of these in our *IMAPIForm::DoVerb* implementation when they are selected, plus a request that the client implement the Forward command on our behalf just as it does for the stub send form. As shown in the following excerpt from the Chap06\Poststub\POSTSTUB.CPP file, the Exchange client will enable all of its intrinsic verbs except for Reply To Sender and Reply To All, each of which the form's configuration file marks with a *2* in the corresponding operations map positions of the *Value* field:

```
⋮
[Extensions]
Extensions1=Exchange_Client

[Extension.Exchange_Client]
Type=30
NmidPropset={00020D0C-0000-0000-C000-000000000046}
NmidInteger=1
Value=112201111
⋮
```

Implementing a Richer Post Form

Many applications do not reuse the schema of *IPM.Post*. Such applications have their own unique properties and their own schema, germane to whatever domain the application occupies: veterinary medicine, gymnastics, inventory control, insurance and actuarial work, business process automation, journalism or publishing, city planning, or building giant robot monsters for total world domination. To track the work taking place in your dinosaur-cloning facility, you don't care about "Subject" or "Message Text": you want to know the number of teeth, the color of scales, the number of RNA base pairs matched, and whatever other properties ("How many scientists did Rex eat last week?") you find pertinent to the work at hand.

To provide a slightly richer example, then, we will conclude this chapter with discussion of the Chap06\Catform example. (See Figure 6-23.) This form does nothing that you couldn't build in half an hour using Microsoft Access; it implements an application for recording the colors and personalities of a group of cats. Nevertheless, the Cat-Tracking Application demonstrates a couple of important techniques to use when implementing a form for an independent message class, such as its *IPM.Goetter.CatForm* schema.

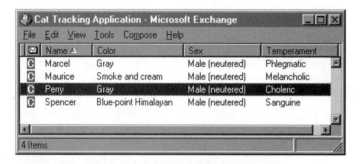

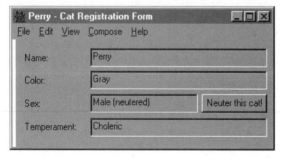

Figure 6-23. *The extremely sophisticated Cat-Tracking Application.*

Named properties

The Cat-Tracking Application shares but few properties with any other message class. It tracks the cat's name, color of fur, sex (if still intact), and whatever passes for the cat's personality type. Because these new property types are unique to my form, they demand unique properties.

One solution involves using the range of message-class defined content properties. Since I have defined the message class *IPM.Goetter.CatForm*, I can define the semantics of any property with a property ID in the range 0x6800 through 0x7BFF. The cat's name could occupy 0x6800, fur color 0x6801, and so forth.

```
#define PR_CAT_NAME PROP_TAG(PT_TSTRING, 0x6800)
```

However, using these per-message-class ranges invites collisions with other message classes that use the range. Imagine searching a message store for a message with the property *PR_CAT_NAME* = *"Perry"*. Now imagine that another custom message class uses a string at property ID 0x6800 to store some other string value. Since the two properties occupy the same slot, they can collide, with views on one class picking up values from another. For this reason, a robust MAPI search should specify the message class as an additional clause in any searches using properties in this range; however, that precludes two or more forms from collaborating and sharing a family of common properties unless the two forms share a common message superclass bearing those properties. In this case, the agency making the query must know that superclass, have its definition, and use its definition in the restriction.

Much of the time, it is easier to work with MAPI named properties. Named properties scope their property definitions within a supplied GUID; the hosting message store resolves a particular named property to a yet unused property ID[18] in the range 0x8000 through 0xFFFE. A form using named properties will typically use its CLSID as the GUID scoping its named properties. Two forms can easily share a body of named properties by agreeing on a common GUID: perhaps the CLSID of one or the other, or perhaps some other suitable GUID.

Obtaining the property tags Since different message stores can carry different messages, the form must resolve its named properties into tags for each destination message store from which it reads or to which it writes. An object hosting named properties supports a property *PR_MAPPING_SIGNATURE*, identifying a particular named property name space that a client can use to determine whether it has its properties resolved correctly. Here the form object keeps the resolved property tags in a number of member variables (*_tagCatName*, etc.),

---

18. The message store hosting the message—or, more precisely, the message store provider implementing the message store object—is responsible for maintaining this name space to avoid exhausting it.

also caching the mapping signature of their name space in the member *_pval-LastMapping*. When the form object needs to use the tags against any message, it calls its *HrCalcTags* member function with the message in question; that function checks the message's mapping signature, returning quickly if it finds a match against its existing remembered signature.

The following *CCatForm::HrCalcTags* function is located in the file Chap06\Catform\FORM.CPP; you will find the declaration of the form object in FORM.H useful as well:

```
HRESULT CCatForm::HrCalcTags(IMessage* pmsg, BOOL fCreate = FALSE)
{
    // Have we mapped these properties already?

    {
        enum { ivalMappingSignature, cvalMsg };

        SizedSPropTagArray(cvalMsg, tagaTest) = { cvalMsg, \
            { PR_MAPPING_SIGNATURE } };

        ULONG cval = 0L;
        SPropValue* pval;
        HRESULT hr = pmsg->GetProps((SPropTagArray*)&tagaTest,
            fMapiUnicode, &cval, &pval);
        if (FAILED(hr))
            return _lasterr.Set(hr, pmsg);

        if (_pvalLastMapping)
        {
            // Compare against the last mapping.

            if (pval[ivalMappingSignature].ulPropTag ==
                PR_MAPPING_SIGNATURE &&
                _pvalLastMapping[ivalMappingSignature].ulPropTag
                == PR_MAPPING_SIGNATURE)
            {
                if (pval[ivalMappingSignature].Value.bin.cb
                    == pval[ivalMappingSignature].Value.bin.cb &&
                    !memcmp(pval[ivalMappingSignature].Value.bin.lpb,
                    _pvalLastMapping[ivalMappingSignature].Value.bin.lpb,
                    pval[ivalMappingSignature].Value.bin.cb))
                {
                    ::MAPIFreeBuffer(pval);
                    return S_FALSE; // No need to remap
                }
            }
        }
    }
```

```
        // Save the mapping signature for the next time around.

        SPropValue* pvalOld = _pvalLastMapping;
        _pvalLastMapping = pval;
        ::MAPIFreeBuffer(pvalOld);
    }
    ⋮
```

If the flow-of-control makes it this far, the form needs to remap its property tags. From a named property perspective, the properties have numbers 1, 2, 3, and 4 within a GUID that is the same as the form's CLSID. This is shown in the following continuation of the *HrCalcTags* function:

```
    ⋮
    // Perform mapping, using following table.

    struct
    {
        int nType;              // A PT_ code of the result
        long nID;          // The MNID_ID code within our GUID
        ULONG*   ptagDest;      // The resting place of the result
    }
    rgNmidTable[] =
    {
        { PT_TSTRING, 1, &_tagCatName },
        { PT_TSTRING, 2, &_tagCatColor },
        { PT_TSTRING, 3, &_tagCatSex },
        { PT_TSTRING, 4, &_tagCatTemper },
#if !defined(ESCHEW_MAPIFORM_ENUM_INDEX)
        { PT_I4,      5, &_tagCatSexIndex },
        { PT_I4,      6, &_tagCatTemperIndex }
#endif
    };
    const int cNmidTable =
        sizeof(rgNmidTable)/sizeof(rgNmidTable[0]);

    MAPINAMEID rgnmid[cNmidTable];
    MAPINAMEID* rgpnmid[cNmidTable];
    int i;

    for (i = 0; i < cNmidTable; ++i)
    {
        rgnmid[i].lpguid = (GUID*)&CLSID_CatForm;
        rgnmid[i].ulKind = MNID_ID;
        rgnmid[i].Kind.lID = rgNmidTable[i].nID;
        rgpnmid[i] = &rgnmid[i];
    }
    ⋮
```

In the concluding lines of the *HrCalcTags* function, note the use of the *MAPI-_CREATE* flag. Lacking *MAPI_CREATE*, a message store will return error rows for any named property that does not yet exist in its name space. Clients should use this flag only when they are preparing to set the property in question. This is shown in the following excerpt:

```
    ⋮
    SPropTagArray* ptagaForm = NULL;
    HRESULT hr = pmsg->GetIDsFromNames(cNmidTable, rgpnmid,
        (fCreate ? MAPI_CREATE : 0), &ptagaForm);
    if (FAILED(hr))
        return _lasterr.Set(hr, pmsg);

    assert(MAPI_W_ERRORS_RETURNED != hr);

    for (i = 0; i < cNmidTable; ++i)
    {
        // Check validity of returned tag, assert notwithstanding.

        *(rgNmidTable[i].ptagDest) =
            (PT_ERROR == PROP_TYPE(ptagaForm->aulPropTag[i]))
            ? PROP_TAG(PT_NULL, PROP_ID_NULL)
            : PROP_TAG( rgNmidTable[i].nType,
            PROP_ID(ptagaForm->aulPropTag[i]));
    }

#if 0 // Forms mistake
    _tagCatSexIndex = PROP_TAG(PT_I4, 32765);
    _tagCatTemperIndex = PROP_TAG(PT_I4, 32766);
#endif

    MAPIFreeBuffer(ptagaForm);
    return hr;
}
```

Reading the named properties   With the named properties resolved against the current message into valid property tags, the form object can read the values of those properties from the message. In the following *CCatForm::HrLoadFrom* function, note the use of the *_tag* member variables when building the property tag array to pass to *IMAPIProp::GetProp*:

```
HRESULT CCatForm::HrLoadFrom(IMessage* pmsg)
{
    assert(pmsg);
```

```
    MAPIFreeBuffer(_pval);
    _pval = NULL;

    // Get the correct tags for the named properties.
    HRESULT hr = HrCalcTags(pmsg, FALSE);
    if (FAILED(hr))
        return hr;

    enum { ivalMsgFlags, ivalClass, ivalFrom, ivalDate,
        ivalCatName, ivalCatColor, ivalCatSex, ivalCatTemper,
#if !defined(ESCHEW_MAPIFORM_ENUM_INDEX)
    ivalCatSexIndex, ivalCatTemperIndex,
#endif
    cvalMsg };

    SizedSPropTagArray(cvalMsg, tagaRead) = { cvalMsg,
        { PR_MESSAGE_FLAGS, PR_MESSAGE_CLASS, PR_SENDER_NAME,
            PR_CLIENT_SUBMIT_TIME, _tagCatName, _tagCatColor,
            _tagCatSex, _tagCatTemper,
#if !defined(ESCHEW_MAPIFORM_ENUM_INDEX)
            _tagCatSexIndex, tagCatTemperIndex
#endif
    } };

    ULONG cval = 0L;
    hr = pmsg->GetProps((SPropTagArray*)&tagaRead, fMapiUnicode,
        &cval, &_pval);
    if (FAILED(hr))
        return _lasterr.Set(hr, pmsg);

    assert(cval == cvalMsg);
    _cvalMax = cval;

    // Set indexes into pval.

    _ivalClass = (_pval[ivalClass].ulPropTag == PR_MESSAGE_CLASS)
        ? ivalClass : IVAL_INVALID;
    _ivalFrom = (_pval[ivalFrom].ulPropTag == PR_SENDER_NAME)
        ? ivalFrom : IVAL_INVALID;
    _ivalDate = (_pval[ivalDate].ulPropTag == PR_CLIENT_SUBMIT_TIME)
        ? ivalDate : IVAL_INVALID;
    _ivalCatName = (_pval[ivalCatName].ulPropTag == _tagCatName)
        ? ivalCatName : IVAL_INVALID;
    _ivalCatColor = (_pval[ivalCatColor].ulPropTag == _tagCatColor)
        ? ivalCatColor : IVAL_INVALID;
```

(continued)

```
    _ivalCatSex = (_pval[ivalCatSex].ulPropTag == _tagCatSex)
        ? ivalCatSex : IVAL_INVALID;
    _ivalCatTemper = (_pval[ivalCatTemper].ulPropTag == _tagCatTemper)
        ? ivalCatTemper : IVAL_INVALID;
#if !defined(ESCHEW_MAPIFORM_ENUM_INDEX)
    _ivalCatSexIndex = (_pval[ivalCatSexIndex].ulPropTag == _tagCatSexIndex)
        ? ivalCatSexIndex : IVAL_INVALID;
    _ivalCatTemperIndex =
        (_pval[ivalCatTemperIndex].ulPropTag == _tagCatTemperIndex)
        ? ivalCatTemperIndex : IVAL_INVALID;
#endif

    return NOERROR;
}
```

Writing the named properties   Because a form might save its state to different
messages, depending on the *IMessage** parameter passed to *IPersistMessage-
::Save*, the cat form resolves its named properties for writing somewhat more
indirectly than it does for reading. It moves data from the user interface object
back to the form object, with tags and values both embedded with a vector of
property values kept in the form object. Therefore, the form must resolve its
named properties before making the move. In the following *CCatForm::Get-
DataFromUI* function, note that the *TRUE* flag is passed to the *CCatForm::Hr-
CalcTags* function, requesting that the calculation use *MAPI_CREATE* when
resolving the properties. This is shown in the following *CCatForm::GetData-
FromUI* function:

```
HRESULT CCatForm::GetDataFromUI(IMessage* pmsgDestination)
{
    if (NULL == _pui) // Nothing to get
        return S_OK;

    const BOOL fDirty = (S_OK == IsDirty());

    HWND hdlg = _pui->GetHwndUI();
    HRESULT hr = S_OK;
    if (_formtype == formtypeRead)
    {
        assert(_pval); // Already set through the HrLoadFrom

        if (!fDirty)
            return S_OK;

        // Until we implement the neutering button, nothing to do
        return S_OK;
    }
```

```
    else // If (_formtype == formtypeCompose)
    {
        if (!fDirty && _pval != NULL)
        {
            // We still need to correct property tags for the
            // destination.

            hr = HrCalcTags(pmsgDestination, TRUE);
            if (FAILED(hr))
                return hr;
            if (S_FALSE == hr) // No need to correct anything
                return S_OK;

            if (IsValidIval(_ivalCatName))
                _pval[_ivalCatName].ulPropTag = _tagCatName;
            if (IsValidIval(_ivalCatColor))
                _pval[_ivalCatColor].ulPropTag = _tagCatColor;
            if (IsValidIval(_ivalCatSex))
                _pval[_ivalCatSex].ulPropTag = _tagCatSex;
            if (IsValidIval(_ivalCatTemper))
                _pval[_ivalCatTemper].ulPropTag = _tagCatTemper;
#if !defined(ESCHEW_MAPIFORM_ENUM_INDEX)
            if (IsValidIval(_ivalCatSexIndex))
                _pval[_ivalCatSexIndex].ulPropTag = _tagCatSexIndex;
            if (IsValidIval(_ivalCatTemperIndex))
                _pval[_ivalCatTemperIndex].ulPropTag
                = _tagCatTemperIndex;
#endif

            return S_OK;
        }


        // A compose form might already have a value array if it
        // came from a saved (but not submitted/posted) message.
        // If not, get a new one.

        if (_pval == NULL)
        {
            hr = ResetPval(CVAL_MAX_ON_RESET);
            if (FAILED(hr))
                return hr; // Cascade
        }

        // Update with the contents of the user interface.

        // Need property tags.
```

(continued)

```
        hr = HrCalcTags(pmsgDestination, TRUE);
        if (FAILED(hr))
            return hr;

        hr = GetStrFromUIEdit(hdlg, IDC_NAME, &_ivalCatName,
            _tagCatName);
        if (FAILED(hr))
            return hr; // Cascade
        hr = GetStrFromUIEdit(hdlg, IDC_COLOR, &_ivalCatColor,
            _tagCatColor);
        if (FAILED(hr))
            return hr; // Cascade
        hr = GetStrFromUILbx(hdlg, IDC_SEX, &_ivalCatSex,
            _tagCatSex);
        if (FAILED(hr))
            return hr; // Cascade
        hr = GetStrFromUILbx(hdlg, IDC_TEMPERAMENT, &_ivalCatTemper,
            _tagCatTemper);
        if (FAILED(hr))
            return hr; // Cascade
#if !defined(ESCHEW_MAPIFORM_ENUM_INDEX)
        hr = GetIntFromUILbx(hdlg, IDC_SEX, &_ivalCatSexIndex,
            _tagCatSexIndex);
        if (FAILED(hr))
            return hr; // Cascade
        hr = GetIntFromUILbx(hdlg, IDC_TEMPERAMENT,
            &_ivalCatTemperIndex, _tagCatTemperIndex);
        if (FAILED(hr))
            return hr; // Cascade
#endif

    }

    return hr;
}
```

Once the _pval_ array contains the correct property IDs, the *HrSaveInto* function can use those entries directly when saving properties onto the message, as shown in the following excerpt:

```
HRESULT CCatForm::HrSaveInto(IMessage* pmsg)
{
    // Get the array that we'll use for outgoing data.

    SPropValue rgvalToWrite[24];
    int ival = 0;
```

```
// From the user interface, set the data into the pval array.
// Corrects property tags for the destination store hosting
// the message.

GetDataFromUI(pmsg);

assert(IsValidIval(_ivalCatName));
assert(ival <
    sizeof(rgvalToWrite)/sizeof(rgvalToWrite[0]));
rgvalToWrite[ival++] = _pval[_ivalCatName];
⋮
hr = pmsg->SetProps(ival, rgvalToWrite, NULL);
⋮
```

How to support systems that won't recognize a custom form

With a message class of *IPM.Goetter.CatForm*, the sample cat registration form doesn't expect any other form to make sense of its messages. Still, since the message class does contain *IPM* as a superclass, the Exchange client will try to use its default *IPM* handler to render these messages.

The default *IPM* form expects at least the following three properties common to every *IPM* message:

■ *PR_SENDER_xxx*[19], naming the identity of the sender. Send forms can defer responsibility for this to MAPI.

■ *PR_CLIENT_SUBMIT_TIME*, naming when the sender submitted or posted the message.

■ *PR_BODY*, containing a block of readable message text.

A custom message class such as *IPM.Goetter.CatForm* does not use the message body in its usual capacity. The cat form itself does not display the message body; therefore, it is free to leave a warning message in this block of text. Any user who, lacking the cat form, attempts to read one of its cat registration items sees this message courtesy of the default *IPM* form. The following lines of code from the *CCatForm::HrSaveInto* function display a warning message for the Catform application.

---

19. This denotes a group of five addressing properties, all prefixed with *PR_SENDER: PR_SENDER-_ADDRTYPE, PR_SENDER_EMAIL_ADDRESS, PR_SENDER_ENTRYID, PR_SENDER_NAME,* and *PR_SENDER_SEARCH_KEY.*

```
        ⋮
assert(ival <
    sizeof(rgvalToWrite)/sizeof(rgvalToWrite[0]));
rgvalToWrite[ival].ulPropTag = PR_BODY;
rgvalToWrite[ival++].Value.LPSZ =
    "You must have the Cat Registration Form to read this.";
        ⋮
```

Other custom forms might take a different approach to displaying the message body. For example, a form might attempt to display its contents in a text-only fashion, allowing readers lacking the form to peruse its contents.

Installation of the Completed Server

Once you have a working form server, you have to get it into a forms library before anybody can use it. Most MAPI clients work with forms libraries indirectly, through the form-oriented services of the *IMAPISession* and *IMAPIFormMgr* interfaces. Adding or removing forms from a library, however, requires direct access of some sort. A setup application could elect to work directly against the destination library, installing the server there through a call to the *IMAPIFormContainer::InstallForm* function. Optionally, the form developer could distribute the form as a number of files, allowing a user or system administrator to install the form through the Exchange Server forms management interfaces.

Specifying the Configuration of the Form

Whatever means of installation the application elects to use, it must describe the form server to the forms library through a form configuration file, or CFG file. CFG files consist of readable text, with a syntax strikingly similar to that of a Windows INI file. By convention, they have filenames with the extension CFG. Through the CFG file, you describe the form, its verbs, the properties on its messages, the files implementing the server, and the entries in the system registry for MAPI to add when installing the server's files on a client.

Let's look at the complete configuration of the cat form sample in the file Chap06-\Catform\CATFORM.CFG.

Description

The description section of the configuration file contains most of the values available as properties on the form information object. Foremost among these are the form's intended message class, its CLSID, and its display name, as shown in the following excerpt from the CATFORM.CFG file.

```
    ⋮
[Description]
MessageClass=IPM.Goetter.CatForm
CLSID={da32e203-97b8-11cf-b6a6-08002b2b3625}
DisplayName=Cat Tracker
    ⋮
```

In the description section of the CFG file, a form sets *ComposeInFolder* to *1* to tell clients that it is a folder-oriented post form. If this field is set to *0* or absent, clients treat the form as a send form. A post form should also supply a string for the client to use as its menu compose command, as shown in the following excerpt:

```
    ⋮
ComposeCommand=New &Cat in the Household
ComposeInFolder=1
    ⋮
```

The Exchange Server organization forms library actually consists of an aggregate of forms libraries, one for each language that the server is set up to support. A form should define its language in the *Locale* field so that it joins the forms of the correct language, as shown in the following line from the configuration file:

```
    ⋮
Locale=enu
    ⋮
```

If a form specifies that it is to be hidden, MAPI will not offer that form in its *IMAPIFormMgr::SelectForm* user interface, thus preventing users from making requests to compose instances of that form. Hidden forms appear in the *IMAPIFormMgr::SelectMultipleForms* function, and the MAPI Forms Manager will still resolve message classes with them. The *Hidden* field is included as part of the Description section of the CFG file.

```
    ⋮
Hidden=0
    ⋮
```

The MAPI Forms Manager user interfaces group displays forms hierarchically into the *Category* and *Subcategory* fields. Although an administrator most often selects the correct categories for the form to use, a form can specify initial defaults for these values, as shown in the following lines:

```
    ⋮
Category=Form Examples
Subcategory=Posted Forms
    ⋮
```

A form must supply two files containing its icons. The large icon appears in various sections of the user interface, such as the dialog box presented by the *IMAPIFormMgr::SelectForm* function. The small icon appears in the icon column of Exchange client views. The CFG file contains pathnames for these files relative to the current working directory of the process invoking the *IMAPIFormContainer::InstallForm* function, as follows:

```
    ⋮
LargeIcon=catforml.ico
SmallIcon=catforms.ico
    ⋮
```

The *Comment, Version, Owner*, and *Contact* fields simply list additional information about the form, which MAPI and the Microsoft Exchange client display in different parts of the user interface. There is no requirement that the version have any particular format—it is nothing more than a string, just like the comment or any other of these fields, as shown in the following lines from the Description section of the CATFORM.CPP file:

```
    ⋮
Comment=Sample catform supplied with DEVELOPING APPLICATIONS
    FOR MICROSOFT EXCHANGE WITH C++
LargeIcon=catforml.ico
SmallIcon=catforms.ico
Version=0.1.0
Locale=enu
Hidden=0
Owner=Angry Graycat Designs
Contact=Ben Goetter
    ⋮
```

Platforms
Since many different clients can share a forms library, the forms library can contain implementations for the form for multiple platforms. The CFG file enumerates each of these in its Platforms section. Each clause of this section indicates a separate section describing some supported platform. The precise values of each field are used to locate a section [Platform.xxx]; they might be mnemonic strings, as the cat form uses, though that is not necessary. This is shown in the following Platforms section of the CFG file:

```
 ⋮
[Platforms]
Platform1=NTx86
Platform2=Win95
 ⋮
```

For a given platform, the form must describe the processor architecture and intended operating system, the files to install and remove, and any values to add to the system registry. Like icon pathnames in the Description section, the CFG must specify the file with a pathname that can be located from the current working directory of the processing, making the call to the *IMAPIFormMgr-::InstallForm* method, since that process will end up opening and reading those files to embed them into the forms library.

The CFG file's *LocalServer* clause for the registry should include "%d" in its named pathname. When it makes the form server local to a workstation, MAPI will expand that value to indicate the true directory housing the form server's files, as follows:

```
[Platform.NTx86]
CPU=ix86
OSVersion=WinNT3.5
file1=catform.exe
registry1=InprocHandler32 = mapi32.dll
registry2=LocalServer32 = %d\catform.exe
```

A form might indicate that one platform uses all the files and registry data of another platform by specifying "LinkTo" in the following platform entry, naming the section with the values to use:

```
[Platform.Win95]
CPU=ix86
OSVersion=Win95
LinkTo=NTx86
```

In the following platform entry, the cat form specifies that it has an Alpha binary available as well. The MAPI Forms Manager installs both the Alpha and Intel binaries into the destination forms library, subsequently extracting whichever version matches the architecture of the client making the request. Different platforms might have different files and registry entries, but they must share all other entries in the CFG file, as shown on the following page.

```
[Platform.ALPHA]
CPU=AXP
OSVersion=WinNT3.5
file1=alpha\catform.exe
registry1=InprocHandler32 = mapi32.dll
registry2=LocalServer32 = %d\catform.exe
```

Properties

The CFG file lists the section of the property schema that the form wishes to publish through the *IMAPIFormInfo::CalcFormPropSet* function. Here the cat form lists four properties, all named properties in a GUID matching the form's CLSID—compare the CLSID field in the Description section above—and all of type *PR_TSTRING*, which represented as a decimal integer is 30.

```
[Properties]
Property1=Name
Property2=Color
Property3=Sex
Property4=Temperament

[Property.Name]
Type=30
NmidPropset={da32e203-97b8-11cf-b6a6-08002b2b3625}
NmidInteger=1
DisplayName=Name

[Property.Color]
Type=30
NmidPropset={da32e203-97b8-11cf-b6a6-08002b2b3625}
NmidInteger=2
DisplayName=Color
```

Two of its properties the cat form presents as enumerations of strings.[20] This is shown in the following sections from the CATFORM.CFG file:

---

20. Because MAPI contains a couple of bugs in its support for such enumerations, the form does not actually save these indexes in its message. The enumeration still serves to list the possible values for their backing properties, however.

```
[Property.Sex]
SpecialType=1
Enum1=Sex_Enum
Type=30
NmidPropset={da32e203-97b8-11cf-b6a6-08002b2b3625}
NmidInteger=3
DisplayName=Sex

[Enum1.Sex_Enum]
;NmidPropset={da32e203-97b8-11cf-b6a6-08002b2b3625}
;NmidInteger=5
NmidInteger=32767
Val.1.Display=Male
Val.1.Index=1
Val.2.Display=Female
Val.2.Index=2
Val.3.Display=Male (neutered)
Val.3.Index=3
Val.4.Display=Female (spayed)
Val.4.Index=4
EnumCount=4

[Property.Temperament]
SpecialType=1
Enum1=Temperament_Enum
Type=30
NmidPropset={da32e203-97b8-11cf-b6a6-08002b2b3625}
NmidInteger=4
DisplayName=Temperament

[Enum1.Temperament_Enum]
;NmidPropset={da32e203-97b8-11cf-b6a6-08002b2b3625}
;NmidInteger=6
NmidInteger=32767
EnumCount=4
Val.1.Display=Sanguine
Val.1.Index=1
Val.2.Display=Choleric
```

(continued)

```
Val.2.Index=2
Val.3.Display=Melancholic
Val.3.Index=3
Val.4.Display=Phlegmatic
Val.4.Index=4
```

Verbs

Just as the CFG file lists all the properties to advertise from the *IMAPIFormInfo-::CalcFormPropSet* function, it lists all the verbs to enumerate in the *IMAPIFormInfo::CalcVerbSet* function as well. The verb section should list every verb with a code of *0* or greater supported in the verb's *IMAPIForm::DoVerb* implementation, as follows:

```
[Verbs]
Verb1=1
Verb2=2
Verb3=3

[Verb.1]
DisplayName=&Open
Code=0
Flags=0
Attribs=2
```

All three of the cat form's verbs are those of the standard Exchange client. Here the verb code comes from that listed in EXCHFORM.H for *EXCHIVERB_PRINT*. Likewise, the following entry uses the code from *EXCHIVERB_SAVEAS*:

```
[Verb.2]
DisplayName=&Print
Code=105
Flags=0
Attribs=2

[Verb.3]
DisplayName=&Save as
Code=106
Flags=0
Attribs=2
```

Extensions

To correlate the above Exchange-compatible verb definitions with those in Exchange, the cat form exports an operations map in its Extension section. Here it declares support for the Open, Print, and Save As commands on the File menu, with everything else disabled. Seeing this, the Exchange client enables the menu commands for those standard verbs when it selects items of this form's class. The Extensions sections are as follows:

```
[Extensions]
Extensions1=Exchange_Client

[Extension.Exchange_Client]
Type=30
NmidPropset={00020D0C-0000-0000-C000-000000000046}
NmidInteger=1
Value=112221112
```

When installed into a form container, the form is ready to serve potential clients. The next chapter will reverse our perspective on form objects by taking the view of those clients.

7

Manipulating and Containing Forms

The last chapter described how to implement the inside of a form; Chapter 7 discusses how to implement the environment hosting the form. Implementing the inside of a form includes describing the proper responses of a form object to the methods of its form interfaces; the interfaces were examined from the fishbowl perspective, as if from within the form object. Implementing the environment hosting a form includes the simple act of reading a message, as well as composing new messages, managing multiple running forms, implementing a viewer window, and writing a form that correctly handles attached messages in its own message's body. This chapter will now examine the interfaces as if they are peer objects.

Clients of Form Objects

In Chapter 4, we divided the top-level windows of the Microsoft Exchange client into two classes: form windows and viewer windows. Chapters 5 and 6 discussed the role and operation of the MAPI form objects that underlay the form windows; now our attention must turn to the clients of those form objects, which, in the Exchange client application, are usually—but not always—viewer windows. As a component object, a form operates in response to some agent that requests its services.

- A viewer window displays a particular view of a group of items; if the user requests to open, print, or otherwise activate one of those items, the viewer requests the correct form for that item from MAPI and then activates the form in accordance with the user's wishes. Sometimes, too, an application needs to activate a form for reasons other than as a response to the user's request. For example, imagine a procedure that prints every message received by the user. Such a routine would most likely operate whenever a message arrived in the user's mailbox by activating the correct form to render the message to a printer.

- An application allows you to both create new messages—invoking a form object to present the user interface—and set the messages' properties before saving or sending the messages. The application can specialize in launching forms for a particular message class, as Exchange does with *IPM.Note* and *IPM.Post* in the Compose - New Message command on its viewer windows, or the application can use the user interface presented by MAPI to allow the user to select the class, as demonstrated in the Compose - New Form. Particular viewer windows can also launch forms from a particular form container—typically the form container associated with the current message folder.

- Messages can contain nested instances of other messages as attachments. If the form of a container message allows the user to examine the nested messages, just as the Exchange standard note form does, that form must be able to locate and activate the correct form for each message within it.

The common thread binding these cases is indirection through a form. In each case, the Exchange client requests the services of a form object rather than interpreting the message itself. With no particular knowledge of a particular form, such a generic viewer can display and activate instances of that form. The standard Exchange note form can contain an attached message of a class that it has never before seen. Through the indirection on its Compose menus, Exchange can launch new message types and can even support external servers implementing the forms intrinsic to Exchange, so long as those servers adhere to the correct schemas for those message types.

This chapter shows how to use the services of forms in this manner.

The Interfaces of the Form's Environment

All of the interfaces discussed in this chapter were also described in the preceding chapter. The difference here is the viewpoint: where the preceding chapter examined everything from within the form object, this chapter looks on them all as peer objects.

Form interfaces

Clients communicate with form objects through the following two interfaces on the form:

■ The *IPersistMessage* interface serves as the initialization interface. Through the *IPersistMessage* interface, the client associates the form with a message and controls when and where the form saves its persistent data. The client can revoke this association at any time.

■ The *IMAPIForm* interface serves as the activation interface. Through the *IMAPIForm* interface, the client tells the form to display itself at a particular location, print itself, or take some other initial action. The client can also force the form to shut itself down through this interface.

Any form object supports both of these interfaces. A client holding one interface can freely query the form for the other interface as needed.

Host interfaces

In turn, the form expects certain information from its client concerning its workplace and expected habits. The client supplies this information by handing the form two objects: the message site and the view context.

■ The *IMAPIMessageSite* interface describes the message site given by the client to the form's initialization method. The message site describes the source of the message against which the client has the form operate so that a form opened from a message attached to another message doesn't try to move that inner message elsewhere, and a form opened from a message saved into a file doesn't try to print the name of the message's parent folder. A form performs all message manipulation, indeed, all session-oriented MAPI activity, through the message site.

■ The *IMAPIViewContext* interface describes the view context given by the client to the form's activation interface and method. The view context describes the operating context of the activated form in terms of the viewer window that launched the form; this enables the form to implement functions requiring knowledge of the state of that viewer window, such as the Previous and Next commands. Form clients other than viewer windows still offer the form view contexts but can create stubs that encompass most of its functionality, marking the view contexts as absent in the status flags returned by the *IMAPIViewContext-::GetViewStatus* method and returning *MAPI_E_NO_SUPPORT* from the methods themselves.

A client gives one instance of each of these objects to any form it invokes. Each object serves only that one form because each represents that form's own relationship with its initialization message and hosting view.

Advise sinks

In addition, both forms and viewers can implement advise sink objects, which each object will give to the other object to keep track of each other.

- The *IMAPIFormAdviseSink* interface describes the form advise sink. A form registers the advise sink with a view context by using the *IMAPIViewContext::SetAdviseSink* method. Just as a view context serves only a single form, the view context holds only a single form advise sink at a time.

- The *IMAPIViewAdviseSink* interface describes the view advise sink. A viewer or other interested party registers the view advise sink with the form by using the *IMAPIForm::Advise* method. A single form can hold many view advise sinks, each relaying information to a separate interested party.

Forms implement form advise sinks. Viewers or other form clients implement view advise sinks.

Viewers and forms and sinks, oh my

Putting all these interfaces together, there are five different objects interacting in a client-form relationship: the form itself, the form's advise sink, a message site, a view context, and a view advise sink.

Figure 7-1 shows a viewer window and a form from the Cat-Tracking Application example of the last chapter (Chap06\Catform). Were the viewer a custom application and the form that of the standard Exchange note, the same architecture would apply.

Figure 7-2 takes a peek under the hood of this running client application to show how all of these objects work together. Through the services of the MAPI Forms Manager, the client has obtained a form object corresponding to the message selected by a user. Since the client owns the viewer window, this diagram shows the client holding a window user interface object for the viewer. The user interface for the form, however, comes courtesy of the form object.

The client itself implements a message site representing the message under consideration, and a view context representing the item's position in the visible sequence of the viewer window. The client hands references to both these objects to the form, which calls through them, where necessary, to get information about its environment. The form's only notion of the message comes from the message site; its only notion of the application that invoked it comes from the view context.

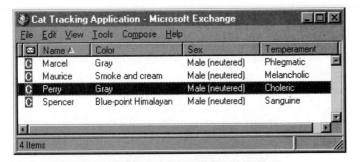

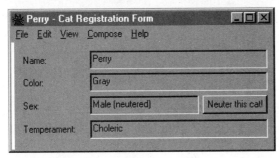

Figure 7-1. *Viewer window and form.*

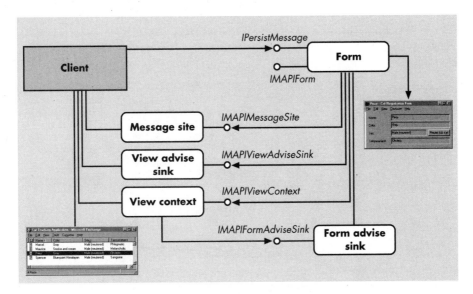

Figure 7-2. *The objects involved in opening a message.*

Because form and view each have their own user interface, they must be able to communicate state changes resulting from user interface activity if they are to remain consistent with each other. The form has registered a form advise sink with the view context to receive notifications of changes therein; likewise, the client has registered a view advise sink with the form. Changes on either end result in one end (form or view) calling the appropriate notification method on the advise sink that it holds. For example, if this form saves its data back to the message site, it would alert the view with a call to the *IMAPIViewAdviseSink-::OnSaved* method on that view's advise sink, held by the form.

Remember that custom forms always use the out-of-process server model. Figure 7-3 shows exactly the same form environment that appeared in Figure 7-2, this time making explicit the interprocess communication necessary to connect the form's server process with the client viewer process. Observe that every path of communication between viewer and form passes through the RPC channel. The client holds an interface to the form, with that interface spanning the gulf between processes. The form holds interfaces on the client host objects, message site, and view context; every form callback on those objects reaches from the form back into the client process. All advise sink notifications, too, cross the process gap.

Note that all session-oriented MAPI activity in the form passes through the message site. This happens either directly, through methods such as the *IMAPI-MessageSite::DeleteMessage* method, or indirectly, through method invocations on the interface handles returned by the *IMAPIMessageSite::GetSession* method,

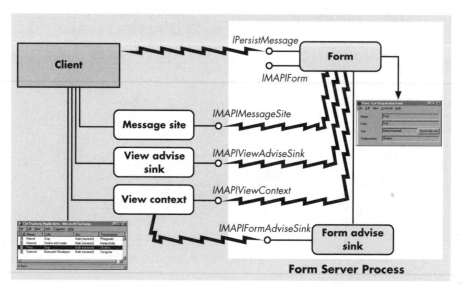

Figure 7-3. *Spanning the gap between viewer and form using RPC channels.*

the *IMAPIMessageSite::GetMessage* method, and the like; the form need not call the *MAPILogonEx* method to get its own session. As a corollary, every MAPI call made in the form process has to travel out-of-process to reach its service providers. When the form calls the *GetSession* method or any other message site interface that returns a supposedly raw MAPI interface, the form gets a proxy object instead, allowing MAPI to remotely invoke all its methods into the correct process.

To Launch a Form

Occasionally, opening an item is referred to as "launching a form." This ballistic turn of phrase seems most natural when composing a new instance of a send form; seemingly out of nowhere, the form springs into life at the user's command and, at the touch of a button, submits its message to the message transports, which take the payload to its destination. With its job done, the form closes. The effect is as if a command shell interpreter had spawned a one-off task. The effect, however, is misleading; there is nothing fire-and-forget about launching a form. The client either creates the new message or opens it from existing storage, giving the message to the form, then saves or submits the message at the form's request. Even with command shells, the word *launch* is misleading because the shell application typically holds a stream, channel, or other IPC construct with which to track error status or perform job control on the spawned process. This is also the case with form clients.

Instead, I prefer the Organ Grinder school of task management: the grinder brings forth the monkey, then holds the leash to control the monkey as the monkey capers and dances, and finally waits for the monkey to come back to the cage with a tin cup full of money. It doesn't help my overactive imagination that the client holds the primary form interface for all the world like that organ grinder holds the monkey's leash, right down to calling the *IMAPIForm::ShutdownForm* method if the monkey doesn't want to go home at the end of the day.

In either case, monkey or missile, the client performs each of the following steps.

- Get the message. For composing new instances of the form, the client must create the new message. (See "Composing a new message" on page 412.) For reading existing instances, the client must open the message from a file, a store, or an attachment. (See "Managing the Open Form" on page 427.)

- Wrap the message in a message site. Clients give message site objects to forms.

- Get the view context.

- Get the form object, either from the MAPI Forms Manager or directly from a class factory.

- Initialize the form object with the message site.

- Set up the form object with the view context.

- Activate the form.

- Manage the active form for its lifetime.

Note that order is not important except when one step requires the results of a previous step. For example, initializing the form requires that the user have both a form object and a message site object at hand. A client can defer many of these steps to MAPI or (if the client is actually an Exchange client extension running within Exchange) to the Exchange client, depending on how much control the client is willing to forgo.

Getting a Message and Client Objects

Whether composing a new message to post or send, or reading an existing message, every form depends on the client to supply a message.

Reading an existing message

Working with an existing message is straightforward. The client has the message to manipulate at hand, selected either by user action or by some other criterion, such as its having just arrived in the mailbox, or its corresponding to a long-term entry identifier saved by another application. Whatever the source of the message—a message in a message store or a message serialized into a disk file, or attached to another message—the client acquires an *IMessage* interface on the message to pass it to the form. The message site object that accompanies the message interface provides a modular abstraction across the different possible origins of the message.

When it opens a message from a folder in a message store, the client has an entry identifier for the desired message. The client usually obtains this entry identifier as a column (*PR_ENTRYID*) in a row of a contents table, where each entry identifier corresponds to a row in a list view or to a tree view control where a command was created. If this is the case, the client benefits by keeping a few additional columns in the table: message class (*PR_MESSAGE_CLASS*), message status (*PR_MSG_STATUS*), and message flags (*PR_MESSAGE_FLAGS*). MAPI can use the values stored in these properties to determine the correct form for the message, thus saving an additional call to *IMAPIProp::GetProps* and the RPC necessary to bring the property values back from the server. The following code fragment outlines how this is done:

```
  ⋮
enum { iprpEid, iprpClass, iprpFlags, iprpStatus, cprpTable };
SizedSPropTagArray(cprpTable, tagaTable) = { cprpTable, \
    { PR_ENTRYID, PR_MESSAGE_CLASS, PR_MESSAGE_FLAGS, PR_MSG_STATUS }
};

// The preceding prop tag array is used to set columns on a
// contents table in the folder.
// That table subsequently yields a row set,
// in which we want the i-th element.

SRowSet* prs = …;
int i = …;
SPropValue* pval = prs->aRow[i].lpProps;

IMAPIFolder* pfld = …;
IMessage* pmsg = NULL;
ULONG ulType = 0L;
hr = pfld->OpenEntry(pval[iprpEid].Value.bin.cb,
    (ENTRYID*)pval[iprpEid].Value.bin.lpb,
    (LPIID)&IID_IMessage,
    MAPI_DEFERRED_ERRORS|MAPI_BEST_ACCESS,
    &ulType,
    (IUnknown**)&pmsg);
assert(ulType == MAPI_MESSAGE);
  ⋮
```

The first part of this code defines the format of our view of a folder contents table, with a local enumeration as an index to the columns in the table; given a particular row in that table—the determination of which I will not discuss here, naming it only as an index into a row set—that index finds the properties in that row's property value array. Thereafter, the client uses the entry identifier column as a parameter to open the message in its folder.

To open a message from a file, the client needs only the name of the file and a MAPI session within which to operate. As you can see in the following code fragment, two standard functions do all the real work:

```
  ⋮
const WCHAR* pwszFileName = …;
IMAPISession* psess = …;
IMessage* pmsg = NULL;
IStorage* pstg = NULL;
IMalloc* pmalloc = ::MAPIGetDefaultMalloc();
HRESULT hr = ::StgOpenStorage(pwszFileName, NULL,
    STGM_READWRITE|STGM_SHARE_EXCLUSIVE,
```

(continued)

```
        NULL, 0, &pstg);
        if (FAILED(hr))
          ⋮
hr = ::OpenIMsgOnIStg(psess,
     MAPIAllocateBuffer, MAPIAllocateMore, MAPIFreeBuffer,
     pmalloc, NULL, pstg, NULL, 0, 0, &pmsg);
  ⋮
```

The function *StgOpenStorage* returns a structured storage interface in the file system; given a filename (expressed in wide characters, as with all other ActiveX interfaces), this function returns an *IStorage* interface on that file's contents. On top of that interface, the MAPI *OpenIMsgOnIStg* utility renders a message object. As befits its hybrid nature, *OpenIMsgOnIStg* uses two different sets of memory allocation functions: both the standard MAPI allocators and the COM-standard *IMalloc*.

Like a message in a file, a message in an attachment has no entry identifier of its own. Instead, the client must open it using its attachment number—the significant column (*PR_ATTACH_NUM* containing a number uniquely identifying the attachment) of the message attachment table—within its containing message. The following code fragment starts with the client having already determined the number of the desired attachment and working with the existing opened outer message:

```
  ⋮
IMessage* pmsgOuter = …;
ULONG nAttachNumber = …;
IAttach* patt = NULL;
HRESULT hr = pmsgOuter->OpenAttach(nAttachNumber, NULL,
     MAPI_BEST_ACCESS|MAPI_DEFERRED_ERRORS,&patt);
if (FAILED(hr))
  ⋮
IMessage* pmsgInner = NULL;
hr = patt->OpenProperty(PR_ATTACH_DATA_OBJ, &IID_IMessage,
     0, MAPI_BEST_ACCESS|MAPI_DEFERRED_ERRORS, &pmsgInner);
if (FAILED(hr))
  ⋮
```

Composing a new message

For a form to compose a new message of its class, the client creates a new message instance for the form's use. This requires nothing more than a call to the *IMAPIFolder::CreateMessage* method in the correct folder, since, unlike reading a message, you do not expect to be able to compose a new instance of a form as an attachment on another message or within a file, or anywhere else.

The client still accompanies the message with a message site object when it initializes the form.

For a send form, the client creates the new message in the Inbox folder, which is the receive folder (the folder returned by the *IMsgStore::GetReceiveFolder* method) for message class *IPM*,[1] the superclass of all user-to-user messages. This lets the user easily find messages that were saved without being sent, because such messages remain in the user's Inbox, marked with the message flag *MSGFLAG_UNSENT*.

For a post form, the client creates the new message directly in the destination folder. This forces the message store hosting the folder to check the user's permissions on that folder immediately, allowing the client to say right away, "You have insufficient privileges to create a message in this folder." As a corollary, once the user saves a post form, it appears within that folder whether the post form is incomplete or not.

Wrapping the message in a message site

Along with the raw message interface, the client offers the form a message site object to provide additional information about the message. Whereas the message interface typically comes from some MAPI message store provider, the client implements the message site itself.

NOTE   Any post form that supports the notion of saved-yet-not-posted must explore various heroic options for differentiating its incomplete item from the complete items visible in the folder.

Most methods on a message site interface fall into one of two categories: access methods and imperative methods. The access methods (shown in Table 7-1 on the following page) provide access to different objects in the message's operating environment, allowing the form to work under the control of the calling client. Particularly significant is the *IMAPIMessageSite::GetSession* method because it allows the otherwise sessionless server process hosting the form object to use the MAPI session of the client. Each access method returns *S_OK* upon successfully acquiring its object, or, with the exception of *GetFormManager*, *S_FALSE* if no such object exists for the particular message site; this would be the case when the *IMAPIMessageSite::GetFolder* method seeks the folder of a message opened from a file on an absent disk.

---

1. Alternatively, the client can create it in the receive folder for the form's own message class if it has that information available.

Method	Object Returned
GetSession	Session
GetFormManager	Forms Manager
GetStore	Message store hosting the current message
GetFolder	Folder hosting the current message
GetMessage	Current message

Table 7-1. *The various access methods of* IMAPIMessageSite *return interfaces to objects in the environment of the client hosting the current message.*

A second category of methods, the imperative methods, requests the client to perform some operation on the message on the form's behalf. These methods allow a form to offer, for example, a Delete button to delete the current message, when in fact the client owns the message rather than the form. This ensures that the delete operation offered by the form is consistent with that of the client hosting the form. Table 7-2 lists the imperative methods available on the *MAPI-MessageSite* interface.

Method	Action
NewMessage	Returns a new message, along with a new message site and view context to go with that new message. Used in implementing Compose commands from within a form.
CopyMessage	Copies the current message to a destination folder. Used in implementing File - Copy commands from within a form.
MoveMessage	Directs the form to consider the next message in the view sequence and then moves the previous message to a destination folder. Used in implementing File - Move commands from within a form.
DeleteMessage	Directs the form to consider the next message in the view sequence and then either deletes the previous message or moves it to a Deleted Items folder. Used in implementing File - Delete commands from within a form.
SaveMessage	Commits all current changes in the form to the current message.
SubmitMessage	Commits all current changes in the form to the current message, relieves the form of the message through a call to *IPersistMessage::HandsOffMessage*, and then submits the message to the message spooler.

Table 7-2. *The imperative methods of the* IMAPIMessageSite *interface allow the form to request client manipulation of the current message.*

Implementing the access methods is trivial; each returns a new reference on its named object, if possible. However, implementing the imperative methods requires some real work. Fortunately, shortcuts exist.

If the client is an Exchange client extension and is composing a new message, it can ask the Exchange client to supply the message site, along with a new

---

FYI

Conceivably, a folder forms library could contain a definition of a send form. A common complaint about the Microsoft Exchange Server corporate forms library construct is that it does not support any means of partitioning its forms into different security classes, with the different classes available only to particular sets of users; once a form is in the corporate forms library, it is visible and accessible to all, unless the form itself implements some sort of privilege-checking scheme. A Microsoft Exchange Server administrator dissatisfied with this might consider keeping certain send forms in public folder forms libraries since the contents of a folder forms library in a public folder are available only to users with access to that public folder. More realistically, a folder application might contain a send form as part of the application: consider a problem report-tracking system supporting a function to notify the original problem reporter of changes in the status of a record.

Be aware, however, that MAPI does not take into account the contents of a folder forms library when resolving a message in the Inbox into a form. MAPI does not know which folder originally hosted the message's form; it sees only the class of the message and the current folder and searches the usual list of forms libraries—local, current folder, personal, and organizational—before determining that it cannot find the form to handle the message. Any message in the Inbox must therefore have a form in a globally visible forms library for MAPI to recognize the message while it is in the Inbox, either when an unsent message is saved or when the message is received at its destination. This makes the use of a folder forms library as a security-enhanced corporate forms library untenable, unless the site is willing to keep read-only versions of each of the protected forms in a global forms library.

Likewise, folder applications with send functions must ensure that their forms are available to their recipients in some manner. Otherwise, a recipient would receive a message of the application's custom message class, but would not be able to locate its form. Similarly, a sender might elect to save the message without sending it; the form would leave its message in the sender's Inbox, where the sender's client originally created it but where the sender would not be able to find the form with which to resume work on the message.

---

message and even a stub view context, through the *IExchExtCallback::GetNew-MessageSite* method on its callback object. This splices the maintenance of the new form object completely into Exchange's usual sequence of operations.

Otherwise, the client can elect to supply stubs for portions of the message site interface, having those methods return *MAPI_E_NO_SUPPORT* in lieu of taking action. If the client knows certain things about the form, for instance, that the form is a post form and hence never needs the *IMAPIMessageSite::Submit-Message* methods, the client can create stubs for any unnecessary methods of the interface. The client can also decide to create stubs for more vital functions. For example, if a client decides that it needs the form only to be able to view the message, that client might create stubs for all of its imperative methods, directing each of them to return *MAPI_E_NO_SUPPORT*. In effect, the Exchange client has decided to invent an environment where the form is launched in a read-only environment (which, mysteriously, also does not support the File - Copy command). The form can't tell whether it is being invoked on a read-only message file or by a lazy client. More compellingly, a message site must refuse to support methods that cannot be used on the current message.

Two methods on the message site have not been discussed. They fit into neither of the two categories—access or imperative—described above. Table 7-3 lists them.

Method	Description
GetLastError	Just like any other MAPI *GetLastError* method.
GetSiteStatus	Returns status flags indicating the operations available on the message site. (See Table 7–4.)

Table 7-3. *The remaining methods of the* IMAPIMessageSite *interface.*

Like many other MAPI objects, a message site supports a *GetLastError* method through which clients of the object can obtain more information about the last error code returned from an interface on the object. The implementation of the *IPersistMessage::GetLastError* method explored in the last chapter will do nicely for the *IMAPIMessageSite::GetLastError* method as well, needing only some alteration in the HRESULT values that it needs to map. A message site describes the methods that it supports through the flags (shown in Table 7-4) returned from its *IMAPIMessageSite::GetSiteStatus* method. A form uses the message site to enable or disable its offered control buttons because there's no point in tempting the user with a Save button if the form already knows that it cannot save changes.

Flag	Description
VCSTATUS_NEW_MESSAGE	The message site creates new messages.
VCSTATUS_COPY	The message site copies the current message to a destination message folder.
VCSTATUS_MOVE	The message site moves the current message to a destination message folder. The *VCSTATUS_MOVE* flag is cleared on read-only messages or on messages not contained in message folders.
VCSTATUS_DELETE	The message site deletes the current message. The *VCSTATUS_DELETE* flag is cleared on read-only messages or is cleared if the *VCSTATUS_DELETE-_IS_MOVE* flag is set.
VCSTATUS_DELETE_IS_MOVE	The message site deletes the current message by moving the message to a deleted items folder. This flag is cleared on read-only messages or on messages not contained in message folders. This flag is also cleared if the *VCSTATUS_DELETE* flag is set.
VCSTATUS_SAVE	The message site commits changes to the current message. The *VCSTATUS_SAVE* flag is cleared on read-only messages.
VCSTATUS_SUBMIT	The message site submits the current message to the MAPI message spooler. The *VCSTATUS_SUBMIT* flag is cleared on read-only messages, messages without the message flag *MSGFLAG_UNSENT*, or messages not contained in message folders. It is ignored by post forms.

Table 7-4. *Site status flags that are returned by the* IMAPIMessageSite::GetSite-Status *method.*

In summary, the state of a message site consists of the values returned by its access functions plus the settings of its status flags. That's not very complicated.

Creating the view context

View contexts are similar to message sites in many ways: objects implemented and passed by the client to the form. Exchange extensions calling the *IExchExtCallback::GetNewMessageSite* method to implement a Compose command obtain a new view context in the bargain. All other extensions have to implement their own view contexts; fortunately, they are easy to implement.

The methods available on *IMAPIViewContext* are listed in Table 7-5 on the following page. Through the *IMAPIViewContext::GetViewStatus* method, a view context offers a set of status flags similar to those returned by a message site. (See Table 7-6.) However, although the message site flags describe the operations available on a particular message site in a method-by-method manner, the view context flags take a more global perspective, describing the overall operation of the form within the view of its host client.

Method	Description
SetAdviseSink	Holds the given form advise sink. This method is called when the form first receives the view context and upon form shutdown to release that sink.
ActivateNext	Activates the next item in the current view.
GetPrintSetup	Returns the current print setup of the client host. This method is called when implementing the File - Print command from within a form and when implementing the verb *EXCHIVERB_PRINT*.
GetSaveStream	Returns a stream to which the form should render its contents. This method is called only in response to the verb *EXCHIVERB_SAVEAS*.
GetViewStatus	Returns status flags similar to those of the *IMAPIMessageSite::GetSiteStatus* method. (See Table 7-6.)
GetLastError	Just like any other MAPI *GetLastError* method, including that of the *IMAPIMessageSite* interface discussed above.

Table 7-5. *The methods available on the* IMAPIViewContext *interface.*

A view context holds a single form advise sink at a time, corresponding to the single form that a particular view context object tracks. Immediately upon its receiving the view context from the client, the form calls the *IMAPIViewContext-::SetAdviseSink* method to register its own form advise sink with the received view context. If a view context has this sink, the form calls the sink's *IMAPI-FormAdviseSink::OnChange* method whenever the settings of the *VCSTATUS-_PREV* or *VCSTATUS_NEXT* flag change, signaling the form that the form should alter the state of its user interface options. (Note that the remaining view context status flags will remain invariant for the life of the object.) Likewise, the form calls the sink's *IMAPIFormAdviseSink::OnActivateNext* method whenever the form calls its own *IMAPIViewContext::ActivateNext* method. If the form decides to register another form advise sink, the view context releases the previous sink and accepts the new sink in its place. A form can pass NULL to *IMAPIView-Context::SetAdviseSink* to have the view release the old sink with no new sink in its place, typically doing this at shutdown time.

Despite their common *VCSTATUS* prefix, site status flags appear only in the status of message site objects and not in the view context. Most of these flags correspond to a single imperative message site method.

The *IMAPIViewContext::ActivateNext* method asks the view context to activate the next item in the view. Forms call it in response to the View - Previous or View - Next command; message sites call it while they are processing their *IMAPIMessageSite::DeleteMessage* or *IMAPIMessageSite::MoveMessage* method.

Flag	Description
VCSTATUS_PREV	The view context contains elements prior to the current item. The form enables its View - Previous command, if any.
VCSTATUS_NEXT	The view context contains elements after the current item. The form enables its View - Next command, if any.
VCSTATUS_MODAL	The view context requires application-modal behavior from the form. The form drops into a modal message loop until the form is closed; if that modal form in turn launches any forms, the setting of the *VCSTATUS_MODAL* flag is propagated. Clients pass view contexts with this flag set as explicit parameters to the *IMAPIForm::DoVerb* method. The view context implemented by the *IMAPISession::ShowForm* method always sets this flag.
VCSTATUS_DELETE	The view context suggests that the form can delete the message.
VCSTATUS_INTERACTIVE	The view context requires that the form suppress its visible user interface. Clients usually pass view contexts with the *VCSTATUS_* flag set as explicit parameters to the *IMAPIForm::DoVerb* method. This is almost always seen when the form is activated with *EXCHIVERB_PRINT* and *EXCHIVERB_SAVEAS*.
VCSTATUS_READONLY	The view context suggests that the form present a read-only interface. This flag should be set on any operation against an unwritable message. If this flag is set, it overrides any settings of *VCSTATUS_DELETE, VCSTATUS_IS_MOVE, VCSTATUS_MOVE, VCSTATUS_SAVE,* or *VCSTATUS_SUBMIT* in the message site status.

Table 7-6. *View status flags that are returned by the* IMAPIViewContext::Get-ViewStatus *method.*

The client, therefore, can stub this call if the status flags *VCSTATUS_PREV* and *VCSTATUS_NEXT* are both clear and if either the view status flag *VCSTATUS-_READONLY* is set or the current message site status is able to disable the File - Move and File - Delete commands. The view context passed to a newly composed form can usually stub this call.

The *IMAPIViewContext::GetPrintSetup* method returns the client's current print settings to the caller. A form uses this method to print the form as if it were an extension of the client, just as it uses the access methods of the message site to perform MAPI operations as an extension of the client. The client can stub this method by having it return *MAPI_E_NO_SUPPORT*, although this prevents most forms from printing altogether.

The *IMAPIViewContext::GetSaveStream* method is valid only when it is called on the view context passed to a form activated with the standard Exchange client verb *EXCHIVERB_SAVEAS*; all other view contexts can return *E_UNEXPECTED* to this call because it is meaningless in any other context. Contexts that implement this method return a stream that results from the client opening a file selected by the user. To do its part, a form implementing *EXCHIVERB_SAVEAS* calls this method on the view context and then appends to the returned stream the contents of its current item rendered as text. Imagine the following sequence of a Save As operation:

1. You invoke the File - Save As command from the viewer. The view makes this command available only if the form of every currently selected item advertises that it supports the verb *EXCHIVERB_SAVEAS*.

2. The viewer presents you with a standard file dialog box. From this dialog box, the user chooses a filename.

3. The viewer opens that filename for creation and writing, or possibly for appending, and gets a stream on the opened file. This is the stream that each view context offers.

4. The viewer sequentially loads the form for each selected item, activates the form with the verb *EXCHIVERB_SAVEAS*, and passes a view context flag specifying modality (*VCSTATUS_MODAL*). These actions ensure that the operation remains sequential and noninteractive (*VCSTATUS_INTER-ACTIVE*) so that a flashing sequence of form windows doesn't distract the user.

5. While servicing its *EXCHIVERB_SAVEAS* verb, each form calls back to the view context for the save stream on which to write and appends the contents of its current item as text on that stream.

6. The viewer commits and closes the stream and the file.

In summary, the state of a view context consists of the position of the current item in the current client view, the printer settings of the application hosting that view, and the advise sink of the form, plus (like the message site) the status flags.

Acquiring a form object

With a message and the various support objects ready, the client lacks only the final ingredient: the form object to receive them all. There are three ways in which a client can acquire a form:

- The *IMAPIFormMgr::LoadForm* method acquires a form for activating an existing message.

- The *IMAPIFormMgr::CreateForm* method requests a form for use with a new message.

- The *IClassFactory::CreateInstance* method creates a form from within a running form.

IMAPIFormMgr::LoadForm   If the client has an existing message of the correct type, the client passes the message (along with a message site and view context object) to the primary MAPI form-loading interface, the *IMAPIFormMgr::Load-Form* method. The MAPI Forms Manager examines the class and state of the given message to determine the correct form to use and loads the form server as necessary to create an instance of the form. Once MAPI has the form object, it sets up the form with the client's message site (using the *IPersistMessage::Load* method) and view context (using the *IMAPIForm::SetViewContext* method) before returning the form to the caller. All that remains for the client to do is to activate the form through the *IMAPIForm::DoVerb* method.

In the course of its duties, the *LoadForm* method checks whether the message is in a state of conflict. If the message is in conflict, the *LoadForm* method checks whether the form can handle such conflicts; if not, the *LoadForm* method supplies a system-standard conflict resolution form in place of the message's own form.

Conflicting Messages

When multiple server replicas host the same message, they introduce the possibility that users at different sites will make simultaneous conflicting changes to the message. Microsoft Exchange Server flags this state by marking the message as being in conflict, using a special message status flag, and attaching the different versions of the message to the message as attachments.

IMAPIFormMgr::CreateForm If the message is new, the client cannot use the *LoadForm* method as described above but instead must give a form information object to the *IMAPIFormMgr::CreateForm* method. The MAPI Forms Manager creates an instance of the form described by the information object and then returns that form object immediately to the caller. The caller takes responsibility for all subsequent initialization of the form, including the necessary call to the form's *IPersistMessage::InitNew* method to associate the form object with the new message.

Clients can also elect to use the *CreateForm* method should they wish to perform the form initialization (calls to the methods *IPersistMessage::InitNew*, *IPersistMessage::Load*, or *IMAPIForm::SetViewContext*) themselves. This is safe if the message is new, because a new message cannot be in a state of conflict. Otherwise, the client risks giving a message in a state of conflict to a form that doesn't know how to handle such messages.

Clients can acquire form information objects in several ways. The client can take a message class value (either defined beforehand or queried off of a message using the property *PR_MESSAGE_CLASS*) and pass that value to the *IMAPIFormMgr::ResolveMessageClass* method to obtain the form information object for the corresponding form. The client can resolve multiple such values all at once or interactively. To resolve them all at once, the client can obtain an array of form information objects corresponding to all the forms in the folders' forms library. This array can be acquired using the *IMAPIFormMgr::ResolveMultipleMessageClasses* method or using the *IMAPIFormMgr::OpenFormContainer* method to get the container and then using the *IMAPIFormContainer::ResolveMultipleMessageClasses* method to get the array of form information objects. To resolve multiple message class values interactively, the client could use the *IMAPIFormMgr::SelectFormContainer* method, specifying *MAPIFORM_SELECT_FOLDER_REGISTRY_ONLY* in the *ulFlags* parameter. Another way in which the client can resolve the message class interactively is to use the *IMAPIFormMgr::SelectForm* method to request the user interface for selecting the form. Regardless of the method, each of these sequences returns a form information object that is suitable for subsequent instantiation using the *CreateForm* method.

IClassFactory::CreateInstance Finally, if the client already has a class object for the desired form, the client can bypass all of the intermediaries and call the *IClassFactory::CreateInstance* method on that class itself. This returns a new, uninitialized instance of the form, just like a call to the *CreateForm* method.

By circumventing the Forms Manager in this way, a client accepts the following restrictions:

- The client must know the precise CLSID of the form it wants and request that exact form every time; rather than having MAPI determine the correct form for handling such-and-such message or message class, the client always receives exactly the form it requests.

- The local workstation's system registry must contain valid entries for the class. The server hosting the form class must be installed locally, either by assumption or by the client calling the *IMAPIFormMgr-::PrepareForm* method to ensure and validate the local copy of a form.

- The client takes all responsibility for locking the server into memory as needed for good performance. The Forms Manager watches requests for forms and caches the most recently used form to speed subsequent form invocations. By avoiding the Forms Manager, the client loses the services of this cache.

This direct approach most commonly appears when the client is actually another instance of the form. Many scenarios require a form to create another instance of itself, such as when a form generates a new form object for one of its Compose - New Message or Compose - Reply to Sender type commands; such a form returns to its class factory for another instance of itself rather than tortuously reentering the Forms Manager.

None of the restrictions listed above should affect an already running form for the following reasons:

- Barring existential crisis on the part of the form, the form knows its own identity. Some client initially loaded it to handle a particular message class; that client should be just as happy to get another instance of the same form for the same message class.

- Because the form is already running, it is already installed.

- Presumably, the agency that initially loaded the class object also called the *IClassFactory::LockServer* method as it deemed necessary; provided that the form returns to its original class object to create the new instance of itself, the server can maintain proper lock and object counts for controlling the server lifetime.

Initializing the form object

All the ingredients—form, message site, and view context—are now ready. It remains only to plug them together into a framework. If the form object was acquired courtesy of the *IMAPIFormMgr::LoadForm* method, then MAPI has already done this assembly and returns a form ready for activation.

With the message site   A new form needs a call to one of its initialization interfaces—either the *IPersistMessage::InitNew* or the *IPersistMessage::Load* method—bearing the message site it will use. If the client wants the form to ignore any data in the message and supply its own default values, the client should initialize the form with the *IPersistMessage::InitNew* method. Otherwise, if the client wants the form to use the data supplied in the message, the client should initialize the form with the *IPersistMessage::Load* method.

Table 7-7 compares the use of the two initialization methods. Note that when the client knows something about the form's message schema and wishes to initialize a new unsent (or unposted) form with default information, the client can set the contents of the new message appropriately and then call the *IPersistMessage::Load* method to have the new form honor those contents. The Compose - Reply verb in the standard note form works in this way: knowing the schema of *IPM.Note* (after all, that's its own message class!), the original instance of the form sets the message body and recipient table of the new message and then initializes the new form instance with that message.

Action	When to Call the IPersistMessage::InitNew *Method*	When to Call the IPersistMessage::Load *Method*
Composing a new message	Use the *IPersistMessage::InitNew* method to give the form a new message in which to write. The form supplies all defaults.	Use the *IPersistMessage-::Load* method to give the form a new message with some default data. This requires some knowledge of the message schema by the client.
Activating an existing message	Never.	Always.

Table 7-7. *Different initialization scenarios require the use of different methods.*

With the default view context   Having received the message site, the form now lacks only the view context. The client gives the form the form's default view context using the *IMAPIForm::SetViewContext* method. This can yield a flurry of calls back into the client; once the smoke clears, the client will probably see the view context holding a form advise sink. The client calls the *IMAPIForm-::SetViewContext* method, giving the form object an interface on its view context object. In turn, the form calls the *IMAPIViewContext::SetAdviseSink* method, giving the view context object an interface on its form advise sink object. At the top of the stack, the client uses the *IUnknown::AddRef* method to obtain a pointer to the form advise sink; fortunately, the *AddRef* method can complete within the scope of the client-side proxy; that is, without requiring a further RPC to some hypothetical server stub for *AddRef*.

Activating the form

Registering a view advise sink   The form is now fueled and ready to launch. However, before the client slings the form into deep space, it considers installing some telemetry equipment so that it can learn what befalls the form. Exchange client extensions that used the *IExchExtCallback::GetNewMessageSite* method to obtain their client support objects need not worry about this, because Exchange takes care of monitoring the form's heartbeat. All other clients must implement a view advise sink and register it with the form using the *IMAPIForm::Advise* method. The form notifies its clients of interesting events through the callbacks on its held view advise sinks, as listed in Table 7-8.

Igniting the form with a verb   A call to the *IMAPIForm::DoVerb* method culminates the launch sequence, converting the stored potential of a merely initialized form into a running form. *DoVerb* invocations specify the form's initial actions—that is, the manner in which the form should activate itself—using an integer

Callback Method	Description
OnNewMessage	A client has reinitialized the form, giving it a new message and message site. Unless the viewer receiving the notification is the viewer that did the reinitializing, it releases its interfaces on the form as no longer interesting.
OnPrint	The form has printed a page. This provides a communication channel for a view to display printing progress. A viewer printing a message registers a view advise sink, then activates the form with *EXCHIVERB_PRINT*, updating its printing-in-progress user interface in response to the form's notifications.
OnSaved	The form has completed committing its changes to the message.
OnSubmitted	The form has completed submitting its message to the spooler and will shut down shortly.
OnShutdown	The form is closing. The viewer should release all interfaces on it.

Table 7-8. *Callback methods on a view advise sink for the* IMAPIViewAdviseSink *interface.*

verb code. A form registers the verbs that it honors in the forms library, and from there the client can access them through the *IMAPIFormInfo::CalcVerbSet* method. The client should display as available options on a form's item any form verbs bearing the attribute *OLEVERBATTRIB_ONCONTAINERMENU.*

All forms share two common ranges of verb values.

- The standard OLE verb values are available to all forms. *OLEIVERB-_PRIMARY* (synonym: *EXCHIVERB_DEFAULT*) specifies that the form take its default action. Other standard OLE verb values are available as well, with *OLEIVERB_SHOW, OLEIVERB_OPEN,* and *OLEIVERB_HIDE* being the ones useful to forms, because the MAPI form user interface model does not support in-place activation. These values start at 0 (*OLEIVERB_PRIMARY*) and decline from there. (Verb codes are signed quantities.)

- The Microsoft Exchange standard form verbs are available to all forms that register themselves as supporting these verbs and that use the extension *PS_EXCHFORM* in their configuration file. These verbs start at value 100 and increase from there.

Between the values 0 and 100 lies the range of custom verb values, each specific to a particular form. For example, three forms might have three different interpretations of the verb value 1. A client with specific knowledge of the verbs of a particular form can activate a form with a specific verb value; otherwise, clients must restrict themselves to offering a form's set of verbs to the user and then relaying the code of the chosen verb to the form.

The client can specify an additional view context to the *IMAPIForm::DoVerb* invocation; if present, this view context overrides any default view context on the form for the duration of the form's execution of the verb. Clients typically use this to specify *VCSTATUS_MODAL* or *VCSTATUS_INTERACTIVE* when invoking verbs that require these settings, such as *EXCHIVERB_SAVEAS, EXCHI-VERB_PRINT,* or the standard open action in an environment mandating modal behavior, such as within another modal form.

A modal *DoVerb* call does not return to the client until its form has closed. Otherwise, the call returns to the client upon activating the form, leaving the form running asynchronous to the requesting client. Figure 7-4 shows the resulting relationship between client and form. The client holds the form interface for controlling the form and listens at its registered view advise sink for news about the form.

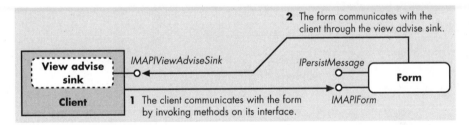

Figure 7-4. *Once a form starts to run, a client communicates with it through the interface that it retains on the form. A view advise sink serves to relay news of the form back to the client.*

Managing the Open Form

Launching the form is just the first step. Clients must continue to track and manage running forms through the interfaces that they hold.

Reactivating the form

The client is responsible for associating entries in its view window with existing form objects. When a user opens an item in the view window, the client does not launch a new form for that item if the item already has a form open and running. Any request to activate an item must therefore check first whether the activated item already exists and, if it does exist, check that it was activated with the same verb. If it is not modal to some other window, the client reactivates it with the *OLEIVERB_SHOW* verb, thus bringing it to the foreground.

Figure 7-5 on the following page shows this in action. The client keeps a list of all of the outstanding form instances that it controls, indexed by the item in the view that each one reflects, and remembers the verb with which it activated each form instance. The user selects an item and requests to open it; the client looks through its list, finds an entry for that item, finds that it was activated with the same verb (*OLEIVERB_DEFAULT*, in each case, for a generic Open action), and so brings the existing instance to the foreground instead of creating a new instance.

Releasing the form

The client is responsible for monitoring the state of the running form through its view advise sink. When the form closes, it announces its demise through all the view advise sinks that it holds; seeing this, a client releases its interfaces to the form and associated objects, allowing the system to clean up the odds and ends of the communication channel. The client also removes any record associating the form with a viewed item so that subsequent requests to open an item work properly.

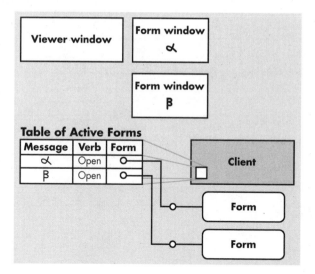

Figure 7-5. *The client reactivates existing form instances in preference to creating new ones.*

Clients also track return codes of value *RPC_E_SERVERFAULT*. These indicate that the server hosting the form object crashed, leaving the form object proxy in the client's address space. If this occurs, clients should call the *IUnknown::Release* method to free the object from memory.

Forcibly closing the form

Finally, there will be times when the client forcibly shuts down a running form. The most obvious case occurs when the client application closes all of the running forms as well. Upon receiving the close query, the client calls the *IMAPIForm::ShutdownForm* method with the *SAVEOPTS_PROMPTSAVE* option for each running form. This option specifies that any dirty forms request what direction to take before closing: should the form save its changes, discard changes, or demand to call off the whole shutdown sequence? If the user wavers in the face of any of these requests, that form refuses the shutdown request with *MAPI_E_USER_CANCEL*, whereupon the client cancels its own shutdown procedure.

Implementing Form Clients

Instead of implementing its own viewer, an Exchange application typically reuses the viewer of the Exchange client. The mechanics of such reuse are discussed in the next chapter. This chapter focuses on more common form client scenarios.

Deferring All the Work to MAPI

The first look at Figures 7-2 and 7-3 made the message clear: implementing a form viewer is hard work—not as difficult as implementing a server, perhaps, but still a lot of effort just to display a single message in its intended form. A client with sufficiently simple message display requirements, however, can take advantage of the higher-level form display mechanism of the *IMAPISession* methods *PrepareForm* (not to be confused with the *IMAPIFormMgr::PrepareForm* method) and *ShowForm*. If the client displays all messages modally, blocking synchronously on the call to the *ShowForm* method until the form closes, and needs no verb other than *EXCHIVERB_OPEN*, these methods save it a lot of effort; they relieve the form's client of any need to implement or interact with form interfaces. *IMAPIForm, IPersistMessage, IMAPIFormAdviseSink, IMAPIMessageSite, IMAPIViewContext, IMAPIViewAdviseSink*—all of these interfaces can remain foreign because MAPI handles them on the client's behalf.

The sample Chap07\Msgopen does little of interest except deliver an Exchange client extension that implements a command Simple Open on the Exchange File menu. The Simple Open command takes the item currently selected in the Exchange view window and displays that item using the *ShowForm* method. Because the *ShowForm* method uses a modal instance of the item's form, it blocks every window in Exchange, making it a poor substitute for the original File - Open command. The *ShowForm* method is most suitable for use either in standalone MAPI client applications or from deep within modal Exchange client extension dialog boxes, where the modal, single-message nature of its operation does not adversely affect user activity.[2]

Getting the information from Exchange

Start in the sample in file Chap07\Msgopen\EXT.CPP, where the extension obtains the identity of the message to open. The extension coordinates its implementation of the methods *IExchExtCommands::InitMenu* and *IExchExtUserEvents::OnSelectionChange* to ensure that Exchange enables its File - Simple Open command only when a user selects a single message in its view window. Once the user selects the extension's menu item, Exchange invokes its implementation of the *IExchExtCommands::DoCommand* method, which is the function *CExtImpl::DoCommand* in the Chap07\Msgopen\EXT.CPP file. After

---

2. Putting it in an Exchange client extension saves me as an author a lot of work; otherwise, I'd have to include some mechanism for selecting the message to display. It also makes a convenient way to test a form server for correct implementation of its *VCSTATUS_MODAL* handling of already-created messages: you can create an instance of the message by composing the form within the Exchange client and then, while still within Exchange, use the File - Simple Open command to check the form again.

assuring itself that Exchange is invoking it for its own menu command, the function turns to the Exchange extension callback interface in order to gather all the information it needs. To start with, it needs a parent window because the *IMAPISession::ShowForm* method always works modally to some window. (*CUICommon* is a class of the application that wraps its window objects—nothing more.) The function also needs an interface on the current MAPI session. This information is gathered in the following excerpt from the *CExtImpl::Do-Command* function:

```
STDMETHODIMP CExtImpl::DoCommand(IExchExtCallback* pmecb,
    UINT cmdid)
{
    if (cmdid != _cmdidStub)
        return S_FALSE;

    HRESULT hr;
    HWND hwnd;
    hr = pmecb->GetWindow(&hwnd);
    CUICommon ui(hwnd);

    IMAPISession *psess = NULL;
    hr = pmecb->GetSession(&psess, NULL);
    if (FAILED(hr))
        ui.Message(IDS_E_NOSESSION);
    ⋮
```

As a safety check, the function ensures that an element is selected and then retrieves everything it can learn about that element: its entry identifier, its message class, and the flags associated with that message. In the following continuation of the *DoCommand* method, the *GetSelectionItem* function is called to obtain this information:

```
    ⋮
    ULONG cElements;
    if (SUCCEEDED(hr))
    {
        hr = pmecb->GetSelectionCount(&cElements);
        if (FAILED(hr))
            ui.Message(IDS_E_EECBGLITCH);
        else if (cElements == 0)
        {
            assert(FALSE); // How was this ever selected?
            hr = E_FAIL;
        }
    }
```

```
ENTRYID* peid = NULL;
ULONG cbeid;
ULONG nType;
TCHAR szMsgClass[256];
ULONG ulMsgFlags;
if (SUCCEEDED(hr))
{
    hr = pmecb->GetSelectionItem(0L, &cbeid, &peid, &nType,
    szMsgClass, sizeof(szMsgClass), &ulMsgFlags, 0L);
    if (FAILED(hr))
        ui.Message(IDS_E_EECBGLITCH);
    else if (nType != MAPI_MESSAGE)
    {
        assert(FALSE); // How was this ever selected?
        hr = E_FAIL;
    }
}
    ⋮
```

Unfortunately, the callback does not return the message status flags from the contents table backing the Exchange client's view. MAPI defines this property *PR_MSG_STATUS* as being available only in contents tables of messages, not necessarily on message objects themselves, since most of its bits apply to the status of the message within the current view.

NOTE   The callback returns the message class as a vector of TCHAR. Message classes actually always use 8-bit characters.

The function also needs interfaces on the message store and folder hosting the message. These parameters are necessary for the *ShowForm* function and allow us to obtain a message interface from the entry identifier more efficiently. In the following excerpt from the *DoCommand* function, these parameters are defined in a call to the *GetObject* function and are used as in-parameters to the *SimpleMessageOpen* function:

```
⋮
IMsgStore* pmdb = NULL;
IMAPIFolder* pfld = NULL;
if (SUCCEEDED(hr))
{
    hr = pmecb->GetObject(&pmdb, (IMAPIProp**)&pfld);
    if (FAILED(hr))
        ui.Message(IDS_E_EECBGLITCH);
}
```

(continued)

```
if (SUCCEEDED(hr))
    SimpleMessageOpen(ui, psess, pmdb, pfld, peid, cbeid,
        szMsgClass, ulMsgFlags);
    ⋮
```

To unwind the above state, release the requested interfaces and return the storage of the entry identifier to the MAPI allocator. As shown in the concluding lines of the *DoCommand* function, the extension callback copies the message class string into a locally scoped buffer, requiring no further cleanup:

```
    ⋮
if (pfld)
    pfld->Release();
if (pmdb)
    pmdb->Release();
if (peid)
    MAPIFreeBuffer(peid);
if (psess)
    psess->Release();


    return S_OK; // Whatever the results--prevent redispatch.
}
```

Additional information not available from the callback

The function *SimpleMessageOpen* called in the *DoCommand* function appears in the file Chap07\Msgopen\WORK.CPP. In the following excerpt from the *SimpleMessageOpen* function, the *OpenEntry* function is called to obtain a message interface:

```
HRESULT SimpleMessageOpen(const CUICommon& ui, IMAPISession* psess,
    IMsgStore* pmdb, IMAPIFolder* pfld, const ENTRYID* peid,
    UINT cbeid, const TCHAR* pszMsgClass, ULONG ulMsgFlags)
{
    // Open message to read.

    IMessage* pmsg = NULL;
    ULONG ulType = 0L;
    HRESULT hr = pfld->OpenEntry(cbeid, (LPIID)&IID_IMessage,
        MAPI_DEFERRED_ERRORS|MAPI_BEST_ACCESS, &ulType,
        (IUnknown**)&pmsg);
    if (FAILED(hr))
    {
        ui.ErrorMessage(pfld, hr, IDS_WHILE_OPENING);
        return hr;
    }
    assert(ulType == MAPI_MESSAGE);
    ⋮
```

Note that in the function call to *OpenEntry*, the *MAPI_BEST_ACCESS* flag is specified to generalize read-write permissions. If the *OpenEntry* function is invoked on the user's own messages, this function returns a writable interface on the message, allowing the user to make changes to the message being read; if the *OpenEntry* function is invoked within a Microsoft Exchange Server public folder and the user lacks permission to modify a message, the function returns a read-only interface.

The function needs to know what kind of interface it obtained—read-only or read-write—as the *IMAPI::ShowForm* function will use that information to determine whether to request a read-only form or not. In addition, the function still lacks the status flags from the message. The *ShowForm* method needs that status property because some message store providers, specifically, Microsoft Exchange Server, track the conflict status of a message in the status property. Deep inside MAPI, *ShowForm* eventually invokes the *IMAPIFormMgr::IsInConflict* and *IMAPIFormMgr::LoadForm* methods, both of which need this status property to handle conflicting messages correctly. Fortunately, those message store providers that keep this important information in *PR_MSG_STATUS* also make the property available on the message object. Hence, this function can request the property from the message interface just obtained, at the same time that it requests the nature of the interface. In the following continuation of the *SimpleMessageOpen* function, the status of the message is obtained using a call to the *GetProps* method:

```
    ⋮
// Need PR_ACCESS_LEVEL from this opening,
// and PR_MSG_STATUS if the MDB provider supports it on message
// objects. In a better world, status would come from the
// client callback.

ULONG ulAccess;
ULONG ulStatus;
{
    enum {ivalAccess = 0, ivalStatus, cval};
    SizedSPropTagArray(cval, taga) = {2, {PR_ACCESS_LEVEL,
        PR_MSG_STATUS}};
    SPropValue* pval;
    ULONG cvalActual = cval;
    hr = pmsg->GetProps((LPSPropTagArray)&taga, 0, &cvalActual,
        &pval);
    if (FAILED(hr))
```

(continued)

```
            {
                ui.ErrorMessage(pmsg, hr, IDS_WHILE_OPENING);
                pmsg->Release();
                return hr;
            }
            if (pval[ivalAccess].ulPropTag == PR_ACCESS_LEVEL)
                ulAccess = pval[ivalAccess].Value.ul;
            else
                ulAccess = 0; // Read-only

            if (pval[ivalStatus].ulPropTag == PR_MSG_STATUS)
                ulStatus = pval[ivalStatus].Value.ul;
            else
                // Status wasn't available, so it can't be important.
                ulStatus = 0;

            ::MAPIFreeBuffer(pval);
    }
    ⋮
```

If the message store provider refuses to return the status property, then the function doesn't need it. In any case, we can proceed to prepare the form for calling the *ShowForm* function.

Preparing the form

To call the *ShowForm* function, the client first transfers ownership of the message to MAPI. Think about the operation of a message site. Since MAPI takes care of all the form interfaces for a client calling the *ShowForm* function, MAPI must implement its own message site to hand to the form object. This requires that MAPI own the message so that it can release all references to the message when submitting it to the spooler.

To give a message to MAPI for use in a *ShowForm* call, the client calls the *IMAPISession::PrepareForm* method and provides the interface to use. In response, MAPI supplies a numeric token representing the message that it holds for the client. This token acts a bit like a coat check in a restaurant:[3] when the time comes to show the form, the client supplies this token to MAPI so that MAPI knows which message to display.

---

3. If coat checks really worked this way, you'd never get your coat back in a restaurant. All you could do is hand the checker your ticket, whereupon the checker would smile sweetly, say "Thank you," and proceed to wear your coat for you. I hate it when that happens.

In the following continuation of the *SimpleMessageOpen* function, the *Prepare-Form* function is called, returning a token in the *nCookie* parameter:

```
    ⋮
ULONG nCookie;
hr = psess->PrepareForm(NULL, pmsg, &nCookie);
if (FAILED(hr))
{
    ui.ErrorMessage(psess, hr, IDS_WHILE_OPENING);
    pmsg->Release();
    return hr;
}

    ⋮
```

When MAPI accepts the message, it increments the message's reference count; correspondingly, the client now abandons its claim to the message by releasing its reference, as follows:

```
    ⋮
pmsg->Release();
    ⋮
```

Showing the form

Finally the client redeems its token ("Good for one form") and tells MAPI to display the message in a form. During the course of the call to the *IMAPISession-::ShowForm* method, MAPI creates the form object, creates all necessary host objects, initializes the form object, and displays the form, all synchronously with the call to the *ShowForm* method. This is shown in the concluding lines of the *SimpleMessageOpen* function:

```
    ⋮
hr = psess->ShowForm((ULONG)ui.GetHwndVisible(), pmdb, pfld,
    NULL, nCookie, NULL, 0L, ulStatus, ulMsgFlags, ulAccess,
    /*unconst*/ (TCHAR*)pszMsgClass);

if (FAILED(hr))
{
    ui.ErrorMessage(psess, hr, IDS_WHILE_OPENING);
    return hr;
}
    ⋮
```

The call does not return until the form shuts down.

Composing a Form from an Exchange Extension

Commonly, an Exchange extension needs to compose a message of a particular class. An application author might want to support a top-level command for the application, similar to the Compose - New Message command, rather than forcing the user to tunnel through the Compose - New Form dialog boxes or enter a particular folder application. Such an extension can use the *IMAPI-Session::ShowForm* method if it can live with the modal operation; otherwise, the extension needs to talk directly to the form.

The sample Chap07\Fwdasatt goes beyond this. It implements an Exchange extension command, Compose - Forward As Attachment, that forwards the currently selected message item as an attachment within a new instance of a message of class *IPM.Note*. If the user selects multiple messages and requests Compose - Forward, Exchange generates a new note form containing each selected message as an attachment. On a single message, however, the Exchange Compose - Forward command activates the item with the verb *EXCHIVERB-_FORWARD*; for the standard note form, that generates a new instance of the form—a response form—with the contents of the original message rendered in its body as text. Instead, the Forward As Attachment command composes a new message and attaches the current selection, with the results shown in Figure 7-6. The outer message is called the envelope because it serves to contain the inner, attached message and conveys that attachment to its destination. The envelope uses message class *IPM.Note*, which is readable and writable by everybody. The envelope does not care about the message class of its contents; it knows only that it carries a message of some type.

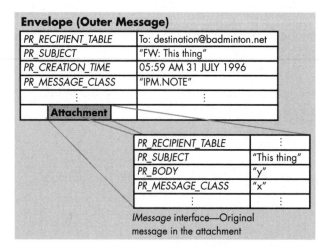

Envelope (Outer Message)

PR_RECIPIENT_TABLE	To: destination@badminton.net
PR_SUBJECT	"FW: This thing"
PR_CREATION_TIME	05:59 AM 31 JULY 1996
PR_MESSAGE_CLASS	"IPM.NOTE"

Attachment

PR_RECIPIENT_TABLE	⋮
PR_SUBJECT	"This thing"
PR_BODY	"y"
PR_MESSAGE_CLASS	"x"

IMessage interface—Original
message in the attachment

Figure 7-6. *Forward As Attachment stores a message as an attachment to an outer message, called the envelope. The envelope delivers its contents to its destination without altering its cargo.*

The extension from a view context

In source file Chap07\Fwdasatt\EXT.CPP, we see an Exchange extension structure very similar to that of the previous sample Chap07\Msgopen\EXT.CPP. However, the Fwdasatt extension differs in that it supports the command both in the view and in the note form contexts. The two contexts supply different sorts of information to the extension and thus require two markedly different bodies of code in their command handlers.

In the function *CExtImpl::DoCommand* of the Chap07\Fwdasatt\EXT.CPP file, the viewer context handler in particular is almost identical to that of the *CExtImpl::DoCommand* of the Chap07\Msgopen\EXT.CPP file. However, the implementation of the *DoCommand* in the Fwdasatt application differs from that of the Msgopen application in that the Fwdasatt implementation is not focused on the message store interface, the message class of the selected item, and the contents of the message flags. Instead, the extension callback *GetSession* is called to describe the currently selected message, and then the function *ForwardAsAttachment* is called to implement the Compose - Forward (as attachment) command. This is shown in the following excerpt from the *DoCommand* of the Fwdasatt application:

```
STDMETHODIMP CExtImpl::DoCommand(IExchExtCallback* pmecb,
    UINT cmdid)
{
    if (cmdid != _cmdidStub)
        return S_FALSE;

    HRESULT hr;
    HWND hwnd;
    hr = pmecb->GetWindow(&hwnd);
    CUICommon ui(hwnd);

    if (EECONTEXT_VIEWER == _context)
    {
        IMAPISession *psess = NULL;
        hr = pmecb->GetSession(&psess, NULL);
        if (FAILED(hr))
            ui.Message(IDS_E_NOSESSION);

        ULONG cElements;
        if (SUCCEEDED(hr))
        {
            hr = pmecb->GetSelectionCount(&cElements);
            if (FAILED(hr))
                ui.Message(IDS_E_EECBGLITCH);
```

(continued)

```
        else if (cElements != 1)
        {
            // How was this ever selected? See InitMenu.
            assert(FALSE);
            hr = E_FAIL;
        }
    }

    ENTRYID* peid = NULL;
    ULONG cbeid;
    ULONG nType;
    if (SUCCEEDED(hr))
    {
        hr = pmecb->GetSelectionItem(0L, &cbeid, &peid, &nType,
            NULL, 0L, NULL, 0L);
        if (FAILED(hr))
            ui.Message(IDS_E_EECBGLITCH);
        else if (nType != MAPI_MESSAGE)
        {
            assert(FALSE); // How was this ever selected?
            hr = E_FAIL;
        }
    }

    IMAPIFolder* pfld = NULL;
    if (SUCCEEDED(hr))
    {
        hr = pmecb->GetObject(NULL, (IMAPIProp**)&pfld);
        if (FAILED(hr))
            ui.Message(IDS_E_EECBGLITCH);
    }

    if (SUCCEEDED(hr))
        ForwardAsAttachment(ui, psess, pfld, peid, cbeid,
            pmecb);

    if (pfld)
        pfld->Release();
    if (peid)
        MAPIFreeBuffer(peid);
    if (psess)
        psess->Release();
}
    :
```

The extension from a note form context

The note form context handler is less complicated than the viewer context handler. Running within an instance of the note form, the note form context handler already has access to an instance of the current message object, which it uses instead of reopening the object through the entry identifier and container (folder) interface. In the following continuation of the *DoCommand* function, the already-existing current message object is used in the call to the *GetObject* function:

```
    ⋮
else
{
    assert(EECONTEXT_READNOTEMESSAGE == _context ||
        EECONTEXT_READPOSTMESSAGE == _context);

    IMAPISession *psess = NULL;
    hr = pmecb->GetSession(&psess, NULL);
    if (FAILED(hr))
        ui.Message(IDS_E_NOSESSION);

    IMessage* pmsg = NULL;
    if (SUCCEEDED(hr))
    {
        hr = pmecb->GetObject(NULL, (IMAPIProp**)&pmsg);
        if (FAILED(hr))
            ui.Message(IDS_E_EECBGLITCH);
    }

    if (SUCCEEDED(hr))
        hr = ForwardAsAttachment(ui, psess, pmsg, pmecb);

    if (pmsg)
        pmsg->Release();
    if (psess)
        psess->Release();
    ⋮
```

If it successfully brings up a form forwarding the current message, this function closes the original message. The member function *CUICommon::Close* does nothing more than send a *WM_CLOSE* message to its window. The Exchange client allows the user to control this behavior by choosing the Close The Original Item check box of the Tools - Options - Read dialog box; because the extension lacks access to that parameter,[4] the *Close* function assumes that this option is always set, as shown in the following lines of the *DoCommand* function.

---

4. Also, the extension author is too lazy to reverse engineer the options settings in the profile.

```
    ⋮
    // Close the current form.

    if (SUCCEEDED(hr))
        ui.Close();
    }

    return S_OK;
}
```

A class definition and safe interfaces

The function *ForwardAsAttachment* appears in the source file Chap07\Fwdasatt-\WORK.CPP. This function takes two different forms, reflecting the different sets of information available to the viewer and note form extension contexts. Each form builds an instance of class *CTargetMessage* to abstract the differences in available information and then invokes the *Forward* member function to create the new form with data from the given message. The *ForwardAsAttachment* function for the viewer context is as follows:

```
HRESULT ForwardAsAttachment(const CUICommon& ui,
    IMAPISession* psess, IMAPIFolder* pfld, const ENTRYID* peid,
    UINT cbeid, IExchExtCallback* pmecb)
{
    CTargetMessage target(ui, pfld, peid, cbeid);
    return target.Forward(psess, pmecb);
}
```

The *ForwardAsAttachment* function for the note form context is as follows:

```
HRESULT ForwardAsAttachment(const CUICommon& ui,
    IMAPISession* psess, IMessage* pmsg, IExchExtCallback* pmecb)
{
    CTargetMessage target(ui, pmsg);
    return target.Forward(psess, pmecb);
}
```

The class *CTargetMessage* holds mostly state information passed to it when the message is constructed. For messages specified directly by message interface, the class holds that interface; otherwise, it holds an interface to the parent folder and the entry identifier necessary to open it within that folder. Privately, it contains a class encapsulating the creation of the note form necessary for containing the forwarded message attachment. Encapsulation of this information is shown in the following excerpt from the WORK.CPP file:

```
class CTargetMessage
{
private:
    const CUICommon& _ui;

    SpIMAPIFolder    _spfld;
    const ENTRYID*   _peid;
    ULONG            _cbeid;
    SpIMessage       _spmsg;

    HRESULT WrapInto(IMessage* pmsgOut) const;

    // Encapsulate resolving and running an instance of the standard
    // note form. NOT safe for reuse as is--needs better
    // resolve/run state control.

    class CNoteFormWrapper
    {
        ⋮
    };

public:
    CTargetMessage(const CUICommon& ui, IMAPIFolder* pfld,
        const ENTRYID* peid, ULONG cbeid)
        : _ui(ui), _spfld(pfld), _peid(peid), _cbeid(cbeid) {}
    CTargetMessage(const CUICommon& ui, IMessage* pmsg)
        : _ui(ui), _spmsg(pmsg), _peid(NULL), _cbeid(0) {}

    HRESULT Forward(IMAPISession* psess, IExchExtCallback* pmecb);
};
```

Throughout this class and elsewhere in this application, the code makes extensive use of so-called safe interface pointers to automate managing reference counts on interfaces. In the following lines from the WORK.CPP file, you see the safe interface pointers used to create the types *SpIMAPIFolder*, *SpIMAPIFormMgr*, and the like:

```
// This file extensively uses the Sp forms of interfaces
// to automate reference counting thereon.

#include "safeiptr.h"

DECLARE_SAFE_INTERFACE(IMAPIFolder);
```

(continued)

```
DECLARE_SAFE_INTERFACE(IMessage);
DECLARE_SAFE_INTERFACE(IAttach);
DECLARE_SAFE_INTERFACE(IMAPIFormMgr);
DECLARE_SAFE_INTERFACE(IMAPIFormInfo);
DECLARE_SAFE_INTERFACE(IMAPIForm);
DECLARE_SAFE_INTERFACE(IPersistMessage);
```

The very top of the WORK.CPP file includes the necessary SAFEIPTR.H header file and builds the templates using the *DECLARE_SAFE_INTERFACE* macro; thereafter, the client code constructs instances of these pointers, trusting them to manage reference counts correctly. For example, look at the first constructor to *CTargetMessage*. By constructing its *SpIMAPIFolder _spfld* member variable, it copies the passed *IMAPIFolder** parameter, incrementing the reference count on the interface through an automatic *IUnknown::AddRef* method. Upon destruction, the *SpIMAPIFolder* destructor releases that reference.

Getting an instance of the form

The embedded class *CTargetMessage::CNoteFormWrapper* manages the instance of the note form needed to forward the target message. *CTargetMessage* uses it by constructing an instance of the class and then using the *CTargetMessage::CNoteFormWrapper::Resolve* member function to have the class bind itself to an instance of a form object. Finally the caller invokes the *CTargetMessage::CNoteFormWrapper::Launch* method to initialize that form object with a message site containing the message data to forward, and sends it on its way. The *CNoteFormWrapper* class is defined in the following excerpt from the WORK-.CPP file:

```
class CTargetMessage
{
private:
    class CNoteFormWrapper
    {
    private:
        const CUICommon& _uiParent;

        SpIMAPIFormMgr _spfrmmgr;
        SpIMAPIFormInfo _spfrminf;
        SpIMAPIForm _spfrm;
        SpIPersistMessage _sppermsg;

    public:
        CNoteFormWrapper(const CUICommon& ui)
            : _uiParent(ui) {}
        HRESULT Resolve(IMAPISession*);
```

```
        HRESULT Launch(IMAPIMessageSite*, IMessage*, IMAPIViewContext*);

        SpIPersistMessage GetInterface()
            { return _sppermsg; }
    };

public:

    ⋮

};
```

NOTE Chapter 1 discussed the *SafeIPtr* template that backs safe interface pointers. In short, the *IUnknown::AddRef* function is called
for the safe interface pointers to the backing interface when
these pointers are copied, and the *IUnknown::Release* method
is called when these pointers are destroyed. They support two
metamethods, *Adopt* and *Abandon*, allowing the client to graft
an existing interface pointer onto a safe pointer or to extract it
without changing the reference count, respectively.

The following *Resolve* member function opens an instance of the Forms Manager, resolves the well-known message class *IPM.Note* to get a form information
object, and then calls the *IMAPIFormMgr::CreateForm* function to create an
uninitialized instance of the form object.

```
HRESULT CTargetMessage::CNoteFormWrapper::Resolve(
    IMAPISession* psess)
{
    HRESULT hr = MAPIOpenFormMgr(psess,
        (IMAPIFormMgr**)_spfrmmgr.Adopt());
    if (FAILED(hr))
    {
        _uiParent.Message(IDS_ERROR_WHILE_LAUNCHING);
        return hr;
    }

    hr = _spfrmmgr->ResolveMessageClass("IPM.Note", 0, NULL,
        (IMAPIFormInfo**)_spfrminf.Adopt());
    if (FAILED(hr))
    {
        _uiParent.ErrorMessage(_spfrmmgr, hr, IDS_WHILE_LAUNCHING);
        return hr;
    }
```

(continued)

```
// From the resolved message class, get interfaces on the form.

hr = _spfrmmgr->CreateForm((ULONG)_uiParent.GetHwnd(),
    MAPI_DIALOG, _spfrminf, IID_IPersistMessage,
    _sppermsg.Adopt());
if (FAILED(hr))
{
    _uiParent.ErrorMessage(_spfrmmgr, hr, IDS_WHILE_LAUNCHING);
    return hr;
}

hr = _sppermsg->QueryInterface(IID_IMAPIForm, _spfrm.Adopt());
if (FAILED(hr))
{
    _uiParent.ErrorMessage(_sppermsg, hr, IDS_WHILE_LAUNCHING);
    return hr;
}

return S_OK;
}
```

Every time the *Resolve* member function acquires a new interface, it leaves the interface in a safe pointer member variable of the class; after the class destructor executes, the safe pointers release the reference in their own destructors.

At the conclusion of this member function, the class has a form object and now awaits the *Launch* function to give that object some host interfaces and activate the object.

Launching that form instance

After calling the note form wrapper's *Resolve* member function, the calling function gets the host interfaces and then hands those interfaces to the form wrapper through the wrapper's *CTargetMessage::CNoteFormWrapper::Launch* function. Since the message contains data—an attachment containing the original target message—for the form to use, the *Launch* function must not initialize its form with the *IPersistMessage::InitNew* function; instead, the *Launch* function calls the *IPersistMessage::Load* method, thus telling the form to initialize itself from the data in the message. If the *Launch* method called the *InitNew* function instead of the *Load* function, the *Launch* function would perform a more traditional Compose - New operation. Ordinarily, a client doesn't necessarily know which message format that a particular form expects; in such cases, the client gives the form a message against which to work and calls the *InitNew* method to tell the form to use whatever defaults suit it. Because the client knows the schema of message class *IPM.Note*, it can supply some additional settings. Note that the call to the *Load* function explicitly specifies the *MSGFLAG_UNSENT* flag as a parameter. The form must know that the message is unsent to bring up the still-under-composition user interface and allow the user to address and submit the message. The *Load* function is called in the following code for the *Launch* function:

```
HRESULT CTargetMessage::CNoteFormWrapper::Launch(
    IMAPIMessageSite* pmsgsite, IMessage* pmsg,
    IMAPIViewContext* pvwctx)
{
    assert(0 != (IPersistMessage*)_sppermsg);

    // Given the new message, associate it with the form.

    HRESULT hr = _sppermsg->Load(pmsgsite, pmsg, 0,
        MSGFLAG_UNSENT);
    if (FAILED(hr))
    {
        _uiParent.ErrorMessage(_sppermsg, hr, IDS_WHILE_LAUNCHING);
        return hr;
    }
    ⋮
```

When the function activates the form, the function plays the role of the client and supplies the coordinates of the rectangle bounding the form's dimensions. Lacking better information about the Exchange client's preferences, the best that this client extension can do is to guess at these dimensions through a series of calls to the *GetSystemMetrics* function, as follows:

```
    ⋮
    const int iOffset = ::GetSystemMetrics(SM_CYCAPTION);
    const int cxMax = ::GetSystemMetrics(SM_CXMAXIMIZED)/2;
    const int cyMax = ::GetSystemMetrics(SM_CYMAXIMIZED)/2;
    RECT rcHere;
    _uiParent.GetRect(&rcHere);
    ::OffsetRect(&rcHere, iOffset, iOffset);
    if (rcHere.right - rcHere.left > cxMax)
        rcHere.right = rcHere.left + cxMax;
    if (rcHere.bottom - rcHere.top > cyMax)
        rcHere.bottom = rcHere.top + cyMax;

    // Tell the form to bring up some user interface.
```

(continued)

445

```
    hr = _spfrm->SetViewContext(pvwctx);
    if (SUCCEEDED(hr))
        hr = _spfrm->DoVerb(OLEIVERB_PRIMARY, NULL,
            (ULONG)_uiParent.GetHwnd(), &rcHere);
    if (FAILED(hr))
    {
        _uiParent.ErrorMessage(_spfrm, hr, IDS_WHILE_LAUNCHING);
        _spfrm->ShutdownForm(SAVEOPTS_NOSAVE);
        return hr;
    }


    // At this point, the running form user interface and the
    // hosting client's view both hold references to the form,
    // so it's safe for this function's caller to release
    // everything by destroying the CNoteFormWrapper object.

    return S_OK;
}
```

After the function successfully executes, the form is running and displaying a window owned by the form's server. This function's caller can then release all of its references to that form by destroying the *CNoteFormWrapper* object, which destroys the *_spfrm* safe pointer, and thus releases the form interface. The form continues to run, with references to the form object held both by the form itself and—as the next section will show—by the Exchange client.

The source of the host interfaces

The instance of the note form wrapper class lives entirely within the scope of the *Forward* method. This method takes its host target message, generates the new form object in which to forward it, obtains the necessary host interfaces, builds the message for the form to use within those interfaces, and finally launches the form.

The *Forward* method uses the Exchange client extension callback to get a new message for its form plus interfaces on the necessary host objects; this saves the method from having to implement those interfaces itself. The callback *IExch-ExtCallback::GetNewMessageSite* method can create a message and interfaces either for a send form or a post form; because the function knows that it is feeding the resulting message site to the standard send note, it specifies the send note behavior. Once the function has a message and a message site, it renders the target message into that message so that the note forwards it. This is why the form wrapper class's *CTargetMessage::CNoteFormWrapper::Launch* member function initializes its form object with the *IPersistMessage::Load* function. Using the *IPersistMessage::InitNew* method (as you might expect for a newly composed message) tells the form to ignore all of the data that the client dropped into the message.

If a modal form launches another form, it must launch that form, in turn, as a modal form. An Exchange client extension has no convenient way of determining whether the form currently hosting the extension is modal. Hence, the *Forward* function first tries to create the host interfaces for nonmodal operation. If the callback complains, the function assumes that it objected to the request for nonmodal operation and tries again, specifying *EECBGNMS_MODAL* for a modal form. The code for performing these actions is shown in the following *Forward* function:

```
HRESULT CTargetMessage::Forward(IMAPISession* psess,
    IExchExtCallback* pmecb)
{
    CNoteFormWrapper form(_ui);
    HRESULT hr = form.Resolve(psess);
    if (FAILED(hr))
        return hr;

    // From the hosting client, get a new message site.
    // We know IPM.Note to be a send form, so we can specify as
    // much without interrogating its form information object.

    IMAPIMessageSite*      pmsgsite = NULL;
    IMAPIViewContext*      pvwctx = NULL;
    IMessage*              pmsgNew = NULL;
    ULONG ulFlags = 0;
    for (;;)
    {
        // We don't know whether this client extension is running
        // from a window that is modal or not. So first, try for a
        // normal form; if the callback refuses that, try again
        // modally.

        hr = pmecb->GetNewMessageSite(FALSE, NULL,
            form.GetInterface(), &pmsgNew, &pmsgsite, &pvwctx,
            ulFlags);
        if (MAPI_E_INVALID_PARAMETER == hr && 0 == ulFlags)
            ulFlags = EECBGNMS_MODAL; // And try again....
        else
            break; // Enough already!
    }
```

(continued)

```
        if (FAILED(hr))
        {
            _ui.Message(IDS_ERROR_WHILE_FORWARDING);
            return hr;
        }

        // Given the new message site, wrap the target message in an
        // envelope within it and then give the resulting envelope to the
        // form.

        hr = WrapInto(pmsgNew);
        if (SUCCEEDED(hr))
            hr = form.Launch(pmsgsite, pmsgNew, pvwctx);

        // Release interfaces acquired from extension callback.
        // These are all now held by the running form.

        if (pmsgsite)
            pmsgsite->Release();
        if (pvwctx)
            pvwctx->Release();
        if (pmsgNew)
            pmsgNew->Release();

        return hr;
}
```

When the *Forward* function returns, its instance of the form wrapper class *CTargetMessage::CNoteFormWrapper* goes out of scope, invoking its destructor. This releases all of the wrapper's interfaces on the form object. The Exchange client still holds an interface to the form object—one that it acquired when this function passed a reference to the *IPersistMessage* interface to the new message site callback. It uses that interface to control the form's lifetime, as necessary. Therefore, the function can return without holding any other interfaces or without concerning itself further with the form's lifetime. If the user shuts down Exchange, Exchange can in turn shut down the running form (using the *IMAPIForm::ShutdownForm* method) for correct overall application behavior.

Clients of the *IExchExtCallback::GetNewMessageSite* callback function pass an interface to the form object as a parameter to the callback function to get the host interfaces from the Exchange client. The Exchange client does not provide a message site interface until it has a form interface with which to associate it. For this reason, such clients always use the *IMAPIFormMgr::CreateForm* method to acquire their form objects, even if they subsequently give those form objects messages through the *IPersistMessage::Load* method, because the *IMAPIFormMgr::LoadForm* method requires the message site interface before returning the form interface.

Attaching the original message

The private member function *CTargetMessage::WrapInto* renders the current message into the passed message as a message attachment, as shown in the following excerpt from the file Chap07\Fwdasatt\WORK.CPP:

```
HRESULT CTargetMessage::WrapInto(IMessage* pmsgOut) const
{
    SPropValue rgval[2];

    // The forwarder wraps its message in a note form.
    // I'm counting on the Exchange extensibility callback to set
    // all the usual defaults on the new message.

    rgval[0].ulPropTag = PR_MESSAGE_CLASS;
    rgval[0].Value.lpszA = "IPM.Note";

    // Build body property.
    // Be sure to change PR_RENDERING_POSITION in sync with this.

    rgval[1].ulPropTag = PR_BODY;
    rgval[1].Value.LPSZ = __T("\r\n    \r\n");

    // Set what we have so far.

    HRESULT hr = pmsgOut->SetProps(2, rgval, NULL);
    if (FAILED(hr))
    {
        _ui.ErrorMessage(pmsgOut, hr, IDS_WHILE_FORWARDING);
        return hr;
    }
    :
```

In the preceding excerpt, the *WrapInto* function sets the message class and body properties of the new message. The message class matches that of the standard note form, which is used as the envelope to carry the attachment. The body contains nothing but white space: an empty line before, an empty line after, and some spaces where the code inserts the attachment.

Next the function opens the source message, both to copy it into the attachment on the new message and to read its subject line so that the subject of the envelope message matches that of the message being forwarded. Recall that *CTargetMessage* has two constructors: one describes the message as an entry identifier within a particular folder, while the other passes an existing message interface. If the class has an entry identifier (here noted by having a nonzero byte count for the entry identifier), then this function opens that entry identifier to reach the message. Otherwise, the function just copies the existing reference, using the safe pointer assignment logic to increment the interface's reference count correctly. Since the safe pointer is a local variable, it releases its interface when the function exits, and the local variable goes out of scope. In the following excerpt from the *WrapInto* function, the *OpenEntry* function is called to open the source message:

```
    ⋮
SpIMessage spmsgIn;
if (_cbeid != 0)
{
    ULONG ulType = 0L;
    hr = _spfld->OpenEntry(_cbeid, /*unconst*/ (ENTRYID*)_peid,
        (LPIID)&IID_IMessage, MAPI_DEFERRED_ERRORS|MAPI_MODIFY,
        &ulType, (IUnknown**)spmsgIn.Adopt());
    if (FAILED(hr))
    {
        _ui.ErrorMessage(_spfld, hr, IDS_WHILE_FORWARDING);
        return hr;
    }
    assert(ulType == MAPI_MESSAGE);
}
else
    spmsgIn = _spmsg;
    ⋮
```

The function then builds the attachment on the output message. By introducing a new level of scope, the function specifies the lifetime of local variables declared within that scope. Here it declares a safe pointer housing an attachment interface, loading that pointer immediately thereafter with the *IMessage-::CreateAttach* function; when this safe pointer goes out of scope, it releases its interface, thus closing the attachment, as shown in the following excerpt from the *WrapInto* function:

```
    ⋮
{
    ULONG nAttach;
    SpIAttach spatt;
    hr = pmsgOut->CreateAttach(NULL, MAPI_DEFERRED_ERRORS,
        &nAttach, (IAttach**)spatt.Adopt());
    if (FAILED(hr))
    {
        ui.ErrorMessage(pmsgOut, hr, IDS_WHILE_FORWARDING);
        return hr;
    }
    ⋮
```

The function warns the message store that it can attach a message by setting the property *PR_ATTACH_METHOD* to *ATTACH_EMBEDDED_MSG*. It also specifies the offset within the message body at which the icon should appear by setting the property *PR_RENDERING_POSITION*. Earlier in the *WrapInto* function, the envelope's message body was defined as consisting of a new line sequence (CR + LF), three spaces, and another new line sequence; now this specifies the offset as 3, effectively replacing the center space character with the icon, to make the envelope message body appear as new line, space, icon, space, new line. The code to set these properties is shown in the following excerpt from the *WrapInto* function:

```
    ⋮
rgval[0].ulPropTag = PR_ATTACH_METHOD;
rgval[0].Value.ul = ATTACH_EMBEDDED_MSG;
rgval[1].ulPropTag = PR_RENDERING_POSITION;
rgval[1].Value.ul = 3;

hr = spatt->SetProps(2, rgval, NULL);
if (FAILED(hr))
{
    _ui.ErrorMessage(spatt, hr, IDS_WHILE_FORWARDING);
    return hr;
}
    ⋮
```

Introducing another level of scope, the function opens the attachment as a message to copy the source message into this attachment. Because the attachment and its data do not yet exist, the function specifies *MAPI_CREATE* to the *OpenProperty* call that obtains the message interface, as shown in the following excerpt from the *WrapInto* function:

```
    ⋮
{
    SpIMessage spmsgAtt;
    hr = spatt->OpenProperty(PR_ATTACH_DATA_OBJ, &IID_IMessage,
        0, MAPI_CREATE|MAPI_MODIFY|MAPI_DEFERRED_ERRORS,
        (IUnknown**)spmsgAtt.Adopt());
    if (FAILED(hr))
    {
        _ui.ErrorMessage(spatt, hr, IDS_WHILE_FORWARDING);
        return hr;
    }
```

(continued)

```
    hr = spmsgIn->CopyTo(0, NULL, NULL, 0, NULL,
        &IID_IMessage, spmsgAtt, 0, NULL);
    if (FAILED(hr))
    {
        _ui.ErrorMessage(spmsgIn, hr, IDS_WHILE_FORWARDING);
        return hr;
    }
    ⋮
```

At each level, the function commits its changes to the object through the *IMAPIProp::SaveChanges* method on the object before releasing the object interface. As each local safe pointer goes out of scope, its destructor releases its interface. At the end, the function has created an attachment on the envelope, with the attachment containing the message data of the original message. Any client can subsequently open this attachment, request a message interface, and host a form on the resulting interface to render the original message.

The *WrapInto* function calls the *SaveChanges* function to save changes on the embedded message and attachment objects in the following excerpt:

```
    ⋮
    hr = spatt->SaveChanges(FORCE_SAVE|MAPI_DEFERRED_ERRORS);
    if (FAILED(hr))
    {
        _ui.ErrorMessage(spatt, hr, IDS_WHILE_FORWARDING);
        return hr;
    }
}
    ⋮
```

Having released the embedded message and attachment objects, the *WrapInto* function still holds the interface to the source message, which the function must use to read the subject of the original message. From that subject, the code derives the subject of the envelope message. It starts with the normalized subject of the original message, which is the subject, less any prefixes such as *RE:* or *FW:*, describing the action that created the current message. On the normalized subject, it prefixes the string *FW:* (here the symbol *SzFW_Prefix*) and then sets the results as the subject of the envelope. The code for constructing the subject of the envelope message is shown in the following excerpt from the *WrapInto* function:

```
    ⋮
enum {ivalSubject = 0, cval};
SizedSPropTagArray(cval, taga) = {1, { PR_NORMALIZED_SUBJECT }};
SPropValue* pval;
ULONG cvalRead = cval;
```

```
hr = spmsgIn->GetProps((LPSPropTagArray)&taga, 0, &cvalRead,
    &pval);
if (FAILED(hr))
{
    _ui.ErrorMessage(spmsgIn, hr, IDS_WHILE_FORWARDING);
    return hr;
}

ULONG cch;
if (pval[ivalSubject].ulPropTag == PR_NORMALIZED_SUBJECT)
{
    cch = _tcslen(pval[ivalSubject].Value.LPSZ);
}
else
    cch = 0;

TCHAR * pszSubject = NULL;
hr = MAPIAllocateBuffer(
    (cch+_tcslen(::SzFW_PREFIX)+1)*sizeof(TCHAR),
    (void**)&pszSubject);
if (FAILED(hr))
{
    _ui.Message(IDS_ERROR_WHILE_FORWARDING);
    MAPIFreeBuffer(pval);
    return hr;
}

*pszSubject = '\0';
_tcscat(pszSubject, ::SzFW_PREFIX);

if (cch > 0)
    _tcscat(pszSubject, pval[ivalSubject].Value.LPSZ);

MAPIFreeBuffer(pval);
// Set the subject on the output message.

rgval[0].ulPropTag = PR_SUBJECT;
rgval[0].Value.LPSZ = pszSubject;

hr = pmsgOut->SetProps(1, rgval, NULL);
if (FAILED(hr))
{
    _ui.ErrorMessage(pmsgOut, hr, IDS_WHILE_FORWARDING);
    MAPIFreeBuffer(pszSubject);
    return hr;
}

MAPIFreeBuffer(pszSubject);
⋮
```

Note that the *WrapInto* function does not commit its changes to the output message. The output message is the prerogative of the Exchange client because the Exchange client ultimately owns the hosting message site. It can commit changes embedded within the message, such as the attachment that it creates, but it cannot commit the message itself. This leaves the hosting message site free to drop the entire message.

Creating a Response Form Within a Form Server

Forms frequently create other form objects themselves, either when they implement a Compose - New command or when they create a response form. A *response form* is a new form created by a form with some relationship to the current item. The command Compose - Reply To Sender on the standard note form *IPM.Note* creates a response form—here a new instance of the same class *IPM.Note*—with a representation of the previous message rendered in the body of the new form and the recipients table preset to contain the sender of the original message. In Microsoft Schedule+, accepting or declining a meeting invitation yields a response form of a different class, bearing the response to the person sending the invitation. A form verb that creates a response form is called, unsurprisingly, a response form verb. Forms implement response form verbs by creating and activating the response forms directly; the item originally activated never appears, creating the illusion that the response form is a different view of the originally activated item.

Creating the form

Returning to the last chapter's sample in Chap06\Sendstub\FORM.CPP, we find that the function *CStubSendForm::HrRespondForm*, called from the function implementing *IMAPIForm::DoVerb*, does almost all the work. In the code for the following Sendstub's *HrRespondForm* function, note the strong similarities to the member function *CTargetMessage::Forward* of the preceding example (Chap07\Fwdasatt\WORK.CPP):

```
HRESULT CStubSendForm::HrRespondForm(HWND hwndParent, LPCRECT prc)
{
    IMAPIForm* pfrm = NULL;
    IPersistMessage* ppermsg = NULL;
    IMAPIMessageSite* pmsgsite = NULL;
    IMAPIViewContext* pvwctx = NULL;
    IMessage* pmsg = NULL;

    assert(_pmsg);
    ⋮
```

The stub send form holds, in a member variable, an interface to the class object that created it. This allows it to return to that class object directly to create a new form instance, because it wants its response form to use the same class as itself. In the following excerpt from the *HrRespondForm* function, the stub send form gets an interface to the class object:

```
⋮
HRESULT hr = S_OK;

// Get the initialization interface on a new form object.

hr = _pfactory->CreateInstance(NULL, IID_IPersistMessage,
    (void**)&ppermsg);
if (FAILED(hr))
{
    _lasterr.Set(hr);
    goto unwind;
}

// Get the MAPI form interface as well.
// We could defer this until immediately preceding the DoVerb,
// but doing it here it simplifies flow-of-control on error.

hr = ppermsg->QueryInterface(IID_IMAPIForm, (void**)&pfrm);
if (hr)
{
    _lasterr.Set(hr, ppermsg);
    goto unwind;
}
⋮
```

The stub send form uses its message site to acquire the host interfaces for the response form that it launches. As did the preceding example, it renders some contents into its new message and then initializes the new form with the *IPersist-Message::Load* function. If this implemented a Compose - New command instead, the form would use the *IPersistMessage::InitNew* function. In the following excerpt from the *HrRespondForm* function, the stub send form acquires a new message and initializes that message to contain response message data:

```
⋮
// Now get a new message (message site, etc.),
// and initialize that message to contain response message
// data.
```

(continued)

```
        hr = _pmsgsite->NewMessage(FALSE, NULL, ppermsg, &pmsg,
            &pmsgsite, &pvwctx);
        if (FAILED(hr))
        {
            _lasterr.Set(hr, _pmsgsite);
            goto unwind;
        }
        hr = HrCreateResponseMsg(pmsg);
        if (FAILED(hr))
            goto unwind; // Cascade error--already set
        hr = HrAddressResponseMsg(pmsg);
        if (FAILED(hr))
            goto unwind; // Cascade error--already set

        // Given the new message, associate it with the form.

        hr = ppermsg->Load(pmsgsite, pmsg, 0, MSGFLAG_UNSENT);
        if (FAILED(hr))
        {
            _lasterr.Set(hr, ppermsg);
            goto unwind;
        }

        // Tell the form to bring up the user interface.

        hr = pfrm->DoVerb(EXCHIVERB_OPEN, pvwctx, (ULONG)hwndParent,
            prc);
        if (FAILED(hr))
        {
            _lasterr.Set(hr, pfrm);
            pfrm->ShutdownForm(SAVEOPTS_NOSAVE);
            goto unwind;
        }


        // At this point, the running form user interface and the
        // hosting client's view both hold references to the form,
        // so it's safe for this function to release everything.


    unwind:
        if (pfrm)
            pfrm->Release();
        if (ppermsg)
            ppermsg->Release();
```

```
    if (pmsgsite)
        pmsgsite->Release();
    if (pvwctx)
        pvwctx->Release();
    if (pmsg)
        pmsg->Release();

    return hr;
}
```

Addressing the form

In the course of building the message for the response form, the stub send form sample preaddresses the form to the sender, Reply style. From the five *PR_SENDER_xxx* properties consisting of (*PR_SENDER_ENTRYID*, *PR_SENDER-_NAME*, *PR_SENDER_EMAIL_ADDRESS*, *PR_SENDER_ADDRTYPE*, and *PR-_SENDER_SEARCH_KEY*) on the source message, the *HrAddressResponseMsg* function builds an entry in an ADRLIST with the five central properties of a messaging recipient object. This sets the form's recipient type to *MAPI_TO* to add that entry to the To list and then blasts the recipients table of the response form message with this ADRLIST.

The code that is required to build an entry in the address list is shown in the following excerpt from the *HrResponseMsg* function of the Chap06\SendStub\FORM.CPP file:

```
HRESULT CStubSendForm::HrAddressResponseMsg(IMessage* pmsg)
{
    enum { ivalType, ivalEid, ivalDisplayName, ivalMailAddr,
        ivalAddrType, ivalSearchKey, cvalSender };

    SizedSPropTagArray(cvalSender, tagaSender) =
        { cvalSender,
        { PR_NULL, PR_SENDER_ENTRYID, PR_SENDER_NAME,
          PR_SENDER_EMAIL_ADDRESS, PR_SENDER_ADDRTYPE,
          PR_SENDER_SEARCH_KEY } };

    SizedSPropTagArray(cvalSender, tagaSenderAsDestination) =
        { cvalSender,
        { PR_RECIPIENT_TYPE, PR_ENTRYID, PR_DISPLAY_NAME,
          PR_EMAIL_ADDRESS, PR_ADDRTYPE, PR_SEARCH_KEY } };

    ULONG cval = 0;
    SPropValue* pval = NULL;
```

(continued)

```
HRESULT hr = _pmsg->GetProps((SPropTagArray*)&tagaSender, 0,
    &cval, &pval);
if (FAILED(hr) || MAPI_W_ERRORS_RETURNED == hr)
{
    // Every property is required.
    return _lasterr.Set(hr, _pmsg);
}

// From the retrieved message properties,
// build a vector of recipient values.
⋮
```

Notice that the *tagaSender* property tag array contained an entry *PR_NULL*. This entry was ignored by the *IMAPIProp::GetProps* call that fetched the sender properties. It exists only to align the sender and destination arrays so that the following simple loop can convert the fetched values into an ADRENTRY:

```
⋮
for (int i = 0; i < cvalSender; i++)
    pval[i].ulPropTag = tagaSenderAsDestination.aulPropTag[i];
pval[ivalType].Value.l = MAPI_TO;

ADRLIST adrlist = {1, 0};
adrlist.aEntries[0].rgPropVals = pval;
adrlist.aEntries[0].cValues = cval;
hr = pmsg->ModifyRecipients(0, &adrlist);
if (FAILED(hr))
    _lasterr.Set(hr, pmsg);

::MAPIFreeBuffer(pval);
return hr;
}
```

With this view of the form server as client of other forms, I conclude form coverage. The following, and final, chapter places post forms in their natural habitat: the designed folder application.

NOTE   A well-behaved MAPI form checks for the *PR_REPLY_RECIPIENTS_xxx* properties, which override the *PR_SENDER_xxx* properties if they are present on a message.

8

Designing a Folder

A synthesis of all preceding chapters, this brief chapter describes how to build folder applications. A folder is a container in a MAPI message store; it can contain not only messages but also the forms defining those messages, plus the structures describing the view for the Exchange client to use when the user browses the folder. In addition, folders on Exchange Server message stores can leverage special features of their host, such as rules, data replication, and security; these special features can also contribute to applications.

In Microsoft Exchange, a folder application is a folder that hosts a set of items so that they are included as the records of a single consistent application. The items can embody documents in a shared library, messages in a discussion forum, requests made to a help desk, sales made to customers, or even moves in a game of chess. When an Exchange Server public folder hosts the folder application, it becomes a public folder application capable of access by many users at once—the hub of a workgroup application.

Previous chapters have described the different ways in which an application author can add a component to a running Exchange system. Client extensions augment and intercept different commands and actions in the Exchange client; form servers add new message types, available both within Exchange and to other MAPI client applications. In each case, the application author implements an object and then registers that object so that the system can acquire instances of that object at the appropriate time.

Designing a folder works differently. The application author does not add components (in the component object sense) to Exchange; instead, the author makes changes to the state of a folder hosted within a MAPI message store. The side effects of those changes yield the application features desired. Therefore, this chapter talks more about copying objects than about implementing them.

Components of a Designed Folder

Folder applications can be thought of as customized folders. The application author constructs the application by starting with a folder in a message store and then by adding components that work together to construct, or design, the folder.

Some aspects of folder design literally reside within the folder. This is the case with a folder's forms and view descriptors, which occupy messages within the folder's associated information contents table. Other aspects of the application exist as MAPI properties on the folder. As a result, a customized folder is inherently self-contained, so that copying the folder copies the complete application. Each folder constitutes a world in itself.

Views

Customized folders work within the user interface of the Exchange client. Users locate folder applications by browsing the store and folder name space in the left-hand pane of the Exchange client, Windows Explorer–style. As the user's focus moves into a customized folder, the client acts as a viewer for the items in that folder, assuming the view designed by the application's author and composing or activating items in the application with their designed forms. The application author is, in effect, reusing the viewer implementation of the Exchange client rather than implementing the interfaces described in Chapter 7.

Exchange determines a folder's views through the persistent *view descriptors* within the folder. A view descriptor describes every configurable aspect of a view in the Exchange client, including the following:

- Its name as it is displayed under the View menu

- The columns appearing in the view, each with its associated message property to display and the dimensions it will occupy

- The column specifying the sort order and the direction of the sort

- Any categorization of the display, per column grouped together

- Any restriction ("filter") applied to the results

An application author creates the view descriptors for the application's views. View descriptors come about through use of the Exchange client's View menu, either directly or as driven through the Microsoft Exchange Application Design Environment. An application author can also specify the default view for a folder.

Forms

The logic for creating and modifying the items of an application and for examining single instances of the item falls to the form. The forms of a designed folder reside in that folder's forms library (described in Chapter 5). From the folder forms library, the Exchange client resolves and activates the forms as user activity dictates.

An application author first develops the form servers for the application's forms, as described in Chapter 6, and then installs those servers into the intended folder. In the Application Design Environment included in Microsoft Exchange Server, the Forms Designer does this for the author. Application authors can also use other form design tools—for example, the Exchange-specific offerings of forms companies such as JetForm and Symantec/Delrina FormFlow.

Comment

By convention, every designed folder bears a descriptive comment summarizing its purpose or expanding on its display name. For example, a designed folder named "Ben's Birthday" might bear the comment text, "Place birthday greetings for Ben Franklin in this folder. Friends of Ben Grimm, please look elsewhere." This text appears when the user or the designer issues a File - Properties command from Exchange.

An application author can specify the contents of the descriptive comment either through Exchange or by calling the *IMAPIProp::SetProps* method on the folder object. Because the folder owner usually resets the folder's comment to a value meaningful in the organization, the value set by the original author isn't too important except as a suggested default.

Exchange Server–Specific Components

A designed folder hosted on an Exchange Server message store can take advantage of the features of that platform. These server features work without intervention on the part of the client; once the client specifies them as part of a folder's design, the server adheres to them until the client changes that design.

Application authors typically edit these server features through the facilities offered by Exchange. Special applications may have recourse to the interfaces set forth in the Microsoft BackOffice 2.0 SDK.

Security

To prevent unauthorized or erroneous changes to data, Exchange Server associates an access control list (ACL) with every folder. The ACL specifies who can access that folder and its contents and to what degree they can do so. Figure 8-1 on the following page shows a sample access control list.

Messaging users identified in the directory	Permissions
Norbert	Create new items, edit and delete own items, read any items
Pierre	Edit and delete own items, read any items
Default entry	Read any items

Applies to all users (not Norbert or Pierre)

Figure 8-1. *Access control lists serve to limit access to a subset of users.*

An application author determines the roles taken by different sorts of users. For example, the author can design a document repository folder to have two classes of users: publishers, who can create and delete documents in the folder, and readers, who can only read those documents. If the author designates a default permission, the author can create that entry in the folder's ACL through Exchange. However, because the contents of the ACL can vary per installation of the application, the author usually allows the installing owner of the folder to specify the ACL.

Rules

Exchange Server can also associate a folder assistant with each public folder. A folder assistant is a set of rules, or condition-action pairs, that the server examines whenever it adds an item to the folder, either when delivering a mailed message or when creating or modifying a posted message. The condition of a rule consists of a Boolean predicate expressed in terms of MAPI properties, as demonstrated in Figure 8-2; the server compares this predicate against the message and, if it finds a match, executes the actions associated with the rule. Some of the many possible rule actions include deleting the message, rejecting the message, forwarding the message to another recipient, and sending a canned response message to the original sender. All rule evaluation and execution take place on the server,[1] without any client action after design time.

Public folder applications can use Exchange Server rules in many ways. A rule can limit the types of messages created within a folder by checking the message class of the new message and rejecting it if it does not match the message class of any form in the folder; this is useful to prevent users from creating inappropriate instances of *IPM.Post* in a dedicated application. A rule can route certain items into another folder for separate processing. A rule can watch for the receipt of messages containing a particular keyword and can reply to the

---

1. The Exchange Server Inbox Assistant supports a mechanism for executing certain actions on a cooperating client; however, this mechanism does not apply to Folder Assistants.

message's sender with a template message that is keyed off of the specified keyword; when used on a public folder that has an associated mail address, this makes the public folder into a document server and sends copies of its documents through e-mail to users who cannot directly connect to the public folder server.

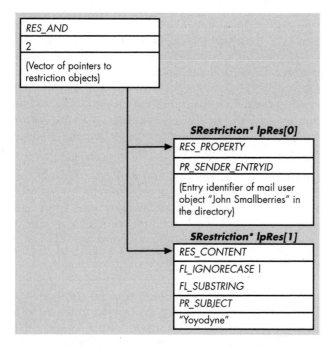

Figure 8-2. *Exchange Server evaluates rules by comparing their condition to incoming messages, executing their action only when the match succeeds.*

An application author in Exchange creates simple rules for a folder through the Folder Assistant interface. For more complex rules, I resort to the interfaces in the BackOffice SDK or delve into the *IExchangeModifyTable* interface directly, as described in the BackOffice SDK header file EDKMDB.H.

Replication

Microsoft Exchange Server allows an organization to replicate the contents of a folder across multiple servers, allowing those servers to keep their data consistent with each other. Replication is usually an administrative issue, not a development issue; site administrators determine the site's data access requirements and replicate a particular folder application in light of those requirements, assuming that the default conflict resolution mechanisms do the right thing when two users make simultaneous changes to an item.

An application author who expects to operate in a replicated enterprise environment can, to a limited extent, control the manner in which Exchange Server resolves conflicting changes.

Folder Installation

The self-contained nature of designed folders makes installing them potentially very simple. Typically, a setup program need do nothing more than copy the designed folder from some source to the destination message store. The folder arrives with all of its designed forms, views, and Exchange Server–specific attributes and, with only a little editing of its access control list, will be ready to run. The installed folder can contain sample items or even online help implemented as items in the folder—for example, instances of *IPM.Note*; instances of *IPM.Document* wrapping Word, Help, or HTML files; or custom forms delivering some application-specific type of help.

In the Exchange client, a simple File - Copy operation suffices to install the application from a designed template folder. For copying from an instance of the application already in use, where the source folder may have an access control list and contained items unwanted in the destination, Exchange offers the Tools - Application Design - Copy Folder Design command.

The source and destination folders can reside on different message stores and even on different store provider types. For the purposes of distributing a designed folder, the Personal Folders (PST) store is convenient because an instance of it can contain a designed folder in a file on a disk. A copy operation between a PST and Exchange Server correctly reconstitutes the folder application on the destination; too, if the folder was originally designed on the Exchange Server store, the copy preserves the Exchange Server–specific attributes such as rules, even though those attributes do not function on PST and, in fact, cannot be designed into a folder on PST.

Per-Client Setup

Many folder applications require no special setup or installation to work on a particular client computer; the user simply locates the application and starts to use it. Any folder application that assumes support outside of that common to all Exchange clients will, of course, require some setup sequence for its participating clients.

If a folder application contains forms that require run-time support on a client, each client must install that run-time support before it can activate those forms. This run-time support might entail a server implementing the *IMAPIFormFactory* interface for a set of forms or might simply consist of the run-time support for a development environment that is used to implement the forms—Exchange Forms Designer, Microsoft Visual C++, or any other development system.

Any folder application requiring the use of an auxiliary Exchange client extension requires a setup sequence to install the extension on each client. Unlike forms, client extensions have no notion of a replicated central distribution point, such as the forms libraries of MAPI.

Obviously, complicated folder applications using facilities outside MAPI might require other setup guarantees. If the forms of an application use ODBC to access a data source on the invoking client, that client had better have both ODBC and its data sources installed before it launches the form. MAPI contains no magic to handle either this case or the case in which the client lacks MFC, Visual Basic, or any other run-time support. The form is nothing more than a bundle of code and shares the same responsibilities for ascertaining its run-time environment as any other bundle of code that can be run on a possibly unprepared client.

Installing Folder Applications

Forms and views are the two visible elements of a folder application. A client can work with either of these elements on any message store capable of hosting a folder application, that is, any message store supporting folder-associated information tables.

Genesis and Comment

Baby folders don't come from the stork; they come from a call into the message store provider requesting a new folder with the *IMAPIFolder::CreateFolder* method on the prospective parent folder. The call to create a folder specifies the display name of the new folder; this must be unique within the scope of the enclosing parent folder to prevent the client from creating two folders with the same name. (Both the Personal Folder and the Exchange Server message stores enforce this requirement and return *MAPI_E_COLLISION* in this case.) In addition, the caller can specify the initial value of the folder comment, although the following example postpones that decision by passing a NULL pointer in the call to the *CreateFolder* function:

```
IMAPIFolder* pfld = …;
TCHAR* pszName = _T("Template for the Cat Tracking Application");
TCHAR* pszComment = NULL;
IMAPIFolder* pfldNew = NULL;
HRESULT hr = pfld->CreateFolder(FOLDER_GENERIC, pszName,
    pszComment, NULL, MAPI_DEFERRED_ERRORS|fMapiUnicode, &pfldNew);
```

If the caller elects to defer setting the comment on the folder, as demonstrated in the preceding example, it is easily set later, as follows:

```
SPropValue val;
val.ulPropTag = PR_COMMENT;
val.Value.LPSZ = _T("Instructions for prospective cat ranchers");
hr = pfldNew->SetProps(1, &val, NULL);
```

The caller should retain the open interface to the newly created folder for subsequent work. If the client elects to release that interface, the caller should first ask the folder for its entry identifier. Note that unlike a newly created message object, the new folder object depends on the *IMAPIFolder::CreateFolder* method returning to the caller. There is no notion of any cognate of the *IMAPIProp::SaveChanges* method being necessary to make the folder data persistent. A call to the *IMAPIProp::GetProps* method at this point returns a valid persistent entry identifier.

```
SPropValue* pval;
SizedSPropTagArray(1, taga) = {1, {PR_ENTRY_ID}};
ULONG cval = 1;
hr = pfldNew->GetProps((SPropTagArray*)&taga, 0, &cval, &pval);
// The entry identifier is in SBinary of pval->Value.bin.
```

Forms

The forms in a designed folder occupy the folder forms library of that folder. Recall from Chapter 5 that folder forms libraries store their forms in messages within the folder's associated information contents table (or FAI). Those messages have class *IPM.Microsoft.FolderDesign.FormDescription*, differentiating them from other pieces of associated information within the folder. Residing within the FAI, a folder's forms travel with that folder whenever the folder is copied or moved, preserving the integrity of the application.

Effects of the set of folder forms

The set of forms in a folder constitutes the most distinguishing feature of a folder application. As component objects external to Exchange, forms can implement the original user interface and features seen nowhere else in Exchange. More to the point, however, the forms define the property schema of the messages within the application, along with any side effects on the folder's contents. Forms define the algorithm and the data; therefore, they must define the program.

By convention, any client resolving a message class passes the entry identifier of the current folder to the *IMAPIFormMgr::ResolveMessageClass* method, specifying that MAPI should look first at the folder's own forms. Alternatively, an application viewer dedicated to work against a single folder can open a form container for that folder's forms library using the *IMAPIFormMgr::OpenForm-*

Container method and then resolve all forms only against that forms library using the *IMAPIFormContainer::ResolveMessageClass* method.

When it is within a designed folder, the Exchange client uses the folder forms library in several ways. Exchange resolves any unknown message classes into form information objects against this library; this yields correct form activation behavior and lets Exchange display the correct small icon in the icon column of its views for custom message classes. Exchange also enumerates every visible, that is, not hidden, installed form in the library and offers to compose instances of that form, which dynamically populates its Compose menu with items for each visible form that it finds. Finally, Exchange calculates the union of all form properties in its forms library and uses the resulting set when it selects possible view columns, restrictions against the entire folder, and other column-specific attributes.

Installing forms in the folder forms library

Let's assume that the folder application's forms are already designed and implemented. (The excessively linear types of persons can comfort themselves by recalling Chap06\Catform at this point.) The folder designer installs the forms in the folder by first obtaining a form container and then invoking the *IMAPIFormContainer::InstallForm* method with the configuration file for each form being installed. (Review Chap06\Catform\CATFORM.CFG for an example of a form configuration file.) In the following example, the designer is installing the form in a new folder and expects all the information it needs to exist in the application form's configuration file; hence, it does not request the form installation dialog box and does not pass *MAPI_DIALOG* in the *ulFlags* parameter:

```
IMAPIFormMgr* pfrmmgr = NULL;
hr = MAPIOpenFormMgr(psess, &pfrmmgr);
if (FAILED(hr))
    ⋮
IMAPIFormContainer* pfrmcnt = NULL;
hr = pfrmmgr->OpenFormContainer(HFRMREG_FOLDER, pfldNew,
    &pfrmcnt);
if (FAILED(hr))
    ⋮
hr = pfrmcnt->InstallForm(NULL, fMapiUnicode,
    _T("catform.cfg"));
```

Upon installing the form, the folder contains a form definition message for the form in its associated information table. Subsequent attempts to resolve the form's message class against the forms library yield the correct form information object.

NOTE Nothing done so far prevents a client from creating a message of an alien class in this folder. To make a folder accept only its designed forms, the folder must reside on an Exchange Server store, where the designer can create a rule to exclude illegal messages.

Views

As previously described, Exchange records the attributes of its view windows in constructs called view descriptors. The current view descriptors are specific to the Microsoft Exchange client; hence, this section manipulates the descriptors in a generic, upwardly compatible fashion.

Brief definition of a view descriptor

View descriptors exist only as a construct of the Exchange client. MAPI provides facilities for manipulating forms but has no equivalent for views. Hence, any folder application or folder application construction sequence that manipulates views must write code that is specific to the view descriptor format.

In many ways, view descriptors resemble the form definition messages that record forms in folder forms libraries. Exchange implements view descriptors as FAI messages of class *IPM.Microsoft.FolderDesign.NamedView*. Each view descriptor bears a number of message-class specific properties that embody the information saved in the view. The only one of these properties that concerns us here is the display name of the view, *PR_VD_NAME*,[2] a PR_TSTRING type with property ID 0x7006.

The folder property *PR_DEFAULT_VIEW_ENTRYID*, if set, contains the persistent entry identifier of the view descriptor for that folder's default view. If this property is not present, the Exchange client uses its default Normal view when first visiting the folder.

Exchange populates its View - Folder Views submenu with the display names (*PR_VD_NAME*) of the view descriptors in the currently viewed folder. When the user selects one of these items, Exchange uses the data in its corresponding named view descriptor to set the view in the window.

---

2. As of this writing, *PR_VD_NAME* appears only in sample code published by Microsoft. It does not appear in any published system header file.

**Using Folder-Associated Information
Messages to Keep Application-Private Data**

Folder-associated information (FAI) messages provide a flexible way for a folder application to keep private instance data about itself. A message store provider cannot implement arbitrary, client-specified properties on folder objects. Any message store provider that supports forms libraries, however, supports FAI messages. This includes the message store providers for both Exchange Server and Personal Folders, although not those for Microsoft Mail Shared Folders.

A client creates an FAI message by setting the *MAPI_ASSOCIATED* flag in its call to the *IMAPIFolder::CreateMessage* method. If the message store provider does not support FAI messages, it returns *MAPI_E_NO_SUPPORT* to this request; otherwise, the provider creates the message in a parallel space within the folder, where the message does not appear in the contents table for that folder. To find FAI messages in a folder, the client must request the separate FAI contents table by setting the *MAPI_ASSOCIATED* flag in its call to the *IMAPIContainer::GetContentsTable* method.

Once the client has an FAI message, the regular custom message type discipline applies. The application gives that application a message class that distinguishes its messages from any others in the FAI table, including folder design messages. Just as Microsoft prefixes folder design FAI messages with the superclass *IPM.Microsoft.FolderDesign*, the application uses its own distinguishing superclass. I might use *IPX.Goetter*, for example. (Strictly speaking, it isn't accurate to use superclass *IPM* on these messages, because they do not implement a human-readable item at all.) The application-specific data might then go into message-class specific properties on the message.

Any application manipulating FAI messages must take care not to interfere with messages other than those of its own message classes, lest it damage the folder design.

Extracting a view from a folder

The best way for an application author to create a view descriptor is to use the Exchange View - Define Views command to create a new view. The author can subsequently copy the resulting view descriptor, as long as it ends up in a folder with the same gross property schema—the same union of all its forms' property schemas—as its source. Otherwise, the view might contain columns that correspond to no legitimate property or that have a misleading column header.

By serializing and deserializing the view descriptor into a disk file, an application can keep the view "alive" outside a folder for later installation. The code sample for the rest of this section, Chap08\Vwinst, demonstrates the rudiments of this process. Implemented as an Exchange client extension for simplicity, it displays all the views defined in the currently selected folder, allowing the user to import and export views to and from disk files, as well as to specify the current default view on the folder. The action all takes place in the file Chap08\Vwinst\WORK.CPP.

At the heart of the program lies the code that enumerates all the views in the folder, listing them as a row set structure in the member variable *CViewDlg-Aux::_prs*. To do this, the code must obtain the associated information contents table, restricting that table to only view descriptors, and must request the three columns pertinent to its work: the message class, ensuring that the message store's database engine has this value to work with when making the restriction; the entry identifier, with which to copy and reference the view descriptor; and the display name of the view descriptor, for use in the user interface. This is shown in the following excerpt from the file Chap08\Vwinst\WORK.CPP:

```
    ⋮
const char SzIPMNV[] = "IPM.Microsoft.FolderDesign.NamedView";
    ⋮
enum {ivalMsgClass = 0, ivalEid, ivalDisplayName, cvalTable};
const SizedSPropTagArray(cvalTable, TagaTable) =
    {cvalTable,
    {PR_MESSAGE_CLASS_A, PR_ENTRYID, PROP_TAG(PT_TSTRING,
        0x7006)}};
    ⋮
```

The function *CViewDlgAux::LoadViews* of the WORK.CPP file starts by releasing any row set that it might already hold, as follows:

```
    ⋮
if (_prs)
{
    ::FreeProws(_prs);
    _prs = NULL;
}
    ⋮
```

The member variable *CViewDlgAux::_pfld* holds an interface to the current folder under examination. In the following excerpt from the *LoadViews* function, the code requests a contents table, specifying that it does not want the usual contents table but specifying the *MAPI_ASSOCIATED* flag to obtain the associated information contents table instead:

```
    ⋮
IMAPITable* ptbl;
HRESULT hr = _pfld->GetContentsTable(
    MAPI_ASSOCIATED|MAPI_DEFERRED_ERRORS, &ptbl);
if (FAILED(hr))
{
    ui.ErrorMessage(_pfld, hr, "Checking for views");
    return hr;
}
    ⋮
```

If the current folder happens to be on a message store that doesn't support folder-associated information, the call to the *GetContentsTable* function returns failure, whereupon the user interface helper object displays the reason for the error to the user. (Subsequent excerpts from Vwinst will not display such calls to the helper function *CUICommon::ErrorMessage*.)

Next the function builds a restriction structure, specifying that it wants to see only view descriptors, and submits this together with the desired column set to the *HrQueryAllRows* utility. The *HrQueryAllRows* function returns a single row set consisting of every row that satisfies the specified restriction and containing the specified columns. The class never sees any row that does not correspond to a view descriptor. The call to the *HrQueryAllRows* function is shown in the concluding lines of the *LoadViews* function:

```
    ⋮
SPropValue valIPMNV; // IPM.blah blah.NamedView
valIPMNV.ulPropTag = PR_MESSAGE_CLASS_A;
valIPMNV.Value.lpszA = /*unconst*/(char*)::SzIPMNV;
SRestriction rst =
    { RES_PROPERTY,
    { RELOP_EQ, PR_MESSAGE_CLASS_A, (ULONG)&valIPMNV }};

hr = ::HrQueryAllRows(ptbl, (SPropTagArray*)&TagaTable, &rst,
    NULL, 0, &_prs);
if (FAILED(hr))
    ⋮

ptbl->Release();
    ⋮
```

With *CViewDlgAux::_prs* containing the row set of view descriptors, the user interface can render that set, allowing the user to select a view and export it to a file. The user interface calls back to the *CViewDlgAux::Export* function, with an index corresponding to the element in the row set to export, as shown in the following excerpt from the WORK.CPP file:

⋮

```
assert(_prs);
assert(iRow < _prs->cRows);
assert(_prs->aRow[iRow].lpProps[ivalEid].ulPropTag ==
    PR_ENTRYID);
```

⋮

Since designed folders typically have no more than three or four views in them, and since other clients can simultaneously access the view descriptors of the folder, working on this sort of static collection of data is acceptable. Contrast this with the requirements of a viewer window rendering a public folder of 2000 items: such a window would never have called the *HrQueryAll-Rows* function unless it could apply a stringent restriction and would not necessarily be as sanguine about having no other agent manipulate its items behind its back. Instead, the message viewer window would retain the table, working with a slice of the table at a time, holding instance keys for rendered items to use in the *IMAPITable::FindRow* function, and certainly tracking table notifications for news of those rendered items.

It's time to get the name of an output file to use. The Win32 User API provides a common raft of utility dialog boxes that do all the dirty user interface work on the function's behalf; the caller needs only to specify that it isn't interested in read-only files and that the function should confirm any selection of an existing file before proceeding. If the user cancels out of the dialog box, the *GetSaveFileName* method returns FALSE, whereupon the function returns without taking further action, as shown in the following excerpt from the *CViewDlgAux-::Export* function:

```
⋮
TCHAR szPathOut[256] = {0};
OPENFILENAME ofn = {0};;

ofn.lStructSize = sizeof(ofn);
ofn.hwndOwner = ui.GetHwndVisible();
ofn.lpstrFilter = ::SzFilter;
ofn.lpstrFile = szPathOut;
ofn.nMaxFile = sizeof(szPathOut)/sizeof(TCHAR);
ofn.Flags =
    OFN_NOREADONLYRETURN|OFN_OVERWRITEPROMPT|OFN_HIDEREADONLY;
ofn.lpstrDefExt = ::SzSuffix;
```

```
    if (!::GetSaveFileName(&ofn))
    {
        // BUGBUG - handle CDERR_BUFFERTOOSMALL
        return;
    }
    ⋮
```

From here, the code moves to an unwind-before-return error-handling pattern as it starts to acquire references to interfaces that it must release in an orderly fashion. All error paths leave a failure code in the local variable *hr*, jumping to the unwind label to perform common cleanup. The *IMalloc* interface is acquired for the OLE structured storage APIs, and then an *IMessage* is acquired on the view descriptor selected by the user. Recall that *iRow* indexed the row corresponding to the selected view. The following eyeball-cracking expression thus names the *SBinary* that contains the entry identifier of the view descriptor:

```
_prs->aRow[iRow].lpProps[iprpEid].Value.bin
```

In the following excerpt from the *Export* function, the *OpenEntry* function is called to open the message:

```
    ⋮
    IMessage* pmsgOld = NULL;
    IMalloc* pmalloc = ::MAPIGetDefaultMalloc();
    IStorage* pstg = NULL;
    IMessage* pmsgNew = NULL;

    ULONG nType;
    HRESULT hr = _pfld->OpenEntry(
        _prs->aRow[iRow].lpProps[ivalEid].Value.bin.cb,
        (LPENTRYID)_prs->aRow[iRow].lpProps[ivalEid].Value.bin.lpb,
        (LPIID)&IID_IMessage, MAPI_DEFERRED_ERRORS, // Read-only
        &nType, (IUnknown**)&pmsgOld );
    assert(nType == MAPI_MESSAGE);
    if (FAILED(hr))
    {
        ui.ErrorMessage(_pfld, hr, "Opening view to export");
        goto unwind;
    }
    ⋮
```

The OLE structured storage APIs all require wide character pathname arguments. For non-Unicode versions of this code, a quick call to the system string conversion API converts the output of *GetSaveFileName* to a suitable parameter for *StgCreateDocfile*. *StgCreateDocfile* will create an *IStorage* interface within an object in the file system, using the system-standard docfile implementation of compound files. On top of this storage, the MAPI utility *OpenIMsgOnIStg* provides a MAPI-supplied *IMessage*-to-*IStorage* mapping. As a result, a message—interface *pmsgNew*—is mapped to a file with the pathname *szPathOut*, as shown in the following excerpt from the *Export* function:

```
⋮
# define wszPathOut szPathOut
#else
    WCHAR wszPathOut[256];
    // BUGBUG handle failure to convert
    ::MultiByteToWideChar(CP_ACP, 0, szPathOut, -1, wszPathOut,
        sizeof(wszPathOut)/sizeof(TCHAR));
#endif

    hr = ::StgCreateDocfile(wszPathOut,

STGM_CREATE|STGM_SHARE_EXCLUSIVE|STGM_READWRITE|STGM_TRANSACTED,
        0, &pstg);
    if (FAILED(hr))
    {
        ui.Message("Failed to create new file");
        goto unwind;
    }

    hr = ::OpenIMsgOnIStg(NULL, MAPIAllocateBuffer, MAPIAllocateMore,
        MAPIFreeBuffer, pmalloc, NULL, pstg, NULL, 0, 0, &pmsgNew);
    if (FAILED(hr))
    {
        ui.Message("Failed to create message within new file");
        goto unwind;
    }
    ⋮
```

Copying the source message to the destination message is a standard MAPI idiom. The variable *pmsgOld* references the source view descriptor; the variable *pmsgNew* references the destination file. After completing the MAPI idiom, the code reverts briefly to the OLE structured storage idiom in which it had nested MAPI and commits the changes to the disk file, as shown in the following excerpt from the *Export* function:

```
    ⋮
    hr = pmsgOld->CopyTo(0, NULL, NULL, 0, NULL, &IID_IMessage,
        pmsgNew, 0, NULL);
```

```
    if (FAILED(hr))
    {
        ui.ErrorMessage(pmsgOld, hr, "Exporting view to new file");
        goto unwind;
    }
    hr = pmsgNew->SaveChanges(0);
    if (FAILED(hr))
    {
        ui.ErrorMessage(pmsgNew, hr, "Exporting view to new file");
        goto unwind;
    }
    pmsgNew->Release();
    pmsgNew = NULL;
    hr = pstg->Commit(STGC_DEFAULT);
    if (FAILED(hr))
    {
        ui.Message("Failed to save message within new file");
        goto unwind;
    }
    ⋮
```

The unwind-on-exit idiom guards its interface pointers with a series of checks. Any pointer set is assumed to hold a reference that the function must release before it returns. Hence, before committing the storage above, the code released the new message interface pointer—to end its life before ending the life of its enclosing storage—then zeroed it. The unwind code looks for a nonzero value in interface pointer variables and assumes that those variables contain interfaces that must be released to unwind the state properly.

The unwind idiom is shown in the concluding lines of the *Export* function:

```
    ⋮
unwind:
    if (pmsgNew)
        pmsgNew->Release();
    if (pstg)
        pstg->Release();
    if (pmalloc)
        pmalloc->Release();
    if (pmsgOld)
        pmsgOld->Release();
}
```

By the end of this sequence of calls to the *LoadViews* and *Export* functions, you have selected a view, entered the desired pathname of a file, and received a view descriptor serialized at that pathname.

Installing a view in a folder

Having a file that contains a view descriptor isn't very interesting unless the process is reversible. The function *CViewDlgAux::Import* demonstrates an interactive version of the action that a designed folder installation program performs noninteractively: taking a previously designed view descriptor and placing it in a folder. In the sample Chap08\Vwinst, that folder is the member variable *CView-DlgAux::_pdlg*, obtained from Exchange client extensibility (the lazy prototyper's friend), whereas an installation folder uses the *pfldNew* returned from the *IMAPI-Folder::CreateFolder* function, as discussed in the section "Genesis and Comment" earlier in this chapter—but the gist of the operation is the same.

After the user presses the Import button, the *CViewDlgAux::Import* function prompts the user for the pathname of the view descriptor file, as shown in the following excerpt:

```
    ⋮
// Set this to refresh table on exit.
BOOL fTableChanged = FALSE;

TCHAR szPathOut[256] = {0};
OPENFILENAME ofn = {0};;

ofn.lStructSize = sizeof(ofn);
ofn.hwndOwner = ui.GetHwndVisible();
ofn.lpstrFilter = ::SzFilter;
ofn.lpstrFile = szPathOut;
ofn.nMaxFile = sizeof(szPathOut)/sizeof(TCHAR);
ofn.Flags = OFN_FILEMUSTEXIST|OFN_PATHMUSTEXIST|OFN_READONLY;
ofn.lpstrDefExt = ::SzSuffix;

if (!::GetOpenFileName(&ofn))
{
    // BUGBUG--handle CDERR_BUFFERTOOSMALL.
    return;
}
    ⋮
```

Again, the code converts any non-Unicode pathnames to wide characters for the benefit of the *StgOpenStorage* function. So far, the function is simply running the *Export* function in reverse. Instead of calling the *GetSaveFileName* function, it calls the *GetOpenFileName* function; instead of calling the *StgCreateDocfile* function, it calls the *StgOpenStorage* function. Finally, it uses MAPI to map an *IMessage* interface for reading on top of its read-only *IStorage* interface. After all of this, it has the message interface for the source of the view descriptor. In the following excerpt from the *Import* function, the *StgOpenStorage* and the *OpenIMsgOnIStg* functions are called:

```
⋮
#ifdef _UNICODE
#define wszPathOut szPathOut
#else
    WCHAR wszPathOut[256];
    // BUGBUG handle failure to convert.
    ::MultiByteToWideChar(CP_ACP, 0, szPathOut, -1, wszPathOut,
        sizeof(wszPathOut)/sizeof(TCHAR));
#endif

    // From here out, "goto unwind" to return.

    IMalloc* pmalloc = ::MAPIGetDefaultMalloc();
    IStorage* pstg = NULL;
    IMessage* pmsgOld = NULL;
    IMessage* pmsgNew = NULL;

    HRESULT hr = ::StgOpenStorage(wszPathOut, NULL,
            STGM_READ|STGM_SHARE_DENY_WRITE|STGM_DIRECT,
            0, 0, &pstg);
    if (FAILED(hr))
    {
        ui.Message("Failed to open the message file");
        goto unwind;
    }

    hr = ::OpenIMsgOnIStg(NULL, MAPIAllocateBuffer,
        MAPIAllocateMore, MAPIFreeBuffer, pmalloc, NULL, pstg, NULL,
            0, 0, &pmsgOld);
    if (FAILED(hr))
    {
        ui.Message("Failed to open message within file");
        goto unwind;
    }
```

Before proceeding, the function ensures that the serialized message is, in fact, a view descriptor. This isn't the only function in Exchange to map an *IMessage* interface onto an *IStorage* .DOC file. Both File - Save As and File - Properties - Forms - Manage - Save As generate such files as well, except with different suffixes. The proof resides in the message class of the message within the file. If the message has class *IPM.Microsoft.FolderDesign.NamedView*, it is a view descriptor; otherwise, it is an impostor. This distinction is made in the following excerpt from the *Import* function:

```
    ⋮
{
    SPropValue* pval;
    SizedSPropTagArray(1, taga) = {1, {PR_MESSAGE_CLASS_A}};
    ULONG cval = 1;
    hr = pmsgOld->GetProps((SPropTagArray*)&taga, 0, &cval,
        &pval);
    if (FAILED(hr))
    {
        ui.ErrorMessage(pmsgOld, hr, "Validating view");
        goto unwind;
    }

    if ((PR_MESSAGE_CLASS_A != pval[0].ulPropTag) ||
        (0 != ::stricmp(pval[0].Value.lpszA, ::SzIPMNV)) )
    {
        ui.Message("The selected file was not a view.");
        ::MAPIFreeBuffer(pval);
        goto unwind;
    }

    ::MAPIFreeBuffer(pval);
}
    ⋮
```

At this point, the function has an open view descriptor. Ideally, it would access the current folder to search for view descriptors with the same name as the new view and delete any matching descriptors; otherwise, the folder could end up with two identically named view objects.

Instead, the function trusts you not to do anything that would result in such a misdesigned folder and charges on ahead. It creates a new associated information message object and then copies the existing view descriptor—*pmsgOld*, from the opened file—onto the new message, *pmsgNew*, as follows:

```
    ⋮
hr = _pfld->CreateMessage(0,
    MAPI_ASSOCIATED|MAPI_DEFERRED_ERRORS, &pmsgNew);
```

```
    if (FAILED(hr))
    {
        ui.ErrorMessage(_pfld, hr, "Creating new view in folder");
        goto unwind;
    }

    hr = pmsgOld->CopyTo(0, NULL, NULL, 0, NULL, &IID_IMessage,
        pmsgNew, 0, NULL);
    if (FAILED(hr))
    {
        ui.ErrorMessage(pmsgOld, hr, "Importing view from file");
        goto unwind;
    }

    hr = pmsgNew->SaveChanges(0);
    if (FAILED(hr))
    {
        ui.ErrorMessage(pmsgNew, hr, "Importing view from file");
        goto unwind;
    }
    ⋮
```

If the function gets this far, it has successfully added a view descriptor to the folder. Before it returns, the function needs to update its user interface to reflect the new entry; it does this by brute force, replacing its row set with a new copy. This approach is acceptable because the set is so small. The concluding lines of the *Import* function are as follows:

```
    ⋮
    fTableChanged = TRUE;

unwind:
    if (pmsgNew)
        pmsgNew->Release();
    if (pmsgOld)
        pmsgOld->Release();
    if (pstg)
        pstg->Release();
    if (pmalloc)
        pmalloc->Release();
    ⋮
    if (fTableChanged)
        LoadViews(ui);
}
```

The *Import* function has run the *Export* function backwards. From a file, a new view descriptor—or rather, a new copy of a preexisting view descriptor—has entered the folder.

Setting the default view to use on a folder

As long as this sample application has a set of view descriptors and their entry identifiers, it might as well offer to set the default folder view. Like the previous example, the *CViewDlgAux::SetDefault* function from the WORK.CPP file demonstrates an interactive version of the action that a designed folder installation program would perform noninteractively: taking a previously designed view descriptor and declaring it as the default view for the folder.

Like the view export sample, the *SetDefault* function starts with the user selecting a view in the user interface and pressing a command button. The function *CViewDlgAux::SetDefault* receives control, with an index *iRow* indicating the element in the row set *CViewDlgAux::_prs*, as follows:

```
    ⋮
    assert(_prs);
    assert(iRow < _prs->cRows);
    assert(_prs->aRow[iRow].lpProps[ivalEid].ulPropTag
        == PR_ENTRYID);
    ⋮
```

The row set contains rows from a contents table. Entry identifiers in contents tables are short-term identifiers, which are not valid beyond the scope of their hosting MAPI session. To assign such a value to a persistent property, the function converts the short-term entry identifier of the selected view descriptor to a long-term entry identifier suitable for persistent storage. It does this by opening the message using its short-term entry identifier and by requesting the entry identifier of the open message interface, as shown in the following excerpt from the *SetDefault* function:

```
    ⋮
    ULONG nType;
    IMessage* pmsgSrc = NULL;
    HRESULT hr = _pfld->OpenEntry(
        _prs->aRow[iRow].lpProps[ivalEid].Value.bin.cb,
        (LPENTRYID)_prs->aRow[iRow].lpProps[ivalEid].Value.bin.lpb,
        (LPIID)&IID_IMessage, MAPI_DEFERRED_ERRORS, // Read-only
        &nType,(IUnknown**)&pmsgSrc );
    assert(nType == MAPI_MESSAGE);
```

```
if (FAILED(hr))
{
    ⋮
}

SPropValue* pvalSrc = NULL;
SizedSPropTagArray(1, taga) = {1, {PR_ENTRYID}};
ULONG cval = 1;
hr = pmsgSrc->GetProps((SPropTagArray*)&taga, 0, &cval,
    &pvalSrc);
if (FAILED(hr) || cval != 1 || pvalSrc[0].ulPropTag !=
    PR_ENTRYID)
{
    if (FAILED(hr))
        ⋮
    ::MAPIFreeBuffer(pvalSrc);
    pmsgSrc->Release();
    return;
}
⋮
```

With a long-term entry identifier for the view descriptor, defining the default view on the folder is now straightforward—merely a process of setting the default view property *PR_DEFAULT_VIEW_ENTRYID* on the folder, as shown in the concluding lines of the *SetDefault* function:

```
    ⋮
    SPropValue val;
    val.ulPropTag = PR_DEFAULT_VIEW_ENTRYID;
    val.Value.bin = pvalSrc[0].Value.bin;
    hr = _pfld->SetProps(1, &val, NULL);
    if (FAILED(hr))
        ⋮
    ::MAPIFreeBuffer(pvalSrc);
    pmsgSrc->Release();
}
```

If only everything were so simple.

Exchange Server Attributes

Exchange Server public folders offer MAPI-amenable interfaces to their application features, such as rules and ACLs. When a client calls the *IMAPIFolder-::CopyFolder* function, the cloned folder inherits all of these features because MAPI sees them as binary properties. Client code can copy these too, either by specifying to the *IMAPIProp::CopyProps* function the property tags that the Exchange Server message store provider uses to encode these features or by calling the *IMAPIProp::CopyTo* function. Table 8-1 lists some of the more significant server feature properties from the header file EDKMDB.H.

Property	Function
PR_ACL_DATA	Copy ACLs to a destination folder
PR_RULES_DATA	Copy rules to a destination folder
PR_DESIGN_IN_PROGRESS	Set to prevent access to all but folder owners
PR_SECURE_ORIGINATION	Set to have copies into folder munge a message in the manner of a forwarded *IPM.Note* message

Table 8-1. *Significant public folder feature properties from the Microsoft BackOffice 2.0 SDK.*

For more information on these and many other Exchange Server–specific interfaces, see the Microsoft BackOffice 2.0 SDK.

PART

THREE

Appendixes

A

A Guide to Sample Applications

The accompanying CD-ROM disc contains sixteen sample applications, each one demonstrating different aspects of implementing a Microsoft Exchange application. For each sample application, this guide answers the following questions:

- What does the sample application do?

- How do you build the sample application from the supplied source files?

- How do you install the sample application?

- How do you run the sample application to see it work?

- How do you remove the sample application to restore your computer's previous state?

- What programming techniques does the sample application demonstrate?

- What might an application author reuse from the sample application?

- What shortcomings should a user keep in mind?

Msess

The directory Chap02\Msess contains MAPI Shared Session, a stand-alone application that either creates a shareable session using the specified profile or inherits the shareable session if that session has already been created. The application runs until the user closes its window or until another application signals to end the shared session. When the application ends, it signals that any other applications using the shared session must end as well.

This sample does not appear in Chapter 2. It is intended for supplementary study only.

Building Msess

To build the Msess application, open a command shell, change its current working directory to Chap02\Msess, and enter the following command:

```
nmake /f Makefile
```

To build a version of the Msess application without debugging symbols, enter the following command:

```
nmake nodebug=1 /f Makefile
```

Users of Microsoft Visual C++ 4.0 can load the workspace file MSESS.MDP.

A successful build generates the executable file MSESS.EXE.

Installing Msess

MSESS.EXE requires no particular installation sequence, although—like every other sample application in this book—it requires a working Windows Messaging Subsystem on the computer hosting it.

As built by Microsoft Visual C++ 4.0, Msess requires the run-time support library MSVCRT40.DLL on the hosting computer. Other development environments might require other run-time support files.

Running Msess

To run the Msess application, launch the executable file MSESS.EXE from Windows Explorer or from the command line and pass the name of the profile for Msess to use when it logs onto MAPI as a command line parameter by preceding the profile name with the /p switch

```
msess /p <profile>
```

where <profile> is the name of a profile.

To use a profile name containing spaces, delimit the profile name with quotation marks, as shown in the following example:

```
msess /p "This Self-Referential Profile Name Contains Spaces"
```

If another application, such as Microsoft Exchange or Microsoft Schedule+, has already logged onto MAPI with a shareable profile, Msess uses that profile as well, ignoring its own command line parameter. Otherwise, Msess logs onto MAPI using the specified profile and creates a shareable session. In doing so, it creates a window on the screen and then minimizes that window when the session is completed.

When an application that uses the shared session, such as Microsoft Exchange, invokes its File - Exit And Log Off command, it signals to all other applications using the shared session that they must log off as well. Msess watches for these events and closes if it sees them. Otherwise, if the user closes the Msess window, Msess, in turn, logs off and informs other applications that they should log off as well.

Removing Msess

To remove the Msess application from your system, simply delete the executable file MSESS.EXE. Msess creates no side effects in the system.

Programming with Msess

Msess demonstrates creating and destroying the shared session, setting up and tearing down a simple notification pump, and responding to the everybody-go-home-now notification on that shared session. To respond to notifications, Msess implements an advise sink object. The symbol *USE_PREFAB_ADVISE_SINK* defined in the file MSESS.CPP demonstrates two different ways to do this: using the MAPI *HrAllocAdviseSink* utility function and implementing the object directly.

Reusing Msess

Msess is the simplest MAPI client application that I could imagine. Hence, it offers little to reuse other than its infrastructure: assertion checking, command line parsing, and the like.

To reuse the trivial assertion checking routine, copy the files ASSERT.CPP and ASSERT.H. Note that they require an external symbol *SzDefaultCaption*, which this sample defines in MSESS.CPP.

The command line parsing code requires some work to reuse. The header file MSESS.H declares the class *CCmdLine*, which includes member variables and accessor functions specific to the flags recognized by this sample. In addition, the functions *CCmdLine::Reset* and *CCmdLine::Parse* in CMDLINE.CPP must be modified to honor any changes in flags.

If you use this application as a template for another project, be sure you change the following elements:

- The name of the application

- The icon

- The contents of the version information block *VS_VERSION_INFO* (in MSESS.RC)

Mfetch

The directory Chap02\Mfetch contains MAPI Download, a stand-alone application that logs onto a specified profile to download pending messages from any transport providers named in that profile. When Mfetch is finished, it logs off of MAPI. This is useful because a task-scheduling application can spawn it at defined intervals, letting it regularly pump pending messages into a message store local to the computer for later offline perusal.

Building Mfetch

To build the Mfetch application, open a command shell, change the current working directory to Chap02\Mfetch, and enter the following command:

```
nmake /f Makefile
```

To build a version of the Mfetch application without debugging symbols, enter the following command:

```
nmake nodebug=1 /f Makefile
```

Users of Microsoft Visual C++ 4.0 can load the workspace file MFETCH.MDP.

A successful build generates the executable file MFETCH.EXE.

Installing Mfetch

Like the Msess application, Mfetch requires the presence of WMS and the run-time support for the development environment that built it.

In addition, Mfetch requires a special profile for its use. This profile should name any message transports from which to download messages and should contain the destination message store specified as the default message store. It should not contain any other message transports or any message stores other than the default. Do not specify remote mail services when configuring those transports.

Running Mfetch

To run the Mfetch application, launch the executable file MFETCH.EXE from Windows Explorer or from the command line and pass as a parameter the name of the profile created for its use as specified above. Precede the profile parameter with the /p switch

```
mfetch /p <profile>
```

where <profile> is the name of a profile.

To use a profile name containing spaces, delimit the profile name with quotation marks, as shown in the following example:

```
mfetch /p "Angry Graycat Delicatessen"
```

The Mfetch application creates a session using this profile and then instructs the spooler to download messages from every loaded transport provider. The spooler moves those messages into the default message store of the session as specified in the profile. When Mfetch finishes, it will exit.

Removing Mfetch

To remove the Mfetch application from your system, simply delete the executable file MFETCH.EXE, plus the profiles created for its use if you want.

Programming with Mfetch

Mfetch demonstrates how to create an independent, nonshareable session (as opposed to the shared session of Msess discussed earlier) and how to log off that session. It accesses the message store table, locates the default message store, and opens that message store, which activates the store and makes it available to the MAPI spooler. Mfetch also accesses the status table by locating the spooler entry within that table. It uses the spooler's status entry to request downloading messages. As part of manipulating the message store and status tables, it demonstrates simple table traversal and extracts short-term entry identifiers from the appropriate column of a table. Finally, it demonstrates calling the *OpenEntry* and *OpenMsgStore* methods of *IMAPISession* on an entry identifier to return the object identified.

Reusing Mfetch

Both the *OpenDefaultMDB* and *DownloadMessages* functions of MFETCH.CPP are suitable for reuse.

If you use this application as a template for another project, be sure you change the following elements:

- The name of the application
- The icon
- The contents of the version information block *VS_VERSION_INFO* (in MFETCH.RC)

Keep in Mind

If you run Mfetch on Windows 95, you might encounter a bug (apparently in Windows 95 Internet Point-to-Point Protocol (PPP) or in an underlying service) that causes the system to lock up when the system breaks the connection. If the system locks up before the file system has had a chance to flush its data to the disk, any messages downloaded will disappear. The following conditions are associated with this problem: naming the Microsoft Internet Mail provider as the transport in the profile and allowing the transport provider to connect and disconnect from the Internet Post Office Protocol (POP) server through PPP.

If you run simultaneous instances of Mfetch, you might learn whether your loaded transport providers can withstand running in multiple MAPI sessions at once. Not all transport providers can endure this gauntlet without crashing.

Mlogon

The directory Chap02\Mlogon contains MAPI Logon, a stand-alone application that creates a shareable session using the specified profile and then launches the Exchange client. Because the Exchange client uses the shared session, it starts on the session without presenting the user with the Logon Choose Profile user interface. The net effect to the user is that the user has started Exchange from a profile specified on the command line—an option that is not supported by Exchange itself.

This sample isn't in Chapter 2. It is intended for supplementary study only.

Building Mlogon

To build the Mlogon application, open a command shell, change its current working directory to Chap02\Mlogon, and enter the following command:

```
nmake /f Makefile
```

To build a version of the Mlogon application without debugging symbols, enter the following command:

```
nmake nodebug=1 /f Makefile
```

Users of Microsoft Visual C++ 4.0 can load the workspace file MLOGON.MDP.

A successful build generates the executable file MLOGON.EXE.

Installing Mlogon

Like the Msess application, Mlogon requires the presence of WMS and the run-time support for the development environment that built it. It also requires the Microsoft Exchange client, which it locates and launches.

To work around bugs in various MAPI providers, Mlogon checks for certain registry settings that force it either to mount the default message store before launching Exchange or to sleep for a specified interval before exiting. See the class *CSettings* in the file MLOGON.CPP for details of these.

Running Mlogon

To run the Mlogon application, launch the executable file MLOGON.EXE from Windows Explorer or from the command line, passing as a parameter the name of the profile created for its use. Precede the profile parameter with the /p switch

```
mlogon /p <profile>
```

where <profile> is the name of a profile.

To use a profile name containing spaces, delimit the profile name with quotation marks, as shown in the following example:

```
mlogon /p "Wallingford, USA"
```

In addition, the command line can specify the /e switch, which passes additional command line arguments to Exchange. Here Mlogon is starting Exchange with the profile name LocalOnly and with the /a flag, requesting that Exchange present the Address Book user interface:

```
mlogon /p LocalOnly /e /a
```

Mlogon logs onto MAPI using the specified profile and creates a shareable session. It creates a minimized window on the screen while it runs. After it creates the shared session, it locates the executable file for the Exchange client and launches that. When the Mlogon application sees that Exchange is running, it quietly exits; unlike Msess, it does not request that all shared session users log off, because it wants to leave Exchange running.

Removing Mlogon

Delete the executable file MLOGON.EXE.

Programming with Mlogon

Mlogon demonstrates a technique for locating and launching the Exchange client executable.

Reusing Mlogon

The internals of Mlogon are fairly messy, with all the actions conditional on the class *CSettings*, which interferes with the basic flow of the program. The functions *FindExchange* and *LaunchExchange* from MLOGON.CPP can be reused.

If you use this application as a template for another project, be sure you change the following elements:

- The name of the application

- The icon

- The contents of the version information block *VS_VERSION_INFO* (in MLOGON.RC)

- The name of the registry key that modifies its behavior (in MLOGON.CPP)

Keep in Mind

Mlogon does not check for a running instance of Exchange before proceeding.

The Microsoft Internet Mail transport hangs the MAPI message spooler when it is invoked by Mlogon.

Eeminim

The directory Chap04\Eeminim contains the simplest possible Exchange client extension, one that does nothing more than let itself be loaded by Exchange.

Building Eeminim

To build the Eeminim application, open a command shell, change its current working directory to Chap04\Eeminim, and enter the following command:

```
nmake /f Makefile
```

To build a version of the Eeminim application without debugging symbols, enter the following command:

```
nmake nodebug=1 /f Makefile
```

Users of Microsoft Visual C++ 4.0 can load the workspace file EEMINIM.MDP.

A successful build generates the executable file EEMINIM.DLL. You can discard the import library file EEMINIM.LIB that is generated during the build.

Installing Eeminim

Copy the source file EEMINIM.REG to a file named INSTALL.REG (or create a file with this name if it does not already exist). Open INSTALL.REG in a text editor. You will see the following text:

```
REGEDIT4
[HKEY_LOCAL_MACHINE\SOFTWARE\Microsoft\Exchange\Client\Extensions]
@=" "
"Stub"="4.0;eeminim.dll;1"
```

Change the second semicolon-delimited field in the right-hand component of the Stub entry to reflect the actual path of the dynamic-link library EEMINIM.DLL by doubling all backslashes in the pathname. For example, if you had this DLL in a directory C:\Exchange, change the line to read:

```
"Stub"="4.0;C:\\Exchange\\eeminim.dll;1"
```

Save the file INSTALL.REG, and exit the text editor. Merge the contents of the file INSTALL.REG into the system registry, either by double-clicking the INSTALL.REG icon in Windows Explorer or by choosing the Registry - Import Registry File command in the Registry Editor (REGEDIT.EXE).[1]

Running Eeminim

Launch the Exchange client. To see the actions of Eeminim, you must run EXCHNG32.EXE under a debugger, watching for debug text (such as a program emits when using *OutputDebugString*) sent to the output window. Eeminim installs an extension object in every context created by Exchange, announcing that object with debug text. When you have finished, exit Exchange.

Removing Eeminim

In a registry editor, open the following key and remove the tagged Stub value.

```
HKEY_LOCAL_MACHINE\SOFTWARE\Microsoft\Exchange\Client\Extensions
```

Programming with Eeminim

Eeminim offers only one interface, *IExchExt*. It demonstrates the most basic attributes of an extension: the entry point into the library, the structure of implementing a vtable, and checking the version of the host in *IExchExt::Install*.

Reusing Eeminim

If you use this extension as a template for another project, be sure you change the following elements:

---

1. The hive-based Windows NT registry editor REGEDT32.EXE does not support this command.

- The name of the application
- The icon
- The contents of the version information block *VS_VERSION_INFO* (in EEMINIM.RC)
- The tag name used by the registry entry (Stub in EEMINIM.REG)

Eeminim checks the version of Exchange by hosting it against a static value. To avoid revising your extension with every Service Pack that updates Exchange clients, consider storing the version number of Exchange in the system registry.

Keep in Mind

Eeminim uses the same tag name as the next sample, Eestub. Therefore, only one of them can be installed within Exchange at a time. You can easily remedy this by changing either EEMINIM.REG or EESTUB.REG so that they use different tag names.

Eeminim complains when it is loaded into any version postdating Exchange Server 4.0 Service Pack 1 (SP1). You can correct this by changing the *LAST-_BUILD_SUPPORTED* manifest constant in EXT.CPP to a value more recent than 839. See also the reuse notes in the previous section.

Eestub

The directory Chap04\Eestub contains an extension that is equivalent to the sample Inetxidm except that it is pruned of all functionality to reveal the structure of the underlying client extension. It has no function beyond its form.

Building Eestub

To build the Eestub application, open a command shell, change its current working directory to Chap04\Eestub, and enter the following command:

```
nmake /f Makefile
```

To build a version of Eestub without debugging symbols, enter the following command:

```
nmake nodebug=1 /f Makefile
```

Users of Microsoft Visual C++ 4.0 can load the workspace file EESTUB.MDP.

A successful build generates the executable file EESTUB.DLL. You can discard the import library file EESTUB.LIB that is generated during the build.

Installing Eestub

Copy the source file EESTUB.REG to INSTALL.REG. Open INSTALL.REG in a text editor. You will see the following text:

```
REGEDIT4
[HKEY_LOCAL_MACHINE\SOFTWARE\Microsoft\Exchange\Client\Extensions]
@=" "
"Stub"="4.0;eestub.dll;1"
```

Change the second semicolon-delimited field in the right-hand component of the Stub entry to reflect the actual path of the dynamic-link library EESTUB.DLL by doubling all backslashes in the pathname. For example, if you had this DLL in a directory C:\Exchange, change the line to read as follows:

```
"Stub"="4.0;C:\\Exchange\\eestub.dll;1"
```

Save the file INSTALL.REG, and exit the text editor. Merge the contents of the file INSTALL.REG into the system registry, either by double-clicking the INSTALL.REG icon in Windows Explorer or by selecting the Registry - Import Registry File command in the Registry Editor (REGEDIT.EXE).

Running Eestub

To run the Eestub application, launch the Exchange client. Because this application has no functionality, you'll see a nonfunctional command on the Help menu called Stub Command (THIS SPACE FOR RENT). Add a nonfunctional toolbar button to the note form toolbar, and observe the empty property sheet pages in each property sheet dialog box. If you run EXCHNG32.EXE under a debugger, you can watch the extension announce its events in the debug text. When you have finished, exit Exchange.

Removing Eestub

In a registry editor, open the following key and remove the tagged Stub value.

```
HKEY_LOCAL_MACHINE\SOFTWARE\Microsoft\Exchange\Client\Extensions
```

Programming with Eestub

Eestub demonstrates an Exchange client extension offering *IExchExtCommands* and *IExchExtMessageEvents* in addition to the primary interface *IExchExt*. It adds a menu command and a toolbar button to every window, and it adds a property sheet page (or two, as noted in Chapter 4) to every property sheet dialog. It is most interesting to study the Eestub application together with an application with more features.

Reusing Eestub

If you use this extension as a template for another project, be sure you change the following elements:

- The name of the application
- The icon
- The contents of the version information block *VS_VERSION_INFO* (in EESTUB.RC)
- The tag name used by the registry entry (Stub in EESTUB.REG)

Eestub checks the version of Exchange by hosting it against a static value. To avoid revising your extension with every Service Pack that updates Exchange clients, consider storing the version number of Exchange in the system registry.

Keep in Mind

Eestub uses the same tag name as the preceding sample, Eeminim. Therefore, only one of these samples can be installed within Exchange at a time. You can easily remedy this by changing either EESTUB.REG or EEMINIM.REG to use a tag name different from that of the other.

Eestub complains when it is loaded into any version postdating Exchange Server 4.0 Service Pack 1 (SP1). You can correct this by changing the *LAST_BUILD_SUPPORTED* manifest constant in EXT.CPP to a value more recent than 839. See also the reuse notes in the previous section.

Eetrans

The directory Chap04\Eetrans contains another skeletal Exchange client extension. This application demonstrates how to implement a command that works on the current selection in the Exchange client. Like Eestub, it has no function beyond its form.

Building Eetrans

To build the Eetrans application, open a command shell, change its current working directory to Chap04\Eetrans, and enter the following command:

```
nmake /f Makefile
```

To build a version of the Eetrans application without debugging symbols, enter the following command:

```
nmake nodebug=1 /f Makefile
```

Users of Microsoft Visual C++ 4.0 can load the workspace file EETRANS.MDP.

A successful build generates the executable file EETRANS.DLL. You can discard the import library file EETRANS.LIB that is generated during the build.

Installing Eetrans

Copy the source file EETRANS.REG to INSTALL.REG. Open INSTALL.REG in a text editor. You will see the following text:

```
REGEDIT4
[HKEY_LOCAL_MACHINE\SOFTWARE\Microsoft\Exchange\Client\Extensions]
@=" "
"Transitive stub"="4.0;eetrans.dll;1;01000000000000;1100000"
```

Change the second semicolon-delimited field in the right-hand component of the Transitive stub entry to reflect the actual path of the dynamic-link library EETRANS.DLL by doubling all backslashes in the pathname. For example, if you had this DLL in a directory C:\Exchange, change the line to read:

```
"Transitive stub"="4.0;C:\\Exchange\\eetrans.dll;1;01000000000000;
1100000"
```

Save the file INSTALL.REG, and exit the text editor. Merge the contents of the file INSTALL.REG into the system registry, either by double-clicking the INSTALL.REG icon in Windows Explorer or by selecting the Registry - Import Registry File command in the Registry Editor (REGEDIT.EXE).

Running Eetrans

Launch the Exchange client, observe the nonfunctional menu command File - Stub Command in the viewer window, and see how Exchange enables and disables the menu command in response to the type of selection in the viewer. When you have finished, exit Exchange.

Removing Eetrans

In a registry editor, open the following key and remove the tagged Transitive stub value.

```
HKEY_LOCAL_MACHINE\SOFTWARE\Microsoft\Exchange\Client\Extensions
```

Programming with Eetrans

Eetrans demonstrates an Exchange client extension offering *IExchExtCommands* and *IExchExtUserEvents* in addition to the primary interface *IExchExt*. These interfaces work together to implement a command that depends on the current selection in a viewer window.

Reusing Eetrans

If you use this extension as a template for another project, be sure you change the following elements:

- The name of the application

- The icon

- The contents of the version information block *VS_VERSION_INFO* (in EETRANS.RC)

- The tag name used by the registry entry (Transitive stub in EETRANS.REG)

Eetrans checks the version of Exchange by hosting it against a static value. To avoid revising your extension with every Service Pack that updates Exchange clients, consider storing the version number of Exchange in the system registry.

Keep in Mind

Eetrans complains when it is loaded into any version postdating Exchange Server 4.0 Service Pack 1 (SP1). You can correct this by changing the *LAST_BUILD-_SUPPORTED* manifest constant in EXT.CPP to a value more recent than 839. See also the reuse notes above.

Mtwb

The directory Chap04\Mtwb contains Janitor In A DLL, an Exchange client extension that implements a new command in the Exchange viewer window, File - Expunge Deleted Items. When you choose this command, it empties the Deleted Items folders on all stores that are present in the current session.

Building Mtwb

To build the Mtwb application, open a command shell, change its current working directory to Chap04\Mtwb, and enter the following command:

```
nmake /f Makefile
```

To build a version of Mtwb without debugging symbols, enter the following command:

```
nmake nodebug=1 /f Makefile
```

Users of Microsoft Visual C++ 4.0 can load the workspace file MTWB.MDP.

A successful build generates the executable file MTWB.DLL. You can discard the import library file MTWB.LIB that is generated during the build.

Installing Mtwb

Copy the source file MTWB.REG to INSTALL.REG. Open INSTALL.REG in a text editor. You will see the following text:

```
REGEDIT4
[HKEY_LOCAL_MACHINE\SOFTWARE\Microsoft\Exchange\Client\Extensions]
@=" "
"Janitor in a DLL"="4.0;mtwb.dll;1;01000000000000;1000000"
```

Change the second semicolon-delimited field in the right-hand component of the Janitor In A DLL entry to reflect the actual path of the dynamic-link library MTWB.DLL by doubling all backslashes in the pathname. For example, if you had this DLL in the directory C:\Exchange, change the line to read:

```
"Janitor in a DLL"="4.0;C:\\Exchange\\mtwb.dll;1;
    01000000000000;1000000"
```

Save the file INSTALL.REG, and exit the text editor. Merge the contents of the file INSTALL.REG into the system registry, either by double-clicking the INSTALL-.REG icon in Windows Explorer or by selecting the Registry - Import Registry File command in the Registry Editor (REGEDIT.EXE).

Running Mtwb

Launch the Exchange client. On the File menu of the viewer window, you will see a new command, Expunge Deleted Items. Select it to empty your Deleted Items folder of all deleted messages. You can place this command on the toolbar if you like.

Removing Mtwb

In a registry editor, open the following key and remove the tagged Janitor In A DLL value.

```
HKEY_LOCAL_MACHINE\SOFTWARE\Microsoft\Exchange\Client\Extensions
```

Programming with Mtwb

Mtwb demonstrates a client extension creating a menu command that does not depend on the current selection in the viewer but that instead derives all of its input from the *GetWindow* and *GetSession* methods of the *IExchExtCallback* interface. The actual work of emptying a folder takes place through calls to the *IMAPIFolder::EmptyFolder* method. This sample also shows how to locate the Deleted Items folder on a particular message store. Finally, when the sample enumerates all of the message stores in the message store table, it uses either *HrQueryAllRows* or a series of explicit table operations against *IMAPITable*, depending on the value of the symbol *USE_EXPLICIT_TABLE_OPS*.

Reusing Mtwb

If you use this extension as a template for another project, be sure you change the following elements:

- The name of the application

- The icon

- The bitmap for the toolbar button (as contained in BUTTON.BMP)

- The contents of the version information block *VS_VERSION_INFO* (in MTWB.RC)

- The tag name used by the registry entry ("Janitor In A DLL" in MTWB.REG)

Keep in Mind

If Mtwb encounters any errors while attempting to empty wastebasket folders, it stops: it does not enumerate or empty any other wastebaskets. It should instead display a message and then continue, so as to handle the case in which the session contains a message store with a Deleted Items folder against which the current user has insufficient permission to empty.

Because Mtwb checks the version of Exchange by hosting it against a static value, it complains when it is loaded into any version postdating Exchange Server 4.0 Service Pack 1 (SP1). You can correct this problem by changing the *LAST_BUILD-_SUPPORTED* manifest constant in EXT.CPP to a value more recent than 839. See also the reuse notes in the previous section.

Rtfguard

The directory Chap04\Rtfguard contains Rich Text Sentry, an Exchange client extension that strips the rich text bits from outgoing messages. The extension examines every outgoing message; if any one-off message recipient (that is, any recipient not from an address book) with an SMTP address has rich text enabled, Rtfguard resets rich text on all such recipients.

This sample isn't in Chapter 4. It is intended for supplementary study only.

Building Rtfguard

To build the Rtfguard application, open a command shell, change its current working directory to Chap04\Rtfguard, and enter the following command:

```
nmake /f Makefile
```

To build a version of Rtfguard without debugging symbols, enter the following command:

```
nmake nodebug=1 /f Makefile
```

Users of Microsoft Visual C++ 4.0 can load the workspace file RTFGUARD.MDP.

A successful build generates the executable file RTFGUARD.DLL. You can discard the import library file RTFGUARD.LIB that is generated during the build.

Installing Rtfguard

Copy the source file RTFGUARD.REG to INSTALL.REG. Open INSTALL.REG in a text editor. You will see the following text:

```
REGEDIT4
[HKEY_LOCAL_MACHINE\SOFTWARE\Microsoft\Exchange\Client\Extensions]
@=" "
"Rich Text Sentry"="4.0;rtfguard.dll;1;00000100001000;0001000"
```

Change the second semicolon-delimited field in the right-hand component of the Rich Text Sentry entry to reflect the actual path of the dynamic-link library RTFGUARD.DLL by doubling all backslashes in the pathname. For example, if you had this DLL in a directory C:\Exchange, change the line to read:

```
"Rich Text Sentry"="4.0;C:\\Exchange\\rtfguard.dll;1;
    00000100001000;0001000"
```

Save the file INSTALL.REG, and exit the text editor. Merge the contents of the file INSTALL.REG into the system registry, either by double-clicking the INSTALL.REG icon in Windows Explorer or by selecting the Registry - Import Registry File command in the Registry Editor (REGEDIT.EXE).

Running Rtfguard

Launch the Exchange client. Compose a note, addressing it to a one-off SMTP address (for example, charon@styx.net); resolve the address using the Tools - Check Names command; open the resolved recipient object by clicking the To button; and set the checkbox Always Send To This Recipient In Microsoft Rich-Text Format to be displayed when you highlight the recipient's name and click the Properties button. After you send the message, Rtfguard interrupts you with a warning, which offers to either send the message as it is, stop sending the message, or eliminate the rich text setting.

Try this again, this time addressing the note to an SMTP address picked from an address book—for example, an entry in your PAB. Rtfguard will not interrupt.

Removing Rtfguard

In a registry editor, open the following key and remove the tagged Rich Text Sentry value.

```
HKEY_LOCAL_MACHINE\SOFTWARE\Microsoft\Exchange\Client\Extensions
```

Programming with Rtfguard

Unlike any other sample in this book, Rtfguard offers an example of a functional Exchange client extension that does not implement *IExchExtCommands*. It offers only *IExchExtMessageEvents* plus *IExchExt*. It hooks the *OnSubmit* event, showing how to torpedo a message submission in progress. In its check, Rtfguard manipulates the *ADRLIST* and *ADRENTRY* structures and examines the format of one-off address entry identifiers, searching them for the telltale flag that suppresses rich text information.

Reusing Rtfguard

The main body of the client extension is so skeletal that you could easily reuse it for another extension hooking message events. If you use this extension as a template for another project, be sure you change the following elements:

- The name of the application
- The icon
- The contents of the version information block *VS_VERSION_INFO* (in RTFGUARD.RC)
- The tag name used by the registry entry (Rich Text Sentry in RTF-GUARD.REG)

Rtfguard checks the version of Exchange by hosting it against a static value. To avoid revising your extension with every Service Pack that updates Exchange clients, consider storing the version number of Exchange in the system registry.

Keep in Mind

Because Rtfguard checks the version of Exchange by hosting it against a static value, it complains when it is loaded into any version postdating Exchange Server 4.0 Service Pack 1 (SP1). You can correct this by changing the *LAST-_BUILD_SUPPORTED* manifest constant in EXT.CPP to a value more recent than 839. See also the reuse notes in the previous section.

If the underlying messaging system does not honor the flag *MAPI_ONE_OFF_NO-_RICH_INFO*, as is the case with the Microsoft Mail transport provider, there is little else that Rtfguard can do to prevent rich text from accompanying the user.

Inetxidm

The directory Chap04\Inetxidm contains Internet Idioms, an Exchange client extension that appends blocks of boilerplate signature text to outgoing messages, sets the font in which the standard note form displays incoming messages with no explicit font attribute, and alters the format of reply messages to use traditional prefix characters such as ">" in the Internet Mail manner.

Building Inetxidm

To build the Inetxidm application, open a command shell, change its current working directory to Chap04\Inetxidm, and enter the following command:

```
nmake /f Makefile
```

To build a version of the Inetxidm application without debugging symbols, enter the following command:

```
nmake nodebug=1 /f Makefile
```

Users of Microsoft Visual C++ 4.0 can load the workspace file INETXIDM.MDP.

A successful build generates the executable file INETXIDM.DLL. You can discard the import library file INETXIDM.LIB that is generated during the build.

Installing Inetxidm

Copy the source file INETXIDM.REG to INSTALL.REG. Open INSTALL.REG in a text editor. You will see the following text:

```
REGEDIT4
[HKEY_LOCAL_MACHINE\SOFTWARE\Microsoft\Exchange\Client\Extensions]
@=" "
"Internet Idioms"="4.0;inetxidm.dll;1;00000111111100;1001010"
```

Change the second semicolon-delimited field in the right-hand component of the Internet Idioms entry to reflect the actual path of the dynamic-link library INETXIDM.DLL by doubling all backslashes in the pathname. For example, if you had this DLL in a directory C:\Exchange, change the line to read as follows:

```
"Internet Idioms"="4.0;C:\\Exchange\\inetxidm.dll;1;
    00000111111100; 1001010"
```

Save the file INSTALL.REG, and exit the text editor. Merge the contents of the file INSTALL.REG into the system registry, either by double-clicking the INSTALL.REG icon in Windows Explorer or by selecting the Registry - Import Registry File command in the Registry Editor (REGEDIT.EXE).

Running Inetxidm

Launch the Exchange client. Visit the Idioms page on the Tools - Options property sheet to configure the various parameters of idioms: whether and with what to append outgoing messages, whether and with what to prefix reply messages, and the font to use for incoming messages.

Removing Inetxidm

In a registry editor, open the following key and remove the tagged Internet Idioms value.

```
HKEY_LOCAL_MACHINE\SOFTWARE\Microsoft\Exchange\Client\Extensions
```

Next, open the following key:

```
HKEY_CURRENT_USER\Software\Microsoft\Windows Messaging Subsystem\
    Profiles
```

Finally, open the subkey corresponding to the profile used, and within that key, delete the subkey 01e232dab897cf11b6a608002b2b3625. (This is *GUID_InternetIdioms*, as listed in GUIDS.H, in Intel byte-order.)

Programming with Inetxidm

Essentially, Inetxidm shows a few things that you can do in *IExchExtMessageEvents* after you get a handle on the rich edit control in the body of the standard note form. This happens in the function *FindREOnNote* in STDNOTE.CPP.

More specifically, the Inetxidm application demonstrates appending pages to a property sheet by passing references to objects to those pages' control procedures. It invokes the standard font chooser dialog box. It appends text to the end of the message body on outgoing messages, synchronizing that text with any rich text present. It maintains a private property on a message to track whether it has already signed a message, thus avoiding double-signing messages that the user reopens, edits, and resubmits from the Outbox folder. It examines the state of opened messages to guess heuristically whether a new note originated from a forward or a reply. It traps the first menu activation in *IExchExtCommands* to get control within new reply forms, where no *IExchExtMessageEvents::OnRead* event ever fires. It changes the default font used within the rich edit control and alters text therein as well. It saves configuration data in the current profile and, in a parallel implementation (marked with the manifest constant *USE_REGISTRY*), shows saving the same data in the registry.

In terms of MAPI operations, the Inetxidm application opens the message body property as a stream and invokes the rich text synchronization engine of MAPI. It defines a new property and sets it on a message. It reads and writes to and from a unique section within the current profile.

Reusing Inetxidm

If you use any or all of this extension as a template for another project, be sure you change the following elements:

- The name of the application

- The icon

- The bitmap for the toolbar button (as contained in BUTTON.BMP)

- The contents of the version information block *VS_VERSION_INFO* (in INETXIDM.RC)

- The GUID identifying the unique property set and profile namespace of Internet Idioms (*GUID_InternetIdioms* in GUIDS.H)

- The tag name used by the registry entry (Internet Idioms in INETXIDM.REG)

Inetxidm checks the version of Exchange by hosting it against a static value. To avoid revising your extension with every Service Pack that updates Exchange clients, consider storing the version number of Exchange in the system registry.

Keep in Mind

The font-mapping function cannot change the displayed font when the message already has an explicit font attribute, as is the case with all incoming messages that arrive through the Microsoft Exchange Server Internet Mail Connector.

The technique by which Inetxidm munges reply text is hideously slow on long messages, working as it does entirely within the rich edit control. The heuristic by which Inetxidm elects to munge replies or not is extremely simpleminded.

The Inetxidm application complains when it is loaded into any version post-dating Exchange Server 4.0 Service Pack 1 (SP1). You can correct this by changing the *LAST_BUILD_SUPPORTED* manifest constant in EXT.CPP to a value more recent than 839. See also the reuse notes in the previous section.

Frminf

The directory Chap05\Frminf contains yet another Exchange client extension; this one examines the currently selected message in the viewer and presents a number of attributes about it, including the following:

- The actual properties on the message

- The verbs published by the message's form, if any

- The properties published by the message's form, if any

- The properties on the form's information object

Building Frminf

The header file EXCHFORM.H is required to compile this program. If the Include directory of your compiler does not already contain this file, copy it from the companion CD-ROM.

To build the Frminf application, open a command shell, change its current working directory to Chap05\Frminf, and enter the following command:

```
nmake /f Makefile
```

To build a version of the Frminf application without debugging symbols, enter the following command:

```
nmake nodebug=1 /f Makefile
```

Users of Microsoft Visual C++ 4.0 can load the workspace file FRMINF.MDP.

A successful build generates the executable file FRMINF.DLL. You can discard the import library file FRMINF.LIB that is generated during the build.

Installing Frminf

Copy the source file FRMINF.REG to INSTALL.REG. Open INSTALL.REG in a text editor. You will see the following text:

```
REGEDIT4
[HKEY_LOCAL_MACHINE\SOFTWARE\Microsoft\Exchange\Client\Extensions]
@=" "
"Form info"="4.0;frminf.dll;1;01000000000000;1100000"
```

Change the second semicolon-delimited field in the right-hand component of the Form Info entry to reflect the actual path of the dynamic-link library FRMINF.DLL by doubling all backslashes in the pathname. For example, if you had this DLL in a directory C:\Exchange, change the line to read as follows:

```
"Form info"="4.0;C:\\Exchange\\frminf.dll;1;01000000000000;1100000"
```

Save the file INSTALL.REG, and exit the text editor. Merge the contents of the file INSTALL.REG into the system registry, either by double-clicking the INSTALL-.REG icon in Windows Explorer or by selecting the Registry - Import Registry File command in the Registry Editor (REGEDIT.EXE).

Running Frminf

Launch the Exchange client. On the File menu of the viewer window, you will see a new command, Form Information. Select a message in the viewer, and then select this command to view all sorts of interesting facets of the current message.

Removing Frminf

In a registry editor, open the following key and remove the tagged Form Info value.

```
HKEY_LOCAL_MACHINE\SOFTWARE\Microsoft\Exchange\Client\Extensions
```

Programming with Frminf

As the Inetxidm application is to Eestub, so is the Frminf application to Eetrans, putting functional muscles on the skeleton of a client extension.

The Frminf application dissects properties, including MAPI named properties, by looking up their property identifier codes and dumping their values by their property type. Frminf enumerates *IMAPIProp* on both messages and form information objects. On form information objects, it enumerates published verbs and published properties. It also acquires an interface on the MAPI Forms Manager and uses that interface to resolve a message class to a form information object.

Reusing Frminf

If you use any or all of this extension as a template for another project, be sure you change the following elements:

- The name of the application

- The icon

- The contents of the version information block *VS_VERSION_INFO* (in FRMINF.RC)

- The tag name used by the registry entry (Form Info in FRMINF.REG)

The Frminf application checks the version of Exchange by hosting it against a static value. To avoid revising your extension with every Service Pack that updates Exchange clients, consider storing the version number of Exchange in the system registry.

Keep in Mind

The Frminf application complains when it is loaded into any version postdating Exchange Server 4.0 Service Pack 1 (SP1). You can correct this by changing the *LAST_BUILD_SUPPORTED* manifest constant in EXT.CPP to a value more recent than 839. See also the reuse notes in the previous section.

The Frminf application contains some code that unsuccessfully tries to avoid bugs in the form information object *IMAPIProp* implementation. See the disabled (#if 0) sequences of code in the function *ListboxFormInfo* in the file WORK.CPP.

Poststub

The directory Chap06\Poststub implements the server for a simple post form.

Building Poststub

The header file EXCHFORM.H is required to compile this program. If the Include directory of your compiler does not already contain this file, copy it from the companion CD-ROM.

To build the Poststub application, open a command shell, change its current working directory to Chap06\Poststub, and enter the following command:

```
nmake /f Makefile
```

To build a version of the Poststub application without debugging symbols, enter the following command:

```
nmake nodebug=1 /f Makefile
```

Users of Microsoft Visual C++ 4.0 can load the workspace file POSTSTUB.MDP.

A successful build generates the executable file POSTSTUB.EXE.

Installing Poststub

Before experimenting with form servers, back up your form cache file \Windows-\Forms\FRMCACHE.DAT to FRMCACHE.OK. (The precise name of the backup file is not important.) This lets you revert to a previous version of the cache.

The symbol *TEST_LOCAL_FORM_LIBRARY* (defined in POSTSTUB.H) enables code in MAIN.CPP that adds the /INSTALL and /UNINSTALL switches to the form server. These switches let you install the form server temporarily in the local application forms library to run a form under the debugger without having MAPI's caching interfere. Change your current working directory so that POST-STUB.EXE, POSTSTUB.REG, and POSTSTUB.CFG are all in the same directory. Edit POSTSTUB.REG to reflect the true path to the executable POSTSTUB.EXE; here you can have the LocalServer32 clause spawn the form server beneath a debugger (for example, C:\Msvc\Bin\MSDEV.EXE POSTSTUB.EXE) for ease of debugging. Merge the contents of the file POSTSTUB.REG into the system registry, either by double-clicking the INSTALL.REG icon in Windows Explorer or by selecting the Registry - Import Registry File command in the Registry Editor (REGEDIT.EXE). Finally, enter the following command:

```
poststub /install
```

To add the form to a real forms library, copy POSTSTUB.CFG to INSTALL.CFG. Open INSTALL.CFG in a text editor, and edit the Platforms fields to reflect the actual platforms for the form server executables that you have. For instance, the following sample shows that the executable references [Platform.xxx] sections for xxx being NTx86 and Win95. Note that I've commented out the entry for the DEC Alpha, thus preventing the installation code from looking for any [Platform.ALPHA] entry that the file might contain.

```
[Platforms]
Platform1=NTx86
Platform2=Win95
;Platform3=ALPHA
```

Now go to each of those [Platform.xxx] sections referenced. There is a single executable, which works on both NT 3.51 Intel and Windows 95 (also synonymous with NT 4.0 Intel). One entry links to the other. Edit the *file1=* clause to reference the actual pathname to POSTSTUB.EXE. You can leave the pathname alone if INSTALL.CFG and POSTSTUB.EXE will remain in the same directory at installation time.

```
[Platform.NTx86]
CPU=ix86
OSVersion=WinNT3.5
file1=poststub.exe
registry1=InprocHandler32 = mapi32.dll
registry2=LocalServer32 = %d\poststub.exe

[Platform.Win95]
CPU=ix86
OSVersion=Win95
LinkTo=NTx86
```

Finally, go to the Exchange client, select a folder to host the folder forms library, and invoke the File - Properties command. Select the Forms tab, and click the Manage button. Beneath the right-hand pane of the Forms Manager dialog box, click the Install button. In the resulting standard file selection dialog box, navigate to INSTALL.CFG, select it and click the OK button, and then dismiss the dialog boxes that follow.

Running Poststub

Launch the Exchange client by opening the folder in which to post the message. If you installed the folder in a folder forms library, pull down the Compose menu and select the new New Useless Posted Note command. Otherwise, select the

Compose - New Form command and do the following: select Application Forms in the combo box, select Stub Post Form in the list box, and dismiss the dialog box with OK. This invokes the command line you specified in the LocalServer32 clause of the registry entry and launches the form server.

If the LocalServer32 clause launches a debugger instead of directly launching a form server, make sure that it doesn't sit for too long without starting its subprocess or COM will time out and return an error to MAPI. (Remember, the System COM Library needs to establish a communication channel between the form server and the requesting Exchange client process, so it is waiting for the server to call *CoRegisterClassObject*.) MAPI will then turn around and try again. You'll end up with multiple copies of your debugger running multiple stalled copies of your form server.

Removing Poststub

If you installed the form in the local application forms library, issue the following command:

```
poststub /uninstall
```

Optionally, you can copy your saved copy of the original form cache file back to FRMCACHE.DAT. Next, in a registry editor, delete the following key:

```
HKEY_CLASSES_ROOT\CLSID\{da32e200-97b8-11cf-b6a6-080022b2b3625}
```

If you installed the form in a folder forms library, invoke the Forms Manager dialog box as described above, select Stub Post Form, and press Delete.

Programming with Poststub

The Poststub application implements a subset of *IPM.POST*. It implements a class factory, supporting multiple forms from a single server—albeit a single-threaded server.

Reusing Poststub

CLastError, *CViewNotifier*, and *CClassFactory* are all reusable with only trivial edits.

If you use any or all of this form server as a template for another project, be sure you change the following elements:

- The name of the application
- The icons

- The contents of the version information block *VS_VERSION_INFO* (in POSTSTUB.RC)

- The GUID identifying the unique class of the form (*CLSID_StubPost-Form* in GUIDS.H and CLSID in POSTSTUB.CFG)

- The message class used by the form's messages (*SZ_FORM_MESSAGE-_CLASS* in FORM.H and Message Class in POSTSTUB.CFG)

- The help file mapping string (*SZ_COMPONENT* in FORM.H)

- Various other descriptive fields in the installation file (POSTSTUB.CFG)

Keep in Mind

As implemented, Poststub does not support conversation tracking, because it does not create the conversation tracking properties *PR_CONVERSATION_INDEX* and *PR_CONVERSATION_TOPIC* on its messages.

Sendstub

The directory Chap06\Sendstub implements the server for a simple send form.

Building Sendstub

The header file EXCHFORM.H is required to compile this program. If the Include directory of your compiler does not already contain this file, copy it from the companion CD-ROM.

To build the Sendstub application, open a command shell, change its current working directory to Chap06\Sendstub, and enter the following command:

```
nmake /f Makefile
```

To build a version of the Sendstub application without debugging symbols, enter the following command:

```
nmake nodebug=1 /f Makefile
```

Users of Microsoft Visual C++ 4.0 can load the workspace file SENDSTUB.MDP.

A successful build generates the executable file SENDSTUB.EXE.

Installing Sendstub

Before experimenting with form servers, back up your form cache file \Windows-\Forms\FRMCACHE.DAT to FRMCACHE.OK. (The precise name of the backup file is not important.) This lets you revert to a previous version of the cache.

The symbol *TEST_LOCAL_FORM_LIBRARY* (defined in SENDSTUB.H) enables code in MAIN.CPP that adds the /INSTALL and /UNINSTALL switches to the form server. These let you install the form server temporarily in the local application forms library to run a form under the debugger without having MAPI's caching interfere. Change your current working directory so that SENDSTUB.EXE, SEND-STUB.REG, and SENDSTUB.CFG are in the same directory. Edit SENDSTUB.REG to reflect the true path to the executable SENDSTUB.EXE; here you can have the LocalServer32 clause spawn the form server beneath a debugger (for example, C:\Msvc\Bin\MSDEV.EXE SENDSTUB.EXE) for ease of debugging. Merge the contents of the file SENDSTUB.REG into the system registry, either by double-clicking the INSTALL.REG icon in Windows Explorer or by selecting the Registry - Import Registry File command in the Registry Editor (REGEDIT-.EXE). Finally, enter the following command:

```
sendstub /install
```

To add the form to a real forms library, copy SENDSTUB.CFG to INSTALL.CFG. Open INSTALL..CFG in a text editor. Edit the Platforms fields to reflect the actual platforms for the form server executables that you have. For instance, the following sample shows that the executable references [Platform.xxx] sections for xxx being NTx86 and Win95. Note that I've commented out the entry for the DEC Alpha, thus preventing the installation code from looking for any [Platform-.ALPHA] entry that the file might contain.

```
[Platforms]
Platform1=NTx86
Platform2=Win95
;Platform3=ALPHA
```

Now go to each of those [Platform.xxx] sections referenced. There is a single executable, which works on both NT 3.51 Intel and Windows 95 (also synonymous with NT 4.0 Intel). One entry links to the other. Edit the *file1=* clause to reference the actual pathname to SENDSTUB.EXE. You can leave the pathname alone if INSTALL.CFG and SENDSTUB.EXE will remain in the same directory at installation time.

```
[Platform.NTx86]
CPU=ix86
OSVersion=WinNT3.5
file1=sendstub.exe
registry1=InprocHandler32 = mapi32.dll
registry2=LocalServer32 = %d\sendstub.exe

[Platform.Win95]
CPU=ix86
OSVersion=Win95
LinkTo=NTx86
```

Finally, go to the Exchange client and invoke the Tools - Options command. Select the Exchange Server tab, and click the Manage Forms button. In the right-hand pane of the Forms Manager dialog box, select the Personal Forms library (using the Set button) if it is not already selected, and then click the Install button. In the resulting standard file selection dialog box, navigate to INSTALL.CFG, select it and click the OK button, and then dismiss the dialog boxes that follow.

Running Sendstub

Launch the Exchange client as follows: select Compose - New Form, select Stub Send Form in the list box, and dismiss the dialog box with OK. This invokes the command line you specified in the LocalServer32 clause of the registry entry and launches the form server.

If the LocalServer32 clause launches a debugger instead of directly launching a form server, make sure that it doesn't sit for too long without starting its sub-process or COM will time out and return an error to MAPI. (Remember, the System COM Library needs to establish a communication channel between the form server and the requesting Exchange client process, so it's waiting for the server to call *CoRegisterClassObject*.) MAPI will then turn around and try again. You'll end up with multiple copies of your debugger running multiple stalled copies of your form server.

Removing Sendstub

If you installed the form in the local application forms library, issue the following command:

```
sendstub /uninstall
```

Optionally, you can copy your saved copy of the original form cache file back to FRMCACHE.DAT. Next, in a registry editor, delete the following key:

```
HKEY_CLASSES_ROOT\CLSID\{da32e202-97b8-11cf-b6a6-080022b2b3625}
```

If you installed the form in the personal forms library, enter the Forms Manager dialog box as described above, select Stub Send Form, and press Delete.

Programming with Sendstub

Sendstub implements a subset of *IPM.Note*.

Reusing Sendstub

If you use any or all of this form server as a template for another project, be sure you change the following elements.

- The name of the application

- The icons

- The contents of the version information block *VS_VERSION_INFO* (in SENDSTUB.RC)

- The GUID identifying the unique class of the form (*CLSID_StubSend-Form* in GUIDS.H and CLSID in SENDSTUB.CFG)

- The message class used by the form's messages (*SZ_FORM_MESSAGE-_CLASS* in FORM.H and Message Class in SENDSTUB.CFG)

- The help file mapping string (*SZ_COMPONENT* in FORM.H)

- Various other descriptive fields in the installation file (SENDSTUB.CFG)

Keep in Mind

As implemented, Sendstub does not support conversation tracking, because it does not create the conversation tracking properties *PR_CONVERSATION_INDEX* and *PR_CONVERSATION_TOPIC* on its messages.

Catform

The directory Chap06\Catform implements a form for a custom folder application.

Building Catform

To build the Catform application, open a command shell, change its current working directory to Chap06\Catform, and enter the following command:

```
nmake /f Makefile
```

To build a version of the Catform application without debugging symbols, enter the following command:

```
nmake nodebug=1 /f Makefile
```

Users of Microsoft Visual C++ 4.0 can load the workspace file CATFORM.MDP.

A successful build generates the executable file CATFORM.EXE.

Installing Catform

Install the Catform application just as you did Poststub, substituting CATFORM.REG for POSTSTUB.REG, CATFORM.EXE for POSTSTUB.EXE, and so on.

Running Catform

Run the Catform application just as you did Poststub, but look for the form Cat Tracker.

After you've added a cat record to the folder, try designing a view (the View - Define Views command of Exchange) in that folder and seeing the new column definitions. Also try the Tools - Find command of Exchange.

Removing Catform

If you installed the form in the local application forms library, issue the following command:

```
catform /uninstall
```

Optionally, you can copy your saved copy of the original form cache file back to FRMCACHE.DAT. Next, in a registry editor, delete the following key:

```
HKEY_CLASSES_ROOT\CLSID\{da32e203-97b8-11cf-b6a6-080022b2b3625}
```

If you installed the form in the folder forms library, invoke the Forms Manager dialog box as described in the installation sequence for the Poststub application, select Cat Tracking Application Form, and press Delete.

Programming with Catform

Catform implements *IPM.Goetter.Catform* to demonstrate named property management techniques.

Reusing Catform

If you use any or all of this form server as a template for another project, be sure you change the following elements:

- The name of the application
- The icons
- The contents of the version information block *VS_VERSION_INFO* (in CATFORM.RC)
- The GUID identifying the unique class of the form (*CLSID_Catform* in GUIDS.H and CLSID in CATFORM.CFG)
- The message class used by the form's messages (*SZ_FORM_MESSAGE-_CLASS* in FORM.H and Message Class in CATFORM.CFG)

- The help file mapping string (*SZ_COMPONENT* in FORM.H)
- Various other descriptive fields in the installation file (CATFORM.CFG*)*

Keep in Mind

The symbol *ESCHEW_MAPIFORM_ENUM_INDEX* keeps Catform from implementing index properties to accompany the strings of its enumerations. Exchange Server 4.0 contains bugs that crash clients referencing index properties, and anyway, the Exchange client does not support them in its views.

Msgopen

The directory Chap07\Msgopen returns to Exchange client extensions, creating on the viewer window a new command File - Simple Open that opens messages in a modal form instance.

Building Msgopen

To build the Msgopen application, open a command shell, change its current working directory to Chap07\Msgopen, and enter the following command:

```
nmake /f Makefile
```

To build a version of the Msgopen application without debugging symbols, enter the following command:

```
nmake nodebug=1 /f Makefile
```

Users of Microsoft Visual C++ 4.0 can load the workspace file MSGOPEN.MDP.

A successful build generates the executable file MSGOPEN.DLL. You can discard the import library file MSGOPEN.LIB that is generated during the build.

Installing Msgopen

Copy the source file MSGOPEN.REG to INSTALL.REG. Open INSTALL.REG in a text editor. You will see the following text:

```
REGEDIT4
[HKEY_LOCAL_MACHINE\SOFTWARE\Microsoft\Exchange\Client\Extensions]
@=" "
"Simple Open"="4.0;msgopen.dll;1;01000000000000;1100000"
```

Change the second semicolon-delimited field in the right-hand component of the Simple Open entry to reflect the actual path of the dynamic-link library

MSGOPEN.DLL by doubling all backslashes in the pathname. For example, if you had this DLL in a directory C:\Exchange, change the line to read as follows:

```
"Simple Open"="4.0;C:\\Exchange\\msgopen.dll;1;
    01000000000000; 1100000"
```

Save the file INSTALL.REG, and exit the text editor. Merge the contents of the file INSTALL.REG into the system registry, either by double-clicking the INSTALL.REG icon in Windows Explorer or by selecting the Registry - Import Registry File command in the Registry Editor (REGEDIT.EXE).

Running Msgopen

Launch the Exchange client. Select a message in the viewer window, and invoke File - Simple Open.

Removing Msgopen

In a registry editor, open the following key and remove the tagged Simple Open value.

```
HKEY_LOCAL_MACHINE\SOFTWARE\Microsoft\Exchange\Client\Extensions
```

Programming with Msgopen

Msgopen demonstrates the use of *IMAPISession::PrepareForm* and *IMAPISession-::ShowForm*. It also serves as a useful test for form servers, invoking their forms modally.

Reusing Msgopen

The *SimpleMessageOpen* function in WORK.CPP can be easily reused.

If you use any or all of this extension as a template for another project, be sure you change the following elements:

- The name of the application

- The icon

- The contents of the version information block *VS_VERSION_INFO* (in MSGOPEN.RC)

- The tag name used by the registry entry (Form Info in MSGOPEN.REG)

Msgopen checks the version of Exchange by hosting it against a static value. To avoid revising your extension with every Service Pack that updates Exchange clients, consider storing the version number of Exchange in the system registry.

Keep in Mind

The Msgopen application complains when it is loaded into any version post-dating Exchange Server 4.0 Service Pack 1 (SP1). You can correct this by changing the *LAST_BUILD_SUPPORTED* manifest constant in EXT.CPP to a value more recent than 839. See also the reuse notes in the previous section.

Fwdasatt

The directory Chap07\Fwdasatt implements Forward As Attachment, an Exchange client extension to supply a new Compose command, Forward As Attachment. This command takes the currently selected message in the viewer window and includes that message as an attachment in a new note form, which the command sets up as a forward-style message.

Building Fwdasatt

To build the Fwdasatt application, open a command shell, change its current working directory to Chap07\Fwdasatt, and enter the following command:

```
nmake /f Makefile
```

To build a version of the Fwdasatt application without debugging symbols, enter the following command:

```
nmake nodebug=1 /f Makefile
```

Users of Microsoft Visual C++ 4.0 can load the workspace file FWDASATT.MDP.

A successful build generates the executable file FWDASATT.DLL. You can discard the import library file FWDASATT.LIB that is generated during the build.

Installing Fwdasatt

Copy the source file FWDASATT.REG to INSTALL.REG. Open INSTALL.REG in a text editor. You will see the following text:

```
REGEDIT4
[HKEY_LOCAL_MACHINE\SOFTWARE\Microsoft\Exchange\Client\Extensions]
@=" "
"Forward as attachment"="4.0;fwdasatt.dll;1;010000110000000;1100000"
```

Change the second semicolon-delimited field in the right-hand component of the Forward As Attachment entry to reflect the actual path of the dynamic-link library FWDASATT.DLL by doubling all backslashes in the pathname. For example, if you had this DLL in a directory C:\Exchange, change the line to read as follows:

```
"Forward as attachment"="4.0;C:\\Exchange\\fwdasatt.dll;1;
    01000110000000;1100000"
```

Save the file INSTALL.REG, and exit the text editor. Merge the contents of the file INSTALL.REG into the system registry, either by double-clicking the INSTALL.REG icon in Windows Explorer or by selecting the Registry - Import Registry File command in the Registry Editor (REGEDIT.EXE).

Running Fwdasatt

Launch the Exchange client. Select a message in the viewer window. Invoke the Compose - Forward As Attachment command.

Removing Fwdasatt

In a registry editor, open the following key and remove the tagged Forward As Attachment value.

```
HKEY_LOCAL_MACHINE\SOFTWARE\Microsoft\Exchange\Client\Extensions
```

Programming with Fwdasatt

The Fwdasatt application demonstrates invoking a new instance of the standard note form, creating an attachment, attaching a message to another message, and generally manipulating a form object from the client's point of view. It also serves as an example of safe interface pointer classes.

Reusing Fwdasatt

If you use any or all of this extension as a template for another project, be sure you change the following elements:

- The name of the application

- The icon

- The contents of the version information block *VS_VERSION_INFO* (in FWDASATT.RC)

- The tag name used by the registry entry (Form Info in FWDASATT.REG)

Fwdasatt checks the version of Exchange by hosting it against a static value. To avoid revising your extension with every Service Pack that updates Exchange clients, consider storing the version number of Exchange in the system registry.

Keep in Mind

The Fwdasatt application complains when it is loaded into any version postdating Exchange Server 4.0 Service Pack 1 (SP1). You can correct this by changing the *LAST_BUILD_SUPPORTED* manifest constant in EXT.CPP to a value more recent than 839. See also the reuse notes in the previous section.

The Fwdasatt application displays obnoxious behavior when a single message is forwarded multiple times.

In such a situation, Fwdasatt—like every other Exchange client extension in this book—presents a message box containing the warning text *IDS_Q_LATER-_BUILD*: "You are loading Forward As Attachment into a version of Exchange (Windows Messaging) that postdates the version released with the Windows 95 Messaging Update. It might not operate correctly. Do you wish to continue?" You then have the opportunity to decline loading the extension. See also the reuse notes in the previous section.

Vwinst

The directory Chap08\Vwinst implements the Folder View Import/Export Utility, an Exchange client extension that saves named folder views as files with the suffix VDM and subsequently restores those views to folders.

Building Vwinst

To build the Vwinst application, open a command shell, change its current working directory to Chap08\Vwinst, and enter the following command:

```
nmake /f Makefile
```

To build a version of the Vwinst application without debugging symbols, enter the following command:

```
nmake nodebug=1 /f Makefile
```

Users of Microsoft Visual C++ 4.0 can load the workspace file VWINST.MDP.

A successful build generates the executable file VWINST.DLL. You can discard the import library file VWINST.LIB that is generated during the build.

Installing Vwinst

Copy the source file VWINST.REG to INSTALL.REG. Open INSTALL.REG in a text editor. You will see the following text:

```
REGEDIT4
[HKEY_LOCAL_MACHINE\SOFTWARE\Microsoft\Exchange\Client\Extensions]
@=" "
"View Imp"="4.0;vwinst.dll;1;01000000000000;1100000"
```

Change the second semicolon-delimited field in the right-hand component of the View Imp entry to reflect the actual path of the dynamic-link library VW-INST.DLL by doubling all backslashes in the pathname. For example, if you had this DLL in a directory C:\Exchange, change the line to read as follows:

```
"View Imp"="4.0;C:\\Exchange\\vwinst.dll;1;010000000000000;1100000"
```

Save the file INSTALL.REG, and exit the text editor. Merge the contents of the file INSTALL.REG into the system registry, either by double-clicking the INSTALL.REG icon in Windows Explorer or by selecting the Registry - Import Registry File command in the Registry Editor (REGEDIT.EXE).

Running Vwinst

Launch the Exchange client. Select a folder in the left-hand pane of the view known to contain named views, and invoke File - View Import/Export. A dialog box appears, listing every view in that folder. By selecting a view and clicking the Export button, you can save the view in a file with the default suffix VDM. Clicking the Import button lets you select a VDM from which to import a view into the folder. You can also change the defined default view of the folder by selecting a view and clicking Set Default.

Removing Vwinst

In a registry editor, open the following key and remove the tagged "View Imp" value.

```
HKEY_LOCAL_MACHINE\SOFTWARE\Microsoft\Exchange\Client\Extensions
```

Delete any views added to folders.

Progamming with Vwinst

The Vwinst application demonstrates trivial manipulation of view descriptors in a folder, setting the default view on a folder, converting a short-term entry identifier to a long-term entry identifier, the use of the standard file dialog boxes, saving a message in a file and reading it back, using a restriction with *HrQuery-AllRows*, and copying a message into a folder.

Reusing Vwinst

If you use any or all of this extension as a template for another project, be sure you change the following elements:

- The name of the application
- The icon

- The contents of the version information block *VS_VERSION_INFO* (in VWINST.RC)

- The tag name used by the registry entry (Form Info in VWINST.REG)

Vwinst checks the version of Exchange by hosting it against a static value. To avoid revising your extension with every Service Pack that updates Exchange clients, consider storing the version number of Exchange in the system registry.

Keep in Mind

The Vwinst application complains when it is loaded into any version postdating Exchange Server 4.0 Service Pack 1 (SP1). You can correct this by changing the *LAST_BUILD_SUPPORTED* manifest constant in EXT.CPP to a value more recent than 839. See also the reuse notes in the previous section.

The Vwinst application lets you create two named views in a folder with the same name.

B

For More Information

In Print, On Disk

Win32 Software Development Kit   This kit includes the hit singles *Win32 Programmer's Reference* (Microsoft Corporation, 1996), *OLE Programmer's Reference* (Microsoft Corporation, 1996), and *Win32 Messaging (MAPI)* (Microsoft Corporation, 1996).

Inside MAPI   This book, written by Irving De la Cruz and Les Thaler (Microsoft Press, 1996), is an essential companion to the Win32 SDK documentation, with many examples.

Inside OLE 2   This book, written by Kraig Brockschmidt (Microsoft Press, 1994), thoroughly explains the Component Object Model, remoted interfaces, structured storage, and persistent objects.

Microsoft Exchange Server 4.0   (Microsoft Corporation, 1996) This information resource contains the informative *Concepts and Planning Guide* and the *Application Designer's Guide*.

BackOffice Software Development Kit   (Microsoft Corporation, 1996) This kit specifies the interfaces for developing gateways, server-side agents, and other software specific to Microsoft Exchange Server, including Exchange Server–specific client interfaces.

On the World Wide Web

The World Wide Web (WWW) is a dynamic resource, where pages come and pages go. Almost anything I list here could disappear by the time this book reaches the market. Instead, I will list a couple of points from which to start your navigation.

Microsoft Corporation

Microsoft's home page address is http://www.microsoft.com. Important sites within Microsoft include the Exchange Server site (http://www.microsoft.com/exchange/), the MAPI site (http://www.microsoft.com/win32dev/mapi/), the For Developers Only site (http://www.microsoft.com/devonly/), and the Internet Site Builder Workshop (http://www.microsoft.com/workshop/).

The Author's Site

My personal home page resides on http://www.angrygraycat.com/goetter/. I maintain a support site for this book on http://www.angrygraycat.com/goetter/book/, where I release additional code samples, late-breaking changes and sheets of errata, and any further information I collect, including links to other resources for MAPI and Exchange developers.

GLOSSARY

access control list (ACL) The construct that specifies the protection level of a folder in a Microsoft Exchange Server message store. Each element in the list is an entry in the Exchange Server directory and describes the set of privileges matching that element that are available to users.

ACL *See* access control list.

activation The operation that takes an initialized but passive object and makes it start interacting with the user. For MAPI forms, this takes place through a call to *IMAPIForm::DoVerb*.

ActiveX A synonym for the diverse Microsoft object technologies—COM, OLE, Automation, ActiveX Controls, and so on.

ActiveX messaging An Automation server that articulates a set of message-related objects to give scripting languages and environments such as Microsoft Visual Basic a means of writing messaging and workgroup applications.

address book In MAPI, an object that manages recipient data from all the address book providers loaded in the current session. The address book interfaces with *IAddrBook* and is available as an attribute of the current session through *IMAPISession::OpenAddressBook*. Also, an address book can be the top-level object of any address book provider. In the Exchange user interface, it is the window that presents the contents of the MAPI address book.

address book container A container object within a MAPI address book. The address book container interfaces with *IABContainer*. An address book container can contain other address book containers (accessible through the hierarchy table) or can contain message recipients and distribution lists (available through the contents table).

address book provider A MAPI service provider that implements a set of address book containers and recipients. The Microsoft Exchange Server address book provider exposes the contents of the Microsoft Exchange Server Directory Service, and the personal address book address book provider lets the user keep a set of names and addresses in a disk file.

advise sink An object implemented by a client for the purpose of receiving notifications. The client hands the advise sink to another object, which subsequently communicates with the client by invoking the methods on the sink. Conventional MAPI advise sinks support *IMAPIAdviseSink*; the client registers them with a MAPI object such as a session or a message store using that object's advise method, specifying the kinds of events for which the advise sink will receive notifications. *See also* form advise sink; view advise sink.

aggregation A technique whereby a component object reuses the implementation of another component object to implement its own interfaces while preserving its *IUnknown* identity.

application programming interface (API) Any well-defined set of routines and structures by which a body of software offers its services to an application. The Win32 function calls and structures compose one well-known API. In MAPI, API is usually used to denote the interfaces available to MAPI clients, as opposed to the service provider interface, or SPI.

attachment A MAPI object that embodies a discrete block of data attached to a message. Attachments interface with *IAttach* and can embody files, OLE compound documents, other messages, or other data.

attachment number A distinguishing attribute of a MAPI attachment that uniquely identifies the attachment within the scope of a particular message. The property of the attachment number is *PR_ATTACH_NUM*.

attachment table An attribute of a MAPI message that describes all the attachments on that particular message.

Automation A standard for interprocess scripting by which Automation clients manipulate objects articulated by Automation servers.

Automation client A program that makes use of other programs' objects through the Automation interfaces. Most Automation clients are scripting languages or other programming environments, such as Microsoft Visual Basic.

Automation server A program that exports a set of its internal objects through the Automation interfaces, allowing other applications to manipulate those objects.

backup domain controller A domain controller that carries a replica of the domain's security accounts database, distributes the load of security validation, and provides fault tolerance in the event of server failure at another domain controller.

binding The process by which a remote procedure call client attaches to a server.

class In C++, a logical grouping of instance data and the functions manipulating that data. A class can be instantiated as a single object. In COM, *see* component class.

class factory The distinguished object in a class that creates instances of that class's objects. The class factory interfaces with *IClassFactory*. To create instances of a class's objects, a client obtains a reference to the class factory and then obtains new object instances through *IClassFactory::CreateInstance*. The library routine *CoCreateInstance* encapsulates these operations within a single function call.

class identifier (CLSID) A UUID that uniquely identifies a particular COM class. Clients use the class identifier to access a particular class and create instances of that class's objects. Beneath the key HKEY_CLASSES_ROOT\CLSID, the system registry indexes, by their class identifier, the servers that implement all available classes on the system.

class object *See* class factory.

client An object that requests services from another object. In COM, a client is any object that holds a reference to an interface on another object. In MAPI, a client is a program that calls the MAPI interfaces.

client application In MAPI, a program that calls MAPI interface methods to interact with the underlying messaging system.

client extension *See* Exchange client extension.

client interface In MAPI, the interfaces intended for client applications, as opposed to the service provider interface.

CLSID *See* class identifier.

CMC *See* common messaging calls.

COM *See* Component Object Model.

command dispatch The process by which the Exchange client locates the body of code that implements a particular command on its menu bar or on its toolbar.

common messaging calls (CMC) An API, developed by the XAPIA, that is intended to provide a messaging interface independent of the actual messaging system, operating system, or hardware used. WMS offers CMC as a layer on top of MAPI. *See* XAPIA.

component A small, reusable program suitable for use in constructing larger programs.

component class The body of code that implements a component object of a particular identity. Every class has a unique class identifier (CLSID), which a client uses to access the class.

component object The instantiation of a component that behaves according to the rules of COM. To access a component object, clients use a pointer to an interface. This pointer is used to call the methods that perform operations or to manipulate the data associated with the object.

Component Object Model (COM) Microsoft's standard component software model.

compound document A document that contains data of different formats from different source applications. An application that renders a whole compound document is called an OLE container application, whereas the applications that render its various elements are called OLE server applications.

conflict The state of a message in a Microsoft Exchange Server message store that occurs when different users have made conflicting changes to the message at different replicas. Microsoft Exchange Server flags messages in this state by setting a flag in their message status (*PR_MESSAGE_STATUS*) and then attaching the different versions of the message as attachments to the message.

container A MAPI object that holds one or more other MAPI objects and possibly other MAPI containers. Examples of containers are address books and folders. Containers interface with *IMAPIContainer*. They describe their contained subcontainers through a hierarchy table and describe their contained subobjects through a contents table.

contents table A table that provides access to information about objects contained within another MAPI object. A contents table interfaces with *IMAPITable*, which is available through *IMAPIContainer::GetContentsTable*. A folder in a message store describes the messages it contains through its contents table; likewise, a distribution list describes its contained mail recipients in a contents table.

conversation index A property on a message (*PR_CONVERSATION_INDEX*) that facilitates ordering a particular message within a thread of conversation. Typically, these consist of concatenated time stamps; any message that considers itself a response to a previous message takes the conversation index of the previous message, appends a time/date value to that index, and saves the result as its own conversation index. Messages bearing a conversation index also bear the property *PR_CONVERSATION_TOPIC*. To sort on conversations, a viewer sorts primarily on a topic and secondarily on an index.

custom interface An interface that does not correspond to any standard interface (MAPI, COM, or the like). A service provider can offer custom interfaces to export functionality unique to that particular provider. For example, the Exchange Server message store provider returns a custom interface *IExchange-ModifyTable* in response to a call *IMAPIProp::OpenProperty* on the special folder property *PR_ACL_TABLE* and, through this table, allows clients to manipulate the ACL on that folder.

DDE *See* dynamic data exchange.

default message store A distinguished message store that bears the property *PR_DEFAULT_STORE* in the message store table. The default message store hosts the Inbox folder for receiving incoming messages, the Outbox folder for hosting outgoing messages, the default views folder, and the personal forms library.

default profile The profile name supplied by *MAPILogonEx* when the client does not specify a profile name and when the *MAPI_USE_DEFAULT* flag is used as a parameter in the function call.

designer run time A fixed body of code that is installed on individual workstations and that implements portions of form servers that were created with a particular development environment (designer). Specifically, designer run time is the body of code that hosts the form factory for a particular form. A particular designer run time is identified by a CLSID that locates it in the system registry, and also by a readable display name; both of these appear as properties on the form information object of a form using the run time.

directory service An Exchange Server service that maintains a database of systemwide administration, configuration, and message recipient information.

directory synchronizer An Exchange Server service that synchronizes the contents of the Exchange Server directory service with external Microsoft Mail global address lists.

display name A printable string intended for display to the user: the property corresponding to the display name is *PR_DISPLAY_NAME*, available on most MAPI objects. By itself, the display name of an object does not provide enough information to open the object; a client must obtain the entry identifier for the object to acquire further access to that object. Display names are for display only.

distribution list A MAPI container object that groups other message recipients in addition to itself acting as a message recipient. A distribution list interfaces with *IDistList*.

DLL *See* dynamic-link library.

DllCanUnloadNow A function used to determine whether a DLL is in use. Not used by Exchange client extension libraries.

DllGetClassObject A standard entry point for COM in-process servers. Not used by Exchange client extension libraries.

document wrapper A message of superclass *IPM.Document* that wraps a document so that the document can appear as an item in a MAPI folder.

domain The logical quantum of security in the Windows NT security model, consisting of one or more servers and workstations sharing a common user and group database.

domain controller A computer that runs Windows NT Advanced Server and keeps a copy of the domain's security accounts database. Every domain has one primary domain controller and can, in addition, have one or more backup domain controllers.

dynamic data exchange (DDE) An ancient Windows interprocess communication convention, based on sending Windows messages and shared blocks of memory.

dynamic-link library (DLL) An executable module that is mappable into a process at run time. DLLs are similar to shared libraries on other operating systems.

EID *See* entry identifier.

e-mail address A string that describes to a transport provider the destination of a message for a particular recipient. The property *PR_EMAIL_ADDRESS* is available on message recipient objects. Goetter@angrygraycat.com and WINDOWS-/CTHULHU/GOETTER are examples of e-mail addresses.

e-mail address type A string that describes the syntax of a particular e-mail address. The property *PR_ADDRTYPE* is available on message recipient objects. A transport provider registers itself as handling e-mail addresses of a particular type, either SMTP or MS, ensuring that the correct underlying messaging system received recipients with that kind of address. An example of an SMTP address is goetter@angrygraycat.com, and an example of an MS address is WINDOWS/CTHULHU/GOETTER.

entryid *See* entry identifier.

entry identifier (entryid) (EID) A binary value that identifies a single MAPI object of a particular type. The property *PR_ENTRYID* is available on most MAPI objects. A client gains access to that object by passing its entry identifier to the *OpenEntry* method on a MAPI object that contains the desired object. Most MAPI objects are identified by entry identifiers, which do not depend on the presence of any code page or language for correct operation; thus, a Japanese environment can pass an entry identifier to an English environment with no danger of data corruption, such as might befall a pathname or similar printable-string construct. Entry identifiers can be compared only by the service providers that implement them using *IMAPISession::CompareEntryIDs*. To compare the identities of two MAPI objects without invoking MAPI or their service providers, use the search key properties of the objects. Entry identifiers come in both long-term and short-term flavors. Short-term entry identifiers appear within MAPI tables and are valid only within the scope of the issuing session and the workstation hosting that session. Long-term entry identifiers appear as the *PR_ENTRYID* property on the object and can persist beyond the current session.

Exchange client The executable program Microsoft Exchange: the standard user-interface application of WMS, an extensible mail user agent written as a MAPI client. In Windows 95, this is called Windows Messaging.

Exchange client extension An object that adds or changes commands in the Exchange client. The Exchange client defines extensibility contexts that correspond to individual windows and tasks in the program and loads client extension objects for each context as windows become active. Client extension objects take advantage of the Exchange client's command dispatch mechanism to work within the menu bar and the toolbar.

Extended MAPI A synonym for the full MAPI interfaces of Win32 API, used to differentiate these interfaces from Simple MAPI.

extensibility context A locus into which the Exchange client loads Exchange client extensions. These extentions correspond to individual windows and tasks in the program. The header file EXCHEXT.H defines the symbols *EECONTEXT_xxx*, which represent each kind of extensibility context.

facility A range of error return codes corresponding to the values generated by a particular subsystem. Within an HRESULT value, the facility appears encoded in the lower 11 bits of the upper word.

flushing a message queue The act of telling a single transport service provider, or the MAPI spooler process, to deliver its pending incoming or outgoing messages.

folder A container object within a MAPI message store. The *IMAPIFolder* interface is used to access the folders. Folders can contain other folders, which are accessible through the hierarchy table, and messages, which are accessible through the contents table. Some message store providers can support folders with two contents tables apiece: the standard contents table, containing the usual messages; and the associated contents table, containing messages that host folder-specific forms, views, and other application data.

folder-centric application Folder-centric applications move information by creating messages in a folder or by interacting with the existing messages in a folder. Folder-centric applications do not need the services of the spooler. They monitor advise sinks for changes in the contents tables of their folder, and they compose new messages and save them to a folder, usually invoking form servers to manage nonstandard message types. Folder-centric applications spend most of their time building and manipulating tables. Examples are traditional database, conferencing, and bulletin board applications.

folder forms library A forms library that uses the FAI table of a folder for storage and provides the forms library for a folder application.

form In MAPI, an object that associates messages of a particular property schema, as represented by the message class property, with a particular body of code for reading and writing such messages. In Exchange, a form is a user interface window manifested by a MAPI form object, either intrinsic or external to Exchange.

form advise sink A variety of advise sink that is implemented by form servers. The form hands this advise sink to the viewer launching the form and registers it with *IMAPIViewContext::SetAdviseSink*. The viewer subsequently will communicate with the form by invoking the methods of the advise sink. Form advise sinks support the interface *IMAPIFormAdviseSink*. Like their cousins, the view advise sinks, they resemble OLE *IAdviseSink* sinks more than they do the MAPI *IMAPIAdviseSink* sinks.

form extension property An additional form-specified named property on a form information object that specifies additional information about the form to clients that know of its presence.

form factory An object that creates multiple class objects for different forms. The form factory object supports the *IMAPIFormFactory* interface. Through the use of form factories, a particular set of forms keeps a fixed run time on participating workstations, storing only the data files unique to a particular form in the forms libraries.

form information object An informational object returned by the MAPI Forms Manager that describes a particular form in a forms library. The form information object supports the *IMAPIFormInfo* interface.

form property enumeration A special type of form property that defines an ordered series of string values for a string property and associates that string property with an integer index property.

form property special type An extension mechanism for form property types, allowing forms and clients to cooperate to define higher-level property constructions. At present, form property enumerations are the only defined special type.

form server The server that implements a form of a particular class. All form servers use the out-of-process server model.

forms library A construct for storing and organizing form servers and their information. Four types of forms library exist: the local, or application, forms library; the folder forms library; the personal forms library; and, in Exchange Server, the organization forms library.

Forms Manager The component of MAPI responsible for organizing, storing, and resolving forms. The Forms Manager supports the *IMAPIFormMgr* interface.

form/view application architecture The standard Exchange application design that implements objects in the application as messages in a folder of a particular message class. This design uses the customizable Exchange client viewer to provide meaningful summaries of those objects.

global atom table A system table, available to all processes on a workstation, that associates a hashed integer value with a string stored in the table. The MAPI Forms Manager expects a running form server to store its class identifier in the global atom table so that MAPI can determine whether the server is running.

GUID *See* universally unique identifier.

GUIDGEN.EXE A simple dialog-based MFC application that generates unique GUIDs. It is included with the Samples/MFC Samples/MFC Programming Utilities of the online books provided with Microsoft Visual C++ version 4. It is functionally equivalent to UUIDGEN.EXE.

Hands Off After Save state The state of a form after the form makes its changes persistent (in response to *IPersistMessage::Save*) and then releases all references to its message in response to an *IPersistMessage::HandsOffMessage* directive.

Hands Off From Normal state The state of a form after the form has released all references to its message in response to an *IPersistMessage::HandsOffMessage* directive.

hierarchy table A table that describes the hierarchy of containers within and beneath a particular MAPI container. The hierarchy table supports the *IMAPITable* interface, which is available through the *IMAPIContainer::GetHierarchyTable* method. For example, a folder describes the tree structure of the folders within it through its hierarchy table.

HRESULT The standard value returned from any interface method.

IDispatch The interface at the heart of Automation.

IID *See* interface identifier.

Inbox folder The default folder to which transport providers and the MAPI spooler deliver interpersonal messages. By convention, the Inbox folder is the delivery folder (as returned from *IMsgStore::GetReceiveFolder*) for the message class *IPM* on the default message store.

information store The server-based message database of Microsoft Exchange Server.

inheritance In C++, inheritance is the definition of a class from a preexisting base class or classes. In COM, it is the definition of an interface that includes all of the methods of another interface with the same offsets in the new interface's vtable as those of the previous interface, so that the new interface can be used transparently as the old interface. All interfaces inherit from *IUnknown* in this manner.

in/out parameter A parameter to a method that references both a value supplied by the caller and a different value upon return.

in-parameter A parameter to a method that expects a value to be supplied by the caller; the method cannot change that value because most methods use roll-by-value semantics.

in-process server An object server that operates within the process of its clients; a server that is implemented as a DLL. *Compare* out-of-process server.

in-proc server *See* in-process server.

interface A group of methods that occupies a single defined virtual function table and that constitutes a single static raft of semantics, such that if an object implements one method of the interface, it must implement all methods. Every interface is defined by its interface identifier, or IID. All client communication with objects takes place through the interfaces of those objects.

interface identifier A GUID that defines the identity of a particular interface.

interface negotiation The process by which a client discovers whether an object supports a particular interface and acquires a reference to the interface. From any interface on the object, the client can call *IUnknown::QueryInterface*, passing that method the IID of the desired interface to obtain that interface on the object if the object supports it.

interface pointer A pointer to another pointer that addresses the first element of the virtual function table of the interface within the object. This is the only token of an object that any client ever holds. A generic way to reference an object is through an unknown interface pointer; in C++, this is type *IUnknown**. Because all interfaces inherit from *IUnknown*, such an unknown pointer can actually refer to any interface.

interpersonal message A message intended for human consumption, which ends its delivery cycle in a user's mailbox folder. Interpersonal messages have message classes with the prefix *IPM*.

IUnknown The master interface in COM that is responsible for reference counting, interface negotiation, and object identity. Every component object supports *IUnknown*, and every other interface inherits from it, including its own methods.

local form cache The set of form servers that the Forms Manager has downloaded from forms libraries to the local workstation. The local form cache tracks these forms, along with any entries in the local forms library, in the file Forms\FRM-CACHE.DAT in the Windows directory.

local (application) forms library A forms library that is co-resident with the database of the local form cache, which provides a place for applications on the local workstation to register themselves as form servers. Unlike the other types of forms library, the local forms library does not supply storage for its forms.

local server *See* out-of-process server.

logoff In a MAPI client, the last call made on a session object (*IMAPISession::Logoff*) or on a message store object (*IMsgStore::StoreLogoff*).

logon In a MAPI client, the call to *MAPILogonEx* that gives the client a MAPI session to use.

mailbox-centric application A mailbox-centric application moves information by sending messages to the mailboxes of mail users or by watching its mailbox for new messages. Mailbox-centric applications always start the spooler unless they limit themselves to running on a system with tightly coupled stores and transports. They monitor advise sinks for new mail notifications and compose, address, and submit new messages to the spooler and to transports for transmission. Mailbox-centric applications might use form servers to send or to read custom message types.

mail client A MAPI client application for sending and receiving interpersonal messages.

mail user A MAPI object that describes an individual, addressable recipient of a message. Mail user objects support the *IMailUser* interface.

MAPI *See* Messaging Application Programming Interface.

MAPI notification window An artifact of WMS: a hidden window implementing the engine that supports clients of *IMAPIAdviseSink*. The MAPI notification window is sometimes called the notification engine. *See* WMS.

MAPI object A component object that supports one or more MAPI standard interfaces, such as *IMessage*, *IMAPIFolder*, and *IMailUser*.

MAPI spooler An artifact of WMS: a process that stores messages in a queue until they are ready to send. The spooler also manages the process of sending messages to and from client applications and messaging systems. *See* WMS.

marshaling The process of converting the parameters of an invoked method to a format amenable to interprocess communication. Any method invocation on an object outside the client's process requires that the proxy marshal the parameters before making the necessary remote procedure call to the server.

message A MAPI object containing information, suitable either for saving into a folder document-style or for transmitting to one or more recipients, using e-mail. Message objects support the *IMessage* interface. Typically, messages reside in folders within MAPI message stores; however, they can also reside as attachments on other messages, or they can be rendered on top of structured storage (*IStorage*) implementations.

message class A string property that identifies the type of message; the property *PR_MESSAGE_CLASS* is available on messages. Messages of a particular message class have the same properties and use the same form.

message class IPM The base message class for all interpersonal messages. Canonically, the delivery folder for messages of this class is the default Inbox.

message flag A bit flag property that identifies a number of interesting states of a message. The property *PR_MESSAGE_FLAGS* is available on messages. Interesting bits within this property include *MSGFLAG_UNSENT*, which a form uses to determine whether to present the under-composition or already-sent flavors of its user interface, and *MSGFLAG_READ*, which indicates that the message has been read by the current user.

message hook provider An installable component used to process messages before the MAPI spooler sends them to the transport provider (called the outbound hook provider) or to intercept and reroute the messages (called the inbound hook provider).

message pump A loop of code within a particular thread of execution that retrieves messages from the message queue and dispatches them to window procedures.

message service A logical collection of service providers used to simplify installation and configuration. Client applications can use message services to interact with service providers without having to deal with each service individually.

message site An object that encapsulates the storage that backs the form's message, in addition to the rest of the form's relationship with MAPI and its hosting client. Message site objects support the *IMAPIMessageSite* interface.

message store The topmost object in a message store hierarchy, containing folders and messages. Message store objects support the *IMsgStore* interface.

message store provider A MAPI service provider that implements a set of message store objects. The Microsoft Exchange Server message store provider exposes the contents of the Microsoft Exchange Server Information Store, and the personal folders message store provider lets the user keep a set of folders and messages in a disk file.

message store table A table that describes every message store available to the current session. Message store tables support the *IMAPITable* interface, which is available through *IMAPISession::GetMsgStoresTable*. Until a client opens the message store using *IMAPISession::OpenMsgStore*, the message store does not appear within the status table.

message superclassing The process by which the MAPI Forms Manager looks for a superclass of the current message class after it fails to resolve the current class to a form. Through message superclassing, MAPI resolves the message class *IPM.Document.Microsoft.Word.6* to the form for *IPM.Document*.

message type A message with a particular message class value.

message viewer A window in the Exchange client that renders the rows of a folder contents table. Upon starting, Exchange creates a message viewer for the Inbox folder. The user can create additional message viewer windows through the View - New window command.

Messaging Application Programming Interface (MAPI) The standard messaging API of Win32. MAPI allows applications to communicate generically with other messaging systems across different hardware platforms. The MAPI subsystem consists of a set of dynamic-link libraries (DLLs) used for managing the interaction between client applications and service providers. These DLLs implement several support objects, including the MAPI spooler, the client interface, and the service provider interface.

method A function that belongs to a particular COM interface.

moniker A naming object that identifies a particular component object so that the name can be used to access the object. The interface for monikers is *IMoniker*. ActiveX uses monikers extensively to implement links within compound documents to other documents.

named properties A mechanism for scoping user-defined property names within a GUID called the property set. Named properties allow multiple components to tag a shared object without the tags interfering with one another and prevent searches for a particular property from returning false positives against the same tag in the context of a different message class. A named property consists of the property set GUID and a subidentifier, which can be either an integer or a Unicode string. From the *MAPINAMEID* structure, *IMAPIProp::GetIDsFromNames* returns a local property tag suitable for use in the other methods of *IMAPIProp*. This property tag has its high bit set.

Normal state The state of a form in which it is interacting normally with the user.

No Scribble state The state of a form in which it has finished making its changes persistent in response to an *IPersistMessage::Save* directive and is now awaiting further instructions.

notification A mechanism by which one MAPI object advises another MAPI object, or a MAPI client, of some event that befell the first object. The interested party receives the notification through an advise sink that it implemented.

object An instance of a class that manifests one or more interfaces and carries instance data specific to the object. Object is short for component object.

Object Linking and Embedding (OLE) A standard for supporting rich compound documents and their applications, built on top of the Component Object Model.

object server The body of code that implements a component class. Object servers can operate either as in-process servers or as out-of-process servers.

OLE Automation A now-obsolete term for Automation. *See also* Automation.

OLE messaging A now-obsolete term for ActiveX messaging. *See also* ActiveX messaging.

OLE object Misnomer for component object.

one-off address An e-mail address that does not correspond to an address book and that is built on the fly for temporary addressing of messages.

one-off table A MAPI table object that describes the templates for legal one-off addresses. A one-off table is implemented by the personal address book.

OpenEntry The operation by which a client acquires an interface on a MAPI object from its entry identifier. MAPI session objects (*IMAPISession*) support an *OpenEntry* method, as do message stores (*IMsgStore*), address books (*IAddrBook*), and containers (*IMAPIContainer*). Containers open entries that correspond to objects that the entries contain. The *IMAPISession::OpenMsgStore* method strongly resembles an *OpenEntry* operation, but it differs by supplying additional information from the client; this information is useful when the message store is mounted.

organization forms library A forms library unique to Microsoft Exchange Server that resides in an invisible public folder. The organization forms library is replicated throughout the messaging site and makes a single set of forms available to all users in that site.

Outbox folder A folder on the default message store that holds outgoing messages between the time that the client submits the message and the time that the spooler transfers the message to a transport provider.

out-of-process server An object server that operates in its own process—that is, it is implemented as an executable. For a client to use an object from an out-of-process server, COM must establish a remote connection between the client and the server. *Compare* in-process server.

out-parameter A reference parameter that directs a method to set a value upon return. When out-parameters return interface pointers, the called object increments the reference count for the interface before returning it. This leaves the caller responsible for releasing the interface.

PAB *See* personal address book.

personal address book An address book provider that stores recipients and distribution lists in a file on the user's local storage. These recipients can be created by the user, or they can be copied from other address book containers.

personal forms library A forms library that uses the default message store on the current session for storage.

personal message store A message store provider that stores folders and messages in a file on the user's local storage.

polymorphism The plug compatibility of interfaces. Because clients see only interfaces, they accept any object that offers the interfaces they seek.

post form A database-style form that saves its message directly into a folder.

primary domain controller A domain controller that carries the master copy of the domain's security accounts database. Every domain must have one, and only one, primary domain controller.

process Quantum of resource ownership in Win32.

profile Configuration data for the message services in a session. The client supplies the name of the profile to MAPI at logon time and in return receives a session constructed from information in the named profile.

profile section Part of a profile that contains information associated with MAPI or with a particular messaging service or service provider. Profile sections identify themselves with a GUID. An application can keep its own configuration data in the current profile by specifying its own GUID.

progress indicator An application-specific user interface that is updated by the client to reflect the completion status of an operation that requires a long time to complete.

property A data attribute of a MAPI object. Objects expose these attributes through the *IMAPIProp* interface. To get a particular attribute on an object, the client specifies the property tag for the property desired. To set the attribute, the client couples the property tag with a property value.

property identifier A 16-bit value identifying a property. Half of this range identifies unique properties defined by MAPI or particular service providers, such as entry identifier, object type, and display name; the other half—the range consisting of the values with the high bit set—is used by the named property mechanism for temporary property identifiers.

property set A particular GUID value that scopes a set of MAPI named properties. A property set is not to be confused with the OLE construct of the same name.

property sheet A complex dialog box that contains a number of lesser dialog boxes and that uses a tab metaphor to allow the user to select the dialog box to display at any time. A property sheet is frequently used to display the properties of the current object.

property sheet page A single selectable subdialog box within a property sheet. Exchange client extensions can add property sheet pages to any property sheet in the Exchange client.

property tag A description of a particular property, comprising a property identifier and a property type, coupled in a 32-bit value. Properties defined by MAPI have property tag constants in the MAPITAGS.H file that take the form *PR_xxx*: for example, *PR_DISPLAY_NAME* for display names.

property type An enumerated value denoting the data type of a property's value, such as string, integer, binary value, or time and date. Together, the property type and the property identifier make up a 32-bit property tag.

property value A structure *SPropValue* that describes the current value of a property.

provider *See* service provider.

proxy A surrogate object, employed when a client uses a remote connection to an object in another address space. A proxy runs in the address space of the client and communicates with a corresponding stub in the server's address space.

published properties The set of MAPI property definitions that a form publishes on its information object.

pygmy marmoset World's smallest monkey, native to the South American rain forest of Brazil, Peru, and Ecuador. Family Callitrichidae: *Callithrix pygmaea*.

QueryInterface The method of *IUnknown* responsible for interface negotiation. It is frequently abbreviated *QI*.

receive folder For a particular message class, the default folder to which transport providers and the MAPI spooler deliver messages of that class. A receive folder is returned by *IMsgStore::GetReceiveFolder*.

recipient An entity that receives a message. Examples of recipients are individuals defined as MAPI mail user objects and collections of messaging users defined as MAPI distribution list objects.

recipient table An attribute of a message, describing the set of recipients to which the message is addressed.

reference counting A count of the number of references—copies of the interface pointer—that access or refer to an object. Multiple references to a single object are allowed. When a reference is removed, the reference count is decremented; the object's space in memory is freed when the count reaches 0. Clients maintain reference counts on objects through the methods *IUnknown::AddRef* and *IUnknown::Release*.

registry A system database of configuration information that stores MAPI profiles and the association of CLSIDs with object servers.

remote connection The communication channel between client and server when the server lies outside the client's process. The client invokes methods on a proxy in its own address space; the proxy marshals the method parameters and calls through the remote procedure call channel to a stub in the server process, which manipulates the object there.

remote procedure call (RPC) An interprocess communication convention that uses a procedure call metaphor. RPC allows one process to call functions that are part of another process on the same computer or on a different computer on the network. The RPC standard is defined by the Open Software Foundation (OSF) Distributed Computing Environment (DCE).

Remote Viewer A window in the Exchange client that renders the rows of a folder contents table as returned by a remote transport provider. It is invoked by the Tools - Remote Mail command.

replica A copy of either a folder or a database at a particular computer.

replication The process of maintaining consistent copies of changing data across multiple computers.

resolution The operation of taking a message type and locating the form, or the form information object, corresponding to that type.

response form A new form instance created in response to a verb that is invoked on another form.

response form verb A verb on a form that examines the current message, creates a new message based on the contents of the previous message, and invokes a form—not necessarily the same form as the one offering the response form verb—on that new message. When the form is different, it is called a response form.

restriction A MAPI structure that describes a logical predicate in terms of a relation of properties and their values. By specifying a restriction on a table, a client limits the rows of that table to rows that satisfy the specified logical predicate.

Rich Text Format (RTF) A format for message text that carries font, color, style, and paragraph formatting information along with the text. Many commercial word processing applications support RTF, as does the Windows Rich Edit control.

RPC *See* remote procedure call.

RTF *See* Rich Text Format.

safe pointer A smart pointer class defined to automate reference counting and cleanup.

schema A particular set of properties assigned by a client to a particular message; the set of MAPI properties and property semantics common to all messages of a particular message class.

search key An attribute of many MAPI objects, a search key is binary-comparable to test for identity. The property *PR_SEARCH_KEY* is available on message, address book container, distribution list, and mail user objects.

search-results folder A folder-compatible object through which message store providers report the results of search operations.

search viewer A window in the Exchange client that renders the rows of a search-results folder contents table. A search viewer is invoked by the Tools - Find command.

send form A message-style form that submits its addressed message to a transport for delivery to its destination.

server An object that offers its services to other objects.

service name A property *PR_SERVICE_NAME* that identifies a particular message service in the message service table. An Exchange client extension can specify that it be loaded only in the presence of a particular message service.

service provider A MAPI component that gives clients access to the resources of a particular messaging system. Service providers implement the service provider interface, or SPI; they cannot act as MAPI clients. Service providers include message store providers, address book providers, transport providers, and message hook providers.

service provider interface (SPI) The set of interfaces that are implemented by service providers. All of the service provider interface methods are defined in the MAPISPI.H header file.

session The root object of the MAPI client experience that embodies client access to all the resources of MAPI and the service providers loaded in the profile named at logon.

shared session A special session shared among multiple clients. By requesting to use the shared session, a client avoids inundating the user with redundant logon requests.

Simple Mail Transfer Protocol (SMTP) Widely used protocol for transferring electronic mail on the Internet.

Simple MAPI A set of functions that are used to add messaging features to client applications. Simple MAPI is compatible with the so-called MAPI interface of Microsoft Mail.

smart pointer A C++ class with its operator -> overloaded. Smart pointers are used in this book to implement safe pointers.

SPI *See* service provider interface.

spooler status object A status object for the MAPI spooler. A client can use this to ask the spooler to deliver messages immediately by flushing its message queues.

status bar text The text in the bottommost window of the Exchange client. When the user selects a command from the Exchange menu bar or toolbar, the status bar text contains a one-line summary of the selected command. Exchange client extensions can use this text to provide a synopsis of their functions.

status object An object for providing information beyond that included in the status table. The status objects support the *IMAPIStatus* interface. To obtain a component's status object, extract the entry identifier from the component's row in the status table and open that entry identifier using *IMAPISession::OpenEntry*.

status table A table listing information that relates to the state of the current session. Every session has a status table, available through *IMAPISession::GetStatusTable*, that includes information provided by MAPI and service providers. MAPI itself provides data for three rows: one for the MAPI subsystem, one for the MAPI spooler, and one for the integrated address book. Because transport providers are required to supply status information to the status table, there is one row for every active transport provider. Address book and message store providers can choose whether to provide status table support.

stream A standard interface for reading and writing data serially. Stream objects support the *IStream* interface.

stub A surrogate object, employed when a client uses a remote connection to an object in another address space. A stub runs in the address space of the server and communicates with a corresponding proxy in the client's address space.

subclass A message class derived from another message class, such that the new message class contains the old message class as a prefix, delimited with the period character. *IPM.Note.Secure* is a subclass of *IPM.Note*.

superclass A message class that is a prefix of another message class.

table A mechanism providing access to the properties for many objects at once. Table objects support the *IMAPITable* interface. MAPI table columns always refer to specific properties of a row. For example, each row represents a particular object, and each column or field represents a particular property on that object. To extract information from a database, clients can specify the columns in a table, restrict the rows in the table to those matching a specific condition, or sort the table on a column.

task allocator object A system object responsible for memory allocation within a particular process. Task allocator objects support the *IMalloc* interface, which is returned by *MAPIGetDefaultMalloc*. By use of a single object, all components within a process can freely manage one another's memory. Most MAPI clients use the MAPI allocation functions *MAPIAllocateBuffer*, *MAPIAllocateMore*, and *MAPIFreeBuffer* instead of the methods of *IMalloc*. These functions access the same task allocator.

TCHAR *See* transmutable character.

tooltip text Text in a pop-up window that appears over an Exchange client toolbar button when the user hovers the mouse pointer over that button. Exchange client extensions can use this text to provide a synopsis of their functions.

transmutable character A logical data type that embodies a traditional 8-bit character in some environments but can optionally be built to support 16-bit UNICODE characters. Programs that use transmutable characters specify their character data as type TCHAR and their MAPI string properties as property type PT_TSTRING, and pass the *fMapiUnicode* flag in all methods that accept the *MAPI_UNICODE* flag.

transport provider A MAPI service provider used to transport messages. The transport provider alters MAPI addresses so that they conform to the format used by the messaging system that delivers the messages.

UNICODE Worldwide character encoding standard that maps the characters of most known languages into a single character set of 16-bit characters.

Uninitialized state The state of a form before its first *IPersistMessage::InitNew* or *IPersistMessage::Load* directive.

universally unique identifier (UUID) A unique 128-bit value that identifies objects such as Automation servers, interfaces, manager entry-point vectors, and client objects. UUIDs consist of both a time identifier and a machine identifier. This format guarantees that any two or more UUIDs produced on the same machine are unique because they are produced at different times. Any two or more UUIDs produced at the same time are also unique because they are produced on different machines.

unmarshaling The process of unpacking the parameters of a received cross-process method call into the format expected by the object. Unmarshaling is performed by the stub.

UUID *See* universally unique identifier.

UUIDGEN.EXE A command-line utility program that creates UUIDs. This program is functionally equivalent to GUIDGEN.EXE.

verb In the Exchange client, a command specific to a message type with which the user can activate the form for the message. All messages support the verb *Open*. Interpersonal note messages (message class *IPM.Note*) support the verbs Reply To Sender, Reply To All, and Forward. In MAPI, a verb is a parameter to *IMAPIForm::DoVerb* that specifies the manner in which to activate the form.

view A group of messages, displayed in tabular form; the set of operations to apply to a folder contents table to yield such a tabular display, including the columns specified, the sort column and order, and any restriction applied to the table.

view advise sink A variety of advise sink implemented by clients of forms. The client hands this advise sink to the form, registering it with *IMAPIForm::Advise*. The form subsequently communicates with the client by invoking the methods of the advise sink. View advise sinks support the interface *IMAPIViewAdviseSink*. Like their cousins, the form advise sinks, they resemble OLE *IAdviseSink* sinks more than they do the MAPI *IMAPIAdviseSink* sinks.

view context An object that encapsulates the form's visual relationship with the view from which the user launched the form. View context objects support the *IMAPIViewContext* interface.

view descriptor A message in a folder's associated contents table that stores a folder view.

viewer In the Exchange client, a viewer is a window displaying a view. Viewers include the message viewer, the search viewer, and the remote viewer. In MAPI, a viewer is the client of a form.

virtual function table (vtable) A vtable is used to keep track of the correct functions that are to be called for every object of a class. It is a table of ordered pointers that point to the address of the actual implementation of the method. The pointers are ordered with respect to the order of the methods in the interface specification.

vtable *See* virtual function table.

Windows Messaging System (WMS) The body of code implementing MAPI, its associated system code, a set of standard service providers, and the standard Exchange client user interface.

WMS *See* Windows Messaging System.

workgroup application Any application primarily concerned with information sharing and exchange among a group of users.

XAPIA The X.400 Application Programming Interface Association.

INDEX

assertions, error paths and, 178
attachments, tables of, 90
Automation, ActiveX/Messaging server and, 79–80
Automation object, MAPI.Session, 79, 80
automation servers, 79–80

B

BackOffice SDK, 262
binary interface standard, 22–25
bulletin boards, 94, 222, 299

C

C++
  COM compared to, 8
  vtables in, 23
caching
  form factories, 298
  server, 298
CalcFormPropSet method, 248, 249, 252, 259, 398, 400
CalcVerbSet method, 253, 255, 400, 426
call-by-reference methods, 27, 28
category of forms, 242
Catform sample application, 514–16
Cat-Tracking Application, 384–94
CCharFormat class, 208
CClassFactory class, 307
CExtImpl class, 147, 148
CFG files (configuration files). *See* configuration files (CFG files)
child windows, Exchange client, 139
ChooseFolder method, 169, 203
classes, 8
  component, 15
class factories (class objects), 15
  form server implementation and, 306–14

class factories (class objects), *continued*
  in-process implementation of, 57–58
  registration of, 310
class identifiers. *See* CLSIDs (class identifiers)
class objects. *See* class factories (class objects)
class scope, 48
Clear method, 154
client applications, MAPI. *See* MAPI client applications
clients, 28–50. *See also* Exchange client
  how interfaces are gotten by, 33
  how interfaces are used by, 29
  how objects are accessed by, 29–33
  in MAPI, 66–67
  object life span and, 15–18
  reference counting rules and, 36–43
Close function, 345, 439
CloseServerCheck function, 312, 314
closing forms. *See* shutting down forms (closing forms)
CLSIDs (class identifiers), 15, 16, 30, 62, 227–30
  of form factories, 298
  implementing a form server and, 299–300
  making a form local to the client and, 267–68
  message classes vs., 229–30
  as a property set's GUID, 236
  scope of valid, 230
CMC (Common Messaging Calls), 73
CmdAddress function, 370–72
CmdPost function, 375–76
CmdSave function, 376
CmdSubmit function, 369–70
CMsgType class, 208

Ben Goetter led a development team that helped create Microsoft Exchange Server. A veteran of a decade of developing Microsoft systems networking and communication projects, including Microsoft Windows NT, he currently consults—focusing on MAPI and workgroup computing development issues—and dabbles in medical informatics. Ben holds a bachelor of arts degree in music from Yale University. He lives in Seattle, Washington, with his wife, Kathryn Hinsch.

For more pointless biographical detail, visit Ben on the World Wide Web at *http://www.angrygraycat.com/goetter/*.

The manuscript for this book was prepared and submitted to Microsoft Press in electronic form. Text files were prepared using Microsoft Word 7.0 for Windows. Pages were composed by Microsoft Press using Adobe PageMaker 6.01 for Windows, with text type in Garamond and display type in FuturaMedium. Composed pages were delivered to the printer as electronic prepress files.

Cover Graphic Designers
Greg Erickson, Robin Hjellen

Cover Illustrator
George Abe

Interior Graphic Designer
Kim Eggleston

Principal Artist
Michael Victor

Principal Compositors
Barb Runyan, Barbara Remmele

Principal Proofreader/Copy Editor
Shawn Peck

Indexer
Maro Riofrancos

INSIDE MAPI— your key to creating robust applications for Microsoft® Exchange!

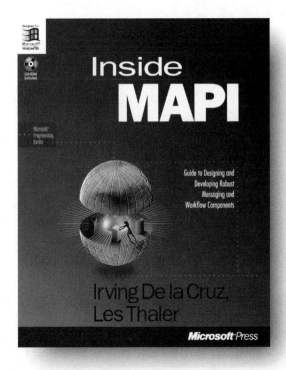

MAPI is more than a library of APIs that a developer can call to create applications for Microsoft Exchange. Beyond the APIs, MAPI is a complex specification to which developers must adhere as they create client applications and service providers. INSIDE MAPI provides the necessary insight and code examples to help developers interpret the specification correctly and create applications that work well and interact smoothly with Microsoft Exchange. This insider's guide is packed with information not available elsewhere and will be a vital, practical resource for developers, MIS professionals, and managers seeking to create robust MAPI-compliant applications.

Put MAPI to work strategically with INSIDE MAPI.

U.S.A.	**$39.95**
U.K.	£37.49 [V.A.T. included]
Canada	$54.95
ISBN 1-57231-312-9	

Microsoft *Press*

Register Today!

Return this
Developing Applications for
Microsoft® Exchange with C++
registration card for a Microsoft Press® catalog

U.S. and Canada addresses only. Fill in information below and mail postage-free. Please mail only the bottom half of this page.

1-57231-500-8A   *Developing Applications for*   *Owner Registration Card*
                                   Microsoft® Exchange with C++

NAME

INSTITUTION OR COMPANY NAME

ADDRESS

CITY   STATE   ZIP

Microsoft®*Press*
Quality Computer Books

**For a free catalog of
Microsoft Press® products, call
1-800-MSPRESS**

BUSINESS REPLY MAIL
FIRST-CLASS MAIL   PERMIT NO. 53   BOTHELL, WA

POSTAGE WILL BE PAID BY ADDRESSEE

MICROSOFT PRESS REGISTRATION
DEVELOPING APPLICATIONS FOR
MICROSOFT® EXCHANGE WITH C++
PO BOX 3019
BOTHELL WA 98041-9946